The Life of Fletcher Blaisdell

In His Own Words

1843-1865

Transcribed & Compiled By

Linda Blaisdell Roosa and John Blaisdell

Published By

Lulu Press Inc
Morrisville, NC

Copyright © 2021 by Linda B. Roosa & John Blaisdell

All rights reserved. No part of this book may be reproduced in any form or by any electronic or mechanical means, including information storage and retrieval systems, without permission in writing from the authors, except by reviewers, who may quote brief passages in a review.

ISBN 978-0-578-89276-4 (Hardcover Edition)

Printed and bound in the United States of America

First printing April 2021
Lulu Press Inc.

Table of Contents

PREFACE	5
TIMELINE	10
OCTOBER 1843	13
JANUARY 1844	16
JANUARY 1845	33
JANUARY 1846	48
JANUARY 1847	63
JANUARY 1848	78
JANUARY 1849	92
JANUARY 1850	105
JANUARY 1851	121
JANUARY 1852	137
JANUARY 1853	155
JANUARY 1854	177
JANUARY 1855	197
JANUARY 1856	215
JANUARY 1857	237
JANUARY 1858	256
JANUARY 1859	274
JANUARY 1860	294
JANUARY 1861	308
JANUARY 1862	322
JANUARY 1863	336
JANUARY 1864	348
JANUARY 1865	363
DEATHS	375
PHOTOS	379
CLOSING ACKNOWLEDGEMENTS	385

Preface

Like most things in the Blaisdell house, the old family diaries were saved. Fletcher's diaries have been read for five generations and their stories told, but until now they have not been transcribed. We wanted to do this to satisfy our interest in family history and to share it with our descendants and others interested in the history of Coeymans and its particular location in the Hudson Valley. We are the last of five generations to call the Fletcher Blaisdell Homestead, "home."

First, a brief family history: Coeymans is a small river town located twelve miles south of Albany, NY and approximately one hundred-fifty miles north of New York City. Fletcher was our 2nd great grandfather. Born in Coeymans in 1817, he was the second child of Levi Blaisdell and Mary Farr Johnstone.

Levi Blaisdell, Fletcher's father, was born in 1757 in Amesbury, MA where his family had lived for five generations. As shown on the first chart at the end of this section, he was the 3rd great grandson of Ralph Blaisdell who immigrated to North America from England in 1635 with his wife, Elizabeth, and son, Henry. He was also the 3rd great grandson of Susannah North Martin who immigrated from England in 1639. Susannah was one of several women who were hanged at Salem, MA in 1692 after being convicted of witchcraft. As the chart shows, the Blaisdell and North families must have been close as we are linked by two marriages.

First Settlers of Amesbury

Family history indicates that Levi's father, Oliver, was a shipbuilder in Amesbury. Levi and his father served in the Revolutionary War. Evidently Levi first came to Coeymans as part of Commodore Jacobus Wynkoop's Revolutionary War shipbuilding force.[1] Apparently Levi met Abraham and Arientje Gardinier during his time in Coeymans as he returned after the war and married Arientje, who had become a widow after the death of Abraham in 1782. Arientje was a wealthy woman as she was the eldest daughter of David VerPlanck and his third wife, Caterina Boom. David VerPlanck's first wife was Arientje Barentse Coeymans, who had inherited a portion of the Coeymans Patent from her father, Barent Pieterse Coeymans on his death in 1710. A portion of the Coeymans Patent was inherited by Arientje VerPlanck when her father died in 1776.

When they married, Levi was 24 and Arientje 29. Although Arientje had 2 children from her first marriage, she and Levi had no children. They lived at the Gardinier farm, which lay north of present day Ravena at a site referred to as the "Old Place" in Fletcher's journal. Levi joined with others in 1789 to build the "Old Stone Church" that is said to have been the first Methodist Episcopal Church building erected west of the Hudson River.[2] It was located near the Gardinier/Blaisdell Farm. In 1814, after 32 years of marriage, Arientje died at the age of 60 leaving Levi significant land

---

[1] Coeymans Conservation Advisory Council, "Town of Coeymans Natural Resources Inventory," July 2019.

[2] Fletcher mentions working at the Stone Church farm and the farm Under the Hill several times in his journal. We think this refers to the property that was the Gardinier/Blaisdell Farm in Levi's time. The Old Stone Church at this location was abandoned in 1836 when the congregation moved to their new location on Church Street (Jean Bush, "Old Stone Church," The Hitching Post, Summer 2014).

holdings.[3] A few months after Arientje's death, Levi married Mary Farr Johnstone, a much younger woman.[4] Levi was 57 and Mary 30 when they were married. The couple had 3 children, Wesley (1815), Fletcher (1817) and Harriet (1821). Levi died in 1833 at the age of 75 when Fletcher was only 15.

Fletcher lived during the years between the War of 1812 and the Civil War. The Erie Canal opened in 1825 providing a water route from New York City via the Hudson River to the Great Lakes. As a result, New York City became the most important city in the country. Its population expanded tenfold between 1810 and 1860 to over a million. Since transportation on land depended heavily on the horse, there was a huge demand for hay, which was the major crop produced by farms like Fletcher's. The demand for farm products led to the development of horse-drawn machines that allowed farmers to transition from doing everything by hand. Although these advances improved productivity, living conditions were primitive compared to today. Homes were heated by woodstoves. There was no plumbing. Drinking water was hand-pumped from wells; baths were a luxury; toilets were outdoor privies, and clothes were washed by hand and hung to dry. There was no electricity and there were certainly no telephones. Indoor lighting was provided by candles or oil lamps. Medical care was primitive, and many died early – especially children. Medicines often contained combinations of arsenic, iron, mercury, opium, cocaine and heroin, which often exacerbated the conditions being treated. Despite it all, they lived full and productive lives – often accomplishing things more quickly than it would seem possible today.

Fletcher's life centered around the farm that he established in Coeymans. The farm was probably part of the extensive property holdings inherited in a convoluted way through Levi's first marriage to Arientje VerPlanck Gardinier. Fletcher had an older brother Wesley, who had a degree in medicine, and a younger sister Harriet, who married Alexander Willis. Wesley and Harriet also lived in Coeymans.

Fletcher married Sarah Ann Houghtaling in 1838 when he was 21 and she was 19. As shown on the second chart, Sarah Ann had a direct tie to the Coeymans family through her 2nd great grandmother Mayke Coeymans, the daughter of Pieter Barentse Coeymans. Fletcher and Sarah Ann lived in the large house on Westerlo Street that Fletcher had completed in 1837, a year before their marriage. The Blaisdell, Willis, Houghtaling and Civill families were close as his journal describes numerous social interactions. Sarah Ann's mother, Maria VanBergen Houghtaling, moved in with Fletcher and Sarah Ann a few years after her husband, Anthony Houghtaling, died.

Fletcher and Sarah Ann were active in the community and church and often entertained friends and family at their home. They relied on paid help for many of the tasks involved with running the house and the farm. Fletcher had significant woodworking skills as you will discover as you read his journal. In addition to constructing their home, Fletcher and his crew built the first Catholic Church in Coeymans, a new home for his mother and the large schoolhouse that housed Coeymans Academy.

Fletcher began keeping a daily journal in 1843 when he was 26, which he faithfully continued until shortly before his death in 1865. In addition to describing the daily activities at the farm, his journal

---

[3] Like many wealthy families in NY in those times, Levi and Arientje were slave owners. It is reported that Levi freed his slaves in 1814 after Arientje's death. Slave ownership was finally abolished in NY in 1827.

[4] Mary Farr Johnstone's parents were from Scotland. Shortly after their arrival in Coeymans, her father returned to Scotland leaving his pregnant wife. He was apparently lost at sea. We believe that Mary was raised by the Cronks and took their last name as she was baptized as Mary Cronk in 1789 when she was 5 years old.

brings to life what it was like in the mid-1800s. His travels by horseback, horse & wagon, stage, steamboat and railroad, took him visiting friends, sight-seeing, attending lectures, museums and many other interesting places. American history, geography and politics were of considerable interest; he and Sarah Ann were fortunate to be financially able to visit many interesting sites. We have added footnotes to elaborate some of the events and circumstances that he encountered during his lifetime.

Daily journal entries usually began with a weather report, followed by seasonal farm work, names of visitors, daily travels and business transactions. Although his writing was quite legible, the lack of punctuation, spelling variances and grammatical differences often made it difficult to transcribe accurately. We took the liberty of adding punctuation and making a few corrections, hopefully without changing his meaning, but we left most of his original spelling. You will note certain passages that are in bold text and an occasional word in brackets. The bold text indicates things we thought might be of interest such as marriages, deaths or something unusual. The bracketed words usually insert what we thought was a missing word or completes an abbreviation that might not be understood.

The map at the end of this section shows the Town of Coeymans as it existed in 1866 – one year after Fletcher died. Fletcher's name and initials appear in at least five places on the map. We know from the journal that he also owned land beyond Coeymans including Greenville, Coxsackie, Herkimer (where he owned a sawmill) and in the state of Michigan. Other names on the map that Fletcher mentions in the diary, although not always spelled the same way, include Ackerman, Armstrong, Briggs, Callanan, Carhart, Colvin, Cronk, Croswell, Crumb, Gedney, Holmes, Houghtaling, Jack, Jolley, Lawson, Lawton, Litchfield, Mosher, Mull, Powell, Pulver, Robb, Robertson, Schoonmaker, Shear, Sherwood, Springstead, Stanton, Sweet, Ten Eyck, Thorn, VanSlyck, VanDerZee, Willis, Waldron, Whitbeck, Wilsey, and Wiltse.

We've included a timeline that begins with Fletcher's 3rd great grandfather, Ralph, arriving in the colony of Maine, on the ship Angel Gabriel, in 1635 and ends with the marriage of his grandson Robert Blaisdell (our grandfather) in 1907. The timeline depicts what was transpiring in Fletcher's life compared to major events occurring elsewhere in the developing young country.

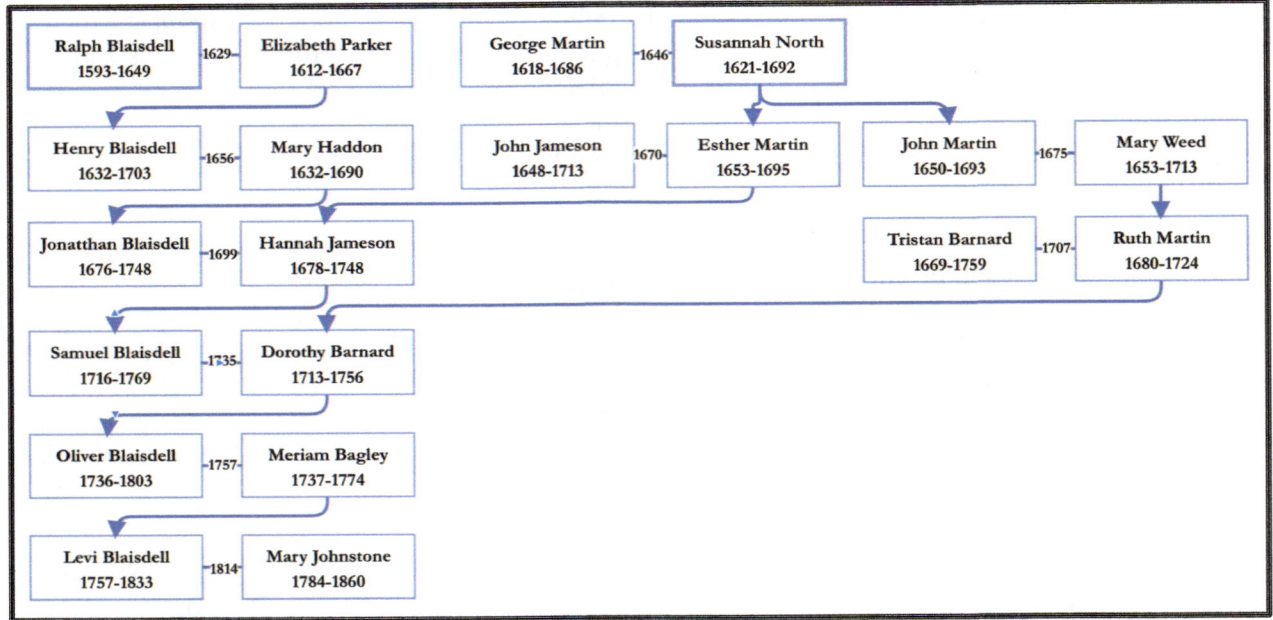

Ancestors of Fletcher Blaisdell

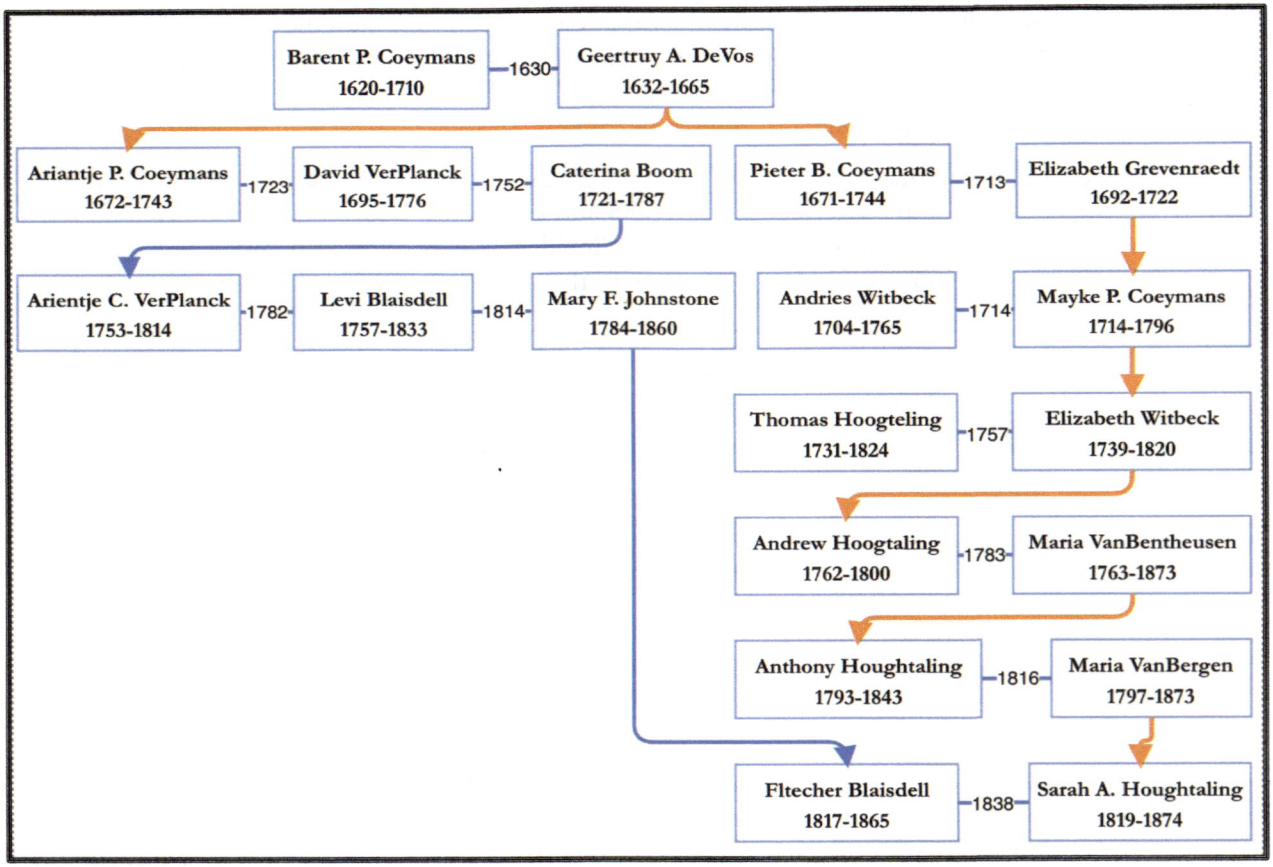

Connection to the Coeymans Family

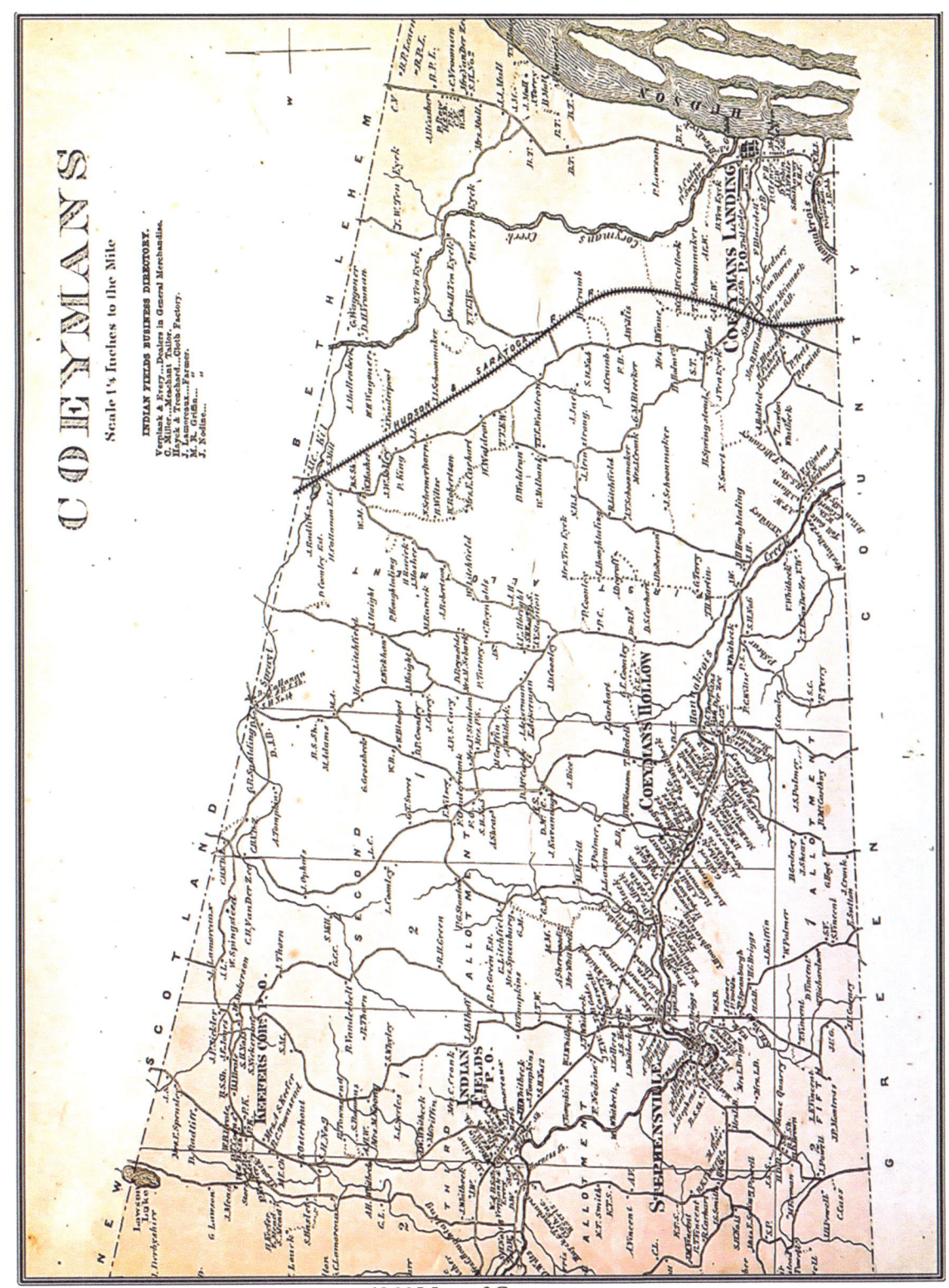

1866 Map of Coeymans

Timeline

Fletcher's Timeline	Year	U.S. Timeline
3rd Great Grandfather (Ralph) arrived from England – 15 Aug	1635	
	1641	Witchcraft became a capital crime
	•	Massachusetts colony legalized slavery
	1664	8 Sep – Dutch surrender New Amsterdam to British
3rd Great Grandmother (Susannah) hanged as a witch – 19 Jul	1692	Salem witch hunts began
	1752	Benjamin Franklin invents lightning rod
	1754	French & Indian War started
	1763	French & Indian War ended
	1773	16 Dec – The Boston Tea Party protest
Father (Levi) & Grandfather (Oliver) & joined the Militia to fight the British	1775	19 Apr – Revolutionary War started
	•	
	1776	4 Jul – Declaration of Independence
Father (Levi) married Arientje Coeymans VerPlank – 15 Aug	1782	20 Jun – Bald eagle became the national bird
	1783	3 Sep – Revolutionary War ended
	1788	21 Jun – Constitution ratified
	1789	30 Apr – George Washington inaugurated
	1791	15 Dec – Bill of Rights ratified
	1797	4 Mar – John Adams inaugurated
	1801	4 Mar – Thomas Jefferson inaugurated
	1807	17 Aug – Robert Fulton's first successful steamboat
	1809	4 Mar – James Madison inaugurated
	1812	18 Jun – War of 1812 started
Arientje VerPlank Blaisdell died at age of 60 – 10 Jan	1814	24 Aug – British soldiers burn the White House
Father (Levi) freed his slaves	•	13 Sep – Francis S. Key writes Star Spangled Banner
Father (Levi) married Mary Farr Johnstone – 23 Oct	•	24 Dec – War of 1812 ended
Brother Wesley born – 12 Oct	1815	6 Feb – First American railroad charter granted
Fletcher born – 20 Jan	1817	4 Mar – James Monroe inaugurated
	•	4 Jul – Construction of Erie Canal began
Sister Harriet born – 27 Dec	1821	10 Jul – U.S. bought Florida from Spain
	1825	4 Mar – John Quincy Adams inaugurated
	•	26 Oct – Erie Canal completed
	1826	17 Apr – First railroad chartered in New York state
	1827	4 Jul – Slavery abolished in New York state
	1828	8 Jan – Democratic Party founded
	1829	4 Mar – Andrew Jackson inaugurated
	•	23 Jul – Typewriter invented
	•	First steam-powered locomotive built in America
	1831	Cyrus McCormick invented the reaper
	•	24 Sep – Mohawk & Hudson railroad opened
Father (Levi) died at age of 75 – 1 June	1833	The Whig Party was formed by Henry Clay
	1835	2 Jan – PT Barnum started first circus
	1836	2 Mar – Texas became independent of Mexico
Completed house on Westerlo St.	1837	4 Mar – Martin VanBuren inaugurated
	•	10 May – Financial Panic of 1837 began
Married Sarah Ann Houghtaling – 30 Oct	1838	
	1839	24 Feb – William Otis patented steam shovel
	1841	4 Mar – William Henry Harrison inaugurated
	•	4 Apr – John Tyler inaugurated
Daughter Harriet born – 30 Apr	•	1 May – First wagon train left for California
Fletcher's diary starts – 20 Oct	1843	21 Jun – Edgar Allen Poe published The Gold Bug
Death of Anthony Houghtaling (Sarah Ann's father) – 22 Oct		
Fletcher & Sarah Ann travel to White Mtns. – 8 Jul	1844	24 May – Samuel Morse sent first telegraph message
Bought the sloop Revenue – 28 Feb	1845	4 Mar – James Polk inaugurated
The wreck of the Steamboat Swallow – 7 Apr	•	Irish Potato Famine started
Maria Houghtaling died – 9 Apr	•	First horse-drawn mowing machine available
Son Levi born – 20 Oct	•	29 Dec – Republic of Texas became 28th state
	1846	25 Apr – Mexican American War started
	•	19 Jun – First officially recorded baseball game

Fletcher's Timeline	Year	U.S. Timeline
	•	10 Sep – Steamboat Excelsior exploded in NY city
Daughter Harriet died at age of 6 – 26 Jan	1848	24 Jan – Gold discovered in California
Son Anthony born – 23 Dec	•	2 Feb – Mexican American War ended.
Completed new house for Mother – 26 Apr	1849	4 Mar – Zachary Taylor inaugurated
Heavy rain washed away portions of Plank Road – 19 Jul	1850	9 Jul – Millard Fillmore inaugurated
Fletcher & Peter Seabridge traveled to Montreal – 25 Nov	•	9 Sep – California became 31st state
Started sawmill in Herkimer – 17 Jul	1851	21 Sep – New York Times first published
Fletcher began discussions with Catholic Church – 20 Apr	1852	29 Jul – Steamer Henry Clay burned on the Hudson
Fletcher & Sarah Ann start trip to Illinois to visit T. Collins – 1 Sep	•	
Fletcher signed contract to build Catholic Church – 29 Sep	•	
Attended inauguration of Franklin Pierce – 4 Mar	1853	4 Mar – Franklin Pierce inaugurated
Visited Shaker Village in Lebanon, NY – 24 Jun	•	14 Jul – Exhibition of the Industry of All Nations
Fletcher completes building Catholic Church – 16 Aug	•	
Attended Exhibition of the Industry of all Nations – 10 Nov	•	
Attended family reunion at Amesbury, MA – 31 Oct	1854	18 Feb – Republican Party founded
Began work on vineyard – 6 Jan	1855	21 Apr – First railroad train crosses Mississippi River
Sister-in-law Margaret Blaisdell died at age of 39 – 17 Feb		
Sold Flat Bush farm – 11 Feb	1856	
Fletcher & Sarah Ann started trip to Michigan – 4 Jun	•	
Fletcher buys 300 acres of land in Michigan – 12 Jun	•	
Starts to build schoolhouse – 9 Aug	•	
Mother (Maria) Houghtaling moved to Fletcher's home – 8 Mar	1857	4 Mar – James Buchanan inaugurated
Attended speech by Frederick Douglas – 16 Sep	•	23 Mar – Elisha Otis installed first elevator
Attended General Worth's Funeral – 25 Nov	•	
Croswell's Papermill burned – 25 May	1858	16 Aug – First telegraph communication across Atlantic
Fletcher, T. Civill, P. Seabridge establish Coeymans Academy	•	21 Aug – First of Lincoln-Douglas debates
Fletcher & Sarah Ann start trip to Mammoth Cave – 27 Apr	1859	16 Oct – John Brown's abolitionists seize armory at Harpers Ferry
Mother (Mary) died at age of 76 – 6 Sep	1860	
Attends Torchlight Parade supporting Abraham Lincoln – 24 Oct		
	1861	4 Mar – Abraham Lincoln inaugurated
	•	12 Apr – Civil War started
	1863	19 Nov – President Lincoln gives Gettysburg address
Brother (Wesley) died at Fortress Monroe at age of 49 – 22 Oct	1864	
	1865	9 Apr – Civil War ended
	•	14 Jun – President Lincoln assassinated
	•	15 Jun – Andrew Johnson inaugurated
Fletcher died at age of 48 – 25 Oct	•	18 Dec – 13th Amendment abolished slavery
	1866	26 Dec – Klu Klux Klan formed
	1868	5 Mar – George Westinghouse invented the air brake
	1869	4 Mar – Ulysses S. Grant inaugurated
	1870	10 Jan – Standard Oil incorporated by J.D. Rockefeller
	1872	5 Nov – Susan B. Anthony (suffragette) voted illegally
Wife (Sarah Ann) died at age of 55 – 23 Aug	1874	
	1876	7 Mar – Alexander G. Bell patented first telephone
	1877	4 Mar – Rutherford B. Hayes inaugurated
	•	2 Jul – President Hayes shot (died 19 Sep)
	•	20 Sep – Chester A. Arthur inaugurated
Son (Levi) built the large hay barn – Jul	1878	19 Feb – Thomas Edison patented phonograph
Son (Anthony) married Mary McConnell – 6 Aug	•	
Grandson (Robert VanBergen Blaisdell) born – 4 Jul	1879	4 Mar – James A. Garfield inaugurated
Granddaughter (Elizabeth Blaisdell) born – 9 Jan	1883	18 Nov – 5 standard time zones established
	1885	4 Mar – Grover Cleveland inaugurated
	•	17 Jun – Statue of Liberty arrived in New York harbor
	1888	11 Mar – The blizzard of '88 started (drifts up to 52 ft)
Granddaughter (Elizabeth Blaisdell) died	1889	4 Mar – Benjamin Harrison inaugurated
	1893	4 Mar – Grover Cleveland inaugurated
	•	5 May – New York stock exchange collapsed
	1895	5 Nov – First U.S. automobile patent
	1897	4 Mar – William McKinley inaugurated

Fletcher's Timeline	Year	U.S. Timeline
•		17 Jul – Klondike gold rush started
	1901	6 Sep – President McKinley shot (died a week later)
•		14 Sep – Theodore Roosevelt inaugurated
	1902	17 Jul – Willis Carrier invented the air conditioner
Son (Levi) died – 24 Mar	**1903**	17 Dec – Wright brothers first sustained manned flight
Son (Anthony) died – 9 Sep	**1905**	
	1906	18 Apr – San Francisco earthquake
Grandson (Robert) married Marguerite Briggs – 19 Oct	**1907**	13 Mar – Financial panic and depression started

October 1843[5]

20 Pleasant day. **I and Wife go to Flat Bush to Father Houghtaling who is sick**.

21 Very pleasant until 4 o'clock in afternoon. Then it rained.

22 Rained all day. **Father Houghtaling[6] died this morning at 5 o'clock & 40 minutes**. James Hawley and Seth Hawley was there who laid him out.

23 Snow 8 in. deep. Father Houghtaling buried. Funeral 2 o'clock P.M. Thomas Houghtaling did not get there till after Father Houghtaling was dead and was affected very much.

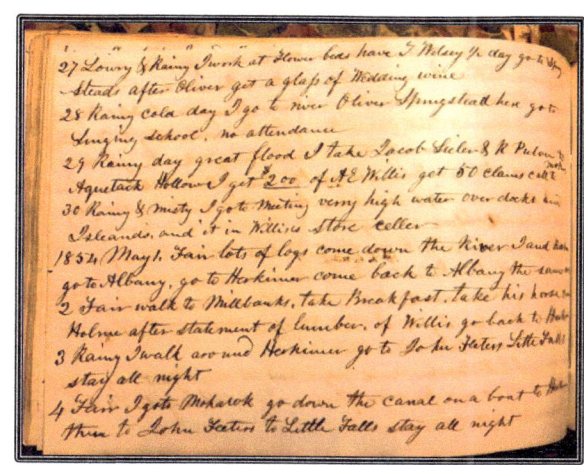

Fletcher's Journal

24 Pleasant. Sun shone all day

25 Rain a little in the morning. Fair rest of the day. I went to Catskill and back holme.

26 South wind. Unpleasant.

27 Rain hail & snow all day. One inch deep at night.

28 Clears off, sun shines.

29 Pleasant. **Go to Flat Bush**. Roads very muddy.

30 Weather fine. I went to **Greenville**.

31 Cold. North wind. Many lose their potatoes.

November 1843

1 Fair south wind.

2 Rainy. I go to Albany. North wind and clears off 9 o'clock.

3 North wind. Clear and cold.

4 Clear & cold north wind. Took my cattle from the Island.

5 Fair, cold North wind.

6 North wind but more mild.

---

[5] We have attempted to present Fletcher's journal similar to the way he wrote it. You will note some missing days; they were left out by Fletcher for whatever reason. Since he often didn't use punctuation, we added it where it seemed to make sense. For the most part we left his spelling as it was, for example 'holme' for 'home', 'sley' for 'sleigh', 'waggon' for 'wagon', 'showry' for 'showery', 'quiry' for 'quarry'… We did change some words such as 'pic nik' to 'picnic' and 'to day' to 'today', etc. You will also note that we bolded some text. This was to identify things that we considered important or unusual. Occasionally we found words that were unreadable. We made our best guess but added (?) to indicate that our guess might be wrong.

[6] Anthony Houghtaling was born in 1793 and was only 50 when he died.

7   Election. Snow all the afternoon. Overcast in the morning.

8   Snow 1½ inches. North wind, very cold.

9   Warmer south wind. I go to Greenville.

10   Foggy south wind. Misty and rainy.

11   Foggy and rainy. Colder in afternoon.

12   Snow 3 inches deep North wind. Squally all day.

13   Warmer south wind.

14   North wind, very cold. Freeze hard.

15   White frost. South wind in afternoon.

16   Rain all forenoon. Mr. Barger here. Afternoon clears off.

17   Foggy and warm all day.

18   South wind pleasant. Sun shines warm.

19   North wind. Cloudy all day.

20   Fine day. Sun shines clear.

21   Rainy and squally and unpleasant.

22   Snow squalls. **I go to Kimmey's to mill**.[7] Very muddy.

23   Fine morning. Cloudy in afternoon.

24   Rainy morning. Clears off in afternoon.

25   North wind. Fair. I go to Mother Houghtaling's.

26   White frost, south wind in morning. Colder in afternoon.

27   Very cold freeze hard. North wind all day.

28   White frost. South wind cold.

29   Snow, south wind. I kill hogs and beef.

30   Colder, north wind. One inch of snow. Salt my pork.[8]

Kimmey's Mill

December 1843

1   Snow all day. I kill my big ox. Beecher goes to Greenville.

2   Fair day. North wind.

3   South wind. Fair

4   South wind. Cold and chilly stormy appearance.

---

[7] Fletcher made many trips to Kimmey's Mill. It was located on the Feuri-Sprayt Kill (Creek) near the town of South Bethlehem. It was both a grist and sawmill owned by Phillip Kimmey.

[8] Salting and smoking was a common way of preserving meat and fish until the middle of the 20th century, when refrigeration became available. Salt inhibits the growth of microorganisms by drawing water out of microbial cells. Smoking adds chemicals to the surface of the meat, which reduces the concentration of salt required.

5	Clear cold north wind.
6	Very cold. South wind.
7	Snow all day, cold north wind. I am not very well.
8	Six inches snow. South wind. Fine weather.
9	Fair day, south wind. Get pig from Flat Bush belonging to Sarah Ann.
10	Colder, north wind. **Steamboats have stopped**. We go to **Meeting**[9] twice.
11	Very cold, south wind. **I sell Turnpike cattle to Peter W. VanBergen**. **A. Willis**[10] took the Flat Bush chickens.
12	Morning fair south wind. Afternoon north wind. River froze hard.
13	Clear cold north wind.
14	Cold, south wind. **Thanksgiving Day**.[11] Barent VanSlyck and Lady here on a visit. **Cornelius Trebout, my boy, run away**.
15	Warmer, south wind. I go to Flat Bush.
16	Four inches snow rain all day. Draw wood for John Hauenstien.
17	Sloppy weather. Rain part of the day. Snow all gone.
18	Stormy day. Snow, rain & hail. I settle with R & J Lawton. **Attend Temperance Meeting**.[12] **Marite**[13] has her teeth fixed.
19	North wind in morning. South in afternoon.
20	Pleasant day, roads bad. I settle with N. Agan.
21	Warm, misty. John Cronk & Lady here.
22	Warm, overcast. **I finish work on Turnpike**.[14] **Attend Singing School**.
24	Warm cloudy day. South wind.

---

[9] Go to Meeting means go to church.

[10] Alexander E. Willis was Fletcher's brother-in-law. He was born in Ballston, NY on 5 May 1812; he married Fletcher's sister Harriet in 1841 and the couple had 11 children. He came to Coeymans in 1842 and entered into the freighting business that became known as Lawton, Willis, Colvin & Co.

[11] Thanksgiving Day wasn't always celebrated on the 4th Thursday of November. Prior to 1863, the date varied from state to state. In 1863, President Lincoln established the date to be the 4th Thursday of November. In 1939, President Franklin Roosevelt changed it to the 3rd Thursday of November to provide more shopping days before Christmas in an attempt to boost the economy following the depression. He changed it back to the 4th Thursday in 1941.

[12] Fletcher was active in the Sons of Temperance Society. It was a brotherhood of men who supported the temperance movement, which was against the consumption of alcoholic beverages. The group was founded in New York City in 1842. As we will see later in the journal, Fletcher had his own vineyard, made wine and was not opposed to the occasional consumption of alcohol.

[13] Marite (Maria Houghtaling) was Sarah Ann's sister who later married Dr. Andrew VanAntwerp.

[14] Turnpikes in the mid-1800's were toll roads. The term 'turnpike' came from the barrier that prevented people from using the road until a toll had been paid [Wikipedia]. These toll roads were usually made with planking laid at right angles to the road and were an improvement over other roads that were usually rutted and full of holes. Evidently Fletcher was one of the investors in one of the turnpikes. This may have been the Albany & Green Turnpike [E.A. Giddings, Coeymans and the Past].

25   Overcast, south wind. **Steamboat pass here for Christmas**.

26   Overcast, north wind in morning, south in afternoon. J. Story & Lady here.

27   Fair and mild. Beecher goes to Greenville. I settle with Nathan Stephens.

28   Cloudy bad weather and muddy.

29   Cold, hard north wind. Freeze hard. John Bushants here.

30   Colder, north wind, squally. Bill Baker's Lawsuit.

31   Cold, squally, north wind. I go to Meeting twice.

January 1844

1   North wind, still times.

2   Pleasant day, north wind. I go Catskill, take Wife to Barent Houghtaling's.

3   Snow all day with hail. 3 inches deep.

4   Fair. Judge Nichols, Mr. Collins, Wm. Hoose, James Gefft here.

5   Very cold day, north wind. I settle with Dennis Tobin.

6   Fine day. Andrew Witbeck & Daughter visiting.

7   South wind, snow in afternoon. I go to Meeting. **Trego's Barn burnt this night**.

8   North wind, cold. I kill my pigs. **Attend the Irishman's trial that set Trego's Barn on fire. Wesley**[15] is sick.

9   Very cold, snows. **Attend Turnpike meeting at Hallock's, Coxsackie**.

10   Snow a little. Trego and Lady here visiting.

11   Clear and cold. **Attend Martin Holme's & Mary Houghtaling's Wedding**. Stay till one o 'clock, have a fine time. All the old folks there.

Wesley Blaisdell's Home

12   Frosty morning, south wind. I and Wife go to Flat Bush. Settle with Uncle Abram, M.G. VanBergen witness.

13   Cold north wind. Fuller, the singing teacher here.

14   Pleasant north wind. I have a very bad cold.

15   Cold & pleasant. E. Millbanks & Lady, Jacob Springstead & Lady here visiting.

16   Snowy morning rain the rest of the day. Beecher come from Flat Bush.

17   Rain all day, south wind till night, then turn north wind heavy. Beecher, E. Holmes goes to Greenville for me.

18   Fair, north wind. I go to John Cronk's then to S. Witbeck's get sweet apples.

---

15   Wesley Blaisdell was Fletcher's older brother. He was a medical doctor and lived on South Main St. in Coeymans. He served as a surgeon in the Civil War.

19 Cold north wind. I go skating on the river, go on the island. **Wife goes to John J. Colvin.**[16]

20 Very cold, north wind. Attend Singing School. Not very well. **Stages**[17] **go on the river**.

21 Colder than ever. I go to Meeting.

22 More mild, 2 in. snow. I kill my ox. Finish flower box.

23 Snow all forenoon. 4 inches at 12 o'clock. I go to Flat Bush. Attend singing party at night.

24 Fair. John Mull, Wife three children here. Mother here & sister. Newman Finch and Lady, Philip Waldron & Lady & child. 12 in all – a good houseful.

25 Very cold north wind. Company goes to Wesley's. I pay off Wm. R. Carroll.

26 Very cold. I send Beecher to Greenville. I settle with **Johnson & Colvin**.

27 Very cold. North wind. **I go to Albany on the ice**.

28 Very cold. **Freeze hard in the house**.

29 Very cold. A.E. Willis & Lady, David Benedict & Lady visit. Emeline Sweet here.

30 Very cold. I go to mill.

31 Very cold, north wind. Mr. Dobbs & son come after the Flat Bush Farm. Beecher's time is up, he goes holme.

February 1844

1 **Very cold, but fair. Go on sley**[18] **ride to Kinderhook. Go to Martin VanBuren's**[19] **residence.** *See him through the glass.* **He stands by the window. Stop to Stenckeem's; have supper. Have 4 horse team. Capsize coming holme**.

Martin VanBuren's Residence

2 A little more mild. Drizly or misty all day.

3 Very cold north wind, but fair overhead.

---

[16] From his obituary Coeymans Herald, 2 Mar 1887, John Colvin was born in Coeymans in 1815 and started out as a shoemaker at the age of 17. He married Catharine Lawton in 1838 and eventually became one of the wealthiest men in Coeymans being involved in a number of businesses. He purchased Wesley Blaisdell's home sometime after Wesley passed away in 1864.

[17] A Stage, or stagecoach, is a enclosed 4-wheeled coach used to carry paying passengers or packages. Evidently driving on the frozen river was preferrable to the rough roadway.

[18] Fletcher's handwriting is beautiful, but his spelling is another story…

[19] Martin VanBuren was the 8th President. He served from 1837-1841. He was a founder of the Democratic party and previously served as the 9th Governor of New York. He was born in Kinderhook to a family of Dutch Americans. He was a one-term president partly due to the financial crisis of 1837.

4	Pleasant day, north wind. Begins to thaw. I go to **Baltimore**[20] **on the ice**. Uriah B. Willis here in the evening.
5	Warmer, snow 3 inches deep, stops at noon. Mr. Lyman & Lady here visiting.
6	Snow forenoon. I go to Albany. **Attempted to go to Schodack to Concert. Could not find the road and come back**.
7	Warm & foggy. S. Nichols call here. Mrs. Trego, Aunt Caty, Mrs. VanSlyck here.
8	Cold north wind. Snow all forenoon. I take Mother to TenEyck Waldron's. Wife go to Andrew Teneyck's. I settle with Robert Pulver.
9	North wind. Martin B. Holmes & Lady, Elizabeth & Henriette Holmes here, visit.
10	Pleasant North wind. **Horse trot on the ice**.
11	Pleasant. **I and Wife go to Albany Universalist meeting**. Pleasant ride.
12	Clear and cold. Marite go holme with Beecher. Picture show in the church.
13	South wind. Blow very heavy. I & Wife go to Athens to G. Nichols.
14	Cloudy, north wind. Mr. Niles, Mrs. Johnson, Mrs. Colvin & Mrs. Lawton here.
15	Fair. I take Mother to Hugh Crumb's. Go to mill. Take Wife to Flat Bush. Afternoon snows.
17	Squally afternoon. Horse trotting. Mother Houghtaling come here with Beecher. He was at Flat Bush with team.
18	Colder. We go to hear Kissam preach in forenoon. Rev. Mr. Rodgers in afternoon.
19	South wind. Child sick. D. Toben here. Alvin Wilber & Saml Gnuth (sp) in evening.
20	Warmer, very thawy. **I go to Baltimore in evening, hear Mr. Lefever, the Universalist minister, preach in schoolhouse**.
21	Pleasant. A. Houghtaling & Lady, Mother Houghtaling & Mrs. Holmes visit here.
22	Warm thaws fast. I have a bad cold. A Temperance party at Andrew Whitbeck's.
23	Some colder. Wife go to river. Mr. Cary here in forenoon. Three Negroes spend the afternoon here on a visit.
24	Cold day. **Negro Nance is gone**. Mr. Fuller and his friend is here, attend Fuller's Singing School.
25	Pleasant. Fuller Dorr, Wife & self go to Meeting. Marite & Cate VanBergen come at night.
26	Mr. Matson & Lady here. I and Matson go to Nathaniel Palmer's pleasant [visit].
27	Rainy forenoon, snowy afternoon. Self, Wife & Ann Bronk go to Hugh Crumb's. Abram VanBergen come with Isiah Roberts to get Flat Bush Farm.
28	Pleasant, 3 inches of snow. I go to Flat Bush. Attend debate at night.

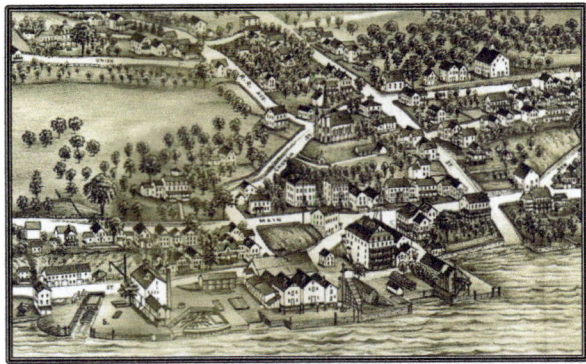

New Baltimore circa 1891

---

[20] Fletcher usually refers to New Baltimore as Baltimore, which may have been common in his time. We left it as he wrote it.

29   South wind, cloudy day. We go visiting to Andrew Teneyck's. Party to Trego's.

March 1844

1   South wind, cloudy & warm. Andrew & Mother Houghtaling here.

2   Warm; thaws very fast. **Close a Bargain for Flat Bush farm with Woolsey Cary**.

3   Warm. I go to Meeting. Wife and Marite go to Wesley's

4   Cold, 4 inches snow, blow all away. I go to river with corn. Wife go to Wesley's.

5   Clear cold day. I and Wife go a visiting to E.E. Sherman's. Wife & Marite go to concert.

6   Warm. I go to Coxsackie, finish drawing my hay, prep timber.

7   Warm, south wind. Mrs. Clement broke her leg last night. Beecher goes to Flat Bush.

8   South wind & rain. I take Wife to river with horse & waggon.

9   Rainy morning clears off. I and Mother go to Albany for witness in case of suit of James Lawson. **I buy child two dresses.**

10   **Riding on river stopped**. I go to Meeting. Quite warm. Wesley here.

11   Pleasant but muddy. Get drill made. Get a letter from Phillip Waldron.

12   Pleasant day. I and Beecher work in quiry. Wife go to see Betsy Teneyck.

13   South wind rain all day. High tides, muddy. Oil my harness.

14   North wind, colder. Get my new pickaxe. River broke up, ice started at 2 o'clock. Temperance Association at Hugh Jolly's, we attend.

15   South wind, overcast, some snow. **Child taken sick**. Ice stops between here & New Baltimore.

16   South wind. **Child sick**. Rain all day. I go to river. Very muddy.

17   North wind, more pleasant. **Child sick**.

18   Cloudy. I go to Flat Bush. Mother here. **Abram Teal's child buried**. Daniel Goldsmith sends us a string of fish. Beecher leave here.

19   Fair. Wesley & Margaret here visiting. I pay off N.H. Johnson. Levi Cronk commence work. **Cornelius VanAntwerp died. Judge Lill (sp) died**.

20   South wind. Three Sloops come lay at the dock. I go to river get return for corn.

21   Colder. I go to Albany. Get my Wife a dress. Very muddy. Get ½ lb. of Spanish tobacco.

22   Pleasant but cold. **We all go to funeral of Cornelius VanAntwerp**.

23   Fair. I go to mill, then to **Widow Houghtaling's Vendue**[21] – buy 4 calves. John Cronk here all night.

24   Pleasant. I and Wife go to see Betsy Teneyck. Wife goes to Meeting. **Betsy Teneyck died at 8 o'clock in the evening**.

25   Fair. I get my cattle from Widow Houghtaling's. Go to river.

---

[21] Vendue is a public auction.

26 Warmer. Wife visit to Beecher. **Holmes & I go to School Celebration in Methodist Church**. David Mosher speak.

28 Unpleasant day. I go to Coxsackie on Wife's business.

29 Unpleasant. **I am in jury in case of Wm. Warner (sp). He is sent to jail 40 days**.

30 I and Wife go to Millbank's with sley. Good sleying.

31 Fair. **Wife goes to Willis's all night. Harriet[22] has a young son**.

April 1844

1   Reynolds pay his rent. 6 inches of snow. Wife & Marite goes to Thomas Houghtaling's visiting.

2   Pleasant overhead, muddy underfoot. Levi Cronk draw wood. I tap sap trees.

3   Fair. **I go to Hollow after 2-inch plank for Hay Press**. John Beacham here.

4   Fair. I draw Sawlogs to the mill. Get horses shod. **Draw out timber for press**.

5   Fair. I go to Albany after castings. Roads bad. Levi Cronk jamb his hand. Get pear trees.

6   Fair. Draw plank from the mill. **Put [hay] press together. Dig hole for the press.**

7   Go to Meeting. Go to Wesley's. South wind. Put eggs under goose.

8   **Raise my hay press**.[23] I and Wife go to Bethlehem. Roads very bad. Go after girl.

9   Wife go to Albany. I go to Town Meeting. Pay off D. Tompkins & L. Witbeck.

10 Prepare my garden. Sow lettuce. Plow & sow some peas & oats. Wife come back.

11 Fair. Plant onions, sow beets. Go to Holmes with seed. **Go sailing in the evening to Barren Island, have a fine time**.

12 Warm. Sow oats. Plow. Go to river. Caroline & Cornelius VanAntwerp here in evening.

13 Hot. I go to Flat Bush to Coxsackie, to A.T. VanSlyck's, Martin VanBergen's, get dried apples, then holme.

14 Hot as summer. We go to Meeting. Wesley Blaisdell & Andrew VanAntwerp[24] here.

15 Fair. Mr. Dewy come here. I go with him to Schoharie. Sell him lease of Barger Farm. Staid first night to Nick Blade's. High Dutch. At Mechanicsville next morning. Go to Schoharie Court House.

Dr. VanAntwerp's Door Plaque

---

22 Harriet is Fletcher's sister who married Alexander Willis.

23 Since shipping loose hay was inefficient, farmers used hay presses in the mid-1800's to compact loose hay into large bales that typically weighed 300-400 lbs. Fletcher describes building his own hay press in this part of the journal. We don't know how his press worked but we've read on farmcollector.com that they could be two-three stories tall and that the hay was compressed by a heavy weight that was raised by a team of horses and then dropped to compress the hay.

24 Andrew VanAntwerp married Maria (Marite) Houghtaling (Sarah Ann's sister) in 1846. He became a doctor with a practice in New York City and was one of Fletcher's close friends.

16 Fair. Took breakfast at Smith's Hotel. Same day started for holme with a teamster. Staid all night to Shutter's Tavern at the top of the Helderberg. Roads bad. Paid teamster 50 cents for riding.

17 Fair. Took breakfast at H. Sloan's Hotel. Got a chance with a man in a one horse waggon to Albany. Took Steamboat holme.

18 Dig ditch, sow oats, put calves on the Island. Willis here.

19. Fair. **Work on turnpike, put in sluice at Wm. Lawton's**. Get ashes to Willis.

20 Work on turnpike. **John Colvin find fault that the water is turning down the street**. I go to Flat Bush. Get Brown Horse.

21 Pleasant & dry weather. Wife and Lib VanBenthuyzen go to Meeting.

22 North wind, warm. Got my horses shod.

23 South wind blows hard. I go to Albany after Irish girl.

24 Work on road in forenoon. Go to Flat Bush in afternoon. Rain. Got wet.

25 Fair. **I and Wife go to Manhattan Hook after Mary Mosher**. Get her.

26 Draw up or raise building. Wife & Lib VanBenthuyzen go to Mrs. Hathaway's.

27 Fair. I go to Albany. Martin G. VanBergen here. Henry VanBergen & Marta here. **I get my dog watch.**[25] **Attend School Meeting**.

28 Fair. All hands go to Meeting. **Cow get cast [?] in barn & died**.

29 I lower the bents of my building draw[ing]. Then holme, get some fish.

30 Fair. Finish drawing up my building. I pay Beecher A. Holmes turnpike bill.

May 1844

1 South wind, very dry. Draw stone for building. Take log to Lawson Mill. **Lay foundation to hay press building**.

2 South wind rain a little. **Raise two bents of hay press.**[26] **Andrew Houghtaling here.**[27] Wife go a visiting.

3 Finish raise my building. Get Old Brown shod. Rain two hours.

4 Fine rain. Blossoms coming out. M.L. Soop & Charles Seabridge here.

5 Pleasant. All go to Meeting in forenoon. Evening go to Br[other] Wesley's.

6 Fair morning. I & Wife go to Albany. Rain very hard. Get very wet.

7 Fair, north wind. Get horse shod. Get 1 lb. flour. Make poll fence. Attend Temperance meeting.

8 South wind. Make fence. Go to John Bushant's in afternoon. See D. Carhart.

9 Fair weather but cold. Beecher furrow out corn ground. I go on turnpike.

---

[25] We don't know what this means. Perhaps he had a dog named Watch.
[26] Bents are the barn timbers running from front to back. If a barn has 4 bents, it has 3 bays.
[27] Andrew A. Houghtaling was Sarah Ann's brother.

10 Fair. Plant corn. **Have lawsuit with Henry Mull.** Adjourn to 15th. I get a peck of corn of John Bronk to plant.

11 Rain in forenoon. I go to Kimmey's Mill. House full of company.

12 Hard north wind. All go to Meeting twice. To Wm. Sherwood & Willis's in evening.

13 Fair. All hands lay wall all day. D. Goldsmith & Peter Cook work at hay press.

14 Raining forenoon. I go to tailor's with cloth. Get my boots mended.

15 Fair day. I settle with Henry Mull. Take his notes – one for 10 the other for 15 dollars.[28] Boys lay stonewall. I make fence.

16 Rain in forenoon. Mr. John Feeter & Lady & Mr. Kelly is here. We go to Island.

17 Heavy rain all night. Mr. Feeter & Lady & Mr. Kelly take Steamboat for New York. Abram Applebee borrow my Coulter & 3 horse whippletree.

18 Rain all morning hard. I go to Flat Bush. Bring Mother Houghtaling. Pay bills.

19 All go to Meeting. John Bronk's & Garret Houghtaling's cattle get on my wheat.

20 Rainy morning. We commence plowing. Rachael Vosburgh & Mrs. Roe here.

21 Fair north west wind. I turn out my cows. Plow. Sell calf to I. Gregory.

22 Fair. Freeze ¼ of an inch ice. Beecher draws stones. **I shingle hay press**. Peter J. Groat & John Haight work at hay press. Andrew Fancher here. Levi Cronk sick. I get chain of Albert Jackson.

23 Fair day. Shingle. Get rack of Barent TenEyck. Plant potatoes. Break plow.

24 Fair. **I and Wife go to Mrs. James Hawley's funeral**. Plant corn, potatoes.

25 Some showery. Boys draw and lay stone wall.

26 Morning fine shower. In afternoon hot. Go to Meeting. A. VanAntwerp and Mr. Jessup here in evening. I & Mother Houghtaling take a ride.

27 Fine shower. **I get 300 herring**. Get horse shod. **Press first bale of hay**.

28 Settle with Daniel Goldsmith & Peter Cook. Press hay. Turn out horses.

29 I go to Flat Bush. Boys lay wall. Lib VanBenthuyzen leave here.

30 Get horse shod forward. Go on turnpike. Make fence in afternoon.

31 Rainy, south wind. Clear out barn. Press hay. Make fence. **Melvin Persons (sp) has his leg take off today**.

June 1844

1 Fair. Plaster corn. Beecher draw hay from Flat Bush. John Finch & his sister Maria here to Quarterly Meeting.[29]

2 Fair. I and Wife go to Meeting. **Mrs. Judson's Grover died.**

3 Fair. I make hay rigging. Levi Cronk draws wood. Wife goes to river.

---

[28] $1 in 1850 would be the equivalent of about $33 in 2020.

[29] An administrative meeting of Methodist society officials within a circuit that was held quarterly.

4	Fair. I and Levi draw two loads of hay from Flat Bush. S. King is here.
5	Fair. Wife & Margarett go to Flat Bush. Sylvester Nichols here. I go on turnpike. Levi Cronk draws wood. Uncle Abram VanBergen here.
6	Fair. I and Levi Cronk work on turnpike. I go to Mossy, take Uncle Abram along. See W.S. Briggs about turnpike. He is Inspector.
7	Some rainy. I go to Albany. **Daniel Goldsmith got hurt at the lowering of Barent Teneyck's barn. Hurt bad. I stay with him at night**.
8	Fair. Levi plow corn. Beecher help John Bushants make road. E. Roberts here.
9	Fair. **Daniel Goldsmith died this morning at 35 minutes past six. I was up with him from the time he was hurt. He was with me when I was sick.**
10	Fair. **Attend D. Goldsmith's funeral**. Dominie Kissam preach. Buried him in Schofield. Two good hearted persons. I go with John Becker. Shut toll gate.
11	Cold. North west wind. I go on turnpike. Boys hoe corn. Draw water for Mary Goldsmith to clean up with.
12	Very dry weather. I and Levi Cronk go to Willis's raising. Beecher go on turnpike. We hoe corn.
13	Very dry. We work in corn. I and Mother go to Greenville.
14	Dry. Boys work on buckwheat ground. I come from Greenville. Get 1 pr. boots of S. Baldwin. My wheel run off of my waggon.
15	Dry. I get my fish. Get horses shod. Levi Bronk sick. Beecher burn brush. Mrs. Pierce here, Old Ginny VanBergen here.
16	Fair. I and Wife go to meeting. Beecher take Mrs. Pierce off with my colt.
17	Fair morning. I go to McCarty's Mill, get plaster. Rain in afternoon. Boys clear up brush. Levi Cronk take Tobias Crumb's turkey holme.
18	Rainy. We make picket fence. Wife & Mrs. Pierce go to New Baltimore. I settle with Jacob W. Story.
19	Dry yet. Emeline Sweet, Deborah Holmes, Miss Tuttle here.
20	All day lay stone wall. Cate VanBergen here. North wind. Hang picket gate.
21	Rainy. **Old Brown kick me in hay press on my thigh**. I take Mrs. Pierce to Andrew VanSlyck's. Bring Marite back with me.
22	Rain all day. Get plow. **Burn chimney**. P. Seabridge here.
23	Fair. Wife go to Meeting. Cate VanBergen here. Wesley, Margarett, his wife, Miss Vela here. Andrew VanAntwerp here.
24	Fair. Get casting repaired. **Draw up Marite's furniture. Draw poles**.[30]
25	Fair. **Weevil destroys my wheat**. Beecher Plows. I & Levi make fence.
26	Fine shower, hot. Fix hay press. Beecher break my plow.
27	Fair. I go to Newburgh on **The Empire of Troy**. Very warm & showery.

---

30   The word "draw" here means to transport, usually by horse and wagon.

28 Fair. **I pay Lawyer Sherman $1118.03 on my Farm**. Get a piece of Sturgeon. Get colt shod. Beecher plow.

29 Fair. Beecher plow. Levi goes holme. Wife & Marite go a visiting.

30 Fair. I and Wife go to Meeting. I go to Wesley's. Cate VanBergen here.

July 1844

1   Fair. Press hay all day. Niles' horses break in my meadow.

2   Fair. I went to Athens. Wife go to Andrew VanSlyck's. Then we go to Flat Bush.

3   Fair. I & Levi Cronk go to work on turnpike. J. Cronk & Lady here.

4   I sow buckwheat. Draw manure. **Go on Island in afternoon. I find a swarm of bees on the Island. Mortica Brogue help me swarm them**. Wife go on Barren Island, attend picnic. Fair weather.

5   I sow buckwheat. Fair weather. Beecher draw wood. Cate Pierce, Miss Gay, Cate VanBergen, Lib Holmes here.

6   Fair. I get m waggon fixed. Lib VanBenthuyzen leaves here.

7   Dry. I go to Meeting. Hear Bloomer & Kissam. John Clement bring my bull holme.

8   Fair. **Go on journey to Vermont, so to White Mountains**.[31]

9   To Troy, Lansingburgh, Reid Hollow, Tom Kimmick Post office. Feed horse. Pittstown then to **Buskirk Bridge**.[32] Staid all night. Linch pin come out of waggon. Travel about 42miles.

10 Travel up Hoosic River, Cambridge Village. Then up the Batten Kill Creek. 14 miles before breakfast. Had good breakfast. Young married people live there. Then to Arlington. 7 miles. To Manchester, 8 miles bad road. Stop to temperance house. Poor picking. Fed horse, then to point, 1 mile. Then up the Green Mountain, a hill seven miles long. Stop and rest at toll gate. Get some spruce beer then to John Batchellor & McMillin's, Mark Batchellor, 8 miles.

11 Stay two nights. Then to Londonderry, small village. Two stores at the foot of two hills. Then to Simonsville, a mere tavern **with a Whig pole**[33] in front, between the mountains. Then to Chester, 20 miles, fed horse. Stop at stage house. Quite a large village, three taverns supported by staging (Winsor Co.)? Then to Williams River, then to North Springfield. Caught in a shower of rain. **Saw a Zanke**[34] **with cuts all over his head**. 8 miles on Black River. Staid all night at river tavern. Had a good supper.

13 Start early through Perkinsville then Weathersfield four corners through Gulf Road, 10 miles. This part of the route has been a very rough country to travel. To breakfast, handsome place, two stores, good roads, sandy & loamy soil. Take glass of Beer, a good breakfast. **Wife getting in better spirits**. Start again, **cross the Connecticut River New Hampshire toll**

---

[31] The original journal did not contain any information for the 9th to the 20th when Fletcher went to the White Mountains. We added the information using Fletcher's notes.

[32] Buskirk Bridge - wooden covered bridge over the Hoosic River, joining Renssalear and Washington Counties.

[33] Flagpole with symbol of the Whig party.

[34] Perhaps the word "Zanke" is misspelled and refers to "Zande," a member of a Central African people of mixed ethnic origin.

	bridge.[35] Up to Windsor Flats then to Lebanon. See eight horse team. Then to Hanover (Dartmouth College) then to Arlington Wales, one mile beyond line, which is a small handsome village with two temperance hotels, fifteen miles. Staid all night at Walises.
14	Then to Oxford, handsome village with numerous maple trees and county seats. Then to Piermont, small village. Haverhill, large village. Fed horse. See where the piazza broke down celebrating the Fourth of July. Then to Newbury, Vt. Then to North Haverhill, took dinner, 21 miles. To Bath, 9 miles, handsome village. North Bath, 2 miles, small place along the Ammonoosuc River. To Lisbon, 7 miles, fine village, to a river tavern. Staid all night.
15	Hard ride to Littleton, 5 miles, 4 small villages surrounded by hills and forests with a stream passing through the village. To Bethlehem, 5 miles. To breakfast. Put out my horse. Hired the landlord, Mr. Spoons, to take us to **Crawford's Tavern Notch House**[36] **in the Notch of the White mountains and the Willey House**,[37] where the great avalanche formerly was and destroyed nine of the family, 20 miles. Then up Mount Clinton, Mount Pleasant and to Mt. Washington,[38] 6 miles. Go back to Crawford's Tavern, 6 miles. Took supper. Go back to Bethlehem, 26 miles. Tired enough. Go to bed twelve o'clock at night. Sleep late next day.
16	Took breakfast. Started for the Franconia Notch. Very rough country. Long hills. **Stop at Notch House see profile**[39] at the head of the Merrimack River. Lake so cold that no fish can live in it. See the Kettle Flume, 14 miles. Have trout for dinner, heavy charges. Then down the river. Staid all night at Temperance House.
17	Then down the river to Plymouth new country, hilly, 2.5 miles. To Hebron, 8 miles, no village except a few houses by a pond rough country. To Canaan, 18 miles, fine village by a large pond. Then to Shaker Village, staid all night at private house, 12 miles, to Mr. Lengrant's house.

---

[35] We believe that this is the Cheshire covered bridge.

[36] The original Crawford House was built in 1825 and destroyed by fires in 1854 & 1858. The hotel was rebuilt in 1859 and became one of the major hotels in the White Mts., accommodating 400 people where city dwellers could escape the sweltering summer heat. It was closed in 1975, burned in 1977 and replaced by a lodge and educational center.

[37] The Willey House was built in 1793 or 1798 as a public house in Crawford Notch. In 1825 it became the homestead of Samuel Willey Jr. and his family. They operated it as an inn for travelers passing through the mountains. In August 1826 a violent storm occurred, and the Saco River began to rise in front of the house. The family apparently left the house to escape the flood only to be buried in a huge landslide. The house was left untouched being protected by a rock ledge on the hillside. The major slide followed two paths that flowed on either side of the house. The news of the tragedy became a national legend resulting in the publication of several poems and a ballad. A fictionalized story was written by Nathaniel Hawthorne entitled the "The Ambitious Ghost." The expression, "a case of the willies," evolved from the Willey tragedy.

[38] Mt. Washington-Highest peak in north eastern U.S. 6,288 ft. It is notorious for its erratic weather.

[39] Franconia Notch - elevation 1,950 ft. is a major mountain pass through the White Mountains of NH. The rough wagon route in the 1800s has evolved into interstate 93 and Route 3 (Franconia Notch Parkway). The area has become a state park and imaginative names denote many of the magnificent geological wonders. Their formations dating back thousands of years to the Ice Age when glacier melt and swirling waters bored deep into the granite rock. "The Old Man of the Mountain," an outcropping of mountain rock which resembled the profile of a man's head has long been a historical site. On May 3, 2003 after years of erosion, freezing/melting and traffic vibrations from Rt. 93, this geological treasure fell. To see this site as it used to be, and other majestic photos of the area go to the web site- Franconia Notch State Park.

18	**Took breakfast at private house among the Millerites**.[40] Took dinner at Mr. Lengrant's in Grantham. 12 miles to Newport. 9 miles to Claremont, fine village had to climb up and down hill for the two last days to Charleston, fine village, 10 miles. Staid all night. Fine village in a valley supported by [coach] staging. Some good land.
19	To Bellows Falls, 9 miles. Large village, quite a curiosity. A natural place for a bridge. 9 miles. Cross over in Vermont to Westminster, 4 miles, to breakfast. To Putney, 10 miles, small village. To Brattleboro, rough country, 10 miles, took dinner at Chandelor Lord's, good style. Then up to Blue Marlboro, 10 miles, all up hill to Middleton, 9 miles, to Bennington, 21 miles, fine village.
20	To Battleground, 6 miles, on Hoosic River. Hoosic Falls, 3 miles, fine village. To Troy, 20 miles, Holme, 21 miles.
21	Fair. I and Wife go to Meeting. Cate VanBergen, A. VanAntwerp here.
22	Fair. I work road. Get in two loads hay. Sell heifer to I. Gregory.
23	Fair morning, showery afternoon. Fix barn for hay. Mother Houghtaling and Mother Blaisdell here.
24	Fair & warm. **Boys mow & rake & bind**.[41] I draw in wheat.
25	Rain all day. Press hay. I get Old Brown shod.
27	Fair. **I go to Democratic Meeting to Schodack**. Boys work at wheat and rye. Go to Schodack in a Siene Boat. Row there.
28	Fair. Go to Meeting twice. A. VanAntwerp here in evening.
31	South wind, rainy. Boys make two swing gates. I go to river, get hooks to hang gates.

August 1844

1	Work hard all day. Clear wheat field. Uriah Willis here. Fair weather.
2	Fair. John Toben come here to work. I go to Albany. **Boys mow & cradle oats**.
3	Fair, south wind. Draw in 7 loads of hay. Wife visits Trego's.
4	Rainy morning. Clears off north wind. Uriah Willis & A. VanAntwerp here.
5	Fair day. Work on turnpike in forenoon. Rake and bind oats in afternoon. Levi draw wood.
6	Rainy day. Boys mow. Uriah Willis here & Elizabeth Holmes. I go to river.
7	Fair day. Boys mow & put up hay. I send a cow to New York.
8	Cloudy morning, but it clears off. **Get in 10 loads of hay**. Mrs. Holmes, Mary Holmes here, visiting.

---

[40] The Millerites were followers of William Miller, who in 1831, publicly announced that the Second Coming of Jesus Christ would occur sometime in 1843/1844. This group was the forerunner of the present Seventh Day Adventists and Adventist Christian Churches.

[41] According to "A Short History of the Horse-Drawn Mower", by L. Miller, the horse-drawn mower started to appear around 1845. The horse-drawn hay rake came later. Fletcher must have been using the latest equipment available at the time. Gathering hay without this equipment was a labor intensive and slow process as hay was cut using scythes and put into haycocks using pitchforks.

9   Heavy south wind. Boys mow. I and Wife go to Millbank's. **The Whigs raise their liberty pole.**[42]

10 Fair. **Whig meeting goes off.** Mrs. Fredenburgh, Miss VerPlank, Miss Oberbaugh, Cate Fredenburgh her visit. Get in 2 loads hay.

11 Fine day. I and Wife go to see Martin Andrews - he is sick. Then to Meeting twice. Uriah Willis here.

12 Fair. Boys mow. Mr. Burdeck & Lady & Uriah Willis here.

13 Fair, south wind. Work hard in hay; work late in evening. Mother here.

14 Rainy forenoon. Get in one load hay. Boys help J.W. Story in afternoon.

15 Fair. I and wife go to John Bushant's. Mrs. Story here. **A woman peddler stopped by here**. Concert this evening.

16 Fair, south wind. Get horse shod. Go to picnic on Barren Island.

17 **Fair. Work on Fallow in forenoon.**[43] I and Beecher attend political meeting in afternoon. **The Old Hunkers**[44] **get 2/3 majority**.

18 Pleasant & warm. We go to Meeting. A. VanAntwerp & Uriah Willis here.

19 Cloudy. **Go to Catskill Mountain House**[45] **with Andrew VanAntwerp, Uriah Willis, Lib Holmes, Marite & Wife**. Some rain. Take dinner to Keith's Tavern in Cairo. Then go on to the Mountain House.

20 Fair. Go to Moses Rock, to the pond, the falls, to South Mountain.

Old Catskill Mountain House

21 Fair. Take breakfast at Osborn's. Stop to Athens, call at Nichols', take dinner at Coxsackie, call at A. VanSlyck's, to Martin VanBergen's. Have pleasant ride.

22 Rainy. I put my bull on the Island. Uriah Willis here.

23 Rainy. Make bridge. Draw stone. Go to river. Get paper & watermark (sp).

24 Fair. I & J.M. Bogardus go a hunting. Boys draw wood, gravel. Peter Cook work at my stoop.

25 Rainy. I go to Meeting. Uriah Willis here to dinner. I take Marite & Mother Houghtaling to Flat Bush. Come holme in evening.

---

42 The Whig Party was active from 1834 to 1854. They were united in their dislike of Andrew Jackson. By 1854, most northern Whigs joined with the newly formed Republican Party.

43 Fields were left unplanted (fallow) for a period of time to allow the soil to regain its fertility.

44 The Old Hunkers were a relatively pro-government faction of the Democratic Party. They were opposed by the Barnburners, so named because it was said they would burn down a barn to get rid of a rat infestation. Martin VanBuren was a prominent Barnburner. The Free Soilers were a short-lived political party that opposed the expansion of slavery. They later merged with the Republican Party.

45 The Catskill Mountain House, which opened in 1824, was a famous hotel in the Catskill Mountains overlooking the Hudson River valley. Much has been written about it and its famous guests, including presidents Grant, Arthur and T. Roosevelt.

26 Fair. Sell heifer to Ira Gregory. Settle with Lawton. Beecher plow, Levi Cronk burn brush. I & Wife go to R. Styles.

27 Fair. Break four plow shares by plowing in buckwheat. Draw wood off my fallow.

28 Beecher plow. Levi draw manure in forenoon. I go to Kimmey's, get seed rye. Wife go a visiting.

29 Beecher plow. I and Levi draw manure. Weather fine. Mrs. Clement visit here. Lib Holmes here in evening.

30 Fair. Sow 2½ bushels of rye. Burn brush. Levi draw manure. I get horses shod.

31 Fair. Sow 2½ bushels of wheat. Levi draw manure. I and Wife go to J.W. Story's. I take gun along, go a hunting.

September 1844

1 Fair. Go to Meeting twice. **Wife taken sick**.

2 Fair. Boys train. **An Irishman hung himself in Sherwood's barn**. I clear off my fallow.

3 Fair, north wind. A. VanAntwerp go after Marite to attend party at Trego's. Have a great time.

4 Fair. I and Br[other] Wesley go to John Bushant's. Beecher plow, Levi draw manure. Marite attend picnic.

5 Fair. Beecher spread manure. I and Levi work on Turnpike. **Silas Wright get the nomination for Governor.**[46]

6 Fair. Sow wheat & rye, I go to Henry Burhaus in afternoon. Get plums to Jacob Story's.

7 Fair. I go to Flat Bush, get peaches & apples. **Go to Baker's to Whig Nomination**. Br[other] Wesley loses the nomination by 3 votes. Leonard Litchfield gets nomination.

8 Fair. I go to Meeting. Mother come back from Quarterly Meeting.

9 Fair. I go out to Wm. Tuttle's. Beecher Holmes' horse run away last evening. He was hurt. Jane Rea get her arm broke. Bring Wm. Lawton's horse holme. Marite & Mary Goldsmith go to Baltimore. Levi draw manure.

10 Fair. I go to Greenville.

11 Fair. I return holme. Get my shoes of Silas Baldwin.

12 Fair. I work on turnpike. Levi draw wood. Newman Finch & Wife here, come in evening.

13 Fair. I attend to Turnpike. Then go to Baltimore to Lawsuit. Pay C. Houghtaling for cattle bought at Vendue.

14 Fair. **I go to Indian Fields to political meeting. Hear John VanBuren**[47] **speak, Mr. Lacy and two other speakers**. They get up a team of 16 yoke of oxen and some others 4 horse teams. **Mother moves on the hill this morning**. I draw one load before I leave for holme.

15 Fair. I and Wife goes to Flat Bush, take dinner to Br[other] Andrew's.

---

46 Silas Wright, a Democrat, defeated Millard Fillmore (Whig) in November 1844 to become the 16th Governor of New York. He was a lawyer from Canton, NY.

47 John VanBuren was the son of Martin VanBuren, the 8th President of the United States. He served as Attorney General of New York in 1845.

16 Fair. Go on Turnpike. Levi draws wood. Mother here.

17 Fair. I attend to Turnpike. Get horse shod. Levi goes after Mother Houghtaling. Elida VanSlyck here. **Peleg Sherman's Boy gets drowned, died today**. Andrew VanAntwerp here.

18 Fair. **I & Wife, Marite & Elida VanSlyck start for New York today on board of Sloop Myrtle**. First night got as far as Esopus Meadows.

19 Fair. Go ashore to Poughkeepsie. All passengers go ashore at Hampton. Get apples and plums.

20 Fair. **We all went ashore at West Point. Group to Fort Putnam came back to see the Cadets parade**.

21 Fair. Sail along slowly. **Go ashore at Fort Lee**. Went up to see the old Fort on breast works. Then went on to New York. Take up board with Charles Hallock. Went to museum in evening, see Negroes dance.

Bowery Theater

22 Fair. Went to St. Patrick's Church & to Methodist Church twice.

23 Went to **Bowery Theater**[48] see play of **Putnam, The Iron Son of '76**.[49]

24 Fair. Do up trading. Go aboard two packet ships with John McMichael and the North Carolina Man of War. Then go to **Croton Water Works**.[50] See Cricket Game, then to Hallock's. Very tired.

25 Rain all day. **We go to Italian opera. Yankee Hill play there.**

26 **Get ready and come holme on North America. Start at 5 pm, get to New Baltimore 3 o'clock am. Walk holme.**

27 I sow rye. Get sugar and flour from sloop. Mother here. Get fresh [?] of Ira Gregory. Applecut to Wm. Sherwood's to night.

28 I sow grass seed in afternoon. I and Wife go to Seth Hawley's, come holme in evening.

30 Fair. I fix grindstone. Mrs. Willis & Harriet here. **Democratic Meeting at Wm. Lawton's**. **Whig Meeting at Aaron Houghtaling's**. Peter Cronk come here to work for me.

---

48 The Bowery Theater opened in 1826 as The New York Theater. It burned in 1828 and was rebuilt as the Bowery Theater. It burned down 4 times in 17 years, a fire in 1929 destroyed it for good.

49 Putnam, the Iron Son of 76 is an 1844 American play by Nathaniel Bannister. The play is about the Revolutionary War hero Israel Putnam. Starting in August 1844, it played for 78 consecutive nights in the Bowery Theater, an astounding success for its time.

50 The Old Croton Aqueduct was a large water distribution system constructed for New York City between 1837 and 1842. It carried water by gravity 41 miles from the Croton River in Westchester County to Reservoirs is Manhattan. It was built because local water resources had become too polluted for the growing population of the city.

October 1844

1   Fair. Get out timber. Get horse shod. Fix my waggon. Get out stone, draw stone. General training today.

2   Fair. **I harness in Old Black. With Robert Pulver, go to Albany to Map Meeting. Hear Michael Hoffman & Bob Tyler & Gen Dix, Mr. Edmunds, Mr. Page Sickels & Kilbourne.**[51]

3   Showry. I and Wife go to A. J. VanSlyck's. He gave wife a box of Honey. A lecture in Methodist church this evening. I took Uncle Abram Holmes.

4   Showry. Buy molasses of John Keller. Elias Dewey & Lady here. I pay Briggs money for John Cronk.

5   Fair. Old Jinny VanBergen came. **Raise my milk room**. Finish digging potatoes. Put up my hogs.

6   Cold, cloudy day. Collins Vielie & Wesley here. Elizabeth Lawton & H. Holmes, we go to Meeting.

7   Cloudy. I draw in corn. Go to School Meeting at night.

8   Fair. I **thresh buckwheat**.[52] Mr. Edward Collins & his Father here.

9   Fair. Beecher go to work. He and Wife go to Flat Bush after apples. I and Levi finish buckwheat.

11   Fair. I go to Greenville. **Take dinner to Uncle Joseph Blaisdell's.**[53]

12   Fair. I pay John Williamson & James Waldron. Get apples.

13   Fair. I, Wife, Doctor & Marite go to Baltimore to Meeting. Cornell preach.

14   Stormy. Thresh oats with machine. **Elias Millbanks, Black Dinah come here to work**.

15   Stormy. Finish threshing. **Whig Meeting at Catskill**. Abram VanBenthuyzen attend.

16   Fair. Go to mill. Put away grain. John Cronk & Wife here, stay all night.

17   Rainy. Boys split slats, make fence in Big Meadow. Husk corn.

18   Rainy. Make Corn Crib. Go to the Hollow. Baltis VanSlyck's party tonight.

19   Pleasant. Beecher go after lumber. **Democratic Meeting in Dutch Church**. Mr. Foster and Doct. Nott speak.

20   I go to Albany. I and Wife go to Wesley's.

21   Fair. I go to Albany. Boys get slats & draw wood to Mary Goldsmith's.

22   Cloudy. **I and Wife go to Funeral of Andrew Houghtaling. His Wife died day before yesterday**.

23   Fair. I work at hay press. Boys draw wood, finish husk corn.

---

[51] Michael Hoffman was a member of the NY State Assembly. Bob Tyler was the eldest son of President John Tyler. General John Dix was a Jacksonian Democrat who served as adjutant general and secretary of state of NY.

[52] Threshing is the process used to separate grain from the stalks.

[53] Joseph Blaisdell was Levi Blaisdell's brother.

24   I work at hay press. Raise Mother's stoop. J. Story bring potatoes.

25   Fair. Press hay in forenoon. Make fence in afternoon.

26   Fair. Make fence. **I and Peter VanAntwerp go to Baltimore, hear Jonas Shear and Frank Wright debate. Hear Mr. King speak.**

27   Cloudy morning. **I and Wife go to Emeline Sweet's Wedding. She marries C. R. Lendder** (sp). Kissam marry them. Then ride to Baltimore.

28   Rainy. Press hay. P.J. Groat here. J.W. Story bring me corn, one load.

29   Rain all day. We press hay. Albert Jackson here.

30   Fair. Wife go to Flat Bush. Press hay. P. Cook left off work here. **Ann Houghtaling married.**

31   Fair, cold north wind. Press hay. **Wife go to Harriet's quilting**.

November 1844

1   Fair. Press hay. **Whig Meeting. H. G. Wheaton and two others speak. Make out but little**. Wife go to Henry Niles.

2   Fair. Mend hay press. Press hay. Mother sick. John Cronk here.

3   Fair. I and Wife go to Meeting. Wesley, Margarett & J. VanAntwerp here.

4   Rainy in afternoon. Boys get out slats, press hay. I go out on Turnpike.

5   Fair. **Election. I attend. Get 22 Democratic majority**. Boys press hay.

6   Fair. Lay stone wall. Get horses shod. Draw 22 bushels of lime from Jerimiah Springstead.

7   Fair. Draw, press hay. **Get cattle of the Island**.

8   Fair. Boys lay wall. I draw lime & go to mill. Go to river.

9   Fair. I draw two loads of lime. Boys lay wall. **I pay off A.N. Briggs**.[54] Buy hoop poles of P. Groat. **Go to Singing School**.

10   Fair, south wind. I and Wife go to Meeting. Wesley, Lib Holmes, Mrs. Scudder (sp) here. U.B. Willis here. Mary Holmes has a young daughter.

11   Rainy, thunder & lightning. I and Beecher draw manure. I go to river.

12   Rainy. Beecher draw manure. **I and Levi make fence between me & Wesley**.

13   Rainy morning. Fix hay press. Make fence. Clears off cold.

14   Fair. Make fence. I fix gutter, draw manure, fix hay press, draw stone, lay wall, buy half a pig.

15   Fair. Work on the road. J.W. Story press hay here.

16   Fair. Work on the road. Mother Houghtaling & Marite come here. Abram VanBenthuyzen here and Mother.

17   Fair, south wind. We all go to Meeting. Doct. VanAntwerp here.

18   Cloudy, north wind. I go on Turnpike. **Mary Goldsmith has a young son and name him Fletcher Goldsmith**.

---

54   Albert Newton Briggs was our 2nd Great Grandfather.

19 Fair. **I go to river get my returns for hay. Attend as Juryman in Lawsuit of N. Carman about a yoke of oxen**.

20 Fair. I go to Athens. Stop at Coxsackie. Sell Old Brown to Martin VanBergen. Almira VanBergen & Cate Houghtaling here.

21 Fair. Wife & Marite go to Albany. Henry VanBergen take away Old Brown. I buy me two hats. John Cronk here.

22 Fair. Levi draw manure. Beecher fix trees. I get colt shod. Martin VanBergen pay for Old Brown.

23 Rainy. Mrs. Scudder here. Levi draw manure from Turnpike. Beecher work in garden. I pay off Peter Groat.

24 Cold, north wind. I go to Meeting. Bronk VerPlank, Martin Andrews take tea here. Doct VanAntwerp here.

25 Cold, north wind. I go to river. Levi draw manure. Beecher work at holme. I kill my beef, fix hay press. Harriet here.

26 Cold, north wind. I go to river. Levi draw manure. Beecher and I work around the house. I buy 15 bushels corn.

27 Cold, north wind. Levi draw wood. Beecher work on the road.

28 Snow all day. I and Levi draw wood. I settle with Dennis Toban. I kill chickens.

29 Cloudy. **Sloops stop going**. I take Elmira VanBergen to Charlotte Houghtaling's.

30 Cloudy, south wind. Boys draw wood. I get horse shod. Nicholas Lantham here. Wife go to Mary Goldsmith's.

December 1844

2 Fair. I and wife go to Greenville. Stay all night at Neuman Finch's.

3 Fair. Go to Andrew Fancher's. Get boots to Baldwin's. Get ½ lb. nuts to J. G. Williamson. Get turnips, (?) cider. **Coming holme horse run down the hill at Stephensville.**[55] **Wife tumble out. I run horse against fence. Horse stop**.

4 Rainy day. **Attend Cornelius Desmond's (sp) Funeral in Dutch church**. Beecher cuts wood. I boil beef's feet.

5 Fair. I go to river. Mason up cellar door. Go to P. Seabridge's in evening.

6 **Lowry**[56] & rainy. Sylvester Nichols here. Beecher help J.W. Story press hay.

7 South wind, rainy. Put Capen (sp) in hay press. Very muddy.

8 Cold, north wind freeze hands. **Two sloops, Myrtle and the Superior, come here yesterday**.

9 Cold, south wind. I buy Mother's sheep. Pay her 25 dollars for them. Press & draw hay.

10 Fair, wind change to the north. Beecher press hay. **[Sloop] Superior leave for New York**.

---

55 Stephensville is now called Alcove.
56 Fletcher uses the word "Lowry" often in his weather reports. Given its context, we assume it means an unpleasant day.

11 Fair, north wind. Beecher press hay. Wife & Mrs. Trego go to John Bailey's. I go take tea, stop at A.E. Willis's.

12 Fair. Put in window glass. Beecher cut wood. **River tight as a jug. Stages run**. Cold weather.

13 Fair. Beecher go to Greenville. I go to Niles, get turkey. Shoot Peter Groats gun.

14 Snowy. I & Dennis Toban go to look at manure. Pile wood. Calvin Carhart call here.

15 Fair. Beecher come from Greenville yesterday; broke down waggon. Borrow another of Daniel Miller. All go to meeting.

16 Fair, north wind. I kill hogs. **Make road down to the creek to get muck**.[57]

17 Cut up my hogs. Beecher go to Greenville.

18 Colder. Andrew Houghtaling here. **I take Mother to Gilbert Cronk's wedding at Hugh Crumb's**. Stay to J.W. Story's.

19 Fair. **I take a skate to Island**. Salt my hogs. Beecher cut wood.

20 Clear & cold. I bring my calf from the Island. Eli Cooper help; he fell in river.

21 South wind, very cold. I go to shooting match. Shoot twice. Calvin Carhart call here.

22 South wind, warmer. Go to Meeting twice. Wesley here.

23 South wind, heavy rain all day and night. I settle with Wm. C. Lawton & J.W. Story.

24 Colder, north wind. I go to Kimmey's Mill; bring my rye from J.W. Story's. A ball at Wm. Lawton's tonight.

25 Fair, south wind. I go to Schodack. I, Wife, Doct. & Marite go to A. Witbeck's.

26 Harriet here. I, Wife & Marite go to Conrad Houghtaling's on a visit. Very dark & muddy.

27 Snowy. Get horse shod. **Celebrate Harriet's Birthday**.[58] Fix hog pen. Attend singing party at Willis's.

28 Cold and pleasant. Finish stable. I go to river. Party at Doct. Fredenburgh's last night.

29 Cold. I go to Meeting twice. Doct. VanAntwerp here.

30 South wind, warmer. Oil my harness. Mr. Matson here. John Cronk & Levi Teneyck, Schoonmaker, Mr. Bloomer here.

31 North wind. I and Jacob Story go to Coxsackie & to Greenville. Beecher cut straw.

January 1845

1 Very pleasant. James A. Witbeck, William Whitman, Jesper Houghtaling here.

2 I settle with Peter VanBuren, Andrew Houghtaling. We all go to A.N. Briggs to a singing party.

3 South wind and cold. I and Andrew go around. I settle with Peter Seabridge.

4 North wind, pleasant. I get pony shod. Fix my well.

---

57 Fletcher often refers to drawing "muck." It usually means the mixture of hay and manure that comes from cleaning out horse stalls etc. But it might have had a different meaning in 1845.

58 Harriet Blaisdell Willis was Fletcher's sister. She would have been 25 years old.

5   North wind, pleasant. I go to Meeting twice. Fine skating on the river.

6   Colder. Peter Brandow pays me $80. **Mr. G. Nichols here & I settle up turnpike debts**. Divide Brandow's rent with Wesley Blaisdell.

7   Three inches of snow. Misty day. I get Big horse shod all around. I pay off Dennis Toban.

8   Fair, warm weather. I go to river. Go to J.W. Story's.

9   Snow a little. I and Wife go to Flat Bush and Woolsey Cary go Martin VanBergen's. Cary bargain for hire Flat Bush Farm.

10 Fine day. I go the river. **Get trace fixed**.[59] Get a pig of William Sherman.

11 Cloudy. Draw muck in forenoon. Go to trotting race in afternoon. The Millbank's mare beat.

12 Fair. I and Wife go to Wesley's. **Mother is sick**. Meeting in the eve.

13 Snow all day 4 in. I go to river. **Mother still sick**. Beecher make a hand sleigh.

14 Fair. **Wife taking care of Mother**. I work at corn crib. I go to river. William Hoose here, pay his rent.

15 Snow in morning. I fix well, go to river. Stephen Witbeck, Mary Goldsmith here on a visit.

16 Rain all day. Beecher make hand sley for Kineer (sp) hill. Levi Lawson horse that got his leg broke and skinned it.[60]

17 Rain all day. I finish corncrib. Beecher finish hand sley. A.E. Willis here.

18 Fair, cold. I go to Coxsackie, going bad. Quarterly Meeting today.

19 Fair and cold. I and Family go to Quarterly Meeting.

20 Fair. **I and Marite go to Albany. A team ran away with a load of ice, knocked my pony over, tip over my sley, came near to killing us both.**

21 Snow all day. I go to river. **Arbitration of Verplank heirs**. I get one pound of tea.

22 Fine sleying. Snow 6 inches deep. Henry Keeler & Lady, Mrs. Baker, Clarisa Houghtaling, George Wolf, Mary Holmes here.

23 Fair day. Go to river. **Go to square**.[61] Go with the Boys draw muck.

24 Rainy day. I go to Martin VanBergen's. **Get Uncle Abram to sign deed for Flat Bush Farm and got it acknowledged**.

25 Rainy day. I go to river. Get a coat of M.G. Bogardus. Buy grindstone of A.N. Briggs. Mr. Jessup here.

26 Fair and cold. A.E. Willis is sick. Little Ben here. We all go to Meeting.

27 Pleasant. I go to Greenville get rents of Edget. Stephens & Roe. Stay at Fancher's all night.

28 Warm. Get logs in sawmill. Put my horse at Henry Witbeck's. Get my boots. Stay all night to Andrew Fancher's.

---

[59] The trace is one or more straps that connect a horse-drawn carriage to the horse.

[60] We can't make sense of this.

[61] Correspondence with Joe Boehlke, President of the Ravena-Coeymans Historical Society, identified the location of the square to be in Coeymans Junction (current day Ravena) near the location of the Congregational Church. This was also near the location of the original Dutch Reformed Church.

29 Colder. I stop at Newman Finch's, get my beehive. Call at Charles Seabridge's at Woolsey Cary's.

30 Colder. Write two letters. Andrew Houghtaling here. Mr. Dewy here.

31 Colder. I pay Willis all his share of Dewy's note. I and Wife go to Milbank's. I bring holme mare from J. Story's.

February 1845

1 Colder. I pay off Johnson & Colvin & John VanDenburgh. Jacob W. Story take my cow and pony holme.

2 Cold; as ever. Judge Nichols pay me off. Go to Meeting twice.

3 Cold yet. Mother here. Beecher go to Greenville. I chop wood.

4 Snow all day. Beecher come from Greenville. Blow hard. I go to river.

5 Snow and blow all day. Abram Sherwood here & Wesley here. Bring my papers.

6 Cold, 8 inches snow. I go to river. **Start to go to Kimmey's, horses fell down in the creek, cut them bad**.

7 Warmer. Shovel snow. Go to river. Willis & Harriet here. Barent Mull pay me off.

8 I buy a **hogshead**[62] of R&J Lawton. Go to Sherwood's, take a ride on river.

9 Cold & pleasant. A whole load from Martin G. VanBergen's here. Bronk Witbeck here. Doct. VanAntwerp here.

10 Fair. I go to Kimmey's Mill, to Elias Millbank's. Mrs. Briggs, Mrs. Trego here.

11 Pleasant. I go to river, get a piece of venison. John Sickler here.

12 Rainy morning, clear in afternoon. I go to Flat Bush, to Mother Houghtaling's.

13 Cold. I go to river. **I, Wife & Elida VanSlyck go to Bloomer's Donation**.[63]

14 Cold. **Make ready go on a general sley ride to Kinderhook to Strueheim's (sp). Have a fine time. Capsize coming holme**.

15 Warmer. I and J.W. Story go to river. Peter VanBergen's Family spend the evening. Rainy.

16 Rainy morning. Martin VanSlyck here. Visitors go holme.

17 Warm, north wind. I go to Kimmey's, get corn & buckwheat. Wife go to Mother's.

18 Warm. I go to Kimmey's Mill. Get a lot of horse feed ground. Levi Cronk here.

19 Warm. I make a feed box. John Bushants & Lady here. Have a singing party in the evening.

20 Warm, south wind. Get a tooth pulled. Get a new broom. Get cheese. Newman Finch & Lady here.

21 Very warm day. I put latch on gate. Go to river. Wife go to John Cronk's.

22 Warm, south wind. I go to woods. I have a bad cold. Drain off barnyard. Mother here.

23 Rainy south wind, very muddy. Wesley & Doct. VanAntwerp here.

---

[62] Hogshead (Hhd.) is a large cask of liquid.
[63] A Donation is a charitable contribution.

24 Very pleasant and warm. They catch 32 (?). Bluebirds make their appearance. I go to river.

25 Warm. **Channel in the river all clear of ice. Steamboat up yesterday.** I get black mare shod.

26 Warm. I got try to catch fish. Steamboat go down.

27 Warm, dry walking. I get 1-bushel clover seed. Pay off Bible man. **Sign contract for Sloop Myrtle.**

28 Some colder, north wind. **I buy sloop Revenue for 2500 dollars.** Go to the woods. Wife go to Henry Niles on a visit.

March 1845

1 South wind cold. Beecher go to Coxsackie. I attend sap trees. Wife go to Widow Houghtaling's.

2 South wind. All go to Meeting. Doct. VanAntwerp & Jesper Houghtaling here. I get sap.

3 Rain in morning. I go to river. Get out timber in afternoon. **Load Sloop Revenue today**.

4[64] Fair. Finish getting out timber. I go to Greenville. Enquire relative to Uncle Joseph Blaisdell's estate.

5 Rainy. I go to Edward Collins, so to Gayhead, then to Newman Finch's.

6 Fair. I go to Coxsackie to Edwin Hubbell's, to Samuel King's, to Woolsey Cary's, then holme. Very muddy ride.

7 **I get my Bill of Sale for Sloop Revenue.**[65] Fine warm day. Go to Wesley's to the woods. Wife go to Betsy Verplank's.

8 Commence rain at noon. Wife go to Martin Holmes. Marite go to Aaron Houghtaling's. I take them with waggon. I am not well.

9 Rain & snow, clears off, north wind. I and Wife go to Wesley's party to Aaron Houghtaling's.

10 Snow and rain all day. Bronk Verplank & Martin Andrews here. I go to river, get my papers.

11 Snow all day. **I take Emetic, am quite sick**.[66] Andrew VanAntwerp here. Beecher gear up waggon & clear out barn.

12 Fair, sun shines all day. **I fix cook house**. Abram Teal pay me. I go to river twice. Get clams & oysters.

13 Fair. I go to Vendue to Mr. Waldron's. Mr. Vandenburgh here. Mother here. A very muddy time.

14 Snow all day hard. Beecher get cut pickets. I stay in house.

---

[64] James Polk, a dark horse Democrat from Tennessee, was inaugurated as the 11th president of the United States. He was a highly regarded president and is credited with expanding the U.S. territory to include most of the South Western states following the Mexican American war.

[65] Fletcher doesn't provide a description of his sloop. But most Hudson River sloops of that era were between 60 – 80 feet long and were used to transport goods to New York City. The price in 2020 dollars is about $85,000.

[66] Emetic drugs were used to induce vomiting.

15 Fair. I go to river. Get chalk line. Get out pickets. Mary Goldsmith here. Lawton's barge come.

16 Colder. I go to Meeting. Mother Houghtaling come back. Margarett Blaisdell & son Edward here.

17 Fair. I get mare shod. Draw out timber. **Joseph Cronk here, he makes it known that John Cronk's house is burnt.**

18 Fair morning, snow in afternoon. I get apples to John Bronk's. I go to river. Charles Seabridge pay me his rent.

19 Fair. **Mary Goldsmith move her things here. I go to river, Revenue come.** Quite cold. **Barbary Carhart died.**

20 Fair. I take Mary Goldsmith to Albany, get 1 keg of nails. See Amos Dean about my note. Roads very bad.

21 Cold, heavy north wind. I go to river twice. Get harness fixed. Jane Stanton, Mrs. Clement here.

22 Cold. **I get my waggon fixed to the square.** Get horse shod to William Carroll's. Elizabeth Holmes & Mary Lawton here.

23 South wind. Go to Meeting. Hear Rev. Mr. Kissam. **Aleas Steenburgh died last night**.

24 Fair, north wind. I go to river. Start to go to Armstrong Vendue. Meet John Bronk, come back.

25 North wind. I am sick all day and night. Beecher & Jacob W. Story go over the mountain after trees.

26 South wind. **Capt. Sherwood here.** Mr. Cary here. I go to river, get medicine of Doctor. **Abram Hazzard's Wife removed here & buried**.

27 Fair. Beecher gets back with trees. I and Willis go to Barley Roe's Vendue. I buy two cows.

28 Fair. **Nomination meeting today. I get nomination for Assessor.** Beecher & Dennis Toben set out trees.

29 Fair. I go to Peter Teneyck's Vendue. Buy two cows & one waggon. John Bushants & John Cronk here.

30 Very warm. Go to Meeting twice. Doct. VanAntwerp here Stephen Houghtaling & Lady here.

31 Fair. **I go to Albany with sloop.** Fetch holme shingles. Joel (?) here, Ezekiel Powel here.

April 1845

1 Squally & rainy. Come back from Albany. Go on Turnpike.

2 Cold, north wind. **I started for New Jersey on board of Sloop Myrtle. Get down as far as Athens, tore sails.**

3 Cold southwest winds. **Sailed down to Highlands. Have there a very Southeast wind & heavy sea. Run back 8 miles**.

4 Cold northwest wind. **Went through the Highlands. Get as far as Hoboken; cast anchor**.

5	Cold southwest wind. I go to Newark with Railroad. Go to Sendders (sp) and come back to New York.
6	Snowy. I go to hear Rev. Mr. Rodgers preach in the morning and to the Odd Fellows in the evening at Duval's Funeral.
7	Fair. I buy wife gold watch. Come holme with Utica. **Steamboat Swallow run on rock at Athens and burnt up.**[67]
8	Fair. Get holme and go to Town Meeting. Mrs. Fredenburgh & Betsey Verplank here visiting.
9	Cold. North wind. **Grandma [Maria] Houghtaling died.** I and Mother Houghtaling, Aunt Gitty go to see her at Garrett Houghtaling's.
10	Fair. I plow ½ day. **Spaulding's Circus here**. William Wilkins & Lady here, spend the day.
11	Cold. Grandma buried. We go to Funeral. I and Mother go to Robert Martin's (sp). Beecher go to Greenville.
12	Cold yet. Make garden; put in onions. **Get my coat from Sloop Revenue**. James Tefft here.
13	More pleasant till 2 o'clock, then north wind blow hard as ever. **I go to Negro Meeting.**[68]
14	Fair, north wind. Plow garden. Lay foundation of barn. Get ½ bu. potatoes of Henry Niles. Draw timber for barn,
15	High wind, fair. **I go to Albany get out Sloop's papers**. Beecher plow. I get 1 bu. Timothy seed.
16	Rain at night. I get horse shod. Finish sowing oats in Big Meadow.
17	Rainy. Get horse shod. Make gate for Big Meadow. Sow grass seed.
18	Lowry. Raise barn, side it up. Thunder in evening. Fix Wesley's fence. I get 1 string of suckers.
21	Fair. I finish carpenter work at Barn. Trim apple trees. Write to Nathan Stephens.
22	Very pleasant. I put my cattle on the Island. Wife and Mother Houghtaling go to Clarisa Houghtaling's. I graft fruit trees.
23	Very pleasant. I cut brush. Beecher plow. I draw timber for Barn. Tides are very high. South wind.
24	Fair, south wind. I go to Baltimore, take Cornelius Brower to Flat Bush. Graft orchard. I get ½ bushel apples to J. Hawley's.

The wreck of Steamboat Swallow

---

[67] This was an era of fierce competition between steamers that often raced each other to reach the landing to get the waiting passengers. An article published 16 July 2016 by Andrew Amelinckx describes the wreck of the Swallow. On the day of the wreck, 3 steamboats left Albany at the same time in route to New York City. At about 8 pm, as the 3 steamers neared Athens, the Swallow was in the lead. The night was dark and overcast and there may have been a snow squall that further reduced visibility. In any event, the Swallow piled into the rocks of Doper's Island. Her wooden hull nearly broke in two, a fire broke out and she immediately began to sink. It was estimated that 15 of the roughly 250 passengers lost their lives. Doper's Island was renamed "Swallow Rock."

[68] Fletcher visited many churches in the area.

25   Rainy forenoon. I go to Woolsey Cary's. Beecher come from Greenville. Catch first shad yesterday.

28   Fair, south wind. Finish grafting to Flat Bush. **Set 1900 grafts in four days**.

May 1845

1   Fair, south wind. Andrew Fancher & Wife here. Pay his rent. I pay R & J Lawton 1000 dollars. Boys draw lime.

2   Fair. Finish sowing oats. I go to river, get 25 shad, get salt.

3   Fair. I plow potato ground in Big Meadow. Andrew Houghtaling here, pay his interest. Wife and Mother go to Trego's.

4   Fair. I and all hands go to Meeting. A lot of company call here this afternoon.

5   Fair. I go to river. Beecher draw manure. I burn brush in afternoon. Wife goes to Albany.

6   Fair. I go to Albany, get dividend. Get peas. Henry Regua here after money.

7   Commence to rain 5 o'clock in pm. I fix barn in morning. Get my hair cut. Get out stone.

8   Very cold. Plow all day. Rain last evening. Henry Regua pay me his note. Mrs. Mull & Mother spend the day here.

9   Fair. I go to Flat Bush, to Coxsackie. Beecher plow. I took dinner to Edwin Hubbell's.

10 Fair weather, hard frost, foggy. Finish plowing. Make bridges, sow peas.

11 Beecher & his Mother go to Peter Tuttle's with my horse. Fair weather. Moses Cary here. I let him have 100 dollars. Aunt Gitty & Cate, her daughter, here on visit.

12 Very warm. I plant corn in forenoon. Go to river. I buy a yoke of oxen of Henry Rarick for fifty dollars.

13 Very warm, fair. Finish plant corn & potatoes. Very tired.

14 Fair. Dennis Toben plow garden in morning. Make fence the rest of the day. South wind, turns north afternoon & shower.

15 Warm morning, south wind, at noon begins to rain turns north. Make fence. Clear out waggon house. Fill in building. Mother here.

16 Fair. I get a jug of sap molasses from John Fetter. Make fence. Send turnpike cart to Judge Nichols.

17 Rain slowly. I go to Coxsackie. Take mortgage of Andrew Houghtaling. Take dinner at his house. I go to river.

19 Fair. Henry Seaburgh help me make fence in forenoon around my grain. Elias Millbanks here, take tea. Paint kitchen floor.

20 Showry. Jacob Story draw away his hay. I and Beecher make fence. I get a letter from Judge Nickolas. Get 30 herring.

21 Fair. I go to Flat Bush. Wife visit to Barent VanSlyck's.

22 Fair morning, rain in afternoon. I go to Flat Bush with 4 cows.

23 Fair. I take John Gibbens to Flat Bush. Mother Houghtaling, Martin G. VanBergen here. Beecher joined issue in his Lawsuit.

24 Fair. I go to Flat Bush & Coxsackie. Draw 5 sticks of timber. Bring holme Marite's bed.

25 Cold, north wind. Go to Meeting twice. Get a letter from N.L. Soop (sp).

26 Fair. Get shad, work on turnpike, get horse shod.

27 Fair. I & Beecher make fence and put up scarecrows.

28 Fair. I go to Flat Bush with Mother Houghtaling & Aunt Gitty. I go to river, get fish.

29 Showry, colder. I go to Albany. Get cheese tub, butter, pail, churn band, clover seed.

30 Fair. Dig out stone. **I go to river, get Sturgeon.**[69] Beecher go to Greenville. Hard frost freeze beans.

31 Fair. Doct. Spoor & Lady here. Take dinner. W. Cary here. I go to J.B. Shear's to hear James Chapman's trial with Mahetable Blodget.

June 1845

1 Fair. I go to Meeting. Mr. Orr & Lady here. Doct. VanAntwerp here. Willis here. Wife go to meeting in evening.

2 Fair. I and Wife go to Schodack to Mr. Matson's. Have a good time. **Deed my island to Matson**. Beecher dig stone.

3 Fair, warm. Dig & draw stone. Go to river.

4 Fair & hot. Mr. John Becker here. Go to toll gate; shut it. I take Marite along to Cedar Hill, get horse shod.

5 Fair. I lay wall in forenoon. Take up assessments in afternoon.

6 Fair. Lay wall. Adjourn Beecher's suit. Judge Nichols here.

7 Fair. Lay wall. I put mare to horse. Oxen on road all day.

8 Fair & hot. Sleep all day. Oxen get out of pasture.

9 Fair & hot. Lay wall. Draw stone & manure. Hard north wind.

10 Fair & hot. I go to Albany. Beecher draw manure & stone.

11 Rainy. **Get signers to petition to have Wm. Parmer turnpike inspector. Take it to Albany. Get introduced to Governor Wright. Present him the petition at his dwelling**. I buy a rocking chair.

12 Heavy south wind. Plow out corn. Commence hoeing. Bronk Witbeck & sister here. I help Dennis Toben.

13 Shower last night, warm & fair. Boys hoe corn. Charles Bruce help. I take up assessment.

14 Rainy. Get horse shod to river. Mrs. Holmes, Mrs. Houghtaling here. **I get chair & cradle**.[70]

15 Fair, south wind. I & Wife go to Meeting. I go to Flat Bush.

---

[69] Sturgeon were both prized for their caviar and meat. Sturgeon can grow up to 15 feet long and weigh up to 800 pounds. In the 18th and 19th centuries, sturgeon meat was so plentiful it was nicknamed "Albany Beef." A 40-year sturgeon fishing moratorium was declared in 1998 in an effort to restore the sturgeon population.

[70] Sarah Ann is expecting a child (Levi).

16	Fair, south wind. I go to river, get oil can of Wm. Sherwood.
17	Fair. Draw stone in forenoon. Take up assessment in afternoon.
18	Fair, dry weather. I dig stone for fence & ditch.
19	Fair, south wind. All work hard, fill in ditch.
20	Fair. A.M. VanBergen & Lady here. **Beecher's Lawsuit goes off today, he gets beat**. Work at stone. South wind.
21	Showry. Work at pantry. Go to Flat Bush.
22	Fair. I go to Meeting twice. Tina VanAntwerp here.
23	Small showers in the morning. I go to Hollow, make out assessment. Boys draw stone; fill in ditch.
24	Shower in afternoon. I go to Hollow. Boys lay wall.
25	Dennis Toben draw timber. I prepare to part my bees. I go to Hollow.
26	Very dry. Finish assessment roll. I go to Greenville, get my wool.
27	Fair. I go to John Cronk's, come holme. Boys work at fence.
28	Showry. I take a load to Flat Bush. Doctor Morris, Mrs. Pierce, Cate Pierce, Lucy Johnson [here].
29	Showery. **Wesley Blaisdell's horse run away. Broke Catharine Niles' leg. Doct. Morris & I go to see her**. Quarterly Meeting to Bethlehem.
30	Rainy. I take Mrs. Pierce and rest of company to Albany. **Celebrate General Jackson's Funeral**.[71] **John VanBuren orator of the day**. Have a good turnout. All orders Military.

July 1845

1	Lowry morning. Boys dig stone. I go to river, get a piece of beef.
2	Showry. Boys get out pickets, get out stone.
3	Rainy morning. I and Beecher draw stone. Wife go to John Clement's visiting.
4	Fair. Draw stone, Go to Island, go on turnpike.
5	Fair. I get waggon tire set to Cedar Hill. Mrs. VanSlyck here visiting. I take John Clement's cross-cut saw holme.
6	Fair and hot. We all go to Meeting. C.R. Scudder & Lady here visiting. Dry weather.
7	Fair & hot day. John Cronk and Peter Cook here. Settle off their account. I go to Aquetuck Hollow. Make out jury list. Beecher cut rye & get wood.
8	Fair. Boys cradle rye; dig stone. I go to J.W. Story's.
9	Fair & dry. Boys hoe corn & potatoes. I make fence. Wm. Sherwood help me work at my bees.
10	Fair & dry. Rake and bind rye. Get a piece of meat. Get new rake.

---

[71] Andrew Jackson, who was the 7th president of the U.S., died on 8 Jun 1845. He was known as "Old Hickory" and his portrait is currently on the $20 bill.

11   Fair & hot. We all work at fence & ditch.

12   Fair. Draw in rye. Fix fence. I pick a mess of peas.

13   Fair, hot – thermometer stands 98. We go to Meeting.

14   Small showers. Rake & bind rye. **Put cattle on the Island**. Make out Assessment Copy.

15   Very warm. Work at rye. Go to Island, go fishing.

16   Fair and hot. I am taken sick. Boys finish rye & wheat, then go to mowing. I am very weak.

17   Fair. I go to Albany. Get clover & timothy seed. Boys work in hay. Little shower.

18   Fair. I go to Hollow. Boys work in hay. Mother, Harriet & Lizabeth Holme here visit.

19   Fair. I go on turnpike. Boys work at hay. Baldwin's School Exhibition goes off.

20   Fair. I go to Sunday School. Then to Flat Bush. Then back at night. Go after cows 9 o'clock in evening.

21   Fair, hot. I get horse rake fixed. **Fix scythe. Catharine Houghtaling**[72] here visiting.

22   Fair, NW wind. All hands work in hay.

23   Fair, north wind. All work in hay.

24   Fair & cold. Work in hay. I get horse shod.

Scythe

25   Fair. Work in hay. Get along finely.

26   Morning fair, shower 6 o'clock pm. Andrew Houghtaling & Lady here visiting. I go to river, get papers.

27   Fair & cool. I go to Meeting. Doct. VanAntwerp & Lizabeth Holmes here.

28   Cloudy & misty. Boys mow hay.

29   Fair. I go to river in morning, get beef. Wife go to Lawyer Temp (sp) visiting. M. Bogardus send me a string of fish.

30   South wind & shower. Mrs. Holmes, Mrs. Crumb, Ann Bronk & Mother here visiting.

31   Work in hay. David Ostram sick. Fair, north wind.

August 1845

1   Fair. All hands work in hay.

2   Finish hay in Big Meadow. Pick wheat & rye. Fair day. I get sturgeon. Isaac Bush leave off work.

3   Fair. I go to Island, get grapes. Martin G. VanBergen here & Nana Uriah Willis here in afternoon.

---

[72]   Catharine Houghtaling was Sarah Ann's sister.

4   Fair. Beecher draw stone. (?) cut bushes. I go to Jerimiah Springstead & J.W. Story. Then to Flat Bush, get cheese.

5   Fair & hot. I get tire sot (sp) at Mr. Burns. **Boys cradle today**.

6   Fair & hot. Rake & bind oats. Draw in oats. I go to Island, salt my oxen.

7   Fair & hot. I and Marite go to Albany I get Timothy seed and Codfish. **Leave deed with Phelps**. Get holme 9 o'clock in evening.

8   Fair, hot. Finish hay. Elizabeth Holmes here. Uriah Willis here. Beecher help his Father.

Grain Cradle

9. Fair. I go fishing; catch a string of fish. See **Acton Civill**.[73] Go to Castleton, stay all day.

10 Fair & hot. Go to Meeting morning. Go to Temperance meeting in afternoon.

11 Fair & hot in morning, fine shower in afternoon. Cradle oats; dig stone & plow.

12 Clears off after raining all night. Dig stone & plow.

Acton Civill Polytechnic Institute

13 Fair. Finish oats. Dig & draw stone, plow. Mother here.

14 Fair. Draw wood. Little shower in afternoon.

15 Fair. Draw wood all day with two teams.

16 Fair. Draw wood all day. Elizabeth Holmes here.

17 Fair & hot I Go to Meeting twice.

18 Fair. Draw wood, clear fallow. Mrs. Story here.

19 Fair. Burn fallow. Have a fine burn.

20 Fair. Burn fallow. Commence threshing. Wm. Bagley & Son William and Br[other] Wesley & son Edward here.

21 Showery all day. Thresh with Machine.

22 Fair & warm. Finish threshing. Pay off hands.

23 A little showery. I and Mr. Bagley & his sons go to Flat Bush, call at Henry Bronk's. Boys plow.

25 Fair & hot. I go to E. Millbank's hunting with Wm. Bagley & his son. Shoot an owl. I get my horse shod.

27 Very heavy showers. **Henry Niles' house struck by lightning**. I take Wm. Bagley to Baltimore. He leave with steamboat.

28 Fair, south wind. Clean up grain. Sow my wheat. Shoot two pidgeons. Dig stone.

29 Fair, south wind. Finish sowing wheat. Dig stone. Elizabeth Holmes here.

30 A little showry, south wind. Draw muck. Sow grass seed.

---

73 Acton Civill built the Acton Civill Polytechnic Institute in 1874 adjacent to Fletcher's farm in Coeymans. It was purchased by the Coeymans Board of Education in 1899 and run as a public school until 1963.

31 Fair & cool. I go to Meeting. A.E. Willis, Doct. VanAntwerp & Wesley Blaisdell here.

September 1845

1   Fair. I & Dennis Toben draw muck. Beecher goes to Training. Mother here. **Maria Cronk died today.**

2   Showry. **I go to Mill then take Mother to Maria Cronk's funeral**, then to river, then to J.W. Story's.

3   Fair, north wind. I sow rye then harrow in rye. Dig out stone.

4   Showery. I go to Albany. Boys harrow in grain.

5   Fair. Draw muck. Make fence. Uriah Willis here. Mr. Mosher here.

6   Fair. Draw muck., make fence, go to river, get beef. Rain last night

9   Fair. Sow seed on fallow. Clean up grain. Go to mill with hog feed.

10 Fair. Draw muck. Cate VanAntwerp here.

15 Fair. I draw wood in forenoon. Boys draw muck.

16 Fair. Draw muck. J. Story's horse sick. North wind.

19 Fair. Draw muck. I go to Flat Bush. Get apples & cheese.

20 Heavy shower in morning. I go to river. Pay A. Sherman. Clean up grain. **Go to Caucus at the Hollow. P. VanAntwerp gets nomination for Assemblyman.**

21 Smart shower last night. Quarterly Meeting here. Doct. VanAntwerp here. I go to Meeting. North wind & colder.

22 Fair. I get plow fixed. Make fence, go to river. Boys plow. Cut up corn, peal apples tonight.

23 Fair. **Get my broom corn seed from the Island.**[74] Boys plow. Cut up corn.

24 Rainy forenoon. Spread broom corn seed. **Transfer Sloop Myrtle to P. Seabridge.** Go to Temperance meeting at night.

25 Fair. Beecher plow. I buy boards; shingle house where Albert Jackson lives. Mother here. Draw plank to bridge.

26 Fair. Patch my roof. Beecher plow. Dennis put up stalks.

27 Fair. I take 3 bu. wheat to mill. Get peaches of R. Pulver. Beecher draw wood & manure. I get posts of I. Vandenburgh. Joseph Bronk & Lady, Andrew Houghtaling & Lady here.

29 Fair. I draw load of sand for hog pen. Go to river. Get iron fixed for Carriage. Get gate post from dock. Draw manure.

30 Fair. I rig out and we all go to Sunday School Celebration to Hollow. Rev. Mr. Hedstrom & Rodgers address the meeting. It rained all the way holme.

---

74 Broom corn is not corn, but a type of sorghum. It is a multipurpose grain crop grown for livestock such as chickens, ducks and turkeys. The sturdy seed heads and stalks are used in making brooms, mats and other items. Joe Boehlke, President of the Ravena-Coeymans Historical Society informed us that there was a broom factory in the Town of Coeymans.

October 1845

1   Fair. I get my winter apples from Flat Bush. Go along with Woolsey Cary to see a wood lot. Hard walk.

2   Fair. Wash rye, sow rye. Draw manure. Work hard.

3   Fair. I go to Flat Bush, to Coxsackie to A.T. VanSlyck's to see Cary on his wood lot, then holme. Beecher draw in rye.

4   Fair. I go to Island; get 100 bushels of broom corn seed at the Island.

5   Rain all day, no meeting. I stir my broom corn seed.

6   Rainy. I go to Albany to attend court as juryman; get excused.

7   Fair. Work in barn. Beecher draw wood. I put in new gate post, hang gate.

8   Fair. I do up cheese. Beecher draw wood. Mrs. Holmes here. Lawyer Sherman call here.

11 Rainy day. Horace Hart here, sell Calder lot. Beecher make gate.

12 Rainy day. **Paper mill dam go away. Wash out stone from turnpike bridge**. I stir broom corn seed.

13 Fair. I fix bridge. Buy a hogshead with molasses from John Keller.

14 Fair. I help Jacob Story get broom corn seed. Open molasses hogshead. Mrs. Story here, Elizabeth Holmes here.

15 Fair, north wind, colder. Boys dig potatoes. I get horses shod. I go to river. Mr. Baldwin here.

16 Fair but cold. **I and Mother go to Albany; I get sloop papers.**

17 Fair, south wind. Draw in corn & pumpkins. Dig potatoes.

18 Fair, south wind. Draw corn, pumpkins & wood.

19 Fair, south wind. I go to Meeting.

20 Fair morning, sleet & hail in afternoon. **Doct. Fredenburgh, Mother & Harriet here**.[75]

21 Fair. 4 or 5 in. snow on Helderburgh. Beecher draw wood. I Go to John Mull's. I am not very well.

22 Fair day. Fix chimney; draw wood; dig potatoes. Pay Peter Gardineer for manure. Potatoes froze in the ground.

23 Fair day. I paint gutters. Go to river. **Gave up the Myrtle papers**. Beecher go to New York.

24 Fine day. I paint all day. Old Ginny VanBergen here.

25 Fair. I go to the Island. I paint at Mother's.

26 Fair. I go to Flat Bush. Wesley & Margarett here.

27 Fair. I go to Island. I bring holme Mrs. Margarett Henry. Marite stay in Albany.

28 Fair. I go to river. I fix hay press. Mrs. Trego, Aunt Caty, Cate Houghtaling and more yet here. House full.

29 Fair. I fix hay press. Draw manure. Settle with John Bushants.

---

[75] Levi Blaisdell was born on this date. His birth is not mentioned in Fletcher's diary.

30 Fair. Work at hay press. Hang swing gate. Beecher draw manure. Get in beets. Willis here. I go to river.

31 Fair. I go to river, make fence. Boys draw manure.

November 1845

1   Fair. I get horse shod at Cedar Hill. M.L. Loop here. Draw manure. Mrs. Holmes and more company here.

4   Clear off, fair. Election today. **Votes stand thus: Dem. for Shaver 12, P. VanAntwerp 94, Watson 2; Whig stand thus: VanSchoonhoven, senator 68, members Ira Harris 59, Crosby 77, Udell 75. No opposition to new Constitution.**[76]

5   Rain all day. Husk corn. I go to river.

6   Fair. **I get cattle off the Island**. Go to Flat Bush.

7   Far. Clean up seed. Get out slats. Go to Mill. Get out hoops. **Old Jan VanBergen died at Black Dick's.**

8   Commence rain. Plow, fix hay press. I take Willis's boys holme.

10 Heavy north wind. Press hay. Beecher come back.

11 Fair, south wind. Plow, press hay, go to river, get hoops.

12 Fair. Press hay. Break press. Plow.

13 Fair. I go to Flat Bush, get cider. Boys clean up broom corn seed. Get hay slats, go to mill. M. VanBergen here.

14 Fair. I go to Albany. Boys draw away hay. **I get potash kettle**.[77]

15 Fair. Draw wood. Fix hay press. I go to river.

16 Fair. Go to Meeting. Bornt VanSlyck & Lady here.

17 Fair. Press hay, draw hay, plow. S. King pay me 100 dollars.

18 Rainy forenoon. I and Marite go to Flat Bush in afternoon.

19 Fair, north wind. Press hay, draw hay. **Catharine Bronk gets married last night. Elizabeth get married right before and they have a horning over it**.

20 Fair. Press hay. **Start for New York; Barge gets detained**.

21 Fair going down the river. Fairly jolly time. Open barrel of apples.

---

[76] The New York Constitution was amended in 1845. It required a Constitutional Convention to revise the Constitution.

[77] Potash is made from wood ashes and used in the making of soap.

22 Fair. Get in New York 3 o'clock **Go to Chatham Theater**.[78]

23 Rainy. Turn around go to Meeting aboard the ship.

24 Fair. **Go to Bull's Head [Tavern]**.[79] Sell my cattle. Pretty tired.

25 Fair. Do up trading. **Start for holme on North America**.

26 Fair. Get holme at 2 o'clock in morning. Put up potash kettle.

Bull's Head Tavern

27 Rain all day. **Finish potash kettle**. Go to river.

28 Fair, cold. I go to river & to mill.

29 Fair, cold. I go to river. **Get things off Barge**. Get calf from Island.

30 Cold. Snow all the afternoon.

December 1845

1 Five inches snow rain all day. Draw hay till noon.

2 Clear & cold. Clean up broom corn seed. Draw pressed hay.

3 Cold. I & Wife go to Flat Bush. Begins to snow at 2 o'clock. Beecher kill our geese. Andrew Houghtaling child born last Saturday.

4 Cold. I get horses shod. **River closed last night. Lawton's Barge detained, heavy loaded**. J.W. Story here.

6 Cold. I get horse shod. Beecher go to Albany. I and Wife go to John Bushant's. Catharine Pierce & her Brother here. Dennis Toben go with Beecher to Albany.

7 Fair Beecher bring holme Mother Houghtaling. I go to Meeting. **Capt. Sherwood lay-up sloop Revenue at New Paltz.**

8 Squally, south [wind]. I kill hogs & beef. Cate Pierce go holme.

9 Warmer. I cut up pork. Settle with R & J Lawton. Fix stable.

10 Fair. I buy sow & pigs of Ira Gregory. Beecher get posts. Salt pork. I sell 131 ½ lbs. to John Keller.

11 Clear & cold. Beecher goes to Greenville. Wm. Sherwood takes my mare to Westerlo.

12 Cold. Beecher gets 1 load of plank. Andrew Houghtaling & John Pierce here. Henriette Holmes here. I go to river.

13 Cold, thermometer 12 deg. below zero. Draw muck, go to river.

14 Snowy. Hanson Scott's burnt last night. North wind & colder.

16 Cold, north wind. Draw muck. Elizabeth Holmes here.

---

[78] The Chatham Theatre was a playhouse on Chatham St in New York City. In the mid-1840s it was primarily a venue for blackface minstrel shows.

[79] The Bull's Head Tavern opened around 1750. It was originally used as a recruitment center where loyalists signed up to fight the British.

17	Fair day. **I go to Nomination to the Hollow. Choose Delegates to be held at A.A. Clark's at a County Convention.**
18	Snowy day. I go to Flat Bush. Beecher chop wood. 3 inches snow.
19	Fair day. I work in **stone quiry**.[80] Wife go to Albany with Willis.
20	Fair. I go to Albany, drive Willis's old mare.
21	Fair. I and Wife go to Wm. Fisher's to Barret Houghtaling's.
22	Fair. I, Wife & Mother Houghtaling go to Baltimore to Andrew Mull's.
23	Fair. I go to river. Beecher draw muck. I settle with I. Story. Wife sick. There is a ball at Baltimore to Andrew Mull's.
24	Cold. I and J.W. Story go to Flat Bush. Beecher draw muck.
25	Snowy. Draw muck. I pay off Peter W. Teneyck.[81]
26	Snowy. I go to river. Beecher cut wood. I buy a watch of Martin B. Bogardus for 8 dollars.
27	Fair. Mr. Brandow here. I and Beecher draw muck.
28	Snowy. I go to J. Story's. Jack VanSlyck here.
29	Fair. Draw muck. I go to Greenville.
30	Fair. Come back from Greenville. Temperance Meeting. Draw muck.
31	Fair. Draw wood. S. Nichols here; pay me off. I draw wood.

January 1846

1	Fair. Mr. Matson here. **I and Wife go to Dominie Jolly to association got up for the benefit of the church.**
2	Rainy & foggy day. Stay at holme. Elizabeth Holmes here.
3	Fair, north wind. I go to the Hollow; pay our tax.
4	Fair. I take Mother Houghtaling to Flat Bush. See J. Story.
5	Fair. Draw wood. I get my hog from John Bronk's.
6	Fair. Finish draw wood. Dig stone.
7	Stormy, snow, rain & hail. Martin Andrews here. Pete Shear here.
8	Colder. Mr. Wm. Hoose here. Mother here. Wash 8 oil lamps.
9	Warmer. I go to Flat Bush, draw out timber. Mother Houghtaling come holme. Singing School at Mrs. Clement's.
10	Fair. I go to Baltimore to J.W. Story's & to Meeting at night.
11	I get horse shod. Mrs. Trego here. Mrs. & Mr. Matson here.

---

[80] Fletcher spells quarry as quiry. He spends a lot of time working in the quarry and drawing stone from it – we don't know its location.

[81] Fletcher rarely mentions a Christmas celebration. Because partying and merrymaking were seen as unchristian, Christmas celebrations did not become widespread until the later 1800's when, in 1870, it was declared a national holiday.

12   **I and Beecher make a road to go to the Dam.**[82]

13   I and Beecher make road. I go to river. Beecher go to Greenville.

14   Fair. **I and J. Clement, Jacob Teal & Hanson Scott go a begging for timber all around the country.**

15   Fair. I and Beecher make road. I and Mr. Matson go to Jacob W. Story's; try to trade horses.

16   Fair. I and Beecher finish road. Beecher go to Greenville.

17   Snow all day I trade horses with John Finch. Beecher come from Greenville. I go to Jacob W. Story's & to Willis's.

18   Cold, north wind. Stay in house all day.

19   Cold, high wind. Stay around & in the house all day.

20   Cold. Beecher draw wood from the Island. **Trotting today on the [river] ice**. A. Jackson pay his house rent up to April 1, 1846. I pay Island tax. Borrow one dollar of Lawton, pay him again at night. Wife visit to Wesley's.

21   Snowy, blow hard. I go to river. Beecher draw wood.

22   Very cold, blow hard. David Benedict & Lady, A.E. Willis & Lady here. Beecher cut wood. **Old Mrs. Ackerman died**.

23   Cold as ever. I go to river. Beecher chop wood.

24   Fair and warmer. Wife go to VanAntwerp's. I and Beecher get wood.

25   North wind and warmer. I go to J.W. Story's.

26   Rain all day. Draw out timber; get holme late at night. Aunt Sarah Ann VanSlyck here.

27   North wind cold. I go to Greenville. Beecher draw out timber. Mother Houghtaling go to her Father's. Andrew Houghtaling here.

28   Fair. I come back from Greenville. Beecher chop wood.

29   I take a load of folks to Hugh Mosher's to the association. Get holme at one o'clock at night.

30   South wind, rainy all forenoon. I go to trotting match.

31   Stormy forenoon, clears off at night. I go to river. Beecher chop wood.

February 1846

1   Fair, cold. I go to Meeting & down to the Dam.

2   Fair. I sold timber to John Clement.

3   Fair. I and Beecher & John Clement go to Flat Bush.

---

[82]   There were two dams on the Hannacroix near Fletcher's farm; both were associated with papermills. "Fields of Reams – The Hannacroix Paper Mills", an article by Chuck Friday in 2009 describes them. The first was the Ravine Mill, which had a substantial timber dam built upstream of the mill. Remnants of the dam are still visible. In Fletcher's time, this mill was operated by William Robb. The second was further upstream and called the Croswell Paper Mill. The timber dam that provided waterpower for the mill was built above the water fall where many of us played as children.

4   Fair. All go to Flat Bush, get out logs. Trego & Lady & Clarisa Houghtaling here, stay all night.

5   Some squally. Go to Flat Bush, get out logs.

6   Fair. Go to Flat Bush, get out logs. Have a sing here tonight.

7   Morning fair, overcast in afternoon. I go to Martin VanBergen, pay Uncle Abram 100 dollars. Go to horse trot to Coxsackie.

8   Heavy wind, NW. Go to hear Cornell preach.

9   Very cold weather, NW wind. I go to river.

10 Fair, cold. I go to Albany on the ice. **Take Margarett King to the Almshouse.**[83] **Nancy White come here to nurse**.

11 Fair morning, snowy afternoon. I and Beecher chop wood.

12 Six inches snow, very light north wind. I go to Houghtaling's sawmill, to W. Cary's wood lot. Beecher go to mill.

13 Fair. I go with Millbanks to Albany. Beecher draw logs to mill.

14 Fair. I and Wife go to Baltimore & to Houghtaling's Mills. Mr. Pierce here. J. Clement fix my saw. I go to river. Beecher draw logs.

15 Snow & blow all day. Snow six inches deep. Stay close [to] holme.

16 19 inches new snow. I go to river. Beecher chop wood.

17 Fair. I and Wife go to Albany. Take Mrs. Pierce holme. **Get Julia to nurse**. Leonard Hathaway come back with us.

18 Fair. I go to river. Beecher draw wood. J. Cronk & Lady here.

19 Coldest morning this winter. I go to Paper mill. Beecher draw wood. **Mrs. Honse Teneyck died yesterday**.

20 Snow all day, wind south. I go to river. Beecher chop wood. **Three ft. of snow and cold**.

21 Fair, moderate weather. I go to river. Beecher chop wood.

22 Fair, warm. Martin VanBergen here.

23 Fair, warm. Beecher draw wood. Thomas Houghtaling here. Andrew Houghtaling here. Harriet, Marite here. Christopher Sickles here.

24 Blows hard, NW wind. Andrew Mull, Mrs. Baker, Mrs. Nichols here. Margarett Blaisdell, Elizabeth & Henriette Holmes here. I pay Ira Gregory five dollars.

25 Clear and cold. Beecher draw wood. **I and Wife go to Lawton's to a Ball. Have a fine time. Get holme 5 o'clock in the morning.**

26 Colder than ever. Beecher Holmes move to Johnstown. I go to river & to Willis's. NW wind, drifts very bad.

27 Very cold, NW wind. I go to river. Beecher draws wood for Dennis Toben. Shovel Turnpike. Doct. Cornell & Ephram VanSlyck here.

---

[83] An Almshouse is a place for poor people to live.

28 Cold & cloudy, NW wind. I go to river. Beecher cut straw. Marite come back. Mother Houghtaling & Wife go to Trego's.

March 1846

1 Cold as ever. Folks all go to Meeting. Uriah Willis here.

2 Very cold. I go to river. Beecher draw wood. J. Houghtaling here.

3 Cold. I go to Houghtaling Mills. I go around by Gurney's (sp) & so holme. Beecher chop wood.

7 Fair. Beecher draw wood. Cary here, Mother here. **Child sick**.

8 Fair. All go to Meeting, hear Cornell. Wesley here.

9 Warm, water runs finely. I go to river. Fix Mother's cask.

10 Fair. I and Wife go to Albany. Get Margarett Beecher. Go to Flat Bush. Mrs. Lawton here.

11 Fair, south wind. Julia go to Albany. I let Wesley have twenty-five dollars. I and Beecher work in stone.

12 Fair. Get out stone. Marite & Margarett go to Albany.

13 Fair. Get out logs. Streams rising fast.

14 Rainy day. Beecher chop wood. Very high water.

15 Fair. **Ice start; throw the Sloop Myrtle on the dock. Higher water than was ever known before.**

16 North wind. I put up Bridge. **Apron goes off the dam**.

17 Colder, north wind. I go to Flat Bush with J.T. Wilsey. Julia Hamilton come back from Albany. Hugh Mosher here.

18 Fair, north wind. I go to John Houghtaling's Vendue; buy four head of cattle. **Two steamboats go up today**.

19 Fair. I go to Story's, chop wood. Wm. Wilsey here. I get my house insured. Willis here. Capt. Sherwood, we make a bargain with Wilsey.

20 Fair. I and Beecher chop.

21 Fair, north wind. I go to Joab Baker's Vendue, to sawmill. Go to river. Hold a caucus. **I am a delegate from this district to go to County Convention**. Mother here. **Myrtle gets loaded**.

22 Fair. Go to Meeting. Wesley & Doct. VanAntwerp here. I go to dam. Dry walking NW wind.

23 Fair. I go to river, to Flat Bush. See Jas. Trego, see Andrew Houghtaling. Beecher chop. Go on Turnpike. Mother Houghtaling here.

24 Rainy. I go to River. Beecher chop wood. **I get Nomination for Assessor for this district. Revenue here**.

25 Rainy day, great freshet. We all go out to Nomination at the Hollow. I get Nomination for Assessor. **Mrs. Albert Jackson died this morning. Waggons go for the first today**.

26 Heavy freshet, very muddy. I and Beecher chop wood.

27 Fair. Beecher chop. **I go to School District Celebration.**

28 Squally. Make fence in the forenoon. **Go out to the Hollow in the afternoon to a meeting to send delegates to the County Convention. Have a general row. Send two sets; I and Hugh Mosher appointed.**

29 Fair. Go to Meeting twice. John Bronk's sheep get on my grain.

30 Fair. I go to river. Fix road. Mother Houghtaling come back.

31 I and Hugh Mosher go to County Convention at Clark's. Wife go to Flat Bush. Have a regular fight at convention. **Old Hunkers get whipped after they backed out. Then they all got drunk and fight among themselves.** Take supper at (?) Mosher's.

April 1846

1 Fair. I go to river. Get wet hay of Henry Niles. Set out trees. Go to Flat Bush. Get potatoes, cheese tub, pail cheese.

2 Fair. Draw wet hay from Henry Niles' hay building. Work hard.

3 Fair. Draw hay. **I buy leach cask.**[84] **Open pressed hay.**

4 Fair. Open hay, plow clay. **Get my leach tub.** Martin Holmes & Lady here and Polly & Aunt Caty visiting.

5 Fair, south wind. Marite go to Quarterly Meeting. I and Wife go to hear Cornell. Go to Mother's.

6 Fair. Draw clay. Get horse shod. Go to Mill, get clams.

7 Fair, south wind. I take Mary Holmes, Wife & Mother Houghtaling to Baltimore. Work in garden. Miss VanSlyck here.

8 Snowy morning. I and Peter Seabridge go to Albany, get trees. Drive my colt & his Dominie horse.

9 Fair. Set out Apple trees. Get a lot of peach trees of John Myers. Elias Holmes come here to work. Wm. Sherwood pay me $25 borrowed money.

10 Fair. Sow oats; put out onions. I go to Flat Bush bargain with David Mead for land.

11 Fair, south wind. Plow, drag, sow peas & barley. Harriet & Jane Lawton here. I pay John Hauenstien $6.25 for hoops.

12 Cloudy & rainy. **Joseph Hazelton died this morning while we were at Meeting.** Andrew Houghtaling here.

13 North wind. Make fence. Boys plow. I go to **J. Hazleton's funeral**.

14 I take team, go to Town Meeting. **R. Reefer gets elected in my place by the Old Hunkers on Stump ticket.**

15 Heavy north wind. I put up meeting notices, go to mill. Boys make fence & plow.

16 Heavy south wind. Sow barley, make fence, plow. I go to river.

---

[84] A leach tub was used to extract potassium hydroxide from wood ashes. Potassium hydroxide was used in the making of soap.

17 South wind. Elias set out trees. I and Beecher go on Turnpike.

18 Showry. Ebenezer Finch & Lady here. Elias work at wall.

19 Fair. Take dinner to Wesley's. **Get news that Cate Collins, Margarette's sister, is dead**. Go to Meeting.

20 Fair. I and Wife go to sawmill, to Woolsey Cary's, to Coxsackie, to A.T. VanSlyck's. Beecher plow, sow, draw stone. I see D. Mead.

21 Fair & warm. Plow garden; plant potatoes. Get 421 ft. of boards from sawmill.

22 Fair. I go to Flat Bush. Sell land to David Mead, then to Greenville.

23 Fair. I and Eben Finch go over the mountain, get trees. Come back to his house, stay all night.

24 Fair. I come holme. Set out trees. Bring Aunt Blaisdell along.

25 Fair. Get out stone. **Attend Democratic Meeting. John VanBuren address the meeting**.

26 Fair and cool. I go to Meeting. Wm. Bissac (sp), Cate VanBergen here. Woolsey Cary pay me forty-five dollars on cows.

27 Fair. Make fence. Beecher plow. I go to river, get shad.

28 Fair. Election for Delegates at C. Needer's. Take in 99 votes. I bring two cows from Cary's. I go to Baltimore.

29 Fair, north wind. I put my cow & J. Story's on the Island. Beecher plow. Done for corn. I set out Asparagus.

30 Fair. I, Wife and Mother Houghtaling go to Coxsackie. Mr. Mead pay me for land. J. Hawley pay me 10 dollars. I pay Uncle Abram 75 dollars. Took dinner & tea at M. VanBergen's.

May 1846

1 A little showry. Beecher get a load of stone from Mud Hill. **Anthony Teneyck died today**. Draw load of hay. Get stone from A.H. Briggs. Draw stone off potato ground.

2 A little rain at night. **I go to Anthony Teneyck's Funeral**.

4 Fair. I and Elias make fence. Beecher furrow out for corn. Mr. Fancher & Wife here, pay his rent. Mother here. I trade my hay press chain with Wm. Sherwood for Rope.

7 Fair. I go to paper mill. Get out stone. Plant corn.

8 Fair. Get out stone, plant corn, get a string of fish.

9 Rainy. Plant corn. Pay Willis 150 dollars. Go to river. **Sell church seats tonight**.[85] Get out stone.

10 Fine rain. I go to Wycoff preach Installation sermon.

11 Colder, north wind. I go to mill, get horse shod, make fence, draw muck.

12 Cornelia VanAntwerp here visiting. Plant corn. Go to Pickaway with J.E. Gibbens; see about building bridge.

Church pew plaque

---

[85] The photo is of the plaque from Fletcher's pew at the Dutch Reformed church in Coeymans. Selling church pews was a fundraiser for the church.

13   Fair. **I go to Albany, start for Herkimer.**[86]

14   Fair. Boys plant corn. I get as far as John Feeter's.

15   Fair. **I and John Feeter go out to Ohio**[87] to H. Schoonmaker.

16   Rain all day. I came holme from Herkimer.

17   A little showery. Fine growing season. Go to Meeting. **Put up scarecrow.**

18   Showery morning clears off colder. Make fence.

19   Cold, north wind. I take two trips to J.B. Shear's. (?) down the license. We put it down. Boys plant potatoes. Frost this morning.

20   Cold. Boys finish plant potatoes. I go to Island, get fish.

21   Fair. **Go to New York on board Coeymans Barge.**

22   Fair. Arrive in New York. **Go to Bowery Theater.**

23   Rainy. Go to Wm. Bagley's to J. Skinner's.

24   Rain. Go to Meeting two or three times.

25   Go a shopping. A little rainy.

26   Fair. **Come holme on steamboat Niagara.** Mr. Hallow's folks come along.

27   Rainy day. I and Elias roll logs in sawmill. Take old Mr. TenBroeck off.

28   Fair. I and Elias draw timber. I and Bogardus shoot crows. Mother here.

29   Cloudy. **Dig foundation for wing of house, east side. Draw sand. Get rope of Capt. Sherwood. Draw timbers I got of A. Jackson.**

30   Fair. I and Elias go on road. Beecher work in garden. I get cloth. Cloudy day.

31   Cloudy & warm. I go to Meeting, hear Cornell. Martin Andrews here.

June 1846

1   Fair day. I and Beecher go on Turnpike. **A boy drownded here last night.**

2   Showery. Boys on road. I and all folks go to paper mill. Mother & Harriet here.

3   Fair, north wind. Boys chop. I and all folks go to A.T. VanSlyck's.

4   Fair, south wind. Mr. Hallock & Family go to New York. Marite go along. I send calf. Pay Mr. Clement 4 dollars night before last.

5   Shower. Plow & hoe corn. **Make corn drag.**[88] Mrs. Willis here.

6   Fair, north wind. Make fence; hoe corn. **Jacob Dorman buried here today.** Mary Goldsmith here. I get strawberries.

7   Fair. I go to Meeting to both churches. Hear Dominie Lull.

8   Fair. Go to Greenville, take Mother along. Go to Fancher's.

---

86   This is the first mention of Herkimer, NY near where Fletcher will own a sawmill.
87   Ohio City, which is now the hamlet of Ohio, is located in Herkimer County.
88   A drag is used to loosen and smooth the surface of a field.

9	Fair. Get shoes of Baldwin. Fine crops growing all over the country.
10	Fair. Work hard at the corn. J. Schoonmaker pay me 2 dollars.
11	Fair. Finish corn. Go to river. Plow for buckwheat.
12	Fair. **Put up foundation for wing**.[89] Get meat of Ira Gregory.
13	Fair. I go to Albany; bring holme her Mrs. Pierce. **Boys lay foundation**. Draw poles. Draw muck last night.
14	Fair. I go to Meeting & to river. Newman Finch here.
15	Fine showers. I go to Flat Bush; draw timber. Make fence. Gave E. Holmes an order to get grain of McGregor. Get a mess of peas from New York.
16	Fair, north wind. Get out timber. Make fence. Draw one load from Flat Bush.
17	Fair. Boys chop. I go to river, get a string of fish.
18	Fair. Get 20 bunches of shingles from Norton Hill. Go a fishing. Plaster corn. Maria Springstead here.
19	Fair morning, rain PM. Draw muck. Plow out potatoes.
20	Heavy showers. **Raise building**. Marite come back. Wm. Verplank & Doct. VanAntwerp here. Pick out hay & straw.
21	Fair. I go to Meeting twice. A. VanBergen & Elida VanSlyck, Doct. VanAntwerp, A. Houghtaling here.
22	Squally. Press hay. Work at shed. Sell my wood to Mr. Robb. L. Crandle here.
23	Showers. Press hay; draw wood. Get Willis's cage from Peter VanBuren's. Almira VanBergen & Elida VanSlyck off.
24	Fair. Draw wood, chop. I take Mother & Mrs. Pierce to Andrew Mull's. Go to Houghtaling Mills. Peter Seabridge let me have 25 dollars. I pay off R & J. Lawton. Draw timber.
25	Fair. I go a fishing. Boys work in corn, draw muck. Have a calf come last night. Finish linter (sp) to hay press.
26	Showery. Hoe corn all day. Draw muck.
27	Fair. I take Mother to Quarterly Meeting. Get a sheep of Calvin Carhart. Beecher sow buckwheat. Elias sick.
28	Fair. I take a load out to Quarterly Meeting.
29	Fair. I take Mother Houghtaling, Mrs. Pierce to Flat Bush. Beecher work in corn.
30	Fair. **I draw 3,000 bricks**. Get (?) of John Keller. Mrs. Fredenburg & Betsey Verplank here. Mrs. Terry here. Finish corn. Black Charly help ½ day.

July 1846

1	Rain hard all day. Put hay & straw on the barge. Fix barn. Cate VanBergen here.

---

[89] This is the start of Fletcher's addition of the east wing of the house.

2	All hands go to Flat Bush. Oren Porter here; **leave horse rake here**, 8 dollars cash or 9 dollars. Note 6 months without interest.
3	Cradle rye. Raise building at Flat Bush. Plow.
4	Showry. Cradle rye. Wife go to A.N. Briggs. I go to river.
5	Fair. Go to Meeting twice. Mr. Howard & Lady here, take tea. Heavy shower in afternoon.
6	Fair. I take Mary Goldsmith to Albany. Bees swarm. Boys cradle rye.
7	Fair. Rake rye. Draw dung. Mr. Batchellor come after Mary Goldsmith's furniture.
8	Fair. Have a lot of visitors. Draw in 3 loads rye. Draw wood.
9	Fair. Cradle wheat. Send away calves. Draw in rye.
10	Fair & hot. I go to John Bushant's. Take Folks to Elias Holmes. Finish rye; rake wheat; get barley forks of E. Millbanks.
11	Get in wheat. Heavy shower in afternoon. Draw manure. Modica Brogue take tea. Go in swimming.
12	Showry. I go to river. Wesley here. I go to Meeting.
13	Fair. Make hay rigging. Get horse shod. I go to river; to paper mill. Mr. Robb pay me 10 dollars.
14	Fair. **My horse gets foundered on wheat**. Go to mill; mow hay.
15	Fair, north wind. Draw wood. Mow, rake hay. Mother here.
16	Morning fair. Put up hay. Shower in afternoon. I go to paper mill.
17	Showery. **Mow & grind scythes**. Cradle barley.
18	Fair. Draw in 5 loads hay. Mother Houghtaling come holme. Martin VanBergen here.
19	Cloudy. I go to Baltimore to meeting. Mr. Wilsey & Lady here. Peter VanWie & Barent Winnie take tea here. I drive my colt.
20	Showry. Work at house. Rake hay. Maria Springstead here.
21	Fair. Cut barley. Mow; draw in hay. M. Bogardus send me a lot of fish.
22	Wet day. Go to mill. Wife go a visiting to Widow Charlotte Houghtaling's. Mother here. I get horses shod. Get in hay.
23	Fair. Mother & Wife go to Hugh Crumb's. We mow, rake barley; put up hay. Write to Oren Porter.
24	Fair. Work in hay & barley. Wife go to J.J. Colvin's.
25	Fair. I take Wife & Mother Houghtaling to Andrew Mull's. Boys chop wood
26	Fair. I go to Meeting. Mr. Orr & Lady here. Margarett Blaisdell & her Children here.
27	Fair. Work in hay. Finish barley. Harriet here.
28	Fair. Work in hay. Get along finely. Mow Little Meadow.
29	Fair, south wind. Lots of visitors. Work in hay.
30	Fair all day, heavy shower at night. Work in hay. Mrs. Willis here.
31	Pleasant & hot morning, shower at noon. I go to Greenville.

August 1846

1. Fair. I come back from Greenville. Get in 1 load hay.
2. Fair, hot. I go to Meeting twice. Mr. Howard & Lady here.
3. Fair. Work in hay. I draw two loads hay for Dennis Toben. Hezekiah Schoonmaker here. Aunt Caty Houghtaling here. Fix turnpike.
4. Fair. Work in hay. Gitty Hathaway here.
5. Fair. Boys get in hay. I and Dennis Toben go to Flat Bush. Wife & Mother go to Thomas Houghtaling's. Raise shed at Flat Bush.
6. Fair. Work in hay. Hogs get out. Get along finely.
7. Fair. Work in hay. Mother here. Crandle here.
8. Fair morning, rain afternoon. Work in hay. Settle with Lawton & Willis.
9. Rain all day. I go to Meeting, hear Cornell. I milk at night.
10. Rainy afternoon. Work in hay. I go to river. Wesley to Albany.
11. Fine day. Get up 500 hay cocks. Wife & Folks go a visiting. **Mrs. S. Harris run away with a Frenchman**.
12. Fair. Work in hay. **Wife go a sailing with the Myrtle.**
13. Fair. I finish haying. P. Phelps & William & Mary Phelps here. Mother here. **I finish hay; have 87 loads in all**.
14. Shower & hot. I and girls go a fishing on the Island. Mrs. Mull, Mrs. Bailey here. Draw sand & brick. Go to Mill.
15. Little showery. Go to river. **Draw brick. Commence building**.
16. Shower in evening. Go to Meeting. Andrew VanAntwerp here. I and Andrew go to Thomas Houghtaling's.
17. Showery, hot. **Work at house**. Wm, McGregor here.
18. Fair, cool. Draw wood. **Work at house. 16 persons here**.
19. Fair, cool. Draw wood. **Work at house**. Mr. Collins here and another man & Mrs. Sherman & Mrs. Houghtaling.
20. Fair. **Work at house**. Draw wood. John Burhaus & Lady here. I settle with him.
21. Showery. Thresh wheat. Get sand. Go to Flat Bush, take Gitty Hathaway along to get her Mother's things.
22. Showry afternoon. Fix fence, work at building, draw lime.
23. Showery. Go to Meeting. Sing in choir with Bronck VerPlanck.
24. Fair. Draw 1 load from Flat Bush. Draw wood. Go to river. Go to mill. Get 1 quarter of lamb.
25. Fair. I go to Flat Bush, get timber. **Go to meeting on Lawton & Willis's Barge**.
26. Rainy forenoon. Thresh wheat. Send to Flat Bush after gutter stick. Go to dam.
27. Fair. Plow, cut brush. Commence bridge. Mother Houghtaling come back. Joseph Bronk here. Margarett and the Misses Angelia (sp) here.

28 Fair. Plow, work at Fallow at building. Draw brick. Go on the Turnpike.

29 Fair morning, showers in afternoon. Dig stone & plow. I go to Quarterly Meeting to Dormansville. Take Mother. Then to Chesterville and then to Greenville.

30 Fair, hot. I come holme. Bring Mother back. Sarah Ann go with Margarett to Dutchess County.

31 Fair. Fix bridge. Draw wood and sand. **Buy Map of Albany County of David Mosher.**

September 1846

1   Fair. Work at bridge. Plow, top corn, go to blacksmith.

2   Fair & hot. Work at house. Burn fallow. Put up corn, plow.

3   Fair morning, lowry in afternoon. Burn fallow, plow. Work hard.

4   Fair. Lewis Crandle quit work. Wife come holme. Draw manure. Fix hog pen. **A fight on sloop between Case Ryan, John Teal and steamboat men.**

5   Fair & hot. Marite come back from Albany. I get horse shod, go to river. Get peaches. I pay J. Keeler 20 dollars.

6   Hot as ever. I go to Meeting. Go to Big Meadow.

7   Hot. Draw dung. **Kissam Houghtaling**[90] & Trego here.

8   Hot. I go to sawmill. See W. Cary. He pay me 8 dollars.

9   Fair and cold. **I go to cave with Phillip Phelps**. Top corn, draw manure from street or landing.

10 Fair, frosty. I send my cow to New York. Top corn. Draw manure. **Attend a Universalist meeting at schoolhouse.**

11 Fair. I draw dung. Sell wood to John Vandenburgh. Top corn.

12 Fair. I go to Flat Bush and attend Democratic Meeting at C. Veeder's. Send delegates to Convention. **Steamboat Excelsior of Coxsackie explode.**[91]

13 Fair and hot Showers last night. I go to Meeting. Doct. VanAntwerp eat almost a basket of peaches.

14 Fair. Fix barn. I go to river. Boys draw manure, work in buckwheat. I send sixty dollars to Henry Parrish.

15 Fair, north wind. I go on Turnpike. Wife & Harriet go to D. Niver's.

16 Fair. Draw in stalks, get timber, draw 3 loads of sand of G. Sherman.

17 Fair. Draw stone. Catharine Houghtaling here.

Kissam Houghtaling

---

[90] Family lore tells us that Kissam Houghtaling [1821-1921] moved to California during the gold rush and became a gold miner.

[91] An internet search indicates that the explosion took place on 10 Sep 1846 at 5:00 pm. The Excelsior, which ran between New York City and Coxsackie, was leaving the dock at the Cortlandt St. Pier in New York City when its boiler exploded. Several of the crew and passengers were killed in the explosion and the boat was burned entirely to the water's edge.

18 Little showery. I kill Willis's bull. The half weighs 150 lbs. Willis had 10 lbs., Margarett a piece. I raise my building. I go to river.

19 Fair. Draw stone. I and Peter VanBuren go to County Convention. Peter VanAntwerp appointed a delegate to State Convention.

22 Fair. Draw stone. Fix turnpike. I go to Baltimore to Rev. Mr. Cornell's, then to J.W. Story's & to E. Millbank's, then to river. Get Boots fixed. Peter VanAntwerp here. **He come up to Marite's Wedding**.

23 Fair. **Marite gets Married by Rev. Mr. Cornell.**[92] **I take the wedding's Bride, Groom and all to Albany**. **Take dinner at the Delavan House.** Boys at Lawsuit at Albany.

24 Fair morning, showery in evening. U.B. Willis here. **I thresh with machine**.

25 Cloudy. I finish threshing. Pay off hands. Wife go to Wm. Southwick's.

Delavan House

26 Fair. Clean up grain. Mr. Finch & Mr. Waldron here.

27 Fair. I, Wife & Mother go to Martin G. VanBergen's, Uncle Andrews & back holme.

28 Fair. I go to Abram Verplank's Vendue. Boys dig potatoes. Wm. C. Robb pays me 9 dollars for wood. Maria VanBergen come here last night.

29 Fair. Dig potatoes, get in buckwheat. **Put up chimney**.

30 Fair. Thresh buckwheat. Wesley cut his foot. Dig potatoes.

October 1846

1 Fair. Thresh buckwheat, dig potatoes, wash rye.

2 South wind. Sow rye; dig potatoes. Four peddlers here.

3 Fair. Finish dig potatoes, sow rye. Take Mother Houghtaling to Uncle Andrew's. Pay James Roberts per his Wife twenty dollars. Fetch holme Mrs. Sherwood's orange tree. Wesley holme for Sea Voyage.

4 Fair. I travel around. Wife go to Meeting. **Child cross**.

5 Fair. Clean up buckwheat. **Get 60 bu. broom corn seed from Island**.

6 Fair. I go to Albany, get lumber. Boys go to general training.

7 Fair. Doctor & Marite come back. I get broom corn seed. I and Wife & Ann Maria go to John Mull's.

8 Fair. Clean up broom corn seed, take it to Bogardus. Draw in two loads of corn. Mrs. Fredenburgh & Mrs. Dorman here.

9 Fair. Get in corn. Go to Honse Wolf's, then to Moses Mead's after girl.

---

92 Marite married Dr. Andrew VanAntwerp.

10   Fair. Get broom corn seed. Draw in corn.

11   Fair. I go to Meeting twice. Have the first frost this morning.

12   Fair, south wind. I go to Island after seed. Draw in corn.

13   Stormy. Get broom corn seed. Draw in corn. **Attend School Meeting**.

14   Fair. Draw & get out stone. Plow & make fence

15   Fair. I go to Flat Bush after girl. Go to river.

16   Fair. Sow rye. Get in Corn. A. Civill pay me 25 dollars.

17   Cloudy. I go to Albany after lumber. Boys sow rye; draw in corn. Wellington Vielie here.

18   Rainy day. Stay about the house and go to Mother's.

19   Fair. Draw up lumber & sand. Go to Greenville. I go to Houghtaling's.

20   Fair. **I go to paper mill** & to the Island. Boys get in beets.

21   Fair. I go to P.W. Brot's to County Convention. Boys get in corn.

22   Cloudy. Attend mason; finish. Get in corn, draw wood.

23   Very cold. Draw wood, make hog pen. Mrs. Willis here. I get lime.

24   Fair. Get logs in sawmill. Draw a load of boards.

25   Fair. Martin VanBergen & P. Mead. I go to Meeting twice.

26   Fair. Go to Flat Bush, get timber. Get Hester Wolf.

27   Fair. **I go to Colvin Carhart's, buy a sheep for 12/**.[93] Bradford R. Wood & Mr. Warren here, disappointed in a Meeting.

28   Rainy & cold. I go to river. Husk corn & put away corn.

29   Fair day. **Put on plastering on the sitting rooms**. Draw wood; go to river.

30   Cold. I go to John Cronk's, to P. Keefer's, to George Soul's, get his note.

November 1846

1   Cloudy. I boil feed. Go to Willis's raising. Uncle Joseph, Waldrom and Newman Finch Meeting at Veeder's tonight.

2   Cloudy. Doct. VanAntwerp here. **I set the tune in the church**.

3   Rainy. I and Wife go to Albany. Boys husk corn. Levi commence work here this morning.

4   Fair. I paint the gutter. Levi clean up around the house. Foggy day. **I attend Election, get 3 majority for Silas Wright**.

5   Fair day. Go to river, get horse shod. Boil beets, work in quiry.

6   Fair day. I go to Aquetuck. Take F.R. Terry & John Vandenburgh along. Boys draw wood.

7   Fair. I take Mother to Quarterly Meeting to the Hollow. Then I go to Calvin Carhart's; get a sheep for 10/. Boys press hay.

---

[93]   Fletcher used this symbol often, which we simulate with /. We think it represents shillings.

8	Fair. I take Mother Houghtaling to Flat Bush. Bring Mother back from Quarterly Meeting. Rev. Mr. Searls preach here.
9	Rainy day. Put on plastering. Press hay. I go to river.
10	Wet. Boys press hay, get out hoops. Discharge Peter Cook; pay him. Get lime of Andrew Teneyck.
11	Cloudy. Press hay; get out hoops. **Put on mortar**.
12	Rainy. Press hay. Attend mason. Get out hoops.
13	Fair. Press hay. Get out hoops. **Finish the wing of my house**.
14	Fair. I go to river. Press hay. **Mother Houghtaling & Marite come holme from Flat Bush. J.T. Wilsey bring them and Andrew brought furniture.**
15	Fair. Go to Meeting. Mrs. W. Blaisdell & Cornelia VanAntwerp here.
16	Rainy. **Draw wood on board of sloop**. Very muddy.
17	Muddy. **Draw hay on sloop. I go on board in evening bound for New York**.
18	**Start for New York. Get down as far as Coxsackie**.
19	**Fair. Get under way, get down as far as Purser's (sp) Reach. Then it commences to rain and as dark as Egypt.**
20	**Fair. Start in the morning. Get down as far as Kingston then go on shore have a very rough time.**
21	Start again. Get down as far as Buttermilk Falls, then come to anchor.
22	Fair. Go through the Highlands. Get down to Dedica Hook, then go on shore alongside of the mountain to dry dock after bread. Have a bad walk, dark & rough. Gale begins about 9 o'clock at night.
23	Fair, heavy sea wind, high. We drag on shore, sea-sick enough. At 4 o'clock pm we strike lay until eleven o'clock then put off.
24	Fair. Get to New York. Tear our jib to pieces. Get bread off Bay sloop.
25	Snowy & Rainy in New York. At holme snow 12 inches deep.
26	Blow heavy. Commence to get off hay. See Doctor VanAntwerp.
27	Blow heavy. Great deal of damage done top of the Atlantic.
28	**Fair & milder. I stay at Peter VanAntwerp all night. Marite and Andrew arrive at New York.**
29	**Pleasant. Get hay off sloop. I attend Book auction.**
30	Fair. I go to Church and Temperance Meeting.
31	Fair do up shopping. **Come holme on the North America**.

December 1846

1	Fair. Some snow. Go to the river & work around holme.
2	Stormy. I kill eleven hogs of my own and then John Toben's.
3	Fair. I kill my beef & my calf. Cut & salt my hogs.

4	Fair. I help the women & go to river. Beecher plow.
5	Fair. I am not well. Beecher plow. I fix my stable.
6	Fair. I go to Big Meadow and to Meeting twice. Some thawy.
7	Cloudy, south wind. I go after a load to McCarty's sawmill.
8	Lowry and rainy. Stay about the house.
9	Cloudy. I get horses shod. **Draw 43 bales of hay on board of the sloop Revenue**. I pay J. Sickles 13 dollars. Wife goes to Meeting in evening.
10	Snowy. J.T. Wilsey here, I settle with him. Mrs. Widow Clement & Mrs. John Clement here.
11	Fair, north wind. Go to mill, draw wood. Mr. Robb pay me 10 dollars.
12	Cold. I work around the house. Beecher draw wood.
13	Very cold. I go to Meeting. **Sister Harriet has a young daughter. Steamboats stop**. They get no further than Catskill. I pay Mr. Ramsdell thirty-five dollars.
14	Cold as ever. I hurt my back. Beecher goes to Greenville.
15	Cold as Greenland. Beecher come back. Bring 12 bunches shingles. I go to the river. Settle with John Bailey. Wife and Mother go to Wesley's.
16	Cold yet. I go to the river. Beecher goes to Flat Bush and draw wood.
17	Cold as ever. I go to river. Beecher draw wood from Flat Bush. Wife goes to Peleg (sp) Sherman's.
18	Snow all last night, heavy wind, a little stormy all day. I go to river. Beecher work at wood rack. Snow about 8 inches deep.
19	Snowy but warm. I get horses shod. Sell ashes. Pay Peter Osterander five dollars. Beecher draw stone on turnpike.
20	North Wind. I go to Meeting three times. Quaker preacher in the evening.
21	Fair. Work around holme. Settle with John E. Stebbins in the evening.
22	Fair weather, little stormy but warm. I go to Mother's, to the river. Beecher draws stone on the turnpike.
23	Colder. Work in stone quiry. Beecher draw wood. Wife & Mother Houghtaling go a visiting.
24	Cold. I go to Albany. There is a ball at Cedar Hill.
25	Rainy afternoon. I go to Peter Coonly's. Beecher draw stone.
26	Fair. **I go to paper mill with 686 feet of boards. Attend a Lawsuit**. Beecher goes to James Robertson's to a party. **Put up notices to sell Flat Bush Farm.**
28	Fine warm day. Get out stone. Shingle hog pen. Draw corn from Big Meadow. Stone comes out finely.
29	Clear and colder. Work in quiry. Fix hog pen. I go to Flat Bush and to James Robert's. Beecher draw corn.
30	Stormy all day. I go to river. Settle with Lawton & Willis.

31   Stormy. I and J.W. Story go out to Abram Verplank's wood lot and to Benjamin Terry's. Beecher husk corn. **Attend watch meeting.**[94]

January 1847

1   Thawy wet day. I go to river and to Wm. Sherwood's.

2   Warm and Fair. I fix hog pen, dig stone, get a pig from J. Bronk's.

3   Cloudy and muddy. I go to Meeting, hear Cornell preach.

4   Cloudy morning, snowy afternoon. Spread manure, chop wood. Maria and Liddy Springstead here. I kill turkeys and chickens.

5   Very thawy day. I fix hog pen. Go to river and go to mill.

6   Clear and warm I fix corn house paint gutter; dig stone.

7   Rainy. Work in quiry and husk corn.

8   Cold, one inch of snow. I go to Doct. Fredenburgh's. Work in Quiry.

9   Cold. I pay my tax. George Nichols here, dig stone.

10   Cold. I go to Meeting and to paper mill dam.

11   Three inches snow. Draw stone ½ day. Schoonmaker's Lawsuit today.

12   Little squally. I go Athens, sell my Turnpike stock. Get dividends. **Donation of the Reverend Wm. Tull's in the evening. About 200 attend**.

13   South wind, cold. I gave Peter VanAntwerp his dividend. Pay off J. Muckelvy.

14   South wind. I get horses shod. Attend a ball at A. Houghtaling's last evening.

15   South wind, thawy weather. **I go to both of the paper mills**. Draw stone. Mr. Brandow here, he pays me 70 dollars. Husk corn.

16   Cloudy, south & north winds. Work in Quiry. Meeting about district road this evening to Aaron Houghtaling's.

17   Clear and cold. Go to Meeting twice. Mr. Harris, Mary & Eliza here.

18   South wind. Work in quiry. Go to river with drill. See Mr. J. Cronk.

19   Cold north wind. Work in quiry. Pay Lewis Crandle. Wesley pay me 15 dollars borrowed money. I go to the river.

20   Fine day. I go to Mill. I pay off Wm. R. Carroll. Cate & Elizabeth Houghtaling here and Mary Jane Lawton. **I go to Dancing School**.[95]

21   Clear and cold. I get my waggon fixed. Get corn taken out.

22   Clear & cold. I go to mill. Cut straw. Cut wood. Take Willis's hog holm. **Doct. Fredenburgh here; bleed Mother Houghtaling & Hester Wolf**.[96]

---

[94] A "watch service" is a time of self-introspection and prayers for the New Year.

[95] Dances popular during this period were the quadrille, the cotillion, the two-step, the waltz and the polka.

[96] Bloodletting is the withdrawal of blood from a patient to prevent or cure illness. This was a common medical practice for over 1000 years.

23 Fair, south wind. Beecher chop. David Mosher run out H. Niles Farm, I go with him. Then to Aaron Houghtaling's to road meeting.

24 Fine day. I go to Meeting then to Wesley's. Beecher takes Mother Houghtaling to Flat Bush.

25 Fine day. I and Henry Niles divide fence. Chop wood.

26 Drizzly & wet. Draw wood to Croswell. Go to Willis's in the evening.

27 Clear and cold. Go to river. Chop wood. Mother here.

28 Clear and cold. I put my pig in Willis's pen. Chop wood. **John Tobin's house caught fire at 11 o'clock today**.

29 Snows finely. **Christopher Sickles buried**. Calvin Carhart pay me off. I go to Aaron Houghtaling's to see Judge Nichols.

30 Snow and blow very hard. Finish to husk corn. Go to Mill. Capt. Sherwood here.

31 Fine clear day. Attend communion in Dutch Church. Wesley here.

February 1847

1 Overcast. I go to Albany. Wm. Hoose here. Beecher draw stone.

2 South wind, thaw. I get crosscut saw from square. Beecher draw stone.

3 Rain hard. Water runs over my bridge. Beecher cuts straw. I get my horses shod, work at grindstone and the corn loft.

4 Cold, north wind. Chop wood. Great freshet in creeks. Bridge near J. Shear's taken off. One at A. J. Teneyck's and one on Sickle's Creek. I lose 2 or 3 cords of wood and two logs.

5 Cold. Beecher goes to Stephenville. **Sons of Temperance organize last evening at Aaron Houghtaling's.** Maria Springstead & Uriah B. Willis here to tea.

6 Fine day, N wind. **Quarterly Meeting. Five Preachers here to stay through the meeting**. Catharine Houghtaling here. Beecher chop wood.

7 Fair. Go to Quarterly Meeting and Dutch Church. U.B. Willis here to dinner.

8 Fair, 4 in. snow in the morning. Mrs. Cronk here. Beecher draw stone. Snow go away.

9 Fair. I get logs from the Island. Clarisa Houghtaling & son Conrad & Wife & Cate Crumb, Deborah Holmes here all day.

10 Cloudy. I get logs from Island. Warm, the roads are muddy.

11 Fair. I and Beecher get wood of the dam. **Attend horse trot in the afternoon**. Wife go to Wesley's. P.W. VanBergen pays me 15 dollars 75 cents.

12 Little squally. Draw wood from Island. Draw stalks. Andrew Houghtaling & John Bronk, I draw wood and timber.

13 A little squally. Draw wood. Get horses shod yesterday. Get notices to serve. R. Mosher. Get new Book.

14 Fair. Go to hear Wycoff in morning. Hear Rev. Jolly in afternoon.

15 Squally. I go to Evert VanSlyck's, to J.T. Wiltsey's, to Hawley's visiting. Beecher draw hay.

16 Very cold, cloudy. I get horse shod. Get $10 of W. Robb. Beecher draw hay and stone to the papermill. I pay John Bronk 3.25 dollars for chopping.

17 Fair. I draw, saw logs. Draw wood. Get horses shod. Pay A.E. Willis 20/ my part of monthly books. Henry Niles very sick with collick.

18 Fair. I go to Greenville with waggon. Boys draw hay in the press.

19 Hazy day. I go to Norton Hill, to Oak Hill, so back to Fancher's. Stay all night.

20 Cold. I come back from Greenville with my John Fitch colt. Settle with Edward Collins. He pays me 85.50 dollars. Bring holme a little girl.

21 Snow all day. I stay about the house. **Henry Niles died last night at a quarter of eight. John Colvin's child died today**. No Meeting.

22 Stormy. **I go to Henry Niles' funeral**. Draw stone, chop wood.

23 Cold. Dig stone, draw wood. **Colvin's child buried**.

24 Clear & cold. Fine sleighing. Work in quiry, draw stone. Jane Bronk and Cornelia VanAntwerp here. Wife go to Dancing School. **I was initiated in the Sons of Temperance last evening**.

25 Fair. Work in Quiry. Draw stone. Go to Meeting, Methodist.

26 Clear and cold. **I go with Doct Huyck & Dr. Mosher. They cut the tonsils out of Betsy Ann Hatch's throat**. I pay John Toben 3 dollars, J. Vandenburgh 4.16 dollars.

27 Storm all day. Get broom corn seed from papermill. Go to mill with it.

28 Fair day. I go to Meeting twice. Willis is quite sick.

Methodist Church

March 1847

1 Cold day. Work in quiry. Henrietta Holmes here. I go to river.

2 Cold day. I get my sledge fixed. Beecher draw wood.

3 Fair, south wind. Draw wood. Get horse shod. Get out stones. Beecher draw wood. Protracted meeting here. I pay Peter VanBuren one dollar.

4 Fair. Get out stone. Beecher draw wood. I go to Peter VanBuren's.

5 Fine, warm. Draw saw logs, draw wood. Get my boots tapped.

6 Fair. I go to wood lot. Beecher draw wood. **I go to New Baltimore to a Universalist debate**. **Sit up with A.E. Willis last night**.

7 South wind, cloudy. Beecher take Wife & Mother Houghtaling to Baltimore to Meeting.

8 Fair, north wind. **Move Mother Houghtaling from Flat Bush**. Draw wood.

9 Cloudy & cold. I draw a load of boards. Take Wife & Mother Houghtaling to Andrew Mull's. Beecher goes to Albany to see the burial of Capt. Morris.

10 Stormy. We draw timber. We settle with Croswell.

11 Very cold, north wind. Draw timber. I go to river.

12 Very cold, north wind. Draw wood. I go to paper mill; get seed.

13	Cold. I and Beecher chop in the forenoon. Draw poles & slats in the afternoon. I go to river. **I endorse a note with Lawton's & Willis of $2000**.
14	Fair and cold. I and all hands go to Protracted Meeting.
15	Fair and cold. Boys draw stone. I go to river. **J.T. Wilsey here. He gives me notice of his going to leave Flat Bush Farm.** Put up bedstead.
16	Fair. I and Wife go to Wm. Wilkins. Boys draw stone. Mrs. Holmes here.
17	Cold, north wind. I go to river. Beecher start out wood. I go to river. Wife go to Mother's. **Very quiet St. Patrick's [Day] on account of Famine in Ireland**.[97]
18	Warmer. Draw stone. Myself, Wife & Cate VanAntwerp go to Cornell's visiting.
19	Warmer. Draw stone. Get out stone. Mr. Pelton here.
20	Heavy south wind. Draw and get out stone. Go to river.
21	Rainy and muddy. I go to Meeting. Mrs. Holmes here.
22	Stormy and sleet. I get horse shod and waggon fixed. Mend harness. J.W. Story pay me 20 dollars on rent. Beecher sick; settle with him.
23	Cloudy, south wind. **Sprout brush**[98] on the Island. J. Roberts here.
24	North wind. I go to Island, cut brush with John Toben & J.W. Holmes.
25	Fair, north wind. I go to Millbank's Vendue; buy one calf. Do business with J.W. Story. Mrs. Briggs, Mrs. Clements & Mrs. Terry here.
26	Cloudy, south wind. Commence snowing at two o'clock. **Snow all day and blow heavy; banks unpassable. Worst day on record at this time of year. I go to Aaron Houghtaling to Caucus Meeting; act as secretary**.
28	Very cold. The lane is full of snowbanks. Team have to go through the fields hard crust. I go to Methodist Meeting.
29	South wind; snow & blow. **I attempt to open the turnpike but cannot on account of the snow blowing.** Some milder in the afternoon.
30	Fair, south wind. Work at shoveling snow on turnpike Go to river. Take Wife to A.N. Briggs. **My horse kick and fall down**.
31	Six inches more snow, cold. Get grist. Get broom corn seed to the paper mill. Pay Calvin Carhart $1.20 for sheep.

April 1847

1	Fine day. Good sleying. Get tea, cheese, clover and timothy seed.
2	Snow till ten o'clock. Beecher draw poles. I & Jacob W. Story go to river.
3	Fine day. **Steamboat Buffalo come to the dock**.
4	Very muddy. I go to Meeting, few out. Fair & warm weather.

---

[97] About one million people died in Ireland and another million left during the potato famine that lasted from 1845 to 1851.

[98] We're not sure what this means, but assume it is a way to reduce the growing of brush in a field.

5	Fair, N Wind. Boys shovel snow. Lanson Carhart here.
6	Rainy in afternoon. I go to the dam. Tie up saw logs.
7	Fair. I go to river. Boys shell corn. Wife go to Wesley's.
8	Fair. I go to river. Wash harness; get out timber. Bridget O'Neil come here to work. Mrs. Clement's people here. Abram Witbeck here.
9	Fair, north wind. Oil my harness. Get out timber. **Secure my lumber at the Dam.**
10	Fair, south wind in the forenoon, N wind in the afternoon. I and Henry look at the line fence. I trim apple trees. Doct. & Marite here last night.
11	Fair, hard north wind. I go to Meeting. Take A. VanAntwerp to Baltimore.
12	Cold, south wind in forenoon, NW wind in afternoon. I get waggon fixed. Boys get out timber. J. Bushants pay his rent.
13	Fair. Dig stone. I go to Town Meeting. Take Mother Houghtaling to Widow Charlotte's to see Aunt Caty. J.W. Story here.
14	Fair. I go to Robert Lay's Vendue, get a Gutter. Abram Witbeck hire my farm.
15	Fair. I go to Flat Bush. Mr. Burrows & Mr. Brandow here.
16	Fair, NW wind, cold. I go to Calvin Carhart's to Daniel Carhart's. Take Mr. Robb's bags holme. Martin VanSlyck & & Henry VanBergen here. Boys get stone; go to mill.
17	Changeable weather, south wind. Get out stone. Go to the river. **Lawton's new Barge come to dock. I let my Island to Josiah Sherman. I pay Willis $500 last night – his part of the Brandow Mortgage**.
18	Cold, N wind, dry backward weather. I go to Meeting
19	Cold, south wind. I trade for mare Cate with Daniel Carhart.
20	Fine day. Put my front stone up. Draw boards. Pay Griffin Holbrook 8.75 dollars for getting out hay hoops. J. Story take my mare holme.
21	Very fine day, little rain last night. Grass starts. **I take to Lawton's 90 bushels of corn**. Lay wall.
22	Showry & south wind. Lay wall. Stake out fence; trim trees.
23	Rain all last night and all day. U.B. Willis here.
24	Fair, north wind. Lay wall. Get clams. Get trees; set them out on the rough hill. **Mrs. Bucklin dies**.
25	Fair, south wind. Mother Houghtaling, Wife & Marite Go to Flat Bush. **Mrs. Bucklin buried today.** Mr. Tombs preach the funeral.
26	Fair morning, little showery in afternoon. Lay sow seed. Mrs. Clement & Mrs. Applebee here on a visit.
27	Fair, north wind. **Attend town meeting on the license question. It stands 14 majority in favor of license. High times**. I take a severe cold.
28	Fair. Lay wall. I go to John Mull's, get my first string of fish.
29	Fair forenoon, rainy afternoon. I go to river. Boys get out pickets.

30   Fair, cold. Backwards weather. I make fence; put out onions. Beecher come holme from Greenville.

May 1847

1   Fair, but backward. I pay Wesley seventy-seven dollars interest money.

2   Rainy. I go to Meeting

3   Fair, north wind. Make fence. I go to Flat Bush and to A.T. VanSlyck's.

4   Fair. I go to Albany. Boys plow & make fence.

5   Fair. Andrew Fancher here. Andrew Houghtaling here & John Bushants here.

6   **I go to New York on the barge.** Boys plow. I get money of B. Teneyck.

8   Showery forenoon. **City of New York was illuminated last evening on account of Battles of Mexico.**[99] Come holme.

9   Fine day, warm. Go to Meeting twice. Cate Houghtaling here.

10 Fair warm day. Plow garden; put out beets. Get a string of fish.

11 Fine warm day. Make fence; plant garden; sow barley. Mrs. Fredenburgh, Mrs. Verplank, Mrs. Houghtaling here visiting. I gave Jackson up his notes. I take mine of him. Deborah Holmes here all day.

12 Fine day. Make fence. Plow; get ready for potatoes.

13 Fine day. Make fence. Plant potatoes; plow. Get a string of fish of John Mull.

14 Fair. Sow barley; plow. Make picket fence down by the house.

15 Fine day. I get 50 shad of John Mull. Make fence; plow. Mrs. Holmes here. Get carpet & hats from the Barge.

16 Fine day. I, Wife & Marite go to Daniel VanAntwerp's.

17 Fine warm day. Make fence; plow. I send tickets to Judge Nichols. Mother here.

18 Fine day. Plow. Make fence, fix for Mother.

19 Misty morning. Plant corn.

20 Fine day. Send off a calf. Wife, Marite and Harriet go to New York. Wm. Lawton pays me for stones. Egbert Stanton pays me for wood. I pay Daniel Carhart off all but $25 on mare Cate. Get papers fixed by T. Trego.

21 Fair, south wind. Dig ditch from swamp. Get corn ground read to plant.

22 Cloudy, south wind. Sprinkle in the morning. Draw out manure on corn ground. Draw wood; plant potatoes.

23 Cloudy day. Go to Meeting. Backward season. Corn just up in the garden; pasture very scarce.

---

[99] The Mexican War, which took place between 1846 and 1847, was caused by conflicts due to the westward expansion of the U.S. into lands occupied by Mexico. The war officially ended in February 1848 with the U.S. acquiring lands that would become Arizona, California, Utah, Colorado, Nevada, New Mexico and Wyoming.

24 Rainy. Hard showers at night. I go to Flat Bush. Woolsey Cary pay me $52.50. J. Story boy bring me holme. I go to river.

25 Fair and warm, growing time. Make fence; plow; draw stone for wall. I pay Lawton's & Willis $300 borrowed money. Andrew Houghtaling and Peter Sylvester here. Take up Andrew's mortgages.

26 Rainy forenoon. Beecher plow for his Father in the afternoon. I go to the river. Mother here. I chop and make fence.

27 Fair. Make fence in afternoon. I go to Levi Lawson's.

28 Fair. **Start for Pennsylvania. Go through Greenville to Potter's Hollow to Strykersville, Rackyres (sp), to Gilboa to dinner. Then to the head of the Delaware. Stay all night.**

29 Fair. **Go to Bloomville, to Delhi, to Mariden, to Walton. Stay all night.**

30 Rainy. **Go to Masonville, then to William Lawson's.**

31 Rainy. **Go to Masonville. Stay around there all day.**

June 1847

1 Fair. **Go to Rum Tavern. Stay around; walk about ten miles, see the country, and then to Equimunk (?).**

2 Fair. **Start for Pennsylvania. Go to Deposit, to Widow Labarte's, take dinner.**

3 Fair. **Start back from Caldass (sp). Cross the Delaware, come near being drowned. Go to Shehawken (sp), so back to William Lawson's.**

4 Rainy day. **Go to Masonville. Stay around there all day.**

5 Fair. **Start for Trout Creek, to Syrenus Betts. Take dinner.**

6 Fair. **Go to Masonville. So near Bainbridge. Buy 14 head of cattle, take them to Wm. Lawson's. Make a bargain with Isaac Lawson to bring them holme.**

7 Fair. **Go to Samuel Carroll's. His boys catch 69 trout.**

8 Fair. **I buy a horse, a mare. Get on her and buy an old saddle and come on for holme. Stay first night at Bloomfield.**

9 Fair morning, rainy afternoon. **Ride as far towards holme as A. Fancher's.**

10 Come holme. Fair weather. Get my wool of Jacob Story.

11 Fair. Make fence around the cow yard. Get sturgeon. Go to river. Beecher come holme from Greenville.

12 Fair. **My cattle come holme. I take them to Flat Bush.**

13 Fair morning, rainy towards night. Meeting till evening.

14 Rainy day. Press hay. Get fish of Wm. O. Lawton. Gave Rev. Lull one dollar.

15 Very cold day. Snow in Catskill Mountains. Visit to Harriet's. Boys chop.

16 Fair, NW. Draw stone. Mrs. Pierce here. Andrew Houghtaling here.

17 Fair. Draw in saw logs. Send to J.W. Story's for my mare.

18 Fair. I get mare from J.W. Story's. Plow out corn. Go to Albany. I pay Doct. Springstead 9 dollars 29 cents for paint, oil etc.

19 Rainy. I take Mother to Quarterly Meeting. Hoe corn. Go to mill. Boys on turnpike. I go to river.

20 Rainy. Go to Quarterly Meeting after Mother. Take Dominie to Mr. Jolly's.

21 Rainy, heaviest on record. Attend the Sawmill. Tinker on the road. J.W. Story, John Finch here. Very muddy.

22 Cloudy, NW. Draw in logs. Draw slats for hay and stone.

23 Fair & warm. I go to Greenville. Boys work in corn and potatoes. A. Teneyck taken sick.

24 Fair, war. I pay C. Sickler 21/. Boys work in corn and potatoes.

25 Hot, SW. Work in corn. I go fishing. J.W. Story here.

26 Heavy shower in afternoon. I go to Albany, get flour, nails. Boys draw stone. **They ride Pat Mooney on a rail.**[100] **Mr. Scribues (sp) died**.

27 Fair and hot. Go to see Andrew Teneyck. Go to Meeting.

28 Rainy at night. We all go to Flat Bush. Boys make fence. Seabridge get barley.

29 Fair morning. All go to Flat Bush. Rainy afternoon.

30 Fair day, north wind. All hands go to Flat Bush; draw timber, make fence. Get W. Blaisdell's Turnpike notice. Mr. Nichols here.

July 1847

1 Fair. Plow out corn. Draw timber. Send calf to New York.

2 Fair, NW. Go to Flat Bush. Hoe corn. Draw last load of timber.

3 Fair, NW. Go to Flat Bush. Hoe corn. Go to J. Robert's. Mother Houghtaling, Mrs. Pierce, Aunt Caty here.

4 Fair & hot. Go to Meeting twice. Mr. Willis here.

5 Fair & hot. **We all go to Hollow Celebration of the Sons of Temperance. Have a fine turnout**.

6 Fair, hot. Plow buckwheat ground. Write to Judge Nichols.

7 Very hot. Draw dung. Hoe potatoes and corn. Owen Porter lend me two horse rakes.

8 Very hot. Work at corn. Draw manure. Make bridges. Temperance Meeting tonight.

9 Very hot. I go to Andrew Mull's & to Elias Holmes after pikes. Tear down barn stable.

10 Fair, hot. Doct. & Marite, Caroline & Mary Hallock [here]. I sow buckwheat, go to river, work in garden.

11 Hot day. I go to Meeting.

---

[100] Riding a rail was a common punishment in the U.S. in the 18th and 19th centuries in which the offender was made to straddle a fence rail held on the shoulders of two or more bearers. The subject was paraded around town or taken to the city limits and dumped by the roadside.

12 Hot, SW, some rain in evening. Get horse shod, draw timber.

13 Rainy. **Lay foundation under Barn**. Wife go to Thomas Houghtaling's. Doct. & Lady come back. Elizabeth Witbeck here.

14 Fair, north wind. I go to Flat Bush, get lamb. Boys work in corn. J.W. Story bring up two of my cattle. **Draw a load of boards here**.

15 Fair. I, Wife, Caroline Hallock, Doct & Marite & Margarette go to A.J. VanSlyck's on a visit. Bring Mother Houghtaling back. Boys work in corn. **I send two cattle to New York**.

16 Fair. Finish corn. Gravel my walk. Get Horses shod. I get lemons and cheese to John Keller's and a pail. **Get my building framed**.

17 Fair, south wind. **Raise my barn, scarce time for hands. Have lots of Lemonade. I pay J. Arnold $13.75. Dedrick Lawton & sister here.**

18 Hot & showry. Bronk Witbeck & Miss Shear & A. Maria VanBergen here.

19 Very hot. **Enclose my barn**. Go to river. Cradle rye. Margarett McMichael here.

20 Little showry. Commence to mow clover. **I go to see J.W. Story to the Old Stone Church Place.**[101] Beecher go to Greenville. Showry all day. Mr. Hallock here. **Work at Barn**. Go to Mother's visiting. J. Story bring up my cattle.

21 Showry afternoon. Cradle Rye. **Put cattle on the barge**. Mr. Hallock and family & Marite leave. I and boys pick 18 quarts of raspberries.

22 Fair. I get scythes of Wesley. Work at barn at hay, rye. Pay off Mr. Parmentier. Shingle the barn.

23 Fair. Draw in 2 loads of rye, 5 loads of hay, take 2 cows.

Scythe in Use

25 Rainy. **Make Affidavit for the purpose of getting rid of P. Cook**. Boys mow.

26 Fair and cold. Draw in hay, mow.

27 Fair day. Rake & bind and draw in rye & hay. **J.W. Story bring up my cattle, 6 in number**.

28 Fair, south wind. **I send off my cattle**. Draw in hay. Henriette Holmes here.

29 Rainy afternoon. I and Wife go to Albany. Boys draw in hay. & grain. **I buy 8 scythes**.

30 Heavy rain last night. Boys mow. Peter VanAntwerp here.

31 Fair. I pay Mr. Parmentier three dollars & eight cents.

August 1847

1 Cloudy. I go to Meeting twice. Ann Maria VanBergen leave here.

2 Fair. Mow and get up hay. Work late in clover lot.

---

[101] There is an article about the Old Stone Church in the Summer 2014 Ravena Coeymans Historical Societies Newsletter by Jean Bush [Vol. 12 No 2] from which the photo was taken.

3	Fair. Work in hay. Finish in clover lot.
4	Fair. I go to Flat Bush. Get Old Cate. Go to Mill.
5	Fair. Work in hay. I and Wife go to Joseph Cronk's.
6	Fine day, cloudy morning, fair in afternoon. Wife & Mother Houghtaling go to Flat Bush to Seth Hawley's.
7	Rainy day. Mow in forenoon. Go a fishing in the afternoon. **Willis's boy, Blaisdell, gets drownded in cistern**.[102]
8	Cloudy day. **I and Wesley go to Old Place to see where to bury Willis's child.**
9	Cloudy & misty day. **All at the funeral of Willis's child.**
10	Fair, south wind. Mow and get in hay. Attend the division. Dominie here. Joseph Cronk give me a new note.
11	Fair, south wind. Showers around. Get in hay.
12	Fair, north wind. Work in hay. I take butter tubs to the river.
13	Fair. Get in hay, bundle oats. Take a load of hay to Dominie Lull.
14	Fair. Get in hay & oats. I go in a swimming.
15	Fair. I go to Meeting twice, then to Big Meadow.
16	Fair. Work in hay & oats. **Get in 9 loads of oats in barn**.
17	Fair. Work in hay & oats. Mrs. Mull here visiting.
18	Rainy last night. Some cloudy north wind. I go to Flat Bush, get a sheep. Finish mowing; put up hay. Rev. Cornell & Lady here.
19	Fair, north wind. **Draw in 18 loads of hay**. Mrs. Clement here. Wm. C. Robb pay me 10 dollars 32 cents. I get horse shod.
20	Fair. **Finish haying. I have 97 loads hay; 6 do. of rye, 6 do. of oats, 2 do. of barley. Go a fishing**.
21	Fair. I go to river. Get buckwheat of Lawton's. Go to see about burying ground. **Commence digging out basement on my Holmestead.**
22	Fair and hot. I go to Meeting. Take tea to Wesley Blaisdell's.
23	Fair. **I go to Albany, get tombstone for Father Houghtaling**. Boys work on Fallow. Draw wood.
24	Fair. I go to Flat Bush. Take dinner to Andrew's. **Take Father Houghtaling's tombstone to where he was buried**. Go to Camp Grounds.
25	Fair. I go fishing. Boys draw wood, work on fallow.
26	Fair. I go to river. See about burying ground. **Go to Flat Bush to the funeral of Andrew Houghtaling's child, named Bronk Houghtaling**.
27	Fair. I go to river. Get horse shod. Beecher goes to Greenville.

---

[102] Harriet and Alexander Willis had 11 children. Blaisdell Willis was their second child and was only 3 when this tragic accident occurred. They named their third child, who was born in 1848, Blaisdell Willis also.

28 Cloudy. **I go to Camp Ground. Make our tent**. Boys sprout brush.

29 Fair day, a little shower at night. Martin VanBergen, Cate, Elida VanSlyck here. They bring back Mother Houghtaling. Wesley & Miss Angevines here. I go to Meeting twice.

30 Fair. I go fishing. Beecher draw wood. Mr. Charles Hallock come here.

31 Fair. **I take all hands to Camp Meeting.**[103] Miss Angevines here. **Wife go sailing**.

Camp Meeting

September 1847

1 Fair. Boys draw wood, burn fallow. I go to Camp Meeting. Take Phillip Phelps' girls along. They come here.

2 Fair. **Take 12 persons to Camp Meeting. Stay all night. Are one of the guards. Jane Phelps hurt her shoulder getting out of the waggon**.

3 Fair. Come holme. Mr. Huddleson here. Beecher draw a load of wood from Flat Bush.

4 Fair. Burn fallow. **Get Daughter's**[104] **Daguerreotype** taken. Martin VanSlyck here. Peter Holbrook have my horse.

5 Fair. I take Phelps' girls to Martin G. VanBergen.

6 Fair. Showers last night. I take Bridget to Albany. Boys sow rye on fallow. I go look for a girl [servant].

7 Fair. **I and Jacob W. Story start for sheep**. Stay at night at Simon (?).

8 Fair. **Drive to Patchin Hollow.**[105] **Stay all night at Sap Bush Hollow to Akerly's Tavern**.

9 Rainy afternoon. **We go to Summit Four Corners. Go to Mr. Story's**.

10 Fair. **Hunt up sheep. Walk all day, get very tired**.

11 Rainy. **Get our sheep together. Get back far as Patchin Hollow**.

12 Rainy day. **I drive holme through the rain. Take cold, quite unwell**.

13 Fair. **I take Physic. Am sick all day**.

14 Cloudy. **I and Wife go to State Fair at Saratoga Springs**. Boys plow.

15 Fair. **Stay last night and all the time to Wm. Cook's. Go to Fair Ground to horse trot; to circus at night. Goes off finely**.

16 Fair. **Attend to Fair Grounds to horse trot. Meet with J. VanBenthuysen. Take tea with Mrs. Fonda**.

17 **Return holme, Railroad and Steamer, Shepherd Knapp**. Boys plow & cut up corn.

18 Fair. **I go to Flat Bush, sell sheep**. Get apples. Take mare holme. J.H. VanBenthuysen here.

---

103 In the early days the Methodist Episcopal Church held multi-day revivalistic Camp Meetings. They were often held simultaneously with the Quarterly Meeting during the warmer months.

104 Harriet was 6 years old at this time.

105 Patchin Hollow, which was named after Freegift Patchin, is on the Schoharie Creek and is now called North Blenheim.

19	Cloudy, south wind. I go to Meeting. U.B. Willis here.
20	Fair. Sow rye. Get horse shod. I work on building.
21	Fair. Finnish sowing rye. **Go to Aquetuck to Democratic Meeting**.
22	Fair. Work on road. I go to Flat Bush. Mrs. Pierce & Catharine here. **Have a large Applecut tonight.**[106]
23	Fair, NW. **I go to Flat Bush. Had about 70 persons here to an Applecut. Have great sport, not much done.**
24	Fair. Work on road. I go to Hollow to Dist. Convention. Take Wm. R. Carroll along.
25	Cloudy & rainy. I go to river. Pay J. Keller 20 dollars. **F.H. Terry take my statement about the thirty acres I purchased of Henry Niles before he died. He agreed to get a deed from the heirs for 40 dollars. I pay one half and half of the reference bill for about one day's service.**
26	Rainy all day. I go to river. Henry Vanderzee, Doct & Marite here. I put up Mother's stove. **Harriet is sick.**
27	Cloudy day. Stay at holme. Mother here. Mr. Perkins & Lady at Wesley's from Illinois.
28	Cloudy & rainy. We work on the road. Julia Hamilton come here to work. U.B. Willis here in the evening.
29	Clear off. **John Schofield buried here today**. Make fence; go fishing.
30	Fair. Take Wife and all hands to Andrew Mull's. I go hunting. Boys work on the road.

October 1847

1	Fair. All hands go on turnpike. Get apples from Niles' place. Wife go to Willis's.
2	Fair day. I and Wm. Bagley go hunting. Boys work on the road.
3	Fair. I go to Meeting, to Wesley's. **Wm. Bagley fell in the papermill dam**.
4	Fair day. Mr. & Mrs. Perkins [here]. Boys cut up corn.
5	Fair. Dig potatoes. The Mr. Collinses here. Miss Ford & Miss Collins, Uriah R. Willis & A.E. Willis here.
6	Fair. I take Mrs. Pierce to Coxsackie & to A.T. VanSlyck's. P. Phelps here.
7	Fair. Finish potatoes. Cut buckwheat. Get Broom Corn seed. Mrs. VanAntwerp here. I take away my butter tubs.
8	Rainy afternoon. We draw logs to mill. Boys go to New York. **John Gibbens work at Old Holmestead.**[107] John Cronk and Lady here.
9	Fair, NW wind. Draw wood, get things of Warren & Steel.

Old Homestead

---

[106] We believe this was to preserve apples for long term storage.
[107] We believe that the "Old Holmestead" is the house on the NW corner of Westerlo St and Main St where Fletcher's father, Levi lived part time, had a store and Post Office. We got the photo from Dennis Whalen who said it was taken ~1880.

10	Hard NW wind. I go to Meeting.
11	Heavy NW wind. Draw posts, wood & gravel. Fix barn yard. **Show tonight in Temperance Hall**.
12	Cloudy, misty. P. Seabridge thresh buckwheat in my barn. We draw gravel.
13	Fair day. Work in quiry. Lay floor in my barn.
14	Fair day. Work in barn. Christina VanBergen & Miss Houghtaling here. We cut apples at night.
15	Fair. I work in Barn. Beecher work at the house.
16	Fair. I go to Albany. Boys draw wood. A lot of visitors here.
17	Fair. **I get sweet fern**. I go to Meeting, hear Dominie Cornell.
18	Fair. Boys thresh. I go a fishing; get some fish and two black ducks.
19	Cloudy. Draw in corn & buckwheat. Draw a load of wood for P. Clancy.
20	Fair. I go to Greenville to Norton Hill. Pay off Mr. Ramsdell. Boys draw wood & thresh buckwheat.
21	Fair. I come from Greenville. Boys draw wood & thresh buckwheat.
22	Cloudy day. Thresh buckwheat. Lay floor overhead in barn.
23	Colder. We all work at barn. Go to Mill.
24	Cloudy & rainy. Cornell dismiss Sunday School.
25	Some rain. I go to Blacksmith's, to Mill, get paint, get **Plowshears**[108] & Pumpkins. Boys get out hay slats.
26	Cold wind NW. Begin to plow. Deborah Holmes here.
27	Fair. Work at house, plow, draw stone.
28	Cold. I go to Albany, get stove. Boys plow.
29	Fair day, cold. Plow, work at House. Give in Affidavit to Sqr. Briggs.
30	Fair. Plow, go after apples, get Carolina potatoes.
31	Fair day. **Albert Jackson & Cornelia VanAntwerp get married today in the Dutch Church by Rev. Mr. Cornell. I kiss the bride**.

November 1847

1	Fine day. Work at house, plow. Mrs. Kilmore & Mrs. Bailey here.
2	Fine day. Election goes off. Work at house, plow. **Whigs get 190 majority in Albany**.
3	Fair, warm day. Work at house, get horse shod. Mrs. Gibbens here.
4	Fair, warm. Work at house. **Mr. Hull's child buried today**. Mr. Ellsworth calls on me about Capt. Sherwood's property.
5	Fair, NW. Work at house, draw in corn. Ira Gregory pay me for my heifer. Mrs. Willis here.

---

[108] We believe Fletcher means "Plowshare," which is the main cutting blade of a plow.

6   Clear & cold, NW. **Get pumpkins from the Island**. Work at house. Draw in corn. Get all corn in barn.

7   Cloudy. I go to hear Rev. Cornell, then to hear Rev. Lull. Beecher have my mare.

8   Cloudy & rainy. Plow & work at house. J. Story pay me 80 dollars.

9   Foggy, south wind. I send Beecher to Albany. Harriet here. **I propose Tobias Crumb for a member of the Sons of Temperance**.

10   Fair. Work at house. **Have a husking bee at night**. Get all done.

11   Fair, NW. Plow. P.J. Groat commence to work this morning.

12   Fair, NW. Plow, work at house. Mrs. Holmes here.

13   Fair, NW. Plow, go to Mill. J.T. Wilsey pay me 54.52 dollars. **A lecture in Dutch Church this evening.**

14   Cloudy & rainy. Mr. Warren preach in Dutch Church.

15   Fair, NW. Draw wood to Capt. Stebben's. Work at house.

Dutch Reformed Church

16   Fair. **J. Muckelroy's child buried today**. Emeline Sweet & Miss Hatch here. I go after Hoop Poles and dig a ditch.

17   Fine day. Work at house. **Tobias Crumb & Deborah Holmes get married. We attend the wedding at E. Holme's.** I get Willis's waggon.

18   Fair. **Work at house & go to wedding to Tobias Crumb's**.

19   Lowry. Work in barn. J.W. Story bring my cider. I go to river. **Sleepy day, the effect of attending wedding two nights**.

20   Cold & cloudy. Go to Greenville. Wife go along. Boys draw manure. A Quarterly Meeting at Dormansville.

21   Fair, cold south wind. Come back from Greenville. I drove my big horse.

22   Fine day. Get out slats, get horses shod. Go to Briggs in the evening.

23   Foggy & rainy. Press hay all day.

24   Rainy, Press hay. David Richard gets out hoops.

25   Cloudy, muddy. **Thanksgiving**. Rev. Wm. Lull preach.

26   Fair, NW. I go to Albany. Boys press hay, get out lumber.

27   Fair. I go to I. Lawson's Vendue, **then to J. Wilsey's leave a counterfeit $10 bill that he gave me. Get another.** Boys press hay.

28   Fair, N Wind, cold. I go to Meeting. Marite & Amira VanBergen here.

29   Very cold. Press hay. Mrs. Aaron Houghtaling & daughter Lib here visiting. I go to river.

30   Clear & cold. **I put hay on board Sloop Revenue**. Doctor VanAntwerp and Marite leave for New York.

December 1, 1847

1   **Finish putting hay on sloop**. Draw wood. Get up stoop at old house.

2	Rainy day. I go to New Baltimore. Boys work around house. **Eliza Lawton died last evening. I go after Minister to preach her funeral sermon**.
3	Snow & rain. **Attend Eliza Lawton's funeral. They take her to New Baltimore and put her in Sherman's Vault. Sarah Camp died last evening**.
4	Fair. Go to Mill, to river. Go after wood for John Toben.
5	South wind, cloudy. Go to Meeting twice. Wesley here.
6	Fair, north wind. Make road. Go to Mill. Work at house.
7	Fair. Make road. Make cow crib. Work at barn.
8	South wind. Work at house. Draw wood to Wesley.
9	Cloudy, south wind. Get out gutter sticks.
10	Rainy day. I get horses shod.
12	Hard rain. I go to Meeting.
13	South wind, misty, in afternoon clears off. I kill my beef.
14	Fair. I kill six hogs. Griffin Holbrook help. Very muddy. **J. Hauenstien's child died**.
15	Cloudy. Cut up my hogs. Go to river.
16	Salt pork. Go to river. They all meet here and make regalia.
17	Sleet & snow. I stuff sausages. I go to river. Pay off A.N. Briggs.
18	Fair. 6 in. snow. I go to river. Boys draw wood. Clear out stone quiry. I get horse collars fixed. River clear yet.
19	Fair. I go to Meeting twice. Good sleying. I call at Capt. Sherwood's.
20	Fair. Draw wood. Other Houghtaling come back. I get sley fixed.
21	Cold. Draw wood. Get turkey of M.B. Bogardus. Sign a note with Lawton & Willis. Fix cellar windows and Barn doors.
22	Fine day. I take Wife to Albany. Get books of R. Garrett.
23	Fine day. Get sley fixed. Get axe handle in new axe.
24	Fair day. I and Harriet go to Flat Bush. Beecher draw wood.
25	Christmas. I & Beecher draw wood all day. **River closed today**.
26	Clear & cold. Dominie Fitch here. I go to Meeting.
27	Clear & cold. Get horses shod. I let J.W. Story have 215 dollars to buy cattle. Story leaves his mare here until he returns.
28	South wind. Draw & saw logs. I and Mother Houghtaling go to Joseph Cronk's. Maria Springstead & Sally Goldsmith here.
29	South wind. I go to Greenville. Beecher draw muck & a load of wood for himself.
30	South wind, fair. Snow all gone. I come back on bare ground.
31	Great thaw, very muddy. Boys chop. I go to river. Mr. Soop here and another man after a farm.

January 1848

1. South wind, very muddy. Wife have Mrs. Fredenburgh, Mrs. Terry, Miss VanAntwerp. Have a turkey supper.
2. Rainy morning, clear at noon. I stay holme.
3. Clear & warm. We chop & work in quiry.
4. Cold, N wind. Dig post holes. **Attend the Division**.[109]
5. Cold south wind. Work in quiry. Wm. Sherwood pay me 100 dollars.
6. Clear & cold. I go to Albany to testify in Terry's & Nike Teneyck scrape. Get Maryett's Novels. Pay R. Garret for books.
7. South wind. **Steamboat Columbia go down today**.
8. Snowy in forenoon. I go to river. Send a letter to David Mosher by Rev. Lull.
9. Fair, north wind. Snow is about 4 inches deep. I go to Meeting. Steamboat come within a mile of New Baltimore this morning.
10. Very cold. I get horse shod. Fetch a sley holme. Draw muck. I pay mine & Wesley's & Beecher & Holmes.
11. Very cold. Draw muck. Harness my colts for first time. Mother here. I get my sley from Peter VanBuren's.
12. Fair. I go to river. Get boots tapped. **Old Mrs. Teneyck died last night**. Boys draw muck. Some thawy.
13. Fine day. Draw muck. Help Stephen Sherwood draw logs in afternoon. I get horse shod. Draw some stumps to Elias Holmes. Go to donation to Rev. Cornell.
14. Misty & stormy. I go to river. Pay H.B. Joslin 105 dollars. Boys cut straw.
15. Cloudy & rain. I go to river. **Get six brooms of Albert Jackson**.
16. Fine warm day – like Spring. I go to Meeting twice.
17. Fine day, but muddy. Work in quiry. S. Carhart & Jeremiah Springstead Lawsuit goes off today. I settle with John Mull.
18. South wind in morning, NW in afternoon. Blows hard & squally. Wife & John Henry goes to Albany. Julia comes back with them.
19. Clear & cold. Boys chop. I go to river. Pay Flat Bush tax.
20. Fair. I and Capt. Sherwood go to buy wood, timber & logs of Wm. Vroman, amount $26.75.
21. Fair, south wind. Boys chop. Get out gutter stick. **Daughter Harriet taken very sick. Doct. Fredenburgh, Dr. Russel & Dr. Youmans here**.
22. Fair day. Chop wood. Beecher goes to take his girl holme. **Harriet is very sick. A great many here to see her**. I get a new coat of Bogardus.
23. Fine day, cold North wind. **Harriet is very sick. I wrote to Doc. VanAntwerp. Up with daughter night & day. Wesley here all the time**.

---

[109] Sons of Temperance meeting.

24	Fine cold day. **Send after Doctor Squires. Harriet very low**.
25	Fine day, warm south wind. Boys draw logs. **Harriet no better**.
26	Cloudy & rainy. **Harriet died at twenty-five minutes past 5 o'clock today p.m. Mrs. Willis here.**
27	Cloudy & rainy. **Beecher goes to Flat Bush to let the folks know of Harriet's death**.
28	Cloudy & muddy. **Harriet buried this afternoon**. Rev. Wm. Lull preach.
29	Clears off. Chop wood. I go to river. Get school district Blank to take up births, deaths & marriages in the district.
30	Fair. Communion today in Dutch Church. I go to Meeting twice.
31	Fair, south wind. Boys lay walk through the lane. I take up the births, deaths & marriages in school district.

February 1848

1	Fair, snow fall 4 in. last night. I take Catharine Houghtaling holme through mud. Boys thresh. It grows colder.
2	Fair. Thresh with horses. I go to river. Cornelia Jackson here. Wesley pay me 24.52 dollars his tax.
3	Fair. Thresh oats all day.
4	Snowy. It melts as it comes. I go to river, get boot mended. **Steamboat Columbia goes up today**.
5	Snow all day. Clean up grain. I pay off Wm. R. Carroll to his son Nelson, amt. 8 dollars besides my bill. Boys draw hay.
6	N West wind blows hard. I go to Harriet's.
7	Cold, N wind. We draw logs I bought of Wm. Vroman.
8	Fair. **Go in woods. Draw 17 hardwood logs, 23 pine ones**.
9	Fair. Draw wood. Rev. Lull's donation at J.J. Colvin's. Mr. Porter here. Cate Houghtaling here, I go with her to donation.
10	Fair. I and Wife goes to Albany. Have Snider. Martin VanBergen, Mr. Chapman, Cate & Almira VanBergen, Elida VanSlyck & Cate Houghtaling here.
11	Clear, cold. Boys draw wood. Mr. Chapman & Eliza Phelps here. Maria Keller here making dresses. **I am vaxinated for kind poc.**[110]
12	Clear & cold. Draw 50 load of muck.
13	Cold. Rev. Wicoff preach in Dutch Church. Elida VanSlyck goes holme.
14	Fair. Draw muck. Newman & Wm. Finch here. Bring me a pair of boots.
15	Fair. I ride to Flat Bush with Newman Finch. Come back with Mr. Bushants. Boys draw muck. Mother here.

---

[110] This could possibly be a vaccination for smallpox.

16	Fair. Draw muck. I attend W.B. Bogardus Lawsuit. Stay until 12 o'clock at night. Am a Juryman. Rev. Wm. Lull quite sick.
17	Fair. Quit drawing muck having drawn 400 loads. Buy a hogshead of John Keller. Cate VanAntwerp here visiting. Draw stone.
18	Fair. Boys go to Flat Bush, draw logs. Cate Houghtaling & Mrs. Terry here. J.K. Terry here in the evening.
19	Draw out logs to Flat Bush. Bring here Cate VanBergen & Aunt Caty.
20	Rainy & Muddy. I go to Meeting. Willis here this afternoon.
21	Fair. I go to Beecher Holmes. **Mrs. John Hauenstien died this morning**. I get turpentine, Beecher chop wood.
22	Rainy. Celebration of Sons of Temperance Coeymans Division, Coxsackie Division & Vesta division turn out. Rev. Wycoff lecture.
23	Fair. **Mrs. John Hauenstien's Funeral today**. Rev. Mr. Lull preach.
24	Squally. **Mr. John Roseboom died**. We go to Thms. Houghtaling; visit.
25	Clear, cold. J. Cronk leave here. Cate VanAntwerp & Joseph Cusdy's Lawsuit goes off today. Abram Witbeck pay me $70. Wife & Cate VanBergen goes to A.N. Briggs.
26	Fair. I take Mother to Quarterly Meeting.
27	Fair, NW. I go to Quarterly Meeting, bring Mother holme.
28	Cold, south wind. Got slat timber. Pay John Keller per Mosher's boy ten dollars.
29	Cold. NW. Draw wood. Go to Mill. Caroline Houghtaling here on a visit. Elias Holmes here. Wife goes to river.

March 1848

1	Cold day. Chop & draw wood. Wife & visitors go to Willis's.
2	Clear, cold. I go to river. Boys chop. Mrs. Peleg Sherman & Margarette here visiting.
3	About 4 inches of snow. I take Wife & Cate VanBergen to river. Cate goes to Dr. Fredenburgh visiting. Boys chop slat timber.
4	Fair. Boys draw logs to Flat Bush. D.R. Convess pay me $8.25. I buy 4 bushels of peas. Harriet here visiting. Mr. Vinton lecture here on Temperance.
5	Heavy N Wind. We all go to hear Cornell preach.
6	Fair. Boys draw logs. Mrs. Fredenburgh, Aunt Betsey, Mrs. McGregor here visiting. I pay off Wm. Lonnon 5.78 dollars, which settles his account.
7	Fair. Boys draw logs. Ephraim VanSlyck & Lady here visiting.
8	Fair. We all go to Coxsackie to Sons of Temperance celebration. Have a fine time. Mr. Gould address the order. I take dinner to E. Hubbell.
9	Cloudy & rainy. I get horses shod. Very muddy.
10	Snow about 7 inches. Clear off in afternoon. I and Boys to Flat Bush. Draw logs; get harness fixed.

11   Fair. I put Henry Mull's notes in E.D. Rlonves's hands to collect. Boys draw logs. I pay Barent TenEyck 18.44 dollars, saw bill.

12   Fair, south wind. We go to church twice.

13   Fair. I go to river. Boys go to Flat Bush. **I get the Myrtle papers of C. Ryan**.

14   Fair, N wind. Boys finish draw logs. I go to river.

15   Fair, cold, N wind. Boys draw wood to Mother's.

16   Fair, cold, N wind. Mary Jane Lawton & Elizabeth Houghtaling here. Boys draw stone. I go to river, get augur.

17   Fair, cold. I go to Barent Mull's Vendue; buy 3 cows, a grain cradle & Saw. Boys draw hay.

18   Fair. I attend H Rasick's Vendue. Buy two calves for $16.13. John Henry draw muck.

19   Warmer, south wind, rainy. U.B. Willis here in evening.

20   Rainy. Draw muck, go to mill. Afternoon is wet.

21   Fair. I attend John Clow's Vendue. Boys draw hay. **River broke and steamboat goes up.**

22   Fair, warm. Boys draw hay & boards from the Sawmill.

23   Stormy. I get my horse shod. Boys chop wood.

24   Fair, north wind. **I go to see J. K. Gerry about my building a room for S.T.**[111] **and about removing Bogardus from my premises**.

25   Fair day. I go to Flat Bush. Boys chop. It is very muddy.

26   Stormy. Andrew & Marite come here from New York. Wesley Blaisdell here.

27   Rainy. Chop wood. P.J. Groat & Beecher go to Flat Bush; get out timber for new Temperance Hall. I get my first string of fish. Very muddy.

28   Rainy day. I go to river. Andrew VanAntwerp goes to Albany.

29   Fair. Clears off pleasant. I get 100 clams today & go to Sawmill.

30   Fair. **I go to Albany with Peter Seabridge. Exchange the title of him. Buy dresses for my Wife. Coeymans Barge comes up today**.

31   Fair, south wind. Barge leave. Quite warm. I sow lettuce bed. Mrs. F.K. Terry here.

April 1848

1   Fair, N. Wind. I go to Hollow to Nomination along with Doct. Russell. Take tea to Widow Andrews. Attend Coeymans Division of S of T.

2   Clear and cold. I go to hear Rev. Cornell preach.

3   Fair, south wind. Work on road & draw in logs in Sawmill.

4   Stormy, south wind. Get in Sawlogs. John Bushants pay me off today.

5   Fair, N wind. Draw lumber from Sawmill. Deborah Carhart here.

6   Fair, N wind. Draw lumber; sow grass seed.

---

[111]   S.T. stands for Sons of Temperance

7   Fair, NW wind. Wife go to N. Johnson's visiting. Maria VanBergen here visiting.

8   Fair. I take all hands to Andrew Houghtaling's; visit. Roads bad.

9   Fair, dry weather. **Mosher's Son buried today**. A. Jackson & A.E. Holmes here.

10 Fair. Commence plowing. Wash barley. I get eight bushels of lime of Jerry Springstead. Wife go to Albany. P. VanAntwerp here.

11 Fair. Attend Town Meeting. Sow barley. Take Marite to David VanAntwerp's. **J.B. Shear get 62 majority over F. Cranston for Town Supervisor.**

12 Cloudy morning, fair afternoon. David Bronk commence work for me.

13 Rainy. **Make a bargain with N.B. Bogardus to put up my Temperance Hall while he occupies my building**. Marite and Mother Houghtaling go to NY with the Barge.

14 Cloudy forenoon, fair afternoon. I clean peas to sow.

15 Fair day. **Survey out Burying Ground**. Draw timber from Flat Bush. Go to Renssalear Hills and to Mr. Vroman's to get my money of him.

16 Fair. I go to hear Cornell preach.

17 Fair, cold. I go to Albany. Boys work in garden.

18 Fair, N wind. French Jo come here today. C. Vroman pay me 13 dollars.

19 Three inches of snow, NW wind. Boys draw timber. I wash harness. I go to river. Take H. Niles' hatchet holme.

20 Fair. Draw stone. Work at barn. Mrs. Andrew Mull here.

21 Fair day. **Raise my barn**. Plow. Mrs. Elias Holmes here. I pay Peter J. Groat 15 dollars.

22 Fair. **Work at Barn down to river by David Baker's**. Get fish.

23 Fair, S wind. Mrs. E. Holmes here. I go to Mr. Willis's.

24 Cold, NW, clear. Draw stone, lumber. **John VanDenburgh broke his leg rolling logs.**

25 Fair. **Work at barn**. Get lime. Plant potatoes. Get iron.

26 Fair, sunny. **Work at barn. Buy an old canal boat of Henry Wilsey for 12/.** Plant beets & onions.

27 I go to Albany to Troy. Get lumber, shingles. **Boys tear old canal boat to pieces and finish barn**.

28 Fair. Fix hay press. Draw up lumber & shingles from dock.

29 Heavy south wind, little rainy. Boys go to Flat Bush. Fix hay press. Gave Rev. Wm. Lull some hay.

30 Fine day. **Mrs. Stacy died this morning. I attend the Funeral.** Cornell preach.

May 1848

1   South wind. Boys work at hay press. Fix fence. Boys go to Flat Bush, draw timber. I go to see J. Vandenburgh.

2   Rainy afternoon. Draw timber, make fence.

3	Fine rain. I help Peter VanBuren roll logs in sawmill. Get horse shod, go to mill. Make fence.
4	Fair. I go a hunting. Make fence. **Wife cleaning house**. Wm. Mead here.
5	Rainy morning. Fix hay press. I, Wife & Mother go to John Mull's.
6	Fair, warm. Make fence; get fish; shoot pidgeons. Joe leave for Canada. Beecher goes to Athens. Mother Houghtaling come back here.
7	A very heavy thunder shower. I go to Meeting twice.
8	Fair. Draw boards & timber. Pick stone. I get my hair cut by R. Keefer.
9	Rainy forenoon. Draw in logs in sawmill. Fair afternoon.
10	Rainy & wet. Boys draw timber from Flat bush. I go to Peter Witmore after him to help. Go to river, **get churn dasher**.[112]
11	Rain hard all day. Wet time.
12	Fair. Draw timber. Attend Sawmill. A. Fancher here, pay his rent.
13	Fair. Draw timber; attend sawmill. A. Fancher here; pay his rent. John Mead here; we gave him a deed for Thompson lot.
14	Cold, rain. I go to Meeting. Cold day.
15	Fair once more. Draw timber, attend Sawmill. Get fish. Send calves to J.W. Story's.
16	Misty. I take Catharine Houghtaling holme. Get fish of John Mull. Draw timber from Mill. Roll in Sawlogs.
17	Fair day. Furrow out corn. Draw manure.
18	Fine day. I and Wife go to Albany. Bridget O'Neil come to work here. Julia Hamilton leave. Wife go to Waterford after Bridget. Boys draw manure & plant corn.
19	Fair, warm. I attend Sawmill. Boys plant corn. My mare has a colt.
20	Showry & hot. Plant corn. Finish drawing timber. I pay N. Agau 11 dollars for turnpike damages. Woolsey Cary pay 42 dollars interest money.
21	Rainy afternoon. I go to Meeting; turn out our horses.
22	Press hay. Rainy. **Get potatoes out of the cellar**.[113] Go to river.
23	Rainy & wet. I take Wife & Mother Houghtaling to Baltimore. Pay off Dr. Newcomb. Get dried apples.
24	Fair. Boys press hay. I take Wife to Greenville. Drive my colts. Get Edgeth (sp) rent.
25	Fair. Come back; take dinner to Mr. Hogan's. Martin G. VanBergen here.
26	Heavy shower. Get lumber from McCarty's Mill. I &Martin G. VanBergen go to Mopy Hill. Mrs. Castle here.
27	Fair. Work on road. Caroline VanAntwerp here. Judge Nichols here. I get fish & get grey mare shod.

Butter Churn

---

[112] A butter churn was used to separate cream into butter and buttermilk. The dasher was the device attached to the pole that agitated the cream.

[113] Potatoes were stored in the cellar to eat during the winter and used for planting in the spring.

28	Fair. I and all folks go to Dutch Church.
29	Fair, south wind. Go to Flat Bush; plow make fence. Notify N Johnson to remove dirt.
30	Fair morning, rainy afternoon. I get in two loads of lime.
31	Fair, NW wind, cold. **Plant potatoes**; draw manure.

June 1848

1	Fair, NW. Plant, draw dirt. I take old mare to J. Springstead to horse. Get some fish.
2	Fair. **Dig at foundation to Temperance Hall. Buy 7 bu. shingles**.
3	Fair. **Dig foundation. I go to Albany after sash & floor plank**.
4	Fair. Go to church. Robert Cronk here.
5	Rain. Draw stone & lumber from dock. Get 14 shad of H. Niles.
6	Draw stone. **Lay foundation to Temperance Hall**.
7	Lowry & misty. **Draw stone and brick**.
8	Fair. Go to Springstead with my mare. Plow out potatoes. Get horse shod.
9	Fair. Work at Hall. I go a fishing with S.F. Cranston.
10	Fair. I go to Baltimore after Marite. **Boys put hay on Sloop Revenue. 125 Bales**. I attend S of T in evening.
11	Fair. NW. I go to Meeting. **My sow has 13 pigs, or 9 this month. Sloop Myrtle takes Folks out on excursion for sail**.
12	Heavy NW wind. I buy bull of Gilbert Cronk. **Finish foundation of Temperance Hall**. Pay Willet Thurston.
13	Fair, NW. **I raise Temperance Hall. Treat with lemonade & cakes**.
14	Fair. I go a hunting. Peter VanAntwerp & Lady here.
15	Fair. I go to Albany. Get Coensad Getsmire (sp) to work for me. Boys work in corn.
16	Fair and hot. Work in corn. A. Fancher send me two loads of boards.
17	Fair. Work in corn. **Auction off lots in cemetery. I buy lot #19**. Abram Witbeck pays me balance on his rent.
18	Fair, SW. I go to Flat Bush; get Marite & Mother Houghtaling.
19	Hot. **I pay Wesley Blaisdell $1,110.41. I get 250 dollars of Ann Bronk. Get $200 of J. Colvin. Lawton & Willis take up note I hold against them**.
20	Fine rain. Dig in cellar. Draw sand. I go to Sawmill. Have lots of company.
21	Fair. Plow buckwheat ground. Draw boards. I take Wife and all hands to Andrew Mull's.
24	Fair day. **Julius Blaisdell died 1 o'clock today**.[114] J. Colvin pays me 148 dollars; I send him his note by B. E. Holmes.
25	Fair. **Attend Funeral [for] Wesley's boy**. Rev. Mr. Tombs preach. Put child in Niles' vault.

---

[114] Julius Blaisdell was Wesley's son.

26 Fair. **I go to Herkimer**. P.J. Groat go along far as Albany.

27 Fair. **Arrive at Herkimer Get affidavit. Get back to Little Falls**[115] **to John Feeter's**.

28 Shower in the PM. **I sell land of H. Schoonmaker and buy it myself**.

29 Fair. Go to see land. Go to Hiram Ayres; take him along, go around the land.

30 Fair. I hire out the land to George Persons. Stay last night to Ohio City.

July 1848

1   Fair. I come holme. Start from Little Falls at half past two o'clock in the night. Get to Albany. Have very bad dysentery.

Painting of Little Falls

2   Fair. Quite sick. Get medicine of Doct. Fredenburgh.

3   Rainy day. Unwell yet. I sign a note with Lawton & Willis of $1000.

4   Fair cold day. Mother here. Boys go to Albany.

5   Cool. Cradle rye. Mrs. Abram Post & Sister here.

6   Fair. I go to Baltimore. Boys work in corn.

7   Fair day. **I go to Albany see the Burial of Cap. Van Olinda**.[116]

8   Fine day, clear. Fallow burn off swamp. **Wife go to get Spinster with Old Mare**.[117] We work late.

9   Showry. Go to Meeting. Hear Rev. Mr. Rodgers. Cate Houghtaling here.

10 Fair. Hoe potatoes; draw water. I pay Jeremiah Springstead twenty dollars.

11 Fair. Draw water; work in swamp; draw in rye.

12 Fair, SW. Cradle rye, hoe corn, sow buckwheat, dig ditch.

13 Fine shower. Sow buckwheat, cradle rye, dig ditch, work in corn.

14 Hot. Work in corn. Dan go to Flat Bush.

15 Fine day. Finish corn; rake up rye. Mother here. I go to river.

16 Fair. I go to Meeting. Hear Rev. Mr. Rodgers. Let Beecher have a horse.

17 Fair & cool. I go to Albany, get trimmings. Boys work in grain & hay.

18 Fair, NW. Work in hay, draw in rye.

19 Fair, south wind. Mr. Hallock & family here. I take Hallock to Baltimore.

20 Fair. Cradle barley; work in hay.

---

[115] Little Falls is a town in Herkimer County. It is built on both sides of the Mohawk River at a point where rapids impede further upstream travel. Fletcher establishes a sawmill here.

[116] Captain Abram Van Olinda was killed in the Battle of Chapultepec on 13 September 1847 (Mexican American War). His Eulogy was delivered at the First Presbyterian Church in Albany on 7 July 1848.

[117] Originated with women who spent their adult years at the spinning wheel rather than raising a family.

21	Fair. Cradle barley, work in hay. I go to river.
22	Fair, hard SW. Draw in barley.
23	Fair, hot showry, south wind. Charlotte Houghtaling here.
24	Fine rain. Quarterly Meeting goes off.
25	Fair. Draw two loads sand. **Aaron Houghtaling serves me with a writ from Bogardus by Terry**. Work in oats. I sell Mc Clancy two pigs.
26	Fair. I go to Flat Bush. J.W. Story pays me three dollars. Boys work in hay.
27	Fine shower. I pay Leonard Hathaway $3.00 for plank. Work in hay.
28	Fair day. Work in hay. H. Niles' cows break in my corn.
29	Fair day. Mrs. E. Sherman, Mrs. Baker, Caroline Hallock and the Gedney girls here from New York. Work in hay. I pay P.J. Groat $15.00.
30	Fair. We all go to Meeting, then to Flat Bush. See Andrew Houghtaling.
31	Rainy all day. I go a fishing. Boys mow, fix scythes.

August 1848

1	Fair. Work in hay. I pay J.E. Gibbens Five dollars.
2	Fine day. Work in hay. I go to river; am not very well.
3	Fine day. Mow; draw in hay & peas. Take letters to the Barge.
4	Fine day, south wind. Work in hay. Take a sail last night to Barren Island.
5	Fair. **Go to see Indians**. Abram Lobden here.
6	Fair, hard NW wind. Mother Houghtaling come holme. Go to hear Cornell preach his farewell sermon.
7	Fair. I go to Albany on Pettet Jury. Boys work in hay.
9	Fair. Boys work in hay.
10	Fair. Boys work in hay. I sick with dysentery.
11	Fair. Boys work in hay.
12	Fair. Beecher is sick. Daniel Bronk go to work.
13	Fair. Frederick & Wm. Bagley here. Phillip Phelps here; he preach. Wife & company go to Baltimore.
14	Fair. I go to Albany on Jury. Boys work in hay.
15	Fair. I come back from Albany. Andrew VanAntwerp & Lady go to Daniel VanAntwerp from here; return today. Boys work in hay.
16	Fair. Work in hay. Doc goes back to Daniel's horseback. Mrs. Mull here. Mr. Civill & guests here. Wm. Bagley & Frederick here.
17	Heavy SW. Wm. & Frederick Bagley leave. We work in hay. Wife, Marite, Doctor go to Coxsackie. Fine rain. **G. Holbrox child died today**.
18	Rainy day. Doc go to N. York. Great freshet in river. Water high.

19 Cloudy. I go to Flat Bush. Martin & Elida VanSlyck come here.

20 Fair day. Martin VanBergen bring Marite & Cate VanBergen here. We go to Meeting.

21 Fair day. **Finish haying; have 121 loads**. I pay Wilkins $4.13 for stone.

22 Fair day. Draw gravel. Wife & Margarett go to Greenville yesterday.

23 Fair day. Draw gravel. Work around the Temperance Hall. **Benzilla Nelson died today**.

24 Fair. Work around Hall. Danl, my hired man, goes to J. Springstead for stone.

25 Fair. I go to Albany; get shingles. Find a parasol. Mr. Stephenson & Lady here. **Old Hunker meeting to Aquatuck**.

26 Fair. Go to Meeting. Have lots of company.

28 Rainy day. Work at Temperance Hall cellar.

29 Fair. Beecher goes to Greenville, plow. I and Teneyck Waldron take inventory to Widow Calvin Carhart's.

30 Fair. Draw wood. I go to R. Pulver's, get apples. Wife and Company go to Garrett Houghtaling's visiting.

31 Fair & hot. Marite & Mother Houghtaling come here.

September 1848

1 Fair. Work at Temperance Hall. **Mrs. Stephenson, child and Servant leave here**. He leave a day or two ago.

2 Fair. Work at Hall. Andrew Fancher's team here.

3 Fair. I go to Meeting. Rev. Mr. Right & Lady here.

4 Fair. I burn fallow. J.W. Story pay me $56.50.

5 Fair. I and Ebenezer Finch go to Albany. I take up my note at the Exchange Bank.

6 Fair. Dan work on fallow. Beecher go on road. I work at Hall.

7 Fair. Work on fallow, at Hall. Wife & Margarett Blaisdell go to Flat Bush.

8 Fair. Boys on fallow. I hurt my back; am very lame. I pay Montrop 15 dollars for stone.

9 Fair. I take inventory. Boys work on fallow. Mrs. Weed & her Mother here.

10 Fair. I have a very lame back. Lay a bed all day.

11 Fair. Beecher goes to Albany. Dan draw stone. We have a fine shower last night. I have a very lame back yet.

12 Little showery. Boys thresh, work on fallow, draw gravel.

13 Fair. Boys work on fallow. I & C.TE Waldron draw off Widow Carhartt Inventory.

14 Rainy. Send things to New York to Mr. Hallock. Boys draw stone.

15 Fair. Work on fallow and Hall. Phillip Phelps here.

16 Fair. Dan goes to Albany. Beecher & John Toben work on fallow.

17 Fair. I take P. Phelps to Baltimore. Wesley here. Bridget goes to Hollow.

18   Clear. Work at fallow. Draw up Abram Post's furniture.

19   Fair, south wind. Work on fallow. **Martin VanBergen married today**.

20   Rainy day. **I discharge Danl Bronk**. Go to river. Thresh rye.

21   Fair. Thresh rye. Go after apples. Harris pays me for wood. I pay Egbert Stanton 15 dollars borrowed money.

22   Overcast, cold north wind. I take Wife & Ruth Ann Finch to Albany. Pay Springstead & Bullock $20. Pay off Tyler & Bullock. Pay P. Groats' man 5 dollars.

23   Fair, NW. Sow rye. John Mead here. He pay me 50 dollars note. Margarett here. I get Broom seed from the Island.

24   Fair. I go to hear Rev. Mr. Pelts preach.

25   Cloudy. Go to Mill and get waggon fixed.

26   Fair, cold NW. Roll logs in sawmill; bring holme a load of slabs. Work in corn. Mrs. Abram Post here.

27   Fair. Plow. Get grist from mill; cradle buckwheat.

28   Fair. Draw manure. I pay Henry Spere $13. Pay P. Reynolds $7. **Acton Civill move to New York.**

29   Lowry. I exchange waggons with H. McDonald; agree to give him Fifty-five dollars to boot[118] now and Five more after he varnishes the waggon and the spring.

30   Fair, SW. Sow rye, work in buckwheat. I pay John Keller. Mrs. Pangburn 2 dollars. Isiah Shawbut come here to work.

October 1848

1   Rainy. I go to hear Rev. Mr. Pelts. Go to Willis's & to Mother.

2   Rainy. Thresh. I go to river. Send notices to VanDalfsen heirs for A.E. Willis. **Attend School Meeting till 12 o'clock. Have a high time**. Set up with Mr. Dorman.

3   Rainy day. I go to river. Boys thresh rye. **I have house plastered**.

4   Appearance of rain. **Barent Ryon died today**.

5   Fair. Draw 5 loads of sand. Mr. & Mrs. Wales, Mrs. Bushnel and Mr. S.A. VanBergen here. Boys make fence. I attend to visitors.

6   Fair. Dig potatoes. **Attend Barent Ryon's funeral**.

7   Fair. I take Mother to Dormansville to Quarterly Meeting. Boys draw up broom corn seed; dig potatoes. I attend Greenville Division of S of T.

8   Fair, NW. I return from Quarterly Meeting.

9   Fair, SW. Draw shingles. Capt. Sherwood pay me ten dollars.

10   Fair. Thresh buckwheat. Work at house. Go to Andrew Mull's.

11   Fair. Thresh buckwheat. Dig potatoes.

---

[118] The idiom 'to boot' means "in addition to." It had nothing to do with footware.

12 Fair. **Free Soil Meeting.**[119] **Bradford R. Wood address the meeting.**[120] Doctor VanAntwerp here. I finish digging potatoes.

13 Fair. Clean up buckwheat. I go to see the **Old Place**.[121] Mrs. Houghtaling & Mrs. Lawton here. Boys draw in corn.

14 Fair. I and Peter Seabridge go to Albany. Boys work in corn. Mrs. Colvin here.

15 Fair. I and Mother Houghtaling, Bridget and Ruth Ann Finch go to Flat Bush.

16 Fair. I take Levi with me to Baltimore. Mrs. Phelps here. Draw in corn; fix bridge.

17 Showers last night and today. Mrs. E. Holmes here. Ordination and Installation of Rev. P. Pelts.

18 Rain all day. Mrs. Phelps go holme. We clean out wood house.

19 Rainy. Wm. Cook & Lady here. We split hay slats. I get 100 dollars of A.E. Willis.

20 Cloudy, NW. I pay off Reynolds for him. Get out slats. Pay 51 dollars to Maria Houghtaling.

21 Misty & wet. **I and F. Mosher go out to the County Convention to Bradt's. The Old Hunkers have a meeting in the Temperance Hall today**.

22 Fair, NW. Mr. C. Hallock here. I take him to New Baltimore.

23 Fair. **I go to Little Falls**. Boys press hay.

24 Rainy. I get to John Feeter's. Go to Ohio. Stay all night to Mr. Bly's.

25 Go with Mr. Persons around the lot. Return to John Feeter's.

26 Fair. Return holme. Bring Margarett Feeter along.

27 Fair. Andrew Houghtaling & Lady here. Draw stone & slats. Fix barnyard.

28 Fair. I go to Meeting & to G. Lawton's. Boys break hay press.

29 Lowry. I go to Meeting in the Dutch Church.

30 Fair day. Fix stone; fix Hay Press; draw manure; pay off Henry Spere.

31 Showry. Fix cellar. Husk corn. Let P.J. Groat have ten dollars.

November 1848

1 Fair SW. Put away corn. Let P.J. Groat have ten dollars.

2 Fair. I go to Flat Bush. Hay press. N.H. Johnson pay me 50 dollars. Mrs. A. Jackson & Mrs. Niles here.

3 Fair. I take Margarett Feeter to Albany and Mother Houghtaling. I pay VanGaasbeck, pay off **Davidson & Viele**.

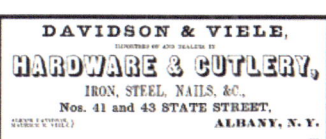

---

[119] The Free Soil party was a short-lived political coalition that opposed the expansion of slavery into the western states. They merged with the Republican party in 1854.

[120] Bradford R Wood was elected as a Democrat to the 29th Congress (1845-1847). He founded the First Congregational Church in Albany in 1850 and was one of the founders of the Republican Party in New York.

[121] We believe that "The Old Place" was his Father Levi's farm, which was north of present-day Ravena.

	Pay Springstead 15 dollars. Take yarn to Abram Koontz. Boys dig beets & fix hay press.
4	Cloudy. Go to mill. Marite come. I get quinces, nuts, cabbages. J.W. Story fetch buckwheat, apples. I fix hay press, get out hoops.
5	Very heavy rain. I go to Mother's.
6	Fair, SW. Fix hay press and press hay. Fix turnpike.
7	Fair. Election. **The Hunkers get but 16 votes in this district, Free Soilers 55, the Whigs get 90.** We press hay.
8	Fair. Go to mill. Get out hoops. Press hay.
9	Fair, NW. Press hay. I go to river.
10	Fair, cold. Press hay. Rev. Mr. Pelts call here. Marite & Mother Houghtaling go to Martin G. VanBergen's.
11	Fair, cold. Put in Mother's Water cask; draw stone. **Abram VanBergen died today**.
12	Snow all day. I take Bridget to Coxsackie to Meeting.
13	Three in. snow. Sleys run. Draw wood. Get horses shod.
14	Lowry. Draw away hay. Draw a cord of wood to C. VanDalfsen's.
15	**Draw 169 bales hay. Attend horse trot upon the Flats. B.E. Holmes died tonight**.
16	Fair, SW. I kill hogs. P. Seabridge & John Toben help.
17	Fair. Cut up port. Work in quiry. Take in carrots.
18	Fair. Work in quiry. Dig carrots. Get letter from A. VanAntwerp.
19	Fair. Go to Meeting twice. Go to Cemetery.
20	Snowy. Draw wood to Mother. Wife & Folks go to Mrs. Clement's.
21	Fair Draw boards from D. McCarty's Mill.
22	Warm, cloudy. Draw stone. **Put on board of barge 600 lbs. buckwheat flour.** Barent VanSlyck & Lady here.
23	Fair, warm. Draw stone. Press hay. Beecher come back.
24	Fair, warm. Press hay. **P. Holbrox sister-in-law buried**.
25	Warm, south wind. **Julion Verplank's child buried today**. We press hay. Wm. Sherwood pay me 100 dollars.
26	Snowy. I take Peter VanAntwerp & Marite to Daniel VanAntwerp's.
27	Clear & cold. North wind. **We put 74 bales on board Sloop**. Plow garden.
28	Fair. **Trego's child Loiza buried today. I go with carriage to funeral**. Boys scrape out cellar.
29	Fair. I go to Albany Beecher draw stone. I pay all off.
30	Fair and warm. Plow in Big Meadow. Go on Turnpike.

December 1848

1. Fair, warm. Plow in Big Meadow. J.W. Story bring me a load of corn and take my mare & colt back with him. **Aunt Luzan VanBergen died**.
2. Rainy. Chop wood and bring up things from Barge.
3. Fair. I go to Meeting and write a letter for Bridget.
4. Fair. I take Mother Houghtaling to Coxsackie. Beecher plow.
5. Rainy & wet. I go to river. Get a letter from Mrs. Stephenson.
6. Rainy day. I go with A.E. Willis to Albany; attend Lawsuit of his against Johnson & Niles.
7. Rainy. I go to Albany on Willis's Lawsuit. Get Isiah Shawbrit a trunk; get Mother Houghtaling's hat – pay two dollars for it. I get 5 dollars of A.E. Willis.
8. Fair. Chop wood; go to river; fix manger for horses.
9. Fair. Attend Sawmill. Go to Grist Mill. Get corn. Get hogshead of John Keller. Get a barrel of flour of Lawton & Willis. Draw lumber.
10. Rainy. Wesley & Margarett here. Stay in house all day.
11. Fair. Work around the house and fix up our Anteroom Chamber.
12. Stormy afternoon. Plow in forenoon. Work at cellar wall.
13. Clear off. I go with Willis to Albany. Boys plow.
14. Return from Albany. Plow and cut brush. Fair day.
15. Fair. I go to Albany with A.E. Willis. Boys plow and cut brush.
16. Fair morning. I come back from Albany. **Attended Lawsuit of George Smith for robbery**.
17. Fair day, warm. I go to Meeting. Pay Hull 50 dollars for Dominie. Write a letter for Bridget to go to Priest to Lansingburgh.
18. Fine warm day. Draw stone, timber; plow; fix shed. Pay John Mosher two dollars.
19. Fine, warm. Plow. Work at shed, fence.
20. North wind, overcast. Dig stone in quiry. Plow. Mrs. Holmes & Mrs. Crumb here.
21. Snow all afternoon. Very bad going. I pay P.J. Groat 25 dollars. Boys wash and oil my lamps.
22. Snow hard all day. Get horses shod; fix wheelbarrow. Send letter to David VanAntwerp.
23. Stormy, snow. I take cutter to McDonald. Boys chop & oil lamps. **Anthony Blaisdell Born. Sara very sick. Child born at 8 o'clock pm**.
24. Snow. I get horses shod. Pay off Doct. Fredenburgh to this date $67.50.
25. South wind, warm. **I go to Black Dick's after negro wench to nurse. She won't come**. Then I go to river. Get Mrs. Shutter. **I let Pat Clancy have my shop**.
26. Fair. I go to Albany. **Get Mary Newcomb to nurse**. Get sley shoes. Boys draw stone.
27. Snowy in afternoon. Boys fix road. I go to river.
28. Fair, North Wind. **I kill my beef. Sell Richard Lawton 1 quarter for 4 cts. per lb, wt. 109**.
29. Snowy & misty. Cut straw, cut up beef, draw muck. Go to river.

30 Snowy forenoon, then clear. I pay Mrs. Shutter 50 cents. Draw Mother's wood; take 1 load to Sally Anderson.

31 Snowy & cold, N wind. I go to Meeting twice.

January 1849

1 Fair. Draw muck. I go to river. Beecher go after his wife & mother.

2 Fair, cold, NW. Draw muck. Capt. Sherwood pay me three dollars.

3 Fair, cold. Draw 3 loads wood. Aunt Catharine & Sarah Ann here. They come with John Nichols. I let Mr. Robb have my tackle blocks. Josiah Theron pay his rent.

4 Fair. Draw muck. Get blanket to papermill. Settle & pay Aaron Houghtaling.

5 Fair, N wind. I take my visitors to T.E. Houghtaling's. Draw muck; fix my pump. Beecher take his Wife to his Father's.

6 Fair. Draw muck. I take Aunt Catharine & Sarah Ann to Charlotte Houghtaling's.

7 Fair. I take Aunt Catharine & Sarah Ann holme. Bring Cate back.

8 Fair. Draw 1 load of wood to W.C. Rob. I go to Albany with Wesley.

9 Overcast. Boys draw muck. Andrew Mull & Lady here. Mr. Collins here, he pay me his rent.

10 Cold. Draw muck. **I subpoena John Roseboom**. J. Wilsey pay me.

11 Cold, thermometer 12 deg. below zero. Draw muck.

12 Little more mild. Draw muck. Mrs. Fredenburgh here. I pay in LW 55 dollars to pay taxes.

13 Warmer, South wind. Draw muck. Margarett here. I go to river. **Subpoena A.N. Briggs to Lawsuit between me & Bogardus**.

15 Rainy afternoon. **My suit called today but postponed by my paying**.

16 Fair. I go to river. Pay F.K. Terry 15 dollars. Get horse shod.

17 Fair. **I subpoena Peter Teneyck, then to Albany after I see him**. Then I go to P. Phelps', then to Enhacon division S of T. Stay all night at Calanan Wilder's Tavern.

18 Fair. Bring Calanan down. **Commence a suit with M.B. Bogardus.**

19 Fair. **Continue the suit. Try to settle but fail**.

20 **Continue suit. George Sickler swore he heard me confess to Bogardus that he, Bogardus, was to have my house for 30 dollars per year, and that I was satisfied with his account, and that I said that it was all right, what is all false. I footed up past of his account against me, but I never did admit the account to be correct, nor never said that 'Bogardus was to have the house for 30 dollars per year. George told a wrong story.**

21 Fair. I take Calanan to Albany, come back & go to Meeting.

22 Fair. I go to river. Get dress for Mary Newcomb.

23 Fair. **Lawyers sum up before Referees, Terry occupy 5 hours**.

24 Fair. I get out timber. Go to Greenville.

25 Stormy. I get my rents, return holme. Boys clean up grain. Donation to A.P. VanSlyck's.

26 NW. I take Wife to Jackson's. Cate VanBergen to W.H. Southweek's.

27 Fair. Mr. Persons of Herkimer here. **The award given against me in Bogardus suit is $142.66.** Draw timber; go to mill.

28 Fair. I take Mr. Persons far as 4-mile point. Let him have 12 dollars, take his note date 27th. I go to Meeting.

29 Overcast, south wind. Draw stalks, hay. Go to river.

30 Overcast. I go to Albany after a load of boards. I pay Dr. LaBask three dollars for Mary Newcomb.

31 Cold. I go to river. Get blank [form] to take up Manager Births and Deaths. Mrs. Garrett Houghtaling & son Anson here. Boys draw hay. I attend to visitors.

February 1849

1 S wind, snowy. Boys draw hay. I take up Manager Births & Deaths.

2 Fair. Mrs. Willis & U.B. Willis here. Boys draw hay. I get 100 dollars of Nelson Agan, gave him my note.

3 Fair. I settle with J.W. Story; he pays me 40 dollars. I take his note.

4 Fair. I and Wife go to Wesley's. I go to Abram Post's.

5 Snowy. Boys chop & draw wood. I go to Albany for A.E. Willis.

6 Cold S wind. I drive Willis's team to Albany. Boys draw wood.

7 Fair. I stay last night to Phillip Phelps. I and Wife go to Troy to Mr. Stephenson's. I then drive A.E. Willis's horse holme. Boys draw wood.

8 Cold S Wind. **I go again to Albany. Testify in Willis's case about Orchard Lot. Return on the ice. Very cold, snow hard. The worst night I ever was out.**

9 Cold, NW. Draw loop poles. I go to river. Pay off Jerry Springstead.

10 Fair. I get 300 dollars of Doct. Fredenburgh. Pay interest to Thms. Houghtaling. Pay Br[other] Wesley 130 dollars. **Get two brooms of J. Sherman.** Beecher take my Grey Mare to bring his Wife holme.

11 Fair, SW. J.H. Holmes take Bridget & Mother Houghtaling to Coxsackie with my team.

12 Snow all day. **I attend funeral of Gardner Sherman's child.** Boys chop wood.

13 Fair. Boys go to Greenville. Bridget sick. Wesley here.

14 Fair. Boys get back from Greenville. Neuman Finch here.

15 Fair. Draw Abram Teal 3 ft. maple wood. Boys go to Greenville. I settle with Peter Seabridge. **My sow has eleven pigs.** I pay John Keller 10 dollars.

16 Fair. Boys get back from Greenville. I pay off John Roseboom & Wm. McGregor.

17 Fair, cold yet. Draw stone. I go to river. Beecher takes my gun; go to see his Wife.

18 Fair, very cold day. Stay in house. **Doct. Fredenburgh draw a tooth for me.**

19 Fair. **Thermometer stands at 21 degrees below zero.** John Bushants here. He pays me 50 dollars. **Daniel Carhart's Lawsuit goes off today.**

26   Thawy. Draw muck. Beecher bring his wife here this morning. Cut wood in afternoon. **The Jews have a sale of goods here today**.

27   Fair. Draw muck and stone. I go to river. Mrs. Hull & Mrs. Sherman here.

28   Fair. Draw muck & work around the house.

March 1849

1   Warm. Fix bin in barn & lay cellar wall.

2   Cold. Clean up barley. Maria Springstead here. I go to river.

3   Clear and cold. Send letter to Albany. Margarett sick. Sprout brush.

4[122]   Fine day, cool. Rev. Mr. Willis preach. Wife & Beecher go to his Father's.

5   Fine day. Draw fence stuff. Lay cellar wall. Mother here. P.J. Groat goes to work at Mother's house.

6   Fair. Lay wall. Draw stone. Elizabeth Holmes here.

7   Stormy, wet. Rev. Mr. Rodgers delivers temperance address in Division Room last evening. We get out hay hoops all day.

8   Cold, NW. I go to Vendue to Maxwell's, then to John Bushants. Boys press hay. William Darling help.

9   Clear cold day. I go to papermill, to river.

10   Clear cold day. I go to river. Get sley tongue fixed for waggon. Boys lay stone wall & draw stone. I get letter from Dr. VanAntwerp.

11   Fair, cold NW wind. Rev. P. Pelts & Lady come to church for first time.

12   Fine warm day. Get out timber. Draw stone. J. Bushants here.

13   Fine day. Lay cellar wall. Get out timber. Sarah Ann goes to Albany. **Rees Whitman died this morning**.

14   Overcast. **I go to Albany; get new nurse. Break waggon tongue. Get waggon of Erastus Corning**[123] **to come holme. Was very thoughtful**.

15   Rainy. I take E. Corning's waggon holme. Boys work at house & get out hoops.

16   Rainy. **All hands work at Mother's**. Capt. Sherwood & John Mosher help.

---

[122] Zachary Taylor, a member of the Whig party from Virginia and Kentucky, was inaugurated the 12th President of the United States on this day.

[123] At age 13 Erastus Corning moved from Connecticut to Troy, NY where he clerked for his uncle's hardware store. He rose through the ranks and became a very successful businessman, educator and politician. He served one term as mayor of Albany 1834-1837 and was a two-term Congressman at the time of the Civil War. He had disagreements with President Lincoln, but always believed in the preservation of the Union. The Town of Corning, NY bears his name. His great grandson, Erastus Corning 2nd, was mayor of Albany for 40 years, 1941-1983.

17	Fair. **Raise Mother's house. Steamboat Columbia goes up**. Mother here.
18	Clear, cold, NW. I write a letter for Bridget & go to Meeting.
19	Fair. **Plane siding for house**.
20	Fair, SW heavy. I go to see Barley Roe's Farm. Take Dinner to J. Bushants.
21	Rainy day. We get out hoops. C. Waggoner here, bring cowhide.
22	Fair. **B.W. Warner here. Take directions to go to see my land in Herkimer**. We get out hoops. I get a letter from Mr. Persons with 12 dollars that I lent him.
23	Fair, south wind. Break hay press. Work at house.
24	Fair, south wind. Fix hay press. Work at house.
25	Heavy rain. Andrew VanAntwerp & Marite come from New York. We go to Meeting.
26	Cloudy, north wind. Press hay & get my boots tapped.
27	Snow and blow all day. Andrew VanAntwerp start for New York. We press hay.
28	North wind & rainy. **We draw 48 bales of hay to Barge**.
29	Fair. Finish press hay. Wife & Marite go to Wesley's. B.W. Warner back.
30	Rainy day. Get out pickets. I go with Mr. Warner to get a house.
31	Lowry & warm. Get out pickets & get a lock fixed.

Fletcher's Plane

April 1849

1	Fair, cold. Go to Meeting. Cate Fredenburgh here to tea.
2	Fair, heavy NW. **Make fence to Mother's house**.
3	Fair day. We all work at house.
4	Fine warm day. Sow lettuce bed. Beecher & Holmes move in my house. **Whig Nomination today**.
5	Rain in forenoon. Draw stone & brick. Mrs. Fredenburgh & Betsy Verplank here.
6	Fair. **We all go to C.F.E. Wife's funeral. Conrad VanDalpsen's child died this morning**. We work in garden.
7	Fair, south wind. I take Mother Houghtaling & Marite to Flat Bush.
8	Fair, NW wind. Andrew bring Marite holme. Rev. J. Cornell preach.
9	Fair day. **Draw 99 bales of hay on board barge.** Dig ditch; work at house. Lib Houghtaling here.
10	Showry. I take Wife & Marite to Daniel VanAntwerp. I go to Town Meeting.
11	Fair, cold, NW. Abram Verplank's Vendue goes off. Beecher buy 1 cow. I pay off John Mosher. I send my calves to New York.
12	Fair, cold. We work at Mother's House. I pay John Keller 10 dollars.

13 Fair, still day. Sow barley, plant potatoes & onions. Plow garden. Work at house. Sell John Keller 64 ft of boards.

14 Very cold. Freezes all day. Draw up gutter stick. Work at house.

15 Two last days snowy and squally. Work at house. Dominie Rite & Lady here.

16 Cold, squally. Go to mill & work in swamp.

17 Fair day. Work at house. Get grist to mill. Leave 1 barrel of rye flour to go to N. York.

18 Cloudy. **I and Wife go to Albany. Get Catharine, our nurse's child.** I pay off James Calanan.

19 Cloudy & rainy. **We take Catharine's child to Mrs. Holmes.**

20 Fair, heavy wind. Mr. Jas. Stephenson here. We work at mortar.

21 Fair. Dig ditch. Our cow has a calf today.

22 Fair. Go to Meeting. U.B. Willis come holme with us. Mother Houghtaling come back from Coxsackie.

23 Fair, south wind. Work in swamp. P.J. Groat here.

24 Fair. I send off my barley. Work at Swamp.

25 Fair. Send off my calf. Get fish to John Mull's. Margarett Blaisdell here. I put out onions.

26 Fair, cold. **My Carpenters finish Mother's House.** I graft my pear trees. Catharine Houghtaling here.

27 Fair. I graft trees; plaster house. Crandle fetch Dominie Rite's daughter here.

28 Rainy, south wind. I go to John Mull's, get fish. I pay him off.

29 Fair, NW wind. I go to Meeting. John Sperl pay me 2.75 dollars.

30 Fair, but heavy south wind. I sow 3 bushels of oats & work in garden

May 1849

1 Fair. Work at fence. Put out carrots. **Attend James Lawton's wedding. He marries Catharine Houghtaling. She is 26 years and he is 47 years old.** Rev. Pelts marries them. We have a fine time and stay until 4 o'clock in the morning. Plenty to eat. Lots of liquor.

2 Fair, cold NW. I pay Thms. Houghtaling 190 dollars. Get fish of John Mull. Make fence. Capt. Sherwood pays me 75 dollars.

3 Fair. I go to Albany, get carpet. Mrs. Sherman, Mrs. Lawton & Harriet here.

4 Fair morning, little shower in afternoon. We make fence.

5 Lowry, rainy. Wife goes to Andrew VanSlyck's with Beecher.

6 Rainy. I go to Willis's. Wife not back yet.

7 Cloudy. I take 2 cows down to Flat Bush; bring back my mare. Take Mother Houghtaling to Widow Carisa's

8 Rainy. **Put up privy**[124] to Mother's. Mr. Warner here; I accept his order.

---

[124] A reminder that there was no indoor plumbing in those days.

9   Clear. **Put in cistern.**[125] **Lay stone. Move Mother to her new house.**

10   Andrew Fancher here; he pay me his rent. David VerPlank here to sell me his horse. I work in garden. Weather fair.

11   Fair. We work in garden. Finish fence to James White's.

12   Fair. I work in garden. Take up note of Thms. Houghtaling. I get 300 dollars of B.B. Fredenburgh. I pay Hugh McDonald fifty dollars. Get fish. Mr. Reynolds fetch me 4 bushels of lime.

13   Rainy day. We go to Meeting & to Willis's.

14   Fair. Go to mill. Lay stone wall. Dig cistern. Pay off A.N. Briggs.

15   Fair, cold day. Beecher go after potatoes. Isaiah go along. I and Wesley go to Greenville. **Uncle Joseph Blaisdell very sick**.

16   Come back, have a lot of painters here. Leave **Uncle Joseph very low**.

17   Fine day. Work in garden; go to mill get bran. **Uncle Joseph Blaisdell died**.

18   Fine day. Move Mother's wood. Fix railing on my stoop.

19   Fair. **I and Wife go to Uncle Joseph Blaisdell's funeral.**

20   Fair, warm. I go to Meeting. Take tea to Wesley's.

21   Fair, warm south wind. Fix a pen for my bull.

22   Fair, SW. I and P. Seabridge go to Albany. I pay off Tyler & Bullock. **Abram Kounts & Peter trade Sloops. I take chattel mortgage**[126] **on his sloop for money he owes me**.

23   Fair, warm & windy. I trade horses with Peter Seabridge. He gave me 10 dollars to boot. Wife go to New York. I send away butter. Turn out horses in pasture. Plant corn.

24   Rainy towards night. **Finish Mother's back house**. Plant corn.

25   Fair. Fix Mother's stairs. Get 1 ¾ lbs. twine of J. Keller.

26   Fair. Plant corn. **Attend lecture in evening on Physiology & Anatomy**.

27   Fair, south wind. Rev. Mr. Serls preach. George Collins here.

28   Fair. Get mare shod. Go to New Baltimore, get Levi's coat cut. Woolsey Cary pay me 20 dollars. Plant corn

29   Rainy. **I go to Albany, then to New York with Steamboat Buffalo.**

30   Get in New York. Abram Post pay me 10 dollars. I stay all night with Peter VanAntwerp. Rainy weather.

31   Clears off. A very wet time. I travel around.

June 1849

1   Fair. Return holme. Mrs. Elias Holmes here. Plant corn.

---

[125] Before indoor plumbing, cisterns were commonly used to collect and store rainwater. Usually they were holes dug in the ground and lined with clay to limit leakage.

[126] A chattel mortgage in which an item of moveable personal property acts as security for the loan.

2	Fair, south wind. I am sick and weak.
3	Fair, south wind. I go to meeting. Wesley & George Collins here.
4	Showry in afternoon. I go to Flat Bush. Help J.W. Story make fence.
5	Fair. I go to Story's. Make fence. Mother Houghtaling & Levi go along.
6	Fair. I go to river. Get sturgeon. Then to Flat Bush. Make fence.
7	Fair. I make fence. I take mare to Jerry Springstead.
8	Rainy all forenoon. I go to river get fish and work around the house.
9	Fair. Work down to Flat Bush. Beecher plows for buckwheat.
10	Rainy all forenoon. I go to Meeting in the evening.
11	Fair day we all go to Flat Bush. Make fence. Maria VanBergen here.
12	Fair. Make fence. **Peter Cook died this morning**. I attend concert.
13	Fair. Draw manure. Work in garden.
14	Fair. Go to river. Draw manure. Work in garden. Wife goes to Holmes.
15	Showery. **I help Acton Civill get his monument.** I make road.
16	Rainy forenoon. **We all go to funeral of Andrew Houghtaling's Wife**.
17	Fair day. **I go to funeral of Martin B. Holmes**. He was brought here from the West.
18	Fair day. Make fence. I go to creek to fish. Andrew Houghtaling here.
20	Fair, hot. I go to Greenville. Stay to Andrew Fancher's.
21	Fair, hot. I come back from Greenville. Eliza Phelps here.
22	Hot weather and small shower in afternoon. I go to mill. I take kettle tub & churn, hoops to J.W. Story and my mare and colt.
23	Fine hot day. We all go to Oak Hill on temperance excursion have a fine time.
24	Warm, showery. **John Bronk died today**. We all go to Meeting.
25	Fair, cool. Work at beets. I take all hands to John Bushant's.
26	Fair. **Go to John Bronk's funeral** and work in the garden.
27	Fair. Work in garden. We all go to Andrew Houghtaling's.
28	Rainy day. Fix around Mother's house.
29	Rainy. I go to river & to mill. Marite and Ann Reedor come here for a visit from New York. **Peter Ostrander's daughter died and was buried today**.
30	I take Marite and Mrs. Reeder to Beecher Holmes. I go to Baltimore.

July 1849

1	Fair day. Go to Meeting. Catherine VanBergen & Elida Van Slyck here.
2	Fair. I take all the folks and Thomas Houghtaling visiting.
3	Fair. I go fishing. Harris pay me 5 dollars. I shoot 3 pidgeons. I get my bull.
4	Fair. I take all hands to Andrew Whitbeck's visiting.

5	Fair. I take visitors & all hands to M. G. VanBergen's then to Andrew F. Van Slyck's. I take P.Q. Groat & John Wheeler to J.W. Story's.
6	Fair. I go to Flat Bush. Put sills under the barn.
7	Fair. Work in garden. Go to river. Bridget O Neil go to Waterford,
8	Fair, hot. Gerry Springstead here. Go to meeting. Rev. Mr. Willis preach.
9[127]	Fair, hot. I go to Flat Bush. Cradle rye. Go in swimming. Settle with James White.
10	Fair, warm. I go to Stephensville after Maria Finch. Cradle rye. Mr. Warner here.
11	Fair, hot. Cradle rye. Go to New Baltimore. J. Story bring Mother Houghtaling holme.
12	Fair. Cradle rye. I send Irish John to Jacob W. Story's.
13	Fair, hot. **Man died of heat at Wm. McCullock's**. I make out writing with Benjamin W. Warner to go out to Herkimer on my land.
14	Fair. I go after berries. William Bagley here.
15	Air cool. I go to Meeting twice & I get horse shod.
16	I draw in Rye. **Go with William Bagley to the cave**. Go on horses.
17	Fair. Draw in rye. I go with Wm. Bagley around. I let B.W. Warner have mill screen to take along to Herkimer. I go to Squire VanDerzee.
18	Fair, south wind. Abram Whitbeck pays me his last year's rent.
19	Fair, South wind. Hot weather. I fix farm bridge.
20	Fair morning, shower in afternoon. Work at bridge.
21	Shower in afternoon. Work at bridge.
22	Showery but not rainy. I go to Meeting. Mother sick.
23	Shower in forenoon. A. Civill, Mrs. Elias Holmes, Mrs. Crumb, Mrs. Beecher, E. Holmes here.
24	Fair, hot. I finish bridge. Set Isaiah to chopping firewood. P. Seabridge pay me off last night.
25	Fair. I go to Little Falls. Take Wife & Harriet along.
26	Shower. I go to B.W. Warner's. Wife & Harriet stay to John Feeter's.
27	Fair. Return back to John Feeter's. Have a dance at night.
28	Fair. **We come holme by railroad & steamboat**.
29	Fair, hot. Mrs. Trego, Cate Houghtaling, Martin Andrews here. I take all hands to Thomas Houghtaling's.
30	Fair, hot, south wind. I go get posts for lot in cemetery. Pay off Jerry Springsted. Get bull.
31	Fair. I help Beecher. I pay John E. Bailey damage for Turnpike Company.

---

[127] Zachary Taylor died on this day of a stomach ailment after having served only 4 months of his presidency. Millard Fillmore, a Whig from New York, was inaugurated as the 13th President of the United States.

August 1849

1   Fair, warm. Commence to work on cemetery.

2   Fair, hot. Bridget O'Neil come back. We work at fence.

3   Fair, hot. I go to Greenville. They have meeting in both churches.

4   Fair, showers. Isaiah work at cemetery. I swear off my tax before the Greenville Assessors Pay James Waldron $5.

5   Fair day. I go to Meeting three times. I gave Mr. Hoyt 2 dollars for church.

6   Showery. Andrew & John Houghtaling here to tea.

7   Fair day. Work at cemetery fence.

8   Fair. I take Mother Houghtaling & Marite to Flat Bush. I get cheese for sample for John Keller. Isaiah help Beecher.

9   Showery. John Sutter here. I work at cemetery fence.

10 Rainy. John Sutter fix my watch & clock. I get check for B.W. Warner for 25 dollars.

11 Rainy. Work on cemetery. Pay off Mariah Finch.

12 Showery. Go to Meeting, go to sleep. Communion. Rev. Mr. Tombs preach.

13 Fair, but muddy. I take Wife, Mariah Finch & Margarett to William Wilkins then to Mrs. Vincent's. I buy sow & pigs.

14 Rain in afternoon. Dig stone attend division. Go to Jacob W. Story's. Get 6 cheeses, 96 lbs. & 16 lbs.

15 Fair. Work at stone. Take letter to barge. Dick Winne here.

16 Fair. Work in cemetery. Lay stone.

17 Fair. Work in cemetery. Lay stone. Marite & Doct. VanAntwerp go to Daniel VanAntwerp.

18 Fair. Work in cemetery. Finish wall. **We caught the Boys stealing corn.** Doct. & Marite come back from Daniel VanAntwerp.

19 Fair. I go to A. Jackson's & to Meeting & to cemetery.

20 Fair. I take Doct. & Marite to Baltimore. Mr. Trego & Lady here, Cate Houghtaling here. Doct. Van Antwerp buys my cemetery lot. **I take up boys for stealing corn**.

21 Showery. **Have a lawsuit with boys for stealing corn. Let them slip**.

22 Fair. Work at cemetery. Go after posts. Wife & Mother Houghtaling go to Civill's.

23 Fair. Work at cemetery. Beecher press hay. I get cot from barge.

25 Fair. Walk at cemetery. Mother Houghtaling go to Albany.

26 Fair. Go to Meeting. Go to sleep.

27 Fair. I take Wife to Albany. Get Marite's watch for 35 dollars.

28 Fair. Mrs. Wilkins here. Frenchman chop wood.

29 Fair. Work at cemetery. Send Marite's watch.

30 Fair. Get horse shod. I am not very well.

| 31 | Rain about all day. I fix road. |

September 1849

1	Fair. **I put up notices to lay out road to cemetery.**
3	Fair. Paint cemetery fence. Have all Hawleys here. Get horse shod.
4	Fair. Paint cemetery fence. Aunt Caty here. Get horse shod.
5	Fair. I take Wife to Flat Bush. Get horse shod
6	Fair. I get broom corn seed. Go to Barent VanSlyck's. Meet Mr. Allen & Lady. Mr. Tolls & Lady & all visit together.
7	Fair, little shower. Draw cemetery posts. Work at fence.
8	Fair. **Get meeting of Freeholders[128] to open road to cemetery**.
9	Go to Meeting. Wife go to N.T. VanSlyck. Get peaches.
10	Fair. Run out the cemetery, that is my lot & grove.
11	Fair. Go to Albany. **Get tombstone for my daughter Harriet's grave**. Get Marite's watch changed. **Dig graves in cemetery**.
12	Get broom corn seed. Mr. & Mrs. Willis here, Mrs. Clement & Mrs. Smith here.
13	Fair, hot. **Paint sloop. Work at cemetery**. Mother Houghtaling came back yesterday. Bring Andrew's son Martin along.
14	Fair. **Remove the remains of my kindred from Old Place, Beecher & hands help**.
15	I take waggons to square. Old Mrs. Willis here.
16	No speaker to Methodist Church – disappointed.
17	Clean up broom seed.
18	Fix walk. Frenchman sick.
19	Fair. Get broom corn seed. Get waggon from square.
20	Fair. **I go to Greenville. See Baptist's Association**.
21	Fair. I come from Greenville. Bring back a load of boards.
22	Fair. I draw muck from widow Lady Teneyck's swamp. I sell my grey mare to Ashmore Grant for 75 dollars.
23	Fair. I go to Meeting. Arthur McClosky here. I go to cemetery.
24	I send Andrew VanAntwerp his title for lot in cemetery. Send grapes to Marite.
25	I & Wife go to Flat Bush. Edward Hubbell & Lady here.
26	Fair. Fix roof. Send plums to barge. **A. Civill move**. I draw muck.
27	Fair. **Dig in cemetery**. Draw muck. Cate wean her child.

---

[128] A Freeholder is a person who owns property. Although owning property was no longer an impediment to vote in New York at this time, evidently it was a consideration in other transactions.

28 Fair. **I bring to our cemetery the remains Father Houghtaling. Our girl Cate leave for Catskill & Gilboa.**

29 Draw muck. Burn fallow. Gave bond to cemetery. Fix M. Bronk's fence. Get holme at 8 o'clock in evening.

30 Rainy & cloudy. **I have a sore finger**.

October 1849

1 **Equinoctial storm.**[129] **Finger sore**. I go chop wood in the woodhouse.

2 Fair. Draw muck and posts.

3 Rainy morning. **Fingers sore**. I go to Elias Holmes.

4 Rainy. I pay off Isaiah $58.05. Get out hoops.

5 Cloudy & rainy. **Very sore finger yet**.

6 Rainy. **Finger sore**. I go to river. Get papers.

7 Rainy. **Finger sore**. I fetch up horses. Very muddy.

8 Fair. I go to river. **Finger sore**. Gardner Sherman pay me 25 dollars.

9 Fair. Lay around. I set John Toben to work this afternoon.

10 Fair. J. Toban dig ditch. John Cutter & son here to dinner. **Wife and Mother Houghtaling go after Negro girl.**

11 Rain hard all day. I go to river. Pay off Wm. B. Hull.

12 Fair. I pay Bridget O'Neil 32.5/100 dollars.

13 Fair. I go to Albany. Take Bridget along. Send a box with things to Herkimer.

14 Fair. **Finger sore.** Go to Meeting. Walk around.

15 Fair. Draw wood. I lend Jonas Bronk three-cornered drag.

16 Fair. J.W. Story bring me a load of corn. I dig potatoes in the garden. Josiah pay me D. Baker's order.

17 Fair. Ira Gregory get two beefs of Jacob W. Story. I get a piece.

18 Fair. Get my building enclosed. Catharine here. I go a hunting.

19 Fair. I put manure around trees. Go to Square & to the barge.

20 I go to river **then a hunting for bees**. Martin VanSlyck & Elida &Cate VanBergen come here.

21 Cloudy. Go to Meeting. Cate Houghtaling & Elizabeth Trego here.

22 Showery & rainy. I go to river. Patrick Clancy & George Sweet's lawsuit is settled. I let Sylvester Harris have my truck.

---

[129] A storm of violent winds and rain occurring at or near the time of an equinox and popularly, but erroneously, believed to be physically associated with the equinox.

23   **I go to J.B. Shear's to Nomination. Cornelius Vanderzee for member of assembly. I and McDonald go together. Callup is beat by 98.**

24   Fair. I go to New York on board of the Barge.

25   I go to Doctor VanAntwerp. **He cut open my finger**.

26   Fair. **I go to Greenwood Cemetery to see Christy's at night**.

27   Fair. Do up-trading. Get a barrel of codfish. **Take Steamboat Manhattan for holme**.

28   Fair but foggy. Get delayed on account of the fog and do not arrive holme until 12 o'clock. Peter VanAntwerp come along up.

29   Rainy. **I am subpoenaed by John Bailey in suit with him and our school district**. Francis Brevenue go to work for me. Saw wood. Work at flower bed. Dominie Pelts here.

30   Clears off. **Fix tombstones in cemetery**. Levi Story leave here.

November 1849

1   Cold, raw day. A.M. VanBergen here. Bring Mother Houghtaling back. I work at corn crib.

2   Fair. **A.E. Willis pay me off his part of cemetery.**[130] I take up my note of him. Mrs. Lawton & Marite come here. I get things from barge.

3   Fair. I go to Albany with Willis's team. Wife & Marite go to Daniel VanAntwerp's.

4   Fair. I go to Meeting, Dominie Jolly preach, then to cemetery.

5   Rainy afternoon. I raise corncrib. Go to river.

6   Little south wind, cloudy. I work at corncrib. Attend Election. Very dull. I receive 4 notes from A.E. Willis by Capt. Sherwood and endorse them in his favor on his bond or bonds I hold against him amt. 464 dollars endorsed for April 1, 1849.

7   Showry. Work at corncrib ½ day. Then I and Peter VanBuren go to Doct. VanAntwerp's Vendue.

8   Rainy. **Finish my corncrib**.

9   Very rainy day. Husk corn. **John Teal lost a child yesterday**.

10   Rainy. Husk corn. Mrs. Elias Holmes here.

11   Clears off. Doct. A. VanAntwerp here. Go to Meeting, then to cemetery.

12   Clear, cold. I & Doct. VanAntwerp go to Daniel's Vendue. Dig up beets.

13   Fair. Mrs. Mary Holmes here, Mrs. Mull.

14   I take carpenter Springstead to Flat Bush. Get cheese, 1 barrel of flour. Go to mill with hog feed. Mrs. Frendenburgh and lots more here.

15   Fine, cool. I take Marite and all hands to Flat Bush. Work at straw shed.

16   Fine day. Work at shed. Get out carrots. **Beecher has a bee to husk corn.**[131]

---

[130] Fletcher and Alexander Willis share a plot in Grove Cemetery in Coeymans.

[131] A bee is a gathering of friends, family and neighbors to carry out a specific time-consuming task. The person who calls the bee is expected to feed them well and to return their workday for day.

17	Fine day. Work at carrots. Go to Stephensville. Sheldon Houghtaling & Lady &Child here, stay all night.
18	Fair. Andrew Houghtaling bring Marite holme. Black Elizabeth & Lafayette & Wife come here.
19	Rain all day hard. I go to river. Get Frank a shirt.
20	Rainy day. Work at shed. Very muddy. I go to river.
21	Clear, NW. Fix shed. Thrash with machine. Marite & Garret VanAntwerp go to New York.
22	Fair. Thrash. I let Beecher have $8.50 to pay Peter Witmore.
23	Fair. Finish pull carrots. Work at Mother's cellar drain.
24	Rainy. Martin VanBergen & Elida, Aunt Caty & Aunt Sarah Ann here.
25	Cloudy, rainy. Visit with company. They leave this afternoon.
26	Fine warm day. Sell my bull to Ira Gregory $11.50. Send a letter to Doct. A. VanAntwerp.
27	Cold & snow squalls. I kill hogs. James White & Peter Holbrox help. Beecher help Joseph Bronk. Send holme my old mare's colt by Story's boy.
28	Fair cold. Daniel VanAntwerp brings his furniture here. He goes on to New York. I gave teamsters their dinners. Finish carrots. Cut up hogs.
29	Fair. Cut up pork and go to Nathan Cronk's funeral. Harriet and Ann Cronk here, and Mother here. I send a letter to B.W. Warner.
30	Fair. **Attend Nathan Cronk's funeral.** Made a mistake in setting it down yesterday.

December 1849

1	Fair, very cold at night. Get horse shod. I take up Isaac Baker's cattle. Attend District Lawsuit.
2	Very cold, freeze all day. Not very well. I go to Meeting. **I call Doct. for Levi.**[132]
3	**Three inches snow. I go after B.B. Fredenburgh 12 o'clock at night. Levi sick.** Rain and snow all day. Beecher draw hay on Barge
4	Foggy & snowy. I am not well. Beecher draw two loads of wood.
5	Clears off. **Sloop Revenue come**. I get ropes to papermill for halters. Doct. Fredenburgh fell and hurt himself yesterday. **Cornelius Ryon's child died last night**.
6	Squally. **I put Daniel VanAntwerp's furniture on board of Sloop Revenue. Attend Cornelius Ryon's child funeral.** Rev. Hoyt preach.
7	Clear & cold NW. Draw wood. Go to river get harness fixed.
8	Clear, cold. Frank chop. I put steps down for mother.
9	South wind, sleet. I go to Meeting hear Rev. Mr. Hoyt & Rev. Mr. Pelts. Stop at A. E. William's.
10	Cloudy. Set out trees in cemetery. **Beecher got new Bob Sley.**[133]

---

[132] A "call" in this time required a personal visit.
[133] Bobsleighs are usually steerable, having two sets of runners – one in front, one in back.

11	Clear cold. I mend harness Go to river. Wife go to Albany with [steamboat] **Shepherd Knapp**.
12	Cold. Set out trees in cemetery. Go to river.
13	Cloudy. Draw wood and stone. I get three Books of Wm. C. Robb.
14	Overcast. Draw stone. Get grist from the mill.
15	Cloudy. Draw stone. **Go after the doctor for Levi**.
16	Rainy. I go to Meeting. **They go after my sloop Revenue.**
17	**I pay Thomas C. Houghtaling one thousand dollars. Go out to coal mine**.[134] Attend meeting in Ante Room. **Jacob Milton's child buried**.
18	Fair. Capt. Sherwood pays me 50 dollars. Draw stone.
19	Fair morning. Commence snowing 3 o clock p.m. Take stove to Mrs. Jeffts. Draw stone.
20	Cloudy, rainy all afternoon. Attend Rev. P. Pelts' Donation. Have a first-rate oyster supper. Cate Houghtaling come holme with us.
21	Clear & cold. Explore new roads. **Go in cave with Oliver Springstead and Samuel Pelts. Take level of Offabarrack Hill and find it 8 inches to the rod on 15 chains and 21 inches to the rod on 5 chains and the new route 15 chains further.**
22	Showry morning. Commence snowing at noon. Draw stone.
23	Fair, 6 in snow. Go to Meeting; hear Rev. Mr. Pelts.
24	Snowy. I kill my beef. Send Beecher to Greenville.
25	Very cold. Boys come back from Greenville. Fine sleighing.
26	Very cold. Rev. Mr. Hoyt's Donation goes off. Boys draw wood. **River closed**.
27	Fine day. I get posts. Frank chop wood. Mr. Curtis lecture in church in evening on Geology. No steamboat today.
28	Fine day. I get horse shod. Draw muck in cow yard. Sell cowhide to Dwight Batchellor 94 lbs.
29	Snowy & misty. Chop wood. Draw muck. **Attend lecture on Geology last evening**.
30	Fair. We all go to Meeting. Hear Dominie Jolly in the afternoon.
31	Fair, cold. **I go out to where they are digging for coal**. Frank draw muck. **Attend Plank Road meeting**.[135] Wife go to Jeremiah Springstead's.

January 1850

1	Cold. Attend shooting match. I take all hands to G. Houghtaling's. John Bushants pay me 50 dollars. I go after folks.
2	Fair. I and Peter Seabridge go to Baltimore. Visit Odd Fellows.
3	Fair. I pay Barent TenEyck his law bill 54 dollars. Newman Finch & Lady here. Wife go to Donation to New Baltimore. Boys draw wood.

---

[134] Evidently there was a coal mine in the area.
[135] This is the first mention of the Plank Road.

4	Fair day. **We survey the Plank Road out to John B. Shear's**. We take dinner to Isaac Skinner's. L.B. Eddy the Surveyor
5	Fair. I go to Meeting. Edward & Mary Blaisdell here.
6	Fair. I go to Albany. I get 4 lbs. tea. **I pay Wm. VanRenssalear Island rent**.
7	Fair morning, snow in afternoon. I send B.W. **Warner 50 dollars to pay for patent dogs**[136] **in sawmill. I and Wesley go to Baltimore to get clothes cut**.
8	Snowy. I take up births, deaths & marriages. Rev. Mr. Hoyt & Lady Mrs. W. Niles & Mrs. Wm. Ostrander here.
9	**Mistake. Cannot tell what went off**.[137]
10	Fair. I go to Greenville get my rents. Stay to Andrew Fancher's.
11	Rain hard all day. I come back from Greenville.
12	Rainy. I take up Marriages Births & deaths. **John Rodgers here. He pay me sloop's bill for moving David VanAntwerp to Westchester Co**. I settle up his business. We have lots of company.
13	I take Mother Houghtaling to Thomas Houghtaling's. I go to Meeting. **I take Wife to Wesley's. Margarett is quite sick**.
14	I go to river. Attend Plank Road mtg.
15	Fair. Draw wood all day. Attend Division in Evening.
16	Fair. Draw wood all day; take Mother 5 loads.
17	Overcast. Draw wood. **Seamstress here**. Draw two logs to mill.
18	Snowy. Draw wood. I go with Beecher to his wood lot. Pay off Judge Nichols 54 dollars.
19	Fair, NW. I pay off Elizabeth Briggs $8.38. I saw wood for Mother. Abram Teal shift her doors. I pay him 5/.
20	I go to Meeting. Cate Hathaway and Elizabeth Post here.
21	Snow & misty day. I go to river. **Get my first papers of the organ**. Talory (sp) come back to work. Rev. Philip Pelts here.
22	Clears off NW. I go to chop wood. Buy some lumber of B.E. Holmes.
23	Fair day. I go to Jacob W. Story's. I take Levi to river. I get letter from B.W. Warner & Doct. VanAntwerp.
24	Fair morning, snowy afternoon. I draw logs from Flat Bush.
25	South wind thawy & rainy. I go to Flat Bush draw logs.
26	Fair & thawy. I go to mill to Phillip Kimmey's.
27	Sleying all gone. **I go to Baltimore after seamstress**.
28	Thawy. I work at Barn. Beecher draw hay.

---

[136] A sawmill dog is a device to hold logs in position on the sawmill carriage.

[137] This is an indication that Fletcher wrote up his journal after-the-fact based upon notes he had saved for each day.

29 Snowy & windy. I go to W.H. Southwick's. Wife go along.

30 Clear and cold. **I go to Albany. Get a girl, Julia Conoly**. Get some cheese and some Fanna. Beecher draws hay.

31 Fair, SW. I take Tailoress holme; pay her off. I go to river.

February 1850

1   Fair. Take sley ride to Coxsackie to Mr. Bucher's. We go with 4-horse team. Dance all night. Have a fine time.

2   Cloudy. I go to Quarterly Meeting. Feel quite sleepy. Get a book of John Stebbens.

3   Clear & colder. I go to Meeting. Hear P.E. Elder preach. Then hear P. Pelts.

4   Very cold day. I help Beecher draw/saw logs ½ day, then to river.

5   Very cold. I help Beecher draw logs ½ day, then to the river.

6   Clear cold day. Wife go to Donation with A.E. Willis.

7   Fair; get a little more snow and milder. Frank thresh. I go to river.

8   South wind. I get a rooster of Granny Sherwood. Wife goes to Holmes.

9   Rainy. **I go to Dan Rice's Vendue. Attend party at A.N. Briggs**.

10 Fair, snow mostly gone. Go to Meeting. Mother Houghtaling go to Andrew's.

11 Fair. I fix door, put in side lights. School meeting tonight. Frank thresh.

12 Fair, thawy. I go to river. Frank thresh. I run around.

13 Fair. Cate Houghtaling here. **We all go to Baltimore to Dancing School**. Take Cate Fredenburgh along.

14 Stormy. Wife & Cate Houghtaling go to Tunis VanSlyck's. Rain all the way.

15 Cold. I settle with Patrick Clancy. Snowy. I get 20 bags of L W & Co. Frank finish threshing.

16 Fair. Clean up rye. **Collect up 1st installment on Plank Rd**. J.W. Story here. Mother Houghtaling come back.

17 Fair. Stay at holme all day. Wife and Mother Houghtaling go to Meeting.

18 Fair. I go to mill with 41 bushels of rye. Work in quiry. Take 7 barrels to mill.

19 Cold, NW. Margarett here. Attend S of T in the evening.

20 Fair. **I go to see new route to Plank Road**. Dine to J. Skinner's.

21 Fair. I go to Flat Bush. Wife & Margarett go to Garret Houghtaling's.

22 Clear, cold, NW. I take Folks out to John VanDerzee's on PR business.

23 Fair. I go to New Baltimore. Make writings for Flat Bush Farm. Wife go along. **I stay at night to Debating School**.

24 Fair, NW. I go to Meeting twice; then to Wesley's, take tea.

25 Fair. Wife go to Revd. Phillip Pelts'. Frank chop wood.

26 Fair and warm. Wife come back from Rev. Pelts. Joseph Bronk here.

27   Colder, fair NW. Get out stone. I lay down a slab walk before Ann Bronk's doors.

28   Fair. Draw stone. Draw boards from sawmill.

March 1850

1   Three inches of snow, muddy. Go to river. Get new pair of clevises of Nelson Carroll.

2   Fair. **Mrs. Phillip Pelts died this morning at 3 o'clock**. I draw plank from mill; fix walk; go to river.

3   Very cold day, NW. Go to Meeting. Go to Egbert Stanton's.

4   Clear, cold. Lay around. Put up notices for Vendue. **Stephen Gould's Wife has a young child last night**.

5   Fair. **I attend funeral of Mrs. P. Pelts**. I go to mill, get feed.

6   Fair. I and James White go to Albany. Get lumber. It rain and snow all the way back. Mrs. Andrew Mull & her Mother here.

7   Snow & rain all day. I take 15 of Lawton's & Willis's bags holme. Go to mill and to river; get Molasses Hhd. of John Keller.

8   Fair, NW. I take Wm. Robb's book holme. **Steamboat go up today**.

9   Fair. Attend Dan Rice's Vendue. Buy stove pipe. **Richard Lawton gets married today**.

10 Fair. Go to Meeting. P. Pelts preach. Wesley here, child sick.

11 Fair. Draw stone. [Steamboat] **Shepherd Knapp make her first trip**.

12 Fair. Draw lumber from mill. Draw stone.

13 Fair. **Coeymans Barge come, Marite come along**. P.W. VanBergen here, take up a note that I hold against him. I draw stone.

14 Fair, hot. Frank help Beecher draw pressed hay on board the barge. I trim trees.

15 Fair. I go to Flat Bush. Attend Vendue of J.W. Story's. I pay Sarah Ann and Marite 5 dollars apiece collected from John Bronk. Frank chop wood.

16 Fair. I pay Aaron Houghtaling $2.75 for register. Take tea at Harriet's. All hands visit.

17 Cloudy. Go to Meeting. Walk around.

18 Snow all day hard, very muddy. J.W. Story here. I lend him 32 dollars.

19 Fair. L.D. Eddy, Anthony VanBergen here. Cate VanAntwerp here.

20 Clear, cold. **I go to survey on Plank Road**. Mrs. Briggs, Mrs. Fredenburgh, Mrs. Andrews and more here.

21 Clear, cold. Go on Plank Road with L.D. Eddy.

22 Clear, cold. Run around. Put seed on cemetery. Frank help Beecher.

23 Snow all day. Phillip Phelps & sister Eliza come here. Frank help Beecher.

24 Thawy day. I take P. Phelps & Eliza & Wife to Baltimore. Very muddy.

25 Fair. I pay Doc. John Squires & Mr. Roseboom. Send a letter to Canada for Adolphus Bievennue. Mrs. A. Jackson here on a visit. My folks go to Doctor Fredenburgh's.

26   Cold for the last 4 days. We go on a visit to Wesley's.

27   Cold. I take up my note held by Marite VanAntwerp. Gave her a new one of 700 dollars. Pay Nelson Agau off. Marite go to New York.

28   Snow all day. Angeline go holme with Thomas Conine.

29   Wife & Margaret go to Beecher Holmes. I divide the fence between me and the John Bronk Farm. I let Lawton's & Willis's have 21 dollars.

30   Fair. **I go to Nomination Meeting**. Lawton & Willis pay me 21 dollars. **Henry Niles gets the nomination for town clerk.**

31   Fair, cool day. Stay at holme. **Baby sick last night**.

April 1850

1   Fine day. I go to Coxsackie get 500 dollars of Newman Finch. I bring holme 3 cows, 1 bull and old mare from Flat Bush. Get cherry trees of Hawley. Attend road meeting at night.

2   Fair and warm. I get 300 dollars of Capt. Sherwood, 30 dollars from Elias Millbanks. Sow lettuce bed, work in garden.

3   Fair, south wind. I pay H.B. Joslin $572.91 [on] note that he held against me. I draw a load of sand, get 1 barrel of flour.

4   I pay Lawton & Willis 300 dollars. Paint sash.

5   Cloudy, rainy, high water. Jonathan McElroy work for me. I pay school tax to George Sweet.

6   Fair. I set glass, plane boards, go to river.

7   Fine day, wind NW I go to Meeting. Rev. P. Pelts preach.

8   Fair. I go to Flat Bush. Three of Houghtaling girls here visiting.

9   Fair. **I get 75 apple trees then attend Town Meeting**.

10   Fair. **I attend to Plank Road. Drive out to George Spannbergh's survey & lay out the road**.

11   Fair. Mr. Eddy here. I plow in afternoon.

12   Fair. I plow. Mr. Eddy here. Mountains covered with snow last night. Henry Spawn contract for our Plank Road.

13   Snow all day. **I get 10 maple trees and set them out at my Old Holmestead**. Beecher help.

14   Squally. Plenty of snow on the mountains. I go to Meeting.

15   Clear, cold. I go to sawmill. Mr. Eddy sends for his tools. **Mrs. John Gay buried today**.

16   Clear, cold day. Draw muck for trees. Heavy wind.

17   Clear, cold. I go to mill. I take Uncle Arthur and Mother Houghtaling to Thomas Houghtaling's. Set out trees.

18   More pleasant. I go to Flat Bush. Cate Fredenburgh, Maria Overlaugh, Hannah Andrews & Eliza Clement here.

19   Showry morning but it clears off. I go to Hollow to make out road list. Frank fix trees & help Beecher.

20 Fair Day. I go to sawmill to get elm lumber.

21 Fair, south wind. I go to Meeting hear Rev. Mr. Hoyt.

22 Rainy. I plow my garden. **Circus to New Baltimore**.

23 Showry but clears off, cold. I go to mill. Bring up cistern. Graft trees. Commence to dig to make cistern for Mother.

24 Fair. Attend to Plank Road. Draw 3 loads of manure from Bushant's. **Draw clay and put in Mother's cistern**.[138]

25 Fine day. Draw 3 loads of manure. Turn out 3 cattle of Raspberry Hill.

26 Fine day. Go to Flat Bush; build stone wall to river. I get 25 dollars of Mrs. Gardner Sherman. Beecher's cow gets hurt.

27 Fine day. I plant potatoes.

28 Rainy. I go to Meeting. Mrs. Elias Holmes, Mrs. Henry Seaburgh & Iva Springstead here in afternoon.

29 Rainy morning clears off in afternoon. Make fence.

30 Fair. I go to Flat Bush. Lay wall. Have lots of visitors. **Mrs. Wm. Wilkins died today**.

May 1850

1 Fair. **Go to Mrs. Wm. Wilkins funeral**; take Rev. Mr. Hoyt along.

2 Fair. **Fix around school room. Gave Mr. Keefer bond to collect taxes on road.** Luther Eddy here.

3 Fine day. **I take Mr. Eddy & Man to lay out our Extended Plank Road.** Wife goes to Albany. **Coeymans Bridge break down. Peter Seabridge horses and Isaac Bush go down with it.**

4 Rainy. I go with Peter Seabridge to Coxsackie. Cate Pierce, Anthony M. VanBergen and Almira here. I pay B.B. Fredenburgh 53.34 dollars.

5 Rainy day. Stay in house. Very wet time.

7 Fair. Rev. Phillip Pelts [here] all the afternoon, take tea.

8 Fair, south wind. I go to sawmill. Make fence down to river. **Down to river buy an old sloop of Richard Lawton for 25 dollars.**

9 Clears off, fair. Work at holme. To river. Make fence.

10 Fair. I take load of brick to Flat Bush. **Mr. Crandle white-wash here.**[139]

11 Fair. I go to Flat Bush.

12 Little rain. I go to Meeting. I & Wife go to Wesley's

13 Fine day. Plow horse kick me. Miss Houghtaling here, Mr. Eddy here, I plant potatoes. Go on the road with Mr. Eddy.

---

[138] Clay was used to line the cistern wall to reduce leakage.
[139] White-washing is the process of covering a wall with a very thin coat of plaster made with water lime and other ingredients.

14 Fair. I go to Albany. **See Spalding's Circus**.[140] Frank plant potatoes.

15 Rainy day. I go to Flat Bush; Wife go along. Andrew Fancher here, pay his rent. Plant potatoes.

16 Very rainy and muddy. I get 100 shad of Leonard Hathaway. Andrew Fancher goes holme. I get horse shod. Salt fish. Get pork barrel of Peter Holbrook.

17 Showry. Dig stone pile. Lumber to sawmill.

18 Cold north wind. Make fence. Marten & Elida VanSlyck & Cate VanBergen here. I let Mr. Spawn have 50 dollars.

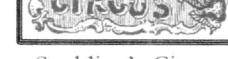

Spalding's Circus

19 Fair. I go to Meeting twice. Rev. Mr. Halloway preach.

20 Hail & rain, very wet I go to river.

21 Fair, cold. Snow on Helderberg [Mt]. Mr. Spawn here this evening.

22 Fine day. Draw manure; put calf on barge. Plant corn. Mr. Spawn's son & team come here. We all go to Jacob Holmes wedding. Temperance meeting in hall.

23 Cloudy, cold day. I take Mother Houghtaling to Flat Bush to Andrew's. I gave her 5 dollars. Frank chop. Beecher plant corn.

24 Lowsy Morning. I go to Flat Bush with a load of boards. Frank chop.

25 Attend Plank Road business. Chop wood.

26 Rainy. I go to Meeting. Wesley bring his cow here to Bull.

27 Rainy. I go to Flat Bush with a carpenter. I notify Commissioner in New Baltimore. Mr. Spawn come back.

28 Rainy. I go to Flat Bush bring holme the carpenter. I pay H. Spawn 50 dollars. Frank pile up lumber.

29 Fair day. **Water very high; our plank goes adrift**. Heavy rain at night. Mr. Eddy & son here. Frank chop wood.

30 Fair. **Work at old sloop**. Draw up 4 loads. Wife & Frank go after a young colored girl.

31 Rainy day. **I pay Andrew VanBergen $1010.05. Draw up old sloop stuff**.

June 1850

1 Fair. I help cut down Casy Hill. Attend to Plank Road.

2 Shower at night. I take Mother & Mr. Spawn to Bethlehem to Meeting. Wife goes along, very muddy.

3 Shower in afternoon. **Work at sloop**. Pay Wm. B. Hull 125 dollars.

---

140 Gilbert Spalding [1812-1880] was an American showman and circus owner. He was the first to send the entire circus on tour on its own railroad cars. Spalding was from Coeymans, the son of Nancy and Guy Spalding.

4	Fair day. **I draw 250 Hard Brick & 250 Pale brick**[141] to Flat Bush and one load of sand. Frank work at old sloop ½ day.
5	Fine day. Mr. Rob pay me up Mr. Golden's note 23 dollars.
6	Fine hot day. Beecher plant corn & draw muck. I pay Mr. Spawn 15 dollars. He leaves off boarding here this morning. I get 500 hard brick of Peter Seabridge. Get 1 sack salt.
7	Very hot. I take a load of brick to Flat Bush. B.B. Fredenburgh pay me error in his Plank Road installment. John Keller pay his first.
8	Fair, warm. I go to Flat Bush. Attend mason. Little showry.
9	Fine warm showers. Go to hear Rev. Mr. Ferris preach.
10	Rainy. I take Frank and two carpenters to Flat Bush. Bring back two of William Fisher's girls; take them to Josiah Sherman's. Angetim come holme; she went away a few days ago.
11	Colder, little showery. **Work at old sloop**. Get first calls of Isaac Witbeck. I pay William Wilkins 25 dollars.
12	Fair. Peter Seabridge raise his barn. Frank draws lumber from the mill.
13	Fair, warm. I go to Albany. I pay Mr. Spawn 600 dollars.
14	Fair & hot. **I fix cistern to Mother's, put in a pump**.
15	I go to Flat Bush. **Sell my gray mare to S.M Pelton for 85 dollars, take a Chattel mortgage on mare & two cows**. Leave the mortgage with the New Baltimore town clerk H.P. Shiller.
16	Fine day. I go to Meeting twice. Mother Houghtaling came back from New York.
17	Fair, hot. Go to Greenville, take Levi along. Get shoes of S. Baldwin & take his note for a balance due me.
18	Fair. Hot. Come back from Greenville. Hoe potatoes.
19	I go to Flat Bush. Mason finish work. I pay seven dollars and fifty cents for lime. Pay B. Garret 2/ for sand.
20	Two heavy showers. I take Wife to Phillip Kimmey's then to Walter Becker's. Put my mare to Elias Melbank's horse.
21	Fair. I put out cabbage plants & turnips.
22	Fair. I pay Mr. Spawn 75 dollars. Go out on Plank Road.
23	Go to Meeting. Take walk with Peter Seabridge.
24	Fair day. I go to Flat Bush. Mrs. Spawn here. I take Stephen Ostrander and James Sherwood to Flat Bush.
25	Fair. **I go to Flat Bush & paint all day**. James Schoomaker gave me 5 dollars for his Father for a roadway. **Mrs. A.E. Willis had a young son last night**.[142]
26	Fair day. I take folks up to Wm. Tuttle's. Julia's mother here.

Hand pump

---

[141] Pale brick lacks weather resistance.
[142] We think this was Alexander Blaisdell Willis.

27 Fair. I put my mare again to Elias Millbank's horse. Frank chop wood. Susan Hawley & Mrs. VanGaasbeck here. **I attend P.R. meeting.**[143]

28 Drizzly & Rainy. Marite & Caroline Hallock come from New York. I & Levi go to W. Serls & to E. Huyck on Plank Road, bumpy.

29 Hot & wet. Frank oil harness. I sell 85 lbs. of pork to G.W. Dorman.

30 Hot. Go Meeting twice then to Phillip Kimmey's after dress maker.

July 1850

1 Fair, hot. I go to J.B. Shear's. Buy turnpike [stock]. McGregor pay me 85 dollars on A. Civill's stock. French woman came here to work. Mrs. Ball leave here for Troy with [steamer] **Shepard Knap**p. Plow & hoe potatoes

2 Rainy. **Draw straw to Mr. Robb.**[144] Attend S of T meeting.

3 Rainy. Put up corn for Peter Seabridge. I pay Henry Spawn 400 dollars.

4 Hot, Fair. **I and all hands attend celebration on Berena Island. Cate Houghtaling here. Mr. Bamber here & Mr. Collins.**

5 Heavy rain & lightening at night. Lay out Gate house. Make out lodge report.

6. Fair. Frank hoe potatoes. Attend the Lodge at night.

7 Fair, NW. I go to Meeting. **Andrew Houghtaling here. He says he is married**.

8 Fair. I go to Albany get lumber for Gate House. Go to Little Falls. Stay all night at the Benton house.

9 Fair day. I go to Salisbury Center[145] then to Mr. Kelly's stay there all night.

10 Fair. I go to B.W. Warner's on foot. Get there before breakfast. Then go to Bennet's Mill. Stay at Warner's all night. **General Taylor died today**.[146]

11 Fair. I come back with Warner to Little Falls. Pay Mrs. Feeter 100 dollars. I let B.W. Warner have 50 dollars.

12[147] Fair. I come holme, bring of Permelia Feeter along.

13 Fair. Lay around the house. Jacob Feeter here.

14 Wife come from A.J. VanSlyck's. Ann Maria VanBergen, Elida VanSlyck & Caroline Hallock come with her.

---

143 Plank Road.
144 In 1850 William Robb was involved with the Croswell paper mill. Straw was used in the paper making process. Mr. Robb was later an owner of the Ravine paper mill located about a mile downstream of the Croswell mill. "Field of Reams – The Hannacroix Creek Paper Mills" by Chuck Friday 2009.
145 A town west of Greenville.
146 Zachary Taylor was the 12th President of the U.S.A. He died in office on July 9, 1850. He was previously a career Army office, rising to the rank of Major General. He was deemed a national hero as a result of his victories in the Mexican American War. He was nicknamed "Old Rough and Ready." He died in office after serving a little more than one year.
147 The 12 July 1850 Federal Census lists the following residents: Fletcher (33), Sarah Ann (31), Levi (4), Anthony (2), Angelina Armstrong (13) Mary Sorels (22), Joseph Sorels (22) Francis Brim (18), Maria Hotaling (56).

15	Fair. Lay around the house. Rake & bind rye. Go to Barren Island in evening.
16	Fair & Hot. John Silcox come after Caroline Hallock. I take them to Baltimore to Steamboat. Visit to Willis's. Frank help on road. We take ride on Plank Road.
17	Fair, hot. Jacob & Pemelia Feeter leave here. I attend to Plank Road.
18	South wind, fine shower. Sow buckwheat. Get in 1 load of rye and two loads of hay. Work at Gate House.
19	**Very heavy rain. Road plank float off. I help take care of plank.** Frank goes after berries.
20	It stops raining. **Work at picking up plank all day. Water high.** I pay Spann 50 dollars.
21	Very high water. **Attend to plank.** Go to Meeting.
22	Fair. **I and John Clement go to Athens after plank that drifts away.** Come back to Coxsackie. Stay all night at Mr. Backuse's.
23	Come holme on **Shepherd Knapp. Frank help dig cellar for toll house.**
24	Fair. **Raise gate house. Work there all day.**
25	Small shower. I am not well. Platte A. Smith pays me $6.62. Take up due bill. I go on road.
26	Fair. I build swing gate. Get 100 dollars of Wm. B. Hull. Pay Wm. Wilkins 50 dollars. Frank work at potatoes.
27	Fair. I make swing gate. Get two logs of Peter Holbrook. Frank work at potatoes. Call on Mr. Civill.
28	Fair. I go to Meeting twice. Pay Frank two schillings for John Toben.
29	Showry & hot. I go to see Wm. Lawton. He is sick. I pay him one dollar for sturgeon. I paint swing gate.
30	Showry. I get letters from Little Falls. Take a ride on Plank Road to New Baltimore. Frank hoe potatoes.
31	Fair & hot. I put up swing gate on Cemetery Road.

August 1850

1	Rainy. I and Wife go to Andrew VanSlyck's then to Coxsackie then after Black Cate. Take sash to Flat Bush. Pay Pelton $3.25 for John Bronk.
2	Fair. I go a fishing. Help on the road. Tuttle's team draw lumber. I dig stone. Dominie Hoyt's two daughters here on a visit.
3	Fair. I go to Aquetuck. See A. Jack about his hogs being in my field.
4	I go to Meeting. **Willis's child very sick.**
5	Fair. I go to Baltimore. Pay off T.H.L. Lockley. Bring Johnson's girls back with me.
6	Little showry in afternoon. Fix a place for my hogs. E. Bonticon pay me toll money.
7	Showry. I go riding with Johnson girls. Excursion to Berena Island today. **A.E. Willis's child died today.**
8	Fair. **Attend funeral of Willis's child.** Frank help Beecher this afternoon. Mother Houghtaling go to Thomas Houghtaling.

9	Fair. I go a fishing. Wife take Johnson girls to Baltimore. Mr. Morrison here.
11	Fair. I go a walking with Johnson girls.
12	Fair. I go to Meeting. Mr. Johnson & Mr. Buss here.
13	Fair. Draw timber for Beecher's house.
14	Rainy. **I take all hands out to Coal Mine to the Gulf.**
15	Fair. Mr. Higgins & his mother here. Take all the girls to Albany. **Beecher has a mowing bee.**
16	Fair. **I go to Waggoner's get 3 bushels of hair.**[148] I take Clarisa Houghtaling and all hands to Thomas Houghtaling.
17	Fair. I go a fishing. Frank help Beecher. Mr. Eddy here.
18	Fair. I take Clarisa Houghtaling holme. **A waggon load of Negroes here**. I go to Meeting.
19	Fair. Hew timber and **go to Dan Rice Circus; take all hands**.[149]
20	Lousy. **Attend George Sickles' lawsuit for stealing flour**. Hew timber. Appearance of rain.
21	Fair day. Get out timber. Go a fishing.
22	Fair. I take Wife & Mrs. Fredenburgh to Isaac Witbeck's and Caroline VanAntwerp. Get out timber.
23	Fine day. Potatoes not in the ground this year. Get out timber. Mother here. **Finish toll house**.
24	Fair. I take Mother & Dominie Hoyt to Dormansville to Quarterly Meeting. Take dinner to Doctor Gibbens. Then I go to Greenville.
26	Showry. Have two hands to work on Beecher's house. Get back from meeting. **John Teal's trial today for stealing flour**.
27	Fair. **Have three men to work at house**. Mrs. Spawn and lots of company here.
28	Fair. Three men work at house. Get out timber. Let Mr. Spawn have 5 dollars.
29	Fair. Draw timber. Work at Beecher's house with two men. Mrs. Shawn leave. Frank draws wood. Peter Seabridge pays me.
30	Fair. I take Wife & Caroline VanAntwerp to Mrs. Matson's in Schodack.
31	Fair. Draw gravel. John W. Cronk & Lady and all the Cronks & John Mull here.

Dan Rice Poster

---

[148] Horsehair was often mixed with plaster to give it better strength.
[149] Born in 1823, Dan Rice became one of the most recognizable names in America. His show business began when he purchased a trained pig named 'Lord Byron'. He started his own circus in 1848 and traveled by wagon and barge from New Orleans to New England. Wild and risqué, the shows were not designed as family entertainment. Counting on the popularity of his name, he launched an unsuccessful run for the Presidency. Heavy drinking became a problem later in life and he died almost penniless in 1900.

September 1850

1 Showry. **I and Wife go to Quaker Meeting.** No preachers come back.

2 Rain all day. David VanAntwerp here.

3 Fair. **Very great damage to roads by rain. Our Plank Road much damaged.** Frank chop wood.

4 Fair. I pay Henry Wilsey. Get toll money. Work in stone quiry. **Aunt Caty Houghtaling died today.**

5 Fair. **I and Wife go to Albany to State Fair. I come back at night it was very dark and rainy. Go to Cedar hill and stop and then led the way holme.** Sara Ann staid all night to Mrs. Johnson's. Frank dig potatoes.

6 Fair. I get one basket of peaches. Marite sent them. **I take Mother Houghtaling to Aunt Caty's funeral.**

7 Fair. **I work at Beecher's cellar.** Mr. Teneyck here.

8 Fair, N wind. I go to Meeting then to A. Jackson's.

9 Fair. I and Beecher lay cellar wall. **Elias Holmes' wife died.**

10 Fair. Work at cellar.

11 Fair. **John Rea move into toll house.** M.G. VanBergen here. Frank draws stone.

12 Clear, cold day. Lay cellar wall. M.G. VanBergen's horse ran away. They found him holme. Captain Morey here.

13 Fair. Lay cellar wall. Dig potatoes.

14 Fair. Raise Beecher's House. Burn fallow. Mr. Pelton here.

15 Fair. Go to Meeting. **Frank take our Negro girls to Coxsackie. [Frank's] Wife has to milk.**

16 Fair. Lay wall. Burn fallow. Send 35 dollars check to B.W. Warner. John McMichael and Lady, Doct. Fredenburgh & Lady call here.

17 Fair. Lay stone. Commence again on Beecher's house.

18 Fair. Shingle house. Mr. Eddy here to survey road.

19 I go to Albany. Get lumber. Rain all the way holme. Peter Livingston go along with me. Mrs. Fondy & Mr. Eddy here. I drive D. Carhart's horse

20 Fair. Doctor & Marite & Henry VanDerzee here. Cate and a lot of [negros][150] come here. I go with Mr. Eddy on the road.

---

[150] This was edited. It is the first of two times that we found of him using the N word.

21 Fair. I pick apples. Mr. Eddy & Spawn have a flare up. I go to **the toll gate** with Abram Teal. Take Mrs. Fonda along.

22 Fair. Go to Meeting twice. Doctor & Marite go a riding with Wesley's horse.

23 Fair. I am not very well. Go out to locate the toll house with A.N. Briggs and William McGregor.

Typical Toll Gate

24 Fair. Draw timber from Creek. Wife, Marite & Mrs. Fonda go to Garret Houghtaling's on a visit.

25 Fair. William Cook and Family here & Andrew Houghtaling here, Mr. Martin & Solomon Tuttle here. I take baskets to barge.

26 Rainy. **David Beach's funeral to our Cemetery today**. I make a swing gate. William Cook Lady & Children & Mrs. Fonda go holme.

27 Lousy. Send 800 dollars, pay James Lawton's note to the bank.

28 Fair. Work at house. Gather walnuts.

29 Fair. **I take a dose Calomel.**[151] Pretty sick; stay holme all day.

30 Fair. **Put on lath all day**.[152] Mrs. Houghtaling here.

October 1850

1 Fair. Work at house. Fair. David VanAntwerp & son here.

2 Rainy. Work at Beecher's House. Go to mill. Marite & Mother Houghtaling go to New York.

3 Fair, heavy NW. I work at house.

4 Fair. Mr. Bonteen pay me toll money. Andrew Houghtaling Wife & Children here. Frank dig potatoes. Draw few loads of sand.

5 I go to Albany. Get cheese. Pay note at bank. Aunt Catherine VanSlyck here Dominie Pelts here.

6 Fair. I go to Meeting twice. Take Mother Houghtaling & Aunt Catherine out a riding on Plank Road.

7 Fair. **I tender Frenchman John**.[153] Pay for saw. **Go out to build Toll house**.

8 Fair. I attend to Plank Road. Get gate ready. Frank gather nuts.

9 Fair. **I and Wife go to New York with the Barge**.

---

[151] Calomel is a mercury chloride mineral that was used to treat numerous illnesses – especially those that impact the gastrointestinal tract. Its use was eventually discontinued when it was discovered that the mercury in the mineral it was poisoning patients.

[152] Lath consists of thin strips of wood. It forms the foundation for plaster walls and ceilings.

[153] Tender means to present payment to another.

10	Fair. **I go to Greenwood Cemetery**[154] and to the **American Institute**[155] & to the museum.
11	Fair. **John Silcox get a team, take myself, Wife and Caroline Hollock to High Bridge.**[156]
12	Fair. I go around New York at night. **Go to Niblo's Garden**[157] with Doctor & Marite.
13	Fair. Go to hear Rev Mr. Balch preach twice.
14	Fair. Go to see Trego and come holme with Baltimore Barge.
15	Fair. Get holme. Pay John Toben off & make mortar.
16	Fair. Make mortar. Go out to Gates; get toll money.
17	Fair. Go out to Hollow. Set Mr. Tuttle to work. Go to mill. Get $17.20 of D. Bonteen.
18	Heavy rain, cloudy. Write to Parker & Pamur at Delhi. Send a check to C.P. Williams for lumber for the toll house & for Beecher's house.
20	Cloudy. Go to Meeting twice.
21	Fair, NW wind. Finish mason work at the house.
22	Fair. Wife come back from New York. **Beecher draw 59 bales of hay**. I put shingles on house.
23	Fair. I go out to gates, get toll money.
24	Rainy. John Silcox & Lady return here from wedding tour, take dinner with us. I take them to New Baltimore.
25	Rainy. I pay off Catherine Hyatt. She go holme. I make hog pen.
26	Rainy all day. I go to river. Convention today at the Hollow.
27	Rainy. I go to Meeting. Cate Houghtaling here.
28	Fair. Wife & Cate Houghtaling go to Charlotte Houghtaling's. M.G. VanBergen here.
29	Clear, cold. I go to Coxsackie, leave notes with Hubbell to collect. Pay Mr. Hubble's bills.
30	Fair. Wife go to Albany. Mrs. Holmes & Henriette, Charlotte Lawton, Mary Houghtaling, Alford Houghtaling, J. Lawton sent Pelts here. I shut toll gates. Work at hog pen.
31	Fair. I take A. Teal & Jonathan McElroy to Flat Bush. Wife come back from Albany. Bring Irish girl along.

November 1850

1	I go to Flat Bush. Carpenters finish there.

---

[154] Greenwood Cemetery founded in 1838 and now a National Historic Landmark is 478 acres of spectacular hills, valleys, glacial ponds, paths and centuries' old trees. Originally a Revolutionary War Site it has an international reputation for its magnificent natural beauty and sculptures. The permanent home of many renowned citizens, it was and is a tourist attraction for family outings, carriage rides and sculpture viewing.

[155] The American Institute of the City of New York for the Encouragement of Science and Invention was a civic organization that existed from 1828-1930. The association organized exhibitions and lectures.

[156] High Bridge, originally Aqueduct Bridge, is part of the Croton Aqueduct and is the oldest bridge in NYC. We have a picture in his September 24, 1844 entry.

[157] Niblo's Garden was a theater in New York City on Broadway

2	Foggy. I go to Albany after lumber. Peter VanBuren's team bring a load. I pay all up then.
3	Foggy. Beecher move in new house yesterday. I go to Meeting. Aunt Calara come here yesterday & stay yet today.
4	Wife, Mother, Aunt Calara go to Dominie Pelts' visiting. I work on house that Abram Teal is to live in.
5	Fair. **Attend election. Robert Babcock gets elected**. Get money to gate. **Leonard Hathaway & Peter Crumb has a regular fight**.
6	Fair. Work at hen house. **Ebenezer Finch bring his girls here to set up business**.
7	Fair. **Finch girls move in my shop**. Frank goes to Canada. I work at hen house.
8	Fair. Work at hen house. **Help Finch girls in the evening**.
9	Fair, cold. I go to Flat Bush get apples. Mrs. Pierce & Phelps girls here. I work at hen house.
10	Fair day. I go to Meeting. **Have a time with Dennis Toben's Geese**.
11	Fair. I work at hen house. Take Peter Ostrander to Flat Bush to paint.
12	Fair. I work at hen house. **Go out to gate & tear up old sloop**.
13	Fair. I work at hen coop. **Bank up Mother's house**.[158]
14	Fair. I go out to measure Plank Road, take John Rea along. Mrs. Pierce & Mother Houghtaling go to Baltimore. **Gardner Lawton died**.
15	Fair. **I take Mother Houghtaling, Mrs. Pierce & Mary Phelps to Martin VanBergen's and attend Gardner Lawton's Funeral**.
16	Fair. Quarterly meeting today. John Bushants and a lot of folks here. Levi is unwell. **I get engravings from Barge**. Dominie Pelts here.
17	Rainy. Maria & Adeline Finch here all day. Go to Meeting.
18	Rainy. I get poles to creek. Get in creek, get wet up to my knees.
19	Fair north wind. Beecher thrash. I do nothing.
20	Fair. Put up gutter on Toll House. Frank come back. I put pump in Mother's cistern.
21	Fair, cold. Travis bring a load of road plank. I draw poles for hen house.
22	Fair, cold. I pay Fraver $137.37. Wife go to Albany.
23	Fair. I go on Martin's Hill, work on road.
24	**Fair under foot, cloudy overhead**. I go to Meeting twice. Cate Houghtaling here.
25	**Fair. I and Peter Seabridge start for Canada. Get to White Hall and take Steamboat United States at 10 o'clock PM**.
26	**Snow all day. We get as far as St. Johns. Stay all night to Mrs. Ezenhart's. We have passed through Benson, Orwell, Ticonderoga, Shoreham, Bridgeport, Chimney Point, Port Henry, West Port, Basin Harbor, Essex, Burlington when we saw a large Fin and**

---

[158] The term 'bank-up' refers to shoveling material along the foundation of a house to prevent the loss of heat during the winter months.

met steamer Francis Saltus, then to Port Kent, Plattsburgh, Chazy, Isle La Motte Champlain, Isle Au Noix then to St. Johns.

27 **Snow & rain. Went to Montreal. Put up to Henny Irish's.**
28 **Rain & sleet. Go around the city. Look at horses.**
29 **Thawy. Peter Seabridge buy the Bursaw horse then we go back to St. John's to Ezenhart's.**
30 **Fair. Go to Stanbridge, Bedford. Stop at Bates Hotel.**

December 1850

1 **Clear, cold. Peter Seabridge go with Mr. Odle to Pidgeon Hill & buy one horse. I stay to Hotel and go to Meeting.**
2 **Fair. We come back to St. John's to Ezenhart's.**
3 **Fair. Peter Seabridge buy one horse. I buy a boas and gloves, mittens.** Start on **Board of Steamer Burlington for White Hall. Get as far as Isle La Motte and lay up for the gale. Passengers afraid to go any farther.**
4 **Fair. Underway again. Arrive at White Hall 5 o'clock pm. Take supper at the Phoenix Hotel. Then start at 7 o'clock on horseback for holme. Get to Little Hartford at 10 o'clock at night.**
5 **Showry & rainy. Come through Arlington. Get as far as Waterford. Ride 47 miles. Have a hard tramp. Stay at Mowry's tavern.**
6 **Come on holme. Very muddy, but no rain. Very tired. Ride on horseback all the way.**
7 Four inches of snow and rainy. I go to river.
8 Fair. I go to Meeting twice. Some sleighs down.
9 Fair, south wind. I pay off Lewis Crandle & kill my hogs.
10 Fair. I cut up my meat. Go to river. Get my boots fixed.
11 Fair. I go out to the Gate. Salt my pork. Wife go to Albany.
12 Rainy. **I attend Thanksgiving**. Frank chop wood.
13 Fair, cold. Mr. Eddy here. I pay him 50 dollars. Frank chop.
14 Fair, cold. I get horse shod & go to Abram Whitbeck's. E. Finch here.
15 Fair, cold. **River froze. No steamboat today**.
16 Warmer. Cherry cow has a calf.
17 Snowy, cold NW. I work around the house. **Old Mrs. Barton died**.
18 Clear, cold. I & Wife go to toll house. River closed. Frank chop wood. River closed.
19 Snowy, cold. **I attend Mrs. Barton's funeral**. Mrs. Fredenburgh, Mrs. Hull, Betsy VerPlanck here; visit.
20 Fair. I go to river. Pass over receipts to Willis & James Lawton for stock P.R.

21 Fair. I & Mother Houghtaling go to Flat Bush. We take dinner to Andrew's. A. Fancher call and pay me ten dollars for Mrs. Rhodes. I pay off H. B. Wilsey. Settle with S.M. Pelton. He owes me $27.44.

22 Cold, cloudy. Go to Meeting. Call at Mother's. **Emma Sherman died about this time**.

23 **Tremendous snowstorm, NW**. Stay about the house all day.

24 Very cold heavy snow. **James Tefft's barns fall in by snow and the Brick Sheds last night**.

25 Cold, south [wind]. **Mrs. Beecher Holmes has a daughter. I go to toll house get tolls**.

26 Fair. G.B. Lansing call on me. **I fix Gate house**. Donation tonight of the Rev. Mr. Hoyt; we attend.

27 Fair. Spend the day to Willis's. Have a turkey dinner. I and Willis ride out to Mr. Bonticon's.

28 Fair. I get check of L&W for 50 dollars. John Burhaus pay me 50 dollars. **I fix churn**. Mrs. Holmes here.

29 Snow all day. **Go to Meeting with sley, 18 inches deep. Very cold. More snow than has been in some years**.

30 Clear, cold. Rev. Pelts lecture before Debating School. Andrew Houghtaling & sister here.

31 Very cold. **Thermometer 22 degrees below zero**. I and Wife & Caroline VanAntwerp go to Albany. **I pay my rent to VanRenssalear**. Buy (?) lots of G.B. Lansing, pay him.

January 1851

1 Fair, warmer. I go to papermill.

2 Fair. Start for Greenville. Meet Edward Hubbell and his family and come back. Mr. Hubbell pay me $97.75 on the notes that I let him have for collection. Wife goes to Dominie Jolly's. Henry Hoag pay me $26.95 balance that he owes me.

3 Fair, NW. I go to Greenville stay all night to Andrew Fancher's.

4 Cold. Collect my rents & come to back from Greenville.

5 Overcast. I go to Meeting. Hear Rev. Mr. Rodgers preach. Finch girls here. Mother sick.

6 Fair. Break roads. Draw wood. Attend Plank Road meeting at Mr. Gregor's.

7 Snow, very cold. Draw wood. Maria VanBergen here.

9 Misty. Attend Pelt's donation. It goes off finely. Raise 146 dollars.

10 Fair. Draw wood. Get 80 dollars of N.H. Johnson for Henry Niles P.R.

11 Fair. I go to Hollow along with Wesley. Pay my tax. Mother, Margaret, Wesley here to spend the day. B.W. Warner here.

12 Fair. I go to Meeting. Mr. Jolly preach in the afternoon.

13 Fair. I pay B.W. Warner 97 dollars. He starts for Herkimer.

14 Fair. I attend P.R. meeting. Wife go to Westerlo to A. Miller's to donation.

15 Warm. I go to toll gates. Wife goes to Thomas Houghtaling's.

16   Cloudy, warm. I give Widow Houghtaling her deed. **James White's child died this morning**.

17   Clears off, cold. Capt. Sherwood here. **We go to Dancing School**.

18   Fair. I get 50 dollars of Andrew VanBergen. Pay him off for Plank Road. Attend Plank Road supper to Aaron Houghtaling's. Frank hurt his eye.

19   Fair. I go to Meeting. Hear Rev. P. Pelts. Call at John Rea's.

20   Fair. Attend P.R. meeting. **Attend Debating School**.

21   Fair. **Work on old sloop**. Beecher draw for me in afternoon.

22   Snowy. I and A.N. Briggs go out to Indian Fields.

23   Fair. I pay Wm. B. Hull lacking 6 dollars. Mr. Matson & Lady here.

24   Fair day. Beecher sell our hay to Andrew Mull.

25   Fair day. Peter Vaulice & McDonald took horses on the ice. I get rocking chair fixed. Get book of Mr. H. Niles Widow.

26   Fine warm day. Eben Finch & Lady & two of his girls & Mother here.

27   Fair. Attend P.R. meeting all day & Debate at night. Frank chop wood.

28   South wind, snow. **I settle with LW&C and gave them my note to balance the account**.[159]

29   Rainy morning. **I go and get toll money. Pay it to A.N. Briggs**.

30   Very cold. Miss Pelts & Mrs. Hull here & Miss Lawton. I go to papermill. Frank chop wood. I kill a rat in the cellar. **Christina VanAntwerp died this morning**.

31   Very cold. **Reuben Dunbar hung today at Albany Jail for murder of two adopted children of his stepfather**.[160] Miss VanLoans, Miss Witbeck & Miss Lawton here. They go from here to Dancing School.

February 1851

1   Very cold. **Mrs. VanAntwerp buried**. Beecher goes to Albany. Frank chop wood.

2   Cloudy. I go to Meeting. Little sun in the afternoon. **Samuel Jolly died**.

3   Fair. **I, Mother & Mother Houghtaling go to Samuel Jolly's Funeral**. Mrs. Sherman, Mrs. Gregory and Ruth Ann Finch here.

4   Fair. I take Willis's Team & take all hands to John Cronk's on a visit.

5   Fair. I go out to Gates, take Levi along. Wife goes to Donation to Baltimore.

6   Very cold. **Old Mrs. Mull buried today**. I settle with Peter Holbrook and take his note for 10 dollars.

---

[159] Lawton Willis & Colvin & Company

[160] "The most foul and unparalleled murder in the annals of crime: life and confession of Reuben A. Dunbar, convicted and executed for the murder of Stephen V. and David L. Lester (aged 8 and 10 years) in Westerlo, Albany County, September 28, 1850," Published by Joh. B. Parsons 1851. It's a sad story of a young man who felt he had been cheated out of his birthright.

7	Very cold day. **Horses & skaters try a race on the ice. Horses beat**. I make leather halter. Frank chop.
8	Colder than ever. Thermometer stand at zero all day. Stay about the house.
9	South wind. Misty & hail all day. I go to Meeting.
10	Rain, south wind all day. I fix hay press.
11	Clear and cold. I fix hay press.
12	Cold. I go to river. Take up Johnson's bill. Go to toll gate.
13	South wind & fair. I take my Wife and Levi to Baltimore.
14	Rain, south wind. I pound my finger, then go to river.
15	Rainy all day. I go to river.
16	Clear off. Cate VanBergen & Elida VanSlyck & Martin VanSlyck and Martin Andrews here.
17	Fair day. I[ce] broke up and lodged from here to Cedar Hill. I go to Abram Witbeck's to see his colt.
18	Fair, cold NW. I go to river.
19	Fair, south wind. I take Cate VanBergen & Elida VanSlyck out to Gate. Attend a party to B.B. Fredenburgh's at night. **Lewis Fatch and Lizabeth Cronk married today**.
20	South wind and rain. I take Wife & Cate VanBergen & Elida VanSlyck to Widow Charlotte's a visiting.
21	Rain all day. I go to river buy spools of John Keller.
22	Martin VanSlyck here. **We have a party; have a jolly time. Lots of boys and girls sing and carry on till about one o'clock at night**.
23	Fine day. Go to Meeting. **Ice move in places and goes out of the river**.
25	Very heavy NW. Martin VanSlyck take the girls holme. **Steamboat Oregon goes up today**. Very muddy. I and Frank make a road.
26	Fair. **Make road to stone quiry**. Wife & Mother go to Miss Finch's.
27	Cloudy, south wind. Work at road to quiry and go to river.
28	Rainy. Stay around the house in forenoon. Go to river in afternoon.

March 1851

1	Fine day. Frank chop. I go to river. Attend P.R. meeting. Abram Whitbeck pay me $75. I pay N.H. Johnson 75 dollars. J.W. Story & his Wife here.
2	Fair, south wind. I go to Meeting twice. Stop at Willis's.
3	Fair cold. Work at cemetery road. **[Steamboat] Shepperd Knapp goes up today**.
4	Fair cold. I settle with J.W. Story. I take Wife & Mother Houghtaling to Grant Houghtaling's. I go there to tea.
5	Fine day. I go to Gate House. Frank work on road.
6	Fair, colder. Work on country road. Make an attempt to settle with Henry Spawn.

7	Cloudy, cold day. Ditch out swamp. A.P. VanSlyck here.
8	Snow all day. I get box fixed by side of desk.
9	Fair. **Attend Dutch Church Communion today**.
10	Snowy forenoon, clears off in afternoon. Get out hoops.
11	Fair, south wind. Wife go to Albany. I trim up cemetery. Pay adjustment on insurance policy. Set out trees. Cate Van Antwerp here. I dig horse radish.
12	Fair, cold. **I go to Baltimore funeral of David Gage**. Wife go to toll gates.
13	Heavy south wind. Snowy all day. R. Garrett's Vendue today.
14	Cold. Frank work at cemetery Road. I work at wheelbarrow. Mother here.
15	Cloudy, south wind. I take Beecher's horses get 1 load of lumber. Frank pile up lumber. Work ½ day on cemetery road.
16	Rainy, cloudy. Go to Meeting. Rev. Mr. Pelts preach.
17	Snow all day. Make wheelbarrow. **Attend Debating School**.
18	Snow 4 in, cold. Send Frank with G. Roseboom get 1 hive of bees.
19	Cloudy & cold. I, Wife & Caroline VanAntwerp go out to John McCarty's, visit.
20	Cloudy. **Jonah Sherman pays me Island rent up to Nov 1, 1850. Amt. 50 dollars**.
21	Fair, cold. I pay LWC & Co over 200 dollars. Frank make basket. I work at swing gate. I send with Simon Garret to pay J. Baker's assessment of insurance.
22	Fine day. Frank work at cemetery road. **Marite come up from New York with Barge**. I walk around. **I have worked 9 days on cemetery road to this date**.
23	Fair day. I go to Meeting & walk about.
24	Fair day. I take Abram Teal go to Flat Bush. Get out gutter stick. Frank go along, he loses his watch. Mrs. John Rea hurt her leg.
25	Clear & cold. I go to Albany. Frank dig ditch. I pay Mr. Heilton 36 dollars. I get a lot of nails, a shovel and a spade.
26	Fair. I get tolls, fix gate, fix rose bushes. Draw one load of lumber from Houghtaling's Mill.
27	Fair day, south wind. Frank help Beecher draw stone ½ day. I fix up my saws and send a letter to Doct. VanAntwerp.
28	Fair day. Pay off Isaac Whitbeck. Plow my garden. Sow lettuce bed. Frank sick all day and ½ day yesterday.
29	We put up Beecher's wood house. Hall & man help.
30	Fair, south wind. I go to Meeting & to see John Bailey, he is sick
31	Fair, south wind. I fix toll gate. George Fancher here.

April 1851

1	Fine day. George Fancher go holme. He takes Abram Teal & James Sherwood along; commence to build. Doct. VanAntwerp come here last night 12 o'clock. He goes out back

	today. Marite & Mother Houghtaling come back from Coxsackie. I & Frank make picket fence around the woods.
2	Rainy. My cow calves. I sell a cow & calf to Josiah Sherman for $27.50. Mr. Casy here. Pays Andrew VanAntwerp 22 dollars. Then Andrew & Marite start for New York. I take them to the river.
3	Showry in the afternoon. I go to John Cronk's in morning, get a lot of chickens & one rooster. Bring Charlotte along. I get 100 dollars of Wm. Hull. I get 50 dollars of John Bushants. I pay G. Sweet $2.05. Make fence. Josiah Sherman take away his cow.
4	Fair day. Make fence and pay off G. Roseboom.
5	Fair. I go to river & to Cedar Hill to Plank Road meeting. I receive a letter from Andrew Antwerp with Rarick's & Casy's notes included.
6	Rain. I go to Meeting and to John Baily.
7	Fine day. Make fences & attend Dist. Road meeting.
8	Rainy afternoon. I fix hen pen and get out pickets.
9	Fair. Get saw logs in dam. Rev. Mr. Hoyt here. Go out to toll gates.
10	Fair. Make fence and drain swamp. Send a letter to Doct. VanAntwerp.
11	Fair. Go to sawmill; get lumber and then plow south of woods. I have Josiah Sherman's mare.
12	Clear, cold. **I go out to Chesterville to meet the people of that place to extend our Plank Road**.[161] Beecher plow for me. Frank dig ditch.
13	Cold as ever. I go to Meeting. Write a letter to J.W. Cronk. Take a walk.
14	Clear, cold. I work in garden. Get sash of G. Roseboon. I get 1 saw of Grant.
15	Misty, cold rain. I put out onions & beans, **get a pie plant**,[162] set out rosebush.
16	Lowry & rainy. I go to Greenville & Norton hill.
17	Rainy. I go to J.B. Waldron's and with Gerry Place in my woods.
18	Return holme by Coxsackie. Go to Thms. Gay's. Put a note that I hold against Mr. Tiffney into J.C. VanSlyck's hands for collection.
19	Lowry & Rainy. I go to Hollow make out Dist. Road assessment. Frank work at trees.
21	Cloudy & misty. A. Teal goes to Greenville 12 o'clock. Go to blacksmiths.
22	Fair, NW. I make fence. **Papermill Dam go off last night**. Wife & Mother Houghtaling go to Thomas Houghtaling's.
23	Fair. Furrow out corn ground. Get horse shod. Go to see Woolsey Cary. Aunt Gitty Hathaway & Deon here.
24	Finest day this spring. I furrow out and plant corn. **Put two calves on board of barge**. Get two shad. Wife & Cate Houghtaling go to Andrew VanSlyck's.
25	Fair. Plant corn and potatoes. Wife & Cate Houghtaling come back.

---

[161] Chesterville is the former name of the hamlet of Westerlo (history.altamontenterprise.com)
[162] In early years, rhubarb was known at the pie plant.

26 Fair. Plant corn. Lots of visitors here. Mr. Pelton come here and pay me part of his rent. I get 5 shad. I break my waggon.

27 Cloudy & Rainy. I go to Meeting twice & call at John Rea's.

28 Cloudy & misty. Mrs. Hall, Cate VanAntwerp & Cate Fredenburgh here.

29 Fair. Make fence. **Appoint G.T. Sweet collector and give him his warrant to collect district tax**.

30 Rainy. I pay check to L. W. & Colvin & Co. 103 dollars. Woolsey Cary pay me 42 dollars. Peter Seabridge pay me 303 dollars and 50 cents. I go out to gates, get tolls. Get cloth of A.E. Willis.

May 1851

1 Fair morning. I go to H.P. Miller's. Leave Pelton's mortgage. **Andrew VanDerzee married to this day or evening**. Then to J.W. Story, then to A. Fancher, then to B. Waldron's Mill, pay him 10 dollars cash and he account for rent of Reynolds Edget.

2 Cold, NW. I come back from Greenville. I buy stone of H.D. Brown. Frank help Beecher.

3 Fair. Settle up with Frank; pay him off. He leave here. Work in swamp. A. Teale come from Greenville.

4 Fair. I go to Meeting. A. Teal goes back to Greenville. A.E. Willis here.

5 Rainy day. I fix basket. Stay around the house.

6 Little showry. I go to Baltimore. Take cloth. Abram Witbeck pay me 25 dollars balance on rent.

7 Little showry. I go to Albany. Get shingles & newel post. Get books & dividends.

8 Fine day. Dig around trees & put manure around them.

9 Rainy. Shingle Beecher's wood house.

10 Fair. **Tear up old sloop**. Get 4 shad & a piece of veal.

11 Fair. I write letters to Warner & to J. Feeter.

12 Clear and then cloudy. Attend P.R. meeting. Almira VanBergen here. **Attend Wesley's lawsuit**. Send a check to Feeter 150 dollars & a letter to B.W. Warner.

13 Hot, fine showers. **I put up notices to sell toll house.** Work around the house.

14 Fair, colder. I take Almira VanBergen riding to toll gate. I pay 62.50 dollars on L W & Colvin & Co. bill on P. Road.

15 Fair. **I sell A.E. Willis butter**. Go to Greenville, take my colt along.

16 Fair. A. Fancher pay me 200 dollars. I go to Menard Stephens', take dinner. Carpenters come holme. I let A.E. Willis have 200 dollars.

17 Fair morning, shower in afternoon. I and all family take tea to Cate Lawton's.

18 Fair. I go to Meeting. Hear Rev. P. Pelts. **Sylvester Harris & Mary Clement get married this evening; we attend**. **Jane Springstead died**.

19 Fair. I shingle house to Abram Witbeck's. Put my mare to his horse.

20 Fair. I shingle house to Abram Witbeck's. Heavy showers in afternoon. **Old Mr. Purdy died today**. I get ¾ bunch of shingles of J. McElroy.

21 Fair day. Finish shingling to Abram Witbeck's. Take all hands to Charlotte Houghtaling's. **Sell old toll house to Wm. Briggs for 25 dollars.**

22 Fair day. **I attend reference suit between James Blodget and the New Baltimore Firm**. Help Beecher. Dominie Ferris stay here all night. Pay L W & Colvin 67 dollars.

23 Rain last night. I help Beecher make fence around the swamp in forenoon. **Hear James M. Smith make speech in the afternoon.**[163]

24 Fair. I hoe corn in the forenoon. Play in the afternoon.

25 Fair. I go to Meeting twice. Lib Houghtaling here.

26 Fair. I hoe corn. Go to river. Work at bridge in afternoon.

27 Showry. Mrs. Houghtaling, Cate & Trego here. I work in garden and go to cemetery. Get meat of Ira Gregory.

28 Fair. I go to Gates get tolls. Help Beecher make fence.

29 Rainy. I saw wood go to river. Get some small fish.

30 Fair. I work around the house in the forenoon. In afternoon I gave Isaac Baker his P. Road scrip. G.T. Sweet pay me 35 dollars of District Road money. I go to Barren Isle, get one shad.

31 Fair. **Henriette Willis died.**[164] I go to river get a piece of sturgeon. Work in garden. Almira VanBergen & Mary Houghtaling here.

June 1851

1 Rainy. **We all attend funeral of Willis's child**. Henry VanBergen here.

2 Fair. Plow & hoe corn. Take masons out to Greenville. **A.E. Willis take his child out of the grave and have her daguerreotype taken here in sitting room**. I pay T. Houghtaling interest on my note, by order on L W & Colvin & Co. Mary Harris, Eliza Clement & Mrs. Clement here to tea.

3 **We all have our daguerreotypes taken**. Mrs. Willis and Mother here all day. **I pay six dollars for them**.

4 Fair. Plaster corn. I take Wife and Mother Houghtaling to George Wolf's. Then go out to Gate to get toll money. I pay P.R. bill of LWC & Co.

5 Fair I put my mare to horse. Put pillows and letters on board of Barge. Write a letter to John Silcox. Mary Ann Lewis here on a visit. Anthony Miller here to tea. Mrs. Briggs call here. **I hopple my mare.**[165]

6 Fair. Work in garden. Settle P.R. bill with Doct. Fredenburgh. Wheel some wood in wood house.

---

163 James M. Smith was born in New Baltimore. He was elected on the Democratic ticket as the Recorder of New York City in 1854.
164 Henriette was about 4 when she died.
165 To hopple is to loosely tie the front feet together.

7	Rainy day. Lawton, Willis, Colvin & Co. send me up one barrel of flour for 5 dollars. I grind my axe. P. Seabridge pay me his bill.
8	Cold rain. Go to Meeting. James Nickerson, a Quaker, preach here.
9	Rainy. I get fish and **send away my dog watch**.
10	Fair. Draw gravel. Attend to Jacob Baker's & Wesley Blaisdell's lawsuit. Go out to toll gate. Pay in A.N. Briggs hands 100 dollars. Sell my account against (?) Spawn to George W. Dorman. Mother Houghtaling come holme. Sarah Ann go to Albany.
11	Cloudy and showers. I go to Albany. Get trimmings. Pay up for Atlas. Pay Davidson & Viele one bill, make another. Get newel post banister caps. I bring Wife & Levi back with me.
12	Fair. **Sit for daguerreotypes to paint a portrait from. Mr. Nichols here**. I borrow a bull of Nyan Sweet. Go after him with a waggon, bring him holme.
13	Fair. Attend Plank Road meeting.
14	Fair. Henry Wilsey bring Fancher's horse. Stay all night. **I get up logs out of Dam**.
15	Cool, fair. Go to Meeting & to cemetery.
16	Fair, cool. Work at bridge. Beecher help.
17	Fair, warmer. I go out to gates, get tolls. Send a letter Ramsdell with check of $69.18. Mrs. Garret Houghtaling here & John L. Rowe's girls.
18	Fair & warmer. Hoe corn. I pay A.N. Briggs 20 dollars making 140 dollars to Barent Teneyck. I shoot one pidgeon.
19	Fair. I work at Plank Road. R. Baker & Beecher help. I pay Andrew Witbeck, Henry Witbeck's bill. Wilsey come from Greenville.
20	Showry & warm. Get fish. Attend work at Plank Road.
21	Rainy. M.G. VanBergen here. Ebenezer Finch here. Mrs. Robb & Mrs. Carroll here. Mrs. J. Lawton here, Mrs. Colvin, Cate Lawton she bump her head. I buy sugar of G.W. Dorman 23½ lb, 3 cts per lb.
22	Fair. I go to Meeting. It is very warm. I call at Widow Clement's.
23	South wind, showry. I furrow out potatoes. Pay Pulver & Rosecrant's saw bill of twenty-eight dollars.
24	Fair. The heaviest showers came last night that has been for years. My bees swarm today. I lay around.
25	Fair. I go to Gate. Send Henry Wilsey and my mare to Andrew Fancher's. I take up my note of Wesley of 25 dollars. I go a strawberrying. I have John Rea hoe my corn.
26	Showry in the afternoon. I go to river. Join issue on horse trial. **Sit for portrait**.
27	Fair. I work in garden. **Go to Wesley's with portrait painter**.
28	Fair. **I sit for portrait**. Fix bridge. Pay John Toben $8.00. Miss Caroline Houghtaling here. Wesley come back from Greenville.
29	Fair, hot day. I go to Meeting twice.

30   Hot and showers in the afternoon. I put **chain pump** in my well. **Go to Hollow for the purpose of getting Barent Teneyck in this school district.**

July 1851

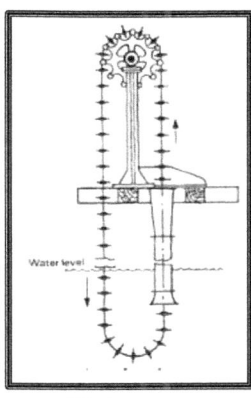

Chain pump

1 Rainy. I gave Henry Wilsey an order for ten dollars. Hoe in the garden. Rev. Mr. Pelts here.

2 Fair. I go out to gates. Pay H.D. Brown. Work in garden. Beecher's bees swarm. Mr. Colborn and Mr. Proceus here.

3 Hot & Showry afternoon. Marite & Mother Houghtaling come back from Flat Bush and Coxsackie. Colburn & Proceus leave by barge for New York.

4 Rainy. **Picnic on Berena Island**. John Bushants & Abram Teal here.

5 Fair. I take Marite out a riding on P. Road. Stop at Baltimore. Load up Abram Teal's tools for Greenville.

6 Fair. I go to Meeting. My bees swarm. Willis & Harriet here.

7 Fair. I go to Greenville. Go part of the way on foot.

8 Fair. I go around among the folks in Greenville.

9 Fair. Come from Greenville part of the way on foot. Shower in the afternoon. I pay off John Rea. Get the Toll funds.

10 Fair hot. **I get hair restoration of A.E. Willis.** Go a fishing. Get lodge papers of N.H. Johnson. I get 4 quarts raspberries.

11 Fair. I go after berries. Lots of little girls here. I hoe in the garden.

12 Fair. I work in garden. Martin VanSlyck, Elida & Cate VanBergen here. Beecher go to Albany.

13 Fair. I go to Meeting. Send John Teal to Greenville. Company leave.

14 Fair. **I buy 100 lbs. sugar of George W. Dorman & 10½ lbs. of cheese**. Mrs. A.N. Briggs, Cate and Lib Houghtaling here.

15 I and Wife go to John Bushants'. Get 1 peck of raspberries. Come back, attend to gates. Get $100 dollars of Lawton W[illis] Colvin & Co.

16 **Fair. I go to Herkimer. Stay to John Feeter's.**

17 **Fair. I go to B.W. Warner's. John Feeter go along. Start my sawmill.**

18 **Fair. I go to Mr. Gray's with B.W. Warner.**

19 **Showry. I & Warner go to Wendover's, take dinner.**

20 **Lowry. Come back to Little Falls. Take up note of Feeter's. Pay Jacob Feeter 2 dollars for O. Springstead. Let Warner have 65 dollars.**

21 **Fair. I and John Feeter go to Salisbury. I buy my Bill horse of Mr. Heller for 100 dollars. Start for holme in cars.**[166] **Get to Schenectady.**

---

[166] The term 'cars' refers to railroad cars.

22	**Fair. Get holme. Ride holme bareback from Albany**.
23	Fair. Get horse shod. Go to gates. I get wool of Ira Gregory. He brought it from Styles.
24	Hot. I patch barn roof. Get 2 gallons of molasses.
25	I go to Coxsackie. Get 50 dollars of J.C. VanDick on Tiffny note. Then to Andrew VanSlyck's. Cate Houghtaling go along.
26	Fair, hot. Go to Meeting. I take Cate Houghtaling holme.
27	Fair, hot. I send by mail to Styles after wool.
28	Fair, cooler. I and Wm. Bagley Junior go to Kimmey's mill.
29	Cloudy. I pay G.W. Dorman off all but $35.46 for checks sent for me to Bank. I pay Sager's interest on P.R. I am quite sick today.
30	Fair. Draw stone, fix bridges. Draw 1 load lumber from sawmill. Dominie Pelts here.

August 1851

1	Fair. I take Wm. Bagley to Greenville. I stay to Andrew Fancher's.
2	Fair. I go around my farm and then return holme.
3	Fair. **I go to funeral of Mr. Titus**. A general turnout of S of T.
4	Fair. Work around. **Notify District to school meeting.**
5	Fair. **I pay Mr. Nichols 32.32 dollars for painting our portraits.**[167] I draw wood and fix my gate.
6	Fair. I go to gates. I get $40 of L W & Colvin. I pay A.N. Briggs seventy dollars. I get hopples fixed. Dominie Pelts and all his folks here. I draw one load of lumber.
7	Heavy shower. I draw one load of lumber from mill. I let John Rea have my horse to go to Coxsackie.
8	Fair. I draw two loads lumber. Mrs. Holmes and Henriette here. Mr. Nichols come back here.
9	Heavy showers. I get pineapples. **I and Nichols go to cave in rocks**. I get apples of A.E. Willis.
10	Fair. I go to Meeting twice. Hear Mr. Halloway & Asa Clements.
11	Fair. Chop in forenoon. Peter Seabridge pay me seven dollars house rent of Louis Clouchy. **Attend school meeting at night**.
12	Fair. Draw wood to self and Mother. I get molasses hogshead to G.W. Dorman's for 4 dollars.
13	Fair, hot. I go to gates and attend **Dan Rice's Circus** in afternoon. Beecher pay me $70.38. I pay G.W. Dorman balance of borrowed money 35 dollars.
14	Rainy morning but it clears off. I pay Abram Teal $40.76. George Sweet pays me 76 dollars Dist. road money.
15	Fair. I am dull & sleepy. Go after berries. Set up last night with Aaron Houghtaling. I go to John Mull's with Mother.

---

[167] See the Photo Section for photographs of the portraits.

16 Fair. Anthony M. & Almira VanBergen, Wife go to John Colvin's. I pay John Toben 15 dollars.

17 Rainy day. Anthony and Almira VanBergen and Mary Houghtaling here. **I get one dollar from Showman last night**. I go to Meeting.

18 Fair. I work at gate posts and the flowers. All visitors leave here.

19 Fair. Hang gates on cemetery road. **Go to Andrew Houghtaling with our Spinster**. Go to Hollow and to S.E. Andrews.

20 Fair. I pay A.N. Briggs 70 dollars toll money for interest due him of Plank Road notes. Wife go with Willis & Harriet to John Cronk's. I get apples and take in onions.

21 Fair. **Beecher finish haying**. Miss Little and Emily VanAntwerp here.

22 Rainy. I and Beecher go fishing. Work around the house. Dennis Toban come to work at noon.

23 Fair. Work on cemetery road. Wife go to Henry Schoomaker.

24 Fair. I go to Meeting. Mr. Briggs & Lady and Miss Andrews call here.

25 Fair, hot. Work at cemetery. Not very well. Go to Mr. Tombs in afternoon.

26 Fair. Work at cemetery. G. Wilsey's & John Lot's horse trot.

27 Fair. I go to gates. Go to Baltimore get pickets. Work at cemetery road.

28 Fair. **I sit up with Aaron Houghtaling last night**. **I was elected Trustee for Cemetery**. Trego's Wife and Cate Houghtaling here to dinner. Mother here. **I finish cemetery road and gate.**

29 Fair. I go to Flat Bush. Go around farm with Mr. Rundell from Greenville. **I hang cemetery gate.**

30 Fair. Quarterly meeting. Casper Witbeck & Lady here, Mrs. Polly Sisk and Mr. Crumb here.

September 1851

1 Fair. I dig potatoes all day. I feel tired.

2 Rainy. I'm not very well. Make gates. Get codfish of John Keller.

3 Fair. I go to toll gates. A.E. Willis pay me 25 dollars last night for rent of Division Room. I pay off Abram Teal today 28 dollars and balance his account. I pay A.N. Briggs 70 dollars interest money on P.R. **John McCarty died today. I hang small gate on cemetery road**. Mr. Pelton here.

4. Fair. **I and Mr. Nichols go to John McCarty, take his daguerreotype and take a sketch of Cave.**

5 Fair. I go to Mr. Tobb's. **John McCarty's funeral today**. Mrs. John Johnson & Mrs. VanEpes here today to visit.

6 Fair. I and Mr. Robb harness horses together and go to Stockport. Wife & Mrs. Robb go along. Stay to George Chittenden's. **I attend the examination of Reuben Gay for a rape committed on Mary __. He is sent to jail at Hudson**.

7   Fair. I attend Universalist Church. Rev. Mr. Collins preach in afternoon. We go to Martin VanAlstine's. Stay all night have a good visit. Eat peaches. Robb & Lady go with us.

8   Fair, hot. Little showry in the afternoon here. We go back to George Chittenden's. Take Mrs. Chittenden. Go to [Valatie]. I take dinner with Wm. Spears. See Samuel & Mary Spears and their father Samuel Spears. He is very old & blind. Leave my team at Mr. Lynch's. Returned by way of Martin VanBuren residence & Stuyvesant Falls.[168] Then cross at Coxsackie.[169] Stop to A.T. VanSlyck's. Get peaches & tomatoes. Then come holme.

Stuyvesant Falls

9   Fair, hot. Do but little. Go to gate house.

10 Fair & hot. I and Beecher & John Henry work at old sloop. Draw lumber & water for Abram Teal. Mr. Colburn & Nichols here.

11 Fair & hot. I send Marite plums. **Make cemetery map**. Get Mr. Colbom things up to his room. **Go to see Indians. They encamp on shore just above the upper dock.** I let Colbom have my Bill horse to go to Baltimore.

12 Fine shower in afternoon. A.M. VanBergen here. Mrs. Bush, Adam VanBergen, Edward Hubbell here. I take Wife and all hands to Weldon. I draw stone. **Lay wall in village. I Draw 3 loads of stone to cemetery road. Commence Beecher's will.** Albert Lester Cronk, I gave him his due bill $13.50.

13 Rainy. **I help Abram Teal raise his house**. I pay off Peter Ostrander.

14 Clear, cold. I go to Meeting. Hear Rev. Mr. Jolly. Then I and Mr. Nichols go to Coxsackie. **I subpoena Mr. Eddy. Find him & his lady at Mr. Hunt's**. I take tea at Edward Hubbel's. Stop at A.T. VanSlyck's.

15 Fair. **Lay out cemetery lots with Bailey & John Hauenstien**. I am not very well. I have a bad cold. I go to river.

16 Fair. **I and Wife attend wedding of Andrew Houghtaling & Caroline Briggs. Have a great time. Stay till one o'clock. Mrs. Briggs made a great fuss on account of my Bill horse jumping & rearing.**

17 I pay A.N. Briggs 70 dollars balance of interest on 200 dollars note against Plank Road. **Attend wedding again to Garret Houghtaling**. Have still (?) time.

18 Fair. I fix hog pen. Go to river. Feel sleepy.

19 Fair. Husk corn. Fix corn crib. Leon Houghtaling here. **I sit up with Aaron Houghtaling**.

20 Fair & warm. Measure and put away corn. I and Beecher & Anthony Bradwell and Elias Holmes go a fishing. Get a fine lot of fish.

21 Commence raining at noon. I go to Meeting twice. Call at Anthony Wolf's.

22 Rainy. Chop wood. **Barge come today**. Stay around the house.

---

[168] Stuyvesant Falls is on Kinderhook Creek in Columbia County.
[169] It is not mentioned how river crossings were made. Evidently there were informal ferries that would take passengers and their horses across the river at various locations along the Hudson.

23 Fair, cold. **I go to Coxsackie to Green County Fair. Take dinner at Edwin Hubbel's. A.N. Briggs & Lady and Hannah Andrews here to sing. Cate Fredenburgh here. Ball at Bushants' tonight.**

24 Fair. I go a fishing. **Mrs. C. Scudder here a dress making.**

25 Fair. Draw wood & stone. P. Phelps & sister here. **I put up school meeting notices.**

26 Fair. I and Nichols go to Albany. I get axe fixed. Get a hatchet. **Get wine, get 1 keg of nails, buy a turning Lathe and vise of Mr. Guyer for 13 dollars.**

27 I go to Meeting. Then inform Mr. Rob about his cow getting in cemetery.

28 Fair. Draw stone. James Hawley, James Allen & Lady Suzan Hawley here to tea. I take grapes to Harriet.

29 Lowry. **Hang cemetery gate.** I get a letter from B.W. Warner. Draw stone for Beecher's well. A.M. VanBergen here.

October 1851

1 Fair. I pay A.N. Briggs 70 dollars. Get meat of Leonard Hathaway. **Go to Seth Hawley's to wedding. His youngest daughter married Mr. Coe. We have a very jolly time; stay until 2 o'clock at night.**

2 Fair. I get Plank Road account of Wm. B. Hull.

3 Rainy. Work around the house. Go to river.

4 Cloudy. **Little John McDonald died.** L.E. Andrews bring down my shingle machine. I gave him my note for 45 dollars.

5 Lowry. I take Nyran Sweet's bull holme. Henry & Cate VanBergen here. Bring Mother Houghtaling holme.

6 Fair. I go to toll gate. Get ready to go to Herkimer County.

Shingle Machine

7 Fair. **I take shingle machine and start for Herkimer County.** Wife & Mrs. Colvin go along to Albany. They go to Oneida lake. I drive to Albany. Get turning Lathe of Mr. Guyer. Pay 10 dollars. Then take the Plank Road for [Fort] Hunter. Go to Lake on the Hill. Go to Minaville, then to Fort Hunter. Stay all night to canal grocery. Get there after dark.

8 Fair. **Cross the Schoharie by scow. A woman ferry me across.** Go to Fonda then to Helderbrant's Tavern to Breakfast. Then to Pleasant Valley, then to Carroga, then to Lacellville, then to Oppingham, then to Salisbury Corners, then to papermill, then to Mr. Kelly's & stay all night.

9 Fair. **Drive to B.W. Warner's to Breakfast. Work at shingle mill all day. The mill goes finely.**

10 Fair. **Saw out pickets. Rig up turning lathe.**

11 Fair. **Make new waggon box. Turn out table & stand legs.**

12 Fair. **Walk around the territory.**

13 Rainy. **Turn out small bedstead. Work in the mill.**

14	Fair. **Start for holme. Came back to Helderbrant's. Stay all night. They had a dance there. They stood up to eat.**
15	Fair. **Start one hour before day & drive holme the same way that I went out. Get holme 10 o'clock at night. Drive 62 miles.**
16	Fair. Unload my pickets. Go to gates. I sign a note L W & Colvin $600.
17	Fair day. Draw wood. Pile wood. Go to river. Attend P.R. meeting.
18	Fair. I go to Samuel Tombs'. Call on Dominie Tombs.
19	Fair. William Phelps & I go to Meeting. A.E. Willis here.
20	Chop wood. Go to river. I break my axe.
21	Fair. Chop wood. Go to river. **Take 86 lbs. of pork to G.W. Dorman. He allows me 8 cents per lb.** Mrs. Elias Holmes & Mrs. Hollenbeck here. **I get citrons from Barge**.
22	Fair. I draw wood. Go to gates. Get horses shod. Get 3 pumpkins of William Tuttle. Mrs. John Rea go along to Gate.
23	Warmer. I send B.W. Warner Davis's deed. Get two barrels of apples. Paint my waggon box and barrel and a swing gate.
24	Fair. Work at hay press. Saw logs. Attend Plank Road meeting.
25	Fair. Go to Greenville. Stop at Newman Finch's. Stay all night at Fancher's. Mr. Nichols, Wife and two children go along.
26	Cloudy. I go to J.W. Story's and then come back holme.
27	Clear, cold. Mother here, stay around the house.
28	Cloudy & rainy. Barge delayed at Cold Springs. Chop wood. Go to Gate. **Notify Mrs. Kinworthy to leave.**
29	Fair. Chop wood. Mother Houghtaling & Marite come from New York trip. A. VanBergen & Mary Houghtaling here. **I write to Mrs. Kinworthy & send her a jug of oil**.
30	Rainy. Chop wood. Stay around the house.
31	Clears off. I work at hog pen. Saw wood. Help Beecher thresh. Pay Wm. Wilkins road bill 12.25 dollars. Get 15 dollars of Lawton. Go to see O.H. Chittenden at Wm (?).

November 1851

1	Fair. Chop wood. Martin & Elida VanSlyck and Cate VanBergen here. Mr. Nichols goes to Stuyvesant. Mary Houghtaling here.
2	Rainy. **P. Pelts preach his farewell sermon.** All the visitors leave. Two ride with Benjamin Andrews.
3	Cloudy. I go to Albany. Pay Acton & George Lawton, pay Davidson & Viele. Get cheese, get pie plant, gooseberry & currant bushes.
4	Clear, cold. **Attend Election. Chittenden has 100 votes, Terry has 71 votes. There was 176 votes polled. Mr. S.J. Nichols returned**.
5	Cloudy. Attend to Plank Road. Adjust our new toll gate gatherer. Mrs. Robertson go to Baltimore after Wife and Marite. Go to Doct. Fredenburgh.

6	Fair. I get in beets. Get horse shod. Wife and Marite go to Doct. Fredenburg.
7	Fair. Draw wood. **Take 21 ½ bushels of rye to the mill**.
8	Cloudy. Go to Andrew Houghtaling's. Take Wife & Marite along to Coxsackie.
9	Cloudy. Stay last night to A.G. VanSlyck's. Stay today until after dawn then go to M.G. VanBergen's to tea, then come holme.
10	Rainy & snowy all day. I gave Doct. VanAntwerp his papers. I go to river. Get beef.
11	Fair, cold. I chop wood for Mother. **I bank up her house**. I get 1 barrel of molasses & one of sugar from G. & A.C. Lawton.
12	Fair. I and Marite go out to the end of the Plank Road. **I buy a stove for toll house**. Take Willis note for 52 dollars toll money. **Have a tooth drawn**. Mr. Williams here. Mother here. Beecher bring in carrots.
13	Fair. Work around. **Start for New York aboard of Barge. Marite and Wife go along**.
14	**Cloudy. Arrive in New York at 1 o'clock. Go to Marite's. Call on C. McMichael**.
15	**Rainy day. Go around go to Christy's at night.**[170] **Then John Silcox and Lady go with us to Taylor's. Treat us with oysters & champagne**.
16	**Fair. I go to Meeting. I go to Tarrytown to Charles Hallock's by railroad**.
17	**Fair. Go to Silcox, to Marite's, to Brooklyn and then start for holme**.
18	**Fair. Get holme about 2 o'clock. Get up things from Barge**.
19	Fair. I go to river. Offer to pay my school tax. Go to gates. Get hinges for cemetery gate for 34 cents, then go to end of Plank Road.
20	Fair. Fix cemetery gates. Pile wood. I am not very well. Put things on Barge.
21	Rainy day. Put velvet on desk. Go to river. Work around the house.
22	Cold. Set out 3 quince bushes got them of Peter Lawson. **I cut my foot chopping down in the field**. Wife, Mother Houghtaling and Anthony go to Lawton's visiting.
23	Fair morning, cloudy afternoon. Stay in house all day. I have a bad cold.
24	Fair, some colder. I hurt my foot with stick of wood. Stay in house.
25	Commence snowing 3 o'clock. John Silcox sent me a barrel of oysters.
26	Fair. I clean my casks. Take lumber to A. Teal. Pay W.M. Wilkins $200. Get salt. Boil out brine. 8 inches of snow fell at this time.
27	Fair. Bridget O'Neil here & Mrs. Hood. I go to river. Pay Willet & Serles 500 dollars for planks. He pay me 100 dollars on stock.
28	Stormy & rainy. I kill hogs. Help Beecher kill beef. First Dancing School.

Christy's Minstrels

---

[170] Christy's Minstrels were a blackface minstrel group formed by Edwin Christy in 1843.

29 Fair, thawy weather. Beecher draw Mother 2 loads of wood for me. Wife & Bridget go to Holmes. I cut up my hogs. **John Bailey's daughter got married today to Dutch John.**

30 Fair, cold at night. Stay in house all day

December 1851

1 Very cold. I salt my pork. Wife go to Albany

2 Fair, cold. Dominie Pelts here. **River froze last night. Barge came as far as Coxsackie and stop.**

3 Cold. I go to mill and to toll gates. Take money to LWC & Co. Take their notes for 77 dollars. Get horse shod. Call at Robert Martin's, buy 1 pig $3. **Steamboats bang away in the ice**.

4 Fair. I received 5 dollars of Robert Martin. Pay him for his pig. Get two pigs of Robert Pulver, pay him 22/. I & John Rea bring them holme.

5 Fair, cold. **I shut up stray pig. Notify town clerk. River shut. No steamboat today**.

6 Fair. **I go to Stephensville. Take W. Warman. Settle lawsuit with Bob Cutter. Leave 3-dollar bill to Gate.**[171] Get 10 dollars to L W & Colvin.

7 South wind, stormy. Go to meeting hear Mr. Gould. Wife go to hear Cornell. **James Sherwood marry E. Ostrander**.

8 Thawy. Beecher & John Rea go to Greenville, take my team. I work at stable and attend first Debating School.

9 Fair. Work at stable. **Make picture frames**.

10 Fair. I go to gate and to Baltus VanSlyck's to New Baltimore. Take Willis's note for 35 dollars. Work at stable.

11 Cold day. I and Beecher work at stable.

12 Draw wood. Work at stable. Lots of company here. I get ½ barrel of soda crackers.

13 Fair, cold day. Work at stable. Go to river at night.

14 Cold, cloudy, south wind. I go to Meeting.

15 South wind, snowy. **I go to Baltimore to get Mrs. Shadden and Miss Houghtaling to make dresses.** I work at stable.

16 Fair, 3 inches snow. I saw wood all day.

17 Fair, very cold. Saw wood. Go to gate. **Negro Prince after stone here from my quiry**.

18 Fair, cold. Draw wood all day. Attend donation of Rev. Mr. Gould.

19 Fair, south wind. I draw wood all day. I lend Beecher 50 cents.

20 Fair, cold. Draw wood all day from dam.

21 Fair, very cold. I go to Meeting. I send Miss Shadden and Miss Houghtaling holme by Peter Rea. Mrs. Holmes here.

---

[171] The U.S. didn't print paper money until 1862. 3-dollar bills were printed by local banks, railroads…

22	Fair. Chop wood. Mrs. Eddy & son here last night. Attend Temperance meeting. Springstead address the meeting. **Mrs. Tombs died today**.
23	Fair. I testify to notes of Daniel VanAntwerp. Lay around.
24	Snowy. I go to Stephensville take W.V. Carman. Attend his case before The Committee on Appeals, then to Cedar Hill to the Odd Fellows Oyster supper. Got holme at 3 o'clock in the morning.
25	Fair, cold. I go to **Mrs. Tombs Funeral, take Wife & Mr. Nichols**.
26	Fair, very cold. I go to river. Take L W & Co. note for 57 dollars. Mr. Willis & Lady here to dinner & tea. **Robert Baker got married last night to Cornelia Andrews**.
27	Fair, south wind. I and Wife visit to A.E. Willis with A. Vanderzee & Lady and Eliza Clement. Mr. Emersson & Lady call then. Cate Lawton call. **15 degrees below zero today**.
28	Sleet, rainy, warmer. I take Wife to Thomas Houghtaling. Mrs. Houghtaling very sick. Mrs. Holmes here.
29	Foggy, south wind. I take Mother Houghtaling & bring Wife back. I put up wood house to the toll gate.
30	Frosty, foggy, south wind. I work to toll gate. **I take my beets out of hole in the garden & put them in the cellar**.
31	Rainy day. I go out to gates & work at toll house on wood house.

January 1852

1	I work over to gate ½ day. **Put my meat in smokehouse**. Let Mr. Nichols have my horse to go to Baltimore.
2	Fair, NW colder. I go to papermill. **The ice break up last night & stop between here & New Baltimore**.
3	Fair. I Paid Doct. Fredenburg 70 dollars interest money. **I paid G. Nichols 30 dollars for painting Children's portraits [see Photos]**. I get $4.95 of A.N. Briggs. Attend installation of officers in lodge. We have an oyster supper to Aaron Houghtaling's.
4	Snow all day. I go to Mother's & to Willis's in snow.
5	Fair, cold. Draw wood. Take gate to Junction and hang it.
6	Snow all the afternoon. Draw wood in forenoon. **Newman Finch & Daughter here**.
7	**Cold as Greenland, snow blows in heaps. Newman Finch & Daughter leave for holme they get stuck in snowbanks**. I get bed pan of Aaron Houghtaling.
8	Fair, cold. I go to Gates. Mrs. Andrews, Mr. & Mrs. E. Sherman here. Plank Rd. meeting tonight. Mr. Lager bring here a bundle from Andrew Houghtaling.
9	Stormy. I take Mother Houghtaling to Flat Bush. I pay Wilken's bill and give it to Mr. Hull. I borrow 26 dollars of J.W. Dorman and pay him again. Peter Seabridge pay me 21 dollars for Daniel Baker. I attend Dancing School. Mrs. Johnson, Miss Johnson, Mary Jane Lawton and Mrs. Stanton here.
10	Cloudy, warm day. **Attend the Lodge. Our Grand Master here from Troy and 6 others all here**. I call at Jemima Houghtaling's.

11	Snowy day. George Bunker here. Stay all day about the house.
12	Fair. I draw wood from dam. G. Bunker leave here.
13	Fair. Chop & saw wood. Take Wife to Thomas Houghtaling's.
14	South wind, fair. I attend annual meeting of Plank Road.
15	Fair. I go with A.E. Willis to gates. Wife visit to W.B. Hull's.
16	Fair, cold. I pay McGregor $11.25. John Cronk here.
17	Fair, cold. John Cronk leave. **We all hands take a sley ride to Martin VanBergen's, have a large party 12 in my sley. Have a fine time. Get back at 1 o'clock in morning. Have Turkey supper it goes off first rate.**
18	Snow all day. I stay in the house. A. Sherwood here. **Betsy Waymen froze to death.**
19	Very cold. **Betsy Waymen buried. She was found dead & froze on the floor by her son.** I take Wife to Thomas Houghtaling's.
20	Fair. Wife come holme. Thomas Houghtaling here to dinner. I go to river. Get a letter from B.W. Warner. Saw wood. A. Sherwood take Lib Rea to Baltimore.
21	Fair, south wind. **John Clement's boy Egbert died this morning.** J. Nichols come back here today. **Genl. Hamilton lecture in Temperance Hall this morning.**[172]
22	Fair, cold as ever. **Attend Egbert Clement's Funeral.** A. Sherwood call here.
23	Fair. Dominie Fenns & Lady here to dinner. I go to Greenville. Benjamin Willis sick. I call at Newman Finch's, then go to Collins get rent, then to G. Baldwin's get 2 pr. Boots, then to Joshua Baker's get his rent & Mr. Hunt pays me his rent.
24	Fair. I settle with Andrew Fancher, Wm. Hoose & Henry Whitbeck, then come holme, stop at Hollow pay my tax and Peter Seabridge's.
25	Cold yet fair. Martin VanSlyck & Elida & Cate VanBergen here.
26	SW, warmer. **I get 50 dollars from L W & Colvin. Get their chk for $1873. Exchange checks with A.N. Briggs. Send the check to Little Falls to Mr. Rust and likewise send to Warner a check for 50 dollars.** Mother Houghtaling come holme. I am not well.
27	Fair. I chop wood to creek. John Silcox & Mr. Moore here to dinner. Thomas Houghtaling take Mother Houghtaling holme with him.
28	South wind, cloudy. I draw two loads of wood from the dam. I take Cate VanBergen & Elida VanSlyck to Thomas Houghtaling, bring mother Houghtaling holme, Peter Seabridge pay me his tax $12.64. Mary Houghtaling here.
29	Fair. **I & Wife go to Troy with Gerry Springstead to Edward Swazzy's to a party, then go with L. Eddy holme. I bear expenses $3.00.**
30	Stormy. **Visit to Eddy's. Take a ride around the country.**
31	Snowy. **Eddy brings us back to Troy then we go to Lansingburgh. See Bridget & Mr. John Whipple. Bridget & her husband take us out to sley ride and at night I & Mr. Hood go get oysters & attend a raffle.**

---

[172] This might have been Alexander Hamilton; whose grandfather Alexander Hamilton was the first Secretary of the Treasury.

February 1852

1. Snowy. Mr. Hood bring us back to Mr. Swazzy's, then Mr. Swazzy take us a riding to Ira Abbot's, then to Luther Eddy's, then we come holme with Mr. Swazzy. Stay all night.

2. Fair. Come holme. Stop at Albany. I go to Bath. Pay Wm. VanRensselaer rent of 5 dollars. Spend 9/. Get holme. **Find Levi sick**.[173]

3. South Wind. **Levi sick**. Work at stable. Israel Lawton pays me 11 dollars. I pay B $74.10.

4. Fair, warm. **Henry Sperle's child died this morning**. **Helen Houghtaling & John Selkirk married this morning**. I work at stable. Saw wood. Go to river. **Margarett very sick**, I see her. Mother here. Cate VanBergen, Elida VanSlyck & Mary Houghtaling here. Edward Thuson lecture in Temperance Hall this evening.

5. Fair, warm day. I take Mother Houghtaling, Elida VanSlyck, Mary Houghtaling to Andrew Witbeck's visiting.

6. Cloudy, rainy. **I take folks to funeral of Henry Sperle's child**. Martin VanSlyck come here.

7. Fair, NW. Coxsackie folks leave. I draw wood & lumber. Wife go to Briggs.

8. Fair. Start for Meeting, but no preacher. I go to Willis's.

9. Fair. I draw muck all day for flower beds.

10. Fair, warm. I draw one load of wood. Andrew & George Houghtaling and Charlotte Houghtaling here & Charlotte Columbus & Mrs. Andrew Houghtaling here.

11. Rain all day, great thaw. Mrs. Holmes & Mrs. Crumb here last night. Peter Seabridge pay me Lewy Cloochy's rent 7 dollars and E.D.R. Converse pay me his rent $1.91 to January 20, 1852. H. Sperl paid me his quarterly rent to February 5th, 1852.

12. Colder, NW. I fix barn occupied by Peter Seabridge. Buy sley, plank, iron of Peter Holbrook.

13. Snowy, south wind. I gave Peter Holbrook up note I have against him of ten dollars and I take away the things that I bought of him yesterday. Wm. & Charlotte VerPlanck, Cate Frendenburgh, Helen Selkirk here.

14. Fair. **B.E. Holmes' child died this morning**. Cate VanAntwerp here all day, Mrs. Robb & Mrs. VanDerzee call. Thomas Houghtaling call. Mr. Elmwood call here. Bridget & Andrew Hood come here.

15. Cold, SW cloudy. Mr. Hood & Lady leave. **I attend Funeral of Backus's child**.

16. Fair, cold, NW. I and Wife go to Albany. Attend lawsuit between Plank Road Company & Henry Spawn. I deposit $30.84 in Mechanics & Farmers Bank. Get certificate of deposit for Mr. Tillinghast.

17. Fair, cold. Wife, Mother Houghtaling & Children go to Beecher Holmes. I saw wood & get out axe. Helve timber for A. Teal.

18. Fair and very cold. I settle with Lawton Willis & Colvin and leave my note with them. Mrs. Holmes here. I am not well.

19. Very cold. I saw wood and get a letter from Phillip Collins and B.W. Warner. Wife go to Wm. Lawton's. I attend auction to G.W. Dorman's.

---

[173] At this point in time, Levi is 6 years old and Fletcher is 34.

20 Fair, very cold. I saw wood. Mother Houghtaling & Wife go to James Lawton's, visit. I go in evening.

21 Very cold, SW. I attend G.W. Dorman's Vendue.

22 Snow, cold ½ day. I go to Meeting; Rev. Mr. Davis preach.

23 Thawy. I & C.T.E. Waldron appraise the property of Widow A. Teneyck.

24 Cloudy, thawy. Mother here. I attend P.R. meeting last evening. Saw wood.

25 Fair, thawy. I put rakes in gate shed. Saw wood. Charlotte Houghtaling & Cate Lawton, her daughter here. I endorse a note for Lawton Willis & Colvin & Co. for 1500 dollars.

26 Fair. I saw wood, go to river. **Am summoned a juror in case of A.N. Briggs & Henry Anderson.** Cate Houghtaling here. **I attend lawsuit all day.**

27 Cold. **I attend lawsuit till 1 o'clock at night. Bring in no cause of action.**

28 Snow all day. I shell corn and go to mill. I get 6/ worth of feed that I had paid for twice.

29 Fair, cold day. Wife go to Coxsackie. I go to Meeting twice & to Willis's.

March 1852

1 Cloudy. I, Wife & Levi go to Edwin Hubbell's & Andrew Houghtaling's. Call at P. Pelts' and Andrew Houghtaling's.

2 Snow all day. Get mare shod. Get boots tap free. Casper Trop pays month's rent $1.25.

3 Very cold. I take Mother Houghtaling to Andrew's. Then I & Wife go to James Hawley's visiting. George Fancher here.

4 Fair. I am quite unwell. G. Fancher leave. Mrs. Clements, Mrs. A.E. Willis, Mrs. Stanton, Miss Stanton here visit. I pay off John VanDenburgh 4.07 dollars. Take a dose of pills of Doct. Mosher.

5 Snowy. I go to river. Am not very well. Split wood. Wife go to E. Stanton's.

6 Cloudy. I hire Elias & John Henry Holmes to chop and draw wood. Pay them 50 cents apiece. Beecher's boy, Acton, here all day.

7 Fine day, clear. Stay at holme all day.

8 Cloudy, south wind. Stay at holme, not well.

9 Cloudy, south wind. I go to Albany. Wesley go along. Miss Susan Cronk here.

10 Fair, colder. Split [wood]. I take Wife, Mrs. Vanderzee, Carroll to Robb's, visit.

11 Very fine day. Split wood. Wife goes to J. Clement's visiting.

12 Cloudy, south wind. Beecher's Wife, Elias's Wife, Mrs. Lawson here visiting. I put jagger knee in wood house & endorse note to LW&C & Co.

13 Fog & Rainy. I go to river. Meet trustees of Coeymans Road Dist. Make out accounts.

14 Rainy. Stay at holme. Go to Mother's in afternoon.

15 Very fine day. I pay off Wm. B. Hull. E. Converse leave my shop. Mr. Grop move in it.

16 Fair day. I get out pickets. Make a walk. Wife go to Hugh Crumb's.

17	Cloudy. High water commences. Cemetery Road. I get ½ barrel apples of L. Hathaway.
18	Snow & thawy. I go to river. Pay S. Vanderbergh 1 dollar that I owed him.
19	Fair. **I & Tuttle measure Dist. Road from gate to my old homestead & find it 121½ rods.**[174] I sharpen pickets. Saw wood.
20	Cold freeze all day. I saw wood. Mother here.
21	Cloudy, cold & snowy. I go to Meeting. Lib Houghtaling here.
22	South wind, fair. John Henry Holmes draw some posts for me. Draw lumber from sawmill. I settle with H. McDonald & pay him off.
23	Snow all day five inches. I saw wood, go to river.
24	Fair. Get out posts. Go to river & to Cemetery Road.
25	Fair, south wind. Margarette & Daughter, Maria Finch & Miss Leburgh here, spend the day.
26	Fair. **Steamboat go to Baltimore. Take barge to Albany.**
27	Cloudy & cold. **I attend nomination to Hollow. I take A. Teall & John Rea along. Great crowd & confusion.**
28	Fair, pleasant. I take a walk to cemetery. Go to Meeting. No minister. Call at Willis's. **Steamboats go. River clear of ice. All glad of it.**
29	Cloudy. I get out stone for a walk. **Attend as Freeholder to lay out a road through Henry lot. J. VanDenburgh lost a small child**.
30	Cloudy, cold. J. Nichols here. I get out stone.
31	Stormy day. Barge come. Nichols leave. Mr. Grop pay me one dollar. I get Marite's basket from Barge.

April 1852

1	Fair, two inches of snow this morning. I let Thomas Penton have my horse. **Chatham Johnson died this morning.**
2	Snow all day. **N.W. Johnson's child, Catham, put in vault today**. I go with Wm. McGregor to toll gate to get Mrs. Robertson to leave. Mr. Elmendorf has moved.
3	Very cold. Freeze all day. Mother & Joseph Cronk here.
4	Fair. I go to Meeting. Cate VanAntwerp & Ackerman Houghtaling here to supper.
5	Cloudy. Make fence. **Attend election of trustees of Coeymans Road District to Aaron Houghtaling's. Have a tight run between Jacob Sickles & Ira Gregory. Jacob beat by one vote.**
6	Snow all day. 6 inches in the morning. **I put my stove that I got of Patrick Chancy in school room**. I split wood.
7	Fair. Wife & Marite go to Willis's visiting. Snow all melt off. I split wood and get a string of fish.
8	Fair. I help Beecher make a fence all day.

---

[174] Approximately 2000 ft.

9	Fair. I and Beecher go to Abm. Witbeck's get posts. I go to river get clams.
10	Fair, cold. **I go and attend appraisal of A.J. Teneyck deceased**. Mrs. Fredenburgh, Miss Verplank, Caroline VanAntwerp, Mrs. Selkirk, Lib Houghtaling and Mrs. Willis here.
11	Fair, warm day. I go to Meeting. Wife & Marite go to Wesley's.
12	Cloudy day. I pay off Wm. K. Caroll Co. Bill $17.79. Get two pairs of shoes of Casper Grop, **pay 18 shillings.**[175] **E. Waldron here, we clear up the inventory of Widow Teneyck**. Marite go to Coxsackie.
13	Snow & rain. I go to town meeting. J.W. Story & Lady here. **Aunt Miriam Waldsome died this morning 4 o'clock**. I settle with J.W. Story, take his note 167.66 dollars.
14	Cloudy & foggy. Story go holme. I get a pair of new hay hooks. Cate Fredenburgh here to tea. I get road book of G.W. Dorman.
15	Rain morning, snow hard all afternoon. I work in wood house.
16	Fair day. Cow has a calf. Mrs. Widow Teneyck here to get her papers. She pay me 4 dollars.
17	Fair. **I make a picket fence between me & Civill**. Wife go to Widow Houghtaling's.
18	Cloudy, SE wind. I and Wife go to Thms. Houghtaling's. Roads bad. My black cow has a calf.
19	Cloudy, NE. I trim trees. Peter Rea work for me ½ day. I sow lettuce. I go to river, get fish.
20	Lowry & rain. **I go with Catholic Priest to look out a site for a church**.[176] I take up my note from Wm. B. Hull that I gave to Ann Bronk. I gave up my notes against Consistory to Wm. B. Hull.
21	Rainy day. **I gave up writings to Catholics for church & cemetery lot. Take a note signed by Timothy Clancy & Michael Dowling and Dennis Toben for 200 dollars.**
22	Clears off once more. I set out current bushes, trees & fix hog pen. Mother here.
23	Cloudy, cold, NW. I take Mother Houghtaling & Little Phillips to Flat Bush. I and Mr. Pelton measure the line fence between Mr. Henry Bronk. He must make 13 panels of 14 ft. fence to be equal to me and Joseph Bronk must make 202 ft. to be equal.
24	Fair, cold. I wheel manure in the garden. **I take Wife to Baltimore to weavers with carpet yarn. Sit up with John Vandenburgh tonight**
25	Very fine warm day. I go to Meeting. I and John Rea go to cemetery for a walk.
26	Fair, south wind. I get Hunt &Netson's check from Gill Pelton for 150 dollars. Leave it with LWC & Co. I send A.N. Bently a check for 15.43 dollars. Help Beecher load hay.
27	Fair, cold. I go to Hollow; make out road assessment.
28	Fair. **I & Jacob Sickles go to W.V. Carmen for advice on District Road. I pay Carmen 50 cents for advice. Then I go out to Herkimer County. Take Steamboat & Railroad get to Little Falls. Take late dinner to John Feeter's. Then start for my sawmill in the**

---

[175] Fletcher often refers to shillings (/). But the US coins of the mid-1800s were half-cent, cent, half-dime, dime, quarter, half-dollar, dollar, quarter-eagle, half-eagle and eagle. Possibly shillings were still in circulation.

[176] Fletcher and his crew built the first Catholic church in the area on land adjacent to the cemetery road (now Blaisdell Ave.). The church stood until 1920 when it was torn down (News Herald – August 6, 1920).

occupation of B.W. Warner. **I find plenty of snow and good sleighing part of the way. I get far as Eben Kelly's & stay the night.**

29 Fair, NW. I walk up to B.W. Warner's, stay all night. Let him have one hundred & fifty dollars.

30 Fair. I come back with Warner. Stay all night to John Feeter's.

May 1852

1 Rainy & cloudy. Come back to Albany. Get dividend to Bank $18.70. Then drive my horse with Wife & Cate Fredenburgh. I pay G. Lawton $27.07, Johnson & Goaly $18.87, H & S Luke $11.72.

2 Fair. I go to hear Rev. McDavis preach his first sermon.

3 Fair, NW. I work in garden. Abram Witbeck pays me $50. I get my horse shod. Amy A. Rea here.

4 Fair. I work in garden. Mrs. Chittenden, Mrs. Carroll, Mrs. Mrs. VanDerzee [here]. North wind. I sow peas.

5 Fair day. I pay Peter Rea 12/. Plow garden, plant corn & potatoes. **Lib Trego came here to board.** Mr. Colburn & Jimmy VanSlyck call here.

6 Fair, hot. Finish plant my garden. Get fish. Take a ride. Attend meeting of Commissioners of Highway. Plank Road lumber come today.

7 Fair. I measure plank for District Road. Wm. Tuttle pay me 25 dollars. **Phrenologist here to examine Anthony's head.**[177]

8 Fair. Quite dry & warm. I measure Plank Road lumber. Get 20 dollars of L.W. Colvin & Co., borrow 5 dollars. I pay Mr. Beebe Cap 108. Get 10 dollars of Peter Seabridge. **Attend the interment of Old Mrs. Civill.**[178]

9 Fair, hot. I go to Meeting. Cate VanBergen here. My mare Rose has a colt this morning.

10 Fair day. **I have two carpenters & put up a new back house privy.** A. VanSlyck commence to occupy my house. She pay me 1 dollar.

11 Fair. Mr. & Mrs. Eddy here. **Survey Catholic Church lot.** Then survey the Plank Road. John Toben & John Rea go along. **Aaron Houghtaling's bush died today.**

12 Rainy day. **Get out bushes Aaron put in the vault.** Mr. Eddy go to Troy. I go to River. Mrs. Eddy stay here.

---

[177] This is the first mention of Anthony since his birth. He would be 3 at this time. Phrenologists believed that the shape of the head could somehow determine one's character. It was dismissed by scientists as quackery in the 1840s, yet it remained popular through the early 1900s. There was a plaster head in the attic of the house that was no doubt related to this visit.

[178] We think this is Mary Flansburgh Civill, the second wife of Lewis Civill, and mother of Acton and Theophilus. She would have been about 82 in 1852. Lewis Civill was a partner of Fletcher's Father (Levi Blaisdell).

13 Fair, cold. Andrew Fancher & Lady here & boy. He pay me $200. I take Wife & Mrs. Eddy up to Gerry Springstead's on a visit.

14 Fair. I go to Schodack. Get Mr. Eddy & Boy. **Then survey Catholic Cemetery**. I go to Gerry Springstead. Get Mrs. Eddy, **then they all go to Troy on the [steamer] Mazeppa**. I trim trees in garden.

17 Showry. I go to river, get fish. Dig in the garden. Send check to J. Feeter 25 dollars. I get check of A.N. Briggs.

18 Fair, cool. I get mare shod, then take her to Jerry Springstead's to the Horse. A. VanBergen here. Mother & Harriet here.

20 Fair, cool. I and Wife go to John Mull's. I go to Mr. Baker's, get three pecks of seed corn.

21 Fair. **I take two barrels of wine to Flat Bush**. I hang a gate on cemetery road.

23 Fair. I take Wife to Baltimore. **Attend the Installation of Rev. Mr. Davis**.

24 Fair warm day. **Judge A.M. VanBergen died last night or yesterday**.

25 Fair. **I take Wife & Mother Houghtaling & Cate Lawton to funeral of Uncle Anthony VanBergen**. Have a job with Mr. Church's horse in starting.

27 Fair. I get a piece of Sturgeon. Work on Dist. Road. Am not well.

30 Fair, heavy north wind. I go to Meeting twice. **Wife go with Cate Lawton after a Negress**.

31 Fair, cool day. I put my mare Rose to Jeremiah Springstead's horse. Work in the garden. Go to mill with corn.

Steamer Mazeppa

June 1852

1 Fair. Mr. Davis & W. Houghtaling here. I make fence.

2 Fair & warm. I get 35 dollars of Lawton Willis & Colvin & Co. Then I pay B.B. Fredenburgh 49 dollars interest money. I get 20 dollars of Samuel Baker. **Thomas Penton clean out my cistern**.

3 Fair. Mr. Fancher here, I give him Mortgage for 666 dollars. I get some cracked wheat from mill. They have Negro Meeting tonight.

4 Fair. I get 70 dollars from Mrs. Sherwood. Thomas & Cate Houghtaling here. I go a fishing.

5 Fair, cool. I Beecher & John Rea and J. Holmes go to Flat Bush. Get out logs & timber. Elizabeth Pelts here. I get holme late in the evening.

6 Fair, cool, SW. I go to Meeting. Cate Hathaway & Vina Rea here. I go to Margarett's see Eben Finch & his girls.

8 Showry afternoon. I draw wood in wood house. Mrs. VanDerzee here. Mother Houghtaling & Aunt Catharine go to Albany.

9	Fair. I put pump in my cistern. Acton Civill pay me for building his half of line fence between me & him $20.63. George Fancher bring me a load of boards. I gave him a new Bond and Mortgage. Mother Houghtaling & Aunt Catharine come back. **Thomas Houghtaling subpoena I & Wife to appear before the surrogate at Albany in a suit brought against him by the heirs at will of Aunt Caty.** Acton Civill & his Sister call here. I set out tomatoes & cabbages.
10	Fair, west wind. I take Wife & Aunt Catharine to Elias Holmes. I work in garden. **Beecher's boy, Acton, ran away**.
11	Fair, cold. North wind. I work in garden. Mother here.
13	Fair. Go to Meeting twice. Hear Rev. Mr. Davis & Rev. H. Jolly.
14	Fair, hot. I take Wife & Mother Houghtaling to Albany. **We all attend the Surrogate Court for witnesses subpoenaed by Thomas Houghtaling**.
15	Hot. I stay at holme. It is the hottest day that there has been in two years. I pay out 1 dollar for P. Ostrander.
16	Fair, hot. B.W. Warner here. Mother here. I go to Baltimore. Take Wife to Jas. Trego. **Attend the funeral of Moses Cary**. I get waggon casting of Peter VanBuren for B.W. Warner. I get a coat cut at Thomas Sockly and pay him.
17	Hot & a little showry in afternoon. I go a fishing to creek. Let B.W. Warner have 50 dollars. Get horse shod.
18	Shower but clears off dry. I go to Flat Bush. **Get Chattel Mortgage of S.M. Pelton**. J.H. VanBenthuyzen & Mrs. Ball here. **I put in fire board for Mrs. P. VanSlyck**.
19	Fair, hot. I and John H. VanBenthuyzen go to river & to papermill. and then in swimming.
20	Little showry. We all go to Meeting, hear Rev. Mr. Davis.
21	Fair. I hoe in garden & go swimming. Mrs. Anthony Bradwell here.
22	Little showry. I take Wife & J.H VanBenthuyzen and Mrs. Ball to Barent Houghtaling on a visit.
23	Fair. I make fence. Wm. Bagley & son & Mrs. Frederick Bagley here & Mr. & Mrs. Willis here in afternoon.
24	Fair. I go to river, get fish. J.H. VanBenthuyzen take Wife & Mrs. Ball to Garrett Houghtaling. I take Jerry's bull holme.
25	Fair. J.H. VanBenthuyzen & Mrs. Ball leave for Troy. Abram Witbeck pays me 50 dollars. I pay him 3 dollars & balance our account. I pay Henry Seburg 3/. Rev. Mr. Davis & Lady call here.
26	Fair, cool. Martin G. VanBergen & Cate come here. I fix Mother's bridge. I go to mill. T.J. Sweet pay me 35 dollars. I pay John Toben 662 dollars.
27	Fair, warm. M.G. VanBergen & Cate leave. Mrs. Castle & Daughter here. Cate Hathaway here. I go to Meeting.
28	Fair. I help Beecher draw manure. I get a piece of sturgeon

30   One fine shower again. Very dry summer. **This hay from 20 to 30 dollars per ton.**[179] Take John Clement & go to Greenville. **Leave Chattel Mortgage against Pelton with Clerk.** D.P. Williams go to A. Fancher's.

July 1852

1   Some rain. I pay Mr. Hassle $9 bill for Fancher's house. I pick 1 bushel of strawberries. I get shoes of S. Baldwin. Mr. L.D. Eddy here. He to take Wife to Baltimore. I come holme.

3   Fair, cool. Doct. VanAntwerp & Lady come here from New York. Mr. Eddy make maps. He leave for Troy. Mrs. Johnson & Mother here.

4   Fair. I take Mother to Aquetuck to Quarterly meeting.

5   Fair, hot day. I go with A. VanAntwerp to Woolsey Cary's, then to K. Cary's, then to see John Calanan, then holme. **Then Doct. take Wife & Marite to Thomas Houghtaling's. Fireworks tonight.**

6   Fair, hot day. Doct. VanAntwerp drives my horse to Coxsackie. Woolsey Cary pay me 42 dollars interest money.

7   Fair, hot day. I go a fishing. Widow A.J. Teneyck here.

8   A little shower. Doct & Marite leave. Thms. Penton pays me $2.33.

9   Fair, hot. I draw stone for walks & go in swimming.

10   Fair, hot. I take Mother to C.T.E. Waldron's. I take children to John Bushant's. Pick ½ bushel of raspberries.

11   Fair. I go to meeting twice. Ann Cronk here.

12   Fair, north wind. **I make out Cemetery Deeds**. Caroline Houghtaling here.

13   Showry. I send to Albany; get 1 barrel of flour by Stephen Knapp. I help Beecher draw rails. Amy A. Rea here.

14   Rainy. I stay around the house cut wood.

15   Fair. I fix the sill & underpin [of] wood house.

16   Fair. I go after raspberries. **Fix stone boat.**[180] Fix door at Tunis Wilsey's.

Stone Boat

17   Cloudy, I hang swing gate & go to Island; take children along. Theophilus Civill take us with his boat. I pay Ira Gregory 6/ for acknowledging a deed. P. Seabridge pay me 1 dollar for 2 bu. oats. I pay Leonard Hathaway 2/ for sturgeon & get things from Barge.

18   Fair. I take Caroline Houghtaling holme. I am sick all day.

19   Fair. I drive up to Peter Seabridge's. Turn over fallow. I take my old waggon to Hugh McDonald, bring my new one holme.

---

[179] The equivalent price today would be $660 - $990 per ton. The actual price of hay today is about $140 per ton.

[180] A stone boat is a type of sled that was used to haul heavy objects such as stone, bales, etc.

20   Fair. I take Wife to Baltimore. Call to Cap. Joseph's. Go to Lockly's. Get pants cut. Get my horse shod.

21   Fair, hot. I get mare shod. Mother here. I go after raspberries.

22   Fair, hot. I oil my harness. Mr. John Rea & Lady here.

23   Fair, hot. I take Elizabeth Trego holme and then take Wesley's children out a riding. Oil my harness.

24   Fair. I go fishing & to Big meadow. Mrs. Houghtaling, Mrs. Wilgus, Mrs. Niles & Mrs. Johnson here.

25   Fair, hot. I go to meeting twice. Take Wife to G. Springstead's.

26   Fine rain. Mrs. Betts, Mrs. Swazey, Abby Springstead & Jerry Springstead here. I and Jerry go to Baltimore. Take my children along.

27   Fair. **I & Wife start for Saratoga** go through Albany then to **the Lower Aqueduct**.[181] Take dinner at Noxeus Hotel. Then go through Jonesville & through Clifton Park so on to Saratoga. Stop at William Cook's. Stay all night and to breakfast & dinner.

28   Fair. Go to Mr. Emmerson. Take supper, stay all night & to breakfast.

29   Fair. Go to Ford's Village then to Glens Falls to Mr. Wood's. Go around Glens Falls through to Sawmills. Shave-up by a darkee. Have a fine shower. **Steamboat Henry Clay burnt today**.[182]

The Henry Clay fire

30   Fair. Go to Sandy Hill & Fort Edward. **See the pine tree that Jane McCrea was murdered under by the Indians in the Revolutionary War.**[183] Go to old Fort. Get 3 musket balls then to a gentleman's where we saw the Relics of the Revolution, then back with Mr. Wood to his house to Glens Falls. Then start for Saratoga again. Get back as far as Mr. Emerson's. Take supper & feed my horse. Then back to Saratoga. Stay to Mr. Fonda.

31   Fair. I and Mr. Fonda go around Saratoga after dinner. Start again for holme, cross Saratoga Lake by ferry. Then go to David Benedict's, take tea stay all night and to breakfast.

August 1852

1   Fair. **Start for holme go to Bemis Heights**.[184] **Then to the Battle Ground**. Stopped at an old Gentleman's who showed me the Relics, Bones, Balls, Swords & Money and described to

---

[181] According to Wikipedia, this was probably the aqueduct that carried the Erie Canal over the Mohawk River in Crescent, NY. It was called the Lower Mohawk Aqueduct.

[182] The Henry Clay was a side wheeler with a walking beam engine. It caught fire on one of its runs on the Hudson. Nearly 50 of its 500 passengers died, making it the worst of the river's steamboat accidents.

[183] Jane McCrea was a Loyalist who was killed and scalped during the American Revolution on the way to meet her fiancé in a British camp. According to the most widely accepted account of her death, Jane was murdered by Wyandot scouts working with the British Army.

[184] The battle of Bemis Heights was called the second battle of Saratoga and proved to be a major turning point for the Americans in the Revolutionary War.

me all about the Battle and how it was fought and the spot where General Frazer was killed. Then we come to Stillwater Village and to Mechanicsville, then to Waterford, then through Troy & Albany to holme. **Then I go to Schodack and bring John Silcox & Lady here. They came with the cars. Get holme 12 o'clock at night.**

2   Fair. I and John Silcox go to the cave and a hunting.

3   Fair. I & John Silcox go a fishing take Anthony along. Then take a walk around the farm and get berries.

4   Rainy. I & John Silcox go after berries.

5   Rainy, I, Wife, John Silcox & Lady go to VanSlyck's. Take children & dogs all on a visit.

6   Showers at night. I let LWC & Co. have Peter Seabridge's note $330.00. I get $250 of them, pay it to A.N. Briggs. Take his check & lend it to John Feeter to pay Warner & James Feeter & Rea. John Silcox go to New York; start from A.T. VanSlyck's.

7   Fair. I go a fishing. Martin VanSlyck & Elida come here and two of J.L. Rowe's daughters, Mary Jane Lawton, Mrs. A. VanDerzee, Alvena Carrol, Mother, & Samuel Pelts & Israel Lawton here.

8   Fair. All go to Meeting twice. Martin & Elida VanSlyck go holme.

9   Little showry. I go to river. Write two letters for P. Seabridge.

10   Fair. I draw wood & stone and go a riding with Mrs. Silcox.

11   Fair. I pick 8 quarts of blackberries; lay around. Wife, Mother Houghtaling, Mrs. Silcox go to Mrs. Clement's.

12   Fair. I draw 3 loads of manure. Then wash off the Plank Road. **Attend to laying out the Catholic Cemetery. The Catholics all here. I gave them their deeds. They took up their old note and gave me a new one. Paid me 4.66 dollars interest.** A.E. Willis here.

13   Fair. I go a fishing. Mrs. Andrew Houghtaling and Caroline & Elizabeth Houghtaling here. Mr. Trego & Lady here. I roll logs out of gully.

14   Fair, south wind. I draw logs. Wife go to Mrs. James Lawton's.

15   Fair. John Silcox come here last night. Brought two lobsters; we cook them for dinner have a great feast. I take Mother Houghtaling to Flat Bush, we all stop to Mr. Hawley's.

16   Fair. I and John Silcox go a fishing. Thomas Penton pay me $2.33 rent. John Silcox & Lady leave for New York. **I gave Levi a good whipping for running away from school and telling lies.**[185]

17   Fair. I wheel muck. Help Peter Rea put on pickets. Mother here. I hurt my foot bad.

18   Fair. I go to papermill, get horse blankets & halters. Go a fishing.

19   Fine shower. I make a fish pole & send a certificate of deposit of 25 dollars to B.W. Warner. **I make Levi a crop gun**.

20   Cloudy. I put out strawberry bed & go a fishing.

21   Fair. I go to Meeting. I & Wife go to Elias Holmes & Abram Witbeck's for a ride.

23   Fair. Do nothing but cemetery business. Miss Pelts & Mother here.

---

[185]   Levi would be 6 at this time. Possibly church school as it is August?

25   Showry. I & Peter Rea go to Flat Bush. Get out logs.

26   Fair, hot. I go fishing; get lots of fish.

27   Fair morning, showers afternoon. I attend Annual Cemetery Meeting.

28   Cloudy. Marite come from New York. Mr. Emerson & Lady, Cate Houghtaling, Eben Finch here. S.M. Pelton send his boy here with $25.

29   Rain last night and all day. I go to Mrs. Willis's & to Mother's.

30   Fair. **I attend John Clement's & S. Warner's & S. VanAntwerp's lawsuit all day until 2 o'clock at night**.

31   Fair. I pick peaches. Mother Houghtaling comes back, Andrew & Sheldon Houghtaling come here, visit. I hire Peter Rea for 7 dollars per month.

September 1852

1   Fair. **I and Wife leave for Illinois**. Peter Rea takes us to Albany with my team. H. McDonald go along. Left Albany 7 o'clock 15 min by railroad. Took a lunch at Syracuse. I buy Wife a vail then arrive at Buffalo at 10 o'clock at night. Then took the **Steamboat Southern Michigan** for Monroe. **Have a great many passengers about 1500 lay all over the cabin or saloon heads and points**. Stop at Dunkirk.

2   Fair morning. Have a great rush for breakfast. Very pleasant on the lake. Have a good Breakfast. Stop at Cleveland two hours. Then leave & have a good dinner and tea. Arrive at Monroe 10 o'clock in evening. Have a squall on the lake. **Then take cars for Chicago by Southern Michigan & Northern Indiana Railroad. Ride all night**.

3   Fair. Ride all day. Pass through some very poor country and get to Chicago. See Lewis Yatch and stop at the Mattesson house. Have a very good dinner. **Then take the packet boat for Morris. On the packet boat all night**.[186] Get into Morris 9 o'clock AM.

4   Fair. **Get a chance with Mr. Wally to ride out to Theron Collins**.[187] They are very glad to see us as well as we are to see them.

5   Fair. **We all go to Phillip Collins where I took my old friend by the hand for the first time in 18 years.** After shaking hands, we all went in the house. His Wife has a young son 4 days old. We stay all night to his house. It is built of logs. We all slept in the same room & had a good night's rest.

6   Fair. Stay to Phillip's until after dinner then go to Joshua Collins and stay all night. Jeremiah go with us. I did not recognize Jeremiah or Joshua, not having seen them in 18 years.

7   Fair. Go to Jeremiah Collins. Take dinner of roast turkey and after tea go to Theron's. I stay there all night.

8   Fair. Theron takes all hands to John VanDalfsen's stay all day. Go with John into the woods. Have chicken for dinner then go back to Theron's. Stay all night.

9   Fair. Go to George Collins. Stay till after Dinner. I and George go shooting. Kill 8 pidgeons then go in the timber. Have a pleasant time with George. Then go back to Theron's. Then go

---

[186]   Packet boats were medium sized boats designed for carrying mail, passengers and freight. They were usually steam powered.

[187]   Theron Collins was Margarett Collins Blaisdell's brother.

to a ball at the public house on the canal at the first lock. Have a fine time, stay all night. **Dance till after daylight and go holme to Theron's in the morning**.

10   Cloudy, rainy. All hands go to Ephraim Bronk's on the ridge, then to Meeting at night at a schoolhouse. I sleep all through the Meeting. Stay all night at Ephraim Bronk's. He has a fine place.

11   Fair. Go to Meeting again. Then after dinner, all hands come back to Theron Collins. Then all the Collins and the Cinder (sp) girls assemble & bid us good-bye. Stay up till 12 o'clock at night. McGlaphlin there also. We had a great time seeing Mr. McGlaphlin with the rest.

12   Cloudy & rainy. Start for holme. Theron takes his Wife and brings us back to Joliet to Mr. Perkins. Stay all night and had another good visit. Go to Deganin artists.

13   Cloudy & Misty. They put us on board the Canal Boat and we bid them all goodbye and start for holme. We came along on the Canal saw thousands of ducks & other wild game and arrive in Chicago at 5 o'clock PM and took tea at the **Sherman House**.[188] Have a first-rate supper. Go around the city then get our tickets and start on the Central Railroad for Detroit. Ride all night in the cars. Get to Detroit in morning.

Sherman House

14   Fair. Get aboard of **Steamboat Ocean** at Detroit and had a pleasant day on the lake. **Negroes perform in the afternoon and the evening it was so rough that they could not dance**.

15   Fair. Arrive in Buffalo 6 o'clock in the morning. Took breakfast at Railroad House and took cars again at 9 o'clock for holme. Arrived in Albany at 10 o'clock in the evening. Stay all night at the Eagle St. Hotel.

16   Fair. I pay G. Roseboom 27 dollars. Do up the rest of the trading and then take the **Steamer Shepherd Knapp** for holme. **Baltis VanSlyck & Maria VanBergen get married yesterday**.

17   Fair. I get 7 bags of broom corn seed of Josiah Sherman. Margarett Blaisdell here today.

18   Fair. I go to Meeting, write a letter to Theron Collins.

19   Fair. **I attend to the Catholics about building their church**. I send to Albany after white lead.

20   Fair. I pick peaches. Draw stone in the afternoon. South wind.

21   Fair. I & Peter Rea go to Flat Bush; get barrels of apples for us. Mr. Fancher & two [of] his sisters and a cousin here. I take them to the Island.

22   Fair. I get horse shod. Draw stone. Send after Wite Brandy. Wife & Mother Houghtaling go to Pulver Rosecrant's.

23   Fair. I draw stone & go to river. Pay Peter Ostrander 10 dollars.

24   Fair. Mother here. I and Wife go to A. VanSlyck's. I go a fishing.

---

[188]   The Sherman House was one of the most impressive buildings erected in Chicago 1836-7. It burned in the Chicago fire 1871.

25 Rainy morning. I, Wife & Elida VanSlyck go to Coxsackie Church, then back to Uncle Andrew's for dinner, then M.G. VanBergen's, then holme. Bring Lib Castle along.

26 Cold. I draw stone. Write to B.W. Warner.

27 Fair. I send B.W. Warner check for 25 dollars. Write to T.W. Olcott to transfer my Bank stock from old bank to the new. Pay into LWC & Co. 75 dollars. I got with Willis up to R. Updike's. Mrs. Fredenburgh and lots of other company here. I pick peaches.

29 Fair, cold. I and Wife go to Aquetuck to Fair. Mr. & Mrs. J. Hawley, Mr. Coe & Lady, Mr. Pelton & Lady, Mrs. Allen, Mrs. Stephens, Mrs. Hoag & Mary Ann Percival here & Pelton's child. Michael Dowling & Timothy Clancy here. **I take the contract for building the Catholic Church. They took up their note of 200 dollars and then pay me 198 dollars for which I gave them a receipt.**

30 Fair. **Attend Town Fair all day. Take out 11 persons bring back 13.**

October 1852

1 Fair. **Hiram Ayres died**. I go to mill, & I pay Montgomery Insurance $4.80. Dig potatoes, draw stone. Send B.W. Warner 110 dollars.

2 Fair. I & Beecher get nuts. John Bushants & Lady & Nicholas Carhart here to tea. I pay J. Springstead $9.58 saw bill of Evert VanSlyck. I pay Elizabeth Rea 10 dollars, she get it to the gate.

3 Fair. I go to Meeting twice. South wind.

4 Rainy. **I make out bill of Catholic Church. Get a copper pail of VanDenburgh.**

5 Fair. Boys go to Island. Cut broom corn stalks. I go up to Springsted's Island to see about broom corn seed. Attend the organization in the Seminary. Thomas Houghtaling & Cate here. I pay Mrs. Bennett 2 dollars. Mother & Miss Jackson & Mrs. Jackson here.

The Copper Pail

6 Cloudy. I take Mother Houghtaling to Andrew VanSlyck's. Get 25 quinces, 6 barrels of apples & one barrel of pears to Flat Bush. I pay Peter Rea 4 dollars.

7 Fair. Draw muck, work at trees. Go to Wesley's take tea. Jerimiah & Joshua Collins has come from Illinois. Rain tonight.

8 Clears off. Peter Rea work at trees. Get horse shod. Get 50 dollars of LWC & Co.

9 Cloudy. Fix trees. Fix cemetery road. Jeremiah Collins Mrs. A. Mull & Miss Lay here, spend the day.

10 Rainy. We go to Mother's.

11 Fair. Mr. Wales & Almira VanBergen here. **I take my team, Beecher take his, we go to Albany, get lumber for Catholic Church.**

12 Fair, south wind. Get nuts, get wood. Put my lumber in A. Teal's shop.

13 Fair. **Work at Catholic Church Foundation. John Toben help ½ day.**

14 Fair. **Draw stone ½ day. J. Tobin work for me ½ day.**

15	Rain last night, clears off cold. I draw wood. Wife go to A. VanDerzee's. I get boots tapped & pick grapes.
16	Fair, cold. I, Wife, Jerry & Josh Collins go to A.T. VanSlyck's &M.G. VanBergen's. Jerry stay.
17	Fair. Jeremiah Collins & Mr. Trego & Lady here. I, Jerry & Joshua Collins go to George Sweet's. **Edward Blaisdell go along.**[189]
18	Fair. I send check 21.54 dollars to H.M. Heath to Little Falls. Gave order to LWC & Co. to let Wesley Blaisdell have 60 dollars. **Cate McCarty & VerPlank Ackerman get married today in Dutch Church, we all attend.** Wife & Collin's boys go to Baltimore to C.L. Rowe's. I fix gate on north side of lot to Mother's. South wind.
19	Fair, cold. I, Wife, Margarett & Joshua & Jeremiah Collins go up to S. Witbeck's.
20	Fair. Wife go to Albany. I pay John Rea 5 dollars that I owed him, then go to Flat Bush and get a load of timber. Wife go with them all visiting.
21	Fair. I go to Albany. Mr. Collins pay me his rent. I bring back ligan, molasses & nails.
22	Fair. I send Peter Rea after pumpkins. I & Wife take tea to Wesley's then spend the evening to James Lawton's.
23	Fair. I get a load of lime from Henry Reynolds; I pay him 5 dollars on it – 26 bu. in the load. Martin & Elida VanSlyck here, Mother here.
24	Fair. Martin & Elida go holme. Go to meeting, go to Wesley's at night. **Daniel Webster died 3 o'clock today.**[190]
25	Fair. Jeremiah & Joshua Collins leave for Illinois. **I draw stone for the Catholic Church & go after Sweet Flag.**[191]
26	Fair & cold. Draw sand and lay around.
27	Fair, south wind. Wm. Mull and Jerome Wilsey work 1 day for me. **Beecher Holmes work at Catholic Church. Peter Rea help Beecher ½ day.**
28	Cloudy. **Work at Catholic Church. Beecher help ½ day.**
29	Fair. **Work at church. Beecher help all day.** Mrs. Clement & Mrs. Willis here.
30	Rainy. I go to River. Abram Teal put up door bell. I make a ladder.
31	Rainy. I go to Meeting & go to Willis's.

November 1852

1	Cloudy. I am not well. Go to river.
2	Rainy day. **I attend Election.** Daniel Baker pay me 20 dollars rent. I pay R. Cutter per B. Holmes. 2.12 dollars for hay hoops.

---

[189] Edward was Wesley's son
[190] Daniel Webster, a skilled orator, served as Secretary of State under Presidents Harrison, Tyler and Fillmore. He was anti-slavery but supported the Compromise of 1850 that defused tension between the slave state and the free states.
[191] Sweet Flag is a medicinal herb. It is a folk remedy for arthritis, cancer, convulsions, diarrhea, dyspepsia & epilepsy.

3	Fair. **Work at Catholic Church all day. Beecher helps all day**.
4	Fair. **Finish Foundation of Catholic Church. Beecher & Jack Wilsey help.** I take Wife down to Baltimore. Take tea to Peter VanSlyck's.
5	Cloudy &rainy. **Peter Holbrook's two wives meet here. He runs away. Great time in the Village.** Mrs. Teneyck, Mrs. VanDerzee here on a visit.
6	Cloudy, misty. Peter Rea help Beecher dig carrots. I fix up windows. I pay Lib Rea ten dollars.
7	Rainy. I go to Meeting & to Mother's. W. Haman came her to tea.
8	Fair. Draw wood to Mother. Draw stone. Trim grape vines. I have a lot of lumber come from Little Falls.
9	Showery & misty. **Attend to lumber from Canal boat. Send B.W. Warner 50 dollars. pay boat Capt. Mr. Rop 144 dollars**. I get chk. LWC & Co. $50 & today $150 cash.
10	Fair. **Draw up lumber all day**. Rev. Mr. Davis & Lady here all day. Mrs. Hull, Mrs. Shimmer here.
11	Cloudy. **Draw lumber from dock all day**. Thomas Penton pay me $233 due. **Wife go to New York on barge.**
12	Rainy. **Draw up lumber**. Clears off in afternoon.
13	Clear, NW. **I get ready and go to New York with Sloop Bristol**.
14	Snow at Coxsackie one inch deep. **Get underway. Go along slowly down from Coxsackie to Kingston so on to the Highlands next morning.**
15	Cold. **Fine breeze through the bays. Sail around New York up to 28th St. Have a fine view of the city. Then go to Doct. VanAntwerp's, stay all night**.
16	Fair. Go to John Silcox to dinner, to theater at night.
17	Snowy & rainy. I go to Brooklyn see Stephen Herminan and around to City.
18	Fair. Go around the city. Do up trading. Then to Uriah Willis's at night.
19	Showery. Do up trading. Go around the city then take Barge for holme.
20	Lowry. Arrive at holme 11 o'clock. Get up things from Barge.
21	Fair, cold. I go to Meeting.
22	Fair morning, cloudy south wind in afternoon. George Bunker here. Wife came holme, Lib Houghtaling here.
23	Two inches of snow. I have a headache all day. I am not well.
24	Fair, cold day. I am not well. Lib Houghtaling here.
25	Fine day, milder. **Thanksgiving Day held in church**. I & Wife go to Flat Bush to S.N. Peton's.
26	Rainy day, sleet in the morning. I pay Peter Rea 4 dollars. John Gibbens pays me 50 dollars.
27	Clears off. I tinker around the house. Mother here.
28	Fair. I go to Meeting & stay around the house.
29	Fair. I kill my beef. Go to river. **Children are unwell. I get 800 dollars of James Hazelton in gold and give him my note**.

30   Fair. I kill hogs. Go to LWC & Co. Get Peter Seabridge's note that I left them. They charge it to me. Seabridge take it up. He pays me $337.44 amt of it. I go to Thomas Houghtaling's take up my note. It amounts to $1076. I go on horseback get holme late in evening. Muddy.

December 1852

1   I cut up pork. Go to river. I send Feeter a check that I get of A.N. Briggs for 100 dollars. I sell a cow hide to Martin Clark. He pay me 2 dollars 25 cts for it.

2   Fair, warm. A. Teal & Jonathan work at Mother's wood house ½ day. **I attend to Catholic Church timber in afternoon**.

3   Fair. **Draw up lumber all day. Pay Capt. John Chapman 69.12 dollars**.

4   Rainy day. Get my colt haltered. Salt my pork & beef.

5   Clears off in afternoon. W.V. Carmen here to tea. I let Beecher have 13 dollars.

6   Fine warm day. I work at Mother's wood house. Beecher help. Peter Rea take Wife to Flat Bush. Miss Crandle here.

7   Fair. I work at Mother's wood house, Beecher help. Wife go to Albany.

8   Fair. Work at wood house to gate. Beecher help Wife come back from Albany. I pay Peter Rea 6 dollars.

9   Cloudy & frosty. Work at wood house ½ day. Garret Houghtaling & Lady here. **Mrs. Dyer died this morning**.

10   Cloudy. I pile up siding. I pay F. Mosher for B.B. Fredenburgh 70 dollars. Leave P. Seabridge bill of account to LWC & Co.

11   Snow. Put up horses and cows. Stay around the house.

12   Fair, NW. I go to Meeting twice. Call at Mrs. Houghtaling. **Get my watch from New York**.

13   Snowy. I draw logs to sawmill. Bring back planks. Lib Houghtaling here.

14   Clear & cold. Work at cow stable all day. Mrs. Trego here.

15   Clear, cold. Work at cow stable all day.

16   Clear cold. I get horses shod, cut wood B.W. Warner & Lady come here.

17   Clear, cold. I get my new harness of Martin Clark's. Ebenezer Finch & Lady here to dinner. **I take children out on a sley ride. Mrs. Thm. A. Houghtaling died**.

19   Fair. Stay in the house. Folks go to Meeting.

20   Cloudy. Cut & draw wood. Attend P.R. Meeting. Warner here.

21   Cold, squally. **I take Wife & Mother Houghtaling & Lib Houghtaling to Mrs. Thm. Houghtaling's Funeral**.

22   Fair, cold. I cut & draw wood for Mother, Peter Rea help. Warner here.

23   Hail & storm. Cut & draw wood to Mother. Warner & his Wife come back here.

24   Lowry & rainy. Cut wood at Mother's & settle with Elizabeth Rea. I pay her 10 dollars. Let Warner have $90. I get $100 of LWC & Co. Mrs. William Tuttle here. **River closed today**.

25   Fair, thawy. I send B.W. Warner & Wife to Albany by Peter Rea. I & Wife go to Baltimore. Get clothes cut. **Then we go to Mr. Allen's & Seth Hawley's to an entertainment for Christmas.**[192] **Levi go along**. Mr. Herman's here. I cut wood.

26   Sloppy. I go to Meeting & to Mother's.

27   Lowry. I cut wood for Mother. Caroline VanAntwerp here.

28   Lowry. Work around the house. Take up notes. I settle with Lawton Willis & Colvin & Co. James Lawton made an assignment.

29   Fair day. Edwin Hubbel & Lady & two children & Almira Van Bergen here.

30   Cloudy. I go with A.E. Willis out to Gates & to L. Witbeck's & N. Niles. He takes up his notes and gives me new ones. I endorse with him. Andrew VanDerzee & Lady here. **John McPherson's child buried today**.

31   Cloudy. I & Levi go to Flat Bush. **Meet Mr. Hermans to sell Flat Bush Farm**. S.M. Petton pay me 17 dollars. Lawton Willis & Colvin & Co. pay me barley bill. I pay Wm. Lawton bill of 8 dollars.

January 1853

1   Stormy. I help Beecher. Gilion VerPlank pay me 5 dollars. Mrs. Tunis Wilsey pay me 2 dollars. I take up due bill against me of G.W. Dorman of $14.91. **Jackson Wilsey & Elizabeth Rea got married**. I & Wife attend the wedding. **I likewise attend an oyster supper of the Odd Fellows**[193] **to Aaron Houghtaling's**.

2   Cloudy. I go to Meeting & I see John Toben about stealing my wood.

3   Cloudy. I help Beecher draw straw. I get horse shod. Beecher pay me 4.29 dollars for straw.

4   Very cold. **I go to papermill, make contract to buy straw for Robb & Milton**. Mr. Wiltsey here to buy wood. **Cattine, the Dutch girl, come here to work. Her sister come with her**.

5   Very cold. I split wood for mother & go to river. **Lawrence Fises died this morning**. Peter VanBuren pays his subscription to Plank Road, 1 dollar. I pay him his blacksmith bill $7.50 cents.

6   Fair, pleasant. I go to Greenville. I stop first to Anthony Miller's, then Nicolas Wingard's, then to Lobden's Mill, then South Westerlo. Stop & take some oysters. Gave horse some oats, then to Silas Baldwin then to Andrew Fancher's. Stay there all night.

7   Fair. I get rent of Mr. Hoose, Mr. Stephens, Mr. Witbeck and 5 dollars cash of Jerimiah Place. Then I pay off I.G. Williamson's bill. Then I get Mr. Hunt's rent and go to Andrew Fancher's, then start for holme. Come back to the Rocky Store. Attend a debate. Put my horse to Michael Dawling's. Spook twice. Then come holme at 11 o'clock at night.

8   Fair & warm for three past days. I go to papermill, then to the river, then holme. Then take Wife & Miss Bennett to Gerry Springstead's.

---

[192] This is the first mention of any kind of Christmas celebration.

[193] The Independent Order of the Odd Fellows is one of the largest and oldest fraternities in the world. They believe that life is a commitment to improve and elevate the character of mankind through service and example.

10	Fair. I cut & draw a load of wood. John Bushant's here. He pays me 50 dollars. I pay his bill 5 dollars 69 cents. Isaac Lawsen come here to look at my mare.
11	Cloudy, muddy. I go to Albany; get 261 dollars at Mechanics & Farmer's Bank. I pay McClure $10.63. Springstead & Bullux 50 dollars, 10 cts. Davidson & Viele $28.14. Get 10 gallons molasses of G.H. Lawton.
12	Stormy, snowy. **We all attend Jenny VanSlyck's & Mr. Colborn's wedding** and Dominie Blake's Donation this evening.
13	Snow all day, knee deep. I attend P.R. Meeting. I send Certificate of Deposit to Mr. Rust at Little Falls for $11.85
14	Cloudy. I attend Plank Road Annual Meeting. There is about 18 inches of snow. I pay Treasurer 73.77 dollars. Take up my note I gave yesterday.
15	Fair. I go to Aquetuck Hollow, pay my tax $54.72. I go to river, get Levi's boots mended. I pay off balance of P. Ostrander's bill 23 dollars.
16	Very cold, heavy NW. I go to Mother's. Snow blows a good deal.
17	Very cold. I go to river. John Hauenstien pay me balance on John Spoor's lot in cemetery, 1.69 dollars above his work.
18	Cold, cloudy. I draw logs from field by Elias Holmes. I take his barrel of flour holme that he left here last night when he got drifted in and almost froze to death. I shovel snow all the afternoon to draw wood from creek. I pay 50 dollars to A.E. Willis for his check to John Feeter to Bassendeile & B.W. Warner. **Elias Holmes & Catharine Crumb gets married.**
19	Fair. I draw wood in forenoon. Mother Houghtaling come back with Martin VanSlyck. I pay John Clement 3 dollars for hanging blinds in Greenville.
20	Cloudy. Peter Rea draw wood for me. I go to Croswell's papermill.
21	Cloudy. Peter Finch draw wood. I pay him off 15/. Caroline VanAntwerp, Cate Fredenburgh, Lizabeth Phoausburgh, Miss Wheelen & Miss Bennett here & Lib Houghtaling.
22	Fair, pleasant. I and Wife go to Andrew VanSlyck's on a visit. The guests were Martin VanBergen & Lady, Baltis VanSlyck & Lady. I go with Baltis to Coxsackie.
23	Cloudy, stormy. I go to river get my new coat and then to Meeting. **Call for Doctor for Anthony. Anthony Bradwell died.**
25	South wind & sunny. I kill 8 turkeys & saw wood.
26	Clear, cold day. Marin & Elida VanSlyck & Cate VanBergen come here. We all attend donation of Rev. Mr. Davis. Have a jolly time.
28	Fair. I saw wood. Mary Houghtaling here to dinner. I gave Charles McAllester lease to put lights up on the Island. **I pay Miss Bennet 2 dollars 25 cents for one quarter schooling for Levi.**[194] I pay French woman 2/.
29	Clear, cold. I take Wife, Cate VanBergen & Elida VanSlyck to Widow Charlotte Houghtaling's house. **Horse-trot today on the ice.**
30	Fair. Martin VanSlyck come after Elida & Cate Houghtaling. We all go to Meeting.

---

[194] Levi is 7 at this time and must have had a private tutor.

31   Fair. **I notify School District of a special meeting** and attend a ball to Aaron Houghtaling. Not a pleasant time at all but a good supper.

February 1853

1   Fair. I and Beecher draw stalks from island. **Mier Fancher draw me a load of timber for Catholic Church**. Mrs. George Wolfe, Mrs. Albert Houghtaling & Mother here.

2   Drizly day. I and Beecher go to Flat Bush, draw 7 logs to mill. S.M. Pelton pay me 20 dollars. **Rachael Ann Gregory has a young child this evening**.

3   Fair, south wind. I & Wife go to Coxsackie. Visit to Andrew Houghtaling. Attend a Festival at Mr. Fichet's hotel. Have a jolly time. Stay all night to Andrew Houghtaling's.

4   South wind, cloudy & rainy. Visit to Edwin Hubbell's. Come holme at night and **find Levi sick**.

5   Rainy, thawy. I go to river & **attend school meeting at night.**

8   Fair. I draw load of boards from sawmill with waggon & saw wood.

9   Very cold. I draw two logs from mill and two loads of boards and then shell 2 bushels of corn.

10   Cold, south wind. I set Thomas Penton chopping wood for me. I go out to Houghtaling's mill, take corn and get 1 load of lumber. Get two shoes set on Bill horse at VanBuren's. Wife & Mother Houghtaling go to Doct. Fredenburgh's.

11   Fair, south wind. **I go with Beecher up to the Stone Church woods**. Get posts.

12   Fair, cold. I go to Albany with A.E. Willis. **I pay Wm. VanRenssalear 5 dollars rent for Island.** Buy Wife a carpet bag for 10/.

14   Blow hard all day. I saw wood and go and get Black Tom and chop a tree that I gave Widow Bronk - 1 dollar for her half. It was on the line. James Wilsey pay me 2 dollars.

17   Snowy & squally. **I go to Island. I go to Albany with Charles McAlister & Josiah Sheron and survey out the Island to put up lights.**

18   Fair morning, snowy afternoon. I draw logs and then let Peter Rea have my horses to get a load of wood. **His Father got the Small Pox. I survey the Island again with Isaac Mosher.** Wife go to Wm. B. Hull's. Martin VanBergen and Aunt Sarah Ann here. Stay all night.

19   Cold. Company leaves after a turkey dinner. I then go to Schodack & meet Charles McAlister & then we again go to Island. **I sell him 1 acre of Island and gave him a deed for it, and he gave me 40 dollars**. I pay Maria Finch 11 dollars 88 cents. I let Miss Bennet have my mare to go a visiting.

21   Fair. I chop wood and **then meet Methodist Church Committee and rent their house north side of Mother's lot for parsonage for 42 dollars per year and am to make the wood house into a kitchen and build a cistern.** I draw two loads of wood and then let Peter Rea have my team to draw 1 load of wood. Mr. Giles Hunt here & Lib Houghtaling here.

23   Rainy day. I get $50 dollars of A.E. Willis, **25 in gold and 25 in bills** that I sent with him for at Albany.

24 Fair and very cold, NW wind. I send a check to B.W. Warner of 25 dollars. I get $32.50 of A.E. Willis & Co. I gave Willis an order for $32.50 on the order of Sons of T[emperance]. I pay Jackson Wilsey 28 dollars 45 cts ball [?] on his Wife's wages due her when she left work here. Rebecca Pelts come here this evening.

26 Fair. I take my mare Rose, take Wife, Doct. Fredenburgh, Cate Fredenburgh & Caroline VanAntwerp & Isaac Skinner, **go to Schodack on the ice**. Call on Mr. Matson. Then take cars & go to New York. Go to Marite's & to John Silcox. Take tea with Marite and stay all night.

27 Fair. I and John Silcox go to Balch's church in forenoon and to Chapin church in evening. **Go to Chrystal Palace,**[195] then to Doct. VanAntwerp's. Stay all night.

Crystal Palace

28 Rainy day. **I and Doctor Fredenburgh, Wife & Cate Fredenburgh & Caroline VanAntwerp start for Washington**. Cross to Jersey, take cars to Newark, then to Trenton, Burlington, Brunswick to Camden. Cross the ferry to Philadelphia. **Got cheated out of an Omnibus**[196] and had to take a coach across town to Depot. Then take cars again; go through to Chester, Wilmington. Cross Mush River, Gunpowder River, Elkton River to Haverdegrass [Havre de Grace]. Cross the Susquehanna so to Baltimore Barnum's City Hotel. Stay all night have a first-rate supper - oysters.

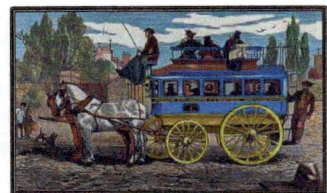
Omnibus

March 1853

1 Rainy day. Take cars to Washington. Pass through several villages. Arrive at 11 o'clock AM. Put up at Mrs. Holriead's on Pennsylvania Avenue opposite the United States Hotel. Then go to the **State House to the Assembly & Senate Chambers**. Then to tea. Then back to State House.

2 Stop raining. **Visit Congress. Then go to President's house. To Jackson's Bronze Statue of brass cast from the cannon he took at New Orleans.**[197] **Then to U.S. Treasury, then to Washington Monument, then to Capitol. Hear Sam Houston's speech.**[198] **Then to dinner, then to hot houses. Play whist in the evening.**

---

[195] The Crystal Palace was an exhibition building constructed for the Exhibition of the Industry of all Nations in 1853.
[196] An omnibus in the 1850's was a horse-drawn carriage that would transport several people at one time for a fee.
[197] A statue of Andrew Jackson at the Battle of New Orleans, War of 1812, was erected in 1853 in the center of Lafayette Square, Washington, D.C. It was the first bronze statue in the U.S. and believed to be the first equestrian statue in the world to be balanced solely on the horse's hind legs. Sculptor - Clark Mills and enslaved apprentice Phillip Reid.
[198] Sam Houston was a soldier, a politician and an active leader in the Texas Revolution against Mexico whereby Texas gained its independence and became the Republic of Texas. He served as its first and third president. After Texas was admitted to the U.S., Houston served as one of its first two senators. He was the only person in the U.S. to be elected as governor of two different states, Texas and Tennessee. The city of Houston is named in his honor.

3   Fair, cold. Take omnibus. Go to steamboat for **Mount Vernon**. Came across Samuel Gedney, who was very polite; gave us free passage, treated us with Brandy Oysters, Champagne. We see the Ship [?]. Pass Alexandria stop there. Then to Fort Washington, stop then to Mt Vernon. Visit tomb of General Washington and others. Then see his Negroes, then pass in the dwelling. View his chairs, pictures, out grounds, dwelling gardens and record my name in their book & Wife spend a good two hours. Then board the boat, stop at Fort Washington on our return come back to Washington. Took coach for the Boarding House & then went to dinner. Then I & and Doctor take a walk and then return to Boarding House. Then all hands take an omnibus and go to Georgetown. Go to convent then return again. Cross Rock Creek then Wife back again to tea. Then Wife go with the Doctor and Cate & Caroline to Mechanics Fair. I go to Cars to look for Doct. VanAntwerp. Don't find them. Then to the Capitol, then to Boarding House to bed.

4   Snow, cold day. **Go to Inauguration. I see President Pierce,**[199] **hear and see him take his oath of office and deliver his inaugural address. It was very good, a great crowd & applause, guns firing, bells ringing, great military display**. I came across Doct. VanAntwerp & Marite. Saw Hiram Litchfield after the ceremonies was over. I went back to Boarding House to dinner. Then I and Doctor go to the National Hotel, then to the railroad depot. The military and people there. Great crowd, some on a spree. Then back to our Boarding House. Then take a coach and visit the **White House** to see the President. Then back to house. Play Whist a spell & go to bed.

Shot Tower

5   Very cold, 1 ½ inches snow. I go and ring up Doct. VanAntwerp; go with him to cars. He leave for holme. Then I go back to breakfast. Take Marite and go again to **Mt. Vernon**. Have a very pleasant trip, see all that I saw before. Return to Washington to Boarding House. Pay up bill and take cars to **Baltimore**. Put up again at **Barnum's Hot**el. Have a good supper and go to bed.

6   Fair, cold. After Breakfast, go to **Catholic Cathedral**, to **Washington Monumen**t and around the city to **Shot Tower,**[200] wharves then to public house. Pay up and take cars at 5½ o'clock pm for **Philadelphia** and put up at **Franklin House**, Chestnut Street. I walk from depot to the hotel on account of no room in the cars.

---

[199] Franklin Pierce was the 14th president of the United States. Born in New Hampshire, he was heavy drinker and against the abolition of slavery. He served one term and is considered by historians to be among the worst of the US presidents.

[200] The Shot Tower, which is 234 ft tall, was built in 1828. It was used to make ammunition. Molten lead poured from the top of the tower formed a perfect sphere before falling into a pool of water.

7   Fair, cool. I go and see Pelts girls then we go to **Fairmount**[201] see the **Schuylkill & Wire Bridge**[202] & **US Mint** and around the city and then go back to dinner. **Fairmount Water Work is beautiful and well worth seeing**.[203] Then we take Omnibus & I go to **Gerrard College**,[204] which is a wonder of art - a magnificent building all marble so are the student's buildings. We passed through them, saw the students then back around the city to supper and then to the theater. **Saw the play of Hamlet. Saw today the Old State Hall where the Declaration of Independence was signed and public grounds in the rear.** Misses Pelts call on us the evening. Then we retire.

Fairmount Water Works

8   Cloudy. Pay off our bills, take coach to cars after breakfast. Cross to Camden and come on through Trenton, Bordentown. **Saw Joseph Buonaparte residence**.[205] So to New York and take dinner at Doct. VanAntwerp's. Arrive at 2 o'clock pm. Then I & Doctor take a ride to Williamsburg. I call on Acton Civill & come back to John Silcox take tea. Then to Doct. VanAntwerp's, stay all night.

9   Rainy. **Come holme by Harlem Railroad to Albany and then meet Beecher there with Aaron Houghtaling's Rockaway and ride holme through the rain & mud. Get holme in evening.**

10   Fair. I cut & draw wood [to] Mother. I pay Peter Rea 9/ that I owe him.

11   Snow all day. I saw wood & go to river.

12   Snowy, 9½ inches this morning. I draw logs. Meet Trustee & Collector of Coeymans Road Dist. J. Sweet pay me $17.75. I pay A.E. Willis 25 dollars on Dist. Note. I settle old bills with A. Teal & Jonathan McElroy. **I pay Abram Teneyck $25 on Catholic Church account**. Take his receipt.

Typical Rockaway

13   Cloudy, NW. I go to Meeting. Wife go to Wesley's & A. VanDerzee's. Very muddy.

14   Snow squalls & cold. I have John Toben to break out stone. We work hard all day.

---

[201] Fairmount park was named by William Penn and was once home to elegant estates.
[202] The Spider Bridge at the Falls of the Schuylkill was an iron-wire foot bridge erected in 1816 over the Schuylkill River and thought to have been the first wire-cable suspension bridge in world history.
[203] Following a series of Yellow Fever epidemics, which were thought to be caused by unclean water at the time, the city of Philadelphia initiated projects to bring clean water to the city from the Schuylkill River. The first project failed. But the second project resulted in the Fairmount Water Works. The industrial facility was disguised by a Classic Revival exterior, which became a tourist attraction. It became the most advanced big-city water supply system in the world.
[204] We think he meant Girard College. It is an independent college preparatory school in Philadelphia that opened in 1848.
[205] Joseph Buonaparte was Napoleon's brother. He was once King of Spain and Naples.

15 Very cold, NW wind. Black Dinah & Cate Hathaway here. I pay off Salmon VanAntwerp. I get my post augur.

16 Fair & cold. I take to the Mill Dam & to the river. I pay Jonas Bronk one dollar for a pine tree I cut on our line.

17 Fair, south wind, cold. I draw a load of boards from sawmill. Margarett Blaisdell here all day. I let Beecher have my horses ½ day.

18 Rainy. I cut wood. I go with Beecher to the Dam.

19 Fair, hard N wind. I chop wood, work around & go to river.

20 Very fine warm day. **Steamboat comes from Albany**. I go to Meeting.

21 Very fine day. Draw stone, work in quiry. Beecher & Peter Rea help all day. Mr. James Trego here to dinner. Drill stone for McAllester.

22 Fair, warm NW wind. Draw & get out stone. S. Tobin & Beecher help all day. Peter Rea help ½ day. Catherine Mannakim comes here to work.

23 Fair, colder. Beecher & Peter Rea help me work at stone ½ day each. Judge Williams & Lady here. Cate Fredenburgh & Caroline VanAntwerp here. Uriah Stephens comer here, stay all night, take supper & breakfast.

24 Fair, cold. I buy a piece of beef. Do but little.

25 Fair. I get mare shod. Beecher get out stone, Mother here.

26 South wind & rainy. I take Beecher, go to Abram Witbeck's, get lumber.

27 Fair, cold day. I go to Meeting twice. Harriet Finch, Mary & Virginia Blaisdell here to supper.

28 Fair, cold. I go to river. George Fancher here.

29 Fair. I go with H. McDonald out to Rosecrant's vendue. I dig in the garden.

30 Fair. A. Teal get out timber ½ day for me. Beecher help. John Gibbens pay me 51.22 dollars, give me his note for $25 more. I take a ride far as Lewis Crandle's. Oliver Springstead & Virginia Blaisdell here to tea.

31 Fair. I make sluice down to Tunis Wiltsey's. Henry Wiltsey move in my house at $2.25 per month. **George B. Lawton tried for a child sworn on him by Rachael Ann Gregory**.[206] Mary Jane Lawton here visiting. Abram Witbeck pay me 95 dollars. I borrow $350 of Mrs. Betsey Sweet. I pay off Newman Finch & Truman Waldsom.

April 1853

1 Rainy. I send by Charles Seabridge 321 dollars to pay a note against me in the hands of Newman Finch and 214 dollars to pay a note against me in the hands of Truman Waldsom. I get 100 dollars more of G.T. Sweet. I take up note I gave him yesterday of $350 and gave him one for $450. I pay A.E. Willis $100 I borrowed of him yesterday. **I attend Lawsuit of G. B. Lawton. It was decided against him.**

2 Fair. I pay H. McDonald $80 on my new waggon. **Attend Nomination meeting. Get nominated for inspector of Election.** Mother here.

---

[206] We're not sure what this means, but probably not good!

3   Fair. Go to Meeting. Mrs. Abby Springstead here to tea. **Catholic Meeting**. Margaret Manaheim & brother here.

4   Rainy. I trade horses with Isaac Lawson. I gave him ten dollars boot money. **Election of Coeymans Road Dist. I and Chunk [sp] run. I beat him 10 majority**. A. Witbeck pay me 5 dollars.

5   Rainy & snowy all day. S.D. Eddy & Lady here. Oliver Springstead here. Mrs. Elizabeth Wilsey here. I get book of district road of R. Houghtaling.

6   Cold, S wind. I, Eddy & John Rea go out finish survey of Plank Road.

7   Fair, NW wind. I work at kitchen over to the Ely or Dominie House. Beecher help ½ day. Gulion Verplank pay me 5 dollars in gold.

8   Fair. I work at kitchen. Beecher help ½ day. Lay foundation ½ day. Miss Bennett & Miss Wheeler call here.

9   Fair. I work at new kitchen. Wife & Levi take my horse, go to New Baltimore.

10   Cold, snow squalls. I & Wife go to Meeting. Wife get dirt in her Eye. Stop at Mother's.

11   Fair. I send Beecher to Albany after lumber. I make fence. Wife go to Widow Houghtaling's. Widow Andrew Teneyck here.

12   Rainy. I Go to town meeting. Take John VanDenburgh along. John Bushants pay me 50 dollars, balance of rent of 10 years lease. Oliver Springstead & his Mother here to dinner.

13   Rainy afternoon. I get letter last night from Jacob Feeter with two receipts from his father. I pay to Mr. Cranston 10 dollars I borrow of A.E. Willis. I work at fence all day.

14   Rainy day. **I send calf & 252 eggs to New York**. Call to Willis's. Capt. Sherwood call here. Mr. Morrison here. Stay all night.

15   Fair, one-inch snow. I draw sand. **Hugh McDonald return me 6 dollars bad money that he said he got of me**.[207] Silas Baldwin here.

16   Fair. I go to Island. Get log & take it to sawmill. **Saw it for a road scraper**. John Nichols bring Mother Houghtaling & Marite and Elida VanSlyck here. Mrs. Wilsey pay me one dollar. D. Fredenburgh here.

17   Fair. I go to Meeting. Mrs. John Cronk come holme with us. I and Marite go take a ride. I call on Wm. Tuttle. Go round on N. Baltimore Plank Road, so holme.

18   Fair. Make fence, draw sand & 300 bricks. I pay Reuben Style $6.38 for cloth.

19   Fair. I make fence. Get a 6½ bu. lime of Mr. Robb. I pay him 13/. I let Miss Bennet have my horse and waggon.

20   Rainy. I make fence, draw one load sand. Draw cistern for Dominie House. Wife & Marite go to Aaron **Hotaling**.[208]

21   Fair. I make fence. Mrs. Fredenburgh, Mrs. Gates & Mrs. Cranston & lots of company here. Aunt Betsey, Mrs. Aaron Hotaling.

---

[207] Counterfeit money was a problem in the decades before the Civil War. Paper money came not from the Federal Government but from a largely unregulated network of private banks – a counterfeiter's hay day.

[208] Fletcher changed his spelling from Houghtaling to Hotaling.

22 Rainy day. Doctor VanAntwerp come here. I work around, go to river. Wife & Marite go to Mrs. Jemima Hotaling's.

23 Fair, cold, NW wind. I get stove tube of Alfred Hotaling, pay 5/. I put on 600 pickets. Dr. VanAntwerp here. Reuben Cary call. Masons finish to Dominie's.

24 Overcast, SW. **I go to cemetery, set out rose bush at Harriet's grave**. **Helen Selkirk has a still-born child last night**.

25 Rainy. I lay walks. I take Wife & Marite to Caroline VanAntwerp's to visit. I get check from Hunt & Nelson $113.12. Leave it with A.E. Willis. He give me credit on his books. I pay Wm. R. Carroll 3/ for fixing hinges. Go with the Doctor around the river. Margarett Manheim leave. I pay her off.

26 One fair day again. I work at Dominie's house & go to Mill. Mrs. Henry Wilsey pay me $1.25. **Doctor & Marite leave for New York by Steamboat Washington**. Mr. Colborn & Lady call here.

27 Fair. **I draw 6 loads of blue clay and one load of stone. We put cistern in the ground**. I pay balance of Doctor Blaisdell's bill of 4 dollars. Wife go to Mr. Trego.

28 Fair. I and Jacob Sickler go to Hollow, make out road list.

29 Fair. Draw one load stone & two loads clay. I take Mother Hotaling to Andrew Witbeck's. Then go to the Hollow make out Dist Road List. **Acton Civill move here today**. Mr. Orr & Beecher Holmes here. Orr buy a lot in cemetery.

30 Showry afternoon. **I and Jacob Sickles go to Albany; get advice of the Attorney General on Dist. Road and Turnpike matter**. Mrs. Elias Holmes here, spend the day. **Mrs. Stephen Gould died today**.

May 1853

1 Fair, cold. **I attend Mrs. Gould's funeral**. Adaline Finch here.

2 Fair. I make garden. Peter Seabridge pay me $110 lumber bill and Gardner Sherman's rent and his rents for Barns lands. I get A.E. Willis check for $113.12. I get Mr. Orr's & S. Gould's cemetery deeds for cemetery lots of Mr. Gregory. Wife go to Mrs. Hotaling's.

4 Fair. I take horse & waggon, go to Albany. Jack Wilsey drive horse back for me. I pay him 50 cts. I go to Little Falls with cars. Take drum to John Feeter's. Then get a chance and go out to B.W. Warner's.

5 Rainy. I go with Wm. McLane & David Bly out in their woods. Stop on our return at Mr. Sirvy's log house. He sat on one side of the table, his little Wife on the other. They had veal soup and shortcake for dinner. House was all open overhead. They had one rocking chair and three common chairs and one bed for the furniture. Then we come back. I went to Warner's stay all night.

6 Took breakfast, took a walk through the woods, walk down to Little Falls to John Feeter's. Took dinner, go see Margarett Feeter, she is very sick. Then take cars for Albany. Stay all night at Eagle St. Hotel. Attend the museum. See James Canole perform.

7 Fair. I walk around get my watch at Hood & Toby's. I pay off G.H. Lawton $40.45. Get some things and take **Steamer Coffin** for holme. I gave Wife $25. Plant peas in the garden. Attend the lodge. I let John Feeter have $25 for Warner yesterday. Turn out cows.

8	Rainy. I stay around the house all day.
9	Fair. Make fence. I pay Doct. Fredenburgh $49 interest money. I get $20 of A.E. Willis. I pay John Bailey $5 for manure. I get balance of $110 I left to A.E. Willis.
10	Rainy. Andrew Fancher here. Pay his rent of $200. I borrow 100 dollars of A.E. Willis. Make fence.
11	Fair. I go to Little Falls. Take dinner to John Feeter's. Then go to B.W. Warner's, stay all night. Settle with B.W. Warner.
12	Rainy day. I and Warner go to Graysville, then to Ohio City, then to Mr. Coppernoll's, then to Norway Corners. **I buy team of Mr. Stebbens, harness & waggon. Let Warner have the team to work.**
13	Fair. I come holme. Stop at Feeter's. Go to see Mr. Waterman. I let Warner have 5 dollars.
14	Fair. **I frame timber, raise the Catholic Church. Have good luck, get it up finely.**
15	Fair. I go to Meeting. Mrs. William Witbeck at Meeting. I was introduced.
16	Heavy rain & hail. Take my colt to Mr. Pelton's to Flat bush. **I draw stuff to Catholic Church**. Get horses shod. I pay H. McDonald balance on my covered waggon 38 dollars. Amy Rea here.
17	Very warm. **I take Wife & Mother Hotaling to M.G. VanBergen's to attend the funeral of Mrs. Bushnel.** I and Wife take dinner to A.T. VanSlyck's. Mary Hotaling come back with us. Lib Wilsey here.
18	Cloudy. **I draw lumber & shingles to Catholic Church**. I make garden. Wife go to Mrs. Robb's visiting.
19	Rainy day. I pay Jerry Springstead 5 dollars Insurance. I pay Wm. B. Hull 13.52 dollars, balance of account.
20	Fair, heavy NW wind. I help Beecher make fence. Go to river. T. Penton to work in cellar. I pay Reynold's $6.16 for lime. P.W. VanBergen here. Pay Mother Hotaling $613.32. Mother here.
21	Fair, cold S wind. I, Wife & Anthony go to Coxsackie. I get twenty shares of stock for Mother Hotaling in Coxsackie Bank. I let her have $39.68; take her note. We stop to Andrew's, take dinner. Bring along Lib Castle's little girl.
22	Fair. I go to Meeting. Take a walk to cemetery. Call to Abram Teal's.
23	I, Wife & Abram Teal go to Albany. I take G. Roseboom's beehive to him. We get lumber bill amt. $77.97. Wife get lots of flowers and rose bushes.
24	Clears off. I help Beecher make fence. I go to Mr. Rob's, call at Jackson's.
25	Rain all day. I pay Dennis Swarthout 3 dollars for bringing lumber from Albany. Get out pickets.
26	Rainy. I draw up lumber from dock. Work hard.
27	Fair, hot. **I work around Catholic Church.**
28	I am unwell with Dyspepsia. **I work around Catholic Church** and in garden. Go to Solomon Tuttle. See Sarah Teneyck's cow. Go to see Mrs. Teneyck, buy her cow for 26 dollars. Call to John Hathaway's.

29   Fair. I go to Meeting. Rev. P. Pelts preach. **I take off my flannels**.

30   Rainy at night. I plow John Mosher's garden. **Draw stuff to Catholic Church**. Get my cow I bought of Mrs. Teneyck.

31   Fair. I am unwell. Run 3 times last night. Mother here. I walk around. Nancy Wilsey pay me 2.25 dollars house rent.

June 1853

1   Fair. I go to Albany. Get 4 bunches of shingles. Thomas Teal go along. I get some beer. Two Black people here.

2   Fair. I work on cemetery road. Go to square. See R. Pulver about working. Tunis Wilsey pay me two dollars. I go to dam. Dig a spring. Go a fishing. Go in swimming. Go to river get two shad.

3   Fair. I work in garden. Work on doing alley street. I pay P. Ostrander 5 dollars. **I take paint to Catholic Church. I am served with summons from Wm. McLane on Warner business in Herkimer.**

4   Cloudy morning, clear afternoon. I stay around. See to Dist. Road. **Elizabeth Hotaling here all-day dress making.**

5   Fair, cool. I take Wife & Eliz. Hotaling to the Hollow to Quarterly Meeting. Richard and Barent Winnie call here. Woolsey Cary pay me forty-two dollars interest money.

6   Fair. **I draw two loads of sand**. I pay to A.E. Willis 30 dollars. I get his check for 30 dollars. Send it to B.W. Warner.

7   Fair. **I draw two loads sand & one load brick for church.** Edward VanOrden bring Almira VanBergen & Mary Hotaling here.

8   Fair. **I draw two loads of sand I got of French Harry. I get a load of posts**. John Mull bring me my fish. Israel Lawton here. I clean my fish.

9   Fair. Widow Charlotte & Heston Hotaling here. Cate Lawton, Mary Jane, Mrs. O. Lawton, Amira VanBergen, Mr. Collins, Slater, McClancy here. **I draw lumber for church**.

10   I hoe in garden. I go with Trego to Hollow, buy a cow for him of Solomon Carhart. Take dinner to J.B. Shear's, then holme. I then go to river, get paper from Waterman. Make affidavit & send them back. Mary Hotaling, Almira VanBergen, Mary Jane & Hellen Lawton here. I pay Wm. B. Hull 5 dollars for Dominie Davis.

11   Fair. I make fence all day to David Baker's. Black Tom help.

12   Fair. I go to Meeting & walk around.

13   Fair. I and Black Tom work at fence at David Baker's.

14   Fair, hot. I hoe in garden, get strawberries. Beecher go to Albany with my team Mary Jane Lawton here.

15   Fair, hot. I go to river, go in swimming, Mrs. Fredenburgh call here, Mary Jane Lawton here.

16   Fair, hot. I make gate. Black Tom work here.

17   One fine shower. I take Mother Hotaling to Flat Bush, come holme in the rain. Set out cabbage plants.

18   Fair. **I settle with the Catholics. Take Bond & mortgage on the Catholic Church for $652**. I pay Mr. Carman 1 dollar & P. Ostrander 5 dollars.

19   Fair. I go to Meeting in the forenoon & to sleep in afternoon. Take a walk.

20   Fair, hot. **I draw stuff for Catholic Church. I pay Teal $50 on Catholic job**. I go in swimming. Mr. Colborn & his Father call here.

21   Fair, hot. I & Tom make fence at Dominie Blake's. **Mrs. McGregor died today**. Mother here all day.

22   Fair, hot. **I work in garden and to Catholic Church**. John Sperl pay me 3 dollars. I go in swimming. Miss Sherwood here.

23   Hot, fair. **I draw 5 loads of stone for Catholic Church. Draw 1 Hh. water 1 Bbl.**[209] lime. **Attend Funeral of Mrs. MacGregor**.

24   Fair, cool. I**, Wife, Doctor & Cate Fredenburgh start for the Shakers**. Stop at Martin G. VanBergen's. Go to Coxsackie. Cross the river. Go through Stuyvesant Falls then to West Ghent, then to William Hansburgh. Stay all night have a pleasant visit.

25   Fair, cool. Go to East Ghent then through Chatham 4 Corners then to Mechanicsville, Canaan, Whitney's Pond then to the Shakers. Go around their village. See them work. They pay great attention to us. **Then go to Lebanon Springs stop at Columbian Hotel**. Take tea & then Doctor and I go to the top of the hill in Massachusetts. **I tumble over the fence, break it down**. Then back to public house, go to bed.

26   Fair cool morning, but showry day. **Attend Shaker Meeting. They dance finely**. Then we come holme same day. Stop at Kinderhook. Take tea.

27   Rain all day. I work at stoop in the wood house. I pay Wesley $20 I borrow.

28   Fair. I help Beecher hang gate. Lay wall & furrow out my garden. I go help Peter Seabridge raise his barn.

29   Warm, cloudy. I go to Flat Bush, see Mr. Pelton. Mr. Morrison here.

30   Warm. I go to Albany get load of lumber. **Go to trial of Hendrickson for the murder poisoning of his wife. He looked very independent.**[210]

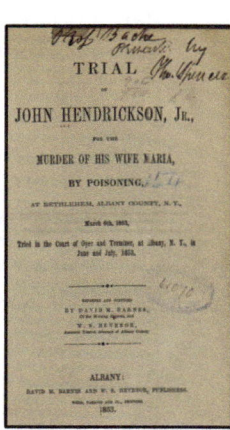

Trial of John Hendrickson

July 1853

2   Fair. I & Levi go to Greenville. Stop at J.W. Story's, take dinner. **Levi fall down the waggon house stairs.**[211] Then go to Jeremiah Place's, he pays me 19.75 dollars. Then to Silas Baldwin's, then to Andrew Fancher's. Stay all night, he pays me 25 dollars.

3   Fair, south wind. We come holme. Wife go to Wesley's.

---

[209] Hh stands for Hogshead (a large cask), Bbl stands for barrel.

[210] This would have been the 17th day of the trial. Mr. Hendrickson was accused of using aconite to poison his young wife. He was convicted and eventually hanged in 1854. He proclaimed his innocence to the last day, when he confessed.

[211] Levi is 7 at this point in time.

4	Fair, hot. **I take Mother Hotaling, Widow Hotaling, Wife & Mary Bland; all go to Aquetuck Celebration.** Come back through New Baltimore. I pay H.B. Wilsey 10 dollars on work. I pay Wesley 5 dollars I borrowed of him. **I spend about 4 dollars; attend fireworks at night.**
5	Fair. Lay around, go to papermill. Cate Hotaling here.
6	Fair. I take Cate Hotaling & Wife to Tunis VanSlyck's visiting. I go to Isaac Witbeck's, buy 5 cedar trees for 3 dollars. Then to Newton Briggs, take dinner. Then to Mossy Hill, then to Wm. Wilsey's, then back.
7	Fair. I take Wife, Cate & Mother Hotaling to George Wolfs. I and Jacob Sickles go back of Gilbert Cronk's get stone for to cover sluices. Jacob break his waggon. I go after the folks at night.
8	Fair. I put up my stoop at John Sperl's. I take Cate Hotaling holme. Draw stone, go in swimming.
9	Fair. **I get timber from Stone Church**. Get policy of insurance of G.W. Dorman. A light rain in the afternoon.
10	Fine shower. I go to Meeting twice. Hear Rev. Mr. Davis & Blake.
11	Fair. I go to mill, draw timber for A Teal, help him raise his barn. **Clean out Catholic Church.**
12	Fair. I take Wife, Mrs. VanDerzee, Margarett Return and go after them at night. **Beecher has Lawsuit with John Rea**.
13	Fair. I and A. Teal go to Albany after lumber. I get 112.20 dollars from Mechanics & Farmers Bank. I pay A. Teal 45 dollars I pay Wm. Headlen 21.54 dollars. Then come holme.
14	Fair. **I lay smoke house foundation**. Go in swimming. Get liniment of the doctor.
15	Fair. I take Lib, Wife & Cate Lawton to Baltis J. VanSlyck's. I and Lib go to A.T. VanSlyck's, then come back to Baltis, take dinner.
16	Little showery. I go get blackberries. I get 63 dollars Dist. Road money. I pay off Willis's note 45.14 dollars against Dist. Road. I pay Peter Ostrander 10 dollars. Attend Exhibition at Temperance Hall. Get 1 dollar.
17	Fair. **I go to Catholic Meeting**. Take a walk up to the meadow.
18	Fair. **I score timber, draw it to church**. Mrs. Castle & two daughters here. I take them to Tunis VanSlyck's. Bring Mrs. Scott's daughters back with me. I take Mrs. Castle to boat. I take company to Mr. Davis's. **I take Mrs. Selkirk & Wife to Catholic church**, then holme. Mr. Trego, daughter & Cate Hotaling here. I borrow 180 dollars of Cate. All take tea here. Lib Hotaling, Mrs. Doct. Mosher here.
19	Rainy. I work at swing gate. Go to river. I take up my 100 dollars note of N.H. Johnson held against me. I pay Will Searles $4.50 for road scraper, turn it with Johnson. Mother here. I and Levi go after berries.
20	Fair day, heavy shower last night. Wife takes Beecher's horse and go with Hotaling girls to Bethlehem. I make swing gate. Widow Thurston here.
21	Fair. I draw stone, lay walk. Two of Rev. Mr. Pelt's sisters here. Eliza Hull here. Miss Bailey here. Cranston's come in my field.

22 Fair. I draw timber and get Blackberries – get 8 quarts.

23 Rainy. Doctor & Marite come here. I get 60 dollars of B. Teneyck for cemetery lots. I and Doctor go in swimming. Dutchman pay me two dollars.

24 Fair. I go to Meeting. Then I and Doctor go to cemetery. Then to Mrs. Hotaling's, see Miss Carson and other company. Jerimiah Springstead & Jonas Bronk here. We have Lemonade. He brings me Oliver's compass.

25 Shower in afternoon. Wife, Marite & Mrs. Thurston go to Doctor Fredenburgh's **I lay foundation for smoke house**. Draw lumber, three load for A. Teal, one for myself. I draw 1 load of wood.

26 Cloudy, rainy. I get compass fixed – pay 50 cts. I, Doctor & Levi go a fishing. Cate Hotaling & Miss Carson here. Gerry call here.

27 Rainy. **I draw 1 load stone, 1 load sand. 400 hard brick, 500 pale [brick] of Seaburgh**. Lib Hotaling, Cate Hotaling, Miss Carson here.

28 Cloudy. **I draw two loads of stone to Church**. I take Mrs. Thurston, Wife, Cate Hotaling & Miss Carson to Coxsackie, then to A.G. VanSlyck's to tea. Call to Martin VanBergen's then holme.   Mr. Colbon & Lady Mrs. Nichols & Elida VanSlyck call here today.

29 Fair. I draw two loads of stone. Mr. & Mrs. Colborn, Mr. Nichols, Elida VanSlyck, Cate Fredenburgh, Cate Hotaling, Mr. Selkirk & Miss Carson here.

30 Fair. **I draw water for church**. Get horses shod. Attend sale of land of Richard Lawton Estate. I take Miss Maxwell & Miss Wheeler to Leonard Witbeck's, then to Stephensville, then holme. Wife, Marite & Doctor go to Widow Hotaling's visiting. **Timothy Clancy pay me 12.87 dollars on Catholic Church.**

31 Fair, hot. Doctor & Marite here. Doctor & myself go to Meeting, then to cemetery. Then I go in swimming.

August 1853

1 Somewhat rainy. I go to Albany with horse & waggon. I take 150 dollars to Samuel Johnson, get his check. I take cars go to Little Falls. I go to see Mr. Waterman. I see Warner, I gave him check for Mr. Legg of 100 dollars. I let Warner have 30 dollars, I buy his potatoes, oats. Then start for holme. Get to Albany at 7 o'clock. I then call on Mr. Buss, he takes S. Johnson 150-dollar check. Pays me the cash I rectify the mistake S. Johnson made in giving the check. Then I take horse & waggon, get holme ½ past 10:00 o'clock. Doctor & Marite take my horse & waggon; go Coxsackie.

2 Fair. I draw up 100 pale brick, 2 bunches lath. Get 1 barrel of flour sent by G.M. Lawton. Lucy Johnson come here. Doctor & Marite come back. Jacob Sickler call here.

3 Fair. I lay around. Doctor leave for New York. **I pay John Ham's bill of George W. Dorman insurance of Catholic Church $14.15**. Go after berries.

4 Little showry. **I draw 1 Bbl. lime & little sand to Catholic Church**. I draw two loads of sand holme. Mr. Charles Buf's two children & Irish girl here. We all take a ride to Pictaway.

5 Fair. I get 20 dollars each of Hull and VanDerzee for cemetery lots. I go to Greenville to A. Fancher's. Stay all night.

6	Rainy & misty. I go to Greenville Village. Meet the assessors, swear off my Peson property. Come back to A. Fancher's, then to Ebenezer Finch's, get pears, then come holme. Anthony & Levi go along. Anthony gets stung with hornets. Mr. Allen & Lady, Barent VanSlyck & Lady, Martin VanSlyck and Elida and two more here besides Mrs. Buss, Mrs. Hays and their nurse & children here.
7	Fair. Martin & Elida leave. Mr. Buss & Mrs. Hays, William Bagley here. Mr. Buss & Hays drive down here with horse & waggon.
8	Shower in afternoon. **I get mortar & stuff from Catholic Church. Levi gets his toe smashed by the horse's foot.** I take Marite, Mrs. Buss & Mrs. Hayes to Thomas Hotaling's for a ride.
9	Hot. I take Mother Hotaling to Coxsackie. Take dinner to A.T. VanSlyck's. He go with us to VanDyck's office on Andrew's affair. I and A.T. VanSlyck go to Landing, see Mr. Sharp.
10	Fair, hot. **I commence to take down cook [house]**[212] & go a fishing. John Sperl pay me three dollars.
11	Fair, hot. I take Mother Houghtaling & Marite to Trego's. I take Mrs. Hays to New Baltimore. **Work at Cook House**. Henry B. Wilsey work at cook house and board here.
12	Fair. I go with Jacob Sickler after posts & polls for District Road. I pay Peter VanBuren's bill against Dist. Road 17.34 dollars and I pay Isaac Witbeck 3.13 dollars. **Mr. Stebbens here from Norway.**[213] Mrs. Hays & Mrs. VanEpps here from Baltimore.
13	Hot and a shower. I take Mother Hotaling to A.T. VanSlyck's then I go to Coxsackie. Then I and he goes to Coxsackie on Andrew's business. I then take Andrew Hotaling holme & come holme myself.
14	Fair, hot. **I attend dedication of Methodist Church & go in swimming**.
15	Fair. **I help Henry Wilsey at smoke house & go and meet the Catholics**. Widow Hotaling & daughter Cate, Mrs. Fredenburgh, Cate, Miss Overbaugh, Mrs. Johnson, Mrs. Niles, Mr. & Mrs. Trego, Martin Andrews, Mrs. W. Blaisdell, Mrs. Jackson and a lot of boys here.
16	Fair, hot. **Catholics pay me 66 dollars. I put fasteners on the windows of Catholic Church**. Marite leave for New York.
17	Rainy morning. I saw wood. It clears off. I, Beecher & Ed Blaisdell go a fishing.
18	Rainy. I put up railing on Dist. Road. Wm. & Frederick Bagley & son here. Charles Buss here. I go to A.E. Willis's.
19	Fair, cool. Mr. Buss & family & girl leave. Mr. Bagleys all here pay. **I pay H.B. Wilsey 5.25 dollars on Catholic job**. Caroline VanAntwerp call here.
20	Fair. I work on Railing Dist. Road. The Bagley's leave. William Phips & sister Mary here. Wife, Levi and Anthony go to Albert Hotaling's.
21	Fair. I and all hands go to Meeting. **Mr. Willis's child died this morning 3 o'clock**. Wm. Bagley here, we walk down to cemetery.

---

[212] We don't know for certain, but this might refer to a summer kitchen that was separate from the main house.

[213] The village of Norway is in Herkimer County.

22	Fair. I take Wm. Phelps & Wm. Bagley to Albany. Abram Teal go along, bring back my team. I go to Herkimer & to Little Falls, then back to Albany. Call to Charles Buss, we go to Hood & Tobey's and around. Then I go to Mr. Buss, stay all night.
23	Fair. **I go to see Mr. Hendrickson in jail, confined for poisoning his Wife**. Then to State Geological Room. Then to Charles Buss, take dinner, so holme. Wife & Mary Phelps go to New Baltimore. **Dutch Frederick's child died**.
24	Rainy. I go to river. **Charles Barrett's child died**. Four of Miss Pelts here. I and Beecher go to Stone Church Farm, get logs & load of wood.
25	Fair. Work at Cook house. **Jonathan McElroy's boy died**.[214] Beecher gets Jonas Bronk's bull. Beecher draw manure 1½ days with my team up to today. Acton Civill & Lady call here.
26	Fair. **Wilsey & Mull finish Smokehouse. I attend funeral of Jonathan McElroy's [son]**. I take Wife & children & Mary Phelps out riding to Willis's farm, get apples & plums.
27	Rainy. I take Wife, children & Miss Phelps to Excursion. We go to Hudson get caught in a shower. Attend cemetery meeting at night.
28	Fair. I take Wife, children & Mary Phelps to Martin VanBergen's. Go to Coxsackie, back again. Take tea to Andrew VanSlyck's.
29	Fair. Beecher take me to Albany. **I go to Herkimer with the cars**. Take dinner & supper to Railroad house. Stay all night at boarding house.
30	Fair. **Attend Lawsuit. Get beat**. Start for holme. Get to Albany, stay all night to Charles Buss.
31	Fair. I pay Wm. Headlam 25 dollars. I call on Henry VanBergen, then I come holme with P.J. Coffin. I go with Abram Witbeck, see John Raymond. Wife visit to Doct. W. Blaisdell.

September 1853

1	Fair. I work around the house. I pay Acton Civill the funds of cemetery 42.53 dollars. Go to cemetery with Wife, Mother Houghtaling, Aunt Catherine & Widow Charlotte.
2	Fair. I pick peaches. Go with Beecher to Island, get 11 bags of broom corn seed. Wife & folks go to John Rea's on a visit.
3	Shower at night. I draw wood. I pay Peter Ostrander 5 dollars. Aunt Catherine leave. Jacob and Gertrude Feeter come here. Cate VanAntwerp here. Tunis Wilsey pays me two dollars.
4	Fair, warm. Cate VanAntwerp here. I go to Meeting. I, Jacob and Gertrude Feeter go to cemetery, then to Wesley's, so holme. John Bushants' team here.
5	Fair, hot. John Silcox here. He brings lobster, sea bass. I and Jacob Feeter go out to Hollow. Jacob leave for New York. Mrs. Ephraim Bronk here. I take her to James Bronk's. Wife, John Silcox, Gertrude Feeter go along. I take Cate VanAntwerp to Jackson's. I pay Gregory for a quarter of land.
6	Rainy. Mrs. Theron Collins here. I & John Silcox go to the Island in the forenoon hunting. Go to dam in the afternoon. **Kill one shitepoke**[215] & one woodchuck. Get nicely wet.

---

[214] Jonathan McElroy was the master builder when Levi's barn was built 1878.
[215] A shitepoke is a bird of the heron family.

7	Rainy. I and John Silcox go hunting, get one woodchuck.
8	Fair. I take Wife, John Silcox, Miss Feeter to Albany. Miss Feeter leave for Fort Plain. I pay H.B. Wilsey 10 dollars.
9	Fair. I and John Silcox goes fishing. He leaves for New York.
10	Fair. Mrs. Ephram Bronk here. I take Wife, Mrs. T. Collins & Margarett to Widow John Bronk's. I go to Kimmey's Mill; stop to Abram Witbeck's.
11	Fair. I go to Meeting twice. Mrs. Trego & another Lady here. Harriet & Adaline Finch here. **I take a walk with John Rea to Catholic Church**.
12	Fair. I go to Kimmey's mill. Get slabs. Put them on Plank Road. Mrs. Ephraim Bronk & Edward Blaisdell here.
13	Rainy. I help Beecher draw manure. Mrs. Casper Witbeck here. I take Mother Hotaling to Flat Bush to Andrew Hotaling's. She has a young Daughter.
14	Rain. I underpin wood house. Plane pickets. Beecher help me.
15	Fair. I work on District Road. Put up railing. Wife go to Wesley's.
16	Lowry. **I go to Old Stone Church. Get posts**. Put up railing. Make affidavit of Island for Charles McAllester. Mother here. Mrs. Henry Wilsey pay me 14/. Mr. W.C. Robb pay me 3.12 dollars for lumber.
17	Heavy rain last night, clear today. I go to Meeting twice.
18	Fair. Work in swamp. Mrs. T. Collins, Mrs. Ephraim Bronk, George Fancher, Mary Jane Lawton here. I pick peaches & plums.
19	Rainy. I send off plums. M.J. Lawton here. N.H. Johnson pay me the old hay bill. I sign note to Bank with A.E. Willis for $500.
20	Fair. I & Beecher get broom corn seed. I have 20 bushels; Beecher has 60 bushels. I get a letter with Mr. Bashite's notes in it.
21	Fair. I work on road. Go after boards to sawmill. Mr. Bogardus here, Mary Lawton here.
22	Fair. **We go to Sunday School excursion. Stop opposite Coxsackie. Come back and have dance at Temperance Hall. Have a fine time**.
23	Shower. I go to Flat Bush. Take Andrew Houghtaling a basket of peaches. I go a hunting in forenoon. Mother here.
24	Fair. **I go to Catholic Meeting**. Mrs. Theron Collins, Mrs. E. Bronk here. Virginia Angevine and another Lady, Margarett & Edward Blaisdell here.
25	Mrs. George Chittenden, Daughter & Husband, Mr. Burdick and another Lady, Mrs. John Bronk, Mrs. Ephraim Bronk, Mrs. T. Collins, Mrs. William B. Hull & Child, Mary Jane Lawton here.
26	Cloudy, cold. I take Mrs. Ephraim Bronk, Mr. T. Collins out to C. Teneyck Huyck's. Draw a load of wood. Mary Jane Lawton here. Mr. Bower & Miss Slater married.
27	One day missed. **Salmon VanAntwerp's child died**.
28	Rainy. I go to Albany attend Temperance Convention. Mary Jane Lawton here.

29   Fair. **I attend funeral of S. VanAntwerp's child**. Mrs. Theron Collins & Mary Jane Lawton here. I send a basket of peaches to John Witbeck.

30   Fair. Go a hunting. Take Wife & Mrs. Ephraim Bronk to Peter Bronk's then to Baltis VanSlyck to Hawley's. I go to Andrew Hotaling's.

October 1853

1   Fair. I dig potatoes. Wife & Theron Collins go to Doctor Fredenburgh's to visit. Mrs. Ephraim Bronk here. I let John Rea have my horse to go after a load of pumpkins. George Sweet pay me $35 Dist. Road money.

2   Fair. I go to Meeting. Take children to Baltimore to Capt. Mull's and back to Wesley's, then holme. I pay H.B. Wilsey 5 dollars.

3   Fair, cold. I & John Rea work on Dist. Road. Mrs. Tunis Wilsey pay me two dollars. Mrs. Henry Wilsey pay me 2.50 dollars. Dutch Frederick's Wife pays me 3 dollars.

4   Fair. John Nichols bring Marite & Elida VanSlyck here. **I go to Schodack before breakfast**. Then back, then to Albany. **Get worsted picture, take it to County Fair.**[216] Then holme, then to Sons of Temperance.

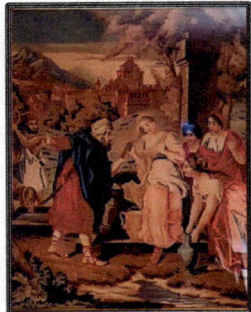

Rebecca at the Well

5   Fair. I take Wife & Elida & Marite to County Fair. Martin VanSlyck here.

6   Heavy wind. **I take all hands to County Fair. I take Marite to Albany; she takes Steamer Isaac Newton for N.Y.** Elida VanSlyck & Lawyer Carmen come holme with me.

7   Fair, cold. I go with Beecher to Flat Bush. He buy beef cow of Mr. Allen. I settle with S.M. Pelton. Mother Hotaling come holme.

8   Fair. **I go to Peter McGee's to Co. Convention. They make out two tickets. The Hunkers bolt the Convention.**

9   Fair. I go to Meeting. Hear Rev. Mr. Blake & Dr. Nott. Then to Dennis Tobin's. **The Catholics pay 69 dollars cash & 10 dollars to come from John Toben & 5 dollars from Dennis Toben.**

10   Fair. I work on Dist. Road. I pay A. Teal $ 60 dollars.

11   Fair. I draw wood all day. B.W. Warner here, Mother here.

---

216   Crewel work is a type of embroidery using fine wool. The word Crewel in the 1700's meant worsted. We believe that the embroidery of Rebecca at the Well is what Fletcher brought to the Fair.

12   Fair. I go with Jacob Sickles, get stone for Dist. Road. I let Warner have 20 dollars. I go to Mother's.

13   Fair. **I black stoves.**[217] Help Beecher draw in buckwheat.

14   Fair. I boil potatoes. **Fix smoke house.**[218] Pick apples.

15   Fair. **I clear away old smoke house**. Clean bricks and draw them away.

The New Smoke House

16   Fair. I go to Meeting. Take walk to cemetery.

17   Fair. I draw away bricks, 4 loads of wood. Andrew Mull here after hay. I go to Mother's. I pay P. Ostrander ten dollars.

18   Fair. I draw away mortar. I fix my trees in peach orchard. Draw wood.

19   Fair. I draw wood. Go to Flat Bush. Take Mother Hotaling and some buckwheat flour to Andrew Hotaling. S.M. Pelton pays me 80 dollars. Wife goes to Dominie Davis's.

20   Fair. I gave Wife 10 dollars. She & Levi go to Albany. I make fence. **Miss Hare buried here in cemetery today**.

21   Lowry. **I go to Old Stone Church Farm**. Wife & Levi come holme. I get $8.94 of Egbert Stanton for grapes. I get check of A.E. Willis $29.20.

22   Rainy. I and Wife go to Lansingburgh. Take tea to Mr. Hood. I leave mortgage at Albany. Stay all night to L.D. Eddy's.

23   Lowry. Go to Meeting, then go to Edward Swazy's, take tea. Then back to Eddy's. Stay all night.

24   Snow & rain all day, hard - 3 in snow at night. stay at Mr. Eddy's.

25   Clear & cold. Come holme. Stop at Albany, got a new coat.

26   Cloudy. I work around. Draw two loads broom corn chips. B.R. Wood speak in church on temperance. I attend.

27   Rainy. I help Beecher husk corn, cut wood.

28   Rainy, cold. I chop wood. Go to river & attend Singing School. I pay Beecher $11.04 plaster bill.

29   Fair. Baltis VanSlyck & Lady & child here. **Mr. Wm. Lawson died**.

30   Fair. We go to meeting. Take Wife, children to Mr. James Trego on a visit. All attend Singing School.

31   Fair day. **Phillip Collins come here**. I work around, go to Singing School.

November 1853

1   Fair. I work around. Have coat cut. Go to Baltimore. Phillip Collins go along. Come back here to tea. Amy Rea here.

---

[217]   To blacken a stove is to refurbish the exterior of the stove.

[218]   We believe the pictured smoke house is the one referred to by Fletcher. It is the one we remember growing up.

2   Fair. I go with Beecher to Flat Bush. I get my calf holme from P. VanBuren's field. Amy Rea here. I fill in brick to Mother's.

3   Fair. I fill in brick at Mother's all day. Phillip Collins & Aunt Sarah Ann VanBergen here.

4   Fair. I visit with Phillip Collins. I take Aunt Sarah Ann to Widow Charlotte's. Jerry Springstead, Henry & Mary here. We have an oyster supper.

5   Fair. I let Abram Teal have 5 dollars to pay out in Albany for me. George Fancher here. Edward Swazy & Jerry Springstead [here]. I and Wife go to Jerry Springstead's have an evening visit.

6   Fair. I go to Meeting. Edward Swazy here.

7   Fair, colder. I take Wife & Mother Hotaling to Thms. Hotaling's. Then go to Baltimore. **William W. Jostin's stove broke open last night**.

8   Snow all day. **Attend Election. Start for New York with Barge**.

9   Rainy. **Get to New York, go to Marite's, stay all night**.

10 Clears off. **I & Phillip Collins & Jeremiah Springsted go to Museum and the tower to see petrified horse & rider and up in the top of the tower. Then go to the Crystal Palace, stay until 9 o'clock at night. I then go to Marite's all night**.

11 Fair. We go to J. Silcox, take dinner. **Then to Barnum's Museum.**[219] Stay in the evening see the play Uncle Tom's Cabin. They have a great crowd and we get well squeezed.

12 Fair. **I, Wife, Jane Stanton, Caroline VanAntwerp, Miss Stanton go to Chrystal Palace stay till the evening. Stay all night to Marite's**.

13 Rain hard. **I go to Rev. Mr. Balch's Church. Then I, Wife & Levi go to J. Silcox in the afternoon. Then I & Silcox go to Rev. Mr. Chapin's Church in the evening.**[220] **Then to Taylor Saloon, get oysters**.

14 Clear, cold. **I, John Silcox & Gerry go to Anatomical Museum and then downtown. Then back to Silcox, take dinner. Then Silcox & Lady, I & Wife go to Buckley's Minstrels then to an oyster saloon. Then to Silcox, stay all night**.

15 Fair. **I and Phillip Collins go around York & Brooklyn and at night. I go to Miss Carson's take tea & play Whist. Then stay all night to Marite's**.

16 Fair. **I pay John Silcox clerk 5 dollars for hat & cap. Then I and Phillip Collins go around Brooklyn to see old Coeymans Boys J. McMichel & Stephen Hains. Then take Barge for holme**.

---

[219] P.T. Barnum's Museum opened in 1842. Its attractions made it a combination zoo, museum, lecture hall, wax museum, theater and freak show. The building burned to the ground in 1865 in one of the most spectacular fires the city has ever seen.

[220] Edwin Hubbel Chapin, born in 1814, was a well-known, preacher, orator and author. He was known for drawing crowds of almost 2000 people every Sunday at the Fourth Universalist Society in New York City, where he served for over 30 years.

17 Cloudy. Arrive at holme at 9 o'clock AM. John Sperl pay me 3 dollars for rent. I draw up Broom Corn chips.

18 Rainy, muddy. I help Beecher draw hay. Go to Singing School.

19 Fair. I work around. Get 30 dollars of John Cronk. Leave 262 dollars with A.E. Willis. I pay N.H. Johnson $200.07, take up my note given for $342.00. Phillip Collins here to tea. I spend the evening with him to Mrs. Clement's.

20 Lowry. I & Philip Collins go to G. Sweet's, take dinner. Come back here to tea. I go to Wesley's with him. Very dark & muddy.

21 Rainy. P. Collins leave for holme. **I make cook house door**.

22 Lowry. I saw wood, draw broom chips. Get Satisfaction piece of N.H. Johnson.

23 Lowry, warm. Beecher go to Herkimer Co. I send 28 dollars to B.W. Warner. I send check to Lantham Gray $91.76. I go to A. Witbeck's & to Nick Carhart's farm with Peter Seabridge. Very muddy going.

24 Fair, colder. **I attend Thanksgiving**. Fill in brick to Mother's. Wife and Mother Hotaling go to Mrs. James Lawton's. Rev. Mr. Blain pays me nine dollars on his rent.

25 Fair, very cold. **I help Peter Rea draw two loads of hay. I capsize and tumble off the waggon. Josiah Sherman pay me Island rent 50 dollars**.

26 Fair. I work around. Buy a pig of Pat Clancy for 5 dollars. John H. VanBenthuyzen here. Beecher get back from Herkimer.

27 Fair. I go to Meeting. John Henry go to Garret Hotaling's.

28 Cloudy, cold, S. wind. Henry here to dinner. He leave for Albany. I and Beecher kill our beefs. I get my pig holme. I pay off H.B. Wilsey in full $23.88. Peter Seabridge pay me Daniel Baker's rent 25 dollars. Mr. Morrison here.

29 Fair, south wind. I take Mother Hotaling to Andrew's. I go around her farm. Take dinner to Andrew. Go to Pelton's & to James Hawley's.

30 Lowry. I cut up my beef. Mr. Morrison leave. I go where Beecher is drawing wood to creek. I pay A. Teal $67.22 balance of account.

December 1853

1 Fair. Draw broom chips. Draw stone, make walk. **Attend wedding of Dewit Mull & Amy Rea and there is another wedding goes off to Rev. Mr. Davis today**.

2 Cloudy. I salt my beef. **Fix front gate**.[221]

3 Lowry. I draw stone, gravel, manure. I pay Ostrander off $18.91 balance of account. G. Sweet here to dinner.

4 Fair, cold day. I go to Meeting. TenEyck Bronk here.

5 Snowy, cold day. I go to John Raymond's. then to New Baltimore. I get my new coat. **I bring back Acton Holmes. He ran away.**

---

[221] We remember our father telling us that there used to be a gate at the end of the driveway. During our childhood all that was left of the gate were two large posts on either side.

6	Rainy. **I go to David Williams. Examine about Pelton's mortgage. Then to Coxsackie get, Constable. Go to Pelton's. Take mare and two cows and then gave them up there. Pelton go with [me] to C. VanDyck's and gave me mortgage for $442 on his personal property. I take it to David Williams to clerk's office then come holme at 10 o'clock at night.**
7	Fair. I saw wood. P. Rea go after my colt to Flat Bush. Mrs. Briggs, Clement & Mrs. Hotaling here.
8	Fair day. I make a halter. Wife go to Troy. **A man here to sell maps. Mrs. James Stephenson died today.** Wife go there at Lansingburgh.
9	Fair day, cold. I go to Albany after Wife. I missed her & come holme. **Andrew Sickler died today.**
10	Fair, cold. Wife come holme. Margarett & Euphema here visit.
11	Clear, cold day. Martin VanSlyck bring Mother Hotaling holme. **I attend Funeral of A. Sickler.**
12	Lowry. I kill hogs. Mrs. Phelps & Mrs. Pierce here.
13	Fair. I take Wife, Mother Hotaling, Mrs. Phelps, Mrs. Pierce to Baltimore. I draw two loads broom chips. George Fancher here get mortgage.
14	Fair. I take Wife, Mrs. Phelps, Mrs. Pierce to M. G. VanBergen's. Mr. Trego & Lady here.
15	Warm, cloudy. I salt my pork. Mr. Trego, Lady & children here all-day visit.
16	Fair. I & John Rea go to wood lot. I let Miss Bennet have my horse & waggon to go to Land Lakes. Lots of children here.
17	Rainy. **I take Wife & Mother to Andrew Hotaling's. She is crazy.**[222] I draw broom chips. Go to mill. Draw 1 load stone.
18	Showry, cold. I write 3 letters & go to Meeting.
19	Fair, cold. I get $62.10 of A.E. Willis. I let him have Mother Hotaling's note.
20	Fair, cold. Draw wood. Get horses shod. Draw broom chips. I pay off Wm. O'Lawton $5.62 manure bill.
21	Fair, cold. I draw posts. **Miss Serles here, work at cloaks. River closed today.**
22	Fair, south wind. Draw two loads wood. John Cronk here.
23	Snow & rainy. I saw wood, plane pickets. I get 25 dollars of N.H. Johnson. I pay Mrs. Rea 5 dollars I borrow of her a few days ago.
24	Very cold, NW wind. I and Beecher go to Albany, drive my team.
25	Fair, warmer. I go to Meeting. Take a walk. Rispan Hotaling call here.
26	Fair. I take Wife & Cate Hotaling to Thms. Hotaling's visit. Miss Serles here.
27	Fair, cold. I take Wife, Cate Hotaling, Miss Letles to Trego's visit. Have a party. Stay late at night. S.M. Pelton pay me 100 dollars.

---

[222] We assume this to be in reference to Andrew's wife as he shoots her later on.

28   Fair. **I skate to Schodack Depot. I then skate to John Bronk's take dinner there**. I pay A.E. Willis 70 dollars. Eben Finch here to tea. Horse stay all night. Miss Serles here. **Thomas Bronk & Miss Witbeck gets married this evening**.

29   Very cold, snow blows. I draw broom chips.

30   Snowy, cold. I pay Alfred Hotaling $5.25. I pay J. Hauenstien $4.92. I pay Wm. B. Hull 1 dollar. **Send for New York Times**.[223]

31   Fair. I work around. Beecher pays me 24 dollars straw bill. Mr. Kimmey brings Marite here. Martin & Elida VanSlyck, Cate VanBergen, we all go to Doct. Fredenburgh's. Have a party. Stay till after 12 o'clock at night.

January 1854

1   Snowy day. John H. VanBenthuyzen & Mr. Ball come here. **I take folks to Meeting with cutter.**

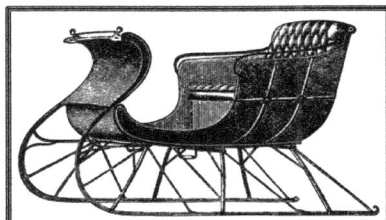

Horse-drawn cutter

2   Fair cold. **We all hands take three cutters go to Garett Hotaling's visit afternoon & evening**. Marite go to Ball Cedar Hill.

3   Fair, cold. J. Henry & Mrs. Ball leave here in morning. M. VanSlyck leave here in afternoon. Mr. Emerson & Lady here. Mother here. I pay my tax $58.71. I take Ladies to S of T in evening. I borrow 25 dollars of Doct. Blaisdell. Doct. VanAntwerp here.

4   Fair, SW. I & Willis go to Albany. He drives his horse & sley. I get 10 percent dividend $37.40 & 4 percent 12. **I attend Albany Agricultural Society**.

5   Fair south wind, warm. I cut & draw three cherry logs to Kimmey's mill. A.A. Hotaling, Lady & children here. Cate VanBergen back here. I draw 2 loads of broom chips.

6   Clear, cold. Doct. VanAntwerp take my team & take folks to Thomas Hotaling's. **Lewa, the Frenchman's Wife died.**

7   Fair, Cold NW wind. I get hand sley shod and ironed. **Have a party here. Betsey VerPlanck, Wm. VerPlanck. Cate Fredenburgh, Aaron Hotaling & Lady, Widow Hotaling, Elizabeth & Ackerman, John Rea & Lady, Doct. Frendenburgh & Jesper Smith, Harriet & Adaline Finch, Cate VanBergen, Elida VanSlyck, Doct. VanAntwerp & Lady here. Stay till 12 o'clock at night.**

8   Fair. I go to Meeting. Hear Rev. Mr. Blake. Folks go to Dutch Meeting.

9   Fair, cold. I take Doct. VanAntwerp & Marite, Cate VanBergen, Elida VanSlyck to Albany. I pay VanRensselaer $8.00. I pay Reuben Styles. I get codfish. Wife go to Aaron Hotaling on a visit.

11   Cloudy, south wind. I get horse shod & saw wood.

12   Rainy. I attend P.R. meeting. A.E. Willis pay me $6.50 P.R. bill. N.H. Johnson pay me balance of acct $37.32. I pay Doct. Blaisdell 25 dollars borrowed money. Wife go to Doct. Blaisdell's on a visit.

---

[223] The New York Times was first published in 1851.

13   Rainy day. I saw wood. Attend Rev. Mr. Blake's donation. **Kissam & Cate Hotaling and Miss Jarvis here, spend the evening.**

14   Fair. I take my saw to Willis's. Attend P.R. meeting. Willis pay me $3.75 Plank Road services. I work at my grain box.

15. Fair, cold. I attend P.R. meeting. Work at Grain Box. **David Dague stole a load of wood of me. Sherwood's team drawed it for him**.

16   Cloudy. Go to Meeting. We call on Widow Hotaling's and to A.E. Willis's.

17   Cloudy. Work around. I send tax to Collector in Herkimer of $10.30. I pay it to F. Cranston for Willis's check. Attend donation of Rev. Mr. Davis or Blake.

17[224]   Fair. I go to Coxsackie, take dinner to Andrew B. Hotaling. Go and see J.C. VanDyck, then to Newman Finch's, then to Silas Baldwin's, then to Andrew Fancher's. Stay all night.

18   Snowy day. George Fancher pay me $2.63. I get the rest of my rents, start for holme. **Stop to Medway, warm.**

19   Cloudy. Abram Witbeck & Lady here, take tea. He takes lease for Bushants' Farm; pays me 75 dollars cash. Mrs. Acton Civill & Daughter here. I go with A.E. Willis to look at brick yard lot.

20   Snow, rain, hail, all. I work at grain box. A. Jackson here.

21   Lowry. I go to mill draw 3 loads broom corn chips. I & Wife go to A. Civill's to a party have a very fine time.

22   Fair, very cold. I go to Meeting twice. Wesley here. I call to Mother's.

23   Very cold. I go to river. Mary Serles here, Willis, Mrs. Holmes and two others here.

24   Fair, very cold. I draw two loads of wood. Mother and Mary Serles here. I go to river. Attend Sons of Temperance.

25   Fair, N wind, very cold. I settle with H. McDonald. I pay him balance of $23.48. Rev. Mr. Blake & Lady to tea. He pay me some rent, making $20.00 in all he paid me. Mary Serles here.

26   Little more snow, warm south wind. H. McDonald [pay] me back error of six dollars of overpaid money that I paid him yesterday. I pay off Witbeck & Seabridge balance $3.56. I draw one load of wood. A.T. VanSlyck call here.

27   Fair. Black Tom work here. P. Seabridge call here. Wife & Mother Hotaling go to L.F. Cranston's. I & Wife go to Aaron Hotaling's to dance last night.

28   Clear, very cold. I, Wife & Peter Seabridge go to Albany. I pay of Davidson & Viele $12.25.

29   Fair, very cold. I go to Meeting. I call to Beecher's.

30   Cloudy, cold, SW. I draw broom chips. I let T. Penton have my horses to get him wood. I take Mother Hotaling's bond. I settle with A.E. Willis. Stormy & snowy night.

31   Fair, warm south wind. I chop wood all day. John Huyck here. I pay my Island tax. **Margarett Blaisdell here. She is taken holme sick. I take her holme with my sley**.

February 1854

1   Warm, south wind. I draw two loads of wood. John Cronk here.

---

224   There were 2 entries for the 17th.

2	Clear, cold at night. Harvy Hodge, Garret Hotaling & Wife & Elizabeth & Widow Charlotte & Hester & Mrs. James Lawton here.
3	Fair, 2 inches more snow. I cut wood, go to river. Lib Trego here. **Elizabeth Hotaling here dress making**. Mother Hotaling go to A.T. VanSlyck's.
4	Clear cold day. I draw saw logs & wood. Lib Hotaling here.
5	Snowy. I call to Mother's. Wife go to Meeting.
6	Fair, very cold. I draw 1 load of wood, two load broom chips. John Sperl pay me 3 dollars.
7	Fair south wind. I draw two load of wood. Edwin Hubbell & Lady & Almira VanBergen here. **Arrange $5 counterfeit bill**. Wm. Allen here. I pay Black Tom $1. Wife go to Willis's & to Rev. Mr. Davis's. Lib Hotaling here.
8	Snow & rain all day. **I and Wife attend oyster supper to brick house got up by Methodists, our bill 12/**. I send papers to A.H. Waterman.
9	Fair, thawy. I cut wood. Mrs. Thomas & Caroline Hotaling here. I draw two logs to sawmill. Wife go to Widow Hotaling's, see Lib.
10	Clear, cold. I draw two loads wood & 1 log to sawmill.
11	Fair, cold. I take Wife & Cate Fredenburgh to Mr. Colborn's. They are gone. Then we go to Baltis VanSlyck's.
12	Cloudy & cold. I go to Meeting in forenoon. Wife go in afternoon. A Negro here to see Dinah.
13	South wind, rainy. I and Peter Seabridge go to Albany. See about the Gedney affair. Get holme. Call to John Clement's and to Mother's & Widow Hotaling's.
14	Foggy, rainy. I & Willis go to toll gates then to Dean's Mills & to A. Garett's, see his colts. **Wife go to funeral of George Mead to Baltimore**. I chop wood.
15	Rainy Day. **I attend Election. Go to Rev. Mr. Davis's Donation. I get sick of smoking cigars**.
16	Lowry, N west wind. I draw logs.
17	Squally. I saw wood. Peter Ostrander here. Wife goes to Wesley's.
18	Clear, south wind. I cut wood, go to river. Pay Leonard Carhart $1.14. I pay Peter Rea $1.00. Doct. Fredenburgh here.
19	Clear, cold. I go to Meeting. Wife goes to Widow Hotaling & to S. Hains's.
20	Fair, cold. I am unwell. I go to **Croswell's paper mill**. I draw 2 loads of broom chips. Mother here.
21	Clear, cold N Wind. A.G. VanSlyck bring Mother Hotaling holme. John Cronk call here. I cut wood.
22	Fair, south wind. I saw wood, go to stone quiry. J.M. Witbeck pay me $4.35 balance due from G. Verplank. I go to Singing School.
23	Fair, N wind, coldest day in 5 years. I go to river. Get boots tapped. Mrs. J. Colvin, Fredenburgh, Niles, Johnson, Vanderzee, Stanton, Clement here visit.

24 Cloudy, cold SW. I go to papermill. Mr. Trego & Lady to tea. T. Penton here. I pay Mr. Deloith Mull one dollar.

25 Cloudy, cold. I, Wife & Cate Hotaling go to M.G. VanBergen's then to Rev. P. Pelts. **Peter Holbrook & Ann Reynolds get married**.

26 Snow & rain. Stay all day & all night VanSlyck's. Had a good visit.

27 Fair, N wind. Plane pickets. Go to river. Give P. Ostrander a (?) loan.

28 Fair, south wind. I go to Albany; bring Anna McKee. I pay off Dina Root $14.28. S.M. Pelton & B. VanSlyck here.

March 1854

1 Fair. I and Peter Rea draw 6 logs to Kimmey's & to Dean's Mill. **I go down the Colakill Road capsize over & over twice; don't get hurt at all**. B. Walsom help me up.

2 Warm. Draw 9 logs to mill. P. Rea help. S. Harris & Lady here. Lib Hotaling here. **Bob Cutler marries Widow Armstrong yesterday**. I draw 3 loads broom chips & I go to Singing School.

3 Great thaw, rain. Wife & Levi go to Seth Hawley's visit to William Allen's.

4 Fair warm thawy day. I walk around. Children go to Willis's to party. I go in the evening. Thomas & Cate Hotaling call here.

5 Fair. Uncle Thomas Hotaling & S. VanSlyck came here stay all night. I go to Meeting.

6 Fair. I and Thomas Hotaling go to cemetery & to river. Thomas leave. Wife go to see Cate Hotaling & Miss Bennett.

7 Fair, south wind. I draw two logs to mill and 19 boards holme. Attend temperance lecture in Division Room. Lib Hotaling here.

8 Rainy day. I work at swing gates. Go to river. **Lib Hotaling here. Jonathan Muckelroy** pay me 32.50 dollars Hall rent.

9 Rainy afternoon. I work at gates. Lib Hotaling here. Wife pay her off.

10 Rainy. I work at gates, go to river. Very muddy. Go to Singing School.

11 Rainy. I go to woods with Beecher then to G. Sweet then holme. I and Wife go to Miss Bennett's. They are gone, then holme.

12 Very fine warm day. I go to Meeting. Then take a walk. **River broke up today, ice go away very easy**.

13 Fair. Beecher start for Illinois. I send 28 dollars with him; pay off G.H. Lawton. I attend concert.

14 Fair forenoon, rainy afternoon. John Bushants pay me $154.00. I pay Wm. B. Hull's bill 26 dollars. Work around the house.

15 Fair. I go to woods cut, saw logs. Then to G. Sweet's. then holme. **P.G. Coffin Steamer go up today**. Children all go to concert at Hollow.

16 Fair. Wilsey's girls all here. Mother here. I get certificate of deposit from Henry Miller 150 dollars. I let Willis have it and 100 more making 250 dollars in all. I and John Toben work in stone quiry

17	Fair. I & John Toben work in quiry. Break my drill.
18	Very heavy NW wind. **Willis had two barns blown down. The heaviest wind I ever knew. Fences, trees, buildings and houses unroofed. Great damage done**. Wife go to Egbert Stanton's visit. Let Willis have 70 dollars, C.C. Bedell's check.
19	Clear cold, NW. I go to Meeting. **John Zeigler & brother here. We take a walk**.
20	Very cold, NW. I go to Flat Bush & to the river.
21	Cold, NW. I take Wife & Mother Hotaling to Gerry Springstead's. I go to Sweet's. Frendenburgh, Jones, Mary & Margarett Hotaling here on a visit, take teas, spend evening.
22	Cold N wind. I & Wilsey draw 12 loads of stone.
23	Snowy. I and Tunis Wilsey cut & draw wood. I take A.E. Willis 194 lbs. Buckwheat Flour.
24	Cold., NW. I and Wilsey cut & draw logs. I go to river.
25	Very cold for last 8 days. I work around. Wm. Tuttle here. Go to river.
26	Very cold Squally day. I go to Meeting & to Widow Hotaling's in eve.
27	Clear, cold. I call to Wm. O. Lawton's & to Widow Hotaling's. Not well.
29	Fair, little milder. I draw broom chips. Take 1 log, bring back lumber. I break axletree. Mother here, Mr. Spencer call here.
30	South wind, cold, squally. Mrs. Harris here visit. Tunis Wilsey here, draw stone all day. Beecher come holme from Illinois.
31	Cloudy & misty. I and Wife go to Flat Bush to M.G. VanBergen, visit. I go to Coxsackie.

April 1854

1	Rainy. I & Beecher go to Flat Bush. He get my mortgage property, bull's waggon. I notify H. Bronk about Tina fence trespass. I and Jacob Sickler go to G.T. Sweet's to settle road account with him. Oliver & Henry Springstead call here. I put up notice to sell bulls.
2	Fair, very cold. I go to Meeting; hear Rev. Mr. Blake.
3	Fair. I attend election of District Road. R. Pulver elected. I pay Sickles balance in my hands of road money. Finch Girls pay me balance of rent money $7.61.
4	Cloudy, south wind. Henry Witbeck here. Mr. Morrison here. I take Mother Hotaling to T. Hotaling. I pay P. Clancy $10.00 for his sow. I go to Bushants' place get 1 load of chips.
5	Fair, SW. I take Mr. Morrison to Coxsackie, then to Greenville. Stop at Newman Finch's, to Baldwin's, then to Williamson's. Get leather of Baldwin. Then to A. Fancher's. I borrow 100 dollars of G. Fancher; gave him my note.
6	Fair, warm. I go to Place's Sawmill then to Story's, then to J.W. Story's, then to J.B. Waldron's, see him about my account. Then to Reynolds Edget, he pays his rent $13.12. Then to Williamson's, I pay him for Baldwin Leather 18/6. Then see J.B. Waldron, I pay him 10 dollars, then to Baldwin's get my boots, then holme. Mary Holmes here.
7	Fair, cold N. Wind. Wife & Mary Holmes go to Cate Lawton's. I go to Gerry Springstead's & to G.T. Sweets. I pay to S.F. Cranston 75 dollars for Willis. Mary Blaisdell here.

8	Fair, cold SW wind. **I and Oliver Springstead & Henry & Mr. E. Holmes go to survey Stone Church Farm. I sell bulls & waggon mortgage property I took of Mr. Pelton.**
9	Fair day. **I and John Rea go to Catholic Meeting. Timothy Clancy pays me 30 dollars.** I go to Dutch Meeting & to Willis's & to Mother's. Beecher has my horse.
10	Cloudy, rainy, SW. **I and O. Springstead & P. Rea go to survey Flat Bush Farm. Get wet. G.T. Sweet move there today.**
11	Fair, cold N Wind. I see Willis. Send Waterman 10 dollars. I and Wesley go to Town Meeting. Wm. Tuttle pay me 6.10 dollars Dist. Road money.
12	Fine still day. Wife &Levi go to Albany. Mother here. I make a lettuce bed. Cate Hotaling here. Isaac Baker here.
13	Fair, cold NW. I pay B. Teneyck Law bill $1.40. I draw wood and chips. Wife & Levi come back from Albany. Mother Hotaling go with Thomas Hotaling to Flat Bush.
14	I, Tunis Wilsey, P. Rea, Beecher go to Stone Church, draw stone all day. Mrs. Hotaling & Mrs. Platt here Mrs. Silcox, Cate Frendenburgh, Miss Groat & another lady here. I paid P. Jackson 6/.
15	Snow 8 inches deep. I go to river twice. K.H. Mosher pay me 12/. **Andrew Teneyck died**.
16	Cloudy, NW. I go to Meeting, then read the rest of the day.
17	Snow & Blow all day - 8 in. I go to river. **Am subpoenaed by Niles to go to Herkimer.** I have a lame arm. **Mrs. Haydock died**.
18	Fair, thawy. **I attend funeral of Andrew TenEyck.** I draw 2 loads of broom chips.
19	Fair, thawy. I work around and go to river. **Henry Carhart buried today**.
20	Fair. I go to Hugh Crumb look for cow. **I attend funeral of Mrs. Haydock.** Willis's horses act bad. Mother & Harriet here to tea.
21	Fair. **I take team, take Oliver & Henry Springstead to Flat Bush. Finish to run out that farm.** Then go to Greenville, stay to Fancher's.
22	Rainy, SW. We run out Fancher's Farm through the rain, get very wet & cold. **Start for holme 5 o'clock pm. Have a bad dark time. Oliver has to walk and pilot me down Coonly Hill with a white flag. Get holme at 11 o'clock at night.**
23	Fair, wind NW. I go to Meeting twice. H**ear Blake & Davis funeral sermon of Mr. Palmeter. He buried in cemetery.**
24	Fair day. I am unwell. **I go to Stone Church place & to river.** Get horse shod.
25	Fair, still day. I go to J. Lisk Vendue & to Flat Bush. Elizabeth & Caroline Hotaling here on visit.
26	Fair. I let Beecher have my horses all day. I put my calf in field. I get out posts for flowers. **Jerry Springstead & Jane Bronk get married.**
27	Snowy & Rainy. **I work at flower beds.** Have T. Wilsey ½ day. Go to Springstead's after Oliver. **Get a glass of wedding wine**.
28	Rainy, cold day. I go to river. Oliver Springstead here. Go to Singing School - no attendance.

29   **Rainy day, great flood**. I take Jacob Sickles & R. Pulver to Aquetuck Hollow. I get $2.00 of A.E. Willis. Get 50 clams. Call to Mother's.

30   Rainy & misty. I go to Meeting. **Very high water over docks and islands & it is in Willis's stone cellar.**

May 1854

1   Fair. **Lot of logs come down the river. I & Beecher go to Albany, go to Herkimer & come back to Albany the same eve.**

2   Fair. Walk to Millbank's, take breakfast. Take his horse, I come holme after statement of lumber of Willis. Go back to Herkimer.

3   Rainy. I walk around Herkimer. Go to John Feeter's, Little Falls, stay all night.

4   Fair. **I go to Mohawk. Go down the [Erie] Canal on a boat to Herkimer**. Then to John Feeter's Little Falls stay all night.

5   Fair. **I go to Herkimer. Attend lawsuit**. Stay there all night at Railroad House.

6   Fair. **I attend lawsuit. Then go to Rome & to Camden, then Richland Depot, then stage to Pulaski, then to Mr. John Tubbs', whose Wife is Elizabeth Uttes, stay all night. They are very glad to see me**.

7   Very cold, NW. **Ice ½ an inch thick. I & Mr. Tubbs go to see Jacob Rupel & Aunt Suzan. She glad to see me, take dinner. Then go back to Mr. Tubbs' to tea. Mr. Robbins, the husband of Nancy Maria Uttes, take me to his house to Pulaski. I stay all night. Peter Seabridge & Charlotte Hotaling get married**.

8   Fair. **Maria Robbins did not know me last evening. I had a pleasant visit. I and Robbins call on Mrs. Matteson, once Betsey Hazzard, and then Mr. Robbins take me to Depot to Richland. Take cars for Watertown, get there 11 o'clock. Call on Mr. Hemek (sp) and his Lady, once Catherine Pierce, go around with me. Take dinner, stay until 5 o'clock PM. Then take stage to Ogdensburg, ride all night. Go through Gouverneur. Go through Bangor. Get to Ogdensburg 8 o'clock morning.**

9   Fair. **Go to Potsdam with Railroad. See T.H. VanBenthuyzen. Go around Potsdam and vicinity. Stay all night to American Hotel. Look at sawmills. Ride with John all day. Fine place; I am much pleased.**

10   Fair. **Take railroad to Rouse Point. Take steamer Canada for Whitehall. Get in fog; lay still all night.** Some rainy.

11   Fair. **Get to Whitehall take cars to Saratoga. Stop two hours. Get to Albany, stay all night to Charles Buss.**

12   Fair. **Come holme on P.G. Coffin**. All well. Am glad to get back.

13   Fair. I work at flower beds, plow garden. Andrew Fancher & George Fancher here. A. Fancher pay me 204.88 dollars. George pay me 44 dollars. Mrs. Jemima Hotaling here. Dutch John come here. I pay A.E. Willis 523 dollars in checks, money & I get one shad.

14   Fair. Go to Meeting. Take a walk. Call on John Rea.

15   Fair. Mother Hotaling & Marite come back from Flat Bush. **Mr. Crandle here whitewashing**. I and Dutchman make fence.

16	Fair, warm. I make fence all day. I pay H.B. Wilsey 1 dollar.
17	Showry, SW. Mr. Crandle here. I pay him 4 dollars & Wife 5 dollars. I plow and plant garden. Mother here, L. Hathaway here. Beecher plow Dominie's garden.
18	Rainy. **I get 17 eggs of Lawson, set them.**[225] Work around.
19	Fair, south wind. Make fence all day. Wife & Marite go to Doct. Fredenburgh visit.
20	Fair. Hang swing gate. Make garden. Beecher has my horse. I turn my horses in pasture.
21	Morning fair, showers at noon. I go to Meeting twice, then go to cemetery. Aceman Hotaling here. We call at Peter Lawson's.
22	Fair, cool. I and Wesley go to Island. Tobias Crumb & Henry Orchard buy my bull for 30 dollars. Mrs. Skinner, Mrs. Hull, Mrs. Andrews here. Mr. Bushants after my colt. Rev. Mr. Blake pay me 12 dollars balance of his house rent.
23	Fair. I & Joe go to Stone Church [Farm], cut posts. Cate Hotaling here. I go to river. Beecher has my team. **I get my hair cut**. I hang swing gate.
24	Fair. Make fence ½ day. I take Mother Hotaling to Flat Bush. Attend lecture this evening. Cate Hotaling here.
25	Rainy day. I get hinges made. Work around the house.
26	Fair. **Eclipse today**. I help Beecher plant corn. Joe help here. John Sperl pay me 3 dollars.
27	Fair. I draw two loads of old plank from road to Stone Church. I, Wife, Mother Hotaling, Marite & Anthony go to Trego holme. A pleasant visit.
28	Fair. I go to Meeting twice. Martin & Elida VanSlyck and Cate VanAntwerp here. Cate Fredenburgh call, Mrs. Rea call.
29	Fair. I & Joe make fence to Stone Church [Farm]. Then go to Tony Teneyck's buy a cow & calf pay $37.50; bring them holme.
30	Fair. Make fence. Wife & Marite go to Albany. Wife has 60 dollars of money paid by Marite for fence. Mother here. Tobias Crumb & Henry Orchard pays me 30 dollars for my bull. Josiah Sherman pay me 24 dollars room rent.
31	Fair. I get log slabs from mill. Make fence. Wife & Marite go to Mrs. Hotaling's.

June 1854

1	Fair. **I, Wife, Mother Hotaling & Marite, go to Henry VanBergen's Weden; he marries Phoebe Botsford**. We take tea to A.T. VanSlyck's. Let Mother Hotaling have 5 dollars for Andrew.
2	Fair. I make fence to Old Church [Farm]. I work hard. Caroline Hotaling, Caroline VanAntwerp. Mrs. Fredenburgh & Cate & Jemima Hotaling here.
3	Fair. I make fence. N.H. Johnson pay me $91.01 balance on hay. Mr. Joslin pay me 1.52 for calf. Kate & Almira VanBergen here. Rev. Mr. Davis & John Rea call here.
4	Fair, SW. Go to Meeting twice. I, Wife, Marite & Children take a ride out to Woolsey Cary's.

---

[225] Presumably Lawson had determined that these eggs were fertilized. Fertilized eggs are then kept warm by setting them under a brood hen until they are hatched.

5	Fair, hot. Draw gravel all day. I go to Barren Island get fish. Mrs. A.E. Willis here. I let my room to Frenchman for 2 dollars per month.
6	Fair, warm S wind. I & Joe draw stone & lay wall all day. **Marite leave for New York with propeller.**[226]
7	Fair, showry. After I go to Kimmey's Mill, take a load of logs & bring back a load of boards. Then go to Hotaling's Mill after boards. I let A. E. Willis have one hundred dollars per S.F. Cranston.
8	Little misty in afternoon. I let Mother Hotaling have 25 dollars. She leave for New York. I draw one load of lumber from Hotaling's Mill. Start up a log from the river here. P. Holbrook call here.
9	Misty. I go on the hill to Stone Church Farm. I get pay of John for my calf $7.81. I pay W.M. Carroll $3 manure bill. I lend John Rea five dollars.
10	Little showry. I work around the [house]. Beecher has my team go to Baltimore; Wife goes along. I get my axe fixed.
11	Cloudy. **I attend funeral of R. Cutler's child**. Leonard Hathoway here to tea. I & he go to cemetery.
12	Fair. I & Beecher draw manure all day. Saul Pelts call here. Wife go to Doct. Fredenburgh's.
13	Fair, warm. I go to Kimmey's Mill get lumber. Take up 3 logs. Draw stone in the afternoon. Wife go to Peter Lawson's. Get horse shod, pay 2/6.
14	Fair. I & Joe go to Stone Church Farm, make gutters lead water for cows. Call on Dominie Macomber. Mother here.
15	Fair. I & Mother go to Flat Bush. Call to G.T. Sweet's. Then go to Greenville to Andrew Fancher's, stay all night.
16	I & Mother go with Fancher to Quarterly Meeting to Old Church Place. Find no meeting. Then go to Charles Seabridge's. I stay to dinner, then I go to Newman Finch's, then to Baldwin's. Then to A. Fancher's, stay all night. John Mull bring my shad & herring.
17	Fair, dry. I leave Fancher's. Call to J.W. Story's, then go to Charles Seabridge's. Get Mother, bring her to Hollow to Quarterly meeting. I bring 46 lbs. of wool from Fancher's. **Bring pidgeon along for Levi. Wife let it go and it flew away**.
18	Fair, warm. I and Wife go to Hollow to Meeting. Bring Mother holme. Mr. Trego here to tea. Miss Teneyck, Serles, Mrs. Johnson, Mr. Willis & Harriet call here. I call on John Rea.
19	Fair, dry. I go to Kimmey's Mill, take 5 logs, get joist. Go to mill, get feed. Help Beecher make fence.
20	Fair, hot, dry. I go to Albany; P. Rea go along. P. Seabridge come back. I get nails, pay 9 dollars for 200 lbs. Get bill goods of G.H. Lawton on credit amt 17 or 18 dollars. Mother here.

---

[226] Fletcher often talks about taking the 'propeller'. He is referring to a steam-powered boat driven by a propeller as opposed to side paddle wheels.

21	Fair. I & Wife go to Flat Bush. Take dinner to G. T. Sweet's. Coming back, stop to Gumey's, raining. Pay John Bronk 4.25 dollars for cutting Marite's posts. Then back to Garret Hotaling to tea, then holme.
22	Little showry or misty. I take 5 logs to Kimmey's Mill. Bring back a load of lumber. Then go to Dean's Mill, get a load of lumber. Wife & Mrs. A. Vanderzee go to W.C. Robb's. I bring them holme at night.
23	Fine rain last night, misty day. I work around the house.
24	Fair. I go to Kimmey's Mill. Take 4 logs, bring holme lumber. I let Beecher have a horse to go to Coxsackie. **I and children go to Hollow and to Isaac Lawson's. I stop to E. Hudson's then to Mr. Pelton's, then holme.** Ebenezer Finch here.
25	Fair, cool. Jacob Laigh pay me 3 dollars. I go to Meeting twice. Peter & Charles Seabridge call here. **MaComber tip over his waggon, hurt his Wife**. Eben Finch leave here.
26	Fair, SW. Peter Roberts & Andrew Hotaling here. I pay Roberts twelve and 9/100 dollars for drawing boards. Miss Serles here. I draw 1 load of logs to Kimmey's Mill. Bring holme boards. I sell my colt & 1000 ft of boards to Peter Seabridge for 85 dollars. Rev. MaComber here.
27	I draw stone, lay wall under building. Peter Seabridge pay me 85 dollars for boards & colt.
28	Fair. I & Joe go to N. Carhart farm, draw 1 load of wood.
29	Fair. Beecher has my team & Joe draw manure. Wm. Bagley & Suzan Hills come here. Mother here. We go to cemetery. Call to Lawson's.
30	Rainy, south wind. I take Wife, Bagley & Susan go to Charlotte Hotaling's. Then to Baltimore. Call to Widow Parson's. They then stop to Wesley's to dinner. Come here and come here to tea. Stay all night. I & Joe make fence for Stone Church [Farm].

July 1854

1	Fair. Sow buckwheat, shingle barn roof. Go to Nathan Cronk Farm, attend Vendue. Rebecca & Mary Pelts here. Mr. Bagley & Susan I take to MacGregor's. See the house. I and Susan take a ride up to Barent Mull's. **Mr. Wood marries Hennetta Holmes** today. I let Mr. Willis have sixty dollars. He sent David for it.
2	Fair. **I and Susan Hills go to Quaker meeting. Then back to Meeting here.** Take tea to Willis's. Wesley & Margaret call here.
3	Fair. **I take Levi, go to S.M. Pelton's after mortgaged horse & waggon. He refuses to let me take it. I then go to H.P. Miller's, Town Clerk. Then to Coxsackie, stop to A.B. Hotaling's to dinner. See lawyer VanDyck, then get officer Chase go and get mare & waggon. Take waggon to G.T. Sweet's. I get copy of mortgage. Bring mare holme. I pay Chase 1 dollar.** Wolsey Cary pays me 43 dollars interest money.
4	**Fair, hot. I take Wife, Anna & children, go to Barren Island. Attend celebration, then take a ride, then attend Sons of Temperance in eve. Then we have a dance in hall. Have a fine time and break up at 10 o'clock at night.**
5	Fair. **I take a load of logs to Kimmey's Mill, cut logs. Then take a ride, Wife go along, with mare to McGee's. Come back, S.M. Pelton meet me at my gate, take away my mare. Henry Harden help him. I call on Beecher, he did nothing.**

6   Fair. I take a door & swing gate, take Beecher go to Flat Bush. Take boards along. Fix barn & I put up gate. **Go to see Crandle about my Pelton affair. Order him to issue a summons against Pelton.**

7   Fair. I take a load of logs to Kimmey's Mill, bring back boards. I pay Anna 10 dollars. Wife go to Albany, then to Rev. Mr. Davis. Sylvester Hams call here.

8   Fair. I go a fishing. **Doct. Mosher put a red-hot iron in my tooth**.

9   Very hot. Mrs. Clement call here. **Levi sick. I call Doct Fredenburgh. I have a toothache**.

10 Fair. I go to Albany, take Wesley along. I buy bedstead & cot for 7 dollars. I pay off McDonald. Get waggon fixed. **Get teeth fixed, pay dentist 2 dollars and come holme. Great fire in Coxsackie**.[227]

11 Fair. **I and Joe make fence to Stone Church [Farm]**.

12 Fair. I lay stone under building in barnyard. Go to river.

13 Fair. I, Wife & Anthony go to Flat Bush, then to Uncle Andrew's to dinner. **Then to Coxsackie [to] see where the great fire was**. I buy nails, get 7 dollars interest money of G. Reed for Mrs. Rea. Then back to Martin G. VanBergen's, then get holme at 9 o'clock at night.

14 Misty. **I take J.M. Harris to Baltimore. Join issue in suit with S.M. Pelton**.

15 Fair. I go to mill, go a fishing. Joe draw dirt.

16 Fair. Go to Meeting, get asleep, come holme. Then go in swimming.

17 Fair, hot. I hang swing gate, make fence. Harriet Finch pays me $6.25 for rent. Joe draw manure.

18 Fair. I take John M. Harris, go to Flat Bush, then to H.P. Millen, get Mortgage. Then to Coxsackie, pay Mr. Hart my bill for nails $5.44. **Attend lawsuit between me & Pelton. Throw them out of court**. Take dinner to C. Bucy, pay him 7/, Then go to C. VanDyck's, the to P.H. Sylvester's, then to G.T. Sweet's leave money. Subpoena George for H. Hoag. I sell Marite's grass to T. Roberts for 50 dollars. He to pay by Jan 1, 1855.

19 Lay around. Fair, hot. **Rev. Mr. Finnegan pays me 80 dollars on last contract of Catholic Church**.[228] I go in swimming

20 Very hot. I lay around, go a fishing. Let Joe have one dollar.

Exterior of Catholic Church

21 Fair, NW, hot. I lay around. Joe dig ditch. Mary Serles here.

22 Fair. Anna go to Lansingburgh. I pay her 2 dollars. I take a log to Kimmey's Mill. Bring boards holme. I help Beecher fix barn. Joe dig ditch. Mother Hotaling come holme.

23 Little shower. I go to Meeting twice. Mother Hotaling pay me 22 dollars, one paid before. **L. Hathaway here; Jane Holmes blows him sky high**.

24 Fair. **I attend lawsuit with S.M. Pelton to New Baltimore**.

---

[227] A disastrous fire destroyed the entire business portion of the village. Forty building were consumed by flames reportedly seen as far away as Albany.

[228] Photos provided graciously by Joe Boehlke. According to "The History of St. Patrick's Church" the building measured 30 ft by 40 ft.

25	Fair. I & Joe go to Wesley's wood lot. Cut 5 logs. Get holme late.
26	Fair. I & Joe go to Flat Bush, peal timber. Anna come back.
27	Fair. **I and John Harris go to Coxsackie, attend lawsuit of Pelton's. Join Issue in one; threw them out of court with the other.** We take tea to A.T. VanSlyck's. Mrs. Hotaling here. **Mrs. Southwick died day before yesterday with cholera. Mrs. Parmentus family of 5 died yesterday & today.** I pay P. Kimmey $16.45 saw bill.
28	Fair Hot. I & Joe start out, logs for timber, draw holme one load of wood. Go without our dinner.
29	Little wet in the morning. **I, John Harris & Beecher go attend lawsuit of Pelton's.** I call on Tregos and to new house of Crandell's. I get 18 pineapples from the propeller.
30	Fair, hot. Go to Meeting, get asleep. Call on Cate Lawton. Call to Doct. Blaisdell & to Widow Hotaling's.

August 1854

1	Fair. **Attend lawsuit of S.M. Pelton's, get beat. Stay till one o'clock at night.** Joe leave here.
2	Fair, N wind heavy. A.B. Hotaling & Lady & Miss Lane here all day. I draw one load of wood. I walk around. Wife go to Doct Fredenburgh's. A.E. Wills send 10-dollar check to Waterman. I make hen house.
3	Fair day, warm. I take Wife, Mother Hotaling & Anthony to Garret Hotaling's visit. I go with S. Harris, look at my farm.
4	Rainy morning. I and John Harris go to Coxsackie. Attend Lawsuit. I pay him $5 to settle two suits at issue. Call to Andrew B. Hotaling's. Take tea to Martin G. VanBergen's.
5	Fair. I go a fishing. Mr. Spraker, Mrs. Spraker, Jane Mitchell, Cate Fredenburgh, Miss Ackerman, Miss Overbaugh, Cate Keller & Ackerman Hotaling, Wm. VerPlanck here, spend afternoon & evening. L. Hathaway here.
6	Fair. I go to sleep, go to Meeting. Go to Wesley's. Go in swimming.
7	Fair. I cut wood & attend party to Doct. Frendenburgh in evening.
8	Fair. I and John Rea take 3 logs to Kimmey's Mill. Fetch back a load of lumber.
9	Fair. **I start for Schroon Lake. Beecher take me to Albany. I send holme a ½ gallon of Brandy. I take cars go to Saratoga to Stuyvesant & Moreau. Then take stage to Glens Falls. Take dinner to Mr. Stemburgh's. Go about the place. Then take stage. Stop at halfway house, see Col. Whiting's monument & Bloody Pond.**[229] **Saw the rock on which he was killed. Then to Lake George. Stop at the Lake House, take a horse, then go to Warrensburg. Change stages, then to Chester, change again, then to Potterville, then to Schroon Lake. Stay all night to Abram VanBenthuyzen. Get there half past 10 at night.**
10	**I and A.B. VanBenthuyzen go to Crane Pond. Look over the property mill's premises. Then back to Schroon to Abram's. Then we attend a party to Col. Ireland's in evening**

---

[229] Col. Whiting was one of the men who fought in the French & Indian War Battle of Bloody Pond. Near Lake George, this battle took the lives of 200-300 men.

	on the Isle of Belle [Isola Bella] in Schroon lake. I dance with Miss Weathurhead, have a fine time. Return to Abram's, stay all night.
11	Fair, warm. **I and A.B. go a fishing.** I then go again in the afternoon. I see them have a boat race on the lake from the Isle of Belle to shore and back. Take tea to Abram's with a lot of company. Stay there until 3 in the morning. Take stage for holme.
12	Fair. **Come to Glens Falls.** I take breakfast to Chester. Take Dinner to Stemburgh's. Go to Fort Edward. Take cars to Saratoga. Have two fine showers, stay two hours then back to Albany with cars. I pay H. Niles 14/ for brandy. Come holme on foot.[230] Get holme 1 o'clock at night. Mr. Weed & Lady, John Silcox & Lady here. **My expense of journey about 8 dollars. Cate Lawton died today.**
13	Fair, warm. **Attend funeral of Cate Lawton.** Take folks out riding.
14	Fair. I take Mr. Weed & Lady to Schodack. Silcox and Marite go along. Come back and I & Levi & John go to Flowing Springs hunting. Put horse to Widow Charlotte's. Come back through New Baltimore.
15	Fair. **I put my bull on barge.** I & J. Silcox go to Mossy Hill. Willis send 12 dollars insurance money to Mohawk Mutual Insurance Company. Gerry Springstead here, Mother here.
16	Fair. I take a load of boards to Flat Bush. J. Silcox & Lady go to New York. Wife & Marite go to Wesley's. I let Gerry Springstead have ten dollars.
17	Fair, very dry. I draw logs & lumber to Kimmey's Mill. Beecher & Peter Rea help. I break my waggon.
18	Fair. **I, Anthony & Levi go to Greenville. Stay all night to A. Fancher's.**
19	Fair. I attend meeting of Assessors. Swear off my tax. Buy a piece of beef, get two pidgeons, two ducks and come holme
20	Fair, very dry. **I take a load up to Negro Camp Meeting at the Old Stone Church Place.** I attend Meeting in morning. Elida VanSlyck here.
21	Fair. I and Marite go to Albany, get dividend $15. **Get 20 lbs. rice, 10 lbs. cream tarter, 5 lbs. soda.** Take dinner to Saul Johnson's. G. Springstead call here. Mrs. Fairchild lecture on temperance.
22	Fair very dry. I cut bushes. **Draw 1 load of wood from Stone Church lot.**
23	Fair, dry. I take a load of lumber to Kimmey's. Draw one load of wood. **Folks go to Negro Meeting.**
24	Fair, very hot & dry. **I take Wife, Marite, Levi & Mary Hotaling, go to Martin VanBergen's to tea. Then go to A. VanSlyck's, then go to Spaulding's Circus, Coxsackie. Stay all night to A.T. VanSlyck's.**
25	Fair. We take breakfast & dinner to A.T. VanSlyck's then come holme.
26	Hot with fine showers. I cut wood, go to Mill, go in swimming. Mrs. Davis, Mrs. Willis & Miss Maxon here visit.
27	Cloudy & smoky. I go to Meeting twice. Gerry Springstead & Lady here to tea. I, Wife & Marite call at Mrs. Houghtaling's & Fredenburgh's.

---

[230] It is a long walk of about 14 miles from Albany to Coeymans.

28   Fair. **I go to Herkimer. Stop at Little Falls, then go up to Herkimer on a Canal boat. Stop at Spooner's Railroad House**.

29   Fair. Lay around, go to Little Falls to John Feeter's to tea & to breakfast.

30   Fair. Go to Herkimer, lay around all day. Stay all night.

31   Fair. Lay around Herkimer. Stay all night.

September 1854

1   Fair morning, rainy afternoon. **Come to Albany, stay all night at C.H. Debois Tavern.**

2   Lowry. **Come holme with [Steamer] Mazeppa.** A.B. VanBenthuyzen here since Tuesday.

3   Fair, hot & dry. I go to Meeting. G. Springstead call here.

4   Fair. I take A.B. VanBenthuyzen & Marite to Albany. P. Rea go along. I go to Herkimer, stay all night to Spooner's. [Law]suit was put over.

5   Fair. I came holme. See Doct. & Marite in Albany. I take dinner to Mr. Browning's, then I come holme.

6   Showry, hot. I draw two logs to Kimmey, making 15 in all. Go with P. Seabridge & Beecher on the hill. Measure wood. Adaline Finch leave my house to river, she pay me 4.57 dollars. She, Wilkins & young Story stay here all night. Put up their teams. Oliver Springstead here. **Richard Hotaling & Cate Drew were married today.**

7   Fair. Draw two loads of wood. Draw poles for Harris. Mr. Little here from Glens Falls, Mrs. W.B. Hull here.

8   Fair, NW in morning, south after. Martin G. VanBergen & Cate and Martin's little girl here. John Cronk here.

9   Rainy. **I & Gerry Springstead take boat to Albany, stage to Troy. Take dinner to Ed Swazy's, tea [to] L.D. Eddy's. Take cars to Moreau, stage to Glens Falls. Stop to Sternburgh's all night.**

10   Fair. **Take covered carriage go to J.J. Harris's. Take dinner to Queensbury then go with Mr. Harris & Mr. Ringsly to Trout Pavilion on Lake George. Take tea & stay all night.**

11   Fair. **Take boat and row to Shelving Rock on lake George to look at Lumber lot. Take breakfast then go into the timber; look about it. It was a bad look. Come back to house. Took dinner, then gave up the job for a bad one. Then come back to Trout Pavilion, took tea. Then walk back to J.J. Harris's. Stay all night, took breakfast.**

12   Fair. **Walk back to Glens Falls. Then come on to Saratoga. Stay all night with John Springstead. They have a fin there.**

13   Fair. **Come holme. Wife go to New York on Tuesday last.**

14   Rainy. Beecher has my team. He pays me 12/. I go to Mull's. I draw Civill 400 pickets. Get horse shod. I pay John Mull 6 dollars for fish. I pay Peter Rose 50 cents. **Then I go to McGee's, have a quarrel and come holme.**

15   Rainy. I draw two logs to Kimmey's Mill. Bring back lumber.

16   Fair. I draw two loads of wood. Wife & Almira VanBergen come back from New York. I get sot with a load of wood.

17   Fair. I go to Meeting, then to Willis's. **Then take Wife, Mother Hotaling & Mother to Bethlehem to Negro Camp Meeting**. Mr. Trego here to Dinner. He takes Almira VanBergen to Camp Meeting.

18   Fair. I and John Rea get broom corn seed. Beecher moved out today. T. Civill pays me 5 dollars for pickets U.B. Willis & Mary Serles here to tea. I help Harris pick apples.

20   Fair, cool. I & Harris pick apples all day. **I bring holme my cow from Stone Church Farm**. Mary Serles here and an Insurance Agent.

21   Fair. I and Beecher lay wall to Mother's ½ day. U.B. Willis & Lady, Mrs. John Colvin, Mrs. A.J. Colvin, Widow Colvin & two boys here. Mary Serles here.

22   Fair. I make fence to Mother's all day. U.B. Willis & Lady here. I buy McGee's pigs for 7 dollars. Mary Hotaling & Sister & Almira VanBergen here, Mary Jane Lawton, Miss Serles & Miss Andrews here. **I get 1 barrel of flour and 50 lbs. sugar**.

23   Fair. I go to Flat Bush, hang swing gate. Go to Andrew Hotaling's, bring back a load of logs & take them to P. Kimmey's. Levi & John Rea go along. Almira VanBergen here.

24   Fair. I go to Meeting twice. Almira VanBergen here, Ed VanArden here. Martin VanBergen & Lady, Henry VanBergen & Lady here. Wife to A. VanDerzee's. His Wife has a young daughter.

25   Fair. I buy Briggs' manure for 3 dollars. I let John Rea have my team. I help S. Harris burn fallow.

26   Fair. **I and Willis harness up horses, go to Albany Co. Fair**. Wife, (?), U.B. Willis & Lady go along. Wife stay. Rev. Mr. Pelts & Lady, Mr. Hubbell, A. Jackson call here. Mr. Dean brings back my map. Widow Mead & Tina Rea here.

27   Fair. **I take Harriet Willis to Albany, attend Fair all day. Come holme at night**. Mrs. Mead here.

28   Fair. **I go to Fair, take Levi along. Coming holme, I capsize and Wife in a stew. Marite & John Rodgers come here from New York. He brings his child here and bury her in cemetery**.

29   Fair. Lay around holme. Caroline VanAntwerp & Anna Overbaugh here. Patrick Clancy call here.

30   Fair. I and Anthony go to Abram Witbeck's. I go to Mr. Rarick's Vendue, then I come back to Witbeck's to dinner. Then I bring holme a load of wood. Wife & Marite visit A.E. Willis's.

October 1854

1   Rainy evening. I go to Meeting & to cemetery & to Willis's. Wife go along.

2   Fair. I & John Rea go to Flat Bush, get out logs, get holme late. U.B. Willis here. Frendenburgh people send girls here for dishes for Cate's wedding.

3   Rainy. I get horses shod.

4   Rainy. I and Tunis Wilsey make fence to Mother's. **Cate Frendenburgh & Frazer Spraker get married. Theron Collins come. Wesley's girls here. We attend wedding. Stay till 4**

	o'clock in morning. Mr. Vosburgh, Mr. Measic and another man and their Ladies stay here, take breakfast on the 5th. **Wedding was grand affair - best ever known in Coeymans. All passed off well.**
5	Fair, NW. I & Tunis Wilsey draw stone. We go to see Bride & Groom off. Temperance Lecture here. Elida and Martin VanSlyck here.
6	Fair. I go to Kimmey's Mill, take gutter sticks, bring back timber. Mrs. George Wolf, Mrs. H. Slingerland here. O. Springstead here, I pay him $20 for my maps. Mr. Andrews & James Trego call here. T. Collins here to tea. I & Tunis Wilsey take and lay foundation under my barn.
7	Fair. I draw timber & wood. Go to Bushants' farm, take P. Seabridge, measure wood amt. 110 cords 1 foot. Mother Hotaling go to Barent Hotaling with Steamer Mazeppa. Miss Andrews & Mrs. Maxon call here.
8	Fine day. U.B. Willis & Lady here to dinner & tea. I and Dinah go to John Raymond's place. I & Wife go to Willis's in evening.
9	Fair. I draw one load of muck. Go to Flat Bush. Get 5 sticks of timber. Lose two linchpins and reach bolts. Andrew Houghtaling, Wife & family here. I pay him 5 dollars on Marite's fencing.
10	Fair. I draw one load of muck. I & Tunis Wilsey go out the hill, get a load of rafters. Willis get boards here. Mr. Hakes get hurt, his horse ran away.
11	Fair. Mother Hotaling & Mrs. Garret Hotaling come back from B. Hotaling's. Widow Ryon & her Granddaughter here. I go to Kimmey's Mill, get gutter sticks. Raise my barn lintes. Draw 1 load muck, T. Wilsey help.
12	Warm. I & T. Wilsey go on hill, get 1 load of logs. I go to Kimmey's, get a load of boards. Mrs. Mead here. We call on Mr. & Mrs. Spraker, play whist.
13	Fair. I & Levi go to Flat Bush. Take boards, bring back Timber. Tunis Wilsey here to work. Widow Mead here.
14	Rainy. I help J. Sherwood around my barn. Attend Temperance meeting. J.H. VanBenthuyzen here. I get clams & Carolina potatoes. Widow Mead here.
15	Fair, heavy NW wind. John VB [VanBenthuyzen] here. I go to Meeting. Call on U.B. Willis & Lady at his Mother's.
16	Fair, cold. **Tunis Wilsey here, we work at carriage house foundation.** I pay Anna 5 dollars. Mother here, Mary Serles here.
17	Rainy. I and J. VanBenthuyzen go to Dean's Mill. Mrs. Gould & Mrs. White here.
18	Lowry & rainy. **I, Wife, Doct. Ben & Wife, D. Witbeck & Wife, Miss Overbaugh go to Albany, take dinner then take cars, go to Palatine Bridge[231] to Mr. Spraker's. Attend wedding. Party very large, have a very grand time, dance till 2 o'clock at night. Then I, David & Doctor go to Tavern, stay all night.** T. Wilsey work for me.
19	Fair. **We come holme in cars. They all see us off at the Railroad Station. Mr. Spraker has a fine house, live in great style. I buy in Albany a keg for put in grape wine.**

---

[231] Small town in Montgomery County, NY.

20	Fair. **I make bolster[232] to waggon. Work at my grape wine.** Edward Blaisdell & Leonard Hathaway here.
21	Fair, cold. T. Collins here. T. Wilsey work here. I and Theron [Collins] go to Dean's Mill. Call to Garret Hotaling. He stay here all night. I pay Harris my school tax.
22	Fair. Mother Hotaling & children go to Flat Bush. I send 3 dollars to Joe Witbeck. I go to Meeting. I go to Willis's. T. Collins leave here this morning.
23	Fair. I go to Albany, get a load of lumber. Mrs. Fredenburgh & Aunt Betsy, Widow Hotaling and lots of company here.
24	Fair. I work at hen house. Mr. Civill pay me back $3.54 cents school tax I paid him. **Theron Collins, Margarett & Uphema start for Illinois. I go to river and see them off**.
25	Fair. I work at hen house, get rafters. Stephen Hotaling & Miss Maxon here.
26	Fair. **Start for New York on Joslin's Barge. Get to Haverstraw Bay, get in the fog. L. Hathaway & Widow Mead get married today**.
27	Fair. **Go on to New York get in 6 o'clock PM. Saw a Balloon go up in Bays. Go to Doct. VanAntwerp's, stay all night**.
28	Fair. **Call to David VanAntwerp's. Call on Wm. Bagley. Buy carving knife & fork. Stay all night to Doctor's**.
29	Rainy morning. **Go to Balch's Church. Then to J.J. Silcox to tea. Then to Restaurant, then to Doct, stay all night**.
30	Rainy. **I go with Theophilus Civill around the city. Call on S. Pelts. He gave us some tobacco. Then back to Doctor's to dinner. Then I & Wife take steamer Commodore to Stonington, then to Boston by Railroad**.
31	Foggy & rainy. **Take coach to Eastern Depot. Then take cars for Amesbury.[233] Get to Frederick Bagley's. Then go around Village and to church in eve. Go to sleep**.

November 1854

1	Fair. **Get a letter from holme. Go to Ferry & to Meeting**.
2	Fair. **I and Frederick Bagley go to Ferry & to Cemetery, then to Nathan Gordon's, then to David Bagley's, then on Po Hill, then to Mr. Hills', then to D. Bagley's to tea, then to Lyceum**.
3	Cloudy forenoon, fair after. **I Wife & Suzan Hills go to Hampton Beach. Then to Exeter to John Goodwin's to Dinner. Then around the Village in factories & Iron works. Then back to tea to Goodwin's. There I view the Prsquataqua [Piscataqua?] River, Squam River. Put my horse to Squam House. We pass through Kensington, is a fine place, then we go back to F. Bagley's**.
4	Fair, very cold. **I, Wife and Mrs. F. Bagley go to Newburyport. I see Aunt Thomas. I miss my folks, walk half way holme, then stage overtook me, and I rode back to F.

---

232 A bolster is the bar placed over the axles of a wagon to support the body.
233 Fletcher's father (Levi) was born in Amesbury, MA. Miriam Bagley Blaisdell was Fletcher's grandmother.

	Bagley's. They keep Pope Day.[234] Burn Bonfire at night. Wife & Mrs. Bagley come on with Stage.
5	Fair, very cold. I go to Methodist Meeting, then to D. Bagley's. Then we go to Cemetery, then to Nathan Gordon's & to Levi Weight's, then to Mr. Standening's in eve, then to F. Bagley's, stay all night.
6	Fair, very cold. Lay around go on Po Hill then to George Hill's then holme to Frederick's. I then go to debating school and then to F. Bagley's.
7	Rainy. We start for holme. Susan Hills come along to Barton. Then we meet Mr. Cary & Lady. Then we go around Boston and take cars for New York 5 o'clock in the afternoon.
8	Fair. Arrive in New York at 6 am. Go to Doct. VanAntwerp. I go downtown see Mr. Wood. He spend afternoon with us. I go to ear Doctor; I pay him 5 dollars. Then I and Wife go to U.B. Willis's, spend the evening. Then back to Doctor's stay all night.
9	Fair. I go to Brooklyn to Wm. Bagley's. We go to Navy Yard then back to his house for dinner. Then to Doctor's, visit with Mr. Wood & Lady, then to Burton's Theater. Cate VanBergen go with us. Meet U.B. Willis & Lady.
10	I call on U.B. Willis & N. Stephens and to A. Civil's, then to Doct. VanAntwerp's. Then we take propeller holme. Cate VanAntwerp died.
11	Rainy. Get to Poughkeepsie, break down. Then get fixed, then run aground on Esopus Meadows. Mrs. Egbert Stanton had a young daughter yesterday.
12	Cloudy. Go on shore to Strattsburg Station. Take cars, stop to Bum (sp) dock. Cronk's boy brings us across holme and glad of it. Last night many vessels run aground and some sunk.
13	Foggy, warm. I work around the house. Aby Applebee & James Anders get married about this time. Mr. Wood & Lady, J.N. VanBenthuyzen & Mr. Ball here while we were gone.
14	Fair. I make swing gate, make fence. Wife & Mother Hotaling go Thomas Hotaling's. G.T. Sweet sends me two barrels of cider by his son. Walter & James Bronk they here to dinner. I help John Rea kill hogs.
15	Lowry, snowy. I make fence to Mother's & work around the house.
16	Cloudy, cold. I finish Mother's fence. Mrs. N.H. Johnson here. We get our things from Steamer T. Durant.
17	Cloudy. I & Dutch John go to Stone Church Place, get out logs. Get horse shod. Wife & Mother Hotaling go to W.B. Hull's, visit.
18	Fair. I draw six logs to Kimmey's Mill. Draw holme lumber. A.E. Willis call here.
19	Fair, cold N wind. I take a walk, go to church. Martin VanSlyck here. Mr. Willis & Lady, Aceman Hotaling call.
20	Fair. I draw one load of wood. Go after hair & lumber to Kimmey Mill. McGee work here.

---

[234] Pope Day is an anti-Catholic holiday celebrated on November 5th in colonial United States. It evolved from the British Guy Fawkes Night. Guy Fawkes was associated with a group of English Catholics who planned to assassinate Protestant King James I and blow-up Parliament. It was also known as colonial New England's version of Halloween.

21	Fair. I and Jonathan McElroy go to Flat Bush, put up gutters. McGee here to work.
22	Snowy day. I work around. Go to river. Get glass, go tell Mr. D. Baker about Ceary.
23	Fair, warm. I go to Dean's Mills, drive one of Harris' horses.
24	Cloudy, rainy. I draw up lumber from the dock. R. Gage bring it from Albany for me. I pay him 6 dollars. Bridget Hood & Miss Berman here. John Sperl pay me 3 dollars. McGee work here.
25	Rainy. I am unwell. McGee here. I and he draw two loads sand. Dutchman's Wife pay me $1.25.
26	Fair, colder. I go to Meeting. Wesley call here.
27	Fair, cool. I kill hogs & beef. McGee here. Wife go to Mrs. James Lawton's.
28	Fair. I cut up by hogs & beef. McGee here. P. Seabridge kill his hogs here today. **My well fails in water**.
29	Fair, cold. I go to Flat Bush with a load of boards. G.T. Sweet pays me 4 dollars for James Hazleton. I go to Dean's Mill get grist; I pay him $5.70. McGee here.
30	Fair, cold. I salt my pork. Bridget and children & Miss Berman leave. I pay James Hazleton 2 dollars. McGee here, work at my trees. **Wife and the rest attend Thanksgiving in the Methodist Church**.
31	One day missed in this month. I suppose I was at Albany.

December 1854

1	Fair, cold. McGee here. Wife & Mother Hotaling go a visiting. I work around the house.
2	Clear, cold. Wife go to Willis's. McGee here. I work around. Salt my beef.
3	Snow all day very cold. I go to Meeting. Propeller loads all day. Plenty of ice in the river.
4	Snow & blow all day. **Harris puts hay on Barge. Don't get it all on board**, very cold.
5	**Fair, cold, lots of snow. I break out road**. Go to river. Draw up broom corn chips.
6	Fair, south wind. I get horses shod. I sign two notes for Willis of $1,000.
7	Snowy, squally. I go to river. I fix hen house.
8	Very cold, NW wind. I and Hubberd Harris start at 9; go to Albany. **Get to Cedar Hill, have my Buffalo Robe stole by two boys. I put after them. Overtake them to Aaron Hotaling's. I get J.M. Harris take them to Bethlehem before Squire Leggett, try them. Send one of them to Albany Jail and other charge of squire and then come holme. Have a cold bad time, try them to Bushants' Hotel.**
9	Fair, cold. **I and Hubberd Harris go to Albany. I try all day to get my reward on the Boys & horse**.
10	Fair, cold. I go to church. I pay John Rea 12/ borrow by Anne.
11	Snowy. I draw one load of wood to Mother's. Abram Witbeck pay me ½ years rent $75 cash and acct. Mrs. L. Hathaway & daughter here. John Nichols here to dinner.

12	Fair, cold. I & Wife go to Albany. I pay Wm. Headlene $59.82, I pay VanRensselaer 5 dollars rent, I pay G.H. Lawton $22.80. I get chicken feed $5.13. **I get Piano for 5 dollars per quarter. I pay 5 dollars advance on it to Myer & Colyes.**
13	Snowy forenoon. I draw one load of wood to Mother's. Tunis Wilsey cut wood ½ day for Mother.
14	Fair. I and Tunis Wilsey draw two loads of wood to Mother. Wife go to Dominie Davis & Wesley's. **Margarett come holme from Illinois.**
15	Fair. Tunis Wilsey draw two loads of wood to Mother. I work around.
16	Fair. T. Wilsey draw two loads of wood to Mother. Miss Maxon here. I cut wood, go to river. I pay into Wesley $290.98 hay money for N.H. Johnson.
17	Fair, cold. I go to Meeting. L. Hathaway here. Wife go to Meeting twice.
18	Fair, very cold. John Clement take me to Albany, his Wife goes along. **I go to Herkimer. Witness in Willis & Richmond [law]suit.** Stay to Spooner's Railroad House.
19	Very cold. Lay around. **[Law]suit goes off. I am sworn.** Start for holme, get to Albany, stay to C.H. Dubois all night.
20	Fair, very cold. **Thermometer reading 19 degree below zero.** I came holme with Peter Shear. Mary Serles here.
21	Fair, cloudy afternoon. I lay around, go to river, cut wood. Mary Serles & Miss Maxon here. **Nelson Agan died.**
22	Snowy day. **Nelson Agan and J. Teal's child buried today.** Very cold. I work about the house and go to river.
23	Fair, very cold for past 8 days. I go to river. Frenchman Squaw pay me $1.50.
24	Fair, S wind. I and Wife go to Meeting. Then go to Thomas Hotaling's, spend afternoon.
25	Fair, south wind. I and Wife go to M.G. VanBergen's and call to A.G. VanSlyck. Bring Mother Hotaling holme. Mr. Spraker & Cate call here. We call to Doc. Fredenburgh's.
26	Fair, warm. Work around. Help John Clement ½ day in quiry.
27	Rainy. I work around, go to river. Almira VanBergen here.
28	South wind, foggy. **I and Tunis Wilsey go to Flat Bush, saw & get out logs. Mr. Willis & Lady, Doct. Fredenburgh & Lady, Mr. Spraker & Lady Ackerman & Lib Hotaling, Caroline VanAntwerp, Martin & Elida VanSlyck, Cate & Almira VanBergen here. Have a very nice party - enjoy it much. Caroline & Lizabeth Hotaling here, have a fine time. Have Colored Waiters.**
29	Clear, cold. Some company here yet. Ed VanOrden here, I take Lib & Caroline Hotaling holme. Get horse shod. Attend a party to Widow Hotaling's this evening.
30	Clear and very cold. Martin & Elida VanSlyck & Cate VanBergen leave for holme. I get 12 bags of broom corn seed of Albert Jackson. Work around, go to papermill.
31	Fair, very cold. I call to S. Harris's. Andrew A. Hotaling & Cornelius here to dinner. I go to Meeting.

January 1855

1. Fair, cold. I draw two loads of wood. I kill 8 turkeys. Henry VanSlyck come here, take Almira holme. Tunis Roberts call here.
2. Fair, south wind. I draw two loads of wood. John Cronk here & son. I pay Cronk 21 dollars interest money. Caroline Hotaling here. She & Wife go to river.
3. Fair, warm south wind. J. Trego & two daughters here to dinner. I hang up my meat. **L. Hathaway & Wife dissolve partnership**.[235]
4. Lowry, south wind. I pay my tax 56 dollars some cents. Mr. Willis & Harriet, Miss MaComber here, visit. James Roberts call. **We all go to show at schoolhouse tonight**.
5. Fair, NW. I, Wife & Mother Hotaling go to James Trego visit. He & I go to Croswell's papermill. Newman Finch here, stay all night.
6. Fair, cold, SW. **I and Dutchman go to Stone Church Place. Look for location for vineyard**.[236] L. Hathaway here. I go to river.
7. Lowry, muddy, warm. I go to Meeting & to Harris's, to Mother's. John Rea call here.
8. Fine day, warmer. James Roberts & A.A. Hotaling call. I cut wood. Go to river. **I fix John Sperl's house**. Pay Wm. O. Lawton $1.59. Miss Maxon, Miss Andrews, Mary Jane & Helen Lawton here, visit.
9. Cloudy, S wind. Tunis Wilsey here ½ day. I and he draw two loads sand for Temperance Hall. L. Hathaway here.
10. Fair, cold. I attend P. Road meeting. Willis pay me $7.50. Mrs. J. Rea here. I & Wife attend Macomber's Donation; I pay him 3 dollars.
11. Cold, snowy, south wind. I go to river. I call at S. Harris's.
12. Little snowy, warmer, S wind. I draw three loads manure & sand in the garden. Frenchman Squaw help. L. Hathaway here. Ball to A. Hotaling's this evening.
13. Rainy, SW morning, North in afternoon, cold. I fix fence attend P.R. meeting. Willis pay me 10/ for today service until 12 o'clock.
14. Fair, very cold. I go to Meeting twice. **I go see my room to river**. Call to Widow Hotaling's & to Mother's.
15. Very cold, south wind. I chop wood, go to river. Wife go to Doct. Fredenburgh's.
16. Snow all day. I lay around. Go to river in evening.
17. Overcast. Mr. Roberts & two boys call here. Mr. Willis & Harriet call. Tunis Wilsey draw me 4 loads wood. L. Hathaway here. I go to Singing School.
18. Fair. I, Wife, Willis & Harriet go to Edwin Hubbel's Coxsackie; visit all day. I go to Bank get $50 on certificate of Robert's. Get 40 dollars Mother Hotaling's dividend; pay it to her at night.
19. Cold, high N wind. I go to Greenville with waggon. I stop to Newman Finch's, to Edward Collins, to G. Place's. I pay him saw bill over 17 dollars. Then to Mr. Witbeck's, then to J.B.

---

[235] L. Hathaway & the Widow Mead were married on 26 Oct 1854.
[236] This is the first mention of the vineyard that Fletcher established with George Rifflin.

Waldron's, pay him salt bill over 34 dollars. Then to Silas Baldwin, then to J.G. Williamson's, then to Mr. Witbeck, pays me his rent. Then go to Andrew Fancher's, stay all night. William Hoose come here with 7 bushels of wheat.

20 Fair, warmer. I and Fancher drive to Williamson's, Mr. Collins, Mr. Hunt, Mr. Whitford pay their rent, then we drive to Mr. Stephen's, then he and Wm. Hoose settle their rent. Then go to Silas Baldwin's get Anthony Boots. Then to Andrew Fancher's. Then over the snowbanks holme by way of Stephensville. Wife goes to Willis's to Singing School.

21 Cloudy, stormy. I go to Meeting, to Willis's & to Mother's. Mary and Uphema Blaisdell here.

22 Very rainy night and this morning streams very high. I go to river. Mr. Roberts, Virginia Blaisdell here. I send Mother a ham and some beef.

23 Fair. I go to river & then to P. McGee's. See him about chopping. Rev. Mr. Macomber here call.

24 Snowy. **I & Dutchman go to Coxsackie to see about grape vines. Call to A.A. Hotaling. Get vines to Edwin Hubbell's.** Go to A.T. VanSlyck's, take dinner. Then come holme through Baltimore. I go to river. I call to Mother's.

25 Still fair, cold. I draw one load of wood & one log off the hill. Wife go to Dominie Davis's & Widow Hotaling's. Mother Hotaling & Anna go to Methodist Meeting. **Mother is quite unwell this winter, keeps her bed.**

26 Snow, all day cold. I go to river & I stay around the house.

27 Snowy, cold. I & Willis go to Albany. I get silver plated forks. **Singing School here**. Wife & Mother Hotaling go to Dr. Fredenburgh's.

28 Fair, cold. **I, Wife & Mother Houghtaling go to Baltimore to Dedication of church**. I call to Mother's. Company at holme.

29 Rainy night, snow all gone, SW. I get horses shod. Go to McGee's; cut timber. Quite a freshet in the creeks.

30 Fair, SW. Mrs. McComber & child and another girl [here]. I go to river. Call to Mother's. L. Hathaway here.

31 Fair, cold. I settle with A.N. Briggs. I pay him 10 dollars, gave him a note for 12 dollars payable in stone & gravel at two cents per load. Rev. Mr. Davis donation goes off; I attend and give him 5 dollars.

February 1855

1 Fair. My Sherwood cow has a calf. George & Charlotte Hotaling here, visit. Rev. McComber here.

2 Fair. George & Charlotte Hotaling, Trego & Lady, Mrs. A. Mull here all day. I help S. Harris draw one load of hay.

3 Fair, cold. A.E. Willis call here. I, Wife & Elizabeth Hotaling go to A.T. VanSlyck's; stay all day & all night.

4 Fair, very cold, NW. We all go to Coxsackie to Meeting. Then back to A.T. VanSlyck's & to M.G. VanBergen's. Take dinner and then holme.

6 Very cold, NW. **Thermometer 14 deg below 0**. I lay around, do nothing all day.

7	Very cold, NW. **Thermometer 18 deg below 0**. I go to river, do nothing.
8	Cold, 5 inches snow. Mother Hotaling come holme. I go to river. L. Hathaway here to tea. A.E. Willis call here. Cate Hotaling here. All go to Meeting.
9	Snowy. I and Gotfriet Yoos draw 5 loads of logs & wood. I pay Cate Hotaling $12.60. Wife & Cate go to Willis's. Snow again 6 in. deep.
10	Fair, cold. Gotfriet draw me 4 loads wood & logs. Cate Hotaling leave here. Trego come after her.
11	Fair, cold. I go to Meeting. John Rea call here.
12	Fair. I and Gotfriet go to Flat Bush draw 4 logs to Kimmey's Mill. A.E. Willis & L. Hathaway call here. I go to river.
13	Fair, SW. I and Gotfriet draw 3 logs from Flat Bush to Kimmey's Mill. I go to Mill with 6 bushels of wheat. I pay Jack Wilsey $15 for mason work.
14	Snow & rain all day. I and Gotfriet draw 1 load wood. Start logs.
15	Cloudy. Fine sleying. I draw 6 logs to Kimmey's Mill. I, Wife and Miss Keeler & Miss Bennet go to Charlotte Hotaling's attend a party. Have a fine time. Get holme at 3 o'clock in the morning.
16	Snowy. Gotfriet take two logs to Kimmey's mill. Draw two loads holme. E. Hubbell & Lady, Mrs. VanDyck, A. VanBergen, L. Hubbell here visit. We go to Willis's.
17	Cloudy. I and Gotfriet work at wood ½ day. I go to John Mull's. Take Wife & children. I and John go to see Mr. Talmage to Castleton. **Margarett Blaisdell died at 7 o'clock today. It was a very solemn time at the house.**[237]
18	Fair, NW. **I go after James Thom to attend Margarett's Funeral. I go to Coeymans Hollow to Meeting; give notice of Margarett's death & Funeral. Then to John Row's, then to Calanan's Tavern. Feed horses, then holme. Wife stay all night to Wesley's. Stay all day to Wesley's.**
19	Fair, cold. I get sley fixed. Go to island. Go to mill; get grist. **Attend Margarett's funeral. James Thom preach**.
20	Cloudy, cold NW. I go to river. A.E. Willis & L. Hathaway call here.
21	Fair. I and Gotfriet draw logs & wood. I go to river; get pension papers of Mark's fixed. I pay J. Moore 2 dollars. Caroline VanAntwerp here.
22	Cold. I and Gotfriet draw timber. I fall & hurt my ear & head
23	Fair, cold. Gotfriet draw wood. James Jack & Lady and Monica Teneyck here. All go to Meeting.
24	Fair, cold. I take Mother Hotaling to Widow Charlotte's. I go to Coxsackie, take dinner to E. Hubbell's. Go to M.G. VanBergen's. Call to G. Sweet's then holme. Wife go to Wesley's.
25	Fair, very cold, NW. I go to Meeting. Wesley & children here. Mary Harris call here I go to Mother's & to Pat Clancy's.

---

[237] Margaret (Wesley Blaisdell's Wife) was only 39 when she died.

26   Fair, very cold, NW. I pay Henry Hoag 2 dollars meat bill. Nett Hotaling here. A.E. Willis here. Frenchman Squaw work here.

27   Fair, very cold. I go to river. Get 50 dollars of A.E. Willis. Gotfriet & Frenchman cut wood all day. I buy two axe helves; pay 2/.

28   Fair, cold. I take Wife & Willis, go to Albany. **I go to Little Falls, stay all night to John Feeter's.** Gotfriet & Frenchman cut wood.

March 1855

1   Fair, cold. **I, Waterman & Judge Benton go to Newport, attend my reference case.**[238] **I pay Martin Luther 40 dollars. I come back to John Feeter's, stay all night. Gotfriet & Frenchman come work for me.**

2   Fair. Come to Albany with cars. Come holme with N.H. Johnson.

3   Fair. Gotfriet work here. I work around the house. Mr. Hogan here.

4   Fair. I go to Meeting twice. Cate Hotaling & Mary Jane Lawton here. John L. Verplank here to dinner & supper.

5   Cloudy, rainy night. Gotfriet saw wood. I get 8 bags broom corn seed of Johnson. I gave Dutchman a piece of pork & beef for trimming grape vines.

6   Fair, cold. Gotfriet chop wood. I make 3 swing gates. Mrs. W.C. Robb & Mrs. A. VanDerzee here, spend the day. I go to river in the evening.

7   Fair. I go to river, go to papermill. Mr. Robb gave me a piece of felt cloth. Dominie Davis & John Rea here.

8   Fair, cold. I help W.M.R. Carroll make hinges. I pay J. VanDenburgh $8.64. Elias Holmes call here. Mother here. Gotfriet & Hill cut wood.

9   Fair, cold. I and Wife go to Andrew Witbeck's attend a party; have a good time, stay till 3 o'clock morning. Gotfriet & George draw gravel, chop wood.

10   Fair, very cold. Gotfriet & George chop wood. I go to river. I pay Blacksmith Bill $4.64 balance.

11   Fair, cold. I go to Meeting. Call to Mother's, Willis's & Mrs. Hotaling's.

12   Snowy morning clears off. Gotfriet & George cut wood. I and Gotfriet go to Old Church Farm, start cut wood. I pay Gotfriet 5 dollars.

13   Snowy. **Gotfriet & George cut & draw wood from Old Church Farm; I go along**. Call at Elias Holme's take dinner & supper to G. Hotaling's. Wife & Mother Hotaling spend the day there. Elizabeth & Caroline come holme with us, they all go to Meeting.

14   Cloudy, 3 inches snow. I draw one log & one load of wood, go to mill. Gotfriet & George cut wood. Elib & Cary Hotaling here.

15   Rainy. I go to river. I pay George 2 dollars. I call on L. Hathaway & Ira Gregory. They are sick. I go to Meeting.

---

[238] Newport, NY is located NE of Utica in Herkimer County.

16 Fair. Gotfriet & Hill chop wood. I go to river, work in wood house. Peter McGee here, we look over our accounts.

17 Stormy. I attend F.H. Slate's Vendue. I pay Mother $174 pension money got of A.E. Willis. I buy Buffalo robe to Vendue. I go to river. Gotfriet & George cut wood, draw 1 load of gravel.

18 Cloudy. I go to Meeting. NW. I go to Harris's. John Rea call here.

19 Fine day, SW. I pay George $2. I let Gotfriet have my team. I go to river. **Steamboat Manhattan goes up today.**

20 Fair, cold, NW. A. Teal fix my hay press ¾ day. I pay J. Sickler $4.63. I pay Miss Wheeler & Miss Bennet $5. I go to river.

21 Fair, cold, NW. I make picket fence. R.H. Mosher pay me $5.63. I go to river and am about the house.

22 Fair, cold. I make fence. Attend Plank Road meeting to A.N. Briggs. Mother, Harriet here, visit. Eliza Roberts, Miss Teneyck here.

23 Fair. I go to Peter W. TenEyck's, see his cows. I make fence.

24 Snowy, NW, very cold. I attend P.W. Teneyck's Vendue, buy Buffalo robe. Go to river. I pay Gotfriet Yoos 3 dollars. **Peter VanAntwerp died today**.

25 Very cold, NW. I go to Meeting twice. Dr. Blaisdell here.

26 Cloudy, snowy. Dr. VanAntwerp & Marite come here. **We all attend Peter VanAntwerp's funeral. I go to Aquetuck to the vault. Sally Teneyck died today.** A. Jackson call here.

27 Fair, cold, NW. I attend A.E. Willis vendue. Andrew VanAntwerp leave for New York. J. Muckelroy pay me $32.50 rent of Division Room.

28 Fair, very cold. **I attend Sally Teneyck's Funeral**. Work around and I pay J.B. Montross 10 dollars on stone.

29 Fair, NW. I go to river. I work around. I see J.M. Harris.

30 Fair, NW. I take Wife & Marite to Trego's. Harris has my team, go to mill. I help S. Harris clean up grain.

31 Fair, SW. I take Wife & Marite to T. Hotaling's. **I & L. Hathaway go to Nomination Meeting to J.B. Shear's.** I pay A. Pulver $9.51 road.

April 1855

1 Cold squally day. I stay holme with A. Hood. Folks go to Meeting.

2 Very cold, NW, fair. **John Sperl died today**. I attend Dist. Road Meeting. Visit to Willis's. Go to Aaron Hotaling's in the evening.

3 Fair, cold. I take Mother Hotaling & Marite to Flat Bush. **I attend funeral of John Sperl.** Mr. George Hills & Mr. Patten here. Wife go to Widow Hotaling's.

4 Fair, warmer. I go to mill. Mr. Hill & Patten leave. I start in logs to sawmill. I bring 21 boards holme. Anne's Sister here. Mr. A. Hood sends us an oil cloth. I get it to H.B. Joslin's.

5 Lowry, rainy. I go to Dean's Mill get a load of boards. Rufus King pays me $169.49 interest & payment on mortgage. I help John Clement shingle my waggon house. I go to river. Call to Woolsey Cary's. Peter Seabridge call here.

6	Clear, NW. G.T. Sweet here. I settle with him. I take his note for 10 dollars & E. Millbank's note $200. Anne's brother-in-law here to tea & stay all night.
7	Fair, cold. I go to river. Get my axe laid. A. Witbeck here to dinner. He pays me balance rent $75. Marite & Mother Houghtaling come holme.
8	Fair day, warm. I go to Meeting. I walk over to cemetery. South wind.
9	Rainy morning clears off. I get $46.96 of S.F. Cranston hay & straw money. I call to Woolsey Cary's. Elizabeth Hotaling call here.
10	I pay Josiah Sherman $819. W. Cary gave me a new Bk. note & took up my old one that he gave me of six hundred dollars. **I take T.F. Cranston & John Minnick to Town Meeting; have a great time.**
11	Snow, blow rain all day. I let Wife have 25 dollars, let Marite have 25 dollars, A. Teal 20 dollars. I get 100 dollars of A.E. Willis. **I take Wife & Marite to Joshua Barge they go to New York, Anthony go along**.
12	I go to Little Falls. Take supper & stay all night to John Feeter's. See A.H. Waterman. Weather fair.
13	Fair. I come holme. I pay A.E. Willis 100 dollars borrowed money.
14	Rainy, SW. I have a bad cold. Go to river. Lay around the house.
15	Fair, still day. I go to Meeting. Lay around, call to S. Harris.
16	Very fine warm day. Work at walks, trim up gardens. I pay Miss Burnett & Miss Wheeler's bill. I go to river. Mother here.
17	Fair for part of day, SW, showry at night. Miss Wheeler, Jane Andrews call. **Henry Applebee died last night**.
18	Fair, warm I lay stone walk. **Attend Henry Applebee's funeral**.
19	Fair, showry, SW. I lay walk. Plow George Rifflen potato ground. Mutual Insurance man here. **I take 11 dozen of eggs to A.E. Willis**.
20	Rain hard all day. I sort out potatoes. Go to river. John Rea call here.
21	Fair, warm, pleasant. I and John Clement shingle carriage house. Harris has my horses. Mrs. N.H. Johnson & Mary Serles call here.
22	Fair, SW. I go to Meeting. John Rea call here. I call to L. Harris.
23	Fair, SW. I and J. Clement shingle all day at my barn linter.
24	Fair, SW. I send 10 dollars to Wife by E. Stanton. I & J. **Clement work at Barn Sleepers**[239] all day. I am very tired.
25	Fair. I draw 5 loads chip manure. I plow garden. Mother here all day. I am very tired.
26	Cold, SW rainy. I lay stone wall, get horses shod. Rev. Mr. Davis & John Rea call here.
27	Fair, cold NW. I go to Ira Gregory's. I go to Kimmey's Mill; get 1 load boards.
28	Fair, cold NW. I help S. Harris make fence at **Stone Church Farm**. Wife comes from New York. I go get things from propeller. **My dog and P. Seabridge's get a fighting**.

---

[239] Sleepers are the horizontal boards serving as support for a large building.

29	Rainy. I go to Meeting. Call to Mother's & to Willis's. **Mother Hotaling faint in church**.
30	Lowry. I furrow out and plant my garden with potatoes. Edward Blaisdell & A. Jackson here. I pay W.B. Hill 60 dollars for manure I got of A. Jackson. I go to Wesley's. I get $95.06 of Cranston, balance on my hay bill.

May 1855

1	Lowry morning clears off. I go with S. Harris to [Old Stone] Church Farm, make fence. Get fish of L. Hathaway, pay 3/6.
2	Fair, NW. Let George Rifflin have my team to go to Rundleville.
3	Fair. I help S. Harris make fence to Stone Church Farm.
4	Fair. I plant corn & beans. I & Peter Seabridge go to J.B. Shear's. Make out road list. P. Seabridge pay me order & cash $66.86. I pay A. Hotaling 11 dollars.
5	Fair, cold, NW. I, Levi & Jim Rea go to Kimmey's Mill, get boards. George Rifflin make my garden. **A. Jackson's child died**.
6	Anne McRea leave here. I pay her $40.50. Wife go with her to Albany. I go to Dean's Mill get 24 slabs, 3 cts each. Lib & Caroline Hotaling here to tea. Mr. McCullock call here.
7	Fair, NW. I go to Meeting. **Attend funeral of A. Jackson child**. Call to Harris. **Catherine Hotaling died**.[240]
8	Fair, cold. I take Wife & Anthony, go to Baltimore then to G. Hotaling's to tea.
9	Cloudy, Rainy. I go on hill, get a load of muck. I get 40 dollars of Willis on P. Seabridge's order. Willis pay me 25 dollars on McComber's rent. P. Ostrander paper here.
10	Rainy. **I attend Cate Houghtaling funeral**. I go to river.
11	Fair. I go to John Mull's get fish. Elizabeth Castle & daughter Elizabeth here, Mother here. **We clean house. P. Ostrander paper here**.
12	Fair. **I take Gotfriet Yoos & family to Albany. Take cars to Little Falls. Then I & Gottefitt go to Eben Kelly's, stay all night**.
13	Fair. **I and Gotfriet go to Graysville, then on my land. Then to Mr. Belcher's to supper, stay there all night**.
14	Fair. I and Linus Belcher go to Gray's Mill. Then I go to Belcher to dinner. Go to see Gotfriet, then to B.W. Warner to dinner to Belcher's. Stay all night.
14[241]	Rainy a little. I and L. Belcher go to Gray's Mill in the woods. Then go to dinner to Belcher's. Then go to Gotfriet's let him have 10 dollars and six I let him have before, making 16 dollars.
15	Rainy. **I go to Gotfriet's take breakfast, then walk to E. Kelly's buy sugar and rest. Then to Little Falls to dinner to John Feeter's. Then see A.H. Waterman, then take cars to Albany. Run off the track at Fonda. Get a going again. Get to Albany at 8 o'clock in the evening. Stay to C.H. Debois all night**.
16	Rainy. Come holme with A.E. Willis in the rain. Wife gave me 200 dollars.

---

[240] Catherine Houghtaling was Sarah Ann's youngest sister. She was only 22 when she died.

[241] There is a mix-up here as there are two entries for the 14th.

17   Fair. I work around. Maria VanSlyck here. I take her to New Baltimore. Mary Blaisdell go along. I let A.E. Willis have 200 dollars, take his note. I pay A. Teal balance $15.25.

18   Fair. I & S. Harris make fence at Old Stone Church Farm. A lot of company is here. **Music teacher stay all night**. John Sickler call. See me.

19   Cloudy, rainy. I get 10 shad, some herring. I go to [Old Stone] Church Farm, take cows along. Mother here, Mary Holmes, widow, here. Frenchman Squaw pay me 4 dollars. Showry at night.

20   Fair. Mary Holmes leave. Wesley's girls here, go to cemetery. **Two burials from Catholic Church today**.

21   Fair. **I, Levi & Anthony go to A. Witbeck's all over rocks, look for a cow**. I buy one of Witbeck's for 30 dollars, bring her holme. Black Dinah here. Wife goes to Wesley's.

22   Fair. **I take horse & waggon go to Albany. Leave there, take box and go on cars to Little Falls. Call on Waterman. I go to Danube, then to Little Falls, then walk to Eaton's Bush. Take supper. Stay all night take breakfast. Then go to New Port.**

23   Fair. **Attend Tompkins' Lawsuit. I then pay Tomkins his Case bill. Then I, Waterman & Judge Benton come back to Little Falls. I eat to John Feeter's, then I start on foot walk to St. Johnsville. Then take cars to Albany.**

24   Fair. **I take my horse, come holme**. Go to island and get 6 shad of John Sickler, 25 herring.

25   Cold, NW. I, Levi & Anthony go to Flat Bush to G.J. Sweet's. Then go to Greenville. Take tea to Newman Finch's, then go to A. Fancher's stay all night.

26   Fair, cold. I go to Place's Mill, then to J. Williamson's. George Fancher pay me 37 dollars. I pay him 7 dollars interest money. Then we come holme. Stop to Briggs & Andrew's papermill.

27   Fair, cold, dry. I and Wife go to Elias Holmes. I go see cows.

28   Fair. I go to Dean's Mill, get logs. I go on hill, fix fence. Mr. White here, stay all night. Eliza Clement here. I get Willis's check $20, send it to Linis Belcher.

29   Fair. I get 75 shad of John Bull. I go to Dean's Mill, get boards. Very dry weather.

30   Fair. I let A.E. Willis have $100 for son David. I & G. Harris make fence, fix gates. I pay G. Peacock 14 dollars for W. Stephens.

31   Fair, SW, dry. I go to Kimmey's Mill, get boards. Go to river & to swamp.

June 1855

1   Cloudy, SW. I lay walk, draw stone. Go to river. **L. Hathaway died**.

2   Cloudy, rainy, misty. I go to river, get 25 herring. A.B. Hotaling here.

3   Rainy. **I attend funeral of L. Hathaway with team**. Mathew Hathaway here.

4   Rainy morning, fair afternoon. I go to river. I work around the house. Mathew Hathaway leave here for Coxsackie.

5   Fair, NW. I go to Kimmey's Mill get a load of lumber & go to river.

6[242]	Fair, SW. I go to Kimmey's Mill, get 1 load fence slats. Go to river. Mrs. Fredenburgh, Betsey Verplank, Doct. Blaisdell call here.
7	Rain all day. Am unwell. Go to river, get sturgeon. **Take 8 lb. 10 oz. butter to Willis**.
8	Fair, NW. I go on the hill, see our rye. G. Harris set out cabbage plants. Wife & Mother Hotaling go to Aaron Hotaling's.
9	Fair. I, Wife, Mother Hotaling & Anthony go to M.G. VanBergen's, take dinner. Call to Martin's, see his twins. Call to A.J. VanSlyck's. The call to E. Hubbell's. I call on T.W. Gay, then to A.B. Hotaling's, then to Andrew A. Hotaling's, then to G.J. Sweet's, so holme.
10	Showry. Wesley Blaisdell, A.E. Willis, U.B. Willis here. I take a walk. Call to Mother's & to A.E. Willis. Mary Blaisdell here.
11	Fair. I work around, go to river. U.B. Willis here, spend the evening.
12	Fair. I work around. A.E. Willis, U.B. Willis, Martin & Jane Andrews here. Mrs. Renny and another lady here. I go to river, am unwell.
13	Fair. I work at picket fence, go to river. James Ostrander call here.
14	Fair, cool. I and A.E. Willis go to Clarksville; attend Agricultural Meeting. I get out pickets.
15	Fair. I make fence. Mother here. I pay Cataline 5 dollars. Willis here. I & Wife go to Wesley's in the evening.
16	Fair. **I fix Old Holmestead**. I give R. Pulver an order on A.E. Willis for 50 dollars. I call to Wesley's. His dog gets cut with a scythe.
17	Fair, NW. I take Wife & Mother to Quarterly Meeting to Hollow. I call to S. Harris's. A.E. Willis call here.
18	Fair. I and G. Harris go to Bushants' Farm, get 2 loads posts. I fix hog pen. Go to river, call to Wesley's.
19	Lowry, rainy. I and Dutch Joe go to Flat Bush, get 2 loads timber. Levi & Anthony go along. G.T. Sweet pays me 10 dollars.
20	Lowry, rainy. I pay Lathan Sickler 34 dollars, P. Sickler 14 dollars. Caroline & Antoinette Hotaling here. Mother here. She & Wife go to T. Harris's, visit. Mary & Uphema Blaisdell here.
21	Fair, warm. I make fence all day. Harriet, Willis & Eleanor VanSlyck here. I go to river.
22	Fair, warm. I go to Greenville. Take dinner to J.W. Story's. I then go to Place's Mill, get a load of pine lumber. It rains hard, get wet. Go to A. Fancher's, stay all night, take supper & breakfast.
23	Fair, warm. Start for holme. Get to J.B. Shear's, take dinner. Martin VanSlyck bring Mother Hotaling holme. I come holme.
24	Lowry. I go to Meeting, then holme, go to sleep. Martin VanSlyck leave. Wesley here.
25	Lowry, rainy. H. Neal & Dutch George here to work. I make fence. Go up P.R., I get 21 3x6 timbers. Get wet, go through a very heavy rain.

---

[242] The 6 June 1855 New York Census lists the following residents: Fletcher (37), Sarah Ann (36), Levi (9), Anthony (6), Maria Hotaling (58), Catharine Biechland (20) servant.

26 Showry, wet. Move wood house to Harris's. Joe Roe sends my cow holme, she runs away, get lame, he sends her back. H. Neil & George work here. Miss Drum here. Wife go to Harris's. I go to river, get fish.

27 Fair, hot. Dominie Blake, Lady & child here. Miss Drum leave. Garret Hotaling & Lady here. Mrs. A. Teneyck call here. Dutch George work here. I lay foundation to kitchen to Harris's. **I was up with Harris's sick horse till 2 o'clock last night**.

28 Fair. I work around Harris's kitchen. Dutch George work here.

29 Fair, hot. I make fence. Dutch George work here. Mother & Henry & Cate VanBergen & Elida VanSlyck, Lib Hotaling [here]. I pay J. Clement 12 dollars, Mr. Bedel's check.

30 **Fair, hot, 105 degrees above zero**. I work at fence. Plow out potatoes and corn in garden. Get 15 dollars of Willis. Dutch George work here ½ day. I go in swimming. Mary Hotaling here.

July 1855

1 Phillip Kimmey here to dinner & tea. Mary Jane Heun & Israel Lawton here. Ed VanOrden call. We all go to Meeting.

2 Fair. I draw 1 load of timber from P.R. I help around building to Harris. James Schoonmaker & Lib Hotaling here. **Wife go to Albany, get Irish girl**. Wesley & D. Lawton call. I get 25 dollars of A.E. Willis.

3 Fair. **I go to Albany get 3,000 shingles, pay 9 dollars**. I gave 5 dollars for 1 gal Brandy & 1 gal of gin. I pay off Springstead & Bullock. Get 10 lbs. tea of L. Lawton.

4 Cloudy, SW. **I, Wife, Lib & Caroline Hotaling, Cate VanBergen, Elida VanSlyck all go to river to go on excursion. Get disappointed, come back. Then Wesley, E. VanOrden, P. Kimmey, H. Waldron come here; stay until 10 o'clock at night. Mary & Charlotte Hotaling here. We have a fine time**. T. Gould pay me $2.53.

5 Fair. I get Harris waggon fixed. Cost me 5/6. Company all leave. I, Levi, Wife, Cate VanBergen go to Widow Charlotte's. I go to river. T. Gould pay rent $2.08.

6 Hot rainy in afternoon. I go to Kimmey's; get 1 load of lumber. **Stop in the rain in Mosher's Barn**. John here all night, leave in morning.

7 Rain all day. I go to river. I work around. Get horse shod. Get meal & I get 150 dollars of A.E. Willis.

8 Fair. Cate VanBergen, Martin & Elida VanSlyck here. Ed VanOrden, A.E. Willis, Uriah Willis & Lady, Wm. MacGregor here. We go to Meeting.

9 Fair. **I start for Herkimer with team. Go to Albany, take P.R. to Fort Hunter, cross wire bridge on Mohawk River. Go to Johnstown stay all night**.

10 Fair. **Start early. Go to Pleasant Valley. Take Breakfast to a mean tavern. Then go to Salisbury Corners. Then to Ebenezer Kelly's, take dinner, feed my horse, have a fine shower. Then go to my land. Take supper to Gotfriet Yoos. Then to Belcher's stay all night**.

12 Fair. Go around, look at new mill. Take breakfast to Belcher's, take dinner to Gotfriet's and supper to Belcher's. Stay all night. **Wm. Southwick died**.

13	Fair. Go around, look at mill. Go to Graysville pay Mr. Parks 20 dollars. Pay Belcher for cows 17 dollars & 30 dollars balance on waggon trade and 10 dollars to Belcher for nails and all labor bills. I pay Patrick 5 dollars for settlement. I take breakfast, dinner & supper to Belcher's, stay all night.
14	Fair. **Start for holme with horse Bill. Leave Charly for Gotfriet. Go to Little Falls. Take dinner to John Feeter's. Pay A.H. Waterman 100 dollars. Start for holme down the Mohawk River to Palatine Bridge see Mr. Hays and Mr. Spraker. Drive 35 miles without stopping; drive 2 hours through the rain. Get to Fonda, stay all night.**
15	Fair. **Drive holme through Tribes Hill to Amsterdam. Came through and take breakfast to Chase's Tavern above Amsterdam. Came through Schenectady to Albany, so holme at 11 o'clock at night.**
16	Fair. **Go to Meeting. Take a sleep.** Call to Willis's & to Mrs. J. Hotaling's.
17	Fair, hot. I drive cow to H. Orchard's to bull. Make fence. Go after cow again at night. I pay Orchard 1 dollar. Heavy shower. I send A.H. Waterman check for 58 dollars. Attend Division. Come holme in the rain. Mrs. Drew here. Mrs. Hathaway pay me 20/ rent & 50 cents for wood. A.E. Willis here.
18	Fair, hot. I work around, go in swimming. I pay Henry Smith 9 dollars for lumber.
19	Rainy, hot. **I, Levi & Anthony go after raspberries; get 12 quarts.** Go to J. Armstrong's & to Abram Witbeck's. Mary Serles here.
20	Rainy day. I work around. I pay Kimmey's bill 16 dollars. **Brent Hallock here with maps.** I go to river. Mary Serles here.
21	Rainy. I work around. Mary Serles here. I pay Mary Serles 1 dollar. I go to river. **Get 18 pineapples and a firkin of lard.**[243]
22	Fair. I take Roe cow to bull. Go to sleep. Go to Meeting. A.A. Hotaling here.
23	Fair. I go to river, work around. I draw Henry Anderson 2 load wood.
24	Rainy. I get wet going after cows. I work around. Get harness of A.E. Willis.
25	Hot, lowry, showers around. I get shoes, boots mended. Mother here. **Mrs. Joslin died last night.**
26	Fair till 4 o'clock. I oil my harness. **I attend Mrs. Joslin's funeral. We have the most terrific thunder shower ever known. Water flow in Johnson's Brick house & in Willis's cellar. Do great damage to Seabridge, to C. Ryon, to John Cronk's garden, carry off their privy. The water flow over my bridge over 1 foot.**
27	Fair, NW. I get harness, get Wesley's horse, go to Albany. C. McCallister here. **Take deed of Calvers (sp) Platt and copy of Father's will.** Wife go to Willis's.
28	Rainy, warm. I take Ellen & Mary Harris to Albany. I pay Ellen 9 dollars, get one barrel of flour & a lot of feed. I drive Wesley's horse. Levi go along.
29	Fair, hot. I go to Meeting. Wife go with Wesley to Mrs. Sarah Ann VanBergen's. A.A. Houghtaling call here.

---

[243] A firkin is a small wooden cask – usually a quarter of a barrel.

30 Showry. I get 5 dollars of John E. Bailey to pay costs against Mutual Insurance Company. Mohawk Valley get sturgeon & eels. Wife go to Rev. Mr. Davis & to Dr. Fredenburgh's.

31 Fair, hot. I and Anthony go to Greenville. Stay all night to Andrew Fancher's. I take flour and meat to A.A. Hotaling's.

August 1855

1 Fair, hot. I swear off my tax. Call to Silas Baldwin's, then come holme.

2 Fair, hot. **T. Civill pays me 5 dollars on Lawsuit of Mohawk Valley Insurance Co**.

3 Fair, SW. Mother here. Mary Blaisdell here. I go to Island. Go in swimming. I get my horse shod.

4 Showry, hot. **I attend Mrs. VanDalfsen's funeral**. Work at apple trees. Lib & Mary Pelts here, visit.

5 Cloudy, south wind. Pelts' girls here. We take a walk.

6 Fair, NW. Rev. Mr. Pelts here after his sisters. I work around. Mrs. Michael Wintin pay $2.57 one month's rent.

7 Shower in afternoon. I go to [Old Stone] Church Farm, get a basket of apples of Willis. Cate Hotaling here. Wife go to Wesley's.

8 Fair, SW. I take Wife & Mother Hotaling to Thomas Hotaling's. Caroline VanAntwerp call here.

9 Heavy rain. I patch my barn roof. Rains hard. I go fetch cows. Miss Drum & Mary Blaisdell call here.

10 Fair, cold, NW. I and Marite go to Willis Orchard, get apples. Lib Hotaling & Miss Boucher here. I take six girls, take ride to Baltimore. Stop to G. Hotaling's & to Wesley's, then holme.

11 Fair day, NW. John Silcox & Lady & two children here. I and John go to P. Kimmey's. I pay Wife $12.37 for Miss Drum.

12 Fair, SW. We all go to Meeting. Willis & Wesley call here, we take a walk.

13 Cloudy. **J. Silcock**[244] & my boys all go a fishing. A. VanSlyck, Lib & Caroline Hotaling call here. Cone pays me 4 dollars rent.

14 Fair day. I take Wife, Marite, John Silcock & his family, we all go to A.T. VanSlyck. Spend the day, get holme at 9 o'clock at night.

15 Fair. **I and J. Silcox go under the Hill**. Elida Miller here. Doct. Blaisdell call. T. Gould pay me $2.08 rent. Lib Sperl pay me 3 dollars rent.

16 Fair. S.W. J. Silcox leave for NY. I go to river, go in swimming.

17 Cloudy morning. Wife & company go to Willis's. I get horse shod, go around farm.

18 Fair, SW. I get apples of A.E. Willis. Go a fishing. **J. Silcox send me peaches & watermelons**.

19 Fair day. I go to Meeting & to sleep. Miss Rea here.

---

[244] Fletcher often switches the spelling of people's names, e.g., Silcox vs Silcock, Houghtaling vs Hotaling.

20   Fair day. I & Wife & all hands go on excursion to Oak Hill. **Have difficulty with Dominie about dancing**. Wesley and Ed VanOrden here. Uncle Garret's girls here. **Helen Hotaling or Miss Selkirk died**.

21   Fair. I work around, go to river. **Mrs. Cate Hotaling has a young son**.

22   Fair, SW. A.P. VanSlyck & Lady, Cate Hotaling & Jenny Trego, P. Kimmey & daughter here. **We all go to Dan Rice's Circus twice. Have a nice time**. I pay Kimmey $5.75 cash & circus tickets. Rain in the evening.

23   Lowry, rainy. I get Willis's horse, go to Albany, take up piano. I pay him 4 dollars, take receipt. I get Mr. & Mrs. Cary & George Bagley and come holme.

24   Fair. Work around. Visit James Trego & Lady & daughter. Lib here.

25   Fair. I take all folks to James Trego's, visit. Then to Baltimore, around out bush, then holme. Then to Willis's., then to Wesley's in the evening. Have music, nice time, dance.

26   Rainy. Go to Meeting. I take George Bagley to Schodack; he take the cars to New York. I call to Josiah Sherman's & to John Cronk's. Willis here. **M.G. VanBergen died**.

27   Fair. **I & Cary go to Albany, get piano to Green Bush**. Attend Cemetery Meeting. **John Harris, Eliza Clement, A. Civil, J.J. Colvin, U.B. Willis here. Have a musical entertainment dance.** I get 150 dollars of John Cronk.

28   Fair. Mr. Cary & Lady leave here. I get 150 dollars of Willis, gave my note to J.J. Colvin for it. I pay Mr. Cary $2.75 for piano; take receipt. **Wife go with Wesley to M.G. VanBergen's funeral.**

29   Fair. John Clement work for me. **I go Under Hill**, get apples. I & Boys go a fishing. Doct. Blaisdell here. Wife & Mrs. Silcox go to Widow Clement's, visit.

30   Fair. I & John Clement work at cow shed.

31   Fair. I and John Clement work at shed. Mrs. Hotaling, Widow here, visit.

September 1855

1   Fair. J.J. Silcox come last night. I get 6 baskets of peaches John bring for me to boat. Wm. Phelps here. Martin VanSlyck bring Mother H. holme. We all go on excursion, have a nice time. Cate Hotaling here.

2   Fair. **I take Wm. Phelps out to Quaker Meeting**. Wesley, A.E. & U.B. Willis here. We take a walk to river. Call to Wm. O. Lawton's.

3   Fair. Work around shed. I and J.J. Silcox go fishing. Trego & Cate Hotaling here. Wife & Mrs. Silcox go to Willis's. Wm. Phelps leave here.

4   Fair. J.J. Silcox & Lady leave. Betsey VerPlank, Mrs. Johnson, Mrs. H. Niles here. I and John Clement work at shed.

5   Fair, SW. I and John Clement work at shed. Mother, Mary & Virginia Blaisdell here.

6   Fair. I, Levi & Anthony get heifer, then go hunting. I help John Clement with shed. Mrs. Gould & Eliza Roberts here, visit. I go to river.

7   Fair. I and boys take old cow up Under Hill. I go to river.

8   Fair, hot. I take Mother to Quarterly Meeting to Bethlehem. Leave her to Mr. Jolly's. **I take cow Under Hill. She come back again.** Mrs. Nichols here, visit.

9   Fair. I take Wife to Quarterly Meeting. Bring Mother holme. Cate & Almira VB [VanBergen], Wesley & Ed VanOrden here.

10 Fair. I go to Herkimer to G. Yoos. Stay all night to L.C. Belcher's. Go in company with P. Rea to Little Falls. **Tom the engineer & Miss Hathaway get married**.

11 Fair, hot. I take breakfast to Belcher's, then go to G. Yoos to dinner. Pay Mr. Manning 21 dollars for shingles. Pay L.C. Belcher 65 dollars, take receipt.

12 Fair, hot. I and Gotfriet start for Little Falls 3 o'clock. I pay Gotfriet 20 dollars. I come holme on cars. I see Mr. Spraker. A. Fancher bring me 2 loads boards.

13 Fair. Wife & Levi go to Bethlehem. Lib Hotaling here. We all attend Singing School.

14 Fair. **I, George Harris go Under Hill get apples**. I brick up Mother's window. Mary Blaisdell & Miss Lawson, all hands go to Singing School last night.

15 Fair. I help J. Clement work at waggon house. T. Gould pay me $2.08 rent.

16 Fair. I go to Meeting. Doct. Blaisdell call. I go up to Willis's orchard.

17 Fair, hot. Wife & Levi go to Coxsackie. I go to papermill. I help J. Clement fix waggon house doors.

18 Hot & rainy, comes of cold. I pay Cate Hotaling $12.60 interest money. Mother here. I help John Clement work at doors. **Mr. H. Renne & Nell Hotaling get married**.

19 Fair, cool. John VanDalfsen here. Timothy Clancy pay me $130.50. Wife & Children go to Singing School. Doct. Blaisdell here.

20 Fair, frosty. I help John Clement. Mrs. Fredenburgh, Mrs. A.B. Verplank here, call. Lib Castle here.

21 Lowry. I help J. Clement work at shed & **apple rack**.

22 Fair. I fill in Brick to Harris's. I go to Wm. Fisher's after boot. Mrs. Hathaway pay me 20/ rent. Doct. Blaisdell here.

23 Fair. Mother Houghtaling come holme. Martin & Elida VanSlyck, Cate VanBergen here. Doct. Blaisdell here. Wife & Levi go to Coxsackie. I & Anthony go to Doct. Fredenburgh's.

24 Fair. I draw brick, fill in brick, draw water.

Apple rack

25 Fair. **I & Wife go to Albany, attend the County Fair**. Lib Hotaling gave me 1 dollar for ticket. Mr. Burdeck gave me 1 dollar for ticket. I came holme. Wife stay all night. I take dinner to Phelps. I gave Wife 5 dollars.

26 Fair, SW. I go to Albany, attend the fair. Take tea to Phelps'. We call and spend the evening with Miss Drum; rainy evening. Go to Phelps' stay all night.

27 Fair, cool. Attend fair. Get premium 2 dollars on cloth. G. Hotaling come with me holme.

28 Fair. I fill in brick, get horse shod. Virginia Blaisdell & Doct. VanAntwerp here.

29 Fair, SW. I fill in brick. I get 60 pale brick of P. Seabridge. Aunt Sarah Ann & Aunt Catharine here visit. Marite come. Almira VanBergen here. Mary & Charlotte Hotaling call. Wife come from Albany, bring Irish girl.

30   Fair, SW. Mr. Renne, Mary Charlotte & Widow Hotaling, Uncle Garret and Caroline Hotaling, Aunt Sarah Ann leave with Widow Charlotte. I get Wesley's horse & I, Wife, Doct. VanAntwerp & Marite & Almira VanBergen go to A. Jackson's visit. Get Holme after dark. Little rainy.

October 1855

1   Rainy day. Our visitors go to Garret Hotaling's. I & Doct. go in evening, take tea, bring Marite holme.

2   Cloudy. I attend mason [work] to Harris's. Doct. & Marite leave for NY. Mother Hotaling, Aunt Catherine, Almira here, Jacob Feeter here.

3   Rainy morning clears off. Aunt Sarah Ann & Widow Charlotte here. I pay Wm. B. Harris $5.12. Mr. Carmen here, sell his horse.

4   Rainy. I work around, go to river. Aunt Catharine leave. Ed VanOrden here, spend the evening. I send $10.50 to Spraker's insure my all by check.

5   Fair. I attend mason [work]. Doct. Blaisdell, Hester Hotaling call here. Wife & folks go to Widow Hotaling's visit.

6   Rainy. Finish mason work. **Go Under Hill, hang swing gate**. Mary Hotaling here. Aunt Sarah Ann & Myra leave.

7   Fair. Wife & Almira VB [VanBergen] go to meeting. Mary Hotaling leave. Ed VanOrden here to tea. Mary Jane, Helen Lawton, Mary Serles call. I and Wife go to Willis's & to Doct. Fredenburgh's.

8   Fair. I go Under Hill, pick nuts, pick apples. Gotfriet Yoos, L.C. Belcher come here, stay all night.

9   Fair. **I, Levi & L.C. Belcher take steamer J.C. Durant for NY**. We go to P dining in forenoon. I let Gotfriet have ten dollars.

10   Fair, warm. **I get to New York at 10 o'clock. Go to U.B. Willis to dinner, then to Chrystal Palace, then to Wallack's Theater. Stay all night to Doct. VanAntwerp's**.

11   Fair. **Go to Navy Yard and around NY. I go to Bowery Theater. Stay all night to J.J. Silcock's**.

12   Rainy day. Do up trading. **Get buzz saw. Leave it to be geared up**. Start for holme.

13   Cloudy, cold, misty. Get holme. **Gottefitt Yoos here since I was gone. Picked my apples & dug my potatoes**.

14   Rainy. We go to Meeting. Doct. Blaisdell & F.H. Slater here. P. Seabridge pay me 28 dollars; he send it by Levi.

15   Fair. I take L.C. Belcher, Gotfriet Yoos to Albany. George Harris go along. I let Beecher have 10 dollars for his own use and $15 to pay off Jonathan Parks. I let Gotfriet have $10. I get mandrill and wrench to E. Corning's; I pay $7.25.

16   Fair, NW. I pick apples, go to Island. Wife go to Wesley's.

17   Fair, cool. Mrs. Spraker, Lib Hotaling, Miss Carroll call here. George Refflin pick apples all day.

18   Fair. I work around house. Pick apples. Mother here.

19	Fine day, Indian summer. I work around, go to river, get boots fixed.
20	Fair. I work around. Have a stiff neck. Boil feed.
21	Lowry. **I get Saw & Mandrill from boat, box them up.** Sarah Ann & Wesley go to Coxsackie. I go to Mother's. John Rea call here.
22	Fair. I go to Albany with waggon. Wife go with boat. I go to Troy, take dinner with L.D. Eddy. **I send Saw & Mandrill [mandrel] to Herkimer**.
23	Fair morning, rainy afternoon. T. Clancy pay me 21 dollars balance on contract. I go to Coxsackie, take tea to A.T. VanSlyck's. Bring Mother Hotaling holme.
24	Rainy day, cold. I go to river twice. Lay around the house.
25	Cold & snow squalls. I go to river & lay around.
26	Cloudy. I go to mill with wheat & buckwheat. Wife go to Wesley's.
27	Rainy. We clean stoves, go to river. John H. VanBenthuyzen here. I pay P. Mull 6/.
28	Cold, rainy, NW. I, Wife, J.H. VanBenthuyzen & Martin VanSlyck go to Garret Hotaling's, spend afternoon and evening. Martin here to dinner, go to Meeting.
29	Fair. I fix tubs for cows, go to river. **I and Doct. Blaisdell go to Hollow to political meeting. Hear A.J. Colvin, Dr. Nott, Mr. Peckham, J.R. Porter speak. Have a good meeting**.
30	Rainy. I fix corn house. Go to river. A.E. Willis & Harriet here.
31	Fair. I gave Wife 15 dollars. She goes to Albany with A.E. Willis. She goes to Binghamton with J.H. VanBenthuyzen. She attends his wedding. Goes from there to NY. Stops to G.T. Nichols Hotel. I help Mrs. Davis move. Fix corn crib. Fix house to Mrs. Hathaway. **Attend No Nothing**[245] **meeting to J. D. Church in evening**.

November 1855

1	Rainy, SW. I go to river. Dig out beets.
2	Cloudy. I fix shed. Go to river. Mother here.
3	Rainy day. I attend Vendue to Widow Charlotte's. Buy Trego's cow and a bull. Go to river have a confab with John Burhaus, No Nothing.
4	Misty, muddy. I call to Willis's & to Mother's. I am sick and I vomit at Willis's. I call to John Rea's.
5	Fair, still NW. I, Levi & Anthony go get cow & bull I bought at the Vendue to Widow Hotaling's. Mrs. E. Holmes here. Mrs. J. Holmes here. **I put Babit Mettle**[246] in boxes. I go to river.
6	Lowry day. **Attend Election**. I'm quite unwell. Settle with A.E. Willis. Send Mr. Storinge bill to him for castings. Mrs. Elias here.

---

[245] The term "The Know Nothings" refers to the political party that was primarily an anti-Catholic, anti-Irish, anti-immigration and xenophobic movement. It was a forerunner to the temperance movement. Adherents to the movement were to simply reply "I know nothing" when asked about its specifics by outsiders.

[246] Babbitt metal is used to make bearings.

7	Cloudy, clears off. I go to Albany, send box to Little Falls. Get my teeth fixed. Very muddy weather.
8	Rainy, clears off. Mrs. Clement here visit. I go to river.
9	Fair, clear day. I go to river. I boil hog feed.
10	Fair, S.W. Mrs. Holmes leave, **Wife come with propeller**. I pay off Woolsey Cary $2.08. Go to river.
11	Fine day. I go to Wesley's & to cemetery. Call to Willis's. A. Hotaling & P. Roberts here.
12	Rainy. **I take a dose of Calomel & oil**. I get horse shod. Go to Charlotte Hotaling's on insurance business. Draw grape vines for G. Rifflin.
13	Fair day. Am better. Go to river. Lay around. Mary come. Mrs. Winters pay me 6 dollars; I pay Mary $1.25.
14	Very fine day. I work at corn crib. Wife go to Wesley's.
15	Cloudy, I go to river. Mrs. Banden pay me 5 dollars rent. Mother here.
16	Rainy. I go to river. Am unwell, lay around.
17	Cold, cloudy, snowy. I sort potatoes, go to river, put potatoes in cellar.
18	Cloudy, some snow, SW. I go to Willis's & to Mother's.
19	Fair morning. **I go to Herkimer. Find snow & sleying. I start on foot from Little Falls, get a ride to Bunvell's, then go on foot 2 miles, then get a ride to Eben Kelly's. Stay all night & to breakfast**.
20	Snowy. **I ride with Willis Kelly on bob sleys up to G. Yoos's**. Take dinner & supper & stay all night to Mr. Belcher's. L. Belcher go to Falls. Get saw & mandrel.
21	Snowy day. I stay around the mill, eat to Gotfriet's. Stay all night to Belcher's. Sawmill runs good. I pay Belcher old sawmill bill & 10 dollars on new mill, I pay Gotfriet $50.
22	Snowy. I go around the woods. Eat to Gottefitt's. Stay all night to Belcher's.
23	Fair. Fine sleying. I come to Little Falls with Gotfriet & Davis. Come on to Canajoharie, stay all night to Mrs. C. Spraker's, fine visit.
24	Fair, very cold. Come holme. Mary Serles here.
25	Cloudy cold, SW, rainy afternoon. I go to Meeting. Doct. Fredenburgh here, spend the evening.
26	Warm forenoon, cold rainy NW in afternoon. I put up crib in barn.
27	Fair, SW. **Wife go to Albany, get girl Anna**. I work around. Mrs. Hathaway pay me 20/.
28	Fair, warm, SW. **I work around women. Miss Schoonmaker, Mary Blaisdell, Elenor VanSlyck here; all go to Singing School**.
29	Cold, NW. Mr. Billings & Elenor VanSlyck leave. I work around, go to river. Get 25 dollars of L.F. Cranston.
30	Cold. I go to Albany, Henry Rilan go along. I stop to Elias Millbank's. I leave box with G.B. Lawton, send it to Herkimer.

December 1855

1 Fine day. I & G. Rifflin work in quiry. Doct. Blaisdell, Mary Almira VanBergen Mary Serles here. I pay Mary 2 dollars. Charlotte Hotaling pay me her insurance money $7.50. We all go there, spend the evening.

2 Fair, SW. Doct. Blaisdell take Almira holme. I go to Meeting. Call to Willis's & to Mother's.

3 Fair, NW. I work around, attend P.R. meeting, to river.

4 Fair. I & Michael Winters get out stone. I & Mother Hotaling go to Garret Hotaling's visit. Elias Millbank here to dinner.

5 Fair. I go to papermill. George & Michael get out stone. I gave Elias Millbank's note to A.E. Willis $213.50. Wife go to Baltimore; bring Elenor VanSlyck here. All attend Mr. Billing's Concert; passes off well.

6 Fair. I, George & Michael work in quiry. Elenor VanSlyck, Miss Davis, Mrs. Trego visit here.

7 Fair, cold, NW. G.T. Sweet & Lady & her Sister & Daughter here. He pays me $200 rent. George Harris come with his Lady.

8 Fair, cold, NW. I work at gravel. Libby Hotaling, Mr. Trego, Wife, Levi, Mrs. Hotaling go to Troy. T. Clancy pay me $23.50 on church. I let A.E. Willis have $200. G. Harris & Lady here. **Chris Sickler died**.

9 Snow & rain all day. I go to Mother's.

10 Fair, cold. I go to mill. Attend lawsuit of John E. Gibbens & H. Neal. **Attend funeral of C. Sickler**.

11 Fair, cold, NW. John E. Gibbens here. Pick out lumber. I go to river. A. Whitbeck pay me $75. G. Harris & Lady call here. I send 50-dollar check to Gotfriet & 50 dollars to L.C. Belcher.

12 Clear, cold, NW. I draw gravel. Mother here.

13 Cold, SW, little snow. I & Dutch Henry kill my beef. I buy a horse of James Jack. I pay $157.50, gave note.

14 Fair, no wind. I cut wood, cut up my beef. I harness horses, take beef hide to Carhart. Draw up plank bought of P. Clancy.

15 Misty, rainy day. I take 6 dollars' worth pork to A.E. Willis. I take Children & Mother Hotaling to Flat Bush. Doct. Blaisdell & Mary here, G. Harris & Lady here.

16 Rainy, misty day. I & Wife call to Willis's to tea. Mary Hotaling call here. I go holme with her.

17 Fair, SW. I get horse shod. I draw plank, pay P. Clancy 4 dollars. Send check to G. Yoos 45 dollars. Call to Willis's.

18 Fair, cold, NW. I work around & in quiry.

19 Fair, SW. I get out stone & draw stone all day. A.E. Willis & Miss MacGregor call here.

20 Fair, cold, NW. I kill my hogs & draw 11 loads stone. **B. Weymouth & Lady arrive here. They are married**.

21 Fair, SW. Cut up hogs. Draw gravel all day.

22 Rainy afternoon. Abram Witbeck pay me 28 dollars for wood. I go to river.

23 Fair. Wesley call here. I & he go to cemetery. I call at his house. Mr. Willis call here. I sign 1000 dollar note with him at bank.

24 Fair, cold, NW. I pay John Clement 10 dollars. I draw wood all day. Wife go to Baltimore.

25 Snow all day. Mr. Willis & Lady & his mother, Doct. Blaisdell & Edward here to dine & Mrs. John Clement. Mrs. C. Hathaway pay me 20/ rent. I salt my pork & hams. Mrs. George Harris & Eliza here. **Mr. Sarell Wood & Lady here. They come from Michigan.**

26 Cold wind, snow & ice. I take Mr. Wood & Lady & Sarah Ann to Garret Hotaling's, visit. Then go to Baltimore so Holme. Mr. Edwin Hubbel, Lady, Almira VanBergen & Leonard here. John E. Gibbens here. Put in my new wardrobe. I play around.

27 Fair, very cold. Mr. S. Wood leave. Mr. Willis, Doct. Blaisdell & Mary, Mr. Hubble here. Mary & Charlotte Hotaling call here.

28 Fair. I draw one load of wood. Garret Hotaling here, visit. I pay of J.E. Gibbens 9 dollars.

29 Cold, snowy, NW. I take Wife, Mrs. Wood, Libby Hotaling to Andrew Hotaling's to Coxsackie. **I get Kip skin**[247] of Bogardus, pay 14/.

30 Clear, cold, SW. I take folks to Meeting; break sley tong. Dr. Blaisdell call here. I go to Mother's.

31 Fair, cold, SW. I draw wood. Martin & Elida VanSlyck and Cate VanBergen here.

January 1856

1 Fair, cold. We dine to A.E. Willis's. Then all go to Garrett Houghtaling's to tea. Spend the evening there.

2 Fair, cold. Doct. Cornell call here. I draw two loads of wood, then all hands go to P. Kimmey's. Spend the evening there have a nice party. Coxsackie folks, Uncle Garret go along. Stormy coming holme.

3 Snow all day. Martin & Elida VanSlyck leave. I go to river. Jacob Leigh pay me 1 dollar rent.

4 Very cold, NW. I go to papermill. Mr. Milton pay me 1 dollar on my straw. Doct. Blaisdell here. I go to river.

5 Snowy, cold day. I take Wife, Mrs. Wood & Cate VanBergen to J.H. Hotaling's, visit. I pay P. Clancy one dollar.

6 Fair, NW. I take children on sley ride. Take folks to Meeting. I & Mrs. Wood go to Mother's.

7 Very cold, SW. **I go to Square** & to river. I pay Dutch Henry 1 dollar.

8 Very cold, SW in morning. Mr. Wood here. **I, Wife, Mrs. Wood go to Albany with Harriet & Willis, have a very cold ride**. I pay off G.H. Lawton, R. McMichael, Davidson & Vielie & VanRensselaer.

9 Fair cold. I take Wife, Mother H, Mr. & Mrs. Wood and Anthony, we go to Garret Houghtaling's spend the day.

10 Fair, cold, SW. I take Mr. Wood & Lady to Albany. Wife & Wesley go to Bethlehem Church; attend concert.

---

[247] Kip skin is leather made from the hide of a calf.

11	Fair, cold, NW. I go to mill. I go to J.B. Shear's, pay my tax $65.18. Cate VanBergen here. I go to Willis's. **Mrs. Thomas Gould died today.**
12	Fair, very cold. I go to mill. Attend P.R. Mtg. all day. I pay Blacksmith John 6 dollars. I pay P. Clancy $4.43 shoe bill.
13	Snowy, cold. Mary Hotaling, Cate VanBergen, Ed VanOrden, Doct. Blaisdell here. I go to Willis's.
14	Fair, cold. **Attend Mrs. Gould's funeral.** I go to Briggs' evening, visit. Draw 24 loads stone to NW Johnson.
15	Fair, cold, NW. P. Kimmey call here, leave his horse. We all go to Coxsackie to Rev. Mr. Pelt's Donation. Work in quiry. **N.H. Johnson pay me $26.31 balance of straw bill of Robb & Milton.**
16	Fair, SW. Lay around, work in quiry.
17	Cloudy, cold. Willis call here. I work in quiry.
18	Fair, SW. I go to Greenville, stay all night to A. Fancher's. Mr. Eddy & Family call here. I get Ed Collin's rent.
19	Fair, cold, NW. I get my rents and come holme. Robert Nelson call here. Wife go with Mr. Eddy's folks to Gerry Springstead's.
20	Fair, cold. Mr. Eddy, Wife, Sister & Children leave. I go to Mother's.
21	Fair. I let Willis have 120 dollars. Mr. Trego, Mast Andrews, Mr. Willis, Mrs. A. Briggs, Wife & Sister call here. I pay John VanDenburgh 10 dollars.
22	Fair, cold, NW. I and Mast Andrews go to Coxsackie, take dinner to J.H., Mr. W. Gay's. **Go to Backuse's, engage entertainment for sley ride.** G.J. Sweet & Mr. White call.
23	Fair, cold, NW. **Judge Anthony VanBergen & daughter call here.** I go to river, lay around.
24	Fair, cold. **Start for great sley ride to Backuse's to Coxsackie. About 100 dance all night. Great blow and drifting. Come holme 8 o'clock in the morning. Very cold. We come back road. Tore down fences. Some froze their ears, noses & feet.**
25	Very cold, NW. Lay around the house all day. **John Mosher died. People got badly froze today.**
26	Fair, cold day. Robert Nelson here. Mr. Matson & Lady visit here. **I attend funeral of John Mosher.** I pay Dutch Henry $11.02. I pay G. Refflin $9.25. I settle off with them.
27	Snowy, SW. T. Civill & Doct. Blaisdell call here. I go to Mother's. Wife go to Meeting.
28	Snowy day. I go to river. **I write Journal.** Get my Buffalo Robes of Peter Seabridge. Mary & Anthony Hotaling here; spend the evening.
29	Cloudy. I go to G.J. Sweet's. A.E. & U.B. Willis, Wm. MacGregor, Miss Nichols, Mast Andrews & two Sisters, Dedrick & Mary, John Lawton, Miss Maxon, Miss Hide here, visit. **Levi Sick.**
30	Fair, cold. I work around the house. Mother Hotaling come holme. Wife go with Willis's folks to Rev. Mr. Jolly's, visit. I send 20-dollar check to G.A. Feeter.
31	Fair, cold. I work around, go to river. **Levi quite sick.** John Mull, Wife & Daughter, Charlotte Cronk here, spend the evening, take tea.

February 1856

1   Fair, SW. We attend party to A.E. Willis's in evening. **My horse get kicked**. I go to mill.

2   Fair, cold, NW. **I go to R. Nelson to sell my Farm**. I go to river.

3   Fair, cold, NW. Garret Hotaling, Lib & D. Nives's daughter here, visit. U.B. Willis here to dinner. I go to Mother's.

4   Fair, NW, cold. I go to river twice. Mother Hotaling here. Widow Charlotte here. George Harris & Lady here. **Granny Sherwood died today**.

5   Very cold, heavy NW. I pay Henry Rilan 1 dollar, let him have 2 bu. potatoes. Stay in house, go to river.

6   Fair, SW. I work around, go to river. **Attend Astronomical lecture in division room. Attend funeral of Granny Sherwood**. Mr. Laigh pay me 1 dollar. **Lyman Baker and Miss Clow get Married.**

7   Snowy, south wind. **I, Wife, Willis & Harriet go to Baltimore, cross to the Island, get in the wood's roads, get lost. Turn around take road down the island. I go to reconnoiter, fall down hurt my head, up again. Then come up the Island to McCabe's road. Get across the Island. Go to John Cronk's, visit all day have a good time. Then come holme**.

8   Fair. I and John McGary cut & draw wood. Mr. D. Shear & Lady, Mrs. Johnson, Mary Serles, Miss Teneyck, Mrs. Hull Mrs. Fredenburgh here, visit in afternoon & eve. Mr. Cranston Lady & Sister here.

9   Fair, cold day. Attend Quarterly Meeting. I pay G. Rifflen 1 dollar. **Jacob Veeder here; he offer me 6000 dollars for Flat Bush Farm.**

10   Fair, SW. I and all hands go to Quarterly Meeting. Uncle Garret & Caroline Hotaling & John Rea call here. Willis's two girls call here.

11   Fair, SW. I, Wife go to Albany, come holme. **R. Pulver here, buy my Flat Bush Farm for his land & house & lot & the sum of $4,900 boot money**. He paid in 300 dollars.

12   Fair, cold, squally after thawy morning. I draw wood. Mother here. Mary Hotaling call. John McGary & A. Seburgh work here. **Attend party to A.N. Briggs, the best party of the season. Get holme at 3 o'clock in morning. Have nice grand time**.

13   Fair. NW, cold. Thermometer stands 10 below zero. I go to river. I pay G. Rifflin 2 dollars. J. Veeder here about Flat Bush Farm.

14   Fair, very cold. Thermometer 12 below zero. I go to Willis and to river.

15   Fair, SW. I, Willis, Harriet, Sarah Ann, Caroline & Eliz Houghtaling go to Andrew VanSlyck's, visit. All have a nice time. **Willis serve notice on G.T. Sweet to leave my Flat Bush Farm.**

16   Fair. Thaws a little. I work in quiry, go to river, Mrs. George Harris [here]. I pay Henry Rilan 3 dollars.

17   Fair, very cold. I go to Meeting. Call to A.E. Willis.

18   Very cold north wind. I go to river. I and Wife go to Garrett Houghtaling's.

19   Cold. Fair, NW. Go to river twice. G.T. Sweet & Wife here. They go to Dancing School. N.H. Johnson pay me 12 dollars stone bill.

20 Fair, cold, NW. **We attend horse trot on the ice, then go to Cedar Hill. Attend to Lady's Leap Year Sley Ride, have a fine time. Get holme at half past 3 in morning**.

21 Fair, thawy. Go to woods, draw out wood. A. Seburgh help.

22 Fair. I work around the house. I and Wesley go to P. Kimmey's to party in evening. **Dedrick Lawton died**. I pay P. Springstead 1 dollar.

23 Snowy afternoon. I go to river, get drill. I pay G. Rifflin 3 dollars. The two Miss Gays and Sarah C VanBergen here. Henry Smith call here. N.H. Johnson pay me 20 dollars on stone bill. I pay him all costs on H. Niles suit of F.R. Terry's getting up.

24 NW wind snow drifts badly. **Attend Dedrick Lawton's Funeral**. A. Sharp here. Martin & Elida VanSlyck, Almira & Cate VanBergen, Mary Houghtaling & John Rea & Doct. Blaisdell call here.

25 Fair, SW. Andrew Houghtaling, Wife & child, Cate VanBergen here. I let Willis have 682 dollars, take his note.

26 Draw 13 loads sand. A.N. Briggs, Wife, Hannah & Jane Andrews, Martin Andrews Doct. Blaisdell here, visit all day. **I attend the breaking of Sons of Temperance. They pay me $86.83 & leave the room**.

27 Fair. I take Mother Hotaling to Garrett Hotaling's. A.B. Hotaling, Lady & two girls here. I take Peter Seabridge to Flat Bush. Settle up my affairs with G.T. Sweet.

28 Fair. Wife & Doct. Blaisdell go to Bethlehem with Willis's horse. I take Wife & Mrs. A.S. Vanderzee, go to Wm. C. Robb's afternoon, spend the evening.

29 Fair. Work in quiry, go to river.

March 1856

1 Fair day, stormy at night. I go after Mother Hotaling. Mrs. Willis & Mrs. Clement to James Jack's.

2 Snowy day. Newman Finch & Daughter, Mary Blaisdell, James Trego & Wife here. A.N. Briggs & Ephram call here. John Rea call. I sign notes with A.E. Willis for 600 dollars, sent by Thms. Penton.

3 Fair, cold. I go to Dean's Mill. I pay him off, $6.94. Wife go to Wm. McGregor in afternoon. I go spend the evening.

4 Fair, cold. Go Under Hill, get wood. I pay off A. Seburgh 1 dollar.

5 Fair. P. Schoduck draw sand for me. Mother Hotaling go to Thms. Hotaling's. Garrett Hotaling & Peter Sickles here.

6 Cold, SW. **I, Wife, Caroline Hotaling go to Barent Hotaling's on the ice, spend all day.** Squally coming back. Go to J.J. Colvin's in evening.

7 Fair, NW, cold. I and wife visit to A.E. Willis's. Attend Singing School in the evening.

8 Fair. I pay off Lewis Crandle $12.54. I pay J. VanDenburgh $7.87 balance. I go to river. Andrew A. Houghtaling, James Bronk here.

9 Fair, cold. **TH 10 deg below 0**. I go with James Trego to John Rowe's. We take dinner to J. Lenden's. Mother, Wesley, John Rea & Wife, Mr. P. Kimmey & Mr. Niven here. Mrs. Jemma Hotaling & Lib Hotaling here. I call to Mother's & to Willis's.

10	Very cold. TH 5 below 0. I go with Willis, have a cold ride. I pay H. MacDonald 8 dollars, get 1 bbl. of flour, get cloth 7 dollars, get knives $4.25.
11	Fair, N and south wind. I lay around. Very cold, go to river.
12	Snow & blow, very cold. I lay around. **I sell my Pulver horse to William Minnick for 600 dollars.**[248] **J. Roe and the Widow Hathaway get married**.
13	Fair, cold, NW. Mother & Mrs. John Cronk here, spend the day. **I write journal**. Go to river. Henry Sniyth pay me $4.84 for calf. I pay Doct. Blaisdell 5 dollars for his stove.
14	Fair. I take Wife, Mrs. J. Clement, Mrs. A.N. Briggs to James Trego's. I and Trego to Baltimore. We attend party to Widow Charlotte Hotaling's in evening.
15	Fair, N & south wind. I take Mother Hotaling to Flat Bush and to see James Roberts at William Cook's. Attend party to A.E. Willis's in the evening.
16	South wind, snowy. H.C. VanBergen, Almira, Martin & Elida VanSlyck, Mary Hotaling call. Wife go to river. John Rea call here. I call to Harris's.
17	Fair. Draw stone, work in quiry, draw stone, draw wood.
18	Fair, warm, SW. Mrs. Garrett Hotaling, Widow Charlotte, Almira VanBergen here. J. Cronk call. I get out stone. **Mr. Chase subpoena me to Greenville**.
19	Snow all day. Draw out gravel. Expect company but they did not come. Willis & Harriet here.
20	Fair. **I, Wife, Mrs. George Harris, Almira VanBergen go with Mr. Willis to Baltimore to a Dedication of M.E. Church. Rev. Mr. Peck preach**. I send letter & check to Gottefriet Yoos. I pay 2 dollars for church.
21	Fair. **I go to Greenville, attend Lawsuit of G. Fancher's and Charles Townsend's**. Go to Fancher's, stay all night.
22	Fair. I go to Greenville, then to Fancher's, stay all night. Am sick all night.
23	Fair. Go to James Waldron's to dinner, then to Meeting, then to Andrew Fancher's. Am sick all night.
24	Go to Greenville. **Attend Lawsuit all day**.
25	Fair. Go to Greenville. Then come holme. **Am in great pain, can hardly get holme**.
26	Fair, NW. **I am sick and have great pain with colic. Doct. Frendenburgh here all night. Wesley, T. Civill, & Robert Pulver here. Great pain all night**.
27	Fair, cold, NW. Mr. Zeller here; bring pictures. Wife pay him 4 dollars. James Jack & Mrs. George Harris here.
28	Fair, very cold, freeze all day. Wife & Levi go to party to A.N. Briggs. John Bushants here. I send J.W. Story's note to T.W. Gay for him to collect the money on it.
29	Fair, very cold. P. Seabridge, John Clement, R. Pulver here. R. Pulver pay me check of 100 & odd dollars. Make out deed to him & Wm. Minnick for property. Mrs. G. Harris here.
30	Fair, very cold. Willis & Harriet call here. Wife go to Widow Hotaling's. I stay in house all day.
31	Fair, very cold. I go to river. Mary Hotaling & Mrs. G. Harris here. **I pay the Mail Man for recording deeds in Albany**. I send 150 dollars by R. Pulver. Pay off G.T. Sweet.

---

[248] That would be approximately $20,000 today.

April 1856

1. Very fair day, SW. Work in quiry. Wife & Mrs. George Harris go S. Harris's.
2. Fair. Mother & Mrs. G. Harris here. Wife & Mrs. G. Harris go to Mrs. J.J. Colvin's visit. I work in quiry.
3. Fair, SW. I go to river. Work around the house.
4. Fair I go to river. A. Witbeck pay me 75 dollars rent. Ms. G. Harris here. I pay $31.50 interest money to Mrs. Sweet.
5. Cold. I go with John Cronk look at land. I work in quiry. I pay off G. Rifflin & H. Rylan. Cate Hotaling here. I and Wife go to A.E. Willis's, spend the evening.
6. Fair. Cate Hotaling, Mrs. G. Harris here. All go to Meeting. I go to river and to Mother's.
7. Fair warm day. **River break up**. Peter Seabridge pay me 48 dollars rent on lots. I pay him 74 cents. J. Leigh pay me one dollar rent. I attend Annual Road Dist. Meeting. Mrs. S. Harris here, visit.
8. Very warm day. I go to Town Meeting with Wesley. Mrs. George Harris here. Very muddy, much snowbanks.
9. Fair, SW. G. Yoos come here. Mrs. G. Harris here. I work around, fix hay press.
10. Fair, cold, NW. **I very sick all night last, in great pain all day**. I go to Doct. Fredenburgh's & to Willis's.
11. Fair, SW. Gotfriet leave. I let him have 25 dollars. I go to Albany with him. I get 1248 dollars out of bank. George Harris & Lady here.
12. Fair morning, rainy afternoon. I work around the house. I get 350 dollars of John Cronk on land.
13. Fair, cold NW. **I go with G. Rifflin to vineyard**. Wife go to Mrs. Hotaling's.
14. Cloudy, SW. I go to river. Work around the house, get fish.
15. Cloudy SW. I go with N. Carroll & Wm. Case. Get press roll. I go to river & lay around the house.
16. I get spike of J. Hazleton, pay $4.75. Let Willis have $1000 last night, take his note.
17. Fair morning, rainy afternoon. G. Yoos hired men here. I pay Philander $50 & Henry 25 dollars. I send check to L.C. Belcher for 50 dollars. Get check of A.E. Willis to send to Belcher to buy shingles for me.
18. Fair. I go to river. Do pension business with Gregory. Doct. and Marite come here from New York. Mrs. Aaron Hotaling, Mrs. P. Seabridge, Mrs. R. Hotaling here. Mrs. John Schoonmaker here, visit.
19. Fine warm day. Sally Teneyck cow has a calf. Mr. A.N. Briggs & Lady, Mr. Willis & Lady, Hannah Andrews, Mrs. Horace Renny, Mary Hotaling, Mrs. A.S. VanDerzee, Widow Hotaling & Lib, Mrs. Wm. Lawton, Mrs. J.J. Colvin here. Mrs. Willis taken sick. I go to river. Doctor & Marite here.
20. Snow & blow. Very tedious day. I stay in house all day. Andrew VanAntwerp & Marite & Mother here.

21 Cold, rainy. Henry Yung, Dutchman come to work. I go to river. Rufus King pay me 40 dollars interest money.

22 Rainy. I lay around, go to river. Lib Hotaling call.

23 Fair, SW. I go to mill. Go under the Hill, fix fence. Lib Hotaling here.

24 Fine warm day. Henry help G. Rifflin. Doct. VanAntwerp take my horse, go to Flat Bush. **Take my deed along to R. Pulver for Farm**.

25 Fair, warm, SW. I, Doctor, Wife & Marite go to Albany. I get hoes & shovels for P. Seabridge.

26 Fair. Work in flower beds. I pay G. Rifflin $7.50 for Big Michael's & Big Dutchman's work. Wife come from Albany. Lib Hotaling here. Mary Holden & Miss Shaddau call. G. Fancher bring my oats from J.J. Williamson's. I pay George $13.88 for Williamson. Mrs. Hathaway pay me 2 dollars today.

27 Very fine day, SW. I go to Meeting. I and Doct. Blaisdell walk over to vineyard & to cemetery. Lib Hotaling & Mrs. Harris here.

28 Fair, very warm. I and Henry work around the house. I go to river.

29 Fair, warm NW. I plow garden, plant potatoes, plow Mrs. Hotaling's garden. Go to river, get one shad. **Old Mr. Tuttle died last night**.

30 Fair, cold NW. I plant garden. I take Wife, Mother Hotaling, Lib Hotaling to New Baltimore. Get my gun fixed by Wm. Carroll.

May 1856

1 Cloudy, cold SW. Reuben Cary here, pay me 132 dollars for Daniel VanAntwerp. I pay the money to N.H. Johnson, take his receipt. He pay it to Andrew or Daniel VanAntwerp. Mrs. Jemima Hotaling here. We all go to vineyard. I plant beets in the garden.

2 Rain all last night and today. I go to river, get 2 shad & 8 herring.

3 Rainy. I pay Widow Charlotte $9.68 for my bull. I pay Doct. Fredenburgh 49 dollars interest money. **Let my Hall to Mrs. G. Harris. Get Marite's Carpet and Band Box** from propeller. Doct. Blaisdell here.

Band Box

4 Cold and wet at evening, NW. I go to Meeting. Call to A.E. Willis's and to Mother's.

5 Fair. **I and Henry Sperl go to Little Falls. Take stage go to Gottefriet Yoos**.

6 Fair. **Go around the lands, woods & sawmill. Charles Barrett died**.

7 Fair. Henry Sperl come holme. I stay around the mill. John Henry VanBenthuyzen & Lady come here. **Mary Harris has a boy and they call him Moses**.

8 Lowry & rainy. **I & Gottefriet Yoos go see Mr. Persons. Buy his farm for Henry Sperl. Stay about mill. I pay off Lines Belcher**.

9 Rain all day. **I stay around the mill with Belcher**.

10 Lowry. **I come to Little Falls with Gottefriet Yoos. Take cars, then come holme**. William & Maria MacGregor, John MacGregor & Lady here, spend the afternoon & evening.

11	Fair. We all go to Meeting twice. Widow Hotaling & Lib call here. We go to Willis's.
12	Fair. I take Wife, J.H. VanBenthuyzen & Lady to William MacGregor's. Then we go to Garrett Hotaling's meet Andrew Fancher. I come back with him. He pay me his rent & wood bill of 56 [dollars] and a few other bills, about 365 dollars. I then go back to G. Hotaling's to tea, so to Baltimore, then holme.
13	Fair, cold NW. Wife, J.H. VanBenthuyzen & Lady, Lib Houghtaling & Levi go to Albany. I work in quiry. I take calf to propeller.
14	Fair, S wind. I and Henry draw gravel. I pay Isaac Brown $7.87. I go to river, get fish. A.E. Willis call here. Mother Houghtaling come holme. T.H. Gould pay me $2.08.
15	Fair, south wind. Draw gravel. Henry help John Cronk harrow & furrow out his land.
16	Rainy. I draw one load sand. Go to the river. Mary Hotaling call here.
17	Rain. I work in quiry Pay G. Rifflin 1 dollar. Mrs. Cate Spraker, Caroline VanAntwerp, Lib Hotaling visit. I go to river. I pay John Rea 3 dollars borrowed money.
18	Fair, SW. Martin VanSlyck here. Mary & Emma Hotaling. I go to Meeting.
19	Lowry, SW. Henry draw 3 loads manure. I pay wife 3 dollars, go to river.
20	Fair, warm. I take Henry Sperl & Family to Albany. I get one pair horse collars. Send files to Herkimer.
21	Fair, cool NW. I work in garden. Draw manure & gravel. I go to river.
22	Fair, cool N wind. Clean house, shake carpets, draw stone. Doct. Fredenburgh call. **Capt. Cobb here, whitewash.**
23	Fair, SW. Draw stone. A.E. Wills call. S. Crandell here.
24	Fair, hot. I work in garden. Go to river. I pay off Jacob $1.75 for G. Rifflin.
25	Very cold, NW. I go to Meeting. Wesley & Euphema Blaisdell, Cate Hotaling here to dinner. A.E. Willis call. Wife go to Widow Hotaling's.
26	Fair, very cold. I go to river. Draw stone & gravel. I pay G. Rifflin 1 dollar. I, Willis & Harriet call to Dominie Gardner's and to Widow Charlotte's. I let Willis have 150 dollars, take his due bill.
27	Fair, SW. Work on road. Mrs. John Rea here, spend the day.
28	Fair. Mrs. C. Hathaway pay me 3 dollars rent. Edward Banden pay me 5 dollars rent. John Cronk pay me $80, gave him his deed. I go to Kimmey's, get plank. Henry goes to Albany.
29	Fair, N wind morning, rainy afternoon. I go to Kimmey's, get plank. Henry come back from Albany. Mrs. Hotaling, Mary Hotaling here. I go to river.
30	Very cold, NW. I am unwell. Miss Brace here. Mr. Civill call here. I go to papermill. I get $480.12 of **Schoonmaker & Johnson.**[249]
31	Fair, NW, very cold. I am unwell. **I go with Mr. Civill to get up school for Miss Brace. She here.** Mrs. George Harris call. I pay Peter Swinne 3 dollars, G. Rifflin 2 dollars.

---

[249] John J. Schoonmaker & Noble H. Johnson ran a freight forwarding business in Coeymans.

June 1856

1   Fair, SW. I go to Meeting. I and T. Civill go to Mrs. Bronck's and to Mrs. Wilson's. I call to Willis's.

2   Fair, very warm. Work at Division Room. **Get ready for school for Miss Brace**. She & Wife go to Albany. I let Wife have 10 dollars.

3   Fair, hot. Fix up Temperance Hall. Miss Brace & Mother here.

4   Fair. **I and Wife start for the West, go to Albany with the steamer P.J. Coffin**. I deposit $800 in Mechanics & Farmers Bank, take certificate. **Start with cars up the Mohawk Country. Very fine, people plowing, grass looks well, stop at Utica, get book for my journal.**[250] Lots of boys around cars selling apples, lemonade & New York papers. Go again, arrive at Rome, country fine. Stop at Rome look around, start again for Syracuse. Country low swampy & poor lands. Arrive at Syracuse, stop again, a short time off, again for Palmyra county. Good except Montezuma Mash corn is up. Some fields of wheat & rye look well. So on to Rochester. Nearly night, change cars for Suspension Bridge. Country looks well, we stop at Braton's American Hotel. Was well pleased, tired & go to bed. Man shot on Bridge.

Suspension Bridge at Niagara Falls

5   Fair. **I walk down to Bridge. Took a drink from Mineral Spring, very strong of Sulphur. View the Bridge; it is a splendid piece of work, the greatest piece of mechanism in the world.**[251] We walk across the bridge. Walk up to the falls on Canada side. Encounter hordes of hackman (one dollar for a ride). We go around, view table rock and a yard of animals; the scenery is very splendid. See the Steam Maid of the Mist make her excursion trip. Passengers have on oil cloth. She goes up to the sheet then around so down to Bridge. We cross below the falls with tiny boat, go around Niagara, then take cars down to Bridge. Then I go to Mineral Spring view the Bridge again. Then to Hotel for dinner. The man that was shot on the Bridge last night died today. Take cars to Buffalo, by way of Black Rock. Take trunk on board steamer Western World, then we call on Pardon C. Sherman. See Mrs. Sherman (Daughter) & Caty VanDalfsin. Then call on Isaac VerPlanck, he is Judge. Then call to Cap Hazzard, take tea with him, he & family entertained us with every degree of politeness. **Harnessed their horses before carriage took us all around the city. Mrs. Hazzard went with us to boat with carriage. We had a very pleasant time. Bade them**

Steamer Trunk

---

[250] The new journal starts on 1 Jan 1856, which indicates he was roughly 6 months behind in updating his journal.

[251] The Niagara Falls Suspension Bridge stood from 1855 – 1897. It was the world's first working railway suspension bridge. It had an upper and lower deck – the upper deck carried trains and the lower deck carried carriages and pedestrians. The initial designer/builder was Charles Ellet Jr, who left the project due to a financial dispute. It was finished by John Augustus Roebling, who designed many other bridges including the Brooklyn Bridge.

Goodbye. We was then in waiting for the boat to start and Martin VanSlyck stepped into the cabin. We was glad to see him. We write back to Coxsackie.

6   Foggy. Steam whistle goes all night. I was in great pain all night with dyspepsia. Eat no breakfast, no dinner. Very foggy. We get aground at 4 o'clock pm. It was a very careless trick. Run ashore in sight of land. Shift freight to aft, send to Malden get 3 steamers, try to pull off, no go. Then we shift baggage on steamer Pearl. Go to Detroit. Go to Public House, get there half past two at night. Stop till morning.

7   Fair. Go around Detroit. Then take Michigan Central RR & Kalamazoo first to Dearborn. Country level, growing corn, oats, a little wheat. Land the same to Wayne. Then to Denton's Mills. Wheat poor saw a little fruit. Then to Yapalanta,[252] a thriving smart place. Then to Ann Arbor, the country is better, grassy & wheat looks well. Then to Chelsea, some very poor, country grass. Then to Jackson, which is a smart place growing fast well located. Then to Parma, land level generally not good, quite sandy, some fair prices of rye, wheat poor, corn small. So on to Marshall to dinner a very dear place, fare very high. Then to Battle Creek. We have a fine shower, ground is higher, crops are much better until we reach Galesburg. it is now better land and the villages are flourishing. Arrive at Kalamazoo. Ride to Kalamazoo House. Pay our fare to Grand Rapids. Take dinner walk around the place. This is one of the finest and most flourishing villages I ever saw. Gardens very forward, corn one foot high. They have plank walks all through the village. Fine horses. One noble stud - as fine a horse I ever saw. Stores have all open fronts and the place is full of teams from the country. Sitting on the stoop at the Hotel, saw an establishment coming with a large two horse waggon covered with a cloth top, a barrel tied behind, a large family of children include men & women driving two bulls, two stags traveling slowly along unconcerned as though they were worth a million.[253]

1868 Map of Ypsilanti

8   Fair morning. I feel well. Pay bill, am well satisfied. Landlord fine man, well pleased, good fare. Take stage for Grand Rapids. Country looks better, fine grass, corn, wheat, fine timber, land lays higher, water clear steam, sawmills along the road. Arrive at Grand Rapids, which is a flourishing city. Go to Sarell Wood's. They are much pleased to see us. This is the most flourishing place we ever saw in Michigan. Soil sandy, a great many fine buildings up and they have extensive plaster beds, fine waterpower of half a mile in length.[254] Fine bridge property high.

Entrance to Gypsum Mine

---

252 We think he meant Ypsilanti. It is currently the home of Eastern Michigan University.
253 Michigan remained a frontier society until the time of the Civil War.
254 Large deposits of gypsum many feet below layers of clay, limestone and hard shale in the Grand Rapids area. Gypsum was first used extensively for fertilizer. As the population and building needs increased, less gypsum was used for farming and more for construction needs: plaster and stucco.

	We go to Meeting in evening, hear Mr. Smith lecture. Have excellent singing. Go back to Mr. Wood's stay all night.
9	Fair. We sleep late. After breakfast, go around the village. Go up to the river, see the boys catch fish - they get Black Fish or Bass & Sunfish. Back to dinner, then go with Mr. Wood to see his farms. The soil is very sandy but productive; wheat & spring rye & grass looks well. Go to see Bridget Hood. Go holme to Mr. Wood's and stay all night.
10	Fair. I & Mrs. Wood take a horseback ride about 5 miles out of town to the lake. The soil is clay & sand. See fine crops of wheat, grass, pass some poor buck, yards fine orchards and a fine nursery. Then back holme to dinner. Mr. Todd & Lady arrived & Mr. Wood. I, Martin & Mr. Wood go view the plaster beds. The plaster is quiried out in blocks and then ground fine. We saw a fine sawmill, which worked well. Then we go back holme to Mr. Wood's. Country low about the plaster beds.
11	Fair Morning. Start for Newago. One waggon, and one horse & saddle. Sandy land for three miles then good - clay loam for more than thirty miles. Take dinner go to Mr. Fairgason's. Leave waggon; take two horses & we ride and walk to Newago. Now we pass through the best pine forest I ever saw. The road is any way through the woods almost impassable. All the houses are built of logs, but very good ones & for 15 miles the road has never been worked. We stay at a boarding house, tolerable good fare, but the mosquitoes are very thick. Newago is a new place; first started three sawmills, one grist mill, one tavern, this bids fair for a large place but two brick chimneys & no foundations to their buildings or cellars. Fine heavy waterpower.
12	Fair morning. We walk around the village, go to steam sawmill, look at timber lots of Mr. Sanders. I & Mr. Woods buy 300 acres near the village then look at grist mill, sawmills. Take dinner. Then I & Martin look again at the lots, get tired, take supper & go to bed.
13	Cloudy morning. Take breakfast, saddle horses & start again for Grand Rapids. Come 12 miles or more through the best pine timber I ever saw. Trees 200 feet high and straight as a rod. Get to Cazenovia, stop to Mr. Furgason's. Take dinner, then come on to Grand Rapids. Country fine, good water. Meet a number of teams going to Newago. One or two loads of furniture - people moving to Newago.
14	Misty, rainy morning. Walk around, take dinner, then I & Wife go to A. Hood's spend the afternoon. Take tea, it is a very cold day; I am quite unwell.
15	Fair morning. I am better. We go hear Mr. Smith preach. Then I and Martin go to see the cemetery. At night I come across Henry VanZant, then we go to Methodist Meeting.
16	Fine, pleasant weather. We all take steamer Olive Branch, go down the Grand River. Country very pleasant, trees hang over the water on the shores, country level and productive. Stop at Granville, start again. Take a good dinner stop at Steel's Landing. Wife & Mr. & Mrs. Wood leave. Martin & I go on to Grand Haven, which is a low marshy place, barren sandy hills. River full of Bayous. There is an Indian settlement across from Grand Haven. Sand blows the buildings under, there is plenty of Steam sawmills and a tannery and a flourishing place but unpleasant. Take steamer Otaway for Chicago.

17	Rainy morning. **Arrive at Chicago. Breakfast at New York House. Call on Henry Witbeck**; see his extensive establishment. Go around the city, take dinner, then go to railroad. Chicago is the city of the West. Buildings are immense as to size of streets. Muddy, walks are bad. Vessels go up almost through the city. We leave by Rock Island RR for Morris. Go through Jolliet country. Looks well, corn looks very well. Arrive at Morris. Meet with John Cronk, go with him holme. Take supper, stay all night, take breakfast.
18	Fair, very dry. **We go to John VanDalfsen's, see him. We come back to John Cronk's dinner.** Then go to Theron Collins, then to George Collins, then we go to Sulphur Spring through the timber to the Railroad. Then back to George's for supper; stay with him all night. His child very sick.
19	Fair, foggy. **Go to Theron Collins for dinner. Then go to Joshua Collins.** Then he goes with us to Phillip Collins where he is breaking Prairie. Then to Joshua Collins to tea, then to Terry Collins. Call then to Theron's; stay all night and breakfast.
20	Fair. **Take Theron's horse waggon & boy and start for Rock Creek. Cross the prairie to Lisbon. Go to Georgetown. Then cross Fox River.** Get waggon tire set. Set time thru to Newark Station. Go to Mr. Marcy's country - all the way very good fine crops of wheat, corn and oats. It is new but improving very fast. It is very dusty, fields are large. Mr. Marcy lives in a double shanty one story high - no upstairs. We take dinner & tea and are made welcome but leave the place and start for holme. Stop to a farmer's house. Stay all night. They keep us for nothing. Very clever people.
21	Start again at sunrise. **Come on to Fox River. Break waggon tire. With it up, come on to bridge**; stop to a tavern, get waggon fixed. Get back again to Jerry Collins to dinner & tea go to bed.
22	Fair, very busy day. **Jerry Hassup take all hands to Beecher E. Holmes. Spend the day.** Martin and myself go with Beecher around to the coal mines with Beecher's team. See his crops. Go back holme to Beecher's, stay all night. We wash off & go to bed.
23	Fair, very hot. **We leave with Beecher for Morris Martin. VanSlyck leave for holme.** Take dinner, then go to Theron Collins, then to George Collins, then back to Jerry's. Meet Phillip Collins and Wife visit them until 12 o'clock at night. Then bid all good night & go to bed.
24	Showry, hot. **Go with Jerry to see his crops. Then Jerry takes me to Morris. I see John Skinner.** Then I go to Jack Wilsey's, stay all night. I call to Levittt Mull's.
25	Showry, hot. **I go around with Dewitt Mull. Then take cars for Chicago. Call at H. Witbeck's shop.** Leave him a letter. Go around the city. Take Steamer Ottaway for Grand River or Grand Haven.
26	Raining. **Arrive at Grand Haven. Could not get any breakfast. Take steamer Olive Branch up the River.** Take dinner on board. Arrive at Grand Rapids. Go to Mr. Wood's, all well. Hear from holme.
27	Fair. **Walk around in afternoon. I & Mr. Wood go shoot pidgeons on Mr. Wood's Farm.**
28	Fair, hot. **Go shoot pidgeons again before breakfast. Come holme, take breakfast & dinner.** Then I go to Bridget's to tea. Her house caught fire upstairs and it made a great bustle. We put it out. Then I come back to Mr. S. Wood's, then we go spend the

evening to Ransom Wood's. Have ice cream and a social party, then back to Mr. Wood's to bed.

29 Showery but clears off. **We go to Meeting to Mr. Smith's Church. Come back to dinner, go to sleep. Spend the evening with Andrew Hood then back to bed.**

30 Fair, pleasant. **Take stage to Kalamazoo. Stop at hotel that we did going out, take tea. Leave for Detroit - ride all night**.

July 1856

1 **Take cars through Canada for Suspension Bridge**. Have a look at Lake St. Clair. Country low & swampy. Go through Chatham. Few crops and small timber - mostly hardwood. Get to Lockport, a low wet & swampy place. So, to London, a large place with a great many large buildings - country good. So to Ingersoll, so to Paris. Country better, higher ground some pine timber, so to Hamilton on the Burlington Bay. Then on and cross the Welland Canal[255] to Mr. Braton's at Suspension Bridge. Country from Hamilton is good ground. Is higher land from 20 to 60 dollars per acre. Walk around and go to bed.

2 Fair. **I go to whirlpool. It is in the form of a basin**. The river turns short at the right. The water is very rough and rapid till it gets to the whirlpool then is whirls to the left round & round. Banks very high and steep. Evergreen & other trees grow on the banks to the river. I go down the back and view the pool & rapids. The water is thrown 10 to 15 ft high. The view is very grand. Then go to the sawmill. The power is got from the river below. 150 feet down below the mill is drove by wires. This is a great curiosity. It is a fine place here to see the cars cross the bridge from the river shore. Then I go back to the hotel to dinner. Then we take the cars cross the Suspension Bridge to Niagara. Country is good but the RR is full of curves and in bad condition. We view Brocks Monument,[256] the Suspension Bridge from the cars. It looks fine. Go on American Boat Ontario have a good supper. Lake is very calm and many vessels in sight. The shore from the lake looks very pleasant & good.

View from the Whirlpool

3 Fair. **Arrive at Oswego - a fine large business place. Leave at 9 o'clock; cross to Sackets Harbor.**[257] **View old battleground forts. Then take stage to Watertown. Go to Mr. Henrick's, take dinner. This is level country, not very good. It is very dry. Go around the place. This is a very fine large village and very pleasantly located. Very extensive water power, large mills and machine shops & factories**.

---

[255] The Welland Canal was constructed in 1829 to connect Lake Ontario to Lake Erie. It provides ships a way around Niagara Falls.

[256] Brock's Monument is a 185-foot-tall monument in Queenston, Ontario dedicated to Major General Sir Isaac Brock, one of Canada's heroes of the War of 1812.

[257] Sacket's Harbor, NY, once a major shipyard to support the war of 1812, with its strategic harbor on Lake Ontario and military installations; the village had national importance throughout the 19th century. At one time it was the third largest city in the state after New York and Albany.

4	Fair. Cannons firing. Attend the celebration. It goes off good. A great turn out of horseman in Indian equipage, all in masks, some in feather dress, some in clownish dresses, some Ragged Regulars. Have a good display of fireworks. In evening bonfire, powder crackers. I get holme at half past ten in evening.
5	Fair. Go downtown to Woodroff House. Take cars for holme go through Adam Center, then Adams, then Pierrepont Center. Soil sandy, crops light, corn & oats very small, some rye growing. Then to Sandy Creek, then to Richland, then to Sand Banks, so to Kasoag, then to Williamstown. Soil sandy. Then to East & West Camden - crops better, sandy yet. Then to Rome, take dinner. Take cars to Palantine Bridge. Go to Mr. Spraker's. Crops look well on the Mohawk. Stop there all night.

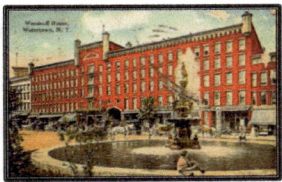

Woodroff House

6	Fair. **We go to Lutheran Meeting in morning and to Methodist Meeting in the evening. Call to Mr. Livingston. Spraker, he is sick. I go around his house & premises. A very extensive house and pleasant place.**
7	Fair. **I go to Little Falls. Wife come holme. I walk & get rides to Mr. Eben Kelly's. Then ride & walk to Gotfriet Yoos to my farm & mill.**
8	Rainy. **I stay around mill. Send & get Mr. Doty & Mr. Truman Yale, millwright make a bargain with them to put my mill in order. Buy a rose wheel to drive my buzz saw. Come back with them to Salisbury. Stay with Mr. Doty all night. Go around Salisbury. Gave Gotfriet check $25 & Belcher check $25.**
9	Lowry. **Come to Little Falls and Mr. Doty. Then come holme with cars & steamboat.**
10	Fair. I sell my Jack Horse to Aaron Houghtaling. Get check of A.E. Willis for Wm. Ladow 32 dollars. Go to river twice. Go around farm.
11	Fair. I go around farm. I go to river. Mrs. Hotaling, Miss Brace and A.E. Willis call here.
12	Rainy. **I, Anthony & T. Civill go to Albany; attend insurance lawsuit. I pay McDonald 54 dollars for defraying expense of lawsuit.**
13	Fair, hot. Go to church, to cemetery, to Elias Holmes.
14	Fair, hot. I and Wife go to Elias Millbank's, spend the day. We go to Mr. Birch's see his mare. Henry work in garden.
15	Fair, cloudy, hot. I go to river. Get horse shod. Mr. Theophilus Civill here. John Bailey pay me check of 57 dollars to defray lawsuit of McDonald's against insurance company.
16	Fair, hot. I send money from Bailey with Willis to McDonald at Albany. Pay up Bailey's part of suit with Mohawk Valley Insurance Company $57.05.
17	Fair, hot, 100 degrees above 0. I take Mother Hotaling to A.T. VanSlyck's. I take up note of G. Fancher, in G. Reed's hands. Take dinner to E. Hubbell's. Take tea to Andrew T. VanSlyck's.
18	Fair, hot. TH 100 degrees above 0. I go to river. **Attend Miss Brace's School. Take children to the Island; take them in swimming.** I gave Mrs. John Rea note for 136 dollars.
19	Cool dry weather. I lay around, call to Wesley's.
20	Fair, dry. I and T. Civill go to Mr. Kimmey's, then to Robert Selkirk's, take dinner. Then holme to Meeting. Mr. A.E. Willis here. We go to cemetery & vineyard.

21	Fair, dry N wind. **J. Muckelroy pay me 4 dollars for rent of The No Nothings.** I pay Israel Lawton 13/ for recording my mortgage against R. Pulver.
22	Fair, warm. I go to river. I pay James Trego $27.75 for cow. He, Wife and son here.
23	Fair, hot. Mother here. I, Wife, Willis & Harriet go and call on Mr. A. Civill. Lib Castle here.
24	Fair. I go to Albany, bring Mary Standring holme with me. I stop to Elias Millbank's. I get Martin VanSlyck's notes at Bank. I take Lib Castle to Albany.
25	Fair, very hot. A.B. Hotaling & Lady here. Caroline Hotaling here. Mother Hotaling come holme. We all go to Stone Church Farm. **Go to school room, hear children speak**. Call at the Widow Hotaling.
26	Very hot, dry. TH at 102 deg. above 0. I go to Gerry Springstead's, then to Blacksmith's. William Phelps here. We all go to Willis's, have a fine time.
27	Fair, hot. I take Mother to Hollow to Quarterly Meeting. Mother here to dinner. Michel Winters pay me 4 dollars. William Phelps, Mr. VanAllen, A.E. & U.B. Willis here.
28	Fair, hot. I go to river. Lay around, go in swimming.
29	Fair, hot. I go to river. **I & Mr. T. Civill go to New York with propeller. Little showry down the river.**
30	Fair, very hot. **Arrive to New York at 9 o'clock am. Take dinner on boat. Go to furniture store. Take tea, stay all night to Doct. VanAntwerp.**
31	Fair, hot. Call on S. Pelts. **Go around city. Take Dinner & Supper to J.J. Silcock's. Go to Niblo's Garden,**[258] **have a fine time**.

August 1856

1	Fair, hot. **Go to Marite's for breakfast, then to Barge, then across town, then to Barge to dinner. Then do up trading and start for Coeymans.**
2	Fair, hot. Get holme 9½ o'clock. Peter Lawson pay me $4.50 stove bill.
3	Fair morning, shower in afternoon. Go to Meeting. Martin & Elida VanSlyck here. We all call at Widow Charlotte's. Ed VanOrden here to tea. Doct. Blaisdell call. Mary Lotte & Tony call here.
4	Lowry, rainy. James Sherwood pay me 10 dollars. **I call in Miss Brace's school**. Call to Willis's. Dominie Selick call here.
6	Rainy day. I go to river twice. I buy mare of Mr. Bush. Am to pay 100 dollars for mare and 12 dollars for the service of the horse if she is with foal.
7	Rainy, cool. Go to river lay around. U.B. Willis call here.
8	Fair after shower in the morning. Mrs. U.B. Willis here. I take Mary Standring to P. Kimmey's & to A. Witbeck's.
9	Shower again. I go to river, take butter. **Fix to build a new schoolhouse. Attend school**.

---

[258] The first Niblo's Garden was destroyed by fire in 1846. The second Niblo's Garden, which Fletcher visited, included a theater that seated 3200 people and had the best equipped stage in the city. The theater was again destroyed by fire in 1872.

10   Cloudy, misty. **I, Wife, U.B. Willis, A.E. Willis, Lady go to Niskayuna to see the Shakers. Stop at Mr. Ireland's, stay all night.**

11   Fair. **Go see Shakers, attend the Meeting. Go to Ireland's to dinner, then come holme. Have a very pleasant ride.**

12   Fair. I and Wife go to Mrs. Springstead's, call. Wife go to Willis's. **I attend to work on new schoolhouse.**

13   Fair. I get my horse of Mr. Bush. Get the money of N.H. Johnson, pay him $100. Work around the house.

14   Fair. **Go to Herkimer to my mill. Pay Truman Yale $100. He and Mr. Doty finish my mill.**

15   **Work around and pay the 100 dollars on the other line to Mr. Yale. They leave**.

16   Rainy. **Work in mill all day. I let L.C. Belcher have 50 dollars chk. Let G. Yoos have 15 dollars cash & 12 dollars for get nails**.

17   Fair. **I come holme. Wife goes to Coxsackie with team**.

18   Fair. I go to Meeting. U.B. Willis here to tea.

19   Fair. I take Mary Standring to Greenville. Leave her to Newman Finch's. I stay all night to J.W. Story's.

20   Rainy. I go to A. Fancher's, stay all night, take breakfast. Then swear off tax. Go to J. Story's to dinner. Call to Eben Finch's, get pears, then come holme. G. Fancher pay me $18.25 for wood Story bought of him. Rainy night.

21   Rainy day. I go to river.

22   Misty. I and A. Teal go to P. Kimmey's, pick out lumber. Aaron Hotaling pay me 98 dollars cash, 2 dollars for Rockaway to go to Shakers. I take the money to Willis's, take receipt of Ben. **Great freshet. Island's under water. Paper mill dam gone. Great losses by the floods. I pay Miss Brace 6 dollars tuition, 25 cents for book**.

23   Fair. **Work around building. Attend examination of Miss Brace school. Goes off well. Children spoke well.**

24   Rainy afternoon. **I and Mr. Wm. B. Hull take N.H. Johnson's horse & waggon, go out Plank Road. See the Bridge and embankment that is carved away by the freshet**. Take dinner to J.B. Shear's. Break fills come holme. Martin & Elida VanSlyck here. Cate VanBergen, Widow Charlotte's girls call. **Work at schoolhouse**.

26   Fair, cold. Doct. Fredenburgh & Lady, Mr. L. Spraker & Lady, Acton Civill & Lady, A.E. Willis & Lady, Mrs. Jemima Hotaling & Miss Cate Spraker here. We have a very pleasant time.

27   Fair, cooler. **I work around schoolhouse**. Go after posts under the Hill.

28   Fair. Excursion from Coxsackie here. I help Mr. Civill at the cemetery, make fence. **Am elected trustee of cemetery.**

29   Fair morning. I let G. Harris have my horse & waggon to go to Albany. I make fence to the vineyard.

30 Fair. I work around. Mrs. Colvin & her niece here. Mr. Spraker & Lady, Betsey Verplank, Ann E. Wilgus here visit. She is my old school mate. **J. Silkerk died.**[259]

31 Fair. **I attend funeral of John Silkerk, take Mrs. James Hotaling & her family. Coeymans Excursion goes off today.** I get checks for 65 dollars, send them to Mr. Cunningham Reddy & to Truman Yale. Mrs. Pierce here.

September 1856

1 Fair. I go to Albany. **Get chairs for school room.** Get plow shares. **Peter W. VanBergen died with Cholera.**[260]

2 Fair. Henry plow. I make fence, go to river.

3 Fair. Cate Houghtaling & Elizabeth Trego here. Mary Hotaling & Anna Sherman call here. Michel Winters pay me 2 dollars rent. I take Mother Hotaling & Mrs. Pierce to Uncle Andrew's.

4 Fair, warm. Go under the Hill to plow. Break plow. I go to river.

5 Fair. I go to river. Go under the Hill to H. Orchard's. Go to river again. Put nails from P.G. Coffin in Johnson Store House.

6 Fair. **I churn in the morning**. Take children, go under the Hill in the afternoon. I call to Willis's in eve. Mary Charlotte Hotaling, Fredenburgh, Jones call here.

7 Fair. Go to Meeting in morning, to Cemetery & to dam in the afternoon. Go hear Mr. J. Thorn preach in evening.

8 Rainy. Get my waggon fixed. I settle with A.N. Briggs. I take up my note to John Andrews given 5 years ago. Briggs pay me 57 dollars balance due me after taken out Briggs & Rummy's account.

9 Fair. **I and Wife go to Albany, get plow casting, get Ambrotypes.**[261] I pay Davidson & Vielie for nails. I get a vise. I take dinner to P. Phelps. Martin VanSlyck bring Mother Hotaling holme.

10 Fair. **I take Willis's horse, go to Dean's Mill, get 309 pounds plaster**. Get salt & grass seed of A.E. Willis. I pay G. Rifflin 4 dollars. Get sugar of Willis.

11 Shower at noon. Draw manure. Let Elida have 5 dollars. Fix cemetery fence. Have a headache and a bile under my chin.

12 Fair. **I go to Albany for lumber for schoolhouse**. Draw manure on Big Meadow. Break waggon crotch.

13 Some showers. Draw manure. Miss Brace come. I go to river.

14 Fair. I go to Meeting. Miss Brace & Lib Hotaling here.

15 Fair. Draw dung, dig stone. I sow rye in Big Meadow. Lib Hotaling here. Miss Brace, Caroline Hotaling, Mrs. Biyack here. Doct. Blaisdell take her to Robert Martin's.

---

[259] He might have meant John Selkirk.
[260] Cholera is an infection of the small intestines, primarily due to the lack of water treatment.
[261] An ambrotype is a negative image that becomes visible when the glass was backed by black material. A daguerreotype produces a positive image when under glass.

16 Fair. Caroline Hotaling here. I draw manure. **We all go to Excursion. Steamboat Anna tow New Baltimore Barges. Martin VanSlyck here. Edward VanOrden here. Have a jolly time. Get back at 11 o'clock at night.** Mother Hotaling come from Albany.

17 Fair. I sow rye, wash rye, drag in rye. Go to river.

18 Fair. I sow rye under the Hill, 9 bushels. A.B. Hotaling Lady, Mrs. Sheldon Hotaling & daughter here, visit. Doct. Blaisdell call here. I pay Willis 20 dollars [for] check sent to G. Yoos.

19 Fair. I sow grass seed Under Hill. I go out to Camp Meeting. Wife go out with Wesley.

20 Rainy. Roll in, wash rye. I and Wife go to Camp Meeting. Michel Winters pay me $1.40. Mrs. China Hathaway pay me 20/ by R. King.

21 Fair. I take Wife, Miss Brace, Mother Hotaling, Lib Hotaling, Mrs. John Rea & Anthony to Camp Meeting. I put my horse to Jacob Coonly's. Mr. Headstrom preach.

22 Rain. Gave Wife 5 dollars. She go to Coxsackie. I go to river twice. Henry Smith call here.

23 Cloudy. **T. Clancy pay me 33 dollars on Catholic Church.** I go to river. I pay Big Michel 1 dollar. I go to vineyard and to dam.

24 Fair. I sow grass seed Under Hill. Henry draw manure & stone. Get 2 pigs of Wm. Clark. Leonard Carhart pay me $7.05 cash. I pay him $4.95 meat bill, square up for cattle.

25 Fair. I and James Bryant go to Albany to the County Fair. I send box to Little Falls. Wife, Elida VanSlyck, Cate VanBergen come back. Levi Seabridge to get holme at 9 o'clock at night.

26 Cloudy, south wind. I go to mill. Caroline Hotaling, Doct. Blaisdell, Mrs. G. Harris here. **I and J.H. Holmes cut bee tree, get a lot of honey.** I pay J. Bryant 3 dollars.

27 Fair. B.B. Belcher here. I go to dam lot. Draw sand, go to mill. I pay J. Barton 18/ for bran. I pay Big Michel 4 dollars for G. Rifflin. I pay P. Swin 8 dollars, pay Elida 9 dollars. **We raise schoolhouse.** Hannah & Jane Andrews, Hester Hotaling, Lib Hotaling, Cate VanBergen here.

28 Fair. I and P. Kimmey go to Coxsackie, call on Mr. Mayo and on Uncle Andrew VanSlyck's. Ed VanOrden here. Levi sick. Doct Fredenburgh here.

29 Cloudy, misty. **Draw lumber to schoolhouse.** Go to vineyard. Plow for G. Rifflin. Miss Brace & Lib Hotaling call.

30 Rainy day. I go to river twice. Mr. Crandle, Mr. Leight here. Put up looking (?) slabs of marble.

October 1856

1 Hail & rain clears off. **I and J.H. Holmes lay cellar wall to vineyard.**

2 Fair, white frost. **Lay cellar wall, J.H. Holmes help.** I pay Michel Swin 10 dollars for G. Rifflin. I borrow 25 dollars of Schoonmaker & Johnson. I take up Mrs. Bronk's horses.

3 Fair day. **Lay cellar wall to vineyard, J.H. Holmes help.** Henry go to Albany.

4 Fair day. **Lay cellar wall, J.H. Holmes help ½ day.** Mrs. McGary pay me $4.50 rent. **I draw up school benches and desks.** J. VanBenthuyzen here. J.W. Story & Wife & Mary Standring here. Mary Jane & Hellen Lawton call. J.W. Story pay me $3 some cents. Gave me a new note $170.

5 Fair. I take Mother to Bethlehem Quarterly Meeting. Take dinner to Dominie Jolly.

6	Fair. Gather walnuts. Henry draw stone. I go to Big Island. Pay Josiah Sherman 2 dollars tax money he paid on my Lower Island. Wesley go along.
7	Fair. Draw stone. G. Yoos here. Wife go to Albany. I go to papermill. **Peter Long's Wife died today**.
8	Fair. I let Willis have my horse to go to Albany. **Attend the funeral of Mrs. Peter Long**. Mary Ann Clancy here.
9	Fair. Aunt Sarah Ann VanBergen here. Gottefriet leave. I lay wall under the Hill. Michel Swinn help.
10	Fair. I go Under Hill ½ day, make fence. My hogs kill one of my pigs. T.H. Gould pay me $2.08 rent. Mrs. Charlotte Hotaling here. **I whip Anthony. Go to Negro Meeting**.
11	Fair. All hand lay wall Under Hill. Boys gather nuts. I pay J.H. Holmes 2 dollars. Old Mrs. VanAntwerp, Doctor & Marite here. I get 1 barrel of flour.
12	I, Doctor, Marite, Mrs. VanAntwerp, Levi & Anthony go to Henry Rarick's. The old lady stay there.
13	Fair morning, rainy in afternoon. **I attend the No Nothing Meeting**. Draw dirt for G. Rifflin. Aunt Sarah leave.
14	Fair, cold. **Unload a boatload of lumber from Little Falls, pay Capt. $107.05 freight money**. I borrow 100 dollars of T. Civill.
15	Fair, cold. Draw up lumber all day. Work around.
16	Fair. Draw up lumber all day, work around. My Bill horse gets kicked by Mrs. Bronk's mare. I get her horse to work.
17	Fair. Draw up lumber all day. Mrs. Briggs, Jane Andrews, Lib Hotaling, Miss Brace, A.E. Willis here. Mrs. J.H. VanBenthuyzen here.
18	Cloudy, rainy. Draw up lumber all day. J. Sickler pay me $1.44 for lumber.
19	Fair. Go to Meeting. Wm. MacGregor, Willis, Harriet, Doct. Blaisdell, Mrs. VanAntwerp, Martin VanSlyck here, tea.
20	Fair, smoky day. Draw up lumber all day. Mary Hotaling and Sarell Wood & Lady here.
21	Fair. Visit with Sarell Wood. Doct, Marite & his Mother leave here for New York.
22	Cloudy, misty. Go around. John Cronk pays me 82 dollars, takes up his notes I have against him. **Attend political meeting at Church's Tavern. Kilbourn & Courtney address the meeting. Good time.**
23	Fair, cold N wind. I take Mr. Wood & Lady, Mrs. J.H. VanBenthuyzen to Uncle Andrew's, then go to Coxsackie. David Willis takes Levi.
24	Fair, cold. Go around. **Attend Fremont Meeting to Aaron Houghtaling's**.[262] J.H. VanBenthuyzen here.

---

[262] We believe this is in reference to the 1856 presidential election, which was a three-way race between James Buchanan (Democrat), John Fremont (Republican) and Millard Filmore (Know Nothing). James Buchanan won and went on to be one of the worst presidents in history. John Fremont was anti-slavery.

25 Fair, cold. Mier Fancher here, pay me 50 dollars on account of his Father's. Mother here to tea. **Barent Hotaling died.**

26 Fair, cool. I go to Meeting. U.B. Willis & Wm. MacGregor here, tea.

27 Lowry, rainy. J.H. VanBenthuyzen & Lady leave. I go to mill. I fix my pump in well.

28 Fair, cool. **All go to Uncle Barent Hotaling's funeral**. Mr. Sarell Wood here.

29 Fair, cool. Mr. Wood, Family and all hands of us go to Garret Hotaling's, spend the day. Willis here in evening.

30 Fair morning, lowry rainy afternoon. I get out timber.

31 Fair. Wife go to Albany. I gave her $5. Work to the vineyard. Mr. Sarell Wood & his brother here. Come in the evening.

November 1856

1 Fair. Caroline Hotaling, Elizabeth Stephens. William Stephens, Garrett Hotaling here to tea.

2 Fine warm day, S wind. Uriah & A.E. Willis here. Go to Meeting twice.

3 Fair, warm. Miss Witbeck here. Mr. Wood & Family leave for NY. **I raise vineyard house. Shingle cow shed.**

4 Lowry, SW, misty. **Attend Election**. Mother here. I get 50 dollars of N.H. Johnson. Barent TenEyck pay me $4.62 for lumber.

5 Cold, NW. I go to Herkimer. **Take P.G. Coffin to Albany. Take cars to Little Falls. Start on foot. Team overtake me. Get a nice ride with them out to Gottefriet Yoos. Have cold snow squalls. Cold ride**.

6 Fair. I pay off Elias Wood, Charles Wood, Lyman Bullock. Go around premises.

7 Fair. Go in woods. Saw timber. Get logs to mill. Saw timber.

8 Cloudy, south. Rain hard in afternoon. Work in barn. Go around the woods in the forenoon.

9 Fair. Go in woods. Take dinner to Henry Sperl's. See Mr. Persons.

10 Fair. **I & Henry Sperl start for Herkimer. Get 3 miles horse break down. Then come on foot 3 miles to Middleville. Then get chance ride to Herkimer. Go to clerk's office. Then I take cars and arrive at Albany half past 10 at night**.

11 Fair, NW. Do up business in Albany, then come holme.

12 Cloudy, SW. I help on vineyard house.

13 Fair. I help on vineyard house. Mother here.

14 Fair. I shingle, plow, attend school. Mary Ann Clancy here.

15 Fair, cold, NW. I work around. I pay girl Bridget four dollars. T. Gould pay me $2.08 rent.

16 Cloudy, SW. I get J. Hazelton splice hay press rope.

17 Fair, cold, NW. I shingle, plow, kill 14 turkeys. I get $500 of B. TenEyck, gave my note one year. I let A.E. Willis have the money, take receipt for same. T. Clancy pay me $5.38 for lumber.

18	Fair, cold north W wind. **I cross river, take cars, go to Albany, get hay press rope. Have a hard time.** Henry plow. Go to river.
19	Fair. N wind. **I work at schoolhouse & to vineyard house.**
20	Fair, cold. I work around. Lawson & Mr. Waldron get lumber. **I take dinner Thanksgiving to Willis's. Levi & Sarah Ann go to Glasgow.** Wm. J. Clark pay me $2.50. Willis call here.
21	Fair, white frost. **Draw two loads of bricks to vineyard house.** I go and get my bull to Mr. Stanton's.
22	Fair. Wife & Levi come holme. I kill little bull. T.E. Waldron pay me $14,84 for fence boards. W.C. Robb pay me $12.84 on his lumber. I go to vineyard & to river.
23	Fair. Have toothache all night. Go to Meeting. Wesley here. Martin VanSlyck bring Mother Hotaling holme.
24	Fair, warm day. Martin VanSlyck leave. **I attend opening of the schoolhouse. I work at vineyard house.** Mr. Tompkins call here. I pay Elias B Holmes 30 cents tax.
25	Fair. I work at vineyard house. Dominie Gardner Lady visit. Mother in law, G. Harris & Lady, Mary Hotaling, Miss Brace here. Rainy evening when they leave.
26	Fair, warmer. Wife go to Albany. I let her have $48.05. Work at vineyard house. I get 15 dollars of W.B. Hull.
27	Fair. **Finish vineyard house**, shingle shed. Get 25 dollars of Johnson & Schoonmaker. Martin VanSlyck here. Installation of Mr. Gardner.
28	Fair. I go to Albany with horse & waggon. Get paints & oil white lead, pants, shirts. **Have my tooth pulled, one filled by Mr. Brockaway. I pay him two dollars**. Pay Bullock 15 dollars for paints & oils.
29	Snow all day. Wife come from Albany. I take tea with Mr. Civill and spend the evening.
30	Fair, cold. I go to Meeting, call to Willis's.

December 1856

1	Fair, cold. L. Carhart kill Harris's two heifers here. Abram Witbeck pay me 70 dollars on rent. **I have a blowup with Sylvester Harris**.
2	Fair, cold. Mother here. Go around. John Cronk pay me $5.63 for corn. Mrs. Hathaway pay me $2.50 for rent.
3	Snow, rain, hail all day. I pay I. Brown 10 dollars. **I let U.B. Willis have twenty-six dollars to send Duncan & Sherman draft to Germany after grape vines**. Fix hay press.
4	Fair, cold. I pay Crandle freight bill on lumber. I pay Swine $3.50 and 10 dollars for Michel Swine.
5	Fair, cold. I go to river. Work around the house. Take pork to Willis. Get 1 barrel flour. Send check to H. Sperl 100 dollars and check to Gottefriet Yoos 10 dollars.
6	Fair, cold. I go to papermill, get horse blankets. I pay off & settle with Mr. Robb. Pay him balance $1.77. Go with A.N. Briggs to Toll Gate No. 3. Stop to Andrew Hotaling's, take tea. Wife & Mrs. Briggs, then they come holme with us.
7	Fair, cold. Go to Meeting. Take a ride. I and Boys call on John Harris.

8	Fair, cold. I kill hogs & beef. G. Rifflin & Henry help.
9	Fair, cold. Cut up hogs & beef. Draw muck in barnyard. Wife go to A.N. Briggs. Mary Ann Clancy here. Dominie Gardner's sisters call. Caroline VanAntwerp call.
10	Fair. Cut around. I borrow 100 dollars of T. Civill. I pay off A. Teal. James Sherwood pays by Teal, 20 dollars rent money. Seabridge pay me 20 dollars. Mary Ann Clancy here. **Mrs. Salmon VanAntwerp died**.
11	Rainy afternoon. Put away beef in snow. Go to river.
12	Fair. **Attend Maria VanAntwerp's funeral. Attend Schoolhouse**. I send check to Lyman Bullock $12.22, one to G.H. Lawton 30 dollars. Salt pork & beef.
15	Fair, cold. I fix well. Put brine on hams & beef. Mary Ann Maclancy, here. I pay her 10/. Lib Hotaling here.
16	Fair, cold, NW. I go to river. Lib Hotaling here. **Israel Lawton & Miss Hotaling get married.** Mother here.
17	Fair, cold, NW. Coldest day. **Boats stop running river**.
18	Fair. **TH 11 deg. below 0.** I work at cellar door. R. Pulver pay me $300. I let Willis have 275 dollars. Garrett Houghtaling & daughter Caroline here. I pay Garret $7.50 for apples, 3 barrels. Mary & Charlotte Hotaling, Lib Hotaling, Cate Hotaling here. I pay Cate 13 dollars interest money.
20	Rainy day. I go to river. Settle with Johnson & Schoonmaker. They pay me off. I let Willis have 250 dollars.
21	Fair, very cold. Go to Meeting. Call to Willis's & to Mrs. Willis's. **Jonathan Muckelroy's child died today.**
22	Fair morning, little snowy in afternoon. I go to river. **T. Clancy here, pay me 18 dollars money on Catholic Church, endorsed & receipt given for 21st Dec. 1856.**
23	Snow all night, all day. I send check to Mr. Cunningham. Mr. Reddy, Mr. Yale, Mr. Doty pay them off. Peter Seabridge kill his cow here.
24	Snow & blow all day. I go to river. Pay off J. VanDenburgh the sum of $8.70. **Mrs. Barent Ryon died**.
25	Fair, cold. Thms. Gould pay me $2.08 rent to Dec 5th. I go to river.
26	Fair, cold. I pay John E. Gibbens tax to A.N. Briggs $11.37. Attend visiting to A.E. Willis.
27	Fair, cold. A.E. Willis & Lady, Miss Brace, Lib Hotaling here, visit. I get check of A.E. Willis $64.67 pay my tax, borrowed. Peter Lawson pay me 10 dollars on his bill. I borrow $150 of Nathaniel Niles, gave him my note. **I ride to Church Farm with Willis**. I get check of Willis of $20. Send to Gottefriet Yoos, borrowed.
28	Little snowy. I call to Mother's. I take dinner to Willis. Henry take Wife, Widow Charlotte Hotaling & Mary Hotaling to Coxsackie to J. VanSlyck's. Mother Hotaling come back holme.

29 Fair. I go Under Hill to Wm. S. Clark's, then to river. Lizabeth Hotaling here to tea.

30 Fair, cold. Willis take I and Wife to Albany. **We take Harlem Railroad for New York. Run our driving wheels off the track at Chatham.**[263] **Get to New York at 4 o'clock PM. Go to Doct. VanAntwerp. Then we call and spend the evening with U.B. Willis, have a very pleasant time.**

New York & Harlem Railroad

31 Little misty. **I go downtown and to Brooklyn. I call to Wm. Bagley's then to Nathan Stephen's and to J.J. Silcox's and to David VanAntwerp's, then to Marite. Stay all night.**

January 1857

1 **Commence for the day, pleasant but cold. I call 1st to P. VanAntwerp's, 2nd to U.B. Willis have brandy, wine &cake. 3rd to Mr. White's grand place, 4th to Acton Civill's, 5th to Mrs. Sumner's, 6th to Mrs. Tam's, very grand places, great show have everything and great splendor. Then Uriah & his friend take me to restaurant, dine have champagne and then I left them to go to Miss DeClyn's 7th for cake, 8th to Dr. Miller's, 9th to J.J. Silcox's. Then go with John and call to a great many more places have a great time. I arrive for more fun than I ever had in one evening. A very great display is made in New York on New Year's Day, I assure you. We call to a great many grand places where there was some very wealthy people. I get holme to Doct, at 11 o'clock at night & go to bed.**

2 Fair. **My head was heavy & dull. Get breakfast & feel better. We go to J.J. Silcox's, then go buy furs downtown - pay $130. Then John Silcock & myself take some oysters, then come across Mr. Toby, take some toddy, then to J.J. Silcock's to dinner. Then holme to Marite's, then to Peter VanAntwerp's to spend the evening. Then holme to bed.**

3 Snowy day. **I & Wife go to Brooklyn to N. Stephen's to tea, stay all night. We have a dance. All hands old & young have a very pleasant visit. Stay all night. They live in good style and entertained us the best they could.**

Plymouth Church (Brooklyn, NY)

4 Clear, about 4 in of snow. **We go to H.W. Beecher's church, hear him preach.**[264] He is a smart man and very talented. Then we go J.J. Silcock's to dinner. Have a fine turkey to dine of. Then to Mr. Charles Hallock's to tea. Very pleasant visit there. Then back to Marite, stay all night.

---

[263] The New York & Harlem Railroad was one of the first railroads in the United States and was the world's first street railway. Horses pulled railway carriages until 1837 when steam engines were used outside of the city.

[264] Henry Ward Beecher was a Congregational clergyman known for his support of the abolition of slavery. He was the brother of the famous author, Harriet Beecher Stowe.

5   Fair. **I go to Staten Island to Sailors' Snug Harbor. I see Capt. James Sherman,[265] S. VanAntwerp, Cat Joseph, I found them all well situated & very comfortable. This is the best institution in the world. The building is pleasantly located, built substantial, warmed all throughout, kept in the very best order and the sailors there are as happy as kings & take comfort. I was well pleased with my visit & took dinner with them. Their living is of the very best.[266] I come back to Doct. VanAntwerp's.** Doctor & I go to Broadway Theater; see Ed Forest play Pythias & Damon.[267] It was well displayed - the best I ever saw. Then we go back to Taylor get some oysters there; take some more oysters in Bleeker St. Then holme to bed.

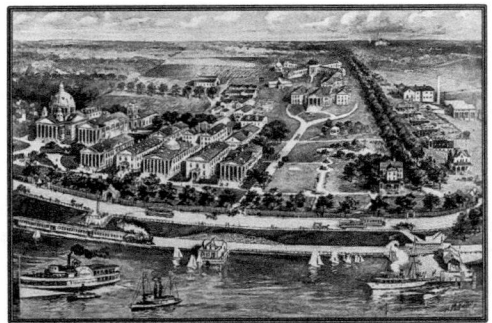

Sailors' Snug Harbor

6   Cold, Fair. **Get up at 5 am go to Harlem Railroad; take cars start for holme. Go along 20 miles, break the axle tree of tender. Get detained 3 hours. Then another train come take us along at a slow rate. Shovel snow all day & get in Albany at 3 o'clock in morning. Stop at Clinton Hotel, go to bed. Very cold, almost froze.**

7   Fair, very cold. **Take breakfast, then I go to Pruyn & Lansing's Furnace. Engage my circular saw. Then to G.H. Lawton's, pay him $20. Then to Davidson & Vielle's, pay him off 6 or 7 dollars. Then to VanRensselaer's office, pay my Island rent, $5. Then I go to Bank, get my dividend $15. Then get ready, take things to Mr. Bullock's, then take the mail stage. Get holme. The roads are badly drifted and very cold.** Attend Donation of Rev. Mr. Selick, gave him 3 dollars.

8   Fair, very cold. Stay about the house, go to river.

9   Fair, warm. Henry Yung go to Albany. I let him have 15 dollars. I go to river. Andrew Sharp come after Mother Houghtaling. She go to Uncle A.T. VanSlyck with Mr. Willis. Miss Brace here.

10 Snow all day. Garrett Houghtaling here. Lib Castle come here in evening. I go to river. **Chris Fike gets married**.

11 Snow blow all day. I go to Mother's. Willis call here.

12 Fair, cold. I sharpen crosscut saw. Lib Hotaling here. Mrs. Hathaway pay Levi 20/ rent for me. Wife take it.

13 Fair, cold. I work around the house. Take hams out of brine. Go to river. Garrett Hotaling & Caroline call here. Wife go with them to the Sewing Society to Wm. B. Hull's.

14 Fair, cold SW. I attend P. Road meeting all day. A.N. Briggs pay me $6.25 directors bill. T. Hotaling here after Caroline.

---

[265] James Sherman was a sloop captain who lived in New Baltimore.
[266] This was one of the first large scale retirement homes for sailors and was in existence from 1833-1976. It is now Sung Harbor Cultural Center.
[267] Edwin Forrest played Damon in the play that was written in 1564 by Richard Edwards. Edwin Forrest was a prominent American Shakespearean actor.

15 Fair, very cold, NW. I go to Greenville. Very tedious day. I stop to Jacksonville & to J.J. Williamson's. Go to A. Fancher's, stay all night. Fancher pay me balance of account $23.16.

16 Fair, SW. I come back to J.J. Williamson's, he pay me my rents as endorsed on my rent book at this date. Stop to A.J. VanSlyck's, take dinner. U.B. Willis here to tea.

17 Fair, very cold. I & Wife attend party to Aaron Houghtaling's. Have a Negro show & dance in evening, we attend.

18 Fair, very cold. **TH 12 deg. below 0 about all day. I go to Meeting to Dutch Church.** Lib Castle leave here. I and Wife call to Mother's & to Willis's.

19 **Snow & blow all day very hard. The worst storm known for many years.** Very cold. I go to river.

20 Fair, cold. Shovel snow. **Mr. T. Civill here. We meet to P. Seabridge's tonight; make settlement on Schoolhouse.** Wife go to Dominie Gardner's. I go in the evening.

21 Cloudy, SW. Lewis Crandle here. I pay him off $12.25. I go Under Hill with Henry. I go to the river.

22 Very cold, NW. I go to river. Work around the house.

23 NW, very cold. **TH 22 deg. below 0 6 o'clock in the morning and ten degrees below all day**. I go to river. Let Willis have $70. Take his for the same for my saw & for G. Yoos. Henry Smith here. Get 9 turkeys. Pay Wife $10.12.

24 Fair, very cold, SW. **TH 24 deg. below 0**. I send letter to H. Sperl & check to G. Yoos 15 dollars. I take Wife, Children & Miss Brace to G. Hotaling's. **Make bargain with Miss Brace for school room.**

25 Fair. S and NW. TH 10 deg. below 0. I go to Meeting. Willis call here.

26 Very cold. TH 10 deg. below 0, SW. I go to Albany with Willis. **Send my circular saw to Little Falls per N.Y.C. I pay Pruyn & Lansing $56.28**. Wife go to Uncle Andrew VanSlyck's with Doct. Fredenburgh. Widow Charlotte Hotaling & Daughter Charlotte here. Mr. Tompkins get plank here. My Witbeck cow has a calf.

27 Warmer, SW. Snow, rain, hail all day. I send check of $15 to G. Yoos. Go to river. I pay Isaac Baker $10.97 for hoops. I get check 15 dollars of Willis, send to Gottefriet Yoos.

28 Fair, warmer. I work around. Attend donation of Rev. Mr. Gardner. Lib Houghtaling come holme with us, stay all night. Have a very pleasant time.

29 Snowy. Draw wood from the Island. I and Wife take tea to Widow Jemima Houghtaling's. Garrett Houghtaling here. Ed VanOrden, Mary & Charlotte Hotaling here.

30 Fair, pleasant, NW, cold. Draw wood from Island. I help boys all day. I lend W.S. Clark 1 dollar.

31 Snow all day, rain in evening. I go to river.

February 1857

1   Fair, cold. I call to Mother's. **Get Dr. Kane's Arctic Expedition, read all day.**[268] Doct. Blaisdell & Willis call here. **Aunt Catharine VanSlyck died**.

2   Fair, sun shines. Caroline Houghtaling here. I and Wife go to river. Andrew Sharp come here from Uncle Andrew's.

3   Fair. I take Caroline Houghtaling, Doct. Blaisdell take Wife. **We go to Aunt Catherine's funeral. Attend Sewing Society to A.N. Briggs in the evening**.

4   Cloudy, rainy, SW. Garrett Hotaling come after Caroline.

5   Cloudy, rainy, SW. I go to river. C. Fike pay me $1.75 house rent.

6   Cloudy, thawy day. I go to river. T.H. Gould pay me $2.08 rent. Draw wood from Island.

7   Thawy, wet sloppy. **Snowbanks slop in the creek; rise so as to come in my cellar.** I and Wife go to Widow G. Hotaling's, visit. John H. VanBenthuyzen here. SW.

8   Rainy, thawy day, SW in morning. Water high in the river. Creeks break up, great thaw. I stay holme all day.

9   Fair, cold, NW. I go to river with John H. VanBenthuyzen. **He crosses river on ice to go to Albany.** Mary Blaisdell here. A.E. Willis here to tea. I call to John Rea.

10   Fair, very cold, little squally. **I and Wife go to G. Hotaling's, attend Sewing Society. Go with A.E. Willis, we break sley, but have a fine time**.

11   Fair, very cold. **Write & execute my will**. I go to the river. **Henry Springstead & Alvira Carroll get married.**

12   Fair, heavy SW. **I go to Castleton on skates to see the great breakup of the ice. Vast amount of lumber come down - ice 2 ft. thick. Have hard time to get back in crossing from Schodack; get back after dark.**[269]

13   Snowy forenoon. I go to river. Afternoon fair. **I attend Miss Brace's school**. Lib Hotaling here. We go out, spend the evening.

14   Fair, warm, pleasant. Quarterly meeting here. **I & boys go to Crosswell's papermill.** Sarell Wood come here. Martin Andrews and another Andrews call.

15   Fair, SW, warm. I go to Meeting. Call to Mother's & to Willis's. Wife, Mother, Mr. Wood go along. John Bushants here & his Wife to dinner. Doct. Blaisdell call. Ackerman Hotaling here to tea.

---

[268] Dr. Elisha Kane was an American explorer and a medical officer in the U.S. Navy. He was a member of two expeditions to rescue the explorer of Sir John Franklin. In the second excursion his party penetrated farther north than any other explorers had done up to that time. He died in Havana in February 1857 (the same month of this journal entry) at the age of 37 while attempting to recover his health.

[269] Hudson River historian, Mark Peckham, when asked how many miles Fletcher skated, said that the distance between Coeymans and Castleton was about 5 miles and at least 4 miles between Castleton and Schodack Landing. There were probably an additional 2 miles finding his way between the islands to cross back to Coeymans and more if he had to backtrack because of river conditions. "He covered more than a few miles on skates and was fortunate to find a place to cross the river when the ice was breaking up."

16	Lowry, rainy, S wind. **I take Sarell Wood to Albany. I pay him my Newago tax.**[270] Very muddy & snowbanks.
17	Cloudy, foggy. I fix hay press all day. Go to river. Mr. T. Civill call here.
18	Fair, SW. I go to mill twice with rye. **Attend Miss Brace's school**. Go to tea to James Jack's, have a nice time, very muddy.
19	Cold, NW. I go to river. Edward Banden pay me ten dollars to March 15th. I go to Dean's Mill, get flour & feed.
20	Snowy, SW. I go to vineyard & to river.
21	Fair, cool at night. Chris Fike pay me $5.50 for a barrel of flour. I owe him 50 cts. Pay him again.
22	Cloudy. Go to Meeting. Call to Willis's. Take walk. J. Rea call here.
23	Fair, SW. G. Houghtaling & Daughter Caroline here. **I work at vineyard house all day. The ice start.**
24	Fair, warm. I go to river & work around the house. **Have Ladies Sewing Society here. Have a large company & a fine time.**[271]
25	Fair. I work around. I go to river. Tobias Crumb pay me two dollars for Wheat. Garrett Houghtaling and his girls here. Andrew Hotaling here.
26	Fair, cold, NW. I go to river. Then I go with Mr. Bush to Rensselaerville, stay all night to Mr. Bush's in company with Mr. Cook. Very squally; go over high snowbanks.
27	Fair, SW. I and Bush go to Mr. Smith's, then go to Mr. Bush brother's, buy mare Chubb; pay him $127.50. Gave Willis check 29th March. Then holme horseback.
28	Fair, SW. I go to river. I and Wife go to A.T. VanSlyck's, stay all night.

March 1857

1	Cloudy, SW. I put my horse to H.C. VanBergen's. We go to Episcopal Meeting, then back to tea, then to H.C. VanBergen's. Spend the evening. Stay all [night] to Aunt Sarah Ann's.
2	Very cold, NW. Snow & blow all day like fury. Go to A.B. Hotaling's to dinner & tea. Go to Methodist Meeting in the evening. Stay all night to Aunt Sarah Ann's.
3	Fair, cold. TH at 0 deg. Call and see Mr. T. H. Gay, then I come holme. Have heavy snowbanks. Wife stay town meeting to Coxsackie today.
4[272]	Fair, SW, warmer. I go to river twice. C. Fike pay me $1.75. I go to stone quiry.
5	Fair, SW. I help I.E. and Ed. Gibbens lay floor to Mother's. They work ¾ day. Henry draw manure.
6	Stormy, cold. **Finish to Mother's**. T.H. Gould pay me $2.08 rent. I make waggon racks.

---

[270] This is a tax on the property he and Sarell Wood bought in Michigan.
[271] We think that this was more of a social gathering.
[272] James Buchanan, a Democrat from Pennsylvania, was inaugurated as the 15th President of the United States on this date. Historians fault him for his failure to address the slavery issue and the secession of the southern states. He is consistently ranked as the worst of the presidents.

7   Fair. I send 5 dollars to Lyman Bullock in a letter. **I and P. Ostrander paint vineyard house.** Martin VanSlyck bring Sarah Ann holme. We go to Meeting.

8   Fair. Go to Meeting. Martin VanSlyck, Miss Brace, Lib Hotaling here to dinner. Doct. Blaisdell call here.

9   SW, snow squalls. Mother here. Willis call. **Finish paint the vineyard house**.

10 Fair, cold. I make waggon tongue. Go to river. Wife go to Garrett Houghtaling's. I go after her in eve. Bring Elizabeth back.

11 Cloudy, SW. Go to papermill. Get due bill of J.T. Milton for 37 dollars. Go to river. I work around the house. Get check of A.E. Willis, 9 dollars for Samuel Bullock.

12 Fair, very cold, NW. Mrs. A.N. Briggs here, visit. A.E. Willis call here. I go to river twice.

13 Fair, south wind. Mrs. Fredenburgh, Mrs. Hotaling, Miss Brace here. I go to river twice. Mr. H. Renny pay me $11.22 for lumber. I pay James Bryant bill 8 dollars for wheels.

14 Fair, SW. I go to river. **I go with boys skating to the dam. I go to Crosswell's papermill & to river again.**

15 Cloudy. I go to Meeting. A. Hotaling call here. I call to Willis's.

16 Rainy afternoon. **G. Rifflin moves on vineyard**. Leonard Carhart in my corner house. I go to river. I pay the Irishman that worked for G. Yoos $7.25.

17 Fair, NW. I attend J. Sickler's Vendue. Lib Hotaling here.

18 Fair. I send my note with G.J. Sweet, 481 dollars with him to Cornelius VanDerzee to take up the note to Mrs. Sweet. I borrow 5 dollars of Willis. I pay Wesley 10 dollars I borrowed of him. I go to vineyard.

19 Rainy. **I work at capstan of hay press.**[273] Go to river. **P.G. Coffin make her first trip today**.

20 Cold, cloudy, NW. I go to river, work around the house.

21 Cloudy, SW. I attend Joslin's Vendue. Take tea to Willis. I borrow 25 dollars of Willis.

22 Fair, cold. Go to Meeting. I call to Willis's.

23 Fair. **R.H. Mosher leave my shops**. I go to river. Bridget Cavender leave. I pay her 21 dollars. Elida Lewis come to work. Mr. T. Civill call here.

24 Cloudy, misty. I work around. Go to Temperance Hall in evening. **Attend Sewing Society; have a fine time**.

25 Cold, NW. I work at vineyard. I go to river. Our Roe cow has a calf.

26 Fair, cold, NW. I put in glass to the vineyard. Vining all day.

27 Fair. I work to vineyard. **Attend a Cotillion Party**[274] **to Temperance Hall. Have a very fine time, pleasant party**.

28 Fair, cold. Work at the vineyard house. Mrs. Wm. O. Lawton here. Wife visit to Willis. I got check of Willis to H. Sperl 10 dollars.

---

[273] A capstan is a revolving cylinder with a vertical axis on which rope is wound.

[274] A Cotillion Party is a version of an English country dance, the forerunner of the Square Dance.

29 Fair, cold, NW. **I work at the hot house to vineyard**. Go to river. Mother here. I call to Wm. O. Lawton's. **John VanDerpool and Miss Brown get married**.

30 Fair, NW. I go to Meeting. U.B. Willis and Mrs. P. Kimmey here. Wm. MacGregor here. We all go to A.N. Briggs in evening.

31 Fair. **Work to vineyard house**. Sow grass seed. Go to the river. Mother & Mrs. Willis here.

April 1857

1   Cloudy. Sow grass seed. Get plaster from mill. Draw manure. John Fike come to work. S. Hany move from my house. John H. Holmes move in my house. **Andrew VanAntwerp here, leave 1200 dollars with me for David VanAntwerp.**

2   Fair, 4 in. snow. I get check of 10 dollars of Willis; send to Lyman Bullock. Wife goes to James Jack visit. Very cold.

3   Fair, cold, SW. **I work at glass house on vineyard**. Draw stone and manure.

4   Fair, heavy SW. Daniel VanAntwerp & Son James here to breakfast. **I pay him 1200 dollars left him by Andrew and take the money of him, let Willis have it**. Take his note, one year. Attend Nomination Meeting to Coeymans Hollow. Get my grape vines from propeller, sent from Germany, and two bottles of Brandy.

5   Heavy SW. I go to Meeting. I call to Mother's. **Newton Briggs died.**[275]

6   Rainy. Go after gate posts for our cemetery. Attend District Road meeting. Rainy day.

7   Fair, 4 inches snow. I get 1865 dollars of William Nodine. Gave him my note. Get the money for Sarell Wood. Wife go to Mrs. Houghtaling.

8   Fair. **I send 1865 dollars with Willis to Albany, get draft on New York for Mr. Wood**. Almira VanBergen here. Mrs. A.E. Willis here. I pay John Clement two dollars for sash. I fix sash.

9   Fair. I get timber for cemetery gate. I work at sash. I take tea, spend the evening to Doct. Blaisdell's. I pay T. Civill 14 dollars interest money.

10 Cloudy, SW. I set glass. Go to Garrett Houghtaling's to tea. Wife, Willis, Harriet, Almira VanBergen go along. Lib Castle's girls here. I go to river.

11 Rainy afternoon. **I and Mr. McKee look at our school rooms. I work at our school building**. All hands visit to Willis's. Rufus King pay me 50 dollars.

12 Rainy day. I call to Willis's & to P. Ostrander's. I go to Meeting.

13 Rainy. I go to John Harris, then work at cemetery. Ed VanOrden, Lib Hotaling, Mary Hotaling, Hannah Andrews here.

14 Rain & snow all day, hard. Creeks full, very wet & muddy.

15 Stormy rain, hail & snow. Work at cemetery. Garrett Hotaling here after Lib. I, Wife & Willis's family go to Wm. MacGregor's to tea. **Wm. C. Robb pay me $37.78 straw bill**.[276]

---

[275] Newton Briggs was Albert Newton Briggs' father. He was our 3rd Great Grandfather.
[276] Wm. C. Robb was involved in running one of the papermills on the Hannacroix. Straw was used in the papermaking process.

16	Fair. **I work at cemetery and schoolhouse lot**. William Minnick pay me 30 dollars, gave receipt and endorsed it on bond.
17	Stormy, snow & cold NW. I work at Stebben's House. Wife go to Albany. Mother here. Let Wm. R. Carroll have 1 bushel ears corn.
18	Fair, cool morning. I work at Stebben's House. Mr. Willis, Harriet, Miss Sage, Aaron Hotaling & Lady Widow & Ackerman, Mrs. Cate Spraker, Betsey Verplank, James Jack & Lady here, visit.
19	Cloudy, SW. Go to Meeting. Miss Brace, Doct. Blaisdell, Mr. Collins, Ed VanOrden here. I go to vineyard & to cemetery.
20	Heavy snow & rain all day. I go to river. I pay John Neagle balance of $11.90. I pay off Wm. B. Hull. He pay me cemetery bill 14 dollars.
21	Cloudy, misty. I go to river. I pay Mrs. Albert Jackson $31.25 for sash & door frames. Miss Brace & Lib Hotaling here. Snow 3 ft. deep in Westerlo.
22	Fair, pleasant, NW. I work at Stebben's lot. Mother, Harriet, Almira VanBergen here. I pay off Henry Yung $42. Mr. H. Niles pay me 42 cents for boards. **I pay P. Lany 75 cents for Schoolhouse hinges.**
23	Fair, cool. **I work at Schoolhouse ½ day and ½ day at vineyard**. J.H. Holmes help. Wife visit to Mrs. John Clement. I go to river.
24	Fair, cool. I work at vineyard, plow some. Wife & Almira go to B.B. Fredenburgh's.
25	Fair, cool. Make letters. Burn brush, plant sweet corn. **All hands go to A.N. Briggs, spend the evening.** I pay Peter Swine one dollar.
26	Fair, cool. I call to John Rea's. Ed VanOrden, Mr. T. Civill, Doct. Blaisdell here. I call to Mother's.
27	Rainy. Almira VanBergen leave for holme. I take her and Wife to the river. I get my waggon fixed, pay 50 cents.
28	Fair, cold, north wind. I make fence. Leave Joslin's note to Willis for him to get the money on for me, the amount is $1146 and some cents. I get 100 dollars of Johnson & Schoonmaker. Mr. Civill, Miss Brace, Beecher Holmes, John Cronk, Miss Bennett, Lib Hotaling here.
29	Fair. **I, John, Chris Fike go to Albany. I go to Herkimer. Get to G. Yoos, stay all night. I ride from Little Falls with Mr. Case.**
30	Fair. **Stay about the mill. Settle with Mr. Bullock. I pay him off.**

May 1857

1	**Fair morning, rainy toward night. Mr. Legg do surveying. Plenty of snow in the woods.**
2	Rainy day. **Stay in the sawmill all day. Settle with Lines C. Belcher, pay him balance $57.07. Pay off Henry Sperl.**
3	Little misty. **Call on Mr. Kelly, he sugars off some maple molasses - have a rich treat. Take dinner to L.C. Belcher's.**
4	Rainy day, high water, rains very hard. **Work about the mill.**

5	Fair. **Survey out my lot. Get very wet, have a hard time. Snowbanks very deep. Am wet knee deep until 3 o'clock in afternoon.**
6	Shower. **Come to Little Falls with Henry Sperl. Let him have 25 dollars. Then I come holme**. Wife go to Widow Hotaling's. My mare Polly has a colt.
7	Cloudy. Make fence; G. Rifflin help. I send Marite and Mother Hotaling to Garrett Hotaling's. I and Wife go after them.
8	Fair warm day. Make fence. **I pay off Miss Brace's school bills**. Andrew Fancher here; pay me his and George Fancher's rent. Charles Cook here. Lib Hotaling & A.E. Willis call. I pay Willis 200 dollars. I take receipt of Ben.
9	Fair. Make fence. Go to river. Doct. VanAntwerp here.
10	Fair, SW. I and Peter Seabridge go under Jill. I pay Doct. Fredenburgh 49 dollars interest money. Capt. J. Sherman, T. Civill, Daniel VanAntwerp here to tea. N. wind in evening.
11	Fair. Go Under Hill, get lumber. Peter Seabridge pay me money. A. VanAntwerp leave. I go to river.
12	Fair. **Clean house, plant sugar cane seed**.[277] L. Crandle here. Tobias Crumb pay me $2.04 for Mr. Wilsey.
13	Fair. I, Levi & Anthony go to Albany. I pay off G.H. Lawton 94 dollars. I get sugar. Pruyn & Lansing pay me $8.29 back on my circular saw. I get fish of John Mull on coming holme. **Mrs. Caroline Scott died**.
14	Rainy. Work at barn. I get checks of Willis, 66 dollars and one 17 dollars, exchange. James Sherwood pay me $8.50 rent due.
15	Rainy. Make fence. Get 3 pigs of Daniel Baker. Mary Ann McClancy here. Work in barn. I pay Peter Long for harrow teeth and snipe bill. **William Lawson died**.
16	Rainy. Work around. Put Polly mare to horse. **A.N. Briggs pay me $37.50 dollars rent; agree to keep the premises at the same rate. This is the house of Harris where David Baker lives**. Lib Hotaling & Cate Spraker call. I pay Daniel Baker 6 dollars for 3 pigs.
17	Fair, cold. **I attend the funeral of William Lawson**. Go to vineyard. Call to B.B. Fredenburgh's & to Dr. Blaisdell's. A.E. Willis call.
18	Fair. Make fence on Church Farm. **Capt. James Sherman here**. Israel Lawton call here.
19	Rainy. Turn cow & calves Under Hill. Make fence.
20	Very rainy day. Go to mill. Lay around, go to river.
21	Showery day. Work at barn. Go to river.
22	Fair, warm. **I and Wife go to Albany. I go on Harris case of citation. Taken sick, get holme half past 10 in evening**.
23	Fair. Make fence all day Under Hill. I put Polly mare to Seabridge's horse again.

---

[277] This is strange as sugar cane isn't grown in the north. There is discussion later of constructing a sugar mill. Possibly this involved using sorghum grass, which was a commonplace sweetener before the use of sugar.

24 Very fine warm day. I walk around. Martin & Elida VanSlyck here. Ed VanOrden call. I call to John Rea's.

25 Fair, warm. Make fence Under Hill. John Rea help.

26 Fair. Plant corn. **Get balance of 3000 dollars of H. Joslin. Send it to Sarell Wood, leave the money and matter with Willis.**[278]

27 Fair, SW. Plant corn. Work Under Hill. Dominie Leluck, Wife & Daughter here, visit. Attend to the matter of S. Wood. I pay Willis Vendue bill of H. Joslin. Rain evening.

28 Fair, SW, warm. All hands make fence Under Hill.

29 Rainy. Go to A. Witbeck's, get stake lumber for vineyard. Get his bull, work at barn. Hail. I send Lyman Bullock check 12 dollars.

30 Fair, cool. Make fence. Work at barn. Go to river. **Get stone for grave of Gardner Lawton**.

31 Rainy. I take Wife, Mother & Mrs. John Cronk to Quarterly Meeting to Coeymans Hollow.

June 1857

1 Cloudy, SW. Work Under Hill ½ day.

2 Heavy showers. Make fence. Attend association in evening. Lib Hotaling here. **Stephen Ostrander died.**

3 Fair. Doct. VanAntwerp here. We all lay walk Under Hill. Mary Ann McClancy & Lib Hotaling here. **Harman VanDerzee died**. I go to river.

4 Fair. **Attend the funeral of H. VanDerzee & Stephen Ostrander**. Garrett Hotaling & Lady, Old Mrs. VanAntwerp, Gittee VanAntwerp & two sisters & Mrs. A. Jackson here, call. Mr. Smith with them. I pay J.H. Holmes 4 dollars. Work at vineyard stakes.

5 Fair, north wind. Get out stakes for vineyard. Go on the Hill, get stake lumber. Company all leave. I and Wife go to Albany.

6 Cloudy. Get out grape stakes. I and Levi go to John Mull's, get fish. Wife come holme from Albany.

7 Rainy. Go to Meeting & to vineyard. Miss Brace, Mrs. G. Hotaling here.

8 Foggy. Work at barn. Mary Ann McClancy & Mrs. E. Holmes here.

9 Fair, SW. Work at barn. Go to river. P. Lawson pay me 40 dollars.

10 Cloudy, SW. Work at barn. Mother here. I pay Mary Ann McClancy 20/. I go to Cemetery.

11 Rainy day. I make and put up swing gate. Go to river.

12 Fair. Work at barn. Make fence. Mrs. A.N. Briggs call and two extra Negroes here.

13 Rainy. Work at barn. Go to J.T. Wilsey's, get seed corn, pay him 3 dollars. Wm. Phelps & Mr. VanAllen here. Miss Brace, Lib Hotaling here. I pay J. Holmes 2 dollars.

14 Fair. Go to Meeting twice with company. Go to vineyard. We call to Mrs. Hotaling's & to Wm. O. Lawton's.

15 Fair, warm. Work all day on barn. Wm. Phelps & VanAllen leave.

---

[278] This might be a payment for the property in Michigan.

16 Rainy day. Work at barn. Mr. Laigh pay me one-dollar rent.

17 South wind, rainy. Work at barn. Lib Hotaling here.

18 Lowry, rainy. Lib Hotaling here. We work at barn.

19 Rainy. Work at barn, make fence. **I take our hearse to barn at brick house**.

20 Fair. **I am 40 years old**. Work at fence, go to river. Call to John Cronk's. I pay J.H. Holmes 2 dollars. **Edward H. VanSlyck died.**

21 Fair, warm. I and Wife go to B.J. VanSlyck's, take dinner and tea. Stop on our return to Barrett Houghtaling. Roads very bad.

22 **Heavy rain. We go Under Hill, get wet. More rain than ever was known for the season throughout.**

23 Fair, NW. I pay D. Tompkins one year's interest on note I gave to Catherine Niles. He pays me my lumber bills of 36 or 7 dollars. **I draw up and lay my plank walk, hard job**.

24 Fair, cool. I work in garden. Go to river, get my horse shod.

25 Fair, NW. Work on my barn. John Cronk & Lady & Charlotte here. I go to river. I call to Willis's.

26 Fair, NW. Work at potatoes. Dominie Selick here to dinner. Wife go to Aaron Hotaling's. **Mrs. John Hazelton died.**

27 Fair. **I go to Herkimer**. Ride out with Mr. Johnson. Stay all night to G. Yoos

28 Fair. I stay to Gotfriet's & to H. Sperl's.

29 Rainy. Go about the place. I pay Mr. Bullock 5 dollars.

30 Rainy. Go about the premises.

July 1857

1 Rainy. I settle with Mr. Bullock and Gottefriet and H. Sperl.

2 Fair. **I walk to Norway & to Newport. Take stage to Herkimer. Meet with David Witbeck to Herkimer. Take cars Holme**.

3 Rainy. Work on barn. Go to river. I call to Wesley. R.H. Mosher pay me off 8 dollars he owed me.

4 One fair day. I pay J.H. Holmes 10 dollars, John Fike 4 dollars. **I go to Island. I attend 4th of July fireworks. Ed VanOrden, Mr. Vosburgh, Martin G. VanSlyck, Lib & Caroline Hotaling, Miss Brace here. The day was passed off very pleasantly**. **Wm. L. Marcy died at Ballstown today.**[279]

5 Fair, warm. I go to Meeting. Martin G. VanSlyck pay me 7 dollars for S. Wood. He and Lib Houghtaling leave.

6 Fair. I draw manure. T.H. Gould pay me balance of $2.08 he owed me. I get Polly mare shod.

7 Heavy shower. I sow buckwheat. I go to John Mull's get fish. Doct. Fredenburgh call here.

---

[279] William L. Marcy was a U.S. Senator, Governor of New York, U.S. Secretary of War and U.S. Secretary of State. He died in Ballston Spa.

8	Fair. I attend picnic at Grove at Stone Church. Call to T. Civil's. Lay sidewalk. Call to Dominie Selick's.
9	Fair, warm. Work at Baker House. Wife go to Albany.
10	Fair, SW, warm. James Hazleton here. I pay him 20/ for plank. Wife come from Albany. Miss Brace here. Mr. VanAllen call. A. Witbeck here. Get 3 bunches of shingles.
11	Fair, hot. Work at barn. Go a fishing. Mary Holmes call.
12	Fair, hot. TH 92°. Uncle Garrett & Caroline Hotaling call. Doct. Blaisdell call. I go to sleep.
13	Fair, very hot. I and J. Henry Holmes shingle barn to Abram Witbeck's. Boys draw manure. J.T. Haley and Mr. Sherill here.
14	Fair, very hot. **Shingle to A. Witbeck's**. S. Winne, boys draw manure. **I sweat about a gallon. Arthur McClasky died 15 July 57**.
15	Fair, hot, SW. Finish barn to A. Witbeck's. Come holme, go to river.
16	Fair, hot. I take my boys, go to Greenville.
17	Fair, hot. Come from Greenville. I pay Mohawk Valley Mutual Insurance Company agent $119.96. Get $60 of Willis and $60 of T. Civill.
18	Fair, hot. I go to Albany, get scythes, cradles. Get my dividend. Wife, Levi, Miss Brace go to Garrett Hotaling's.
19	Fair, hot. Mr. Civill call. We go to vineyard. **I go to Catholic Church**. Mr. VanAllen here to tea. Mr. Willis & Harriet call.
20	Fair, hot, SW. Commence haying and my grain. **Ziegler men come to work**. I borrow 60 dollars of John Reed, gave note. Henry Springstead pay me shingle bill $28.88. Gave him bill dated 17 receipt at that date. Get in 2 load hay.
21	Rainy. Work at mowing. I go to river. I pay T. Civill 10 dollars cash. Leave 50 dollars with Ben Kelly for him, which pays him 60 dollars borrowed of him.
22	S wind, little rain at night. Work at my rye.
23	Rainy day. Clear out barn. Mr. T. Civill & A.E. Willis call here.
24	Rainy. **I attend Miss Brace school**. I go to river. Boys work at matters around house.
25	Rain, heavy shower. I and boys go fishing. Wife & Miss Brace go to Coxsackie. Men work in barnyard.
26	SW, showry. Mr. Civill call. I and he call to Widow Bronk's. **My cows get in my garden, destroy corn.** I go to Meeting. I and Levi go to Uncle Andrew VanSlyck's. Bring Wife, Mother Hotaling, Miss Brace holme.
27	Fair SW. Get in hay & rye. Mary & Charlotte Hotaling here. Mrs. A.E. Willis & Children here. We work hard.
28	Rainy. Work in hay & rye. Mr. Civill & Mother call here.
29	Fair, NW, heavy rain last night. We work in hay. Willis call.
30	Rainy all day. Draw in 4 loads. Go to river.
31	Lowry. Work at J. Henry's cellar drain and hay. Mr. N.H. Johnson & Lady, Mrs. H. Niles, Mary Serles, Miss Brace [here]. John take them holme in waggon.

August 1857

1. Cloudy, clears off. I get 10 dollars of Ben Keller. I go to Albany. Get Dividend No. 5. Come back, pay money back to Ben. Mrs. A. Jackson & Christina Tefft call. **Marite bring Harry VanDerzee here to board.**[280]

2. Fair. I go to Meeting & Marite go to vineyard. **Wm. MacGregor & Mrs. Terry married**.

3. Fair, NW. Miss Brace, Mr. Porter here. We work in hay. Wife and Marite go to Doct. Fredenburgh's.

4. Fair, SW. Work in hay. Mr. Israel Lawton & Lady here. Mary Jane Heller & Miss Drew here.

5. Rainy. Make fence. Mow some. Wife go to Albany. Mary Hotaling call here.

6. Fair. Work in hay. **Get 25 loads ready for barn**. Wife go to Widow Jemima Hotaling's.

7. Fair. **Get in 10 loads hay**.

8. Fair, SW. Work in hay. Henry VanBergen come here. I and boys go in swimming. **Get 11 loads of hay, 58 in all**.

9. Fair. Go to Meeting. Mr. Civill, P. K. Runiny (sp), Willis & Harriet call.

10. Rainy afternoon. Get in my wheat & mow. I pay Mrs. John Rea 10 dollars interest money. I get 25 dollars of Johnson & Schoonmaker. Willis take up my 100 dollars in hands of Dr. Blaisdell.

11. Fair. Work in hay. Henry VanDerzee & Martin leave. Wife go to Wm. MacGregor's.

12. Fair. Work in hay. Mother here. Charlotte & Mary Hotaling here. Wife visit to John V.A. Witbeck's.

13. Rainy, hot. We mow, I go to river.

14. Fair hot day. **Work hard. Have 76 loads hay in barn, 15 out**. Dominie Selick, Wife, Mother-in-Law, two daughters, Mother, Mrs. G. Harris here. All visit; have a fine time.

15. Fair, NW. John Silcock, Wife, 3 children & a black woman come. We work in hay. **John Sickler died.**

16. Fine day. All go to Meeting. I and J.J. Silcock go to vineyard. Mary Hotaling & Cate Hotaling here.

17. Rainy day. James Sherwood pay me 10 dollars. Peter Swinn pay me 2 dollars. **I attend funeral of John Sickler**. I go to river. Get pay for G. Rifflin calf. I pay the money to him $7.18.

18. Cloudy, NW. I and Wm. MacGregor go to Greenville. We stop to U.B. Willis's at Coxsackie to Futchet's. **I attend Mrs. Harris's Concert in the eve at M.E. Church.**

19. Fair. Work in hay. Mrs. Colvin, Miss Hill, Mary Jane Lawton, Mr. J.J. Colvin, Miss Brace, Lib Hotaling and another girl here.

20. Fair. I, Wife & company go to A.E. Willis, get apples. I cut my oats.

---

[280] Harry VanDerzee was the son of Henry VanDerzee who was a friend of Marite & Doctor VanAntwerp and Fletcher & Sarah Ann. He was the same age as Anthony and spent considerable time boarding with Fletcher & Sarah Ann.

21 Fair. Work in hay. **Attend Miss Brace School. I pay her tuition, 6 dollars. She pay me $5.22 rent.** Lib Hotaling & Miss Brace here. C. VanDerzee & Doct. Blaisdell here. **Wm. Springstead and Lib Waldron married.**

22 Cloudy, SW. Work in hay. Mrs. A. Mull & Daughter, Mr. Trego, Baltis J. VanSlyck, Lady & Child, Cate VanBergen, Widow Charlotte, J.J. Silcox & Family here. I go to river.

23 Showry, thunder & lightning. I take Mother to Bethlehem to Quarterly Meeting. Take dinner to Dominie Jolly's. Mother here. Cate VanBergen, Mary Hotaling, Mr. Civill call here.

24 Cloudy, NW. Mow all day. B.J. VanSlyck here. J.J. Silcox leave for New York.

25 Fine day. Work in hay. Mrs. Garrett Hotaling Mrs. N. Stephens, Lib Hotaling, Mr. Stephens here, visit. Miss Angevine, Mary & Euphema Blaisdell here. Levi take Mrs. B.J. VanSlyck to Mr. VanOrden.

26 Fair day. Work in hay. Company here yet. They leave for Garrett Houghtaling's.

27 South wind blow hard. Work in hay, work hard. **John Rix and Mary get married.**

28 Showry. I go to river. Mrs. Banden pay me 10 dollars rent. I pay J.H. Holmes 5 dollars.

29 Rainy. Commence hay in Big Meadow. I go to Mr. Soop's, get 3 pigs. **I use Willis's mowing machine.**[281] H. VanDerzee here.

30 Beautiful day. H. VanDerzee & I go to Elias Holmes' & to vineyard.

31 Fine day. **Work in hay in Big Meadow until dark.**

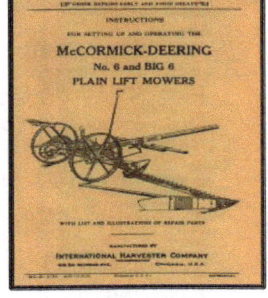

Mowing machine

September 1857

1 Fine day, no wind. Silcox & family leave. Mrs. Livingston Spraker, Mr. Spraker, Mrs. Cate Spraker here visit. Miss Brace, Mr. Acton Civill & Lady call & two daughters.

2 Fair. Work hard in hay. Get stung with bumble bees.

3 Fair, SW. Finish mowing in Big Meadow. Wife go with Willis to Camp Meeting. Mrs. L.D. Eddy & Son call here.

4 Fair. Work in hay Under Hill. Mr. Baltis VanSlyck call here for shingles.

5 Fair. I and T. Civill go to Schodack to Mr. Reed's. P. Swinn pay me 2 dollars. I pay J.H. Holmes 3 dollars. **Finish up my haying, am glad of it. I cut 202 loads of hay, 10 loads of rye, 3 loads of wheat, 3 loads of oats.** Wife go to Baltimore to James Trego's.

6 Rainy morning clears off again. Go to Meeting & to vineyard. Cate VanBergen here.

7 Fair NW. Commence plowing. I go with S. Hathaway to P. Kimmey's, to Mr. Stanton's, to Mr. VanDerzee's, to J.B. Shear's to dinner. Then to P. Bronk's, then to John Teneyck's. **Saw two funerals – Getty Blodget's and James Rankin's child.**

---

[281] The horse-drawn sickle bar mower didn't come into common use until about this time. Prior to their use, hay was cut by hand using a scythe, which was time consuming and brutal work. We don't know exactly when Fletcher began using the mowing machine.

8   SW, Fair, first frost. **Yernick Ziegler come to work again for 3 months at 10 dollars per month.** I have headache, lay around.

9   Fair, SW. Lay around, am unwell. Boys plow; cut brush.

10 Fair. I go to Island. Cate Hotaling, I gave her a note for 200 dollars. I take up my old one 180 dollars.

11 Fair. **Go after timber for sugar cane press**. Take it to Kimmey's, get it sawed & turned out. Get holme 10 o'clock at night.

12 Cloudy, little rainy. Lay around, go to river. Get 5 dollars of Wiley, leave it with A. VanDerzee. Have peaches & melons come with propeller. **Get a roller from papermill**. Mrs. Sarell Wood come here.

13 Fair. Go to Meeting. I take Mr. Wood and the folks to Garrett Hotaling's, spend afternoon, take tea.

14 Fair, warm. Mr. S. Wood leave. **We work on Sugar Mill. James Hazleton's boy get drowned.** Samuel Pelts, Mary Jane Lawton, Israel Lawton & Lady here.

15 Fair, NW, cooler. **Attend funeral of J. Hazleton's boy. I work on sugar mill.** Caroline Hotaling here. I go to Mr. Robb's. I pay J.H. Holmes 3 dollars. S. Carhart pay me 1 dollar. Miss Brace here.

16 Fair. I & Wife go to Coxsackie. I take dinner to U.B. Willis's. **Attend a Negro Convention, hear Frederick Douglas speak. He is a coppered colored Negro with some degree of intelligence, spoke well.**[282]

Frederick Douglas

17 Rainy. **I harness horses with A.E. Willis and all hands go to Albany, attend our County Fair. It rain all the way holme**.

18 Fair. Plow. **We work at Sugar Mill**. Attend rehearsal at the Methodist Episcopal Church.

19 Rainy. Elida VanSlyck here. **I work at Sugar Mill**. Peter Swinn pay me two dollars. I call to Mother's.

20 Cloudy & misty. Ed VanOrden & Mary Hotaling here.

21 Fair. **I work at Sugar Mill**. Cradle my buckwheat. Wife & Elida go to Albany. They come back again. Hiram Briggs here. Mr. T. Civill & Mr. Hoag here call.

22 Cloudy, cold, SW. Wife & Elida go to Thomas Houghtaling's. I work at hay press & go to Thomas in afternoon.

23 Fair, cool. Work at press. Go on the hill, get hoop poles. Levi go after Levi & Elida VanSlyck to Thomas Houghtaling's.

24 Fair, frost, SW. I work at hay press. Wife & Elida come back. They go to Widow Charlotte's.

---

[282] After escaping from slavery in Maryland, Frederick Douglas became a national leader of the abolitionist movement in Massachusetts and New York, gaining note for his oratory and incisive antislavery writings. He was also active in the women's suffrage movement with Elizabeth Cady Stanton and Susan B. Anthony. Douglas was born in 1818 and would have been about 39 at this time – 1 year younger than Fletcher.

25 Fair day, SW. Draw manure. Levi take Wife & Elida to Garrett Houghtaling's. **I attend McKee's school and to rehearsal.**

26 Fair day. Draw brush. I, Wife & Elida go to Mr. Croswell's. Henry VanDerzee, Doct. VanAntwerp, Marite, Martin VanSlyck, Doct. Fredenburgh here.

27 Warm fine day. Stay about with Henry VanDerzee & Doct. Mary & Charlotte Houghtaling here.

28 Showry, NW. I stay around with Doc. & Henry VanDerzee. **I take boys to the Indian Show in evening.**

29 Cool. Stay around with Henry VanDerzee & Doct. VanAntwerp and Caroline VanAntwerp. She is here. They pay me 68 [dollars] for cemetery lots. I let Willis have 60 dollars, get his check for 100 dollars, send it to H. Sperl.

30 Fair, frost & cold. I take Mother Houghtaling & Marite to Uncle Andrew's. Mother Hotaling stay Andrew's. I sow my rye.

October 1857

1   Lowry. Work at rye. Go to cemetery with G. Rifflin. Go to river. Fix Baker's stoop.

2   Rain all day. Uncle Andrew & Marite come here. I take Uncle Andrew to vineyard. I go to river. P. Lawson send me 25 dollars. I pay the same to Willis.

3   Lowry. **I and Uncle Andrew go to Erastus Corning's Nursery.** I pay J. Soop $4.50 for 3 pigs I bought of him.

4   Fair. Go to cemetery & to vineyard. Go to Meeting. Mary Hotaling & A.E. Willis call here.

5   Fine day. Press hay. **Timothy Clancy pay me $96.50 on debt of Catholic Church.** I pay Willis 95 dollars. Mrs. A. Jackson & Miss Tefft here.

6   Fair. **Work on graves for Doct. & H. VanDerzee.** Widow Hotaling, Mrs. F. Cranston, Mrs. A. VanDerzee, Mrs. Samuel Gedney, Mrs. Gedney, Mr. W.B. Hull here. Mrs. Swinn pay me 2 dollars. I pay G. Rifflin 2 dollars.

7   Fair. Marite & Mother Hotaling go to N. York. **I attend removals of the dead for H. VanDerzee & Doctor.** I take Mother & Marite with team to New Baltimore.

8   Fine day. Wife go to John Mull's. Eliza Phelps and her Boy here. We dig potatoes, go Under Hill get apples.

9   Fair, dry. Draw timber & muck for G. Rifflin. Draw in buckwheat and slat timbers.

10 Fair. Go after hoop poles, press hay. Mare Polly hurt her head. P. Swinn pay me 1 dollar.

11 Fair. Wm. Phelps & Mr. VanAllen here. Baltis VanSlyck. We go to Negro Camp Meeting.

12 Fair. Press hay. P. Swinn pay me 6 dollars. I pay John H. Holmes 3 dollars. I borrow 20 dollars of A.E. Willis.

13 Fair. I go under the Hill, then to Greenville. I stay all night to Andrew Fancher's.

14 Rainy. I come holme. Wm. Tuttle pay me $3.62. I pay Willis 25 dollars. I and Willis go Under Hill.

15 Rainy afternoon. **I work at the sugar cane.** I pay Elida five dollars. I go to the river.

16   Rainy. Press hay. **I attend McKee's school**. Miss Brace here to tea. I send H. Sperl check for 25 dollars.

17   Fair. Press hay. I go to Schodack to Mr. Reed's. Mary Jane & Helen Lawton call.

18   Fair. Go to Meeting. Almira VanBergen, Mary Hotaling here. Mr. T. Civill call. I and he go to vineyard and to cemetery.

19   Rainy. **Work at sugar cane. Put hay on board the propeller**. Timothy Clancy pay me $36. I pay J.H. Holmes 2 dollars.

20   Cold, NW. **I work at sugar cane**. I go to river.

21   Cold, NW. Snow squalls, freeze, ice. I go to Albany. Martin VanSlyck here.

22   Fair, cold. I get 10 dollars of Willis. Go to Corning's with M.G. VanSlyck. Stop to J. Soop's, get 4 pigs. Martin leave. Dominie Selick & Daughter here.

23   Cloudy. **Work at sugar cane. Go to Singing School. Lots of folks here to see me work.**

24   Lowry, rainy. Work roads & **boil molasses**.

25   Rainy day. Go to Meeting. Call to Willis's.

26   Rainy day. Go to river. Bad storm. Work at hoops.

27   Rainy day. **Work at molasses**. Press hay.

28   Lowry, little rainy. **I attend Miss Brace's school**. **Work at sugar cane.**

29   Lowry. Work at barn & to woodhouse to vineyard. Willis here.

30   Cloudy. **Work at sugar cane**. George Harris here. James Sherwood pay me 10 dollars rent.

31   Cloudy. **Finish sugar cane**. Mother & Harriet here. Dominie Selick, Miss Brace, Lib Hotaling call. Henry VanDerzee. I borrow 10 dollars of A.E. Willis. I pay Dutch Lewy $20 & to John H. Holmes 1 dollar.

November 1857

1   Fair. Gilbert Budd here. I take him to Mrs. P.W. VanBergen. Call to Martin VanBergen's & to Baltis J. VanSlyck. A.E. Willis call here.

2   Fair. Work on hog pen. Caroline VanAntwerp and Aunt Betsey Verplank here.

3   Fair. **Election. I vote then go to Low Point.**[283] **Take Steamer Eagle, go to Poughkeepsie. Take cars to Hamburg. I get 90 dollars of Johnson & Schoonmaker. I pay J.H. Holmes 10 dollars. Get to Low Point 12 o'clock morning. Stay to J. Hart's.**

4   Fair. **Go to Mr. G. Budd's to breakfast. Get my vines dug up and, on the dock, ready to start for holme. Stay all night with Gilbert Budd. Charlotte Hotaling visit.**

5   Fair. **Come holme with my vines on Steamer Constitution. Henry VanDerzee here.**

6   Cloudy. **Work on vineyard.** Andrew Houghtaling, Wife and Children here.

7   Fair day. Work on vineyard. I take Andrew Houghtaling, Wife & Child holme. I take Children and Cranston's Girls along to Coxsackie.

---

283   Low Point, now called Chelsea, is a hamlet in Dutchess County, NY.

8	Cloudy. Go to Meeting & to cemetery. Lib Hotaling and Elizabeth Stephens here.
9	Cloudy, misty, SW. **I lay wall on vineyard and work hard**. Girls all here.
10	Rainy, clears up. Work ½ day on vineyard. Girls here. Wife go with them to Albany. Widow Charlotte pay me 3 dollars for corn.
11	Fair. Work on vineyard. Mr. Brandow here.
12	Cloudy, cold, SW. Work on vineyard. I get 50 dollars of Platt A. Smith. Gave me note payable April 1, 1858. Eliza Roberts & her niece call here.
13	Cloudy, cool. I work on vineyard. **Attend Miss Brace's School. Miss Brace here.** Wife & Lib Hotaling & Miss Stephens come back.
14	Fair, NW, cold. **I go to Herkimer**. Stop to Eben Kelly's. Stay all night.
15	Fair, NW. I walk to G. Yoos & to H. Sperl. Go around in the woods.
16	Stormy, snowy. Work around the mill & in the woods. I pay Gottefriet 30 dollars & H. Sperl 5 dollars.
17	Cloudy, little stormy. I go to Wm. Kelly's to breakfast. Come with Willis Kelly to Little Falls. Stop to John Feeter's. I pay off Wm. Kelly, take his receipt, I pay Johnny Rix ten dollars, then I come holme.
18	Fair. Plow, work around, go to vineyard.
19	Rainy, SW. Measure up corn with Henry Smith. Go to river.
20	Squally, snowy, N.H. Johnson pay me $1.50 for 6 grape vines. I go to river twice. Chris Fike pay me $3.00 balance due me.
21	Fair, cold. Press hay. **I and Wife go to New York with Baltimore Barge**.
22	Fair. **Arrive at New York. Go to J.J. Silcock's. Go to Hear Mr. Chapin preach**.
23	Stormy. **Go to Doct. VanAntwerp's and around the city. Doctor pay me 13 dollars balance of account.**
24	Fair. **I and J.J. Silcock go to Sing Sing. Go around the State prison and see the prisoners dine; so through the prison. Then we take horse & waggon go to Tarrytown, see Andres monument at the place where he was taken prisoner.**[284] **See the old Dutch Church dated 1679. Then to Silcock's farm. Then back to Sing Sing. Take cars for New York. Then go to political meeting at the Academy of Music, great crowd there.**[285] **Then to an eating house, got refreshments. Then to John's. Stay all night at Andrew VanAntwerp's.**
25	Fair, cold. **Go to see the procession of Major General Worth funeral, 4 miles long.**[286] **Saw Gov. King, then to the burial place. Then to Mr. Weed's to tea.**

---

[284] John Andres was a Major in the British Army. He was hanged as a spy by the Continental Army for assisting Benedict Arnold's attempted surrender of the fort at West Point.

[285] One of the largest popular gatherings in New York that opposed the re-election of Mayor Fernando Wood.

[286] William Jenkins Worth was born in Hudson, NY. He served in the War of 1812, was commandant of cadets at West Point and was active in the Mexican American War (1846-48) where he was given his highest rank, Major General, in 1846. Following the war, Worth commanded the Army's Department of

26	Fair. Go around. **Attend Thanksgiving**. Dine to J.J. Silcock's.
27	Fair. Go around town. **Start for holme with our propeller**.
28	Fair. Get holme. Plenty of ice in the river. **Put my hay on boat**.
29	Fair, warm. Mr. T. Civill call here. I and he go to vineyard. Mr. P. Kimmey and Mr. Winne call.
30	Cloudy, cold. Mr. Civill pay me $1.80 for Sp plank. P. Seabridge, **Civill & myself have our Daguerreotypes taken and gave them to Miss Brace**.

December 1857

1	Rainy morning clears off cold. Press hay. I pay Jonathan Muckelroy 28 dollars interest money. Buy order on Johnson & Schoonmaker.
2	Cloudy, SW. Press hay. Abram Witbeck pay me 75 dollars rent. I pay Willis 65 dollars. I pay Mr. Winne 5 dollars for J.H. Holmes.
3	Fair. Press hay; draw it on boat. NW, colder.
4	Fair, cool. Mrs. A.E. Willis, Mrs. H. Springstead, Mrs. C. Fike [here]. Mrs. George Slater have daughter last night.
5	Cold snowy day. I go after slats, go to river. Call for Wife to Widow Houghtaling's.
6	Cold, snowy, rainy. I bring my calves holme. Go to Meeting. Call to A.E. Willis.
7	Fair, warm, foggy. Press hay. Lib Hotaling here. I go to river. Get iron for hay press.
8	Fair, warm. Press hay. I go to river. Very muddy.
9	Fair, warm. Press hay. I go to river. Rainy day. Garrett VanAntwerp here.
10	Fair, warm. Draw stone. Mr. Wiltsey pay me 75 dollars.
11	Colder, NW. Work in quiry, plow. I pay H. Rilaw 5 dollars vineyard bill.
12	Fine day, SW. Dig & draw stone. Lay walks. Miss Brace here.
13	Fair. Go to Meeting. Mr. Civill call here.
14	Fair, warm. I go to J. Baker's woods. Go to river. Wife go to Coxsackie with Mrs. A.N. Briggs.
15	Fair. I go to Baker's woods with John, draw chips. I pay Mr. Peacock's teamster 10 dollars, 7 dollars for J.H. Holmes and 3 dollars for myself. I pay J.J. Colvin balance of interest about 7 dollars. Draw two loads chips to Mother.
16	Fair day. Draw 3 loads chips. Caroline Hotaling here. Yernick Ziegler leave here at noon for C. VanDerzee's.
17	Cloudy, SW. I put hay on Barge. Draw 1 load chips.
18	Rainy. George Houghtaling here. **I go with him to vineyard and to cemetery, to papermill & to Miss Brace school & to Singing School.** Mrs. Willis call here. **Barent VanDerzee gets drownded in Big Creek tonight.**

Texas and while there died of cholera in 1849. His body was temporarily interred in Brooklyn before being buried on Evacuation Day at his monument's location in New York City. The burial followed an elaborate processional, which included 6500 soldiers.

19   Fair, colder. Wife come holme. I fix windows. Garrett Hotaling & George here. George leave for holme.

20   Fair, colder. Garret Houghtaling here. Mr. T. Civill call. **All hands attend the funeral of Barent VanDerzee.**

21   Fair, cold. Draw stone. Fix windows. Dominie Gardner call.

22   Rainy, SW. **Work at glass house**. I get 50 dollars of Johnson & Schoonmaker. Send check 30 dollars to H. Sperl. Let John Fike have 10 dollars.

23   Fair. Draw stone. Pay tax of over 70 dollars. I pay J.D. Chuck $8.94 for hay hoops. I pay Wm. O. Lawton's fish bill. I get 50 dollars of Johnson & Schoonmaker.

24   Fair, cold, NW. I go to Island with Smith, draw stone. Mother here.

25   Fair, cold. Am unwell. I go to river.

26   Fair, cold. **Go with Boys to skate to Dam. I go to Croswell's. Levi fall down, gets a black eye. Attend concert of Mrs. George Harris. Mr. Seloc & Lady arrived, just married. I am quite unwell.**

27   Fair, cold. Stay about the house all day. Folks go to Meeting.

28   Cloudy, SW. Draw stone, get horse shod. **Get two books from district library**. Almira VanBergen here.

29   Snow. Draw stone. John go to Dean's Mill. Take Wife & Almira [to] Garrett Hotaling's. I get 50 dollars of Schoonmaker & Co.

30   Cloudy, snowy. Draw wood. **Pay Miss Brace Schooling. Attend Dominie Selick's Donation. River closed**.

31   Rainy. I pay G. Rifflin 2 dollars. I pay Jonny Dutch $3.66. I pay Barent Teneyck 35 dollars interest money. Willis call here.

January 1858

1   Fair. I borrow $200 of Nathaniel Niles. I take up his note against me of 150 dollars; I gave him new note for 350 dollars. I take up note of A.N. Briggs of 92 dollars, which I gave to H. Harris. Martin & Elida VanSlyck here. I take Wife & Elida to Garrett Houghtaling's.

2   Fair. Draw posts to Martin & Elida VanSlyck, Mary Hotaling & Almira VanBergen here. I go to river.

3   Fair, NW. Martin & Elida leave. P. Kimmey call. We go to Quarterly Meeting. Mr. Civill call.

4   Fair, warm, SW. Mrs. Garrett Houghtaling & Mrs. VanOrden here. I go Under Hill Farm, get posts. Stop to W. Clarks to dinner. I pay Willis 50 dollars for check to H. Sperl.

5   Fair, very warm. Mrs. A.N. Briggs here. I get 300 dollars of N. Niles, gave note, leave 200 dollars with Willis. I take up my note in Civill's hands of 64 dollars. Harris & Briggs gave me horse Charley.

6   Snow all day, cold. I stay in house, am unwell.

7   Fair, about 8 in. snow, north wind, cold. I put 25 dollars in Willis hands, get check to John Feeter, send it to him. Draw one load of wood. Fix my stable. Mary Hotaling call. Wife go to Doct. Fredenburgh's. **Two steamboats go down today**.

8	Fair, NW. I and G. Rifflin go to Albany. I pay to VanRensselaer 5 dollars. Get dividend 15 dollars. I pay Koontz 25 dollars & get beef.
9	Cloudy, snowy, SW. Draw wood, go to river. I pay Mrs. G. Harris 3 dollars. Lib Hotaling here.
10	Fair, pleasant. Go to Meeting. I and Mr. Civill go to vineyard. Elizabeth Houghtaling leave. **Attend Quaker Meeting**.
11	Rain all day. Mr. Civill call here. I go to river, attend PR meeting to A.N. Briggs. Very sloppy & foggy.
12	Fair, SW. Go to Greenville. Stop to J.W. Story's & to Mr. Collins', then to Wm. Stephen's, get rents. Then to A. Fancher's, stay all night.
13	Fair SW. Get rents of Witford, Edget, Hunt, Witbeck then go to Greenville. Then to South Westerlo, see Mr. Phinney, then to Mr. Lamb's, buy a colt for 50 dollars.
14	Fair. Boys draw wood. I attend PR meeting all day. Briggs pay me $3.75. I attend Donation for Mr. Gardner at J.D. Church. I pay Willis 25 dollars for check to G. Yoos. Martin & Elida VanSlyck here.
15	Fair, SW. Go to Hollow, get my colt of Mr. Lamb. Boys go to woods. I pay Mr. Lamb 50 dollars. Go to J.J. Colvin's in evening, have party there.
16	Rainy day. I go to river. Boys chop wood in wood house.
17	Fair, NW. I go to Meeting. Call to Willis. Cooler.
18	Fair, cold. Boys thrash wheat. I go to river. I let Mother Hotaling have 10 dollars. I get the same again of Willis. I take Mother Hotaling to G. Hotaling's. Miss Brace here.
19	Fair, NW. Boys thrash. I settle with Johnson & Schoonmaker. They pay balance $81.73.
20	Fair, NW. Boys thrash. **I take 9 bu. wheat to Dean's Mill. I pay Mr. Dean plaster bill $1.63. I pay him 80 cts. for grinding**. Wife visit to Doct. Mosher.
21	Boys thresh. I go to river. Get 200 dollars of Wm. B. Hull, from R. Pulver. Let Willis have the money. **I and Mr. Civill go to Steam Mill**. Then to J.T. Witbeck's; see his horses. Then back to J.B. Shear's; take some brandy. Caroline VanAntwerp & Miss Selick here.
22	Fair, very cold. Boys thresh. I fix horse blankets, go to river.
23	Fair. **I go to Papermill Dam and mill. Skate with Boys**. J.H. VanBenthuyzen & Sarell Wood here.
24	Fair. Go to Meeting. Mr. Civill call. Garrett Hotaling, Lady & Elizabeth call & Caroline here to tea. Mr. A.E. Willis & Harriet call. John Fike & Levi go to Uncle Andrew's, get Mother Hotaling.
25	Fair, SW, very warm all winter. Mary Hotaling call. J. Henry & Sarell Wood leave.
26	Rainy, SW. Work in quiry. Stay about the house.
27	Lowry, rainy. I and Wife go to Albany. I pay Koontz $10.75, get feed. Very muddy weather.
28	Cloudy, colder. Fix stable. Boys thresh. Wife come from Albany. I gave Willis 10 dollars, send his check to H. Sperl.
29	Cloudy, cold. Em Brace here. I get tripe & tongue of L. Carhart. I go to river.

30 Clear, cold. **I go skating with Boys to dam**. Mr. Willis, Miss Brace, Miss Johnson, Mary Serles call. I go to river.

31 Fair, cold, NW. I let John have team, he go to Bethlehem. I go to Meeting. Mr. T. Civill call.

February 1858

1 Fair, SW. **I go to Schodack on skates**. Get my sole leather. I take cars, go to Troy to Co Treasurer's Office. **Come back with cars, skate holme again**.

2 Misty, rainy. I go to river. Sell my sole leather to C. Fike. He pay me some, leave balance due me $11.88. Paid $10 after.

3 Fair. **I attend examination of Miss Brace School. Children do well**. I go to river. Work around, go to river.

4 Fair. I go to river, draw wood. Wife visit to Wm. B. Hull's.

5 Fair, NW. **I get pump of P. Seabridge, put it in my well**. T. Civill call. Wife visit to Cranston's. I go to river.

6 Cloudy, cold. I go to river. We all spend the day to Willis's.

7 Cloudy, cold, SW. Mr. Civill call here. I go to Meeting. James Sherwood pay me 7 dollars on rent. John draw wood.

8 Cold, NW. Mary Ann McClancy here. Widow Teneyck call. **I attend Dist. School with J. VanDerzee, the Co. Superintendent.** John draw wood.

9 Snowy, SW. Boys thresh. I go to river. Mary McClancy here.

10 Fair, N & SW. I go Under Hill, draw 3 logs to P. Kimmey's.

11 Fair, cold, NW. TH 2 deg above 0. I go to James Armstrong's to a Vendue. John draw wood. I go to river.

12 NW & SW, fair. I go to river. TH one deg. below 0. I go to Island with John, draw wood. **Attend horse trot on ice**.

13 Fair, NW, very cold. TH one deg. below 0. Draw cornstalks from the island. Draw muck on vineyard. I go to papermill & to river. C. Fike pay me balance on leather $1.88.

14 Snow all day, cold. TH one deg. above 0. Miss C.A. Brace & Doct. Fredenburgh here. I call to J.H. Holmes.

15 Cold, fair, NW. Mr. Willis call. I go to river. John draw muck on vineyard. **Miss Brace here. I pay them their school bills, Levi $5.25, Anthony $3.25, Harry $3.25**. I pay J.E. Gibbens bill $2.25.

16 Snowy, cold, NW. I and Wife go with Willis & Harriet to Coxsackie to U.B. Willis, visit. Widow Charlotte & Daughter Mary here. TH one degree below 0.

17 Very cold, NW. Draw muck. I go to river. TH at 0.

18 Cold, NW, TH 8 degrees below 0. I go to papermill, to vineyard & to river. Draw muck. I buy paper, pay one dollar. I pay Elida 5 dollars.

19 Cold, SW, cloudy. Draw muck, go to river. Attend Dance to Aaron Houghtaling's. Wife visit to J. Jack's, we have a pleasant time.

20   Snow all day, NW. **I & Wife go to Albany. Have our daguerreotypes taken. Come back on the ice**.

21   Fair morning, snowy afternoon. Mr. Civill, Mr. Veeder, Mr. Keith. Miss Brace here. I go to Meeting. I visit with the folks in afternoon.

22   Fair. I go to river. Draw wood from Island. J.E. Gibbens call here.

23   Fair cold day. Mr. Edward Beers, Lady & Child [here]. Draw wood. Go after a stick of timber in J.J. Colvin's woods, have a hard time. Go to river. W.S. Clark call here.

24   Fair, SW. TH 10 deg. below 0. I take Miss Brace to Wm. Tuttle's. I go to J. Whitbeck's. Call to Willis's.

25   Fair, SW. **I take Wife & Mrs. Willis to Baltimore to Henry Slingerland's, visit.** I take tea to James Trego.

26   Fair, warmer, NW. George & Caroline Hotaling, Barent Lane & Martin VanSlyck here. I go to river. Boys draw wood.

27   Fair. I take John, go to Albany. Miss C. Brace go along. **We go on the ice**. I pay Island tax to Mr. Hoose. **Have a horse trot on the ice**. Anthony take Mother Hotaling & Caroline holme. Thawy day.

28   Fair, thawy, SW. I go to Meeting twice, then to vineyard. Ed VanOrden & Bill Keller call here. I call to Willis's.

March 1858

1   Fair. I go to river. J.W. Jolly & Lady & Sister, T. Harris & Lady, Miss Selick, Mrs. John Clement, Miss Brace, Mr. Willis here. Boys thresh.

3   Fair. I take Wife, Lib & Caroline Hotaling, take Uncle Garry's horse, go to Widow Barent Hotaling's. Visit George. **Take us to hear E.H. Chapin in the evening lecture to Coxsackie. His subject was Social Forces. It was very good lecture, the best I ever heard. Go back, stay all night. We have a very pleasant visit.**

4   Fair, cold. Come back, go to Uncle Andrew's, take dinner & tea, then holme. Miss Brace here. Have a very good visit and a very nice time.

5   Fair, very cold. TH at 0. Martin VanBergen & Henry VanBergen Lady's here. We all attend Cotillion party to Aaron Houghtaling. Have a very nice time. **Dance until 4 o'clock in the morning**.

6   Fair. Miss Brace here. I go to river. Mr. Civill call here.

7   Fair, very cold, NW. I go to Meeting in morning. S.F. Cranston, Mr. Willis call in evening.

8   Fair, SW, warmer. Draw hay, go to river, sell lumber to M. Donahue.

9   Cold, NW, two inches snow. Wife go to J. Cronk's visit. Boys draw hay, cut wood.

10   Fair, cool. I and Wife go to Mr. Matson's to Schodack. Mother here. Boys draw hay. **I am subpoenaed to attend lawsuit of McGregor & B. Teneyck**.

11	Fair, warm, thawy, SW. I and Sarah Ann go with Willis & Harriet to Baltimore, visit to J. Reynolds. We have a pleasant visit. **Willis's horses break whippletree act bad**.[287] I get check of Willis, sent to H. Sperl, 25 dollars.
12	Fair, NW. **I and Willis each take a load of company, go to J.W. Jolly's in evening, have a very pleasant time. I fall out of the waggon coming holme.** Boys draw hay.
13	Fair, SW. I walk around. Go to Doct. Fredenburgh's, he cut my hair. Boys draw hay. Wife & Harriet go to Gideon Lawton's. Miss Brace here. Willis call.
14	Cloudy, SW. I am holme all day. Wm. MacGregor here to dinner.
15	Cloudy, SW, rainy. Draw hay. Go to river. **Negress Dean here.**
16	Cloudy. **I go to Albany with the mail stage. Attend as a witness in the case of Teneyck & McGregor.**
17	Fair. **Attend court. Go around the city. Put up at the Empire House.**
18	Fair. **Am around the city. Attend court. Go to see Buckley's Minstrels.**
19	Fair. **River break up. Go around city, attend court.**
20	Fair, very muddy. Come holme. Mr. Willis & Lady. Mr. & Mrs. Reynolds here.
21	Rainy, SW. I go to Meeting. Mr. Civill call. I call to J. Rea.
22	Fair, cold, NW. I go to river. **Fight with Donahue & Blacksmith today takes place**.
23	Fair, cool, NW. I work at vineyard. Mother Garrett & Elizabeth Houghtaling, Mrs. Keefer here I borrow 10 dollars of A.E. Willis cash. **Little Olly Lawton died.**
24	Fair, NW. I go to mill. **I work at glass house to vineyard**. Go to mill, get my grist.
25	Rainy, squally. **I attend funeral of Olly Lawton. Work at glass house to vineyard**. Mrs. Wilson, Mr. Wilkins, Old Deauchy here. I go to mill, get grist.
26	Fair, cold, NW. **I fix leach tub**. Go to river. Take up my note of C. VanDerzee of A.D. Tompkins. Gave him a new note of 52 dollars due April 1, 1859.
27	Fair, NW. I attend Seabridge's Vendue all day. I buy boards & wheelbarrow. Abram Whitbeck here to dinner.
28	Fine day. NW clear. Mr. T. Civill here. I go to Meeting. Stop to Willis's. Miss Brace call.
29	Fair. I go to Albany, was witness to Lawsuit of Mrs. Bronk & Wm. Gregor. Go around city.
30	Fair. Go around city. **Go to Penitentiary, Alms House, Lunatic Asylum, to Legislature**,[288] attend court room.
31	Fair. Go around with Martin VanSlyck to nursery, then to lumber district. Stay to Empire House.

Buckley's Minstrels

---

[287] A whippletree is the swinging bar to which the traces of a harness are fastened, and by which a carriage is drawn.

[288] The Alms House farm was situated on the Plank Road south of Washington Park and west of the Penitentiary. The buildings included the poor house, the lunatic asylum, hospital, pest house, etc. The average number of paupers was 250 with more in the winter. Men and women were separated.

April 1858

1. Lawsuit put over. Get clover & timothy seed, peas. Then come holme.
2. Fair. I sow timothy seed. Go to river. Cate VanBergen here.
3. Fair. Plow; work around. **Attend Nomination at the Hollow. J.B. Shear nominated for Supervisor, R.S. Hotaling for Clerk**. Abram Whitbeck pay me $15 rent. **Mrs. Robert Martin died**.
4. Fair, S wind. Go to Meeting. **Attend funeral of Mrs. Robert Martin**. Go to cemetery. Pay John Fike 10 dollars. Mr. Civill here.
5. Cloudy, little rainy. Attend Dist. Road meeting. Sow oats in Big Meadow. Mr. Reynolds here. Uncle Garrett Hotaling here.
6. Fair, cold, NW. I and Garrett Hotaling go to Mud Hollow to Addison Reynold's vendue. Stay to Mr. Reynold's all night. Take dinner, supper & breakfast.
7. Fair, cold, NW. We go to Chesterville, then to Greenville. Take dinner to Andrew Fancher's. I and Fancher go to Mr. Botchford's, see his colts. Come holme at 8 o'clock in the evening.
8. Fair, cold. Work at cemetery fence. Wife go to Coxsackie. A.E. Willis call here.
9. Cloudy, little rainy. Work in garden. Go Under Hill, fix fence.
10. Fair, cold, NW. I plant potatoes, work at cemetery fence. Martin VanSlyck bring Mother Hotaling holme. **Mr. Reynolds bring me 21 calves**. Abram Whitbeck pay me 50 dollars. Wife come from Albany.
11. Fair, NW. **I pay Mr. Reynolds 185 dollars in checks and cash**. Gave him due bill of 100 dollars. I take Mr. Reynolds to Mr. Tompkins. I stay to dinner. I call to P. Kimmey's. Mr. Civill & Miss Brace here. M. VanSlyck leave.
12. Fair morning, rainy at night. I sow peas. Go to river. Robert Pulver pay me $59.50. I pay George with 2 dollars.
13. Rainy. I attend Town Meeting. Abram Whitbeck pay me 10 dollars, balance of rent.
14. Cloudy. Make fence. Go to river. I pay Israel Lawton 25 dollars, take receipt. Mary Ann Clancy here. **Martin VanBergen & Michel Niven died**.
15. Squally. **I & Wife attend funeral of Martin G. VanBergen**. I sow my spring wheat.
16. Fair. Plow, work around. Wife go to Johnson's. I go to river.
17. Fair. I work around, go to river. Chris Fike buy my black heifer for 25 dollars, pay me 15 dollars cash.
18. Fair. I go to river. Miss Brace & Eliza Clement here. Theophilus & Acton Civill here. I take tea to Mr. Civill's.
19. Fair. Plow. I pay H. Stiley one dollar. Go to river. Lib Hotaling here.
20. Rainy day. Lib Hotaling leave. I go to river.
21. Rainy. **Attend Miss Brace's School Exhibition. It goes off well**. Mr. Civill & Miss Brace here, call. **I pay school bill $11.50**.
22. Fair. I go on Hill, make fence. Get potatoes of Henry Springstead, amount for potatoes 25/. Chris Fike pay me $7 balance due yet on cow is 3 dollars. I pay A.S. VanDerzee $7.95 interest

	for Cornelius VanDerzee. J.H. VanBenthuyzen & Lady here. Mother here. I go to river, get a string of suckers. Wife go to Albany.
23	Rainy. Plant potatoes. **I and J.H. VanBenthuyzen go to Mr. Robb's papermill**, then to village. R. Pulver pay me $59.50, which lacks 3 dollars, which is to be sent to J. VanDenburgh on Monday. I pay A.E. Willis 15 dollars, borrowed money and 2.75 dollars for feed. Roller (sp) get Power of Attorney of Israel Lawton for Mr. Tompkins.
24	Fair, cold, NW. Turn 14 head of yearling calves on the Hill. Snow on Mountains east. Wife & J.H. VanBenthuyzen & Lady go to Garrett Hotaling's and come holme in evening.
25	Cold, NW, icy. I go to Meeting & to vineyard. Mr. Civill here, call.
26	Cold, NW. Work around house, go to river. **Get Boys teeth drawn**. Pay G. With 5/. Call to Willis's. J.H. VB & Lady leave.
27	Cold, overcast. Send one calf to New York. Go Under Hill with hay for calves. I pay Henry Riley 8 dollars.
28	Cold, heavy NW. I go to Dean's Mill. I pay Lewy Bare's Wife balance 2 dollars. I pay A.N. Briggs 10 dollars. Chris Fike pay me 3 dollars balance on cow. I get raspberry vines of Johnson & Schoonmaker. Go to vineyard. Mary Ann McClancy here.
29	Fair. Plant garden; cut brush. Go to river. **Talk matters over with A.N. Briggs about house rent**. J. VanDenburgh pay me balance of 3 dollars of R. Pulver interest.
30	Rainy. I go to river. Mrs. Clement, Mrs. Ostrander, Mrs. Willis here. I plow to vineyard.

May 1858

1	Fair. I work around house. I pay J.H. Holmes 2 dollars. Pay Wife 4 dollars. Furrow out corn land. Mary Ann McClancy here.
2	Fair. Attend Quarterly Meeting. Go to vineyard. Mr. T. Civill & Mr. Willis here.
3	Plant corn. Fair weather. Mother & Ann Marie Selick & Miss Lawson here.
4	Fair. Plant corn. Go Under Hill. Mother here. Mr. H. Rennie pay me $150 and due bill of A. Reynolds, making in all $250. I pay P. Long $2.40 cemetery work.
5	Fair. I plow. Go to river, get fish. I pay boys 10/ apiece.
6	Rainy. Work around house. Go to river. Get Willis check 25 dollars to H. Sperl, pay him the money for it. Send him check. Mr. Civill here. Mrs. James Sherwood pay me $13.50.
7	Fair. Make fence all day to swamp & Bush lot.
8	Fair. Make fence. Take Children to John Mull's, get 8 shad, pay 1 dollar. E. Bandon here in evening, pay me 10 dollars on rent to March 15th, 1858. Mr. Civill call.
9	Cloudy, SW. I go to Meeting. John Wright here. Mr. Civill call. I go to vineyard.
10	Fair. Work at cemetery. Plant corn.
11	Misty & rainy. Plant corn. Go to river. Put my Bull in pasture. He goes to Sally Teneyck cow.
12	Rainy. Work at fence. Fix around house. Peter Seabridge pay me balance of bill $97.12. Mother here.
13	Fair, heavy north wind. Work at fence. Mr. Civill call here. Go to river.

14	Fair. Turn cattle Under Hill. Make fence. Caroline Hotaling here.
15	Cloudy, rainy, warm. I take Caroline Hotaling, Wife & Levi, go to Albany. I pay Atlas & Argus, Lawton & Taylor bill $32.22, get chicken feed.
16	Fair, cold, NW. Mother, John Rea, Mr. Mr. Civill here. I go to vineyard.
17	Rainy. **I draw brick & sand, fix cistern**. Go to river. Mr. H. Rennie pay me 30 dollars. I take J.J. Colvin's note $500. I let Colvin & Rennie have 100 dollars, take their note. J. Schoonmaker pay me 10 dollars for cemetery lot. I leave the money with A.S. VanDerzee.
18	Rainy. I lay around. Go to river.
19	Fair. Turn out colts. Work at cemetery. J.J. VanDerzee here, survey cemetery. I go to river.
20	SW, rainy. Make fence in Big Meadow. I pay W.H. Johnson $1.50 for tuning piano. I let J.H. Holmes have 7 dollars.
21	Fair, cool, NW. **I was up with George Rifflin last night, he is sick**. I make fence. I go to river. Mother & Rebecca Holmes & Children here.
22	Cold, snowy, NW. I go to river. Join issue in [Law]suit with myself & A.N. Briggs. Go Under Hill, fix fence. Go to John Mull's, get fish. Miss Selick here.
23	Fair morning, rainy at night. Marite come from New York. A. Fancher here. Mr. Civill call. I go to Meeting & hear Mathews.
24	Fair, NW. Work at house. H. Harris here. I go to river. I sign note with A.E. Willis to D.C. Tompkins, $400.
25	Fair, warm, SW. **Make cistern to Old Homestead**. Wife & Marite go to Uncle Garrett's. Call to Willis's. **Croswell's papermill burn**.
26	Rainy day. Work around the house. Mr. Civill here. Go to vineyard & to river. H. Harris plaster our rooms.
27	Little rainy. Go to river. Attend boatload of lumber. Plant potatoes. Wife & Marite leave for Stuyvesant.
28	Fair. Onload and draw up lumber. Tobias Crumb pay me balance of rent on pasture lot 33 dollars by order on Johnson & Schoonmaker. I pay Capt. Carroll $151.10 freight on lumber. Willis's team help draw up lumber.
29	Fair. Draw lumber. Mr. Church pay me 50 ct. for 26 ft. of lumber. Miss Brace come, Mr. Civill come.
30	Fair. **Go to Meeting. [Go] to Croswell's Mill, which was burned**. Martin & Elida VanSlyck here, bring Marite along. Mr. Civill, Mr. Cranston call.
31	Fair, SW. Finish draw lumber. Willis's team help 2½ days. **Attend Lawsuit with A.N. Briggs, get beat**. Mr. Aaron Houghtaling here. Martin & Elida leave. Almira VanBergen here.

June 1858

1	Fair, warm. Mr. Civill call. I and Willis get draft of Civill, 535 dollars. Gave him note for $500. Miss VanDerzee & Miss H here. Marite leave for New York.

2	Fair, warm. Polly mare has a colt. **I put stone on cistern at Holmestead**. Work around house.
3	Fair. **I go to Herkimer. Buy saw & files to Corning's. Send them by express. Stop to John Feeter's. Stay all night to H. Sperl's.**
4	**Settle with G. Yoos. Go to Graysville, take supper with V. Tompkins. Stay to Henry Sperl's.**
5	Stormy at night. **Stay around the mill. Get my mortgaged property of G. Yoos.**
6	Rainy. **Go to L.C. Belcher's, then to Graysville, call on Mr. Tompkins, stay all night with C. Johnson.**
7	Fair. **Come with Mr. Johnson to Herkimer. Then take cars for holme.** Mr. Civill call.
8	Fair. David VanAntwerp & Joseph Cary here. Uncle Garrett Houghtaling & Aunt Hannah & Mother here. I go to vineyard & to river. I pay David VanAntwerp $84 interest money.
9	Overcast, little rainy. Draw manure. I am not very well. I go to river & to Willis's. J.W. Harris & Thms. McKee call.
10	Fair, SW. Work at building on house. A. Teal, Jonathan Muckelroy work here. My colts get out on road.
11	Rainy. I put my colts in pasture. Work on road Under Hill. I borrow Willis's check 10 dollars for H. Sperl. Get fish of Wm. O. Lawton.
12	Rain all day hard. **John Mull bring me 69 shad. I clean & salt them**. I go to river.
13	Cloudy. I take Mother, Miss E. Brace, Mother Hotaling to Hollow to Quarterly Meeting. Mr. Civill call. Go to river. Put Polly mare to Seabridge's horse.
14	Cloudy. Fix fence, cut wood, go to river. I pay A.E. Willis $10. John E. Gibbens pay me 5 dollars. Aaron Hotaling pay $6.51 for lumber.
15	Cloudy. Work at house. Fix cistern. J.E. Gibbens pay me $4.
16	Fair afternoon, cloudy morning. Go Under Hill, fix fence. **I let Mr. Wilsey have my barn lot, orchard lot, Crumb lot for $60.** Thms. Houghtaling call here.
17	Fair. Work at potatoes. Go to river. Aaron Hotaling pay me $3.57. Mrs. McClancy pay me 80 cts.
18	Fair, warm, SW. I go to P. Kimmey's, get lath. Mr. Civill call. I work at house.
19	Fair. I furrow & cultivate my orchard. Boys hoe corn. I put my cattle in new pasture. I take Miss B[race] along.
20	Fair, hot. I go to Meeting. Mr. Civill here, we go to vineyard. We call to Willis's. T. McKee & B. MacGregor here.
21	Fair, hot. We work at building. I get load of sand. I go in swimming. **Eli Long come near drowning**.
22	Warm. All hands work on my barn. John get 1 load of sand. I go to river. Get my turnip seed of Lawton.
23	Fair, SW. I go to Albany. Lay out 15 dollars for shingles & feed & rigging for house. Widow Charlotte & Aunt Sarah Ann here.

24 Fair, hot, SW. Work at barn. Wm. Bagley & two Daughters here.

25 Fair, hot. Mr. Bagley, self & Wife go to Willis's to tea. Work at waggon house.

26 Fair, hot. I get an order of Mr. Robb on Johnson & Schoonmaker for $65. I draw the money and get their check for $75 in favor of John Feeter, which leave me their debtor 10 dollars.

27 Fair, N. wind, hot & dry. Go to Meeting. Thms McKee & B. MacGregor here. All go to vineyard.

28 Fair, hot. I take folks all out riding Under Hill. We work at barn. Mrs. C. Spraker call here.

29 Fair, warm. Press hay. Anthony is sick. Mother here.

30 Fair, cooler, NW. Press hay. Andrew Fancher here. I settle with him, he pays his rent 200 dollars for D. Baker. **I and Mr. Civill take all our folks sailing. Mrs. Cate Herrick and her Son come here. We are full of company**.

July 1858

1 Fair, cooler. Press hay all day. Aunt Sarah Ann here.

2 Fair, dry. Press hay. I pay Mary Ann McClancy $5.31. Mrs. Herrick and Son, Aunt Sarah Ann leave. J.M Harris here. I pay P. Kimmey's bill $6.45.

3 Showry, rainy at night. I take Boys to go in swimming. Get caught in a shower. **A horse of Mr. Martin's run off of Briggs' dock**. I pay John Fike 5 dollars, John Maxwell $1.50, G. Rifflin 1 dollar. I let Wife have 10 dollars. She and Bagley's folks go to Albany.

4 Fair, hot. Go to Meeting & to vineyard. Mr. Civill call.

5 Fair day. **All hands go on excursion on steamer TC Durant. Have music, dancing. Have a fine time.**

6 Fair. **Draw 23 loads hay**. Wm. McGregor here. I go to river.

7 Fair, S wind. Work at corn. Go Under Hill, get two brooms. Mrs. A.E. Willis here. I hire Dutchman for $25 dollars per month.

8 Fair, hot, SW. I sow turnip seed. Boys hoe corn. Bagley's folks leave. Levi take them to Baltimore.

9 Fair, hot, S wind. Press hay. Almira VanBergen & Miss Stoutenburgh here. Charlotte Houghtaling pay me my lumber bill $27.94 by hand of Almira VanBergen.

10 Fair, SW, very dry. Press hay. Aaron Hotaling pay me $1.32. All hands go in swimming.

11 Hot, heavy shower. Cool after. I go Under Hill, then to Meeting. Get check of Willis for H. Sperl. Gave Willis 20 dollars for check.

12 Rainy, draw hay. Fix for haying. Settle with J.H. Holmes, take receipt of settlement. I pay him 5 dollars. E. VanOrden pays me 8 dollars for lumber. U.B. Willis here to dinner. Anthony Bullock come to work.

13 Very heavy rain. Fix around house. Go to river. Israel Lawton pay me 18 dollars rent of Baker's.

14 Cloudy. **Commence haying all hands**. I and boys & Mr. Civill go Under Hill, shift cattle in new pasture. Elizabeth Hotaling here. **Mrs. Teal died**.

15 Fair. Work in hay. **Get mowing machine of S.F. Cranston, try it**. Caroline Hotaling here. **Child of Danl. Shear died**.

16 Fair. Work in hay. Go to river. Cows break out.

17 Fair. Pay P. Ostrander 5 dollars. I [pay] Maxwell 2 dollars, G. Rifflin one dollar. Cows break out. Work at rye & oats. Get along finely.

18 Fair. I take boys, go to Mrs. Nikinson's to get Mrs. Keefer. She did not come, we go to vineyard. Mr. Civill here. I and Wife call to Willis's. I get his check to John Feeter for 20 dollars. Pay him money, send it to Feeter.

19 Fair. **Mow with machine**. Work in hay.

20 Fair, SW. All hands work in hay.

21 Fair, SW. Work in hay. Mrs. Fredenburgh, Mrs. Spraker, Mrs. Akerman, Betsey Verplank, Mrs. F.G. Mosher, Mrs. A.L. VanDerzee, Mrs. Renne, Mrs. Jack, Mrs. Niles, Mrs. Johnson, Mrs. Hull, Mrs. R. Hotaling and others here. Wife go to Meeting.

22 Showry, rainy. Fix around barn.

23 Fair. Work in hay, all hands. Mother, Mrs. A.E. Willis, Charles Bagley here.

24 Fair, cool. Work in hay. I pay Tony 5 dollars, J. Maxwell 5 dollars. **Attend Nebraska lecture at Temperance Hall**. Fix house to D. Baker's.

25 Fair. Go to Meeting. Mr. Civill, Mr. Willis & S.F. Cranston here.

26 Fair, heavy SW. Work at wheat & to Big Meadow. Mr. Civill call.

27 Fair, heavy SW. Work at wheat & hay. Mr. Civill call.

28 Fair. I mow in vineyard lot. All work in hay. I and Miss Brace go Under Hill, salt cattle. I pay G. Rifflin 1 dollar. I pay Mrs. John Rea 10 dollars interest money.

29 Warm. Work in hay. Heavy shower at night. Mother here. Mr. Civill call.

30 Rainy day. I call to Willis's. Lay around the house. Mary Serles & Brother, Mrs. Reynolds, Mr. Civill call.

31 Cloudy, little rainy. Work in hay. Mrs. Keefer & Daughter, Mr. Nickerson here. Mrs. Willis & Mrs. Bevy call. I pay John Reid 5 dollars, J. Maxwell 5 dollars & Tony 2 dollars.

August 1858

1 Martin VanSlyck bring Mother Hotaling holme. We go to Meeting. Mr. Civill call here.

2 Cloudy. I mow till 5 o'clock. Miss McCabe here. I pay Elida 2 dollars.

3 Rainy. Work in hay in forenoon. Go to river. Mr. Civill call.

4 Rainy. Go to river. Mrs. Martin VanBergen here, Mr. Civill call. I go to Johnson & Schoonmaker's, get their check for $43.27 to P.H. Stancusy.

5 Clears off, but rains again. Work in hay. Take timber to W. Croswell. Mr. Willis call.

6 Fair. I work in hay. Mr. Civill call. Elizabeth Hotaling here.

7 Fair. Work in hay. Henry VanDerzee, Marite come here. Mother, Mrs. Israel Lawton & Helen, R. Hotaling & Lady, Miss Buck, Miss Drew and a lot more call. I pay John Maxwell 2 dollars, G. Rifflin one dollar.

8	Fair, warm. T. Clancy pay me 74 dollars. Mr. Civill call. I go to Meeting and to vineyard.
9	Fair. Work in hay. I pay off A. Bullock 13 dollars. H. VanDerzee leave. Mother Hotaling go to Andrew's. Yerrick Ziegler come to work.
10	Fair. I finish haying. I pay John Maxwell 5 dollars. Attend a party to Aaron Hotaling's. Have a dance, have a fine time. Mr. T. Civill call.
11	Rainy morning; clears off again. Israel Lawton & Lady, Helen Lawton, R. Hotaling & Lady, Miss Drew, Miss McKinstry, Miss VanDenburgh, Lib Pelts, Laura Buckley, Laura Colvin & lots more here. I go to river & I work around the house.
12	Fair. **I attend Miss Brace school exhibition**. I pay I. Brown $2.38 for G. Rifflin. Mr. McKee, Mr. Civill call. I pay Willis 10 dollars for check for H. Sperl.
13	Fair. I pay John Fike 10 dollars, he go to Albany. I take Wife, Harry & Anthony to Albany. I get my dividend of 15 dollars.
14	Fair. G. VanAllen, Wm. Phelps & Lady here. L.D. Eddy here. Mr. Civill call. A. Teal & J. Hauenstien call.
15	Fair. Miss Brown come here. I go Under Hill, see the colts. **Mr. McKee, Mr. Seabridge, Mr. Civill here.** Caroline & Gitty VanAntwerp call. **We make a bargain with McKee for schoolhouse.**[289]
16	Fair. I go to Greenville, swear off tax. I stay to A. Fancher's all night. Levi & Harry go along.
17	Fair. I go to J.W. Story's, try to trade horses. Come holme. Fix stoop to Carhart's. **Have a freight of lumber come.** Shower all night. Go to Willis's. Pay Mr. Civill $204.38 on mine & Willis's note. I gave my note to Mr. Civill for $100.
18	Fair. **Unload & draw up lumber**. I get 11 dollars of Mrs. James Sherwood. I and Wife go to Troy. Stay all night at L.D. Eddy's.
19	Fair. **Go around Troy. Take cars, go to Saratoga. Eddy & Phillip Teats & Lady go along. Wife stay there, I come back with Eddy & Teats, stay all night with Eddy**.
20	Fair. **I and Eddy take cars to Pittstown to Buskirk's Bridge, then to Hoosick, then take a waggon, go on line of Boston RR twelve miles to Paton's. Take dinner, then come back to Troy. Stay all night with Eddy**.
21	Fair. **Go to Albany Cemetery and about Troy**.
22	Fair. **Go to Arsenal at Troy then come holme**.[290]
23	Fair. Work in hay.
24	Fair. Work at cemetery & around house. Mrs. A. Civill call. Wife go to Willis's.

Buskirk's Bridge

---

[289] According to "Bi-centennial History of Albany: History of County of Albany", Fletcher, Theophilus Civill & Peter Seabridge established the Coeymans Academy in 1858. Misses Caroline and Emma Brace were teachers at the school. Control of the school was later turned over to Thomas McKee. The building still stands at the corner of Blaisdell Ave and Westerlo St.

[290] We believe Fletcher is referring to the Watervliet Arsenal, which is on the west side of the Hudson directly opposite Troy. It was founded in 1813 to support the War of 1812. It is the oldest, continuously active arsenal in the United States.

25 Fair. I take Mother to T.E. Waldron's. I go to Abram Whitbeck's, then to Waldron's to dinner. **Then take Mother to Negro Camp Meeting to Bethlehem**. Wife go to Aaron Hotaling's. Mrs. Wilson call. I pay John Reid 5 dollars. Mr. Smith call.

26 Fair. Levi go get Mother Hotaling. Mr. Budd here. I go Under Hill.

27 Rainy. U.B. Willis & Lady & guests. Miss Dickey, A.E. Willis & Lady here visit. I attend Cemetery Meeting at Aaron Hotaling's.

28 Rainy. Miss Dicky & company leave. **I make fence to trim yard**. Go to river. Pay G. Rifflin 1 dollar.

29 Miss Brace return. **I take all hands to Negro Camp Meeting to Bethlehem**. Mr. Civill call. Fair weather.

30 Fair. I take timber to Mr. Robb. Work at cemetery. Take a ride with Willis to vineyard. Take tea to Willis's.

31 Fair. T. Clancy pay me 26 dollars. I borrow $50 of N.H. Johnson. I gave him $17.50 for checks to Joseph Spraker, $5.50 & 12 dollars to H. Sperl. Sarell Wood here. We all go to Garret Hotaling's.

September 1858

1 Fair. **Great Celebration of Atlantic Cable at Albany.**[291] **Wife, Miss C.A. Brace, Mr. Wood go there**. I work around, draw manure. John Fike go with his brother Chris to Poestenkill to look at Farm.

Trans-Atlantic Telegraph Cable

2 Fair. Draw manure. Trade horses with Abram Whitbeck. Gave him my note for 95 dollars boot money. Mr. S. Wood here. Wife & Miss Brace come holme. I go to Island with Smith, get sweet corn. Mr. McKee call here. We call to Willis's.

3 Rainy in afternoon. Mr. Wood leave. Mr. Civill call. We draw manure.

4 Fair. Mr. H. VanDerzee here. Draw manure. Go to vineyard and to cemetery. Mrs. Keefer leave. I pay her 6 dollars.

5 Fair. I go to Meeting. I take Wife, Levi, Mr. H. VanDerzee, go to Flat Bush. Call to Uncle Andrew's then holme.

6 Fair. I and J.H. Holmes lay floor in Baker house. Uncle Garrett Hotaling & Lady, Mrs. N. Stephen's & Daughter here. Caroline Hotaling & Jasper Smith here. We go to vineyard. Mr. Civill call. I go to river.

---

[291] This was one of many celebrations around the country of the first telegraph communication (16 Aug 1858) between North America and Europe, an accomplishment largely due to the efforts of Cyrus Field. From the Albany Evening Journal, August 31, 1858: THE CABLE JUBILEE: Celebration in Albany, a Great Day! "Albany has never witnessed so enthusiastic and universal celebration…"
The cable ran between Trinity Bay, Newfoundland and Valentia, Ireland, a distance of almost 2,000 miles across the Atlantic at a depth of often more than 2 miles. It didn't work very well and failed completely in September 1858. A second cable, made with improved materials, was laid in 1865, and was more successful.

7	Fair. I sow rye, go Under Hill. H. VanDerzee leave. Mrs. J.J. Silcox come, bring 3 children. Mr. Civill call. I and all hands go to Willis's, spend the evening.
8	Fair, warm. **Settle with Miss Brace, pay her off. Then we all go to Albany. I and Mr. Civill go to Hinsdale, Mass. Stay there all night. Go through Schodack, Kinderhook, to Chatham Corners, To Pittsfield, Dalton.**
9	Fair. Get Mr. Adams, go to see Mr. Stanton's Farm, then take cars back holme. Mr. Civill pay all the bills.
10	Fair. J.J. Silcock come here. He take his Wife & Children and leave for New York. Mr. Civill call, go to vineyard.
11	Rainy. Work around. Go to vineyard with Mr. Civill and Mr. N. Niles. Levi take Miss McCabe holme.
12	Fair. Go to Meeting. Mr. Civill call. Wife stay to Willis's all night. Mr. Niles here.
13	Fair. Make fence in Big Meadow.
14	Fair. Make fence. Go to Leonard Whitbeck's, borrow his cider press. Mr. Civill go along.
15	Fair. I go Under Hill. **Sell 4 head of cattle to J.A. Wilsey for 100 dollars**. A. Hotaling, Lady & Child, Mrs. Ralfe Briggs & Child, Mrs. Jones & Child, Old Mrs. Briggs here visit. I put my cattle in Big Meadow. Go to vineyard.
16	Rainy. Miss McCabe here. We press our grapes. Mr. Civill call. I pay John Reid 8 dollars.
17	Fair. Sow rye. Work around. Go with J.J. Colvin to cemetery. Attend Cemetery Meeting in evening.
18	Fair, NW. Make fence, plow. Get a letter from Mr. Wood with Kellog White & Co. Send it back to have Mr. Wood sign it.
19	Fair. I take Mother to Quarterly Meeting to Bethlehem. Take dinner to Dominie Jolly's. A. Jackson call here.
20	Fair. Leigh & Wiley pay my rent due from them to Sept. 1. **Willis's child died**. I fix stoop to Old Holmestead.
21	Fair. **Attend funeral of Willis's child**. U.B. Willis call. Plow, pick stone.
22	Cold, NW. Work at Stebben's house. Draw manure. Willis call.
23	Fair. Go to Albany, attend Co. Fair. Come holme with cars to Schodack, cross river. Boys draw manure.
24	Lowry, rainy. Wife go to Fair. I work around house, go to river.
25	Fair, frost. Dig potatoes. Elida VanSlyck here. Mary Ann McClancy here. Go to river.
26	Fair, frost. I go after Mother Hotaling to Flat Bush. Mr. Civill call. Elida VanSlyck here.
27	Fair. I go to Albany, get note of Sarell Wood discounted at Merchants Bank $500. I take out of it my 150 dollars interest money. Pay 10 dollars to Dr. Gilbert. **I send the balance less**

the discount by American Express Co. to Mr. Wood.[292] I leave 140 dollars with Johnson & Schoonmaker.

28 Fair. I, Wife & Elida go to Barrett Hotaling's. Caroline Hotaling come holme with us. James Trego & Cate Hotaling call here. I get 25 dollars of Johnson & Schoonmaker. I let G. Hotaling have 5 dollars.

29 Fair. I take Wife, Elida VanSlyck, Caroline Houghtaling. **Go to Albany. John Fike and my boys go along. Attend Fireman's celebration. A woman gets killed by the coping falling from the top of a building. A negro fell dead in the street. 69 companies celebrate the day**.

30 Fair, very warm. Garrett Hotaling here, pay me 5 dollars he borrowed of me. He takes Caroline holme. I pay Elida Lucas 20 dollars. I pick peaches. Get 15 dollars of Schoonmaker & Johnson.

October 1858

1 Rainy day. Fix barn, press hay. Turn cattle in cemetery lot, in vineyard lot.

2 Fair. Press hay. Take cattle Under Hill. Pick apples. Henry VanDerzee come. Elida VanSlyck leave. Mrs. R. Hotaling & Mrs. J. Witbeck call.

3 Fair, SW. Go to Meeting. Mr. Civill call. We go to vineyard and to cemetery. Call to A. Jackson's.

4 Fair. Draw hay. Go to Mill with corn. Dig potatoes. Mr. Civill, Mr. Willis call. I take E. Stanton's grapes to vineyard.

5 North wind. I go to mill. I go to vineyard. Mr. Condor call. I get 25 dollars of Johnson & Schoonmaker, $10 of D. Baker, $3 of C. Fike. H. VanDerzee leave here.

6 Fair. **I, Wife, Mr. Civill go to Syracuse to State Fair. Stop to Mr. Brace's find things very pleasant**.

7 Rainy. **Attend fair & see the salt works**.[293]

8 Cold, windy. **Go attend the fair all day**. Squally day.

Syracuse Salt Works

9 Rainy. Leave for holme. Stop at Little Falls, dine to John Feeter's. Then go to Henry Sperl's, stay all night. Settle with Henry, pay him 10 dollars and two dollars to get string leather.

10 Cloudy. Stay about Henry Sperl's all day.

11 Cloudy. **Start at one o'clock am with Henry Sperl, drive to Little Falls, get there 7 o'clock, gave Henry 1 dollar, then take cars for holme. I pay John Fike 5 dollars**.

12 Fair. Work around house morning. **Then take Wife & children & go to New York with propeller T.C. Durant**.

---

[292] American Express started as an express mail business in Albany in 1850. In 1858, they expanded their shipment services by opening the first transcontinental stage line carrying mail from Missouri to California.

[293] Syracuse was once the main producer of salt in the country. It is known as the salt city.

13 Rainy. **Get to New York at 2 o'clock pm. Go to A. VanAntwerp's. Stay all night.**

14 Clears off. **Go with Henry VanDerzee to museum, then go to hear Mr. Balch lecture on Syria. Stay all night to J.J. Silcock's**.

15 Fair. **Go to Black Well's Island with Mrs. Drew & Doct. Fredenburgh.**[294] **Then at night go to see Wood's Minstrels**.

16 Fair. **Take the folks to Nathan Stephens at Brooklyn. Then start for holme**.

17 Get holme. Call to Willis's. Mr. Civill call. Martin VanSlyck here.

18 Fair. **Put hay on boat**. Make fence. Go to Dean's mills, pay Dean 7 dollars. E. VanOrden pay me $12.35. Attend a lecture at the hall. **Call to see Salmon VanAntwerp**.

19 Fair. Clear meadows of stone. Mr. T. Civill call.

20 Fair. Very warm. Work around the house. Daniel Baker pay me 15 dollars. D. Wiley pay me 2 dollars. I go to vineyard.

21 Fair. **Wife, Children & Henry VanDerzee come holme**. Mr. Peacock's teamster pay me 5 dollars. We work at manure and the fence. **Salmon VanAntwerp died.**

22 Cloudy. **Attend funeral of S. VanAntwerp. Attend the Political Meeting at the Hall**. Hear Mr. Courtney & John I. Burton. Mrs. Wilson pay me 2 dollars.

23 Lowry, rainy. Press hay. **I and Henry VanDerzee go to Briggs & Andrews papermill at Stephensville**.

24 Lowry, rainy. I go to Meeting, call to Willis's. Mr. T. Civill here. Uncle Garrett here, take Mother Hotaling holme with him.

25 Fair, cold, NW. I take Henry VanDerzee to Walter Becker's. I go to Albany. I pay $2.16 for fish, $5.96 to Mr. Brooks for cutting files, $6.00 to **Pruyn & Lansing** and 1 dollar for oil cloth.

26 Fair. Ice this morning. **Go to river, to Mr. Robb's papermill**. I kill beef. Mr. Civill call. Mother Hotaling come holme. **Andrew Whitbeck died.**

27 Fair. Work around. **Go to William Tuttle's swamp for muck**. Settle with Peter Ostrander. Mr. T. Civill call. Gave P. Ostrander order on **Colvin & Rennie** $59.42.

28 Fair. **Attend the funeral of Andrew Whitbeck. Attend political meeting at Temperance Hall. Hear Mr. Casidy, Mr. VanDerpool. James Hilbourn speak**. Boys dig out muck at Wm. Tuttles Swamp. Garret Hotaling call here.

29 Lowry, rainy. Work on barn to vineyard. **Attend examination of McKee's School**.

30 Rainy. Press hay. H. VanDerzee come. I sell Uncle Garrett two heifers.

31 Fair. Go to Meeting. Mr. Civill call. Go to vineyard. Spend the evening to Mr. Willis's.

---

[294] New York Historical Society, Museum and Library: "Located in the East River Black Well's Island was renamed Welfare Island in 1921 and Roosevelt Island in 1973. In the past the city built a number of institutions on the island, including a prison, an insane asylum and hospitals. Some hospitals remain but the island began to be developed for residential use in 1968."

November 1858

1. Fair. Press hay. I go to river.
2. Fair. I work around house. **Attend Election. Henry VanDerzee leave.** Sell 3 cattle to Dutchman from Albany. Work around.
3. **Lay foundation for barn to vineyard.**
4. Rainy. Press hay. Anthony sick. Doct. Fredenburgh here.
5. Cloudy. Press hay. Fix barn to vineyard. Mother here.
6. Rainy. Work at barn to vineyard. Press hay; take timber to A. Jackson.
7. Fair. Go to river. Go Under Hill. Call to Mrs. Wilson's. Spend the evening to Willis's, take tea.
8. Fair. Draw hay. Fix hay press. Take lumber & timber Under Hill. Wife go to Baltimore, bring Miss McCabe here. Mr. Civill call. Albany butcher take away 4 cattle.
9. Fair. Plow, work on barn to vineyard. **I am subpoenaed to attend Lawsuit of TenEyck & McGregor.**
10. Fair. John plow, work at carrots. **I go to Albany to attend Lawsuit between Teneyck & McGregor.**
11. Fair NW. **Am sworn in suit between Teneyck & MacGregor. Israel Lawton & Mr. Elsworth return by steamer P.G. Coffin.** Martin VanSlyck here. Boys work at turnips and carrots.
12. Fair, cold. I fix windows. Go to vineyard. **Attend McKee's School.** Mr. Civill call; bring picture frames. Henry Jackson here.
13. Cloudy, snow, SW. Work at turnips. Go to river. Mr. Civill call. **Make a bargain with Dutch Shoemaker for my shop and house at 40 dollars per year.** Snow fall tonight.
14. Fair, cold. I bring Marite from boat. I and John bring my colts holme from Under Hill. Put them in Big Meadow. Mr. Civill call. I call to Willis's in evening.
15. Fair, cold. I pay off Yernick Ziegler. Draw hay. Get horses shod. Mrs. A.E. Willis & David here. John & Yernick Ziegler here.
16. Fair, cold, NW. **Cut & bury turnips.** I gave Colvin & Rennie order on Johnson & Schoonmaker for 100 dollars. Go to river. Wife & Marite go to B.B. Fredenburgh's.
17. Cold, heavy NW wind. Work at turnips, split hay slats. **Wife & Marite go to Canajoharie.** Mother here.
18. Fair, NW. **I take Thanksgiving dinner to A.E. Willis's.** Mr. Stanton call here. I go with him to vineyard. Mr. Civill call. Press hay. I go to river.
19. Cloudy, cold, NW. Press hay.
20. Cold, NW. Press hay. H. VanDerzee come. **Wife & Marite come from Canajoharie.** Mrs. Fredenburgh spend evening here.
21. Cloudy. I am unwell, stay about house till evening. Then go to Doctor's, get medicine.
22. Little snow, still weather. **Draw 65 bales hay on boat.** Mr. Curle call.

23   Snowy day. H. VanDerzee & Marite leave with propeller. I take them to boat. Then I take Martin Anthony Houghtaling to Flat Bush with cutter. About 10 in. of snow fell. **Cate Robb & Walter Hotaling get married. Abram Verplank died**.

24   Still cloudy. Press hay. Addison Reynolds here, press hay to Dr. Fredenburgh.

25   Clear, cold. Press hay. **Abram Verplank's funeral today**.

26   Cloudy, cold. Press hay, go to river. Mother here. **I send two chains, 2 horse blankets, horseshoes, rope, 6 axe helves & 10 dollars with John Ozle to H. Sperl**.

27   Warmer, NW. Press hay. Miss Meriam here, call.

28   Snowy. I go to Meeting. Call to Willis's. Mr. Civill call.

29   Fair, still day. **I put 75 bales of hay on propeller and 42 bushels of rye**. Mr. Sherman here. I go to river, call to Willis's.

30   Cold, NW. I go to river. Abram Whitbeck here. Mary Ann Clancy here. I go to river.

December 1858

1   Fair, NW. Press hay. U.B. Willis & Lady here, call. Mr. Civill call. I go to river.

2   Cloudy, SW. Get horses shod, go to river. George Wolf & Lady here.

3   Fair, SW, warmer. **I put 50 bales hay on boat**. Go to river. Put my cattle & colts to haystack.

4   Stormy, rain, snow. I get my mare shod. Wife go to New Baltimore, take Mrs. Sherman.

5   Rainy, SW. I and Wife go to Garrett Hotaling's, get wet. Mr. Civill call.

6   Fair. I go to Barent Teneyck's, pay interest on $500 note. Go to river. Mother here.

7   Cloudy, stormy. Addison Reynolds here with buckwheat flour. He take dinner. I go to river. I attend show at Temperance Hall. Mr. Civill call.

8   Fair, warm. **I draw two loads timber to Stone Church [Farm] for barn**. I then go to river, get my new harness of Mr. Wicks.

9   Cloudy, cold. **I husk corn all day in the barn**.

10   Cloudy, SW, cold. **I have a tooth pulled**. Call to Willis's. Am quite unwell. R.W. Stanton get bull he bought of me. Aunt Hannah Houghtaling here.

11   Fair, SW. Go Under Hill twice, fix barn. Aunt Hannah leave. Uncle Garrett call.

12   Cold, NW. I call to Willis's and to Doct. Ben Fredenburgh. **Have toothache all day**.

13   Cloudy, SW, rainy. Go Under Hill. Get mare shod. A.E. Willis here. Call to Elias Holmes. A.E. Willis here.

14   Foggy, rainy. I send wheat to mill, kill my beef, go to river. Peter Rea help me today.

15   Rainy. I kill 5 hogs and beef. John Rea & Peter help.

16   Fair, warm. Cut up meat. **Thresh with machine**. I go Under Hill with lumber. Call to Willis's.

17   Fair, NW. Thresh, salt pork, go to river.

18   Fair, NW. I go Under Hill twice with lumber. Thresh, go to river. Miss McCabe here.

20   Fair. I finish threshing. Addison Reynolds, Mr. Tompkins here to tea. I go with them to Mr. Tompkins', stay all night. **Rev. Hugh Jolly died**.

21 Snow & blow hard all day hard. I and A. Reynolds start go to **Mud Hollow.**[295] Go through Reidsville. Stay to Reynolds all night.

22 Snow & blow hard. Go to Mud Hollow. Stay about there all day.

23 Cloudy, still N wind. **Start for Otsego. Go through Swich Kill, Peora, Gallupville, then to Schoharie; stop at Mr. Parrot's tavern, have a good dinner. Then take P.R. go through Punch Kill, then to Minorville, then to Richmondville. Take tea to Mr. Crandle's then to Carleville & Wooster Corners & Wooster. Then Schenevus Village. Stay all night to Richard Wilson's – fine people.**

24 Fair, cold. **Start west through a number of villages to Cherry Valley & Schuylkill Valley. Cross the river, go through Cortland Ville. Cross Elk Horn Hill & Drake Hill then through Maryland back to Mr. Wilson's to tea. Then go to William Bronk's to a Ball. They have about 80 couples. Stay there a short time then back to Mr. Wilson's, stay all night.**

25 Fair, still very cold. **Start for holme. Come through Minorville & through Cobleskill then past Howe's Cave to Central Bridge then stop and call to Wm. Young's. Then to Widow, stay all night.**

26 Fair. **Come back to Addison Reynold's stay all night. Have best sleying I ever saw all the way.**

27 Fair NW. Come holme. Mrs. Henry VanBergen, Cate VanBergen, Widow Charlotte Houghtaling here, visit. I go to river.

28 Fair. I go Under Hill, draw wood. Call to A.E. Willis, Mr. N. Niles here. I go to river.

29 Cloudy, cold, NW. I shell corn. Harness & drive mare Topsy, go to Dean's Mill. Call to G. Hotaling's; call to Wm. O. Lawton's in evening. Draw wood today.

30 Cold, SW. I work around the house. Mr. Civill call. I go to river. I take Mary Jane Lawton a bottle of wine.

31 Snow, stormy. Draw wood. Work at harness room. I go to river. Mr. Civill call. **Attend Watch Meeting tonight**.

January 1859

1 Fair, SW. I harness with Mr. A.E. Willis, go to Coxsackie. Visit to U.B. Willis's, have a good visit. John Fike go to Poestenkill. Mr. Civill, Martin VanSlyck call.

2 Fair day. Mr. Civill call. I go to Meeting.

3 **Fair. I and Mr. T. Civill take School Boys & Girls out to John B Shear's sley riding. We have a good sley ride.** John Fike come holme, go to Willis. He gave me 17 dollars to deposit for him at Merchant's Bank. I lend him 3 dollars. He pays me 3 dollars again 4 Jan 1859.

4 Snowy day. I go to Albany. I take up S. Wood's note at the Merchant Bank Albany by his draft on N. York. I get things for Family. I get Willis's dividend and deposit 20 dollars for him at Merchant's Bank. The money he gave me yesterday. Come holme and pay him his money.

---

[295] According to our cousin, Laura Palmer, Mud Hollow was near the Town of Westerlo. It disappeared when they installed a dam on Mud Hollow pond to create Onderdonk Lake to support the South Berne Mill.

5	Fair. I return Johnson & Co check $500. I harness up mare Topsy, take Wife to G. Hotaling's. Smith bring me my turnips. John draw muck. Go with Dutchman to Bethlehem.
6	Fair. **I and Levi go to Greenville.** Call to J.W. Story's, then go to A. Fancher's, stay all night.
7	Stormy or foggy. **I go around among my tenants**. Come holme by way of Coxsackie. A.E. Willis & Lady, Mrs. J. Reynolds & Mary Holmes here, spend the day. John draw muck.
8	Fair, cold, NW. I go to river. Settle with S. Harris. Mr. Sarell Wood here. Mr. Civill call.
9	Fair, cold. Go to Meeting twice. Call to Willis's. Wood here. Mr. Civill call.
10	Fair, very cold. **TH 18 deg below 0 all day**. I go to river. **I draw one load hay to Mr. Robb. Gross wt. 2520, sley 990.**
11	Snow, cold. **TH 15 deg below 0**. Johnson Smith & Mike Hoos here. Wm. Phelps & Lady, Garrett VanAllen visit. Dominie Wood here.
12	Snowy, cold. I call to Willis's & B. Teneyck. I take Harris my note of him. I pay him 25 dollars. I gave him my note for 100 dollars. Martin VanSlyck bring Mother Hotaling holme. Elida VanSlyck, Elizabeth Hotaling here. **Two Dutchman call here.**
13	Warmer, SW. Martin & Elida VanSlyck leave. John draw muck.
14	SW, rainy. Attend P. Road meeting all day. I take Elizabeth Houghtaling holme.
15	Cloudy, misty. Work at waggon house. Harness Topsy, go Under Hill, go to river. Settle with Johnson & Schoonmaker.
16	Fair, SW. Stay about house. B.E. Holmes here to dinner.
17	Cloudy, SW. Work around, go to river. C. Fike here, draw muck.
18	Fair. **Work at Holmestead. Attend Negro Meeting at Temperance Hall in eve**. John clear out barn, hang up my meat.
19	Fair. I go to Croswell's Papermill & to river. Dominie Gardner here. I go to Meeting in the evening.
20	Fair, SW. Draw stone. Jackson get timber. I go to Willis's, then to river. Wife, Mother Hotaling & Anthony go to Dominie Gardner's Donation.
21	Rainy day. Mr. Rennie call. I go to river. John Tryon here to dinner. I pay him 63 dollars on 63 bunches of shingles he left with me for sale. **Mr. Civill returned from Syracuse**. He call here.
22	Cloudy. Work at harness room. Go to river. Attend minstrels. Mrs. Springstead, John Bushants, David Jerolomon here.
23	Fair, cold. Go to Meeting & to vineyard. B.E. Holmes & Mr. Civill here to dinner & tea.
24	Fair, cold, SW. Work around the house, go to river.
25	Fair, SW. **I take Wife to Albany on the ice**.
26	Fair, SW. **I & Wife go to A.T. VanSlyck's, spend the day, stay all night.**
27	Fair, SW. **We go to E. Hubble's, spend the day. Then to A.T. VanSlyck's, stay all night.**
28	Rainy. **Dine to A.T. VanSlyck's, then go to R.H. VanBergen's to tea. Then go to E. Hubble's, stay all night.**

29	Lowry, warm. **Start for holme. Stop to A. Houghtaling's & Seth Hawley's, then holme. Jemima Hotaling here, visit. I go to river.**
30	Fair, cold, NW. I go to Meeting, call to Willis.
31	Fair, NW. **I take boys skating on Dam. I go to Croswell's.** Call to Peter Seabridge's, then to river. Call to Willis's & to G.H. Harris's.

February 1859

1	Fair, SW. I go Under Hill. Attend to mark trees to S. Tuttle. **Attend horse trot on ice in afternoon.**
2	Cold, cloudy, NW. I go Under Hill. Take 3 bu. shingles, bring back 4 cedar trees I bought of S. Tuttle.
3	Snowy. Draw hay. I and Wife go to A. Hotaling's, visit.
4	Fair. Fine sleying. Draw wood, go to river. Mr. Civill call.
5	Fair. I take A. Borkman to Albany, get him leather. **I send 15 gallons of oil & one barrel pork to H. Sperl to Little Falls**.
6	Cloudy, SW. I go to Meeting. Mr. Civill call. Martin VanSlyck here.
7	Fair, cold. **Copy journal**. Draw wood, go to river.
8	Cloudy, S wind. Draw wood. Visit to Willis's. U.B. Willis there. I go to river.
9	Lowry, misty. Mr. E. Hubbell & Lady & two Boys here, spend the day. A.E. Willis visit here. I go to river. Call on Mr. Powell this evening.
10	Fair, cold, NW. I go to papermill. Settle with Mr. Robb, he pay his bill & N. Carroll's bill. I call to Johnson & Co. Leave Mr. Robb's order on him of $75.25. I draw on him $25.25. I pay G. Rifflin bill to Colvin & Renne. Go to hear Mr. Wycoff preach in the evening.
11	Fair. I draw logs from on the Hill. Mr. A.B. Hotaling & Lady here. Sarell Wood here. I go to river.
12	Fair. Draw posts. I take Mother Hotaling to A.A. Hotaling's to Flat Bush. Visit in afternoon to Uncle Garrett Hotaling's. Miss & Mrs. Spraker call.
13	Fair, cold. I go to Meeting. Lib Hotaling call. **Our folks go to Meeting 3 times**.
14	Fair. I get stake timber. Benona Clapper & Lady & Miss VanSlyck, Ephraim VanSlyck, Mrs. Cate Spraker, Miss Spraker, Mr. Matson & Lady & Daughter here, visit. All go to Meeting in evening. Lib Hotaling here.
15	Rainy. I go to Kimmey's, draw posts. Mr. George Hotaling & Charlotte Hotaling here. I and George go to Aaron Hotaling's, attend a ball, have a good time.
16	Fair, warm, thawy, SW. I, Wife, George & Charlotte Hotaling go to Garrett Hotaling's visit. I call to D. VanOrden's, we bring Mary Hotaling holme with us.
17	Fair, SW. **Mr. Zeller bring fire board**. Mr. Willis call. I draw posts. I work around, go to river.
18	Cloudy, SW. I work around, go to river.

19   Fair, SW. We saw posts, go to mill. Quite muddy. Anthony Wolfe here, settle with me for lumber. I take his note $44.82.

20   Rainy. I go to Meeting twice. Wife 3 times.

21   Cold, squally day. Cut wood, go to river. I call on Mr. McKee. Wife go to Meeting.

22   Fair, sun-shiny day. Draw posts to Kimmey's Mill. I go to river. J.E. Gibbons here. **We look at timber for to build new School Room**.

23   Fair still. **I draw timber & stone for School Room**. Wife go to Meeting.

24   Stormy, clears off again. **I hire Lewy Ziegler for one year for $140. I go to Johnson & Schoonmaker's office, then to Colvin & Rennie store. Get money of them**.

25   Cold, NW. Work hard. Open stone quiry. Go to river. A.E. Willis call. Mr. Civill call. Widow Anna Teneyck here all day.

26   Snow all day, about 6 in. deep. Go to river. Make out writing for P. Long for house.

27   Fair, SW. Go to Meeting. Call to Willis's. **Sign notes for N.H. Johnson for $2000 at Union Bank Albany**.

28   Fair, NW. I, G. Rifflin & Stiley work in quiry.

March 1859

1   Cold, NW. Draw stone, work around house. Wife go to Widow Charlotte's & to Meeting. I go to river, kill my calf. **Dan Sickels shoot Mr. Key at Washington**.[296]

2   Fair. Work around, draw stone. Mr. Civill here. I go to river. Mrs. Jeminia Hotaling here, visit.

3   Fair morning, snowy afternoon. Draw posts, draw manure, pump the water out of the well. Mr. Willis & John Rea here. Wife go to Eliphalet Ackerman's.

4   Fair. Work at stone. Martin VanSlyck here. Mr. Civill call. Mr. McKee call. I am unwell, go to river.

5   Fair, wind N & south. Draw hay from Big Meadow. Peter Rea here. John D. Verplank, A.A. Hotaling, Mother here. I go to river.

6   Fair, thawy. Mr. Civill call. I go to Meeting. J. Fike go to Cedar Hill.

7   Fair still day. Draw hay, P. Rea help. Almira VanBergen here. Mary Hotaling here. **George Harris' child died**.

8   Rainy, muddy. Draw hay. I go to river, work around the house. Almira VanBergen & Mary Hotaling here.

9   Fair, cold, NW. Draw hay, go to river. Mr. Civill call. Almira VanBergen here.

10   Fair. Work in quiry. Wife & Almira go to Willis's. B. Waldron get a load of lumber, pay cash.

11   Fair, SW. I send John Fike Under Hill with shingles. He pick stone. Lib Hotaling, Mr. Civill call here. I work around house, go to river.

---

[296] Daniel E. Sickels, a first term Congressman from NY, shot and killed Phillip B. Key II after finding out that he was having an affair with his wife, Teresa. Key was the son of Francis Scott Key who wrote the "Star Spangled Banner."

12	Fair, warm in forenoon, rainy afternoon. Ice break up. I work at pickets. Almira VanBergen leave. I go to river.
13	NW. I go to Meeting twice, then to vineyard. Mr. Civill call. **Henry Niles' child died.**
14	Fair. John Fike oil harness. **I work at schoolhouse**. Go to Meeting in the evening.
15	Rainy day. Work around. Mr. Civill call. Wife go to Meeting.
16	Fair. Dig stone, work around the house. **I execute deed for Grove Cemetery**.
17	Fair. **Draw stone, work at schoolhouse**. Mrs. Geo. Harris call. Mrs. A.E. Willis here all day.
18	Rain hard all day. Uncle Thomas Hotaling here. We get out slats, I go to river.
19	Wet & stormy. Uncle Thomas Hotaling leave. I work around house. Wife go to Widow Clement's.
20	Cloudy, cold, NW, freezing. I go to Meeting.
21	Fair, cold. **Work at schoolhouse. Lay stone**.
22	Fair morning, rainy afternoon. Wife go to Albany. **I raise my schoolhouse addition**. I go to river, call to Willis's. Mother here. Addison Reynolds here.
23	Fair, NW. Wife come holme. A. Reynolds leave. Draw lumber.
24	Fair morning, rainy afternoon. Work at fence on the Hill. Get cherry trees. G. Rifflin, Peter Rea help. I go to river.
25	Rainy. Press hay, P. Rea help. G. Hotaling & T. Civill call.
26	Fair, cold. I, Civill, Borkman go to Albany. Mr. S. Wood, A.B. VanBenthuyzen, Mrs. Wood here.
27	Cloudy. I send John Fike to Cedar Hill, bring Borkman back. A.E. Willis & Lady & Mother here. All go to Meeting, call to Willis. Tony Hotaling here.
28	Fair. Mr. Wood & A.B. VanBenthuyzen leave. Wife & Mrs. Wood go to Garrett Hotaling's. I go Under Hill. Dutchman come here. John work at manure & the trees. John VanDenburgh pay me 100 dollars for R. Pulver.
29	Rain. I and Wife go to Albany. I go to Waterford with Mr. Wood & A.B. VanBenthuyzen. We go to D. Leonard's at Lansingburgh, take dinner to Morgan House, Waterford. Go to Mrs. Bailey's to tea, stay all night.
30	Fair. **Go to Lansingburgh to D. Leonard's. Make contract with him for lands in Michigan**. Take dinner to Troy House, then back to D. Leonard's, then to Waterford, take cars. Come to Albany, stay all night to Mr. Style's.
31	Fair. Come holme. Lib Hotaling here. I get Willis's waggon, go to see Mr. Tompkins, meet him Under Hill, then holme. Mr. A.D. Tompkins here. I pay him $3.46.

April 1859

1. Fair, cold, NW. **I saw wood with horse power all day.**[297] Get $100 of Johnson & Co. Settle & pay off John Fike.
2. Fair, SW. Finish swing. **Attend Nomination Meeting to J.B. Shear's**.
3. Rainy, hazy day. I go to Willis & to Meeting. Mr. Civill call.
4. Squally. Draw hay, manure. Go to river, draw timber, boards.
5. Fair, heavy NW, cold. Work around house, go to river. Call to Willis's. Wife visit to Hull's. Ann McCabe here. Cut wood. **Send contracts of Michigan Lands to Mr. Wood & A.B. VanBenthuyzen**.
6. Fair, heavy NW. Draw manure make fence to vineyard. Mrs. Kate Spraker here, visit.
7. Fair NW. Make fence to vineyard. Go to river. **Prayer Meeting here this evening**.
8. Cold, NW. I work at vineyard all day. Snow squalls.
9. Cold, NW. Go to river. Mr. Civill call. Commence to plow. **Mrs. VanAntwerp died, Doctor VanAntwerp's mother.**
10. Fair, NW. I go to Meeting. Mr. Civill, Aaron Hotaling call. I call to Willis's.
11. Rain all day. **Attend the funeral of Mrs. VanAntwerp**. I take team, go to Baltimore after the relatives. P. VanAntwerp & Lady, Doctor & Marite & Daniel VanAntwerp all here.
12. Fair, warm, SW. Go to Town Meeting. Dr. & Marite here. I go to river.
13. Fair. I draw posts & slats to vineyard. Take G. Rifflin one barrel of flour. Dr. VanAntwerp leave. Wife & Marite go to D. Fredenburgh's. Lawrence plow.
14. Rainy. Press hay. Fix Mother's cistern. Wife go to Albany.
15. Fair. **I & Mr. Civill go to Albany. Boat gets aground**. **Get clothes and things for new schoolhouse.**
16. Cloudy morning. Press hay. **Attend my Lawsuit to Baltimore with Reynolds Edget**. Work at vineyard. Go to river.
17. Fair, cold NW. Marite & Elida VanSlyck come here. I go to Meeting & to vineyard. Mr. Civill, Doct. Fredenburgh & Mr. Spraker call here.
18. Fair, cold. Draw hay. **Work at schoolhouse**. Mr. Civill call.
19. Fair, cold NW. Send away two calves. Marite leave. **Work at schoolhouse**. Mrs. Geo. Harris call.
20. Fair, cold NW. **Work at schoolhouse**. Mother, Harriet Willis, Mr. Wm. Allen & Lady here. Elizabeth Tubbs here. I go to river.
21. Fair, warm. I take Elizabeth Tubbs to Albany. Levi sick. I am unwell with headache.
22. Rainy. Set my leach, press hay, go to river.

---

[297] Fletcher doesn't describe how this worked. Our research identified a couple of ways horses were used to power a small sawmill. One involved the horse walking in a circle to turn a wheel that drove the mechanism. Another involved the horse walking on a treadmill that drove the mechanism.

23   Rainy. Press hay. I go to Albany. **I move Mr. Mckee in new school room**. Mr. Willis & Mr. Civill call.

24   Fair, heavy NW wind, cold. I go to Doctor's. Call to Mr. Civill's & to vineyard. **Lots of [people] call here to see Lev**i.

25   Fair. **Draw hay on propeller**. Mother here. Mr. Civill call. Minick Boys here. **I graft grape vines**.

26   Rainy day. Make fence Under Hill. Go to river. Call to Willis. Leave Sarell Wood note with Willis to get discounted. Mr. T. Civill call.

27   Fair. **Wife & self leave holme with Mr. T. Civill with Steamer PG Coffin to Albany. Take cars to Syracuse. Stop to Mr. Brace's, take tea, stay all night**. Weather fine.

28.   Fair, pleasant. **Mr. T. Civill & Miss Caroline A. Brace gets married.**[298] We have a fine party. Three ministers present and about 30 guests. Entertainment good, all happy & cheerful. Marriage takes place at 10 o'clock am. I present the bride, on behalf of her husband, the sum of two thousand dollars. We, that is, Mr. Civill & Lady, Wife & myself then take cars at 1 o'clock pm go to Niagara Falls, go through snow banks. The spring looks backwards, grain looks green, streams are much swollen. We arrive at Niagara Falls at 7 o'clock pm. Stop at the American Hotel.

29   Fair, pleasant. **The buds of the trees begin to swell. Walk down to American Falls & back to Breakfast. Take a carriage, cross Suspension Bridge. Go to Table Rock. We go down under Falls then up and go through museum. Then go to see two live buffaloes & two live wolves. Then leave and go to Burning Spring. The gas from this water burns very much, as gas that we see in our cities.**[299] **Then we view the Three Sister Islands. Then go to Landy's Lane. Go up to the top of the Observatory, view the celebrated Battleground and have it described to us by an old gentleman who was in the action. Then start again. Go through Drummondsville so back again across to Niagara. Then to Goat Island on the Observatory so around the island and back again to dinner. We, this time, cross the suspension bridge on foot. The view was beautiful almost beyond description. We again get ready to take cars to Buffalo. Arrive there at 7 o'clock pm. Go around some. Then take sleeping cars for Cleveland. Ride all night, arrive at Cleveland in morning at 3 o'clock amid confusion and the rattling of baggage, and a great hurrah.**

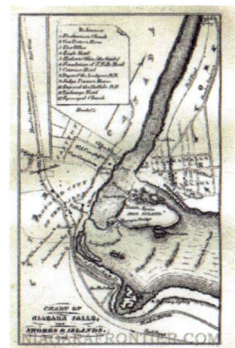

---

[298]   Theophilus Civill would have been about 57 at this point. Caroline Brace was about 27.

[299]   First discovered by Native Americans, Burning Springs was charted on the earliest maps of North America after the French explorer Robert Cavelier deLaSalle's visit in 1669. The burning spring was fed by natural gas created by decaying material captured in the rocks below.

30   Fair, warm. **Take cars for Cincinnati via Columbus. A fine pleasant smart place. Country from Cleveland to Columbus is new and timber principally white oak. Land not very good.** At Columbus, land is fine, level beautiful flat meadows & winter grain and the land is good along the Little Miami river and it is a pleasant country all the way to Cincinnati. Arrive at Cincinnati we dine at the Galt House. Do not like the place and leave for the Burnette Hotel, a good house. Go around the city, take tea. Go to the theater then back to hotel. Retire for the night, some tired.

Burnet House

May 1859

1   Fair, warm. **Trees out in bloom, full of leaves.** Breakfast, then I take omnibus go to Yateman's Vineyard. This is the finest place and view in the country. Go in to see his wine press and wine cellar. Take some of his wine, view his premises. It fronts the Ohio River & White's Borow Canal and Mississippi Railroad. Beautiful dwelling, fine ornamental trees, splendid garden, fine fruit grounds laid out in a beautiful manner. On the whole, this is the finest place I have yet been. Take cars back to Burnett House to dinner. Then walk down to steamboat wharf. The water overflows the wharves and up to the second story of their stores shops and they have floating wharves that boats are tied to which they move out in the river as the water goes down. Here I encounter hogs, dirt. See great many bare-head women & girls running here & there. A great many children. People loading and unloading vessels, vessels undergoing repair, great many drunken loafers. Plenty of Negroes, which does not leave a very pleasant sensation on the mind of a stranger on a Sabbath day. Great quantities of flood wood and whole trees go floating down with the rapid current of the river. On looking at the scene before me, I make up my mind that this city exceeds everything I ever saw for dust, smoke, filth, hogs, and immorality about the wharves I ever saw, and I then turn back. Go to Hotel to our room and am satisfied to take supper and look for something else. We all start again out in the city & go to the Protestant Methodist Church. Poor attendance. Fair sermon then back to the hotel to retire for the night.

2   Fair. **Take morning walk about town,** then back to breakfast, then go to steamboat & telegraph office. Then I go to Mr. N. Longworth's Residence, then to his wine cellars which are a great sight. Casks are marked 2400 gallons. Bottles piled up in stacks. The cellar is very large, and persons constantly engaged bottling wine. Leave the cellars, go to the office. Partake of some Sparkling Catawba. Have a talk with the clerk, who is a fine fellow. Then leave for hotel, pay up bills. Take coach to Steamer Telegraph for Louisville. This is a fine boat, good accommodation, excellent dinner and good speed. We stop at Lawrenceburg. Pass Blennerhassett Island. Stop at Carrolton at mouth of Ohio River & many other places. [The] Ohio River has fine lands on both sides of the river. Some high elevations, numerous orchards, fine grain & grass looking well. But no wharves and the sides of the river often are washed away by the current at landing places, sometimes carrying dwellings along with it and doing other damage. Arrive at Louisville 12 o'clock midnight. Take carriage to Mr. Lewis Civill's. Stay until morning, find them very pleasant & agreeable people.

3   Fair morning. Hear from holme by dispatch. Write holme. We go to Mrs. Clute's; find them very glad to see us and very friendly. Take dinner, then he takes his carriage &

we all go to Artisan Well. This is a sight. It is 2,086 ft. deep and it throws the water about 40 feet high. Then go around the city, then to Cave Hill Cemetery. This is a beautiful place. Then around the country, which is the finest I ever saw. Wheat is two ft. high. The land is rolling, soil a sandy loam and the best soil and most highly cultivated land I ever saw. Louisville is a prosperous city; a large business and the prospects are that this will be one of the most flourishing cities of the West. Fine churches, well attended, and very little immoral conduct perceptible to a stranger to be seen. Population are Germans and people from different states & Irish laborers and some Negroes of the number of 70,000 persons. Negroes have easy times in this city. Then go to Mr. Lewis A. Civil's, stay all night.

4   Fair morning, quite warm. Take omnibus early. Go to Depot, take cars for Mammoth Cave.[300] Country level, wet heavy timber with hard wood. Our cars are the Nashville cars. On this route there is some fine villages. Country pleasant until you reach the highlands. Then it is rough and plenty of poor uncultivated land. Leave cars to Munfordville. Take stage, go across Green River, cross in a scow. Walk up & down the hills. This is a hard road and hard ride. Arrive at Woodland to dine. Have good dinner. Mr. Ridder the landlord owns plenty of Negroes. All go on board stage again and drive through forests of oak timber to Mammoth Cave. See snakes & wild turkey on the route but little farming or enterprise through this route and few roads and very bad ones at that. Sometimes you could not tell whether the road went any farther or not. Saw quails, partridges, then arrive at Cave House. Quite a number of guests here. This house is built of logs 1½ stories high with a large piazza floor the entire length of the building. They have a large ell on the west end used for rooms and a fine lawn in front. Some shade trees, fine gardens. I walk around down to the mouth of the cave and then we take super & soon retire for the night - very tired.

5   Fair, warm. A little black barber charge me 2/ for shaving. This commences the day's operation. Take breakfast, dress for going in the cave. Start out of the back door, see two white opossums near the mouth of the cave. At once we take our guide and seven lamps. Nick Brensford, guide, leads, we all follow in Indian file. At the entrance, there is a fine clear fall of water, cool and refreshing. The air rustles out of the cave, nearly blowing out our lamps. This water was used for procuring salt peter in 1812 when they made a great deal of it.[301] The cave grows large as you enter 70 ft. height & 50 ft wide. All the routes of cave and avenues is 90 miles. The direct route is 14 miles. We went to the river, saw one of the boats used for navigating. It was wedged up between the rocks. The water had fell off and left it there. We saw Grand Dome, which is a very interesting sight, so is the Bottomless Pit, also Registry Hall. Matrimonial Hall we drink at a fine spring of water take a little cake & Brandy. Come back through different route. Saw representation of stars, clouds, men and animals of different kinds - dogs, trees in a petrified shape, side saddle, domes, natural wells, the church, giant coffin, dwelling used by invalids, their dining rooms, salt peter pits, innumerable to describe and, at length, reach the entrance quite tired. Come out again & see daylight, well satisfied with seeing one of the greatest curiosities in nature. Return to hotel, shift our clothes, go to dinner feel rested, but not very well. Roam about the place, see

---

[300] The world's largest known cave system.
[301] Salt peter is potassium nitrate – once the main ingredient for gun powder.

	about the country, attacked with cramps. Some it passes off with Diaboca. Take supper. Hear Mr. Rany, the horse trainer, make a speech. Then go to bed.
6	Fair. Rany perform with horse taming, the women attend. I take a walk to Whiles' Cave then around a few miles through the forests. Saw quantities of hogs that inhabit these woods. Then back to Cave House. Take whiskey sling. Take dinner then pay up and leave for Mr. Bell's Hotel – 9 miles. This is another bad & lonely road. Our ladies ride, the men ride and walk and, at night, reach Mr. Bell's Tavern very tired. We see a few houses and only one that seemed to be occupied. The rest all deserted. The land poor, no springs of water. Hardwood timber principally oak and a limestone country altogether. We take a little bourbon sling have a good supper and go to bed. We have seen but little good land in this part of the state. They raise tobacco, corn, mules and hogs.
7	Fair. Take stage at 4 o'clock am; go to Woodland House again, take breakfast. Then start again to Mulfordsville [Munfordville], take dinner. At this place was a gallows erected. A man was hung some time since on it and a wag had wrote on the gallows "50 miles to hell." It was Election Day in Kentucky and people were mostly out on horseback and no waggons. Not many slaves in this part of the country. Take cars for Lewisville [Louisville], arrive at evening. Take tea with Mr. L. Civill. This was a very dry dusty day and very warm. We stay at night with Mr. Clute.
8	Fair & warm in morning. Go to Meeting with Mr. Clute & his family to the Episcopal Church, then back to dinner. Very hot. We have a heavy shower of rain & hail, heavy wind. I take a walk down about the wharves then back to tea & then visit with family & play with the children and then go to bed.
9	Warm & rainy. Call to Mr. Civill's then to his store. Walk about town. Go to Mr. Clute's to dinner. Then Mr. Clute takes his carriage and gives us a ride down on the Lexington road past the Blind Asylum. Go to the fair grounds. This is a place worthy of imitation and the best arrangement I ever saw. The Amphitheater all covered 900 feet in circumference, well seated, a fine Flora Hall. Great numbers of sheds & stables. Ground in fine grass, well shaded and the best country of land around here I ever saw. Then we go back to Mr. Clute's. The Mr. Civills all invited there, have a good supper. Spend the evening very pleasantly, then go to bed.
10	Fair. Go to see all the friends. Bid them goodbye with regret, having been so kindly treated by them. I saw more friendships manifested by the people of Kentucky than any people I ever saw. It seemed to be a pleasure to them to do all they could to entertain you. We leave in the steamer Jacob Strader, a fine boat and the best fare and accommodations for Cincinnati. Stop at Madison, Jeffersonville, Ghent all fine villages. Arrive at Cincinnati in the morning.
11	Fair. Take breakfast at the Spencer House and take the omnibus for the cars. Leave the land of vineyards, come back to Columbus, arrive at 20 minutes past 10 am. Dine here and then take Ohio Central RR, go through Newark, a smart place, then to Zanesville, country not good. Cross the Muskingum River. Zanesville is a fine village - fine waterpower. Follow the great National Road.[302] Cross a part of the Allegheny

---

[302] The National Road, also known at the Cumberland Rd., was the first federally planned and funded interstate highway crossing 6 states: Maryland, Pennsylvania, West Virginia, Ohio, Indiana and Illinois - 620 miles. It served as a main transport path to the West.

Mountains, arrive at Bellaire, take supper. Cross the Ohio River in a ferry boat, take the Baltimore & Ohio RR - ride all night.

12 Come over a mountainous country. Arrive at Cumberland, large place, to breakfast. This is a vast coal region. No land for cultivation. Strike the Potomac River, it runs through a poor mountainous country. Pass Sir John's Run, poor place, North Mountain, the country begins to look better, land more tilled, some crops growing. Stop at Martinsburg, fine crops of wheat, grass is poor. Arrive at Harpers Ferry. This place is where Old Brown tried to get up an insurrection and he and all the party 21 in number got killed or was hung in Dec. 1859.[303] Cross the bridge, come to Washington Junction. Here is a fine bridge and a monument in honor of the proprietors of the Baltimore and Ohio Railroad Co. Dine here then go to Washington. Stop at United States Hotel. Take supper, walk around and retire for the night.

13 Fair. Take Omnibus to Steamer Collier. Go to Mount Vernon, view the premises, then go to Fort Washington, view the fort. Then back to Washington for dinner. Then take Omnibus to boat again to Alexandria to Samuel Gedney's, stay all night.

14 Fair. Take Omnibus to boat again. Come back to Washington - lots of fisherman on board, and a rough looking jolly set they were. Then take breakfast and go to Georgetown. Visit the Catholic College & Convent. These are good Institutions, well conducted. We saw books at the college written on parchment in the 1376 and a vast amount of old Bibles, a great quantities of old coins Roman & Italic. There was about 100 girls at the Nunnery - all young well dressed and good looking. They are instructed in all manner of painting and educated. The chapel is a sight - it is kept very neat and many figures producing a singular feeling on the visitor. We return again to hotel to dinner, then take a coach call to Mr. Peal's. Take Mrs. Peal call to the President's Mansion. Go through the rooms and about the grounds, which are very beautiful. Then go to Washington Monument, then to Smithsonian Institute and through the building and were much interested. Then to the Capitol. There is a large assemblage of people, Bands of music and children dancing around the fountain. Then go through the Capitol and visit all parts of the building. Then back and take supper & then retire for the night.

15 Fair. Mr. Civill is sick. We take Breakfast. I walk to Lafayette Square where Dan Sickles shot Phillip B. Key. Looked at the tree where Key fell. Then back, take dinner, then we all take a walk down to Lafayette Square. Call to Mr. Peal's. Then back to supper. Then attend church at the Wesleyan Chapel and go back to bed.

16 Fair. We go to the Capitol, then to the patent office. Look at camp chest & sword for General Washington, then go to Book Stores. Then attend anniversary of the Sabbath School Children at the Capitol yard. They have a good display and fine music. Then to Hotel. Pay bills & take cars to Baltimore, so to Philadelphia. Stop at St. Lawrence Hotel, a good house.

17 Lowry rain a little. We go in the Mint, then to Girard College, then to Fairmount Water Works, then take Steamer Wissihikon. Go up the Schuylkill River to Laurel Hill

---

[303] Abolitionist John Brown lead a small group on a raid against a federal armory in Harpers Ferry in October 1859 in an attempt to start an armed slave revolt and destroy the institution of slavery. He was convicted of treason, murder and conspiring with slaves to rebel and sentenced to death. Note that this occurred after Fletcher's visit indicating that he updated his journal after the Harpers Ferry raid.

Cemetery, the prettiest and most expensive place I ever saw.[304] **A visit here is very interesting. Saw Dr. Kane's tomb, pass Thomas Moore's residence, Benedict Arnold's residence, then to hotel, then to Independence Hall, then retire for the night.**

18 Cloudy. **Take breakfast & then take cars for New York. The country looks fine, grain forward. Arrive at 10 o'clock am. Go to propeller, then to Dr. VanAntwerp's stay all night.**

19 Cloudy. **Take breakfast. Call to John J. Silcock's. Buy Anthony a drum. Then go to boat and about the city. Take dinner to J. Silcock's, then to Dr. VanAntwerp's, stay all night.**

20 Cloudy, rainy. **Go to boat. Walk around town, then start in propeller for Coeymans.**

21 Rainy. **Arrive holme; find apple trees in blossom. And where I have been, trees have been out of blossom for 6 weeks, this looks strange. All well and people glad to see me. Mr. Civill & Lady come here in the evening and Sarah Ann comes with them. They have a wonderful horning for the benefit of Mr. Civill & Lady.**[305] **Keep us up until 12 o'clock at night. Mr. Civill & Lady and kind girl boarding with us.**

22 Rainy. Mr. Civill & myself go to vineyard.

23 Fair. Alter my colts. I go under the Hill. Uncle Garrett here. Lawrence go after posts to P. Kimmey's.

24 Fair, warm. Go to vineyard. Get horses shod. Take potatoes out of the cellar.

25 Fair, warm. I work to vineyard, draw manure.

26 Fair. I cut brush. Work to vineyard, go to river, call to Willis's. Mrs. Aaron Hotaling here. Lib Hotaling, David Niver, Thms. McKee call here.

27 Fair, warm, SW. Go Under Hill, make fence. Draw boards to Kimmey's for pickets, draw posts. Fanny & Sarah Cramer, Mother here.

28 Fair, cold. I go to Herkimer to H. Sperl's, stay all night.

29 Fair, cool, rainy afternoon. Go around the place.

30 Fair, frosty. I work around the mill. Settle with H. Sperl.

31 Fair, frosty. I walk to Little Falls. Stop to John Feeter's to dinner, then take cars. Get to Albany 5 o'clock pm. Rainy evening.

June 1859

1 Fair. Walk around Albany, then come holme.

2 Fair day, shower in evening. I lay wall, work to the vineyard, draw manure. Mrs. John Harris here. I call to see John Rea.

---

[304] Founded in 1836, this is more than a cemetery, it is a sculptural garden, a horticultural gem - one of the few cemeteries in the U.S. to be designated as a National Historic Landmark.

[305] Horning is an old country custom popular when couples got married. Making noise and engaging in disorderly conduct.

3	Fair, hot SW. **Clean house, shake carpets**. I work to vineyard. Mr. Lewis Crandle & Hubberd Harris here and whitewash. Lawrence draw pickets. Get straw of Mr. Robb's. I pay H. Harris 10 dollars.
4	Cloudy, very cold. I take Mother to Hollow to Quarterly Meeting. Lawrence work on road under the Hill.
5	Very cold. I take Mother to Quarterly Meeting to Hollow. I go to vineyard. Lawrence go to Albany.
6	Fair. Frost this morning. I make fence all day, go to river, get barrel flour, get fish.
7	Fair. I go after timber for grape poles Under Hill. Take my colts along, drive Mare Topsy. Mr. T. Civill & Lady & Wife go to New York.
8	Rainy. Draw manure, make fence, go to river & to vineyard.
9	Fair, cold. Take colts to pasture, make fence, go to river, work on vineyard.
10	Rainy. Furrow out potatoes, draw manure, make steps.
11	Fair. Work at vineyard, lay wall, draw manure. Mr. T. Civill & Lady & Wife come back from NY.
12	**Frost again, it kills the beans, SW.** I go to Church, attend Bible class.
13	Rainy. Work in garden, put down carpets.
14	Warm, foggy. I lay walk, work at potatoes, go to river, get some mutton.
15	Fair, warm, SW. Draw manure, get horses shod. Levi go Under Hill. I lay wall, furrow out G. Rifflen's potatoes. Mrs. G. Harris here.
16	Fair. I lay wall. Go Under Hill, bring holme my bull. Go to river.
17	Fair morning, NW. Rainy afternoon. Draw manure. I take Mr. Civill & Lady & Wife riding down to Widow McCabe. Then we go up the turnpike.
18	Fair, cold, NW. **Mr. Civill & Lady & girl leave here and go to housekeeping.** I go to river, call to Mr. Civill's & to Willis's.
19	Fair, cool. Wm. Phelps & G. VanAllen, Martin VanSlyck here. Mother Hotaling come holme. Go to Meeting, call to Mr. Civill's.
20	Rainy day. Press hay, go to river. Wm. Phelps & G. VanAllen leave.
21	Rainy. Press hay, SW. I take up my note in hands of J.J. Colvin. He pays me his note $500 in my hands. I let Johnson & Schoonmaker have $376.
22	Fair. Lay wall all day. Go to river, **get shad and sturgeon.**
23	Fair. I take Wife & Mother Hotaling, Mrs. Civill to Baltimore to Baptist Meeting. Dr. Spoon & Mrs. R.H. VanBergen here. Mr. Civill & Lady here to tea.
24	Misty & rainy. Lay wall, work at corn, go to river, work in garden.
25	Fair. Lay wall, work in garden. We visit to Mr. Civill's.
26	Fair. **Go to Baltimore, see the immersion of Mr. Mead.** Go to vineyard. Mr. Civill call.
27	Fair. I take Wife, go to Albany, lay out 40 dollars. I receive Sarell Wood's note from A.B. VanBenthuyzen to send to Mr. Seymour at the Waterford Bank.

28   We have a shower, very hot. **Shingle hay press**. Send note of S. Wood to Mr. Seymour. Draw in hay. Lib & Caroline Hotaling here. Wife go to Horace Renne, visit.

29   Heavy Shower; **TH 108 degrees above 0, very hot**. Work at potatoes, go to river.

30   Fair, cool, heavy N wind. Work at barn, go Under Hill. Sell cattle to Peter Seabridge. Mrs. J.J. Colvin & Aunt Lucy here. Garret Hotaling here. I go to Mother's.

July 1859

1   Fair, frosty. Henry VanDerzee come here. **We attend McKee's school; it goes off well.** Work around house.

2   Rainy. H. VanDerzee leave. Draw hay, go to river, settle with John Hauenstien.

3   Rainy. Go to Meeting, take tea to Willis's. Andrew A. Hotaling's 3 children here.

4   Fair, cold NW. **I take Wife & Children to Baltimore to celebration. Goes off well**.

5   Fair, cool. Henry Lawrence's Brother come here to work today with Lawrence. I go Under Hill, fix fence. Draw hay, send calf to New York. Draw manure. Sell some grass to Mr. Halstead.

6   Fair. Draw manure. Go Under Hill. Grind scythe. **Have a trial of Mr. Crumb's mowing machine.**

7   Fair. Draw in a little hay, draw manure, go to river.

8   Fair, warm, SW. **I mow with machine. I take Boys to Island, go and swim.** Mother Hotaling come holme.

9   Fair, NW. Work in hay. Henry VanDerzee & Mary come. Marite come along. Mary come to live with Lib Hotaling, come here to tea. Go to river.

10   Fair, warm. I go to vineyard. Call to Mother's. Elizabeth Hotaling here.

11   Fair dry day. I mow, draw in hay, go to river.

12   Fair, very warm. H. VanDerzee leave for N. York. Work in hay. I sell grass Under Hill to Danl. Baker for $40.

13   Fair. Work in hay. Go to river. Bind up rye.

14   Fair. Work in hay. Wife & Marite go to Uncle Garrett's.

15   Heavy shower, SW. I draw in 7 loads rye & two loads of hay. Miss McCabe here.

16   Rainy. I go to river. Mr. Civill & Lady, Miss Ann Brace here. Doct. Fredenburgh call. **I & Civill buy out Seabridge share of Schoolhouse for 400 dollars.**

17   Rainy, hot. Doct. Fredenburgh call to see Marite.

18   Cloudy. Go Under Hill, fix water troughs, mow a little.

19   Cloudy. Draw stone, lay wall. Go to river & to vineyard.

20   Fair. Work in hay. Mr. Civill & Lady, Mr. McKee call. I go to river.

21   Fair, NW. **I mow all day**. Widow Charlotte & Widow P. VanBergen here. Miss McCabe here for 4 days. Mother here.

22   Heavy shower in afternoon. Work in hay, go to river. Wife & Mary go a riding with Mr. Civill.

23	Fair, cool NW. Work in hay. Mrs. Budd, Mrs. Adams & their three children, Mrs. P. Phelps, Eliza Phelps and Dr. Jones Daughter here. H. VanDerzee & Marite here.
24	Fair, NW. Go to Meeting & to vineyard.
25	Cloudy, clears off. **Henry VanDerzee pays Harry's bill to this date**.
26	Fair. I go to Albany, get 500 dollars out of Merchant's Bank. Go to Waterford to Saratoga Co. Bank, take up S. Wood's note pay $501.04.
27	Clears off, misty morning. I go to river. Mow all the afternoon. P. Phelps here.
28	Fair. Work in hay. Wife & folks go a riding with Mr. Civill.
29	Fair. Work in hay. I let P. Phelps have horse, he go to Baltimore.
30	Fair. Take all the folks to Uncle Andrew's. Then go to Mr. Fick's vineyard with Uncle Andrew. Boys work in hay.
31	Fair. **Go to Dutch Church to Meeting then attend Meeting of Baptist at Temperance Hall**.

August 1859

1	Fair, SW. Work in hay. Rev. P. Phelps & Lady, Eliza Phelps & Miss Jones leave.
2	SW, heavy shower. Work around. Willis call.
3	SW, showry. Work in hay. Mr. Civill & Lady & Miss Brace here.
4	Showry, SW. Draw in hay. Go to vineyard and to river.
5	Cloudy, SW, warm. Work hay, warm.
6	Fair, NW. Work in hay & oats. H. VanDerzee, Mary Bagley here. Mr. Civill & Lady, Miss Brace call.
7	Fair morning, SW, shower in afternoon. Go to Meeting & to vineyard.
8	Fair. Work in hay. Anthony sick. Wife & Mary go with Mr. Civill a riding.
9	Fair. Work in hay. H. VanDerzee leave. Mary Bagley come. Mrs. Thomas & two children, Caroline Hotaling, Elizabeth Stephens here.
10	Fair. Mow all day, get in hay. Go to river.
11	Cloudy morning, SW. Mr. Casey & Lady come here. Work in hay.
12	Fair day, rain in evening. Work in hay. Mr. Fitch here to tea. Mr. Civill & Lady, Miss Brace here, call. Rainy night.
13	Clears off. Work in hay. Attend P. Road meeting to Briggs.
14	Fair morning. Go to Meeting, then go Under Hill. Oil my colt's feet.
15	Fair, NW. Work in hay. I go to Greenville. Stay all night to Andrew Fancher's.
16	Fair. I go to Greenville, swear off my tax. Then come holme. Go to river. Call to T. Civill's.
17	Fair, NW. We go to mowing Under Hill. Have a party to Mr. Civill's & Lady's. G. Harris & Lady, besides ourselves, have a fine time. Mary Bagley leave.
18	Fair. **Finish hay - 118 loads**. Henry Casey & Lady leave. I and the Boys work under the Hill.

19 North & SW, little shower. **I take children fishing, have poor luck**. Miss Virginia Angevine and her little Boy here. Mother here.

20 Fair, dry, NW. Start plow. I take George Rifflin, go to Mr. Fitch's Coxsackie. Stop to Uncle Andrew's. Henry VanDerzee come.

21 Fair. H. VanDerzee & I take a ride Under Hill, so to Stile Barrack.

22 Fair. I put a new pump in cistern. Make fence to vineyard. Mr. Niles, Thomas Calanan call. Boys & H. VanDerzee go hunting.

23 Fair SW. Make fence to vineyard. Mrs. William Bagley & Daughter here. I go to river.

24 Fair. Thresh rye. Go to river. Wife & Levi go to Uncle Garrett's. John G. VanDerzee & Mr. Civill call.

25 Rainy morning. Boys Thrash. I help Henry VanDerzee stake out Cemetery ground.

26 Fair, SW. We all attend Camp Meeting out to Bethlehem. We plow in Big Meadow.

27 Fair. Attend Camp Meeting. Elida VanSlyck & Sarell Wood here. They go along.

28 Fair, cool North wind. Attend Camp Meeting. Take Mother out. H. VanDerzee come back with us.

29 Fair, cool NW. Sarell Wood leave. Elida go holme. I work around. Boys plow; cut brush.

30 Fair, SW. H. VanDerzee leave. I and J.H. Holmes work at barn. Plow, draw stone.

September 1859

1 Fair, NW. Shingle barn and stoop, hay press. Mother Hotaling go to Coxsackie. Two Mr. Roberts call here.

2 Fair, cool NW. Shingle. Mother here. Draw manure, go to river.

3 Fair, SW. Go to Kimmey's Mill & to Dean's Mill after plaster. **I let Mr. Tompkins have Temperance Banner.**[306] Wife go to Coxsackie with Willis. Sarell Wood here.

4 Fair, NW. Mr. Wood & G. Houghtaling here. We all go to Meeting. Timothy Clancy here, gave me his note for $50. He pay me 155 dollars cash.

5 Fair. Sarell Wood leave. I sow rye, go to river.

6 Fair, cool. I dig potatoes. Go with Willis to S. Tuttle's. Go to river.

7 Far, cool. Go to Stephensville after stone. Call to Willis. **Mrs. Cornelius Demond died, 90 years old.**

8 Fair, cool. I take Wife & Children to Albany. Lawrence plow.

Temperance Banner

---

[306] The temperance banner was found in 1999 in the attic of the Blaisdell home when we were setting up for an auction. It was sold at the auction to the Ravena-Coeymans Historical Society. The banner was restored and is one of the artifacts on display. This photo was taken prior to its restoration.

9	Fair, cold. I sow grass seed. Mr. T. Civill & Lady, Mr. Reynolds & Lady here. We go to vineyard.
10	SW, rainy. **We attend school celebration to Aquetuck.** Martin VanSlyck bring Mother Hotaling holme. **We have a fun time today. I take out 23 in my load.**
11	Shower, SW. Go to Meeting & to vineyard. Martin VanSlyck leave.
12	Fair. **Mr. Switzer come here. I sell him my grapes at 8 cts. per lb. Mr. McKee here, settle his ren**t.
13	Shower. Draw stone. Send off grapes, go Under Hill.
14	Fair, cold, heavy NW. I pick apples & peas. Go to the boat with grapes. Mother here. Wife go to Willis's. Mr. Civill & Lady call in evening.
15	Fair, cold. Send off grapes. Go Under Hill, gather apples.
16	Fair morning, SW. H. VanDerzee come. Work at manure. I fix hay press, go to river.
17	Rainy day. Send off grapes. Go to river.
18	Fair, NW. I and H. VanDerzee go around. Mrs. U.B. Willis here.
19	Fair. I send off grapes, go Under Hill. Take Mr. Civill & Lady get butternuts. Go to cemetery & to vineyard.
20	Rain. **Classes meet at Dutch Church. We go in evening**.
21	Rainy. Send off grapes. Press hay, go to river.
22	Rainy day. Press hay, fix barn.
23	Rainy. Draw chips, fix fence. Mr. Civill & Lady here.
24	Fair. **I go to Herkimer. Stop to John Feeter's, go to H. Sperl's.**
25	Little shower. **Go around place, go to Meeting to Western's.**
26	Fair. **Stay around mill and the farm.**
27	Fair. **I, Henry Sperl, Lyman Bullock go to Graysville, then to Cold Brook, then to Russia, then to Graves Hollow, then to South Trenton, then to Holland Pattent. Here is six churches. Take dinner, then to Floyd, then to Rome. Go to Seymour & Adams Furnace. Then take cars to Albany. Stay all night to Mr. Styles. Mr. Wash & Miss Neal married.**
28	Fair. **I come holme. Squeeze grapes.** Go to Garrett Hotaling's to tea.
29	Fair. **Dig potatoes, fix for drying apples in wood house.** Go to river.
30	Fair, SW. Work at potatoes. Go to C.T.E. Waldron's. **Bring wine from vineyard.** Saml. Smith's children here.

October 1859

1	Rainy afternoon. **Mr. Barnum died.** Henry VanDerzee & Marite come. I gather apples. R. Pulver here. Edwin Hubbell here. I call to Civill's, go to river. William Bagley send me a cow. **Jacob Sickles died**.
2	Fair. I go to vineyard. Go to Meeting. Call to Aaron Hotaling's.

3	Fair. I take G. Rifflin & John Rodgers, go above Teneyck Waldron's, get stone for H. VanDerzee. Mr. Hartwell here to tea. Mr. Civill & Lady, Emma Brace and Boy Charley here. Lawrence go to Albany.
4	Fair. Work for H. VanDerzee on cemetery. Go after stone.
5	Fair, SW. Draw stone, Lawrence come. Wife & Marite go to Civill's.
6	Fair, cold NW. **I take Children, go to Albany attend State Fair. It was a great display of everything. The best I ever saw. Get holme 9 o'clock pm**.
7	Fair. Draw stone. Work about cemetery. Henry, Marite & Wife come back. Mr. Fredenburgh, Betsey Verplank, Caroline VanAntwerp here.
8	Rainy. Andrew VanAntwerp horse come here. **I get nuts, work at potatoes & buckwheat. Attend show at Temperance Hall**.
9	Fair, cool NW. Henry, Boys & self go to cemetery. T. Civill Lady & Charley, Mr. Mackee call here in evening.
10	Fair, cool NW. Draw stone for H. VanDerzee to cemetery. Cate VanBergen, Mary Hotaling call here.
11	Fair. I work at cemetery, draw lumber. Mrs. Pierce & Mrs. Dr. Jones here.
12	Fair. Draw stone. Go to J.B. Shear's Attend Meeting of Coeymans Mutual Insurance Co. I take Marite along. I send Henry VanDerzee to Walter Becker's. Go to river.
13	Fair. Draw stone, go to river, dig potatoes.
14	Rainy. **I go to Albany, get cauldron**.
15	Fair, cold NW. **Set cauldron in smoke house.** Doct. VanAntwerp come. I go to river.
16	Fair, cool. I take all hands, Marite & Children, go to Harman VanDerzee. Martin VanSlyck here. Henry VanDerzee come back with us.
17	South wind, cloudy. I take Mrs. Pierce, Mrs. Jones to Uncle Andrew's, Marite go along. I go to river.
18	Rainy. Doct. & Marite leave. **I get coal**.
19	Fair, cold. H. VanDerzee leave for Albany. I work at ditch, draw stone, go to mill. Mrs. Clement & Eliza here.
20	Cold. I work around house. Draw dirt, go to river. **Mrs. Wm. Bushants died.**
21	Very cold, freeze, heavy NW. **Draw coal, stone & sand**. Have a headache all day. Go to river.
22	Fair. Work at ditch, sow rye, draw stone.
23	Fair, cold. Go to river. Mr. Civill, Lady & Charley here.
24	Fair, cool. Press hay. Attend lecture in evening.
25	Fair, cool. Draw hay & leaves for G. Rifflin. Mother here.
26	Fair, cool NW. Draw manure. Miss Haswell, Miss Terry, Mr. McKasy here. Attend lecture in the evening.
27	Fair. Draw manure, cabbage. **Attend School Convention and Lecture**. Mr. Terry come here with Miss Terry & Miss Haswell.

28 Cloudy, cold NW. Press hay all day.

29 Fair, cold NW. I take Wife & Mary, go to Albany. I take up my note at Merchant's Bank $500 with Johnson's check.

30 Cloudy. I go to Meeting and to vineyard. Mr. Civill & Lady, Mr. Fletcher Bangs & Lady here.

31 Cloudy. Draw hay, work in quiry.

November 1859

1 Cloudy. Draw manure. **Take out beets**. Wife go to Four Mile Point to Mr. Adams.

2 Fair still day. I split slats. Aunt Hannah Houghtaling here. Uncle Garrett call.

3 Fair, cold. Go after slat timber and call to N. Carhart's. Take dinner to Abram Witbeck's.

4 Fair. Press hay. Mother here.

5 Fair. Press hay; draw hay. H. VanDerzee come. Wife come back. I go to river.

6 Fair, NW. I go to cemetery & to vineyard & to river.

7 Fair. I, Wife, H. VanDerzee & Mary go to Albany.

8 Fair. **Attend Election, work around**.

9 Fair. I send box to Herkimer. Work around, go to vineyard.

10 Cloudy, warm SW. Draw stalks. Press hay.

11 Fair, cold NW. Press hay all day.

12 Rainy. Draw stone for G. Rifflin. Draw hay & press hay.

13 Rainy, cloudy, snowy. H. VanDerzee, Peter & Maria VanDerzee here, stay all night.

14 Fair, cold. Draw hay, go to mill. Wife & Mary, H. VanDerzee go to Albany.

15 Fair, pleasant. I go to mill, plow. H. VanDerzee leave for New York. I go to river. Elizabeth & Cary Hotaling here.

16 Fair, SW. Plow. I split slats, work at barn.

17 Fair, SW. Plow, press hay. **Prayer Meeting here tonight. Martin VanSlyck take Mother Hotaling to Aunt Sarah Ann's to attend Ed VanOrden's Wedding**.

18 Rainy. Press hay, go to river. Call to Civill's. Willis call here.

19 Rainy day. Work in barn, go to river.

20 Cold NW. Go to Meeting, call to Willis's.

21 Fair. Draw hay. Go to Gerry Springstead's. Aaron Hotaling call here.

22 Rain, some snow. Press hay all day.

23 Cloudy, NW. Press hay & plow.

24 Cloudy, cold. **All hands go to Coxsackie to U.B. Willis's. Spend Thanksgiving, have a good time. Mother Hotaling come back with us**. Road very bad.

25 Cloudy, cold. Go after slats, draw leaves. Ed VanOrden here. Go to river.

26 Cloudy, muddy, thawy. Draw & press hay. H. VanDerzee come.

27   Fair, NW. I and H. VanDerzee go to cemetery. Stay around the house.

28   Fair, NW. Draw hay, plow, go after hay slats.

29   Fair. I and all hands go to Albany. **R. Pulver died**.

30   Fair day, warm. Split slats. **I and H. VanDerzee go to Mr. Robb's & Mr. Croswell's paper mill.** Finish plowing.

December 1859

1   Rainy day, a little sun. H. VanDerzee leave. I go to river, work around. **Washington Irving died.**[307]

2   Rainy. **I finish press hay.** Call to Civill's in evening.

3   Cold. I fix around for G. Rifflin. Send to Mill, go to river, to Singing School.

4   Snowy day. I call to Mother's & to Civill's. Go to Meeting, call to Willis's, Willis's call here. I let Willis have 100 dollars and gave him an order on Schoonmaker for $200 more. He get a draft for me, I send it to P. Collins.

5   About 4 in. snow this morning. I and Lawrence go Under Hill, fix for my colts. Peter Ostrander here, I settle with him. Wife to Albany.

6   Misty. Draw hay to propeller. Fix for killing hogs.

7   Stormy, rainy. I kill beef, work in cellar, go to river.

8   Cold, 4 in. snow. I kill hogs & beef.

9   Cold, NW. I cut up hogs & beef. Go to river, send to mill.

10   Cold, NW. I and Lawrence go Under Hill, finish barn stable. Cut up hogs for Mr. Blodget. Go to Gregory's to Singing School.

11   Little snowy, SW. I go to Meeting, call to Willis & to Civill's.

12   Cold, NW. I salt beef & pork, cut wood.

13   Fair, cold. I get horse shod, go to river. Mrs. James Jack, Mrs. Rea here.

14   Fair, cold. Get horses shod. Work in stable, go to river.

15   Fair. Cornelius VanDerzee call. Mr. T. Civill & Lady & Charley here, visit. I work at stable, draw brush on vineyard.

16   Fair still day, cold. Work at stable, go to river.

17   Fair day, storm in evening. **Work at stable, go with Boy a skating.** Elida VanSlyck, Mother here. Mrs. U.B. Willis call, we attend Singing School to Ira Gregory's in evening.

18   Stormy, warmer. Go to Meeting. Martin & Elida VanSlyck leave.

19   Thawy. Draw manure, work at stable, go to river.

20   Snow all day. Work at stable, go to river.

21   Fair, cool. Work at stable, call to Willis, go to river.

---

[307] Washington Irving, known as the first American Man of Letters, achieved international fame for his short stories *"Rip Van Winkle"* and *"The Legend of Sleepy Hollow."*

22 Fair day. Work at stable, go to river.

23 Fair. **Attend photographs**, go to Barret Teneyck's, pay interest money.

24 Fair, cold. Take Wife & Children to Albany.

25 Cold, SW. Call to Civill's, go to Meeting, go to G. Rifflin.

26 Cold, cloudy, SW. U.B. Willis & Lady, A.E. Willis & Lady, Andrew Hotaling & Lady & Child and Black Joe here.

27 Very cold, NW. I take Mother Hotaling to Baltimore. Go to river, work around house. James A. Wilsey here. I settle with Peter Seabridge. **Anthony VanBergen Died.**

28 Very cold, NW. Draw muck. I settle with Mr. Civill. Wife & Children attend Donation to Dominie Mathew's. **William Civill died**.

29 Very cold, NW. **TH 12 deg. below 0.** I work at Temperance Hall, am around house. Wife & Mother Hotaling go to Jacob Holmes.

30 Snowy, about one foot deep, cold. Go to river. **Go to the funeral of William Civill. Garrett Hotaling, Caroline, Miss McCabe, Willis, Harriet call to exchange photographs.**

31 Fair, cold. **TH 12 degrees below 0. I Work at Temperance Hall. Attend there to see Minstrels in the evening**.

January 1860

1 Very cold. Call to T. Civill's, go to Meeting. Stephen Hotaling here.

2 Very cold NW. I, Wife & Mary call to Garrett Hotaling's, then to Gerry Springstead's, then to Baltimore. Then we go to T. Civill's to tea, have a nice time.

3 Fair, very cold. **TH 14 deg below 0**. Martin VanSlyck, A.E. Willis here. I go to river.

4 Fair, SW. Miss McCabe here. I work around, go to river. Go to P. Long's house, settle with him.

5 Fair. Go to river. Clean up grain, pay Teneyck Heiss & Mrs. Lott. Call to Mr. Civill's.

6 Fair. Draw wood, go to river. P. VanBuren here, call.

7 S Wind, little rainy. I and Wife go to Greenville to Andrew Fancher's, stay all night.

8 Foggy, thaws. We go to Cornwallville to Quarterly Meeting, then back and then go to Greenville to Meeting in evening.

9 Fair. Go around collect my rents, then come holme. Attend show at Temperance Hall in evening.

10 Cloudy, thawy. Pay tax $82.56 to R. Hotaling.

11 Cloudy, rainy, SW. Draw wood, go to river. Wife to Bethlehem with Willis.

12 Snowy day; clears off. Spend the day to Willis's. Attend Plank Road Meeting.

13 Fair, NW, cold. Work around. Hang up meat. Attend P. Road Meeting.

14 Cloudy, warm. I take a ride to papermill. Go to Mr. Gregory's to sing in evening.

15 Fair, SW. Call to Civill's, call to Blodget's. Go to Meeting.

16 Fair, SW. Mr. Civill, Miss Brace, Mary Clancy here. Martin VanSlyck here. I go to river.

17   Fair. I and Mr. Civill go to Albany. **Gilbert Cronk was at Style's, very much hurt.**

18   Cloudy. I help Willis get logs. Go to river. Attend Negro dance.

19   Fair, cold NW. Go to river. Call to Mr. Blodget's.

20   Fair, SW. Go to river. **Attend McKee's School**. Mrs. Clancy here, pay me $1.08.

21   Fair, warm. **I take our Mary & Fanna Cranston out sleigh riding on the river. Go to Stuyvesant and Schodack. My horse step through the ice up in the Got**. Attend Singing School in the evening.

22   Fair, warm, SW, muddy. We go to Meeting. Take dinner to Mr. Civill's. I call to Mr. Blodget's.

23   Fair, warm. I make two swing gates, go to river.

24   Fair, SW. I work around, go to river. Attend a Ball to Aaron Houghtaling's. **Mrs. T. Civill has a young daughter.**[308]

25   Fair. I go to the square to Peter VanBuren's. Then I and VanBuren go to Cornelius Baker's. Roads very muddy. **Edward Baker died.**

26   Cloudy, NW. Work around house. Go to river. Mrs. Gerry Springstead, Widow Charlotte & Mary Hotaling here.

27   Fair. Boys thrash. I attend funeral of Edward Baker.

28   Snowy. I take Euphema Blaisdell out riding. Attend Quarterly Meeting. Go to Ira Gregory's to Singing School.

29   Fair, cold. I attend Quarterly Meeting. Call to Mr. Blodget's.

30   Fair. I work around house. Go to J. Tuttle's, then to river. **Attend Boys' debate in the evening at McKee's School**.

31   Snowy afternoon. Mrs. Mary Holmes, Mrs. Mathew's here. I let Smith have my team to draw logs. **Attend School exhibition in evening at McKee's. It goes off very well. House well full.**

February 1860

1   Fair, very cold NW. I go to river, call to Mother's. Take 1 bu. corn and 48 bu. rye to Dean's Mill.

2   Cloudy, cold. TH 11 deg. below 0. I go to river.

3   Fair. Go to Coxsackie, take tea to U.B. Willis. **Attend Lecture of Rev. Mr. Fitch at the Dutch Church. Very good lecture.**

4   Snowy. Work around the house. Go to river. Attend Singing School.

5   Snowy, cloudy. Go to Meeting. Call to Mr. Blodget's.

6   Rainy. Work at Swing Gates. Go to river. Attend debate.

7   Fair grows colder. I and Wife go to Garrett Hotaling's. I call to Doctor VanOrden's.

8   Fair, very pleasant. I go to stone quiry & to river. Quite muddy.

---

[308]   This would have been Sarah Ann Blaisdell Civill.

9   Fair, SW. I and Wife go to A. Hotaling's to Coxsackie Landing, visit, take dinner. Then to Edwin Hubbell's to tea, stay all night. Very heavy NW.

10 Very cold. Visit to Hubbell's all day. Stay all night again.

11 Cold, NW. Come holme, then go to a party to Gary Houghtaling's, have a fine pleasant time.

12 Cold, NW. Go to Meeting. Call to Mother's & to T. Civill's.

13 Fair, SW. Send to mill, get rye flour. Sarell Wood here. Attend Debating School.

14 Fair, NW. I and Mr. Wood go to James W. Jolly's, then to Garry Houghtaling's, then to Johnson & Schoonmaker's.

15 Fair morning. Snow at night. I take Mr. Wood to Schodack. Stop at Mr. Matson's.

16 Snow all day I go to river. Boys clean up oats.

17 Cold, NW. I get horse shod. Call to Willis, go to river.

18 Cold, NW. Go to river. Harness horse, break cutter.

19 Heavy, NW. Go to river. Draw cedar posts. Call to Willis & to Civill's.

20 Fair, SW. Garrett Hotaling, Elizabeth & Caroline here. A.E. Willis & Lady here. Draw cedar posts.

21 Fair, S wind. Martin & Elida VanSlyck here.

22 Rainy day. I go to John Cronk's. **Saw Dr. March operate on Gilbert Cronk's leg**. We all take tea to Mr. Civill's.

23 Fair, SW in morning, change in afternoon. I take Wife & Elida VanSlyck to Dr. VanOrden's, spend the day. I go to river. Call to John Cronk. I send check 50 dollars to H. Sperl.

24 Cloudy. Elida leave. Mr. Civill & Lady & Child here. Miss Brace here, visit. I go to river twice **Old Mrs. Gibbens died**.

25 Fair, NW. I go Under Hill, then to Singing School. Elida come back.

26 Fair, NW. **Attend funeral of Mrs. Gibbens**. Elida VanSlyck here.

27 Fair, SW. I take Wife, Elida VanSlyck, Elizabeth Hotaling to Tunis B. VanSlyck's. Attend Debate in the evening. **Mrs. Thomas Penton died**.

28 Fair warm. I go to river & to vineyard. **Party here tonight. Martin & Elida VanSlyck, Jollys, Kimmeys, Radleys, Tuttles, Nevers, Willis & Lady, Mr. T. McKee here. All stay till one o'clock at night**.

March 1860

1   Very rainy, foggy, muddy. I go to river.

2   Fair, NW. I trim trees. I go to river. **Ice break up & stop here**.

3   Cloudy, warm. I go to river. Sarell Wood here.

4   Fair, NW part of the day. I call to Fredenburgh's office.

5   Fair, NW. **I and Mr. Wood go to A.N. Briggs, make a bargain for lands in Michigan. Attend debate**.

6	Fair. Mr. Wood leave. I take Wife & Mother Hotaling to Coxsackie, visit to Henry VanBergen's. Go hear Mr. Scudder lecture. Stay all night to A.T. VanSlyck's.
7	Stormy, snow, rain. Visit to A.T. VanSlyck. Come holme, very muddy.
8	Fair. I go Under Hill and to river.
9	Fair. I go to Albany. Stop to R. Styles, see A.B. VanBenthuyzen.
10	Fair, cool. Go around Albany. A.B. VanBenthuyzen come holme with me. I go to Gregory's to Singing School.
11	Cloudy, stormy. Draw hay, go to river.
12	Fair, cold. Draw hay, go to river.
13	Fair, NW cold. Mrs. Lasher & Emma Root here.
14	Fair. Draw stone. Make fence to G. Rifflin's all day.
15	Fair. Make barnyard fence Under Hill.
16	Fair. Charles Johnson here. Walk around, call to Civill's.
17	Fair. I and Mr. Johnson walk around, go to Meeting.
18	Fair. Mr. Johnson leave. Wife go to Coxsackie. I lay wall Under Hill. Attend Debating School.
19	Rainy. Work to vineyard. J. Fike help.
20	Snowy, SW cold. I go Under Hill, make fence. J. Fike go along. Mrs. John Rea, Wm. J. Bullis here.
21	Snowy, cold day. Lay around, go to river. Mr. Bullis leave.
22	Fair. Work in quiry all day. I send hay & colt to Walter Millbank's. John Fike help ½ day.
23	Fair, cold. Work at vineyard, J. Fike help. Attend Singing School. Call to Willis.
24	Squally, cold. Call to Willis, go to Meeting.
25	Fair, cold. Work around, go to river. U.B. Willis here.
26	Fair, cold. Go to James W. Jolly's Vendue, buy a hog of Dutchman. Go to river. Mr. Civill & Lady call here.
27	Fair, SW. Go Under Hill. Lay wall all day.
28	Fair. Work to vineyard. Go to river, call to Willis's.
29	Fair, very warm. Lay about holme, am not very well.
31	Fair. Lawrence leave. John Fike commence work. I help Willis draw logs with my team to mill. Ann McCabe here. I go to river. Get check of Johnson $374.34.

April 1860

1	Smoky morning. Go to Meeting, call to Willis's & to Mother's. Go to vineyard. Rainy afternoon.
2	Fair, cold. **I and A.N. Briggs go to Lansingburgh, arrange business with Dr. Leonard.** I stay to R. Styles supper & breakfast.
3	Fair. **I go to Herkimer. Stay all night to H. Sperl's.**

4	Fair. **Stay around mill. Settle with H. Sperl**.
5	Fair. **I come to Little Falls. Stop to John Feeter's. Take cars to Albany. Ride down holme with Mr. Vroman.**
6	Fair, NW. I dig stone all day. **Girl's Association meet here this evening**.
7	Fair. Take hay Under Hill, cut brush, lay wall. Marite come from NY.
8	Cloudy, rainy. Go to Meeting & to vineyard.
9	Cloudy, rainy. Go to river. Make fence. Wife go to Albany. **Gilbert Cronk died**.
10	Cloudy, rainy. Make fence. Go to Town Meeting.
11	Cloudy, rainy. I go to Albany on Pulver affairs. Come holme unwell.
12	Fair. Make fence. Sow grass seed. Visit to Mr. Civill's. Martin VanSlyck here.
13	Fair, cold, NW. Go to river. Draw manure to vineyard. **Albert Hotaling died**.
14	Fair, cold, NW. Dig ditch and stone. Mr. Gregory, Mr. Civill here. **Attend inquest of woman drowned at the dock.**
15	Fair, very cold, SW. Mr. Spraker & Lady [here]. I call to Mr. Blodget's.
16	Fair. I sow oats. Go to river. Cate Van Bergen & Mary Hotaling here visit.
17	Fair. I go Under Hill in forenoon. **Help Irishman remove the drowned woman from cemetery**. Go to vineyard. **Heenan & Tom Sayers prize fight**.[309]
18	Fair, cold. Sow oats. Go to river. **Get 1654 lbs. plaster**.
19	Fair, cold. Sow oats. Go to river. Sow grass seed. Call to Mother's.
20	Fair, still day. I graft & trim trees. Wife come from Albany.
21	Rainy. Work in cellar & to vineyard.
22	Rainy. Go to Meeting. Call to Mother's & to Willis's.
23	Fair. Lay wall, plow. Work on vineyard. Go to river.
24	Fair, cold. I go to John Mull's, get fish. Work to vineyard. Go to river.
25	Snowy day, ground covered. I work to vineyard. Go to river.
26	Cold NW. I work on vineyard. Go to river.
27	Fair. Work at vineyard all day. Call to Willis's.
28	Fair. Plow garden & orchard and vineyard.
29	Fair, SW. Go to Meeting. Take a ride Under Hill.
30	Fair day. Plow, work at vineyard, draw stone.

May 1860

1	Fair. Go Under Hill. Send off two calves. Work on vineyard. Plant potatoes.

---

[309] Tom Sayers was an English bare-knuckle prize fighter. John Heenan was an American bare-knuckle prize fighter, born in Watervliet, NY. The two fought in England on 17 April 1860. The fight went on for 42 rounds before the referee ended it. The controversial fight was finally called a draw.

2	Fair. I settle with G. Tuttle. Go on Hill, make fence. Go to river.
3	Fair. Lay wall. Go Under Hill, make fence.
4	Fair, warm. Go Under Hill. Help Willis. Uncle Andrew VanSlyck here. Eliza Clement, Miss Stanton here.
5	Fair, warm. **Sow plaster**. A. Fancher here, pay rent. Mrs. S. Gould and Child, Miss Parker here.
6	Fair, very warm. Go to Meeting. Call to Mr. Blodget's.
7	Fair, dry NW. Sow plaster. Make fence. Turn out cows, go to Blacksmith.
8	Cloudy, SW. Sow plaster. Go to John Mull's get fish. Make fence.
9	Cloudy, SW. Make fence round house. Call to Wills. Clean house. Go to river.
10	Cloudy, SW. **Work for Willis all day. Raise his barn.**
11	Fair, SW. Work around, go to river & to vineyard. J. Fike sick.
12	Fair. Work around, fix fence, go to river.
13	Fair, warm. Go to Meeting. Call to Civill's, go to vineyard.
14	Fair, SW. Work around house & cellar. Go to river.
15	Fair. **Draw lumber all day from river.** Martin VanSlyck here. Wife & Mary go to Albany.
16	Fair. **Draw lumber all day.**
17	Fair. Draw up lumber. Wife & Mary go to Albany. Martin VanSlyck here.
18	Cloudy, SW. **Pile lumber all day.** Dominie Stillman & Lady here. Walk to vineyard & to cemetery.
19	Rainy & hail. **Handle lumber**. I take Wife to Hollow to Quarterly Meeting. Go to river. S.D. Smith here, settle his rent, pay me off.
20	Fair, cold, NW. I take Wife & Mary to Hollow to Quarterly Meeting. Go to vineyard, call to Mother's & to Willis's.
21	Rainy. **Work at wine & lumber.** Go to river.
22	Cloudy, clears off. I and John Fike dig stone all day.
23	Fair, SW. Go Under Hill, get grape poles. Go to river.
24	Fair. **Work to vineyard & to Schoolhouse**.
25	Fair. **Work to Schoolhouse**. Go Under Hill.
26	Rainy day. **Work to Schoolhouse & to vineyard**. Miss McCabe, Helen Briggs, Cate Johnson, Miss Bushants [here]. Call to Blodget's.
27	Cloudy. Go to Meeting twice. Dominie Gardner's last sermon.
28	Cloudy. Go to John Mull's with Miss Clement & Children. T. Clancy call here.
29	Fair. **Work at Schoolhouse ditch**.
30	Shower at night, SW. **Work at Schoolhouse**. Abram Whitbeck take away two swing gates.
31	Showery afternoon. **Work at Schoolhouse**.

June 1860

1   **I work at Schoolhouse**. Go to Isaac Baker's.

2   Fair. I work around. **Attend the burial of Mr. Lee at cemetery**.

3   Fair, warm. Go to Meeting & to vineyard.

4   Fair, SW. Work in garden. Put out cabbage.

5   Cloudy, SW. Make fence Under Hill.

6   Fair. Work on road. Make fence. Take Wife to Baltimore, then to Uncle Garret's to tea. I go to Wm. Tuttle's.

7   Fair, rainy. Go Under Hill. Work around house. Call to T. Civill's.

8   Fair, NW. Press hay, **sell lumber**.

9   Fair. Go to Albany. John fix fence. Go to river.

10   Fair, cold NW. Go to Meeting. Call to Mother's, go to vineyard.

11   Fair. Make fence Under Hill all day.

12   Fair. Make stone bridge. U.B. Willis & Lady here. I call to Mother's, Willis & Dominie Stillman's.

13   Fair warm day. I work around, plow out potatoes, go to river.

14   Fair. Work around, go to P. Kimmey's, visit to James Jolly's. Martin VanSlyck call here.

15   Hot, shower, hail. **I take a load of lumber to Kimmey's, have it dressed**.[310]

16[311]   Rainy. Press hay, go Under Hill, fix up gate. Ephram VanSlyck & Lady here, visit. I call to Mother's.

17   Fair. I go to Meeting. Take tea to Willis. Go to vineyard, Willis go along.

18   Fair. Press hay. **Help Willis raise his barn on Peneniol Farm**.

19   Showery. **Work to river on Holmestead**. Press hay. Wife & Mary go to New York.

20   Cloudy. Press hay all day. Call to Mother's.

21   Cloudy, rainy. **Work at Holmestead all day**. J.H. Holmes help.

22   Fair. **Work at Holmestead and to cemetery all day. Teachers Association meets at Hall**. Mr. Jerry & Sister here.

23   Fair. Work at cemetery. Draw lumber for Mr. Niles. Hoe Potatoes.

24   Fair. Go to vineyard. Call to Blodget's & to Civill's & Willis's.

25   Fair, warm. I go to Kimmey's twice, get lumber dressed.

26   Fair, warm, SW. Work around, go to river, draw manure. James Huyck & Son here, go to vineyard.

---

[310] Dressed timber is timber that has been run through a planer and jointer to make the surfaces smooth on one or two sides.

[311] The 16 June 1860 U.S. Census list the following residents: Fletcher (42), Sarah Ann (40), Levi (14), Anthony (11), Harry Vanderzee (11), Mary Vanderzee (9), Maria Hotaling (63), Alida Lewis (35) servant.

27 Fair, SW. Lay wall to vineyard all day. Go to river.

28 Fair. Work at wall to vineyard all day. Go to river.

29 Showry. Draw manure. **Attend McKee's School**. Go to river, call to Mother's. Willis here.

30 Fair, warm. Wife & Mary come from NY, bring Elizabeth Silcox along. I work around house, go Under Hill.

July 1860

1   Fair. I go to Meeting twice. Go to vineyard. Mr. T. Civill & Mr. McKee here to tea.

2   Fair, NW, very dry. I draw stone on the Hill. **Fall off the waggon; hurt me very much - came near to breaking my neck**.

3   Showery. I go to vineyard. Not well.

4   Fair. I go to Hollow, then to Harman VanDerzee's to tea. Then to Kimmey's. Wife, Mary, Elizabeth Silcock go along. **Barby Rifflin & Henry Yung get married**.

5   Rainy day. Go to river, get mare shod.

6   Fair. William Wright come to work here this morning. **I work around, draw straw to papermill**.

7   Fair. Lewy Ziegler here. I borrow $80 of him, gave him my note. Henry VanDerzee came here. **Cradle rye, mow in cemetery.** Go to vineyard & to Island.

8   Fair, SW. Go to Meeting. Mr. & Mrs. Thomas here. Lib Hotaling, Mrs. N. Stephens [here]. I go to Mother's.

9   Little shower. **Attend Albany excursion in my grove**. Willis call here. I go to river.

10 Rainy. H. VanDerzee leave. I go Under Hill. **Get my mowing machine & horse rake**. Go to river.

11 Fair, cool, NW. Work to vineyard. Mow. U.B. Willis & Miss Jones here to dinner. I and Wife take tea to Willis.

12 Fair. **Work in hay all day**. Mow with machine. **Richard Lawton died**.

Horse drawn hay rake

13 Fair. Mrs. E. VanOrden, G. Hotaling, Mary & Charlotte Hotaling here. I take them to vineyard. Work in hay.

14 Fair. **Draw hay on propeller**. Work in hay.

15 Fair. Go to Meeting. Call to Mother's. Willis here.

16 Fair. Cradle rye, work in hay.

17 Fair. Miss McCabe here. Work in hay.

18 Fair. Work in hay. U.B. Willis & Dr. Spoor here.

19 Cloudy, hot SW. Work in hay. J.J. Silcock & Lady, Mr. T. Civill & Lady here.

20 Fair, hot. Work in hay. Cate Hotaling here. Willis & Dominie Stillwell call.

21 Rainy day. J.J. Silcock & Family leave. Henry VanDerzee, Dr. VanAntwerp & Marite come. Work around, go to river.

22 Fair, NW. Go to vineyard, to Meeting. Dr. Spoor leave.

23 Clears off. I go Under Hill, draw in hay. Uncle Garrett & Aunt Hannah here.

24 Fair. Work in hay. H. VanDerzee leave here.

25 Fair, NW. I take Wife & Mary to Garry Hotaling's. Work in hay, go in swimming.

26 Work in hay. SW, shower at 5 o'clock. Go to river. Call to Civill's & to Willis's.

27 Fair. Work in hay. Go to Uncle Andrew VanSlyck's. Wife, Doctor VanAntwerp go in morning.

28 Fair. Work in hay. Go to Uncle Andrew VanSlyck's.

29 Rainy. Come holme. Bring folks and Miss McCabe along.

30 Fair. Work in hay. Mow for John Cronk. Mr. A. Civill and Family, Lewis A. Civill, Theophilus Civill & Family here.

31 Hot, SW showery. Work in hay. Doctor & Marite leave.

August 1860

1 Fair, cool. Work in hay all day.

2 Fair, cool. Work in hay all day.

3 Fair, cool. Finish in Big Meadow. Work till after dark.

4 Rainy. Cradle oats. Henry VanDerzee and I go to vineyard and to the river. **Mrs. Willis break her leg**.

5 Fair. All go to Meeting.

6 Fair. Work in hay Under Hill. Lady & child here. Mr. Willis call.

7 Fair, very warm SW. Work in hay Under Hill. T. Civill call.

8 Hot still day. Work in hay Under Hill. **Break my machine**. Shower at 4 o'clock in afternoon.

9 Fair. Work in hay. Go to the Island.

10 Cooler, heavy SW. Work in hay Under Hill.

11 Rainy. Go to Baltimore & to river. Take Wife & Mary.

12 Foggy. Go to Meeting twice. Go to vineyard. Mrs. Jemima Hotaling here.

13 Rainy, thunder & lightning.

14 Rainy, clears off in evening. Mrs. Thurston here.

15 Fair. Go to Albany. Take Harry along.

16 Fair. Work in hay. Mr. T. Civill & Family here. Mrs. J. Witbeck and another Lady here. Go to vineyard. **Mr. Willis's Daughter Sarah died**.

17 Fair. **Attend Funeral of Willis's child**. Finish hay & oats.

18 Fair morning, shower in afternoon. Henry VanDerzee come. He and myself go to Coxsackie to U.B. Willis's, then go to Mr. Fitch's. See his vineyard, drink brandy.

19 Fair warm. Go to vineyard & to Meeting.

20 SW, Cloudy. I take Anthony, go to Greenville. Stay all night to Andrew Fancher's.

21 Rainy, SW. Go to Greenville village, swear off my tax. Come back to James Trego's to Baltimore, take tea then holme.

22 Fair. **Work at Schoolhouse**. Martin VanBergen & Lady, Mrs. Persons here, and their children.

23 Cloudy, rainy. **Work at schoolhouse**. U.B. Willis & Mrs. Bevy here.

24 Rainy. Dig blind drains. Go horseback riding with Mary Under Hill.

25 Showery. Go to river. Oil harness; work around. Garrett VanAntwerp here.

26 Rainy. Go to Meeting. Newton Briggs, Garry VanAntwerp & self go to vineyard.

27 Rainy. Dig ditch. Attend cemetery meeting. Call to Mother's.

28 Fair. Dig blind drain. Go with Wm. Bagley Under Hill.

29 Fair. Work at blind drain. Visit to Acton Civill's in evening.

30 Fair. Our folks go on excursion. Rev. P. Phelps Sister & Son here. **I lock up Mother's papers**.

31 Fair, little showery. Work at ditch. **Bring Mother's trunk holme. I found her bureau drawer burst open**. A. Borkman died.

September 1860

1 Fair. I have a load of lumber come. Draw lumber all day.

2 Fair. **Attend funeral of A. Borkman**. Walk around.

3 Fair. Finish draw up lumber. Rev. Mr. Brace & Emma Brace, Mr. Civill & Family here. We go to vineyard.

4 Fair. Work at lumber. Make fence to G. Rifflin's. Boys go to show. Uncle Garry's girls call. P. Conin (sp) gets lumber.

5 Fair, cloudy, SW. Work at lumber. Mr. Switzer here. **Old Mrs. Bronk died. Sam Teneyck died, John Teal's child died**.

6 Rainy. **Mother died.**[312] I take team go to Greenville. Start at five o'clock PM; get to Fancher's, stay until 3 o'clock am.

7 Fair. **Take Fancher's team. I & Wm. Fancher go to Durham Village after Rev. Mr. Matthews to preach Mother's funeral sermon. He was from holme – disappointed. Call on Mrs. Moore then come back holme.** Cate Hotaling here. I go to river.

8 Very heavy rain. I and Willis go to Baltimore and around the house & to Mother's.

9 Rainy morning clears off very pleasant. **Attend Mother's funeral. It was very large & interesting. Rev. Mr. Stillman preach. Congregation all follow to the grave.**

---

312 Mary Farr Johnstone Blaisdell was born in Coeymans about 1784. We believe that her mother, also Mary, was taken in by the Cronk family before Mary was born. Her father, who had sailed back to his home in Scotland, was apparently lost at sea and never returned. She was Levi Blaisdell's second wife whom she married after Levi's first wife, Arientje VerPlank, died.

10 Fair. Put grapes on the boat. Theophilus and Anthony Civill call. H. VanDerzee leave. Work at ditch.

11 Fair SW. Cate VanBergen, Mary Hotaling, Mr. Brace & Lady, Mr. & Mrs. Civill visit here. I pile up lumber.

12 Rain blow hard all day from NW. **I and Wife go to Theophilus Civill's. Rev. Mr. Stillman christen their child Sarah Ann Blaisdell**.

13 Fair. Mrs. Bedell & child leave. Dig ditch, pick apples. I meet Willis & Wesley at Mother's house. Martin & Elida VanSlyck here.

14 Fair. Mr. J. Jack & Lady, Mrs. John Rea here. Go to the vineyard, go to river. **See J. Lawton on will business**.

15 Fair. Pile lumber. Fix roofs, go to river. John go Under Hill pick apples.

16 Fair. Go to Meeting. Anthony is sick. Go to vineyard with Mr. Civill and Mr. Reynolds & son. Mrs. Ostrander & Hester Hotaling call here. I call to Mr. Blodget's.

17 Rainy. Send off grapes, work around the house.

18 Fair. Pick plums. Mr. Civill & Lady & Child, Miss Brace & Charley here, spend the day. **My Wine Press come**.

19 Rain. Send off grapes. Work around. Willis & Dominie Stillman here, we go to vineyard.

20 Rainy. Go to Albany, get casks, go to the Fair. Come holme with H. Smith, get caught in the rain.

21 Fair. Wife go to Albany. I work at grapes.

22 Fair SW. H. VanDerzee come. I work at wine. Elizabeth Hotaling & Elizabeth Stephens here. I go to the river.

23 Fair. Go to Meeting. Go to vineyard, walk about.

24 Fair, SW. Go to Leonard Witbeck's, get cider press. Break waggon. Press grapes. Attend circus in evening.

25 Rainy. Fix up wine. Handle lumber, go to river. Mrs. Clement call.

26 Fair NW. Work at lumber. Go to Greenville, stop to A. Fancher's. H. VanDerzee leave.

27 Fair. Go to Durham. Take dinner to Mrs. More's. Bring Mrs. More holme with me. Mrs. L. Gedney, Mrs. Josiah Sherman, Mrs. & Mr. Civill here, visit.

28 Fair NW. **Go to Albany with Dominie Selick and Mrs. More. Prove Mother's will**. Uncle Andrew VanSlyck here.

29 Fair, frosty north wind. I go to vineyard with Uncle Andrew. Then I take Mrs. More to Durham. Then I come back to A. Fancher's, stay all night. **Drive 40 miles in a half day with mare Topsy**.

30 Fair. Come holme. Go to vineyard, call to Willis.

October 1860

1 Heavy frost, SW. Foggy morning rain all day. **Grapes froze bad**. Go to vineyard. See Johnson, he take up my note at National Bank at Albany.

2	Cloudy rainy. Press hay. Harman VanDerzee & Lady & Henry VanDerzee here. We go to cemetery & to vineyard.
3	Fair. Make fence, fix wine press. H. VanDerzee leave. Miss Bailey call.
4	Rainy. **Take inventory of Mother's things**. Dig potatoes.
5	Rainy morning. Clears off. Press hay, go to river, call to Civill's.
6	Fair. I take Wife & Mary, go to Albany & Troy. Do business with Marcus Ball. Bring my horse Charley holme with me. He comes from H. Sperl.
7	Fair warm heavy frost. Go to Meeting.
8	Rainy. **J.J. Colvin burned by lightening**. I draw hay on propeller.
9	Fair cold. Work at potatoes, go to river.
10	SW. Work at grapes, go to river.
11	SW rainy in evening. I and Wife go to Coxsackie to U.B. Willis. I call on Mr. Fitch have a pleasant time.
12	Fair. Work at wine, go to river.
13	Fair NW. Press hay. Finish up wine. Rosy Church here.
14	Cloudy cold SW. Go to Meeting. Go Under Hill to Mrs. Wilson. I call to William Winne's.
15	Cloudy. Draw hay, lumber. Pick apples.
16	Fair. I get in my potatoes & apples. **Prince of Wales pass here**.[313]
17	Cloudy rainy at night. Mr. Fitch & U.B. Willis [here]. There is **torch light procession out this evening**.[314] I press out apples & pick apples.
18	Fine day. I work at cider & wine. **Go with Little Giant Club to Baltimore**.[315] Martin & Elida VanSlyck here. Attend Installation of Rev. Mr. Collier.
19	Fine smoky day. Work at wine. Miss Teng here to tea.
20	Cloudy. Divide up things to Mother's house, bring them holme. Go to river.
21	Rainy day. Go to Meeting. Call to Civill's.
22	Cloudy rainy. Split hay slats. Get out wire.
23	Fine day. Go to river. Settle with Elida Lewis, pay her off.

91 Gun HMS-Hero

---

[313] Edward, Prince of Wales, the eldest son of Queen Victoria and Prince Albert was only 19 when he was sent on a goodwill mission in the Fall of 1860 to Canada and the U.S. He was the first member of the British Royal Family ever to visit North America. He went on to become King Edward VII after the death of his mother Queen Victoria.

[314] The torchlight parades of 1860 were presidential demonstrations in favor of Abraham Lincoln, the Republican candidate for president.

[315] The Little Giant Club supported Stephen Douglas who was one of the Democratic Party nominees for president in the 1860 election, which was won by the Republican Abraham Lincoln. Douglas believed states should be allowed to determine whether to permit slavery within its borders.

24   Fine day. Split slats. Caroline & Lib Hotaling here. **I go with torch light procession to Catskill. About 1200 torch light and 130 horsemen go with Steamer Rip VanWinkle. Have a fine time.**

25   Fair day. Lay wall, dig ditch, go to river. L. Hotaling help.

26   Fair. I let John Fike have team. He go to Albany. Martin VanSlyck here. I fix up apples, stay about house.

27   Fair. Plow; fix around. Marite come here from New York.

28   Fair. I go to vineyard, go to Meeting. Call to Mr. Blodget's.

29   Fair. Draw hay. Fix around. Wife, Marite & Levi go to Coxsackie.

30   Wife & Marite come holme. Cloudy & rainy. Plow; go to river.

31   Rainy. Plow; press hay. **Go to Hollow to political meeting**.

November 1860

1   Rainy. Press hay all day. Go to river in evening.

2   Fair warm day. Press hay. Draw leaves & gravel. **Wide Awake Meeting here this evening.**[316]

3   Cloudy SW. Work around, plow. I go Under Hill and to river. Elizabeth Hotaling and two other ladies call.

4   Fair. Go to vineyard & to Meeting. Call to Willis & to Civill's. Cate VanBergen & Mary Hotaling here.

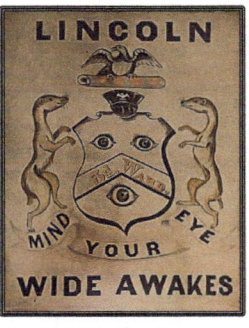

Wide Awake Banner

5   Fair. Draw hay on boat. Go to river.

6   Rainy day. **Attend election**.

7   Fair NW. I go to Albany. John plow. Wife & Levi go to Coxsackie.

8   Fair. Plow. Put up Minick's cows. Go to river.

9   Fair. Make fence, plow, go to river.

10   Rainy day. J.D. Verplank here. Press hay.

11   Rainy. Go to Meeting, call to Willis. Martin VanSlyck here.

12   Cloudy. Press & draw hay. Sell my Bill horse to Wm. Fancher. He takes him holme with him.

13   Cloudy. Draw hay. Richard Wilson & Lady here. Martin VanSlyck & Mary Hotaling here.

14   Fair. **Attend wedding of Martin VanSlyck & Mary Hotaling. Ben Keller & Helen Lawton get married today**.

15   Fair NW. Make fence, plow. Mr. Civill's folks here.

---

316 Abraham Lincoln spoke in Hartford, CT in March 1860 opposing the spread of slavery and advocating for the right of workers to strike. Five store clerks, who had started a Republican group called the Wide Awakes, decided to join a parade for Lincoln, who delighted in the torchlight escort provided for him after the speech back to his hotel. Over the ensuing weeks, the Lincoln campaign made plans to develop Wide Awakes throughout the country and to use them to spearhead large voter registration drives, knowing that new voters and young voters tend to embrace new and young parties.

16	Fair. **Attend school examination**. Plow; make fence.
17	Cloudy. Make fence. Henry VanDerzee come. I go to river. **Wide Awake meeting tonight**.
18	Cloudy rainy. I go Under Hill. Call to Willis. A. Rogers preach today.
19	Fair SW. Draw hay, split slats, make fence.
20	Fair, cold NW. Make fence. H. VanDerzee leave. Two Black women come here to work.
21	Fair cold. Plow take in cabbage, draw leaves.
22	Fair. Draw manure, work to vineyard.
23	Rain & snow all day. Press hay, go to river.
24	NW, fair, very cold. Freeze all day. Press hay.
25	Fair NW, very cold. Go to Meeting. Get two grape vines sent by William Ward. Call to Willis. Go to vineyard, freeze.
26	Cold SW. Draw hay. Call on B. Keller, treated with cake & wine.
27	Rainy. Go Under Hill, get slat timber. Send Bagley's cow to New York.
28	Cold NW. Press hay, go to river, get oysters.
29	Fair. Draw wood from Mother's house. Draw leaves. **Attend Thanksgiving here. Mr. Willis & Lady, Mr. Stillman & Lady, Mr. Civill & Lady here.** I call to Willis's.
30	Rainy. Go Under Hill, draw leaves. Wife goes to Albany.

December 1860

1	Cold cloudy NW. Press hay. Wife comes holme from Albany.
2	Cold cloudy NW. Go to Meeting. Mr. McKee call here.
3	Cloudy. Draw hay, go to river. A. Witbeck here, pay me 75 dollars. **Mr. Hill & Ann Jane Schoonmaker get married**.
4	Snowy cold. **Draw up coal**. Go to river.
5	Cold, 6 inches snow. Work around house. Get horses shod. Go to river.
6	Fair cold. Get horses shod. Mrs. Civill here. Go to mill. Go to river.
7	Fair cool. Set glass, work around house. Go to river.
8	Fair. Work around house. Fix stable. Mrs. E. VanOrden, Mrs. Mosher, Mrs. Hotaling call. I and Wesley call to Civill's.
9	Fair. Go to Meeting Call to Mr. Blodget's.
10	Snow & rain. Work around the house. Go to river. S. Tuttle here.
11	Fair, cold NW. Wife & Children go to Albany. Work around house.
12	Fair cold. Aunt Sarah Ann, Mrs. VanOrden, Ed VanOrden & Lady, Widow Charlotte here. I draw clay from barnyard.
13	Very cold. Work in barnyard. Mr. Civill call. I go to river. Pay Doct. Fredenburgh $70 interest money. Aunt Sarah Ann VanBergen here.
14	Very cold NW. Work in barnyard. Aunt Sarah Ann here. I go to river.

15   Fair very cold. Finish draw dirt in barnyard. Wm. Fancher bring me two cows for 50 dollars. James Trego & Elizabeth call here.

16   Fair very cold. Call to Willis's & to Blodget's. Aunt Sarah Ann leave here.

17   Fair. Go to river, chop wood. Ann McCabe here.

18   Fair very cold. Go to river. Draw wood & brush.

19   I make a set of Whippletrees.

20   Rainy. Kill hogs & beef.

21   Fair warm. Cut up hogs & beef. Draw brush, go to river. Mr. Civill call.

22   Stormy. Salt my pork. H. VanDerzee come. Clears off cold.

23   Fair very cold. Go to Meeting. Call to Willis. Civill call here.

24   Fair very cold. Go to Albany, take Civill & Wife. Bring Miss turner back with us. **Attend Festival in evening. Draw a box**.[317]

25   Cold. Work around. Go to river.

26   Cold cloud. Work about house, cut wood.

27   Cloudy cold NW. I call to Willis, to N. Niles. B. Teneyck pay my interest money. Dominie Stillman here to dinner. Donation to Mr. Collier this evening.

28   Cloudy cold NW. Work at timber. Go to river. Take tea and spend the evening to Mr. Civill's. His coat gets stolen.

29   Cloudy cold. Work at shed. Miss Turner and Mr. Lansing here, make a call.

30   Cloudy snowy. Go to Meeting. Call to Blodgett's. Caroline Hotaling here.

31   Very cold NS. Work at shed, go to river.

January 1861

1   Fair pleasant. Spend the day at Egbert Stanton's. Go to P. Kimmey's. Attend the Association.

2   Fair. Work at lumber. A.B. Hotaling & Lady here. We go to vineyard. Elizabeth & Caroline Hotaling & Elida VanSlyck here.

3   Snow & blow all day. Work at the house. I go to river. Attend concert in Dutch Church in evening.

4   Snowy. Cap Schoonmaker & Lady here, spend the day. Mary VanSlyck call here. I go to papermill.

5   Fair. Pile lumber. Spend the day to Charlotte Hotaling's. Go to river.

6   Fair. Go to Church. Call to Civill's. Ed VanOrden & Lady, Martin VanSlyck & Lady H. VanBergen & Lady, we all take a ride to Baltimore. **Call to Trego's, his child died**.

7   Rainy wet. H.C. VanBergen Lady & Boy, Sarah, Cate VanBergen, Elida VanSlyck, Martin VanSlyck & Lady, Charlotte Hotaling here. I work at shed, draw wood.

---

[317] This is Fletcher's first mention of a Christmas Eve celebration.

8	Fair cold NW. I work around barn. Mary VanSlyck, Mrs. Henry VanBergen & Boy, Cate VanBergen here.
9	Cloudy cold. I go to Albany with Henry. Get feed, **subscribe for semi-weekly Atlas & Argus.**[318] **Get up club for 5 copies**.
10	Snowy. Draw wood, attend Plank Road meeting. Have party here: Mr. McKee. Mr. Harris, Miss Harris, Mrs. S. Harris, Mrs. E. Stanton, Miss Clement, Mrs. Clement, Miss Cranston, Mr. McDean here. **Barent Mull died.**
11	Fair NW, very cold. I take Mother Hotaling to Flat Bush. Go to Greenville, stay all night to A. Fancher's.
12	Fair, very cold. I stop to J.J. Williamson's, get my rents, then come holme. John Fike's Wife has a young son. He is holme all day.
13	Fair, very cold. **TH 14 degrees below zero at 8 o'clock AM and it is 21 deg below 0 at J.B. Shear's**. I go to Meeting, call to Mr. Civill's.
14	Cold NW. Attend PR meeting. Call to L. Blodget's, pay my tax.
15	Cloudy. **I work to river on Holmestead**. Attend Association to A.J. Take out a load.
16	Rain all day. Go to river. Get out pickets.
17	Little misty. I take Wife, J. Jack & Lady, go to Widow Andrew Witbeck's, spend the day. Draw wood. **Old Mrs. Jolly died**. My Boys draw wood.
18	Little snow. Work around, go to river. **Fix Holmestead**.
19	Fair, pleasant. Work at stable. Attend Lecture in Hall.
21	Fair. Go to Meeting. **I take J. Jack & Lady, attend funeral of Mrs. Jolly**. Call to Willis & to Mr. Civill's.
22	Fair, cold. **Commence threshing**. L. Hotaling help.
23	Fair, cold NW. **Copy journal**. Go to river & to papermill.
24	Fair, cold. I go to river. Pay Briggs $400 & my Island tax.
25	Snow all day. Clean up oats, go to river.
26	Fair. Get out pickets. Take a ride to Mr. Robb's, then around to Baltimore. Wife go along.
27	Fair. Go to Wm. McCullock's. Spend afternoon & eve with Willis & Mr. Jack. Levi take black girl Betsy to Coxsackie, bring Mother Hotaling holme.
28	Fair. Work at pickets, thresh, go to river.
29	Fair. I take Willis & Lady, J. Jack & Lady go to John Callanan's, spend the day. Attend the Association to Henry Calanan's. Stormy coming holme.
30	Fair. Baltis VanSlyck & Lady here, spend the day. I get out pickets.
31	Fair. I take Wife to George Wolf's, spend the day. **Attend show of Coeymans Boys in evening**. Thresh rye.

---

[318] Newspaper published in Albany with articles about city, county and state.

February 1861

1   Fair. Work around. Go to Schodack. Call to Mr. Matson's. Bring H. VanDerzee holme **Attend McKee's School Exhibition; went off well, large audience**.

2   Rainy thawy. Work around house. Peter VanBuren here, pay rent. P. Hubbell here. McKee call in evening.

3   Fair, cold. Attend Quarterly Meeting. Stay about house.

4   Fair, cold. Work about house. Go to river, draw wood.

5   Cloudy, SW. Draw sand. I take H. VanDerzee, go Under Hill, so around to Stile Barrack, so holme. Get out pickets, go to river.

6   Fair. Get out pickets, draw sand, spend the evening to Willis's. J. Reynolds & Lady, T. Civill & Lady, Ann Brace there.

7   Snowy morning. Clears off very cold with snow & N wind. I go to river, draw sand, get out pickets

8   Very cold, NW. I take H. VanDerzee, he take cars for N. York. Thermometer 20 deg below 0. **Ira Carhart and Miss White get married last evening**.

9   Fair, cold. TH 10 deg. below 0. Draw sand. Willis call. I and Wife spend the evening to Capt. Colvin's.

10 Fair, warm SW. Go to Meeting. Call to Willis & Charlotte Hotaling's. **Rachel Gregory's Boy died.**

11 Cloud. Draw sand & manure. **Rev. Mr. Fitch here. Attend his lecture in ME Church in evening on Geology.**[319]

12 Fair warm. Get out pickets. I take Wife, J. Jack & Lady & Eliza Clement to James Jolly's to Association. Have a good time.

13 Fair. **Water is very high. Ice broke up down to VanWie's Point**. Andrew A. Hotaling, Henry Hotaling, Mr. Willis & Lady, Mr. Civill & Lady, Miss Brace here. I get out pickets, go to river.

14 Fair. **Great freshet in Albany**.[320] Get out pickets. Go to river. Leave note of R.A. Alger with N.H. Johnson to collect. Attend Lecture of Mr. Fitch at ME Church.

15 Stormy SW. Get out pickets all day. Go to river in evening.

16 Very warm SW. Get out pickets. Attend concert. Levi take Jane Harrison to Coxsackie.

---

[319] The ME (Methodist Episcopal) Church had its beginnings in England and was brought to the colonies by its founder, John Wesley. Methodism emerged as an evangelical revival movement within the Church of England that stressed the necessity of being born again and the possibility of attaining Christian perfection. Early Methodism was anti-elitist and anti-slavery.

[320] On the evening of 13 Feb 1861, the New York Times reported that a thaw in the tributaries of the Hudson River, including the Mohawk, sent tons of fast-moving ice down the river where it eventually collided with solid ice. The floating mass of huge ice chunks created havoc for the port city of Albany. Docks were destroyed causing devastation to canal boats, barges and steamboats. Bridges lifted from their moorings and either sank or floated away. The high water and ice made travel impossible, and roads and railroads were forced to close.

17	Fair cold. Stay in house. Call to Blodget's. Martin VanSlyck & Lady here, call.
18	Fair. Wife, Levi & Jane come holme. I and John Fike build bridge in Big Meadow. Go to river. Sarah Cranston call.
19	Fair. Draw hay. L. Hotaling help. I work at pickets, go to river. Attend Lecture of Mr. Fitch at ME Church. **William Bushants died**.
20	Snowy. Draw hay ½ day. L. Hotaling help. Willis call. I go to river.
21	Snowy, squally SW. I and Wife go to Martin VanBergen's. John & Stephen Hotaling draw hay.
22	Cold NW. Draw hay. We go to Uncle Andrew VanSlyck's, then come holme.
23	Cold, rain SW. Some sun. I go to river. Call to J. Lawton's. Get G. Bullman's money. Call to Johnson's office, get a check for H. Sperl. Leave P. Road dividend to Briggs $56.62. Draw hay, L. Hotaling help.
24	Fair, cold SW. Go to Meeting. Call to Willis's. Willis call here. **Dr. Ben call here, Levi is sick with measles**.
25	Fair, cold SW. Draw hay. L. Hotaling help. I fix barn, go to river, get out pickets.
26	Fair, S wind. Draw hay. Go to river. Willis & Barent Teneyck here.
27	Fair SW. Get out pickets. Draw 5 loads manure from Minick's. Go to river. Mr. P.R. Casy call here.
28	Fair, very warm. Go to Willis's woods. Get 11 buts for grape poles. Go to river, get out slats. **Attend School Meeting**.

March 1861

1	Heavy NW, fair. I go to river. Take tea, spend evening to Mrs. Clement's.
2	Cloudy. S. Wivanu work to vineyard. Make fence. **Ice broke up in river last night**. I go to river. John cut wood.
3	Very warm wind every way. Mr. T. Civill & Lady here. I go to Meeting and to cemetery.
4	Fair. Work at stone wall. L. Hotaling help get out slats. I go to river. **Abraham Lincoln inaugurated**.[321]
5	Fair, cold NW. I take Ann Brace to Albany to cars. Roads bad. Mr. Sweet come holme with me.
6	Fair, cold. Draw stone, go to river, work at gates.
7	Fair, very cold. TH at 0 at holme & to river.
8	Very cold SW. Draw stone, go to river twice.
9	Rain & snow, wind changes. I work in carriage house, go to river.
10	Cold NW. Icy. I go to river. Mr. Willis & Lady, Mrs. Stanton, Doctor B.B. Fredenburgh call.
11	Fair, cold NW. Draw stone. I work in shop, go to river.

---

[321] Abraham Lincoln was the 16th president. He led the nation through the Civil War. Historians consistently rank Lincoln as one of our best presidents. He was assassinated in April 1865 at the beginning of his second term.

12	Fair, cold. Work in shop, go to river.
13	Rainy, SW. Work in shop. Clears off, go to river.
14	Snowy, cloudy. Draw stone.
15	Fair, cold NW, 4 in. snow. Cut wood, go to river.
16	Fair, NW pleasant. I work in shop. **Negro Johnson Dominie here**. I go to river.
17	Fair, very cold. I go to Meeting. Call to Blodgett's.
18	Fair, very cold. TH 3 deg. above 0. Go to river. John cut wood.
19	Cloudy morning, very cold. I work around, go to river.
20	Fair, very cold. I go to vineyard & to cemetery. Willis go along.
21	Snow & blow all day hard. I work in shop. Cold.
22	Fair. About 20 inches of snow. I work in shop. Go to river.
23	Fair SW. I go to Phineas VanDerpool's. Go to river. I buy calf to Phineas VanDerpool's for $6.25.
24	Fair, cold NW. I go to Meeting. Call to Willis's. Martin VanSlyck here in evening.
25	Fair, muddy. I work in shop. Go to mill & to river.
26	Cloudy, rainy SW. Very muddy. I and John go Under Hill take feed for cows. Work around, go to river.
27	Rainy day. I work around house. Go to river. Call to Civill's, pay interest, **settle Schoolhouse rent**.
28	Fair NW. Work at stone. Go to river. Mr. Civill and Charlotte Stilwell call.
29	Fair. Draw stone. Attend Mrs. Bushants' Vendue.
30	Cloudy SW. I go to P. Row's Vendue. Buy 1 skiss of bees and a cow for G. Rifflin $26. Gave note due Nov. 30. **Then go to Hollow to Nomination.** Stop to Mr. Hardin's. Lib Hotaling & Theophilus and Acton Civill call.

April 1861

1	Cloudy, SW snowy. I work in shop. Send lumber Under Hill. John move. Attend District Road meeting.
2	Snow all day about 1 foot deep. I fix house for Gregory.
3	Cloudy & fair. I press hay, go to river.
4	Fair. I go to Albany, attend to Pulver business. Get $121.29 pay it to Wife. Henry VanDerzee come.
5	Fair. **Draw 42 bales hay on boat**. Go to river after.
6	Fair, pleasant. **Press 42 bales hay**.
7	Fair, pleasant, warm. Go to vineyard. Martin & Mary VanSlyck here.
8	Fine day. Draw hay, work around, go to river.

9	Fine day. H. VanDerzee leave. I go to Town Meeting. John Rodgers come here. Visit to Dominie Stillman's. David A. Witbeck & J.W. Jolly run for Supervisor.
10	Fair, warm. **Tear down my shop, draw it holme. Mr. Enos & Lib Hotaling married. Daniel Carhart died.**
11	Fair, warm. Draw manure. Fix for hog pen. Visit to A.W. Willis.
12	Fair SW. Mrs. Aaron Houghtaling, Widow Houghtaling, Betsey VerPlanck, Mrs. Spraker, Mrs. Johnson, Mary Serls, Miss Johnson, Mrs. A.E. Willis, Mrs. T. Civill here visit. I work at hog pen. **War commence to South.**[322]
13	Rainy day. Go to river, press hay.
14	Fair, NW. I go to Meeting. Mr. Civill call. I go to vineyard.
15	Cloudy, NW. Work at hog pen. Draw hay, go to river.
16	Snow all day. Press hay, go to river.
17	Snow all day. Press hay, go to river. About 3 in. snow.
18	Fair SW. Snow & mud. I fix house to Gregory's. Go to river.
19	Cloudy NW. Work at hog pen. John Fike bring his cow here. I work to Gregory's.
20	Fair NW. Work at hog pen. Go to river. Fix to Gregory's.
21	Fair NW. Go to Meeting & to Civill's & to Blodgett's.
22	Fair. Work at hog pen. Draw stone.
23	Fair, NW very warm. Go Under Hill. **Attend Union meeting or demonstration to Acton Civill's.** We have lots of Coeymans Company: Mrs. Briggs, Mrs. Charlotte Hotaling, Mrs. VanDerzee, Mrs. Harris, Mrs. Ven Keller, Mrs. J. Holmes, Eliza Clement, Mrs. Colvin and some more.
24	Fair morning. Go Under Hill, make fence. Get caught in a very heavy rain. **Attend a Public meeting in Hall. Mr. Smith & Mr. Shaver speak. Great enthusiasm of the war at the south.**
25	Fair, cool NW. Work Under Hill. J. Maxwell help.
26	Fair NW. Harness colts; get them shod. Go to Uncle Andrew's, get grape vines. John draws stone.
27	Fair. Graft trees. Take pigs Under Hill and calves. Go to river.
28	Rain all the afternoon. Attend Meeting. Mr. Elis preach. I call to L. Blodget's.
29	Fair NW. Lay wall all day. I go to river.
30	Rainy afternoon. Lay wall. Dominie Stillwell & Lady, Dominie Ellis, A.E. Willis here. I go to river.

---

[322] The Civil War began on this date when Confederate artillery fired on Fort Sumter in Charleston, SC. President Lincoln issued a proclamation 3 days later calling for 75,000 militiamen. The war between the states lasted 4 years.

May 1861

1	Rainy. Make fence. **Have a tooth drawn; have a hard time**.
2	Fair, very cold, freeze hard. I draw off wine, make fence, go to river.
3	Fair. Go to river, make fence.
4	Fair, cold NW. Make fence.
5	Fair, SW. Go to Meeting. Call to Willis & Blodget's. Mr. Civill call.
6	Rainy, very wet. Sort potatoes, go to river.
7	Fair, NW. Call to Josiah Sherman's, make fence.
8	Fair, shower. Lay wall. **Attend concert in evening, have a rich treat.**
9	Fair NW. Go Under Hill. Doctor & Marite come. **Raise a Union Flag to river.**
10	Fair. I fix old Holmestead, Plow. **Doct. VanAntwerp shot off his finger**.
11	Rainy day. Work around. Go to river. Settle with P. Long.
13	Rainy. I work at hog pen, go to river.
14	Rainy. Work around. Send off calves. Mrs. Hotaling call.
15	Fair day. Lay wall, draw manure. A. Fancher here, go to vineyard.
16	Fair, cold. I take Wife, Mary, Levi & Anthony - go to Albany. Roads bad.
17	Cold hard NW. Work in field, plow.
18	Cold NW. Plow, draw manure, go to river.
19	Fair NW. Go to church. Call to Civill's.
20	Cloudy NW. Plow & harrow.
21	Heavy shower. Draw manure. Plot. Go to Wm. McCullock's, get seed wheat. Elib & Garry Hotaling & Mary Bronk here.
22	Fair, NW. Draw manure all day.
23	Fair. Draw manure. Get ½ ton plaster.
24	Fair, heavy SW. Sow wheat. All hands visit to Garry Hotaling's. Willis & Harriet go along.
25	Showery, warm. Make fence, go to river.
26	Fair. Go to Meeting. Mr. Civill & Lady, McKee, Dr. Fredenburgh, we go to vineyard.
27	Rainy, showery. Boys make fence Under Hill. Folks go to Albany. I am around holme.
28	Rainy, cold NW. Doct & Marite leave. John cultivate corn ground. I and John Rodgers make fence. Take colts Under Hill to pasture.
29	Rainy. I take boys, go Under Hill, fix around there.
30	Fair NW. Make picket fence. Furrow out corn lot.
31	Fair. Furrow out corn lot. Draw manure. Ira Gregory help draw manure, plant corn. Work hard.

June 1861

1. Fair, warm SW. Go to Meeting & to vineyard. Call to Civill's. Elida VanSlyck here.
3. Rainy. Go to mill, make fence. Elida VanSlyck leave.
4. Cloudy. Plant corn. John work on road. I. Gregory help.
5. Fair. Work at vineyard ½ day. Set out cabbage. Wife go to Albany.
6. Rainy. I go to river. Fix up corn. Plow.
7. Fair. Lay wall; make fence. **Attend school concert at the Methodist Church - it went off well.** Wife come from Albany.
8. Cloudy. Make fence all day.
9. Very warm. Go to Meeting. Call to Civill's & to Blodget's. Go to vineyard.
11. Fair SW. Wife go with Mr. Civill & Lady to Syracuse. I make picket fence all day. John plow. Sarah Rea call.
12. Fair SW. Make picket fence; plow. Mrs. Ostrander here.
13. Fair. Draw 34 loads of stone & gravel on Road District.
14. Fair. Draw stone & gravel. A. VanSlyck here, we go to vineyard. Mother H. go holme with Uncle Andrew.
15. Fair, hot. Work at hog pen. Go to river. Widow Hotaling & daughter Charlotte here. Mother Hotaling come holme.
16. Fair, NW. I take Mrs. Gregory to Hollow to Quarterly Meeting. Go to vineyard.
17. Fair. Draw manure. Plow for I. Gregory. Go to vineyard.
18. Fair. Furrow out potatoes. Draw manure, go to river.
19. Shower last evening. Fair morning. Work at fence, draw manure.
21. Cloudy SW. Cut brush, go to river.
22. Fair NW. **I go to Herkimer. Stay to H. Sperl's all night. Call to John Feeter's**.
23. Rainy SW. **Go around the place. Call to Belcher's, take tea. Call to Davy Bly's. Settle with H. Sperl, stay with him all night**.
24. Fair NW. Come holme. Go to vineyard.
25. Fair. Work at vineyard. **Attempt to go to New York - get overboard. Come back holme**. Boys work in corn.
26. Little shower. Wife come holme. Hoe corn. Go to river.
27. Fair. I go to P. Kimmey with a load of boards. Get 28 dressed, come holme with them. Cate & Mrs. H.C. VanBergen, Elida VanSlyck here. I draw ground in lot of H. VanDerzee & Dr. VanAntwerp.
28. Fair NW. Make fence. Take boys to Ephram VanSlyck's. Take a ride over rocks to hunt up bull, then holme. **Attend Teachers Association**. Mr. Jolly, Mr. Johnson, Miss Slingerland, and another lady here.

29 Fair. Sow buckwheat. Get horses shod. Go Under Hill. Miss Slingerland, Miss Simmons, Mrs. Tuttle, Miss Bennet here.

30 Fair, SW. Little shower. I go to vineyard. Call to Civill's. Dr. B.B. Fredenburgh call here.

July 1861

1 Cloudy, little showery. I take a ride Under Hill.

2 Rainy. **I go to New York with Barge, T.C. Durant.**

3 Fair. **Arrive at New York. Stay to A. VanAntwerp's.**

4 Fair. **I go with Dr. & Marite to Long Branch. Have a fine time, go with boat. Then come back by railroad through Jersey. Some fine country; some very poor.**[323] **Come Back, stay with J.J. Silcock all night. Go to a fire.**

Long Branch Beach

5 Fair, hot. **Buy a carriage in Brooklyn.**

6 Fair. **Get carriage, start for holme.**

7 Fair. Arrive at holme. Go to vineyard.

8 Fair. Little shower. John sick. I go Under Hill. **I draw 15 bales hay on barge.** Go in swimming.

9 Little shower, very warm. I plow to vineyard. Go to Ephraim VanSlyck's, get bull.

10 Fair SW, very warm. Work in corn. Go to river. Call to Widow Hotaling's. See Mr. Enos & Lib. Call to A. Civill's & to T. Civill's, to Willis's & Ann Civill's. Rain in eve.

11 Fair. I take Wife, Mary & Anthony, go to Albany. **My horse fall down in ditch.** Boys work at corn.

12 Fair. I go Under Hill. **Get Rake and Mowing Machine.** Hoe corn, work at barn.

13 Fair. Hoe corn. Take Wife, Willis & Harriet, Mr. T. Civill & Lady, go to Baltimore for a ride.

14 Rainy all day. Mr. Civill call. I call to Blodget's.

15 Rainy. I go to river. **Am sick with dysentery**.

16 Fair SW. **Am still quite unwell**. Go to Dr. B.B. Fredenburgh's.

17 Fair NW. **Am still confined to house.** Boys work in hay.

18 Shower last night. Fair morning. **I am still unwell, stay in house.** Lib Hotaling, Miss Thomas, Mary Hotaling, Widow Charlotte, Cate VanBergen here.

19 Heavy shower. Joseph Bronk & Lady here visit. Mary Ellis, Mrs. Muckelroy, Mr. McKee & Willis call. Rainy in eve.

20 Clears off. **I am still sick around house all day.** VanSlyck's bull taken from here. Mr. Willis call. Mrs. Wilson here. Work a little in hay.

21 Fair, cool NW. I go to vineyard with waggon. **Am some better.**

22 Fair. **Mow with Machine. Work in hay**. Wife go to Ed VanOrden's. I go after her.

---

[323] The development of Long Branch, NJ as a summer coastal resort began in the 1780s. By the 1830s, gambling and horse racing brought an influx of visitors.

23	Fair. Mow, work in hay. **Attend school celebration in my woods**. Mr. Enos & Lady and a lot of people from Albany here, Caroline Houghtaling, Miss Thomas.
24	Fair. Work in hay. **Wife & Tony go to Albany, bring Jones children along**.[324]
25	Fair. Work in hay. Mr. Trego & Lady, Mr. Andrew Mull here.
26	Fine day, SW. Work in hay.
27	Fair, SW. Henry VanDerzee come here. Take a carriage ride in evening.
28	Fair, SW. Go to vineyard. Take a walk in big meadow.
29	Rainy. Go to river. Boys go in swimming.
30	Fair SW. Work in hay. H. VanDerzee leave. Mrs. Doctor Jones come here.

August 1861

1	Warm, SW. Rainy at night. Work in hay. Rachel Gregory here.
2	Fair. Work in hay. Commence in Big Meadow. **Catharine Hotaling died**.
3	Fair. Work in hay. Mrs. John Rea here.
4	Fair, SW. Mrs. J.J. Silcock & 3 children, Mrs. C. Hallock come here. Work in hay.
5	Fair, SW. Go to Meeting. Call to Civill's & to Blodgett's. Mrs. T. Civill & Mr. Jenkins call here. We go to vineyard.
6	Fair, SW in morning, shift to NW. Work in hay, take tea to A.E. Willis. Ride out with company with my carriage.
7	Fair, NW. Work in hay. Mr. Hallock's folks leave. Mr. Phillip Phelps & Mrs. Dr. Jones here.
8	Cloudy & rainy. Work in hay ½ day. P. Phelps leave. AE. & U.B. Willis & Lady here.
9	Rainy. Do but little. Go to river.
10	Rainy. Do but little. Go to river.
11	Fair, NW. Work in hay. Quite warm. Mrs. Dr. Jones & Son leave. Go to river.
12	Fair NW. Go to Meeting & to vineyard.
13	Cloudy & rainy at night Work in hay. Wife go to Coxsackie with Willis.
14	Rainy. Go to river twice. Do little or nothing.
15	Little showry. Work in hay. Mrs. Garrett Hotaling, Miss Dickey, Mrs. A.E. Willis here.
16	Fair. Commence haying Under Hill.
17	Fair, SW. Work in hay.
18	Fair. **Finish haying**. Mr. Trego & Lady & daughter call, Mrs. J.J. Silcock and three children here. **Party of children to Willis's. I spend the evening there**.
19	Fair. Go to Meeting. Call to Gregory's.
20	Fair. Cut my oats. I go to Greenville. Stay to A. Fancher.

---

[324] We believe that Tony is the nickname of Anthony Blaisdell

21	Fair. Bring my wool to C.T.E. Huyck's. Come holme. Draw in oats. Swear off my Greenville tax.
22	Fair. I take Mrs. Silcock and Wife & Uncle Garry's girls, go to A.T. VanSlyck's. I call to Stephen Calanan's.
23	Fair. I cradle wheat. I take Mr. Civill & his [?] a riding. Go around by Kimmey's & to Bethlehem, then holme here to tea.
24	Fair & warm. I go to Kimmey's, get dressed lumber.
25	Fair warm. I go to vineyard. I and Sarell Wood call on Briggs.
26	Fair, SW. L.D. Eddy here. Draw in wheat. All hands go a fishing, get nothing.
27	Fair. H. VanDerzee leave. **Mrs. Helen Keller died**. Go to river. Attend cemetery meeting. Mr. Civill call.
28	Fair SW. Lay wall & stone on cemetery. **John Ziegler's child died**.
29	Fair. **Attend funerals of Mrs. Ben Keller & John Ziegler's child**. Eliza Phelps and Bedell's Boy here.
30	Fair. Work at cemetery. Attend the excursion. Go to river.
31	Fair, cool NW. **I and Levi go to Albany, buy him a saddle**. Mr. Lansing & Mr. Civill's guests, two Syracuse women, here.

September 1861

1	Fair. I go to Meeting. J. Hilton & Lady, Thomas Hotaling here to dinner. Mr. Civill & Lady call.
2	Fair SW. Make fence. Go to river. Call to Mr. Civill's.
3	Showry. Dig stone. **Wife & Children go on excursion**. Elida VanSlyck here. Mrs. Silcock & children leave.
4	Fair, NW. Dig stone. Marite & Elida leave. Mr. Civill call.
5	Fair. Dig stone, Make fence. Mrs. A.E. Willis here to tea. Mr. & Mrs. Civill call.
6	Fair. I let John Fike have horse & waggon to go to Albany. **I work at Holmestead**. Wife go to Albany.
7	Fair. **I work to river on Holmestead**. Dr. & Daniel VanAntwerp come here.
8	Fair. I take Dr. & Daniel VanAntwerp & Levi, go to Uncle Andrew VanSlyck's. Bring Marite & Mrs. Martin VanSlyck back with us.
9	Cloudy, SW. **Work at Old Holmestead**. Draw stone.
10	Fair. **Work at Holmestead**. Draw stone.
11	Rainy. Go to river. Fix around the barn.
12	Fair, NW. **Mr. Simmons here; buy my grapes for 10 cts per lb.** Mrs. Charlotte Hotaling, Mary VanSlyck, Mr. Enos & Lady, Carrie Hotaling here.
13	Fair. Draw hay & stone. Teneyck cow goes to bull. Send off grapes.
14	Fair, SW. Press hay ½ day. Go to river.

15	Fair, SW. Go to Meeting. Mr. McKee, Mr. Willis call. Go to vineyard.
16	Fair. Draw & press hay. Get out slats. Mr. Willis & Lady, Mrs. Civill, E. VanOrden & Lady call.
17	Cloudy. Press & draw hay. P. Rea help. Dr. VanAntwerp & Daniel leave for NY.
18	Cloudy. Draw hay. Work around, go to vineyard.
19	Fair & hot. **We shingle our bedroom. Levi take Mother Hotaling to Baltimore. They go to New York.**
20	Fair hot. Draw stone. Shingle hen house.
21	Rainy afternoon. Dig ditches. Wm. Fancher came here, take my Charley colt. I and boys go with him part of way holme.
22	Cloudy. Go to vineyard. Call to Gregory's & to Willis. T. Civill call here.
23	Fair. **Make a stoop to Baker house.** Work in buckwheat.
24	Fair. Cut bee tree. Go to river & to vineyard.
25	Fair. Cut buckwheat. **Measure fence for Teneyck heirs**.
26	Fair SW. **Work at fence for Teneyck heirs**. Go to vineyard, dig ditch.
27	Cloudy. Send grapes to Simmons. **Attend funeral of John Niles**. Bring Civill's folks from dock. Dig potatoes.
28	Fair NW cooler. Dig potatoes. Go Under Hill to Mrs. Wilson's. Mrs. John Hotaling. Widow & Martin VanBergen's child here.
29	Fair. Go to Meeting & to vineyard & cemetery. Call to Willis's & to Mrs. Clement's. J.M. Harris sick.
30	Cloudy misty. Mrs. & Mr. Brandow & child call. I dig potatoes. Send off grapes.

October 1861

1	Fair. Finish dig potatoes. Pick apples, go to river. Set up buckwheat.
2	Fair, SW. Shingle to Gregory's. Send off grapes, fix wine press. Wife go to Ed VanOrden's.
3	Fair. **Thrash buckwheat with machine. Press grapes.** Draw one load buckwheat for Willis.
4	Work for Willis. Fair. Draw buckwheat.
5	Rainy. Get out slats. Go to river. Mr. Enos & Lady here. **George Wilson died**.
6	Cloudy, rainy. Go to Meeting & to vineyard.
7	Cloudy. Cut up corn. Send off grapes.
9	Fair, cool NW. I and Willis go to P. Kimmey's. Then I go to vineyard; then to tea to Mr. Civill's.
10	Fair. Pick apples. **Bring beef cow holme**. T. Civill & Lady, Lewis A. Civill & Lady here & son. Send off grapes.
11	Rainy day. Work about stable. Go to mill. Get 1-barrel flour.
12	Rainy Forenoon. Press hay. Clears off. H. Yung help. I pay Donald Borhouse note.

13 Showery. Go to Meeting. Call to Willis's & to Gregory's.

14 Fair. Draw hay. Send off grapes. Mr. [?] here to dinner. Wife go to Albany. I go to mill.

15 Fair day. Pick apples. Go to Crosswell's Mill & to vineyard. A.E. Willis call. Wife come holme.

16 Fair, SW. **Pick grapes; send them to Albany. Pay Mrs. Ostrander; make settlement 15 dollars for attending Mother**.

17 Fair, SW. Work at blind drains. Send off grapes. **Old Mr. Teats died**.

18 Rainy, foggy. I go to Albany. Get hogs from Under Hill.

19 Rainy. Press hay. H. Yung help. Go to river.

20 Fair, cool NW. I go to Meeting & to vineyard. Call to Blodget's & to Willis's.

21 Fair, cool. I take harness up with Willis. **We all go to Albany see the Ellsworth Regiment start for the war**.[325]

22 Fair. First frost. Press hay. H. Yung help. Call to T. Civill's.

23 Rainy. Fix cellar windows. Draw hay. Elizabeth Stephens, Carrie & Lib Hotaling & a School Mistress here.

24 Fair. Draw hay. Break down truck. Draw ground. **Attend lecture.**

25 Fair SW. Froze hand. Draw manure & ground. **Go to Circus**.

26 Fair SW. Press & draw hay. H. Yung help. The Misses Bailey here.

27 Fair, cold NW. Go to Meeting. Stop to Blodget's. **Johnson & Co. robbed last night. Their safe blown open, money taken**.

28 Cold NW. Draw wood & pumpkins. Work at shed & stable.

29 Fair, pleasant NW. Work at shed & buildings.

30 Rainy. Work at shed, clean up hayseed.

31 Fair NW. Work at shed buildings. Draw manure.

November 1861

1 Fair, pleasant. Work at buildings. Draw manure & corn.

2 Rainy. Wife & Levi go to Coxsackie. Draw corn, fix truck.

3 Rainy. Go to Meeting. Call to Willis's & to Civill's.

4 Cloudy cold. Draw & press hay. H. Yung help.

5 Cloudy SW. Make fence. Cut trees in Big Meadow.

6 Cloudy NW. Rainy at night. Work at shed buildings.

7 Cloudy, heavy NW. Dr. Spoor & Lady come here. Split slats. Mother Hotaling come holme.

8 Cloudy. Work at shed building. Plow. **Attend concert at Methodist Church.**

---

[325] The 44th Regiment was known as the Ellsworth's Avengers. It was, to the extent possible, comprised of one man from each town and ward, unmarried, not over 30 years of age or under 5 feet, 8 inches in height, and of military experience. The regiment, numbering 1,061 men, left Albany on 21 Oct. 1861 for Washington.

9	Cloudy. Plow; draw rafters from Under Hill.
10	Fair NW. Go to Meeting. Call to Blodget's.
11	Rainy SW. Plow; work at hay press. Take tea to Willis's.
12	Cold, heavy NW. Work at hog pen. Get in turnips. Mrs. Wm. Lawton, Mrs. Jemima Hotaling, Widow Charlotte, Mrs. Willis, Mr. Willis, Mrs. Fredenburgh here, visit.
13	Fair. Work at hog pen; plow. Company go to Dr. Fredenburgh's.
14	Fair cold NW. Work at hog pen; plow. Take tea to Widow Charlotte's. **Give a tea party**.
15	Fair cold NW. Work at shed building.
16	Fair cold NW. Work around. **Take in beets & cabbage**. Take tea to Jemima Hotaling's.
17	Fair cold NW. Go to Meeting. Call to Civill's & to Blodget's.
18	Fair cold. Work at ditches, draw stone.
19	Fair cold. Work at ditches, draw stone.
20	Fair cold. Go to Albany. Dig ditches, get shingles. **Edward Gibbens died**.
21	Fair cold NW. Work at ditches.
22	Snow all day. Work at stables. Husk corn. **Kit Sickels died**.
23	Fair NW. Snow & mud. Go to Meeting, call to Blodget's.
24	Fair. Press hay. H. Yung help.
25	Fair, N wind. Draw hay. Split slats; fix for pressing.
26	Cloudy. Press hay, H. Yung help. Go to river.
27	Cloudy. **Attend Thanksgiving dinner to Willis's**.
28	Cloudy SW. Work around barn.
29	Snow & rain. Press hay. John Ozle help.
30	Cloudy, snowy. Go to Meeting. Call to Willis.

December 1861

1	Fair, cold NW. Draw hay. Shingle granary.
2	Fair, cold NW. Work around house. **Knitting Society meet here**.
3	Fair cold. Draw hay. Go to river. **I. VanDerzee died**.
5	Fair, warmer. **Attend funeral of I. VanDerzee**. Harman VanDerzee & Lady here. **Finish press hay.**
6	Cloudy SW. Draw hay. Wife & Mary go to Albany.
7	Fair SW. Draw leaves.
8	Fair, very warm. Go to Meeting. Mr. Civill call. We go to vineyard. I call to Blodget's.
9	Cloudy & foggy. Draw leaves. Ann McCabe here.
10	Foggy SW. Work at blind drains.
11	Fair, cold NW. Work at blind ditches. Very muddy.

12	Fair, cold NW. Work at blind drains. I kill a pig. Go to river.
13	Fair. Cut wood, plow. Get pigs Under Hill. Attend tea party to Mrs. Clement's.
14	Fair. Cut & draw wood. Visit to Aaron Hotaling's.
15	Fair. Go to Meeting. Call to Gregory's & to McKee's.
16	Fair. Cut & draw wood. Go to mill.
17	Fair. Cut wood, plow. Mrs. T. Civill, Miss Brace, Misses Blodget call.
18	Fair. Cut & draw wood. Go to vineyard. **Attend a party to James Jack's. We have a good time.**
19	Cloudy SW. Dig ditch. Mrs. & Mr. Blodget, Mrs. Clement here, spend the day. I go to Mill & to river.
20	Fair cold NW. I and Wife go to Albany. Boys dig ditch. I get spade. Coat the grape boxes.
21	Fair cold. I go to river. Fix my gloves. Boys draw stone & cut wood.
22	Fair SW cold. Go to Meeting. Call to Willis's & McKee's.
23	Rain & snow all day. I work at granary.
24	Fair cold. I go to river. Boys chop. I work at the granary. **Attend Soldiers Friend Society at McKee's**.
25	Cold NW. Attend surprise party at I. Gregory's.
26	Cold S wind. Go around. TH 6 deg. below 0. **Lawford Hathaway marries Harriet Wilsey**.
27	SW morning, changes to NW cold. I call to Willis's. Rachel Gregory here.
28	Fair and cloudy. Go to Meeting. Call to Widow Charlotte's.
29	Fair cold NW. Work at granary. Boys cut wood.
30	Milder SW. Go to river. Work at granary. Rachel Gregory here.

January 1862

1	Warm SW. Go to river. Work at granary.
2	Very cold NW. I kill hogs, 6 of them & two for John.
3	Fair, cold NW. I kill my beef. Dominie Stillman call.
4	Fair cold. Cut up hogs & beef. Go to river. Andrew A. Hotaling here.
5	Fair cold. Go to Meeting. Call to Civill's & Blodget's.
6	Snow all day. Salt pork & beef. I go to river.
7	Fair, cold. I go to Schodack. I pay Josiah Sherman and my Island tax. James Trego here to dinner. **Mrs. Theophilus Civill has a young son**.[326]
8	Fair. I get my colts shod. Go Under Hill, get a log. Get a boar of P. VanBuren.
9	Cloudy SW. Go to Baltimore morning. Attend Road Meeting in afternoon.

---

[326] This would have been Acton T. Civill.

10	Cloudy SW. Draw logs. Go to Greenville. Rainy warm. Stop to J.G. Williamson. Stay to A. Fancher's all night. Get my rents mostly.
11	Fair cold NW. Go in wood lot. Come holme. Pay my tax.
12	Snow S wind thawy & rainy. Go to Meeting. Call to Civill's.
13	Fair cold NW. Martin VanSlyck here. Husk corn.
14	Fair, pleasant. Attend P. Road Meeting. Draw logs. Our folks attend Donation at Rev. Mr. Stillman's.
15	Snow all day. Settle with A.N. Briggs.
16	Fair, cold NW. **Go to Albany with sley**.
17	Cloudy. Snow all afternoon. Mrs. Robert Henry VanBergen here. I go to river.
18	Snow all day. Work about house. Go to river.
19	Cloudy. **Sarah Ann very sick. Doct. Ben here twice**. Mr. Willis & Harriet, Mrs. Stanton, Mrs. Clement, I.M. Harris call.
20	Snow, rain. **Lots of folks here to see Sarah Ann**. We husk corn. I go to Uncle Garry's, get Caroline. Go to river.
21	Fair pleasant. Go to river. Get a boar of P. VanBuren.
22	Cloudy. Children go to Coxsackie. I go to river. Work around. **Sarah Ann very sick**.
23	Pleasant & warm. **Lots of people call here to see Wife**. Uncle Garrett's folks here. They go to donation Mr. Collier.
24	Fair cold. Draw 13 loads stone for A. Civill. Work around, go to river.
25	Snow & hail all day. I go to river. Sarell Wood here. I and Levi take him & Carrie Hotaling to Uncle Garrett's.
26	Cold NW. Plenty of snowbanks. I shovel out and break road. Mr. Wood & Carrie come back.
27	Fair, cold NW. I and Mr. Wood [go] to Schodack. Mr. James Trego & Lady here.
28	Fair cold. Boys thrash. Mrs. McCullock here. I go to river. Mrs. George Wolf & Mrs. Slingerland call.
29	S wind, hail and misty. Go to river, stay about the house
30	Cloudy warm NW. Shovel snow off roofs. Go to river.
31	Pleasant NW. **Attend McKee's School**. Go to river.

February 1862

1	Cloudy SW, turns NW. **I go to see horses trot to Baltimore**. Stop to H. Stiley's. Call to Israel Lawton's office
2	Cold Fair NW. Go to Meeting. Call to Ira Gregory's. Mr. Willis & Lady, Mr. Civill call here.
3	Snowy afternoon, cloudy. Mrs. Gregory & Widow Hotaling [here]. I go to river, draw sand.
4	Snowy day. Go to river. **Copy journal**. Aunt Hannah Hotaling here. J.H. Holmes fix desk.
5	Fair. Go to Albany. Caroline Hotaling come here.

6	Snowy. **I take Barbary Yung to Albany on Lawsuit between me & Elida Lewis.** Mr. Civill & Lady & Ann Brace, Mrs. Stillwell here visit. Levi bring Mother Hotaling from Flat Bush. **Andrew's child buried today.**
7	Fair NW. Draw sand & wood. I go to Baltimore to Mrs. Sherman's. Mr. Leet call here.
8	Fair. Mr. T. Civill & John Rea call. I go to river. Draw wood & sand. Black Sam work here.
9	Fair cold. Go to Meeting. Call to Willis's. John Harris & Eliza and Jane Eliza Clement call here.
10	Fair. Draw sand. Cut wood. **Copy journal**.
11	Fair. Some cloudy. Draw sand. Hang up my hams. I go to Albany. Take dinner with Dr. Jones.
12	Snowy, clears off. Draw sand. Mr. Matson & Lady here. I go to Albany, take dinner with Fredrick Swarts.
13	Cloudy cold NW. I and Willis go to David Calanan's. Stop to P. Kimmey's. Rachel Gregory here.
14	Snowy. Mr. Civill & Lady here, visit. Dominie Stillwell call. Draw sand, go to river.
15	Fair. Go to Meeting. Call to Gregory's & to Willis's. A. Hotaling call.
16	Cloudy. Draw sand, go to river.
17	Fair. Draw wood. I go to river. Mrs. Gregory & Rachel here. James Jack call.
18	Fair, snowy in evening. Cut & draw wood. Doct. & Marite come. I take Wife out riding. A.B. Hotaling & Lady call.
19	Snowed 6 in. last night, cold cloudy NW. I go to river.
20	Fair cold NW. Not very well. Go to river, draw wood.
21	Cloudy SW. I go to river. Draw wood. Call to Mrs. Rea's. Hire Mother's house to her. Cate Hathaway here.
22	Fair morning SW. Cloudy afternoon. I take Dr. VanAntwerp, go to L. Litchfield's, then to Harman VanDerzee's. Ed VanOrden & Lady call.
23	Rainy morning. Clears off cold. Very heavy wind from NW. Go to river, draw two logs to mill. **My chimney blown down this evening.**
24	Clear NW. Go to river. Mr. Civill, Mr. Willis call here.
25	Cloudy NW cold. Draw wood. James Trego & Lady & daughter Elizabeth call here. Cate Hathaway leave.
26	Snowy. Draw wood. Go to river.
27	Very cold NW. I go to river twice. Blows very heavy.

March 1862

1	Cold NW. Blow hard. Roads all blown full. I take Wife, go to Uncle Garry Hotaling's.
2	Fair, cold NW. Go to Meeting. Mr. Willis call here.
3	Rainy. Go with Willis to Calanan's Corners & to river.
4	Fair, cold NW. Fair about 9 o'clock. I go to river. **Fix windows to Mrs. Maxwell's.**

5	Fair. Draw wood. Elida VanSlyck, Aaron Hotaling & Lady, Mrs. Jacob Holmes & daughter here. Draw wood, go to river.
6	Cloudy NW. **I and Dr. VanAntwerp go to Albany on the ice**. I get lath & shingles for Dr. Fredenburgh.
7	Fair. Draw hay. Snow melts finely. Go to river.
8	Fair NW. Draw hay. **I and Dr. VanAntwerp go to Dean's Mill. Attend christening of Mr. T. Civill's son, Acton, to Ann Civill's. Have large party & tea to T. Civill's.**
9	Fair. Go to Meeting. Mr. McKee call in evening.
10	Cloudy SW. Draw stone. **Work at Holmestead**. H. Wilsey help. It thaws very much.
11	Fair. Draw stone. **Work at Homestead**. Very thawy weather.
12	Fair SW. Turns to north. **Serve notice on G. Bullman to leave my house. Work at Holmestead.** Mrs. Jane Stanton [here]. Draw stone & lumber from the mill.
13	Fair NW. Draw hay. Work at pickets. Go to river. Dr. VanAntwerp leave.
14	Cloudy. Draw hay. J.W. Jolly & Lady here & sister Martha visit. **I work at the stable.**
15	Rain all day. Go to river. Work in shop. Get my bills of Johnson & Co.
16	Snowy day. Go to Meeting. Call to Willis & to Mr. Civill's & Ira Gregory's.
17	Snowy NW. Mother Hotaling go to Flat Bush. I and Wife go to Henry Springstead's, visit. Uncle Garrett and Aunt Hannah here visit & Miss Parsons. Lotte Stillwell here. Heavy shower in eve.
18	Fair NW. Fix stable. Work in shop. I go to river & to vineyard.
19	Fair. Work in shop. Minick cow has a calf.
20	Fair. Draw manure. Go to mill. Wm. Nodine call. David Whitbeck & Lady here visit.
21	Snow & rain all day. Go to river, work in shop.
22	Snowy. I and Levi go to Mrs. Wilson's; I hire William for $10.50 per month.
23	Snow all day. Go to Meeting. Call to Widow Charlotte's & to Willis. He and Eliza Clement call here.
24	Fair. I take J.M. Harris, go to Albany. Take up my note in favor of Cate Hotaling. **Bring Dr. VanAntwerp holme with me. Tip over in the snow**.
25	Fair. Work in shop. Visit to Dominie Stilwell's. Have a party there.
26	Fair cold NW. I take my men, go Under Hill. Get out saw logs.
27	Fair SW. Work in shop, go to river.
28	Fair cold NW. Work in shop, go to river. Oil harnesses. Freeze hard. T. Civill & A.E. Willis call here.
29	Fair cold NW. **I take Gregory, go to Town Caucus to J.B. Shear's**. Plenty of snow & ice.
30	Fair NW. Go to Meeting. Mr. Willis & Martin VanSlyck call.

April 1862

1	Fair warm. Work around house. Settle with John Fike. Wm. Wilson come here to work.

2	Cloudy foggy SW. Mr. Henry Hotaling here. Take up mortgage. I go with him to Baltimore. **I attend School Meeting in evening**. Dig out stone, go to river.
3	Fair. Go to vineyard. Lay wall. Dominie Stilwell & Lady, T. Civill Lady & children here.
4	Fair cool SW. I make bee house. Lay wall. Go to river. Take up my note to J.J. Colvin. Leave $150 with Johnson & Co.
5	Snow all day. I go to river. Sort out apples. John Rea here.
6	Fair cold NW. Go to Meeting. Call to Willis's & to Gregory's. Mr. Willis & Martin VanSlyck here.
7	Fair cold. **River open.** Cold NW. Work at garden fence. Go to river. Mrs. Pearce come here.
8	Cold NW. Attend Town Meeting. I take Dr. VanAntwerp and Marite to the Barge. They start for New York. Elizabeth & Caroline Hotaling here.
9	Fair cold. **I make fence to Old Holmestead.**
10	Fair cold. **I work to vineyard and to Old Holmestead.**
11	[no entry]
12	Fair. Work around house. Wife & folks go to Ed VanOrden's.
13	Fair cold NW. Go to Meeting in Dutch Church. Call to Willis & to Blodget's.
14	Fair. Work on road Under Hill. **Work at Holmestead**. Mrs. Pierce & Mother Hotaling go to Coxsackie.
15	Fair SW. I, Wife & Tony go to Albany; Wife stay there.
16	Fair SW. I work in garden. Plant potatoes; plow. Wife come from Albany. Charlotte Stillwell & her brother here.
17	Fair SW. Shower at night. **Work at blind drains.**[327] Go to river.
18	South wind cloudy. Little rainy. Work at blind drains. Fix fence. Dominie Stilwell & Family & I. Lawson here.
19	Fair cold. Fix front yard. Dominie Stilwell's Family leave. I and Wife take tea to Ira Gregory's.
20	Fair cold. Go to Meeting. Very high water.
21	Rainy. I go to river. Work at blind drains.
22	Clears off. Work at blind drains.
23	Cloudy cold NW. Snow squalls. **Put up Monument in Cemetery**. Work at blind drains.
24	Fair very cold NW. Work at blind drains. Draw 4 ½ loads of manure from J. Hazleton's. **Send 3 barrels of apples and butter, cow & calf to New York**.
25	Fair NW. Work at blind drains. Plow.
26	Fair NW. Plow, plant garden. Wife go to Schoonmaker's.

---

[327] A blind drain is a trench filled with gravel or rock that redirects surface and ground water away from an area. For Fletcher, it was a way to prevent a tilled field from becoming too wet from standing water making it impossible to be worked.

27　Fair. Go to Meeting & to cemetery. Call to Blodget's. Mr. A. Civill here to tea. **A.A. Hotaling shot his wife yesterday**.

28　Fair SW. Work to vineyard & blind ditches.

29　Rainy. Press hay. Go to river.

30　Fair. Work at blind ditches. **I take Mother Hotaling to A.A. Hotaling's to Flat Bush.**

May 1862

1　Cloudy SW rainy. Work at blind drains. Fix wheat to sow.

2　Rainy. Work around the house. Go to river.

3　Fair. Wind N & S. Sow wheat. Dig stone & ditches.

4　Fair. Go to Meeting & to cemetery, then Under Hill.

5　Some rain at noon, fair again. Harrow wheat. **Draw 48 bales of hay to boat**. Mr. J. Clement here.

6　Fair, but some May showers. Cold NW. Dig & fill ditches.

7　Fair, cold heavy NW. Work at blind drains.

8　Fair. Sow oats, peas, wheat. Harrow it in. Levi & Wife go to Albany.

9　Fair, heavy NW in afternoon. I sow grass seed. Make fence, plow. A. Fancher here.

10　Fair, heavy NW. **I roll land, make fence, plow. Pick stone**.

11　Fair, heavy cold NW. Mr. T. Civill & A.E. Willis call. **Robert & Lyman Baker's children buried today**.

12　Fair. I take Mother Hotaling to Catskill. Stop to George Hotaling's. Take tea to A.T. VanSlyck's, then come holme.

13　Cloudy, rainy. 3 calves, one from under the Hill [something left out]. Plow, go to river.

14　Fair, warm pleasant. Plow, plant. Draw sand. Work to vineyard. Go to river.

15　Fair. Wife go to Albany. Mr. T. Spraker call. We go to vineyard.

16　Fair SW. Draw manure. Willis call.

17　Fair. Finish sow oats. I and Wife go to Hollow to Quarterly Meeting. Go to river.

18　Fair. I go to Mr. Winnie's & McCullock's. Willis & Civill call, we go to vineyard.

19　Cloudy & cold. Plant potatoes. I plow them in. N & S wind.

20　Fair. Very cold morning; gets warm. Plow, plant potatoes.

21　Cloudy & rainy. Work at my roller.

22　Fair. Make fence. I and Rachel Gregory go to Albany. Boys split out slats.

23　Fair NW. Wife go to Stuyvesant. Work at roller. Get a new stove.

24　Fair. Work at roller. Make fence. Wife take Anthony to Albany. Mrs. Albert Hotaling here.

25　Fair. I take Mrs. Hotaling to Flat Bush. Take dinner to Martin VanSlyck's. Mr. Willis & Mr. Civill call.

26   Fair. Make fence. Work at roller. Go to river.

27   Fair. Draw up lumber. Mr. Willis & D. Baker help.

28   Fair cool. Draw up lumber. Willis help. Mr. Thomas & Lady, Caroline and Anson Hotaling go to Exhibition.

29   Fair NW. Roll land. Alter colts. Make fence.

30   Fair. Make fence. Go to river. Get check of Colvin & Rennie of $6.71 for Mother Hotaling. Send it to George Hotaling. She pays me the money back.

31   Fair very dry. Draw off wine. Sow plaster. Go to river.

June 1862

1   Fair. I call to Tunis Roberts & to Willis's.

2   Lowry. **I go to Catskill for Mother Hotaling. Put up at the Old Catskill Stage House. Go to see Andrew Houghtaling at the jail. They get a bill of indictment against him**.

3   Fair. Commence to rain in the evening. **Am all about the court**.

4   Rain hard all day. **Andrew Houghtaling gets his sentence by Judge Peckham of two years in Sing Sing Prison.**[328] **Then I attend a rape trial**.

5   Clears off. I come holme. Go to vineyard.

7   Make fence in Big Meadow. Take colts Under Hill. Send lumber to Kimmey's. Make waggon box. Trade horses to Blacksmith shop. Press hay. Set out cabbage plants.

8   Fair. Dominie Stillwell & Son here to dinner. Go to Meeting and to G. Hotaling's.

9   Fair. Work in barn. Take colts Under Hill. Work in Big Meadow.

10   Fair. Make Picket fence. Uncle Garrett & Lady call.

11   Fair. SW. Make picket fence. Plow. Mrs. Clement here.

12   Rainy, wet. Press hay, pile lumber. Go to river. Wife go to Albany.

13   Fair, warm. Work in garden. Plow. Go to river. Dig around the house.

14   Fair. Plow. Dr. VanAntwerp here. Send a load of lumber to Kimmey's.

15   Fair. Go to Meeting. Call to I. Gregory's & to Civill's & Willis's.

16   Fair. Work in garden. Draw lumber to Kimmey's.

17   Fair. Draw two loads of lumber to Kimmey's. Work at potatoes. Dr. VanAntwerp leave.

18   Rainy. Send plank to Kimmey's. Work about the house.

19   Rainy afternoon. Make waggon box. Send lumber to Kimmey's. Go to river.

20   Fair & hot. Work at Holmestead. Go Under Hill. Draw lumber from P. Kimmey's.

21   Rainy afternoon. Handle lumber. I and Levi go to Abram Witbeck's. William Phelps & his Daughter here.

---

[328] Sing Sing Prison is located along the Hudson River in Ossining, NY. It is one of the oldest prisons in the U.S. (1826). During the 19th and 20th centuries, it was well-known for its harsh conditions.

22 Fair. Go to hear Rev. Mathews preach. Go to vineyard & to cemetery. Mr. McKee call here.

23 Fair. William Fancher and Mr. Fiero here. Trade horse to Blacksmith's Shop.

24 Rain all day. Press hay. G. Rifflin help.

25 Rainy day. Go to river. Set out cabbage plants.

26 Rain. Press hay. Go Under Hill. Get logs. Mr. Fiero and William Fancher exchange horses. He takes Chub & her colt holme. I take his mare Fanny, gave him $22.50.

27 Calm, hot. Make road. Get plank from Kimmey's. Wife & Marite go to Albany. My bees swarm.

28 Calm, hot. Go Under Hill. Draw lumber from Kimmey's. Dr. VanAntwerp come. Mrs. Hotaling come with Wife & Marite.

29 Fair, hot. Go to vineyard. Call to Civill's & Dr. Fredenburgh's.

30 Rainy day. **I attend funeral of Uncle Andrew VanSlyck**. Break down with Mr. Lawson's waggon. Get Mr. Colborn's. Dr. VanAntwerp leave.

July 1862

1 NW Fair, cool. **I go to Albany with Dr. Fredenburgh in his waggon. Go to the Barracks. See the sick and wounded soldiers**. Draw lumber from P. Kimmey's.

2 Fair, cool. Work around. Swarm bees. Anson & Caroline Hotaling here, visit. **Attend school exhibition at McKee's**.

3 Fair, NW. Work at hay rigging. Take old mare & colt Under Hill. **Bring Levi's colt holme, have his wolf's teeth knocked out.**[329]

4 Fair pleasant SW. Am holme all day. Go to river in eve. Send Levi to Flat Bush, bring Mother Hotaling holme and one of Andrew's children.

5 Fair SW. Very hot. Work at road west of barn. Draw gravel and sand.

6 Hot SW & N wind. Go to vineyard. Dr. Fredenburgh here.

7 Fair, very hot. Hoe potatoes. Cultivate buckwheat ground.

8 Fair. Cap Budd Lady & child here. Hoe, plow.

9 Rainy, cloudy. Dig stone. Plow. Send colt to Henry Springstead's.

10 Fair. Work at stone. Sow buckwheat. Go to Hollow. Take Wife, Civill's family & Marite to Dominie Stilwell's.

11 Fair pleasant. Top out chimneys. Sow buckwheat. Go in Swimming.

12 Fair. Draw manure. Take Wife & Marite, go to Coxsackie. Stop to Flat Bush to Andrew Hotaling's. Stay all night to Martin VanSlyck's.

13 Fair. Go to Coxsackie to Meeting, then come holme.

14 Rainy. Break out stones. Draw out manure. William Wright come to work for me this morning.

---

[329] The wolf teeth are small, peg-like horse teeth that are often removed as they can interfere with bit placement and can cause pain for horses during training.

15 Fair. Draw manure. Work in quiry. Charley Jones here.

16 Fair hot. Draw manure. Dominie Stilwell Lady and Child here.

17 Fair cool. Draw stone for A. Civill. Mrs. Jemima Hotaling here.

18 Fair. Plow for turnips. Draw manure. Draw lumber for Civill.

19 Fair. Draw lumber & hay. Commence to mow. Dr. VanAntwerp & Marite come. Dr. Jones Children here.

20 Rain all day. Call to Willis's.

21 Cloudy. Go to Albany. Harry VanDerzee go along.

22 Cloudy. **Go Under Hill. Bring my machine, work in hay.**

23 Cloudy rainy. Draw up lumber all day.

24 Cloudy. Fix machine. Pile lumber. Mow a little.

25 Fair. Work in hay. Aunt Hannah, Anson & Elizabeth Hotaling here. Old Mrs. Jones & Emily here.

26 **Shingle Old Holmestead**. Work in hay.

27 Fair. Go to Meeting & to vineyard.

28 Fair SW. **Shingle Holmestead**. Work in hay.

29 Rainy. **Shingle at Holmestead**. Work in hay.

30 Rainy. **Work at Holmestead**. Work in hay.

31 Fair. Rain in evening. Mrs. Lucy Colvin, Mr. T. Civill & Lady, Mr. Brace here.

August 1862

1 Fair. Work in hay. Shower in evening.

2 Fair SW. Work hard in hay. Elizabeth & Caroline Hotaling here. Mary Bagley come here.

3 Fair SW. Go to Dutch Meeting. Rev. Mr. Pelts preach. Take all hands on a ride Under Hill.

4 Fair, showery. Work in hay. **Mow with machine**.

5 Fair. Work in hay. SW, very heavy rain. Thunder & lightning. Take tea to Mr. T. Civill's.

6 Fair, NW, pleasant. Work in hay. Elizabeth Pelts, Dr. Spoor, Mrs. A. VanDerzee here.

7 Fair SW. Work in hay. Dr. Spoor leave.

8 Fair hot. Work hard in hay.

9 Rainy afternoon. Work in hay. Mary Bagley leave.

10 Fair. Go to Meeting. **Leonard Blodget died. I go there; help lay him out**. Marite goes to Coxsackie.

11 Fair. Work in hay. Call to Blodget's.

12 Fair. Work in hay. Dr. VanAntwerp call here.

13 Fair. Work in hay. Lend I. Gregory 3 dollars.

14 Fair. Work in hay & oats. Rain in the evening.

15 Fair. Work in hay & wheat.

16 Fair. **Draw in 13 loads of wheat & 7 loads of hay.** Dr. Spoor here.

17 Fair. Go to Meeting. Call to Blodget's. Wm. Bagley here.

18 Fair. Work in hay. I and Wm. Bagley go to Greenville. Stop to A. Fancher's.

19 Fair. Come holme. Work in hay.

20 Fair. Work in hay.

21 Fair. Work in hay. J.H. Holmes help.

22 Showery SW. Draw in hay. Mr. N. Clute & Lady & two daughters come here.

23 Fair. Work in hay. U.B. Willis & Lady call here.

24 Fair cool NW. Walk around. Go to Meeting. Levi take the visitors a riding.

25 Fair. Work in hay. Dr. Spoor & Lady here. A.E. Willis here. Spend the evening.

26 Fair. Finish mowing in Big Meadow. Draw in hay. Marite leave for New York.

27 Fair SW. Work in hay. Mary Ann, Daughter of Daniel Goldsmith [here]. I break down my waggon.

28 Showery. Mow Under Hill. Harley Jones leave. Mary and Emily Jones come from Albany.

29 Fair. **Finish mowing with machine.** William Bagley and Aunt Sarah Ann here. **Willie Stilwell died**.

30 Fair cool. **Finish hay Under Hill.** Wm. Bagley and Mrs. R.H. VanBergen here.

31 Fair. **We attend funeral of Willie Stilwell**. Go to cemetery & to vineyard with Mr. Clute & Wm. Bagley.

September 1862

1 Cloudy & rainy. I take Wife, Emma Jones and Mr. Clutes Family to Albany. Come holme in the rain.

2 Fair, cold NW. I take boys and J.H. Holmes to Henry Waldron's to cut hay for Billy Wilson & John Henry. Miss McCabe here.

3 Fair, little frost. **Finish haying.**

4 Fair. I help J.H. Holme & Bill Wilson get their hay.

5 Fair. Mr. Clow & Lady call. I and all the folks go to Mr. Civill's spend the afternoon & evening. Martin VanSlyck call.

6 Fair. I go Under Hill after slats. Lay wall.

7 Fair. I go to Meeting. Mr. T. Civill call. Go to vineyard. Mr. McKee call in evening.

8 Fair. I take Wife & Mr. Clute's Family to Coxsackie. I sign a bond for Martin VanSlyck. Send off apples.

9 Fair SW. Go after slat timber. Get peas from Island. Get grape boxes from Albany. Mrs. Jemima Hotaling call.

10 Fair. Get hay slats on the Hill. Draw in beans.

11 Fair SW. Get hay slats. Draw in beans.

12 Rainy. Get flour. Go to river.

13 Fair SW. Draw lumber. I and Levi go to Mr. Fitch's to Coxsackie. Mother Hotaling go along to Flat Bush. Take a barrel of flour to A.A. Hotaling's.

14 Fair SW. Go to Meeting. Mr. McKee call. I go with him to the vineyard. I call to Seabridge's.

15 Cloudy SW. Draw wood & logs.

16 Fair. I work to vineyard. Boys draw slat timber.

17 Fair SW. Split slats. Work around the house.

18 Cloudy SW. Mr. Clark & Ischar Bates and another Shaker here. I take them to vineyard. Mrs. John Rea visit here.

19 Fair. **I shingle on Mother's house. J.H. Holmes help.**

20 Fair SW. Finish shingling. Go to river.

21 Fair. Go to Meeting. Call to T. Civill's. Go Under Hill. I and Wife take tea to Uncle Garret's. Mrs. Jemima Hotaling here.

22 Fair. Make waggon tongue. Cut buckwheat.

23 Fair. Dig potatoes. Go Under Hill. Rake buckwheat.

24 Fair. Fix barn. Press hay. Mr. Moseley & Conoly here. I take them to vineyard. They dine here.

25 Fair. Press & draw hay. Work to the vineyard.

26 Fair. Press hay I. Gregory help. Walk about.

27 Fair. Go to Albany. Take dinner with Mr. Mosely. Go to see Mr. Conoly or Conard, **go to Dudley Observatory**.[330]

28 Cloudy S wind, little rainy. I take Mother Hotaling to Flat Bush. Go to Meeting. Call to T. Civill's, he call here. **Mrs. Capt. Miller died**.

29 Fair. Press hay. I. Gregory help.

30 Cloudy. Pick apples. Send two loads lumber to Flat Bush. Mother Hotaling leave for New York.

October 1862

1 Rainy day. Press hay, go to river.

2 Rainy. **Draw hay on boat.** Go to river.

3 Foggy & rainy. **All hands go to Flat Bush. Draw stone, raise barn**.

4 Cloudy, S wind. Wife come holme. **We go to Flat Bush, work at barn**. Willis call here in evening.

5 Fair. Go to Meeting and to vineyard. Mr. Civill & Lady call.

---

[330] The Dudley Observatory was originally chartered in 1852 by New York State Senate; first located in Albany, but later moved to Schenectady. It is no longer an operating observatory but remains the oldest non-academic institution of astronomical research in America.

6	Cloudy SW. Go to Flat Bush. **Work on barn, stay all night.** Call to Flansburgh's.
7	Fair. **Take down lumber. Shingle barn to Flat Bush**.
8	Fair. **Go to Flat Bush, work there.** Wife & Levi go to R.H. VanBergen's, visit. Miss McCabe here.
9	Fair. Dig potatoes. Take tea to T. Civill's. Mr. Charles Brace & Lady then the Bride & Groom.
10	Cloudy & rainy. **Go to Flat Bush, work there & finish barn**. Come holme in rain, get very wet. **Mr. T. Civill & Lady, Mr. Charles Brace & Lady, Mary Civill here, visit**. Pick apples.
11	Rainy. Press hay, go to river.
12	Fair. Go to Meeting. Mr. T. Civill & Lady, Mr. Brace & Lady, Martin VanSlyck call. We go to vineyard.
13	Rainy day. Mr. Clute & Family here They leave again. Press hay, Gregory help.
14	Cloudy. Draw hay. **Help Seabridge raise his barn**.
15	Cloudy, wet. Press hay. Wife goes to Albany. **Mr. Clute & Family leave for Louisville**.
16	Cloudy. Pick apples. Bill help Mr. Gregory.
17	Rainy morning. Split slats. Work at corn crib. Go to river.
18	Fair. Dig potatoes. Mrs. Jane Hotaling, Elida VanSlyck here. Finish to dig my potatoes.
19	SW, rainy in evening. N.H. Johnson call. We go to Meeting.
20	Fair cold NW. Thrash buckwheat. Draw hay.
21	Fair. Pick apples, go to river.
22	Fair, very cold SW. Pick apples Under Hill.
23	Fair, very cold. Pick apples. Go to river. Draw up buckwheat & potatoes.
24	Cold cloudy SW. Go to Albany. Bill Wilson go along.
25	Cold SW. I and Wife go to R.H. VanBergen's to Coxsackie. Boys press hay.
26	Cold SW. Nancy come holme from her visit.
27	Cold rainy. Press hay. Gregory help ½ day.
28	Fair. Draw & press hay. Go to river.
29	Fair morning. **I and Levi start with horse and waggon for Herkimer. Stay all night at Amsterdam**.
30	Fair. **Start on through Tribes Hill, Fonda, Caroga and Salisbury. Stay all night to Eben Kelly's**.
31	Fair. **Drive to Henry Sperl's. Take a tramp through the woods. Very tired, go to bed**.

November 1862

1	Fair. **I keep in Sawmill. Levi goes to Graysville**.
2	Fair. **Start for holme. Stay to Perth Center**.
3	Fair cold NW. **Come holme. Drive 60 miles**.

4	Fair cool. **Attend Election. Vote for H. Seymour[331] & Ticket, which gets 24 majority**. Take tea to Mr. T. Civill's. Mrs. Stilwell, Miss McCabe here.
5	Fair SW. Go Under Hill. Get hoop poles. Mr. Civill & Lady, Rev. Mr. Gorse & Lady, Miss Gorse here, visit. Miss Fuller, Mrs. Weymouth all here.
6	Fair cold. Split hoops.
7	Cold heavy NW. Snow ½ day. Bring in apples & potatoes.
8	Cold. 4 inches snow. Fix stable, saw wood.
9	Snow & blow all day. Call to Willis's, Cranston's & Gregory's.
10	Fair NW. Shave hoops. Fix around barn. Go to river.
11	Fair SW. Split slats. Press hay ½ day. Gregory help.
12	Fair SW. Press hay, Gregory help.
13	Fair NW. **Shingle house to Daniel Baker's**.
14	Fair SW. Finish shingle. Daniel Hudson Dairy man here. **Willis & Harriet spend the evening here**.
15	Fair. Go to river. Dr. VanAntwerp & Marite come. Split slats, draw hay, go to vineyard.
16	Fair. Go to Meeting. Call to Willis.
17	Rainy cloudy. Draw leave, hay. Get out hoops.
18	Changeable. Press hay; get out hoops.
19	Rainy. Press hay; get out hoops.
20	Rainy. Get hoops. Split & shave hoops. **Dr. Fredenburgh call here. Gave us portrait of Horatio Seymour**.
21	Rainy day. Press hay. Get out hoops. Gregory help.
22	Cloudy, muddy. Press hay. Get out hoops, go to river.
23	Cold NW. Freeze hard. Go to Meeting. Call to Willis's.
24	Fair. Draw hay. Get slat timber.
25	Fair. Get out hoops & slats. **I cut the cord off of my third finger. Go to the Doctor's**.
26	Rainy, cloudy. Press hay. Work around.
27	Fair. Press hay.
28	Fair. Press hay. Get slat timber. Widow Charlotte Hotaling here.
29	Cloudy. Rain & snow in evening.
30	Fair. One inch of snow. Go to Meeting. Mr. Willis, Martin VanSlyck call here.

---

[331] Horatio Seymour was a two-term Governor of New York 1853-1855 and 1863-1864. He was a Democrat and not a strong advocate for the Civil War as he did not believe the Federal government had the power to regulate slavery.

December 1862

1. Rainy. Press hay. Get out hoops.
2. Fair cold. Press hay.
3. Fair. Press hay. Get out hoops.
4. Little cloudy. Kill hogs. G. Sickels, P. Jackson & Gregory help.
5. Fair. Press & draw hay. P. Jackson help.
6. Fair. Heavy NW, very cold. Press hay. Get out hoops. R.H. VanBergen & Lady here.
7. Fair cold. Freeze very hard. Mr. VanBergen & Lady leave. I go to vineyard. Mr. Willis & Mr. Civill call.
8. Fair. Still cold. Draw wood. Get horses shod. Cut up my pork. Misses McCabes here.
9. Overcast, cold. Levi, Anthony, Wife, Mrs. T. Civill, Mrs. Gorse go to Albany. I go to river.
10. Fair SW. Levi take Mother Hotaling to Flat Bush and then go and bring Cornelius from R.H. VanBergen's here to work for me. Misses McCabe here.
11. Fair. Work around the house. Go to river and then to Barent Teneyck's, pay interest money.
12. Fair. Chop wood. **Work at schoolhouse**.
13. Cloudy SW. **Go after wood for Ira Gregory, break down, come holme. Draw hay on the Barge**.
14. Cloudy SW. Go to Meeting. Call to Ira Gregory's.
15. Fair. Press hay. Go to river.
16. Rainy morning clears off. I and Wife go to Albany. Very muddy, bad going.
17. Fair cold NW. **Work at schoolhouse. Draw two loads of hay on boat**.
18. Fair. Cut & draw wood. Go to river.
19. SW fair. Wind turns north and very cold. **I and Levi go after Christmas Tree.**
20. Fair, very cold NW. I go to river then to New Baltimore.
21. Fair, very cold. I go to Willis's. Mr. T. Civill & Lady call here. I call to Mr. Wallas's.
22. Cloudy. **Work to church and to schoolhouse**.
23. Cloudy. Go to Albany then to church and to Mr. Civill in the evening.
24. Fair. Draw wood for Mr. Gregory. **Attend Christmas tree celebration at the Methodist Church in the evening, it went off well. Anthony spoke his piece well. I get two presents**.
25. Cloudy SW. Go to river and around the house.
26. Rainy. Go to river. Take tea. Spend the evening to Rev. Mr. Gorse's. Pleasant visit.
27. Cloudy. Work around the house, go to river.

28 Fair. Go to Meeting. Call to Mr. Willis's.

29 Fair warm. Get out timber. Draw leaves.

30 Cloudy. Draw leaves. Work at waggon house.

31 Snowy. **Thresh with machine**. Levi go to Donation to Rev. Mr. Stilwell to Coeymans Hollow. Gregory help thresh. **Elizabeth Sherman & David Witbeck get married**.

Threshing Machine

January 1863

1   Fair day. Mr. T. Civill Lady & Children here, visit. I go to river.

2   Fair pleasant. Thresh, Gregory help. Go to river.

3   Fair. Finish threshing. Go to river.

4   Fair SW. Go to Meeting. Call to Willis's.

5   Fair. Go on Hill. Get logs. Go to river.

6   Fair morning, rainy afternoon. Work at carriage house. Go to river.

7   Fair NW. Very cold. Work at carriage house. Clean up grain. Attend a surprise party to J.E. Gibben's.

8   Fair SW. Clean grain. George & Henry help. Rev. Mr. Stilwell here.

9   Fair & cold. I and Anthony go to Greenville.

10 Snow. Collect lease money. Come holme. Charlotte Stilwell here.

11 Fair. Go to Meeting. Call to T. Civill's. John Rea call here.

12 Fair. Go to Ephraim VanSlyck's. **Halter break my colt**. Kill my beef.

13 Fair. Go to Ephraim VanSlyck's, get timber. Get it sawed, bring it holme. Go without my dinner.

14 Rainy day. Attend Plank Road Meeting. **My colt died**.

15 Rainy day. **Skin my colt**. Go to river. A.E. Willis here.

16 Rainy day. Work in shop. Go to river.

17 Cold. Fix waggon box. Go to river.

18 Cold. I am sick, go to Doctor's. Stay about house. A.E. Willis call. Sick all night.

19 Very cold. Mrs. Cook & Mrs. Jacob Holmes call.

20 Cold cloudy. Am unwell. Go to river.

21 Snowy. Go to river. Mary Ann Hotaling come here with Joe Witbeck.

22 Cloudy. Little snow. Draw logs to mill.

23 Foggy, clears off cold. I am quite unwell. **Mrs. Jemima Hotaling died**.

24 Fair warmer. **Attend the funeral of Mrs. Jemima Hotaling**. John Mull & Lady, Mr. Lasher & Lady here.

25 Fair. Mr. Willis call. Attend church. Call to T. Civill's.

26 Cloudy rainy. I take Ira Gregory and his girls, go to Albany. Rain all the way holme.

27 Snow & rain all day. Go to river.

28 Cloudy snowy. Draw logs & manure. Go to river.

29 Snow all day. Go to river twice.

30 Fair. Draw logs to mill. Go to tanners to Bethlehem. Attend **Mr. McKee's Examination**. Misses VanSlycks here.

31 Fair. Quarterly Meeting. Go to river twice. Misses VanSlycks here.

February 1863

1   Fair. Attend Quarterly Meeting. Dine to Mr. T. Civill's. Mr. Civill, Mr. Turner call here.

2   Fair. Cut & draw wood. Levi go to Coxsackie. Take Cornelius along. Two Negroes here. I go to river.

3   Fair very cold. Go after timber. E. Hubbell & Lady, Mr. Spoor, Miss Fairchild, R.H. VanBergen & Lady, A.E. Willis & Lady & Leonard Hubbell and their driver here, visit. Three Negroes here all day.

4   Very cold. **TH 12 degrees below 0**. I take Wife and Uncle Garry's Girls to Coxsackie to A.B. Hotaling's, visit.

5   Fair very cold. Go to river twice.

6   Rain all day. Saw wood.

8   Fair pleasant thawy. Go to Meeting. Call to Willis's.

9   Cloudy go to the Carhart farm, get out slat timber. Uncle Garry's girls go to J.W. Jolly's visit.

10 Cloudy cold. Draw slat timber. I take Wife, Mrs. Gorse and Uncle Garry's girls, go to J.W. Jolly's, visit.

11 Fair warmer. Draw wood & slat timber.

12 Snow all day. Draw slat timber.

13 Fair. Draw slat timber. George Wolf & Lady here. Martin Andrews call.

14 Fair very cold. I draw two load of wood for Gregory. Go to river. Draw up beans.

15 Fair thawy. Go to Meeting. Dine with T. Civill. Call to Gregory's.

16 Fair cold. Cut and draw wood.

17 Fair. Draw & cut wood. Work at press.

18 Fair. Draw and chop wood. **I go to Croswell's papermill**.

19 Rainy. Work at hay press. Clean out barn.

20 Cloudy. **I and Wife go to Albany with a waggon**.

21 Very cold NW. Martin VanBergen & Lady, Cate VanBergen and Emma Hotaling here, visit.

22 Snowy cold. Go to Meeting. Martin VanBergen & Lady leave.

23 Fair, NW cold. Draw 1 load straw Under Hill and a load of wood for Nick. I am unwell. Go to river. Levi take Nickolas & Mother Hotaling to Coxsackie.

24 Cloudy cold. Wife go with Dominie Gorse & Lady to Andrew Teneyck's. **I draw timber for ice men**.

25 Fair. I take Wife, go to Martin VanSlyck's, visit. Stay all night. Very pleasant.

26 Rainy. I go to Flat Bush, then to Martin VanSlyck's with Mother Houghtaling. Then I & Wife go to Martin VanBergen's, visit. Then come holme. Sley goes hard.

27 Fair. Work at [hay] press. Go Under Hill. Get timber.

28 Fair. Work at hay press. **Draw 1 load of lumber for ice men**.

March 1863

1 Snow all day. Go to Meeting.

2 Fair. Draw manure. Fix hay press.

3 Snow. Work at hay press. **Go to dam, see them get out ice**. Mr. Civill & Lady, Dominie Gorse & Lady and Child here visit.

4 Fair cold. Draw hoops. Go to river. Take tea to John Clement's, spend evening. Mother Hotaling come holme.

5 Fair cold. **Write lease for Mother Hotaling**. Go to river.

6 Cold cloudy. Heavy SW. Go to River. Nick & Cornelius draw poles; cut wood.

7 Snow all day. Go to river & to **Robb's mill dam**.

8 Snow all day one foot deep. Stay in house.

9 Fair NW. Draw hay. Work around the house. Willis and Mr. McCarg call.

10 Fair. Work at waggon tongue. Draw hay.

11 Fair. I take Mrs. Civill to Albany then go to Troy. Good sleying.

12 Fair very cold. Draw hay. George Hotaling here to dinner. I go to river.

13 Fair cold. TH 6 deg. below 0. Draw hay. Edward VanOrden here, visit. **I go to river and to Mr. Robb's dam**.

14 Fair, cold. I and Wife go to G. Hotaling's, visit. Draw hay. Gregory help.

15 Fair, very cold. I call to T. Civill's & Willis call here. I am unwell.

16 Fair. Draw straw & poles to Mr. Fitch. I take Mr. T. Civill & Lady to Aquetuck to Dominie Stilwell's.

17 Fair. Draw poles & hay. Mrs. Dr. Jones & Miss Rice, Lib Hotaling here. I go to river. Work at straw.

18 Fair, cold. Wm. McCullock & Lady here. I go to river twice. We draw hay.

19 Fair. Draw hay. Go to river. I take Wife, Mrs. Jones, & Miss Rice to Mrs. James Thorn's. Dominie Patterson here, visit, take tea & stay all night.

20 Fair, very cold NW. I take Wife, Mrs. Dr. Jones, go to Uncle Garry's, visit.

21 Fair. Draw manure. Go to river. Send feed under the Hill. Miss Rice return holme.

22 Fair. Thaws very much. Go to Meeting. Call to Willis's & to Gregory's.

23	Fair, cool. I go to river twice. Work around the house.
24	Fair, cool. Go to river twice. Mrs. Jones & Miss Rice leave.
25	Rain all day. Mr. T. Civill call. I go to river.
26	Fair cool NW. Work at waggon house. Mother Hotaling go to Uncle Garrett's.
27	Fair cold NW. Work at waggon house. Go to river. Am quite unwell.
28	Am unwell. Snow all day. Stay in house.
29	Snowy morning; clears off. Snow 6 in. deep. Mr. T. Civill call. I go to river.
30	Fair NW. Work at waggon house. Go to river.
31	Snow all day. Work at waggon house. Clean up beans. Go to river.

April 1863

1	Fair, cold NW wind. I take Wife, go to Coxsackie, bring holme two Negroes. Take dinner at U.B. Willis.
2	Heavy South West. Go to Mr. Tompkins & Nodine's. **Pay $2028, i.e., $400 to A. Tompkins, $1600 to Wm. Nodine**. Go to river.
3	Fair NW. Work at waggon house. Go to river. Take [tea] to Willis's.
4	Cold cloudy SW. I go to river twice. Work around.
5	Snowy. I call at T. Civill's. Go to Meeting. Call at Gregory's & at E. Stanton's.
6	Pleasant morning. Cloudy at night. Work at waggon house. Go to river.
7	Rain & snow all day. Go to river. Take tea at Mr. Stanton's.
8	Snowy. Work in shop. Take tea & visit at A.N. Briggs.
9	Fair. I go under the Hill. Get Levi's cow. Work in shop. Go to river. Cornelius come back this evening.
10	Fair. Go to Albany. **Get Anthony's compass**.
11	Fair SW. Press two bales hay. Go to river.
12	Warm, morning SW rainy. NW afternoon. Gregory call, we go to vineyard and to cemetery.
13	Fair NW. Get out hoops, press hay. Gregory help.
14	Fair. **Attend Town Meeting**. **Draw 3 loads hay to Barge**.
15	Fair SW. **Set out Civill's trees**. **Plant 66 hills of potatoes**.
16	Rainy day. Get out hoops and press. Dick help ¾ day; Gregory help. I go to river.
17	Cloudy misty. Press hay. Gregory help ½ day, Dick all day. **Catharine Hathaway died**.
18	Fair. Press hay; get out hoops.
19	Fine [day]. **Attend funeral of C. Hathaway**. Mr. Willis & McKee here.
20	Cloudy SW. Press and draw hay. **Mr. Gregory get hurt by my press sweep**. Nick help.
21	Fair and pleasant. Mr. Jack & Lady, Mr. Civill & Lady, Mrs. Fredenburgh, Mrs. Spraker, Mrs. A. and R. Hotaling, Mrs. Stanton, Mrs. Clement & Eliza here. Press hay. Nick help.

22 Fair. Go to Albany with waggon.

23 Fair and still. Sow seed Under Hill. Graft and trim orchard. Visit and take tea at Mr. T. Civill's.

24 Cloudy. Go under the Hill. Sow seed. Make fence, trim orchard, go to mill.

25 Cold cloudy NW. Trim orchard. Draw manure & hay. Cornelius go to Coxsackie.

26 Fair and cold NW. Go to Meeting. Mr. Civill and Willis call, go to vineyard.

27 Fair NW. Plow in orchard.

28 Fair SW. Plow & plant potatoes. Work in garden.

29 Fair. Plant potatoes and plow.

30 Fair. Draw manure. Plow. Work at carriage house.

May 1863

1 Fair. Sow oats. Plow. **VanOrden move in my house**.

2 Fair. Plow. Draw stone. Elida VanSlyck here. Draw manure. Dominie Gorse & Lady & Miss Gorse here.

3 Fair. Go to Meeting. Mary Civill's girls here. I call to Walleen's.

4 Cloudy, rainy. Plow. Plant beets. Get out hoops. Take tea to Mr. Civill's.

5 Cold NW. Plow. Draw manure. Go to river.

6 Rain all day. Get out hoops.

7 Rain all day. Get out hoops. **Work at privy for Holucester.**

8 Fair. Go Under Hill. Make fence. Work around holme.

9 Fair. Make fence Under Hill. A. Fancher here.

10 Fair very warm. Go to Meeting twice. Go to vineyard. Call to VanOrden's. **Old Trip died 17 years old**.

11 Fair. Finish sowing oats. Charlotte Hotaling, Elizabeth & Carrie Houghtaling here.

12 Warm SW. Put calf on boat. Plow. Roll oat ground. Sow grass seed. Go to Dean's Mill, get balance of lumber.

13 Rainy misty. **Make fence in front of the house**.

14 Rainy. Make fence. Plow. Turn out cows.

15 Fair, cold NW. Press hay. Mrs. B. Weymouth here.

16 Fair SW. Draw hay. Make garden fence. Wife & Mary go to Baltimore.

17 Rainy. Call to Willis's & to Civill's & Gregory's. Go to Meeting.

18 Fair. Press hay. Put up apples. Go to river.

19 Fair. Draw & press hay. Plow Under Hill. **Send off 7 barrels apples**.

20 Fair. Plow. Make fence on the Hill.

21 Fair. Make fence. Plow. Martin A. Hotaling here.

22 Fair NW. Plow. Plant potatoes Under Hill.

23 Fair, very hot. Plant potatoes. Go to Hollow to Quarterly Meeting. Take Wife, T. Civill & Lady & Mary Jenkins.

24 Fair SW. Cloudy in evening Go to vineyard. **Call to John Ziegler's**[332] then to I. Southard's & T. Civill's. Go to Singing School.

25 Rainy. Make fence. Plow. Make gates.

26 Fair. Plow. Harrow. Plant sweet corn.

27 Fair. Plow. Plant beans. Go to McCullock's raising.

28 Fair. Fix waggons. **Draw ice**.[333] Harrow corn ground.

29 Fair. Finish plant corn. **Draw ice**.

30 Showery. Go to Meeting. Willis call. I call to VanOrden's.

June 1863

1 **Draw ice**. Make fence. Hot, rainy. Clears off cold.

2 Fair very cold. **Draw ice**. Make fence. Go to river.

3 Fair, very cold. Work at potatoes. **Draw ice**. Go to river.

4 Fair, cold. **Draw ice**. Make fence.

5 Fair, cold. **Draw ice**. Make fence.

6 Rainy. **Draw ice**. Go to John Mull's get fish. William Phelps Lady & Child here.

7 Fair cold NW. Go to Meeting. Mr. Civill & Lady, B. Weymouth & Lady here. We all go to vineyard.

8 Cloudy cold NW. **Draw ice. Work to Old Holmestead**.

9 Cloudy cold. **Draw ice** & manure. Fix fence. **Wife & Anthony go to New York on Barge.**

10 Fair. Draw manure. I, Levi & Mary go to Albany with waggon.

11 Fair. Draw off wine. Plow to vineyard.

12 Showery. Draw manure. Paint fence. I go Under Hill.

13 Rainy. I work in shop. Go to J. Mull's, get fish.

14 Fair, warm SW. Go to Meeting. Call to Wallase's.

15 Fair, cool NW. Plaster corn. Fix around house. Go to river.

16 Fair, cool NW. Work in garden. Fix up clothes rack. **Go to raising to Cornelius Slingerland's**.[334]

17 Cloudy. Draw dirt out of barnyard. Willis call.

---

[332] An article in the Ravena-Coeymans Historical Society's Newsletter (summer 2015) indicated that the Ziegler brothers (John & Lawrence) purchased land in Coeymans in 1863 on which they built a broom factory. Broom corn was the material used to make brooms.

[333] This is the first mention of drawing ice. As it is warm weather, we suppose it comes from one of the ice houses by the river. We don't know where or how it was stored.

[334] We believe that this was Cornelius H. Slingerland (1826-1921) who was married to Adelia Mull. He would be Betsy Slingerland Blaisdell's great grandfather.

18	Fair SW. Dig out barnyard.
19	Fair. Draw stone, sow plaster. Plaster & hoe corn. Aunt Sarah Ann VanBergen & Widow Charlotte here.
20	Cloudy SW. Work at road. Sow buckwheat. Wife & Anthony return from N. York. Widow Charlotte & Aunt Sarah Ann call. Mr. Petersman come fix my clock.
21	Rainy. Mr. Petersman & a Dutchman here. Go to vineyard. Willis call.
22	Showers. Draw slabs. Press hay. Go under the Hill.
23	Fair. Press hay. Work road Under Hill. Fix up barn.
24	Fair. **Go to Herkimer. To Albany with waggon. Stay all night to Henry Sperl's.**
25	Fair. **Go around the woods with H. Sperl.**
26	Fair. **Start for holme. Stop to Mr. Kelly's. Go a fishing for trout. Stay all night to Kelly's.**
27	Fair. Come holme. Uncle Garry here. Go to cemetery with him.
28	Fair & hot. I and Harry go to Stephensville to Mr. Vincent's, then holme, then to Meeting.
29	Fair. Make fence Under Hill. Martin A. Hotaling here.
30	Fair SW. Make fence Under Hill. **Send cow & calf to NY.**

July 1863

1	Fair. **Make fence around my Tenant House.**
2	Fair hot SW. Make fence. Hoe corn. Go in swimming. Charley Jones here.
3	SW. Very heavy rain. Dig stone. Creeks very high.
4	Cloudy & rainy. Work at bees. **Attend picnic on Barge. George Sickler and John Rondout get hurt with cannon.**
5	Misty & rainy. Go to vineyard. Go to sleep. Go to Meeting.
6	Cloudy hot SW. Make fence. Go to river. Mrs. Civill & E. Brace call.
7	Fair hot. Send off my Witbeck cow & calf.
8	Cloudy. Heavy shower. Hoe corn & potatoes. Call to Willis's.
9	Hot SW. Showery. Cut wood. **Fix around my Holmestead.** Miss McCabe here.
10	Hot SW. Little showery. Cut wood. **Fix Holmestead.** Go in swimming.
12	Cool cloudy. Go to Meeting. Call to Willis & to VanOrden's.
13	SW rainy. **I and Levi go to Albany, get barometer.**
14	Rainy. I go to Island with Mrs. Payn. **I. Southard died.**
15	Cloudy hot. **I go to Coeymans Hollow, meet the Internal Tax Revenue Collector.** Dine to Dominie Stilwell's. Mr. T. Civill & Lady & Emma Brace here.
16	Fair once more. **Attend the funeral of I. Southard.** Fix gate to bean field. **Go and see boat launched to New Baltimore.**[335] Mr. Stillwell & Lady here to tea.

---

[335] Ship building was a major industry in New Baltimore the 1800s.

17 Rainy day. Make fence. Go to river twice.

18 Fair NW. Make fence. Go to river.

19 Fair. Go to Meeting & to vineyard. Go to Wallas's.

20 Rainy. Work at corn. **Bring holme my mowing machine**.

21 Very rainy. **Creeks higher than I ever saw before**. Cornelius go to Albany.

22 Fair NW. Make fence. Make road. Nick & John mow. Emma Brace here. Levi take her & Wife out riding. Go to mill.

23 Fair SW. **Mow with machine**. Work in hay.

24 Rainy morning. Clears off SW. Work in hay.

25 Rainy afternoon SW. Work in hay. Marite come. **Go to Albany, attend Golden Wedding of Mr. P. Phelps & Lady at Dr. Jones. Have a large company & pleasant time, stay all night.**

26 Fair. Come holme. Widow Charlotte's folks call.

27 Fair. Wife come holme. Bring Emma & Libby Jones with here. We work in hay.

28 One fair day. Work in hay. Go to river. Warm.

29 Rainy. Am unwell. Go to river. Do but little.

30 Rainy. Mow. Work a little. **George Sickler died**.

31 Rain forenoon. Clears off. Work in hay. Martin VanSlyck & Lady call.

August 1863

1 Fair SW. Work in hay.

2 Fair, very hot. I take Wife & Marite, go to Martin VanSlyck's, spend the day. Little rain.

3 Fair NW. Work in hay. Fine day, hot.

4 Fair, pleasant. Work in hay. Wind N & S.

5 Fair SW. Work in hay.

6 Rainy morning; clears off. Work in hay.

7 Fair NW. Work in hay. U.B. Willis & Lady here. Charley Jones here.

8 Rainy cloudy day. Do nothing. Go to river twice.

9 Very warm SW. Stay about the house. Call to VanOrden's.

10 Very warm SW. Work in hay. Rev. P. Phelps, his child and Edward Bedell here. We work very hard.

11 Fair SW. Work hard in hay. **James Sherman drownded**.

12 Fair. Work hard in hay. Rev. P. Phelps here. NW.

13 Fair. Work hard in hay. Go in swimming.

14 Fair SW. Work in hay and oats.

15 Fair. P. Phelps & Children leave. Work in hay.

16	Rainy. Go to Meeting. Go Under Hill. Call to T. Civill's.
17	Rainy. Clears off. I and Wife go to Greenville. Stay to A. Fancher's. Boys work in hay.
18	Fair. I go to Greenville village. Meet assessors. Then take my wool, go to Teneyck Huyck's, then holme. Boys in hay.
19	Fair. Work in hay. Mrs. A. Civill & Valera, Mrs. Thomas and Carrie Hotaling call.
20	SW. Shower in afternoon. Work in hay.
21	Rainy. Work ½ day in hay. **Am not well.**
22	Shower in afternoon. Work in hay.
23	Showery morning; clears off. **Not well.** Mr. Willis & T.H. McKee call here. **Am in house all day.**
24	Cloudy SW. Work in hay.
25	Cloudy rainy day. Do nothing. Go to river. Cornelius sick. Wet weather.
26	Rainy. Clears off. Work in hay.
27	Fair NW. Work in hay.
28	Fair SW. Work in hay Under Hill.
29	Rainy SW. Do nothing. Go to river.
30	Fair, cold NW. Take Mother Hotaling to Flat Bush, then take Anthony to R.H. VanBergen's. Take dinner, leave him and come holme.
31	Fair, cool NW. Work in hay Under Hill.

September 1863

1	Fair. I, Wife & Levi take boat to Albany, dine with Mr. Thomas. **See the return of 10th regiment.** Go to Saratoga, stop at the Cressent.
2	Fair. Go around Saratoga, see what is going on.
3	Fair. **Go about village drink Congress Water.**[336] **Visit all the springs. Go to the fair.**
4	Fair. **Go around, then take cars and stage to Glenn's Falls. Dine, then stage to Schroon Lake.** Stop to A.B. VanBenthuyzen's.
5	Fair. **Go about Schroon.**
6	Fair. **Go to Meeting. Call to Mr. Fowler's and Alvy Robbins.**
7	Fair. **Go to Ireland Island.**
8	Fair. **Go to Garret VanBenthuyzen. Go fishing.**
9	Fair. **Go to Andrew VanBenthuyzen. Go fishing.**
10	Fair. **Come to Fort Edward with Mrs. A. VanBenthuyzen. Stay to Fort Edward all night.**

Congress Bottle

---

[336] Water from Congress Springs in Saratoga supposedly to have a curative effect. The water came in embossed green bottles.

11	Fair. **Come holme. Harriet VanBenthuyzen come along.**
12	Fair. **I and Levi go to Mr. Mead's, get flag stone for schoolhouse.**
13	Cloudy SW. Go to Meeting to Dutch church.
14	Fair. Draw dirt. Pick apples. **Lay stone to schoolhouse**.
15	Fair. Draw dirt and manure. **Am unwell with headache and toothache**.
16	Fair. Draw manure. Get horses shod. Draw timber from Under Hill.
17	Fair SW. **Go to Westerlo after flag stone**.
18	Rainy day. Lay around. Go to river.
19	Cloudy, little rainy. Go after flag stone. **Wm. F. Cronk brought holme dead. Call to J. Cronk's in eve.**
20	**I attend funeral of Wm. Cronk**. Cloudy, cold. Call to T. Civill's.
21	Fair. **Cradle buckwheat**. Go after flag stone.
22	Fair, cool. David Mead call here. We rake up buckwheat, cut up corn. **I lay stone to M.E. Church ½ day.**
24	Fair. Set up corn. Lay walk in New Street.
25	Rainy. Go to river. Sheldon Houghtaling visit here. Dominie Stillwell & Lady, Captain Colvin & Lady, T. Civill & Lady, Lucy Taylor & Laura Calder visit here.
26	Cloudy NW. Work at hay slats and stable. Mrs. J. Rea, Mrs. Gorse, Mrs. A. Teneyck, Monica & Mrs. Jack here.
27	Fair, pleasant. Go to Meeting. Go Under Hill. Call to Acton Civill's in evening.
28	Fair. **Lay walk to church**. Dig potatoes.
29	Fair. **Dig potatoes, thresh buckwheat, clean up beans**.
30	Fair, foggy. Get horses shod. Draw & thresh buckwheat. Cornelius and Nick help Gregory ½ day. **Mrs. John Sickles died**.

October 1863

1	Fair. **I take folks, go to Albany County Fair. Start to come holme, go back & stay all night to Dr. Jones. Break my wagon.**
2	Cloudy. Attend Fair. Then come back holme.
3	Cloudy. I go to river. Work at stable. Go to Mrs. Rea's & to E. Bandon's.
4	Fair, warm SW. Go to church. Call to Willis's & to I. Gregory's.
5	Fair NW. Dig potatoes. **Put 7 barrels of potatoes on boat. Pick 11 barrels apples**.
6	Fair. Finish potatoes. **Send off 9 more barrels & one for I. Gregory**.
7	Fair. Pick apples. Cate VanBergen, Emma Hotaling, Mary Ann Hotaling and Mr. P. Conely here.
8	Cloudy SW. Pick apples all day. Rainy in evening.
9	Fair SW. **Pick apples. I take 75 bushels to J. Springstead for cider**.

10 Fair morning, cloudy afternoon. Husk corn. Dominie Patterson & Dominie Slater, Elida VanSlyck here. **James Schofield died**.

11 Cloudy. Go to Meeting. **Attend funeral of James Schofield**.

12 Fair cold. Husk corn. Go to river.

13 Fair. Finish husk corn. Take tea to T. Civill's. **Attend school meeting**.

14 Fair SW. Draw holme corn stalks. Take cider barrels to J. Springstead's.

15 Fair, warm. Take E. Stanton's wine to Baltimore. Get timber Under Hill. Mrs. John Rea here.

16 Rainy day. Go to Westerlo, get a load of stone.

17 Fair SW. **Bring holme cider. Press hay. Martin VanBergen & Lady here. I take them & Mrs. T. Civill & Elida VanSlyck go to Niskayuna to Shaker's. Stay all night at the family of Mr. Bates. Take supper & breakfast.**

18 Fair SW. **Go to Shaker Meeting.** Come holme. Wm. Bagley here.

19 Rainy. Draw & press hay. A.B. VanBenthuyzen here.

20 Fair. Press hay. A.B. VanBenthuyzen & daughter leave.

21 Fair. Work at stable. Press hay. Mr. Frothingham and another gentleman here. We take Wm. Bagley, go to Uncle Garry's to tea.

22 Fair cool. Press & draw hay. Wm. Bagley here.

23 Fair. Press hay. Go to Albany & Troy. Wm. Bagley go along.

24 Cloudy & rainy. Marite come. **We press 40 bales of hay from 8 o'clock AM till sundown**.

25 Fair, cold NW. Go to Meeting. Call to T. Civill's.

26 Cloudy, cold. I take T. Civill & Lady, Lewis Civill & Lady and children, go to Baltimore for a ride. Then they visit here the rest of the day. Draw hay on boat.

27 Cloudy, cold NW. Press hay. Cornelius come holme. I go to town meeting. Levi get hoop poles. I get Topsy shod forward.

28 Fair, cold NW. Press hay.

29 Fair NW. Press hay and draw it away.

30 Fair, warm SW. Draw hay & coal. Work at stable. Dig beets.

31 Rainy SW. Dig carrots. Press hay. Work at stable.

November 1863

1 Fair, cold SW. Walk around. Am unwell.

2 Fair NW. Work at stable. Dig beets & turnips.

3 Fair. **Send off 17 barrels apples. Press hay; send off 3 loads. Marite leave for New York. I attend Election.** Elizabeth & Jenny Trego here.

4 Fair. Go after stone. Boys press hay. **Mrs. John Anderson's children burned to death**.

5 Fair SW. Put up apples. Draw hay and one load of wood for old Dick.

6   Cloudy. Get out slats. Press hay. **I start for Herkimer. Get as far as Eben Kelly's. Stay all night.**

7   Fair. Boys press hay. I get to H. Sperl's.

8   Cloudy. I go to Mr. Bly's.

9   Fair. I come back as far as Mr. Kelly's. Stay all night.

10   I come holme. Boys press hay.

11   Fair. I press hay. Take in apples.

12   Fair warm. **Fix cellar door. Draw hoop poles. Press hay. Shingle stable**. Mrs. Maria VanSlyck & daughter and Elizabeth Hotaling here.

13   Fair. Work at stable. Press hay. Go to river.

14   Fair. Draw hay. **I & Wife go to New York**.

15   **Rain all day on passage**.

16   Rainy. **Go to Andrew VanAntwerp's.**

17   Rainy. **I go to Brooklyn to Wm. Bagley's. We go to funeral.**

18   Rainy. **I go to Brooklyn. Buy Levi a cutter & self a hat**.

19   Fair. **I go with J.J. Silcock to Central Park**. **Mrs. Widow Gedney died**.

20   Fair. **Stay around Dr. VanAntwerp's, then start for holme.**

21   Rain all day. Arrive holme.

22   Fair. Go to cemetery. Call to I. Gregory's.

23   Fair. Draw stone. Break out stone. Plow.

24   Rain all day. Work in waggon house.

25   Fair. Plow. Draw timber for stable. Go to river.

26   Fair. Plow. Work at stable.

27   Fair SW. Plow. Work at stable. Wm. Bagley call here.

28   Rainy. Plow. Fix stable. Wife come holme.

29   Fair cold NW. Go to Meeting. Call to Seabridge. Wm. Bagley here.

30   Very cold NW. Work at stable. Plow.

December 1863

1   Fair. Cold NW wind. Work at stable. Draw wood. Settle with Peter Roberts. Pay him off.

2   Fair. SW cold. I kill my 5 hogs & two for P. Seabridge, 1 for Wallas.

3   Fair cold. Draw manure. Cut up hogs. Fix my stable.

4   Fair SW. Draw manure. Work at stable.

5   Cloudy. Draw manure. Work at stable. **Tommy Colvin died**.

6   Fair, cold NW. Stay at holme. Call to Mrs. Clement's & to P. Seabridge.

7   Fair cold. Draw manure. Go on the Whitbeck Farm with Mr. Robertson.

8	Fair cold. **Attend the funeral of Tommy Colvin**. Draw manure. Albert Hotaling & Mr. Lisk here.
9	Cloudy morning SW. Turns to north. Cornelius sick. I am unwell.
10	Very cold NW. Stay around the house. Mrs. B. Weymouth here.
11	Very cold NW. Draw leaves. Draw wood for I. Gregory. Cornelius sick. River freeze up.
12	Rainy. Go to river. Work around the house. **Wm. Winnie died**.
13	Rainy day. Stay about the house. Mr. T. Civill call. I call to Wallas's.
14	Rainy day. Work at stable. Mrs. McCabe here.
15	Fair. Lay cross walk to Peter Seabridge's. Albert Hotaling & James Lisk here. **I take Mother Hotaling to New Baltimore. She executes a deed of her farm to Albert Hotaling he pays her $950. I deposit the money with Johnson & Co.**
16	Fair SW cold. Cornelius sick. We draw leaves.
17	Snow all day. I kill my beef.
18	Rain & sloppy. Clears off. I cut up my beef. Fix my stable. Attend a tea party to James Jack's.
19	Fair NW cold. Get horses shod.
20	Fair cold. Stay at holme. Call to A.E. Willis. **U.B. Willis died**.
21	Fair cold NW. Make sley box.
22	Fair cold. **We take a load, go to Coxsackie. Attend the funeral of U.B. Willis. Bring him to our cemetery**.
23	Fair NW cold. Go to James Comers. Take my beef hide to the tannery to tan for one half. Call to Mrs. Clement's.
24	Fair. Saw wood. Go to river. **Attend to making out cemetery deeds**.
25	Fair. I and Levi go to T.E. Huyck's, get cloth. Boys go skating.
26	Cold pleasant. Cut & draw wood. Go to river.
27	Fair. Stay around house. Levi go to Coxsackie, bring Wife holme.
28	Snow all day. I get horses shod. I take Wife, call to J. Muckelroy's in evening. Mr. A. Hotaling & Mr. Lisk here.
29	Cloudy. **I and Wife, Gerry & Jane Springstead go to Albany to John N. Cutler's. Have a very pleasant visit. High time**.
30	Fair SW. Thawy. Cut & draw wood.
31	Cloudy SW. Cut & draw wood.

January 1864

1	Stormy, clear off, cold. **I take a load of children, go a sleigh riding to Coeymans Hollow. Call to Dominie Stillwell. Attend a festival to McKee's school room in the evening. Have a very pleasant time.**
2	Fair, very cold. Cut wood. Go to river.
3	Fair, SW cold. Call to Wallas's.

4	Fair, cold NW. Very cold. Cut & draw wood all day. **Elias Holmes died**.
5	Snow all day. Attend the funeral of Elias Holmes. Saw & split wood. **Barent Teneyck & Miss Wyncoop get married**.
6	Fair, cold NW. Cut wood. Martin VanSlyck bring Mother Hotaling holme. Levi goes to New Baltimore.
7	Fair very cold. Pay my tax. Am not very well. **Ischer Bates and two Shaker women, T. Civill & Lady here visit & dine**.
8	Fair, cold. Draw wood. Attend P.R. Meeting.
9	Fair. Chop and draw wood. **Dominie Patterson here to Quarterly Meeting**.
10	Fair, very cold. Attend Quarterly Meeting. Casper Whitbeck & Lady, Dominie Patterson here to dinner.
11	Fair SW. Go to Greenville. Stay to A. Fancher's all night.
12	Fair. Collect my rents. Come holme. Levi go to Albany for Mr. Holstead.
13	Fair SW. I take Mary to Albany. Go to D. Jones to dinner. Attend to her teeth.
14	Fair SW. Attend P.R. Meeting. B.E. Holmes here. Donation of Mr. Goss.
15	Stormy. I go to Castleton with Josiah Sherman. Boys draw hoop poles.
16	Fair, cold NW. Draw hoop poles. Go to Uncle Garry's. Go to river.
17	Fair SW. Go to Meeting. Call to Wallas's.
18	Rainy. Draw wood & poles. Go to river.
19	Rainy. Cut wood. Go to river.
20	Fair, cold. Wm. Bagley, Andrew B. Hotaling & Lady here. We cut and draw slat timber. **Charles Sager and Agnes Schoonmaker and James Schoonmaker and Miss Hill get married**.
21	Fair, cool NW. Draw wood. Aunt Sarah Ann & Cate VanBergen here. I go to Baltimore. **Go skating in the evening**.
22	Fair, warm. Cut & draw wood. Attend a party to Willis's in evening.
23	Fair SW. Fix barn Under Hill. Uncle Garry & Lady here. **We put up our large new Buck Stove**. Mr. McKee call.
24	Fair, warm SW. Go to Meeting. Call to J. Ziegler's. **Mr. Davis and Elenor Ostrander get married**.
25	Fair, warm. Work at stables Under Hill. Go to river. **Wife & Levi go to Coxsackie flats after girl**.
26	Fair NW. **I, Wife & Levi go to Casper Whitbeck's, visit, then to Dominie Patterson's donation. Have a large party. They gave him $350**. Come to Mr. Whitbeck's, stay all night.
27	Fair. Take breakfast, come holme. Put up beans for H. Sperl.
28	Fair SW. Fix up new axe. Go to river.
29	Fair SW. Boys thresh. I go to river, do nothing.
30	Cloudy SW. Boys thresh. I go to river.

31 Cloudy. Go to Meeting. Call to T. Civill's. Call to Wallas's.

February 1864

1   Snow & hail all day. Finish threshing. Go to river.
2   Cloudy a little. Draw manure. Take tea to Wallas's and spend the evening to A.N. Briggs all hands.
3   Fair NW. Go to Albany for Mr. Holstead. **John Gibbens' Daughter died**.
4   Fair SW. Work around. Go to river. Spend the evening to Mr. Civill's.
5   Fair SW. **Attend funeral of Miss Gibbens**. Go to Schodack, get Mary's skates. Attend party to T. Civill's in evening.
6   Fair SW. Clean up oats. Go to river.
7   Fair NW. Go to Meeting. Call to I. Gregory's.
8   Fair morning. Clean up oats. Squally. Draw hay. Go to river.
9   Fair NW. Draw hay. Go to river.
10 Fair, very cold NW. Draw hay. Go to river.
11 Fair NW. Draw hay. Go to river My horse Topsy get kicked.
12 Cloudy NW. Draw hay. Fix stable. Go to river. Mrs. John Rea here, visit. Dominie Colier call.
13 Fine day SW. Draw hay. **Fix schoolhouse. Have a party here.** Mr. A.N. Briggs & Lady. Ephraim & Newton & Elizabeth Briggs, Hannah Andrews, Miss Witbeck, Mr. T. Civill & Lady, Capt. J.J. Colvin & Lady. I.M. Harris & Eliza Clement here. **Peter Holbrook died**.
14 Fair, cold NW. Go to Meeting. Go to cemetery. Call to Wallas's.
15 Fair. Draw hay. Attend funeral of Peter Holbrook.
16 Very cold NW. Finish draw hay. Go to river.
17 Very cold NW. Snowy. Go to river twice.
18 Very cold SW. **Sylvester Teal Married**. Go to river.
19 Fair, cold. Go to river. **Have a party of Sunday School Teachers here**.
20 Fair SW. Work around. **Go to river. See horses trot**.
21 Fair SW. Go to Meeting.
22 Fair SW. I take Mrs. Jack, Mrs. T. Civill, Wife, go to Hollow to Dominie Stilwell's. Break my waggon tongue.
23 Fair. Draw stone. Go to Uncle Garry's
24 Fair. Fix waggon tongue. Carrie Houghtaling here.

25 Fair. **I take Wife, Mrs. Civill, Carrie Hotaling to Albany. Go to the Bazaar.**[337] Dine to Dr. Jones. Levi Seabridge & Mary Blaisdell get married.

26 Snow all day. Go to the river twice.

27 Fair. I take Mary & man, Cornelius & Ephraim Briggs, go to Albany. Dine to Dr. Jones. S. Wood come back with us.

28 Cloudy. Stay in the house. Mr. Willis call.

29 Fair NW. Work around the house. S. Wood here.

March 1864

1 Fair morning, snow in afternoon. Draw stone. **Attend Cornelius Lawsuit. Sickles Family arrested for stealing chickens**.

2 Fair. Little do nothing. Go to the river.

3 Fair. Work to Holmestead. Cut wood.

4 Fair, pleasant. Work at Holmestead. **Patrick Minick died**.

5 Fair SW. Rainy in evening. **Survey N.H. Johnson's Farm**. Take tea to Tom Rosecrant's.

6 Fair SW. **Ice start a little**. I go to Meeting

7 Snow 4 inches deep. Go to river. **P. Minnick buried**.

8 Fair. **Attend election allowing soldiers to vote in the army.**[338]

9 Fair, pleasant. Attend Cornelius Lawsuit. **Ice goes out**. Attend a party to Egbert Stanton's in evening.

10 Fair. **Help Anthony survey. Steamboat goes up**.

11 Cloudy & wet. Go to river. Cut wood.

12 Fair. Work around. Uncle Garret, Caroline & Elizabeth Hotaling, Mrs. Thomas, Maria VanSlyck & daughter here.

13 Snow, mud & rain. Go to Meeting. Call to Willis's.

14 Fair NW. Pleasant cold. **Our Barge comes**.

15 Fair, cold NW. Make up and sign writings with Gerry Robertson. A.E. Willis & Lady, Dominie Gorse & Lady, J. Jack & Lady, H. Springstead & Lady, Mrs. B. Weymouth, Mrs. T. Civil, Mrs. E Stanton & daughter, J. Muckelroy & Lady here.

---

[337] In February and March 1864, as the Civil War raged on, the Army Relief Bazaar opened to raise money desperately needed for the US Sanitary Commission to aid sick and wounded Union soldiers. Military hospitals were understaffed, with limited medical supplies or decent food. The Bazaar was organized by individuals from all walks of life from Albany and the surrounding area. Carpenters erected a large temporary structure, staffed with cooks, crafters, clerks and many others, mainly women who gave of their time and talents. Over $100,000 was raised, a huge sum for that time. It was so successful that it carried over into March.

[338] 1864 was the first time since 1812 that a presidential election took place during a war. President Lincoln won re-election, but not without allowing the soldiers' votes. This was the beginning of mail-in voting.

16 Fair very cold. Go to river. **Attend wedding party of Levi & Mary Seabridge**. Have a good time.

17 Cloudy. Go to river.

18 Fair SW. Work at boxes for trees. **Attend Teachers Association to James Jack's**. Have a fine time.

19 Fair. Work at tree boxes. Miss Gorse, Miss Ward, Miss Miller, Charlotte Stilwell & Brother here.

20 Fair, cold. Freeze all day. Go to Meeting.

21 Fair, cold NW. Cut wood. Go to river. Miss VanDerzee & Mrs. Hull call.

22 Fair, very cold. Cut wood. **Jane Eliza Clement died**.

23 Cloudy NW. Very cold. Cut wood. Go to river.

24 Fair, hard NW. **Attend funeral of Jane Eliza Clement**.

25 Fair, warmer. Draw two load hoops from E. Roberts.

26 Cloudy. Draw hoops. Draw manure. Work in shop. Go to river.

27 Fair NW. Go to Meeting. Go to McCullock's & to Mrs. Wilson's & to Mrs. Holmes & to Wallas's.

28 Fair. Draw two loads sand. **Work at house where Mother lived**.

29 Cloudy. Work at house. Go after trees.

30 Snowy & stormy. Work at house. Go after trees. Peter Seabridge & Lady, Levi Seabridge & Lady, Jane Seabridge, Mrs. Cornelius Ryon & Daughter here.

31 Snow & rain all day. Work at Mother's house.

April 1864

1 Cloudy and rainy. **Work at Mother's house**.

2 Cloudy. **Work at Mother's house. Attend Nomination at J.B. Shear's**. J.W. Story here.

3 Fair NW. Go to Cemetery & to vineyard. Go to Meeting. Mary Seabridge, Miss Ryon call. Willis call; gave me a gold pen.

4 Fair SW. Draw two loads sand & two barrels lime. Go to river. Graft trees. Our girl come to work from Coxsackie.

5 Cloudy SW. Make mortar and fence under the Hill.

6 Fair cold NW. Make fence Under Hill. Wife go to Albany.

7 Fair. Lay wall Under Hill all day. Gregory & John Jackson help.

8 Fair. Draw manure. Dig stone Under Hill. **Mrs. Stilwell died**.

9 Fair. I & Levi go to Albany, Troy & Lansingburgh. Buy a watch for Levi & Anthony, buy oilcloth.

10 Rainy day. Go to Meeting.

11 Snow & rain all day. Make a swing gate & fence.

12	Snow & rain all day. Work in shop. Put down oil cloth.
13	Cloudy & rainy SW. Plaster house. Make fence. Help I. Gregory.
14	Cloudy, rainy. Work at stables.
15	Fair NW. Make fence. Fix up gate near road.
16	Fair cold NW. Fix gate. I take Wife to J. Mull's. Get fish.
17	Very cold NW. Call to Civill's, to Gregory's & Wallas's. **Mr. Baldwin's Steam Mill Burned last evening**.
18	Fair. Make fence. Plow. **Band here this evening. Gives us music**.
19	Cloudy NW. Draw manure. Go Under Hill.
20	Cold NW. Harrow land. Plant 1½ bushels potatoes.
21	Fair, pleasant. Sow 9 bushels of oats. Harrow. Plow. Draw stone.
22	Pleasant. Plow all day. Miss McCabe here.
23	Cloudy SW. Cut wood. Lay wall under barn. Plow Under Hill.
24	Fair, pleasant. Go to Meeting. Call to Willis's & to Wallas's & to Peter Seabridge's. D. Witbeck, Mr. Rennie, Ack Hotaling call.
25	Rainy SW. Sow & harrow oats & grass seed. Call to Willis. Mr. Goss & Wife & Children, Mrs. T. Civill & Mrs. Weymouth visit.
26	Cloudy morning; clears off. Go to Meeting.
27	Rainy. Dominie Patterson here, stay all night. Miss Goss leave.
28	Cold, cloudy. I am unwell. Stay in house all day. Gregory call.
29	Fair. Attend to income tax. Make fence. Go to river.
30	Fair. Make fence. Harrow oats. Mary Seabridge here

May 1864

1	Cloudy. Clears off. Go to Meeting.
2	Fair SW. Make fence. Mrs. Mary VanSlyck, Mrs. J. Trego & others here.
3	Rainy day. Wife & Mary go to New York. I go to river. Work around.
4	Fair SW. Make fence. **Mrs. Stephen Drew brought dead here from New York**.
5	Fair. **Levi attend funeral of Mrs. Drew**. We make fence.
6	Fair. Plow all day Under Hill.
7	Fair. Plow. Dig stone. **Mr. Requa barn burned**.
8	Shower, warmer. Go to Meeting. Willis & McKee call. Go to vineyard.
9	SW, very warm. Press hay.
10	Fair, heavy SW. **Sow 21½ bushels of oats**.
11	Cold cloudy rainy. Harrow oats. Fix fence.

12 Cloudy SW. Cultivate potato ground. Plow ½ day. **Levi sells his colt to Mr. Schoonmaker for $150.**

13 Cloudy SW. Call to Willis with Wm. Minick. He orders Willis and he pays me 50 dollars. Lay wall. Make garden. Levi sow 1 bushel of oats. Gregory help.

14 Cloudy SW. Make fence. Cultivate potato ground. Draw hay. Wife & Mary come from NY. Bring Lizzie Silcock along and a dog.

15 Cloudy SW. Go to Meeting. Call to Wallas's. T.A. Hotaling & Emma Hotaling call here.

16 Plow. Harrow. Draw manure. Rainy afternoon, get wet.

17 Little shower. Plow. Harrow. Draw manure.

18 Shower in forenoon. Draw manure. Furrow land. Plant potatoes for I. Gregory. **David Holbrook and Lib King get married**.

19 Fair, cool NW. Plant potatoes. Harrow & furrow corn ground.

20 Fair SW. Plant corn Under Hill.

21 Fair, hot SW. Alter colt. Plow orchard. Pick stone Under Hill.

22 Fair, cool NW. Go to vineyard. Wallas call.

23 Fair SW. Dig blind ditch. Dig stone. Plow. Mrs. Maria VanSlyck and daughter here.

24 Showery. Mrs. Herrick here. Plow. Harrow. Fix road. Go Under Hill with my calf.

25 Fair warm SW. Plow. Help Gregory plant beans.

26 Cloudy rainy. Plant beans. Plow. Cut brush. Press hay.

27 Sunshine, warm, rainy. Press hay. Break press. I lose a hog.

28 Fair NW. I & Levi go to Albany. I come back right off on account of my lumber being shipped.

29 Fair. Go to cemetery. Call to Willis's. McKee call.

30 Fair. Draw away 47 bales hay. Plow. Burn brush. Go to river.

31 Fair, warm. Hoe potatoes. Burn brush. Dig ditch.

June 1864

1 Cloudy SW. Make blind drain. **Have a freight of lumber come.**

2 Fair. Draw up lumber. **Phillip Winnie get killed. Attend Lawsuit of Capt. Crest and Gil Cronk.**

3 Fair. Finish drawing and piling lumber.

4 Fair. Press hay. John Cronk & Lady and Charlotte Cronk here. Doct. VanAntwerp and Marite come.

5 Fair. Go to vineyard & Under Hill to Mrs. Wilson's.

6 Warm, small shower. Pick stone Under Hill. Draw hay. Dominie Stilwell and Family here.

7 Fair. Split slats. Lay walk. Dominie Ackerly & Lady here.

8 Fair. Levi take folks to Martin VanSlyck's. Elida come here. I split slats.

9   Rainy morning. Clears off. Mary Seabridge here. Press hay. **The Hudson Boat gets blowed up.**[339]

10 Cold NW. Work in corn and blind drain. Mrs. Ed VanOrden here.

11 Fair. **I go to Herkimer. Stay to H. Sperl's all night**.

12 Fair. **Work around. Have a little shower**.

13 Fair. **I go to Weston's, see them make cheese. Settle with H. Sperl**.

14 Fair. **Come holme.** Very dry weather.

15 Fair. Draw lumber. Very warm.

16 Fair NW. Finish draw up lumber. Go out to P. Roberts. Get hoops. Hoe corn. Put cement on cistern.

17 Fair. Hot and dry. Hill potatoes. Go to Dean's Mill, get plaster.

18 Plaster corn. Lay barn floor. Mrs. J.J. Silcock & Children here.

19 Fair. SW hot. Sleep; lay around. Willis & Wm. Bagley call.

20 Fair. No wind. Hot. Lay barn floor.

21 Fair. Work at barn. Sell cemetery grass to I. Newman for $25.50.

22 Fair SW. Work at barn. Uncle Garry & Daughters here.

23 Fair N & S. Work at barn.

24 Fair, hot. Draw manure. Wm. Bagley here.

25 Fair NW. Very hot. Draw manure.

26 Fair, hot NW. Lay around the house.

27 Fair, cool. Press hay. Wife & Tony go to Albany.

28 Fair. Go after stakes. Make fence in the orchard.

29 Fair. Make fence. Draw water. Miss Coonly here.

30 Fair morning, rainy afternoon. Hoe corn. Fix cistern.

July 1864

1   Cloudy. Hoe corn. Wallas help ½ day.

2   Cloudy, rainy. Hoe corn. Go to river.

4   Fair, cool. **Go on excursion of Coeymans Band to West Camp have a good time**.

5   Harrow buckwheat ground. Draw manure.

6   Fair. Sow Indian wheat. Draw manure.

---

[339] From the NY Times 10 June 1864, bails of hay stowed on the main deck of steamer Berkshire, of the New York and Hudson Line, caught on fire at about 10:00 pm a few miles below Rondout. As the fire was impossible to extinguish, the pilot headed toward shore at maximum speed and ran her aground two miles below Hyde Park. Thirty to forty people, many of them children, perished in the accident. The cause of the fire was never determined.

7   Cloudy. Drive two cows to bull. Harrow Indian wheat. Henry Sperl and David Bly here. Levi take Wife and a load, go to Albany.

8   Fair. Go around with D. Bly. Finish buckwheat ground.

9   Fair. Take D. Bly to Albany. Get sugar and scythes.

10 Fair SW. Go to Meeting, take a walk.

11 Fair SW hot. Commence mowing. E. Bandon get horses shod.

12 Fair NW. Draw away hay. Work in new hay. Charlie Jones here.

13 Fair. Work in hay.

14 Fair, hot SW. Work in hay.

15 Fair. Work in hay. Virginia Blaisdell here.

16 Fair SW. Very hot. Lay around. Mrs. Harriet, formerly Miss TenBrock, here.

17 Fair SW. Work in hay.

18 Fair. Work in hay.

19 Fair SW. Work in hay.

20 Fair, hot SW. Work in hay. Take Wife to Uncle Garry's.

21 Fair, cool NW. Work in hay and oats.

22 Fair, cool NW. Work in hay. Emma Jones here.

23 Fair, cool SW. Work in hay. Very smoky.

24 Fair, hot. Go to Meeting.

25 Rainy. Work ½ day in hay. Wm. Bagley here.

26 Cloudy morning; clears off. Work in hay.

27 Fair NW. Work in hay.

28 Fair. Work in hay.

29 Fair. Work at oats. **Discharge my men**.

30 Fair. Finish hay and oats. Go to river. Go in swimming.

31 Fair, hot. Go to Meeting. Call to Willis. Go to vineyard.

August 1864

1   Go a fishing. Have a little shower.

2   Cloudy rain in evening. Fix shop to J. Hazleton's. Go Under Hill, get lumber for barn.

3   Rainy day. Go to river. Mrs. Lucy Colvin here.

4   Cloudy. Dig out under corn crib and under hay press.

5   Fair. Draw stone. **Survey island**. Go to E. VanOrden's to tea.

6   Fair. Buy 3 pigs of Mark Row. Attend appraisal of land for James Hotaling, George Wolf, Gerry Springstead. E. VanOrden & Uncle Garry.

7   Fair, hot. Go to Meeting. Mr. McKee & Willis call. Maria Hotaling here.

8	Fair. **Go after 2 load stone for cemetery road**. Get out stone. Plow.
9	Fair, smoky. Plow. Draw coal and stone.
10	Fair, hot. Plow and cut brush.
11	Fair, smoky. Fix house. Plow. Mrs. Jones & Children come here.
12	Fair. Plow. Work at sluice. Take our folks & Mrs. T. Civill out riding.
13	Fair. Mrs. Dr. Jones & Eliza Phelps leave. Shower in evening.
14	Fair. Go to Meeting & to vineyard.
15	Fair. Plow. I and Wife go to Greenville. Stop to John Neill's, stay all night. Take supper & breakfast.
16	Fair. Come holme. Stop to John Smith's. Take my wool to TenEyck from A. Fancher's. Swear off my tax.
17	Rain all day. Fix stable. Go to river.
18	Fair. Plow all day. Mr. A.N. Briggs & Lady call. Dr. Spoor here.
19	Fair. Plow. Go to river. Mrs. T. Civill call.
20	Cloudy. I and Anthony go to Albany. J. Silcock & Elizabeth here. A.E Willis call.
21	Fair. Go to vineyard. All hands take a ride to Ben Hotaling's.
22	Cloudy, little rainy. Draw stone for Civill. Draw stone for T. Civill. Draw gravel. Dominie Stilwell & Children here.
23	Fair. Stilwell & Children leave. Draw gravel and brush. Settle with Barent TenEyck.
24	Fair. Plow & harrow all day. J.J. Silcock leave.
25	Fair. Plow. Draw manure. Get seed, rye, to Henry Springstead's. 16 bushels.
26	Fair SW. Sow rye & harrow. Take Wife & Folks to Gerry Springstead's.
27	Fair. Draw manure Under Hill. Mrs. Goss, Mrs. Colvin, Marite here.
28	Fair. Go to Meeting & to vineyard.
29	Fair. **Attend Lawsuit of Hudson River & Saratoga RR at N. Baltimore**. Go on their farms.
30	Fair. Draw manure. Sow rye.
31	Fair. Sow rye. Draw stone. Harrow.

September 1864

1	Fair. Pick stone. Roll land. Mr. Stilwell here. Take his horse and leave. Go to river.
2	Fair. Clean up hay seed. **Attend railroad suit of James Hotaling to New Baltimore**. Dr. VanAntwerp come here.
3	Fair SW. I take Peter Seabridge to Albany. Wm. Bagley Jr. here. Miss Goss call.
4	Rainy. Go to vineyard. Lay around.
5	Rainy. Sow grass seed. Dig out under corn crib. Dr. Spoor & Wm. Bagley Jr. here.

6   Fair, cloudy. Work at corn crib. David VanAntwerp, Dr. Spoor, William Bagley & Miss Goss here.

7   Fair. Work at corn crib. **Go to Universalist Meeting in evening**.

8   Fair. **Send 8 barrels of apples to New Baltimore Barge**. Work at corn crib. Wm. Bagley Jr. here.

9   Fair. Work at corn crib. Dr. VanOrden & Lady, Mrs. Ed VanOrden & Child, Aunt Sarah Ann & Cate VanBergen, Widow Charlotte [here]. Acton Civill call.

10 Fair. Work at corn crib. Go to river.

11 Cloudy. A little shower. **Attend the funeral of Mary Jane Crothier**. Go to vineyard with G.F. Cranston. Have lots of calls.

12 Cloudy. Clears off. Work at corn crib. Pick apples.

13 Fair. **Attend Lawsuit of George Wolf with R.R. Company at Baltimore**.

14 Fair. Get horses shod. Go to Bethlehem. **Get tan bark**.[340] Mr. T. Civill & Lady, Mrs. Lewis Civill here, visit.

15 Fair. **Draw tan bark for icehouse**. Capt. Jackson, J.W. Jolly here. Mr. Brook's girls call.

16 Far. Work at corn crib. Mrs. John Rea & Mrs. Nichols here.

17 Fair. **Draw one load tan bark**. Cut up corn. Spend the evening and take tea to Mr. T. Civill's. Lots of company.

18 Fair. Go to Meeting. Mr. Civill's folks here. We all go to vineyard.

19 Fair NW. **Cut up corn. Pick plums**.

20 Fair. Pick plums & apples. **Work ½ day with team on Catholic Hill with team**. Mr. Hill & Lady here.

21 Fair. Cut up corn.

22 Fair. Pick apples. **Work ½ day to Catholic Hill**.

23 Fair SW. **Work at icehouse and ½ day on cemetery road**.

24 Fair. Work at hay press & ½ day to cemetery road. Showery. J.J. Silcock & Children here.

25 Fair, cold NW. Go to Meeting. Call to Willis's. Go to vineyard.

26 Fair, cool. Work at Indian wheat & apples.

27 Fair. Work at Indian Wheat. Silcock Family leave & ½ day at 2:00.

28 Cloudy. Work at Indian wheat and cemetery road. ½ day team.

29 Lowery, rainy. Cut Indian wheat and around the house.

30 Rainy. Work at Indian wheat and waggon box.

October 1864

1   Cloudy. Rake Indian wheat. Send cider apples to Jerry Springstead.

---

[340] Tan bark is the bark of certain species of trees used for tanning leather. We don't know the purpose of using tan bark in an icehouse.

2	Rainy day. Go to vineyard.
3	Rainy. Work at grapes & grape boxes.
4	Mrs. T. Civill, B. Weymouth, Wife & children here. Fair. Help G. Rifflin pick grapes. Work at cemetery road ½ day.
5	Fair. Work at cemetery road ½ day. **I go to Herkimer**.
6	Fair. Levi work at cemetery road ¼ day. I settle with H. Sperl.
7	Fair. I. Gregory work at cemetery road ½ day. Levi get Broom corn seed. **I make a contract with D. Bly for NW part of Lot 8 Jersey Field patent**.[341]
8	Fair. Boys get broom corn seed from Island. **I come holme from Herkimer**.
9	Cold. Snow on the mountains. Go to Meeting. Civill's girl Mary here, we pick grapes.
11	Fair NW. Work at grapes. Thresh Indian wheat. **Attend School Meeting**.
12	Cloudy, frosty, rainy. Work at cemetery road. **Attend RR Suit to Baltimore**.
13	Cold NW. Cloudy. **Attend RR Suit to Athens**. Levi pick apples. Gregory work with team on cemetery road. I take dinner in Athens. Come on holme. Take supper to Baltis T. VanSlyck's.
14	Cold, cloudy NW. Lavina Rea & her Husband here, visit. We work at Indian wheat.
15	Rainy. **Go to Athens attend RR Suit for Gerry Springstead**.
16	Fair. Go to Meeting. Call to A.N. Briggs & to Willis & Gregory's.
17	Fair. **Anthony & I start for Michigan. Take boat to Albany, take cars. Arrive at Suspension Bridge at 1 o'clock am. Was too late for the connecting train & had to stop for 6 hours. We went on Suspension Bridge and looked at Niagara Falls & the country**.
18	Fair. **Take cars again 7 o'clock am, go through Canada. Arrive at Detroit at 5 pm. The country from Suspension Bridge is very fertile, but a great deal of uncleared land. Wheat looks well. Take cars at 9 pm, arrive at Grand Rapids 5 am. Went to S. Wood's; were cordially received.**
19	Fair. **We went across the river and saw Mr. Stockings who described Briggs & my land very accurately. Then went to see Mr. Canada & Son who occupies some land of mine, which is low land but good. His son is in Canada. The soil is sandy, the trees are large and mostly elm. They had only a small clearing and that is very stumpy. In fact, wherever you go, you find stumps in great abundance. Nearly all the farmers have**

---

341 We were unable to find much information about the Jersey Field Patent except that it is in Herkimer County. Lot 8 is on the southern boundary.

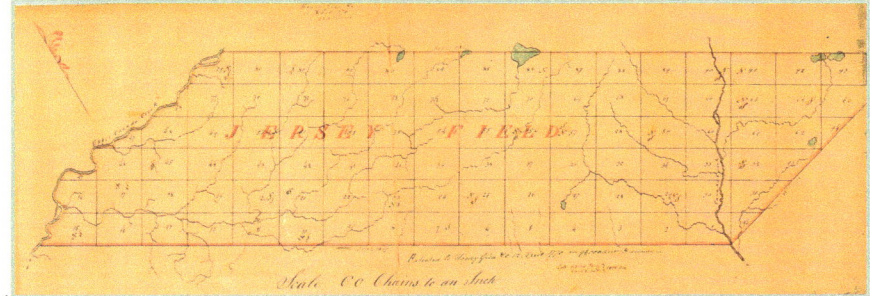

sheep. We went to see some city lots of mine. Lots 11 & 12 in Block 5 and found stumps in abundance.

20   Fair. **S. Wood & I start for the land of Briggs & Blaisdell. Anthony stay to Wood's. The road from Grand Rapids is good as far as Ferguson's. Take dinner. Roads bad to Newago. Part of the way, the road was stumped out. Stay all night at the Brooks house. Newago has two public houses, two sawmills and a number of stores.**

21   Fair. **Start again up the river. Road to Croton sandy and poor soil. Timber: pine coarse & poor. Croton is a smart village. The buildings are new. It is situated on the Junction of the West Muskegon. Sawmills and shingle mills. Land poor & sandy. Then go up the river. Road good until you cross Stearns Prairie, which is worn out land. Then strike through woods. Timber coarse and large. Roads partly cut out but not stumped. Some good pine timber. Land sandy and poor. Cross the Muskegon at Mr. Rogers Acosta Co. Take dinner with Rogers. He has a hewed log house. I hire Mr. Rogers and he goes with us. Go through Big Rapids, a fine place. Growing country is better from Rogers up. Some very fine farms and it is hardwood timber. Bridge at Big Rapids crosses the Muskegon. Then we go on for D.A. Blodget's. Some parts of the roads are good, some very bad. Farming most of the way to Blodget's. Mostly log houses. Arrive at Blodget's at 8 o'clock PM. His farm is 400 acres. Has a large clearing and large business. Man has a sawmill, Grist Mill, Blacksmith Shop, log & frame house and good barns. Hay worth $50 per ton here.**

22   Fair. **Leave Blodget's, go 16 miles through the forest to Mr. Power's Shanty; dine. All woods and pine mostly. Leave team, take dinner. Pack up and start for the land. Call to Benjamin's Shanty so on up the town line. Pass through one part of section of our land. It is very good timber. Then strike the corner of the large tract. Follow the line. Timber is good pine, some hard wood. Mark B&B on the corner. Land is gently rolling. Encamp for the night. Mark FB on the encamp tree.**[342]

23   **Start again. Strike on Section 6 & 5. Land rolling. Pine more scattering, but very large and some hard wood oak & maple. Pass over knoll where Indians had buried their wheat & corn. Then leave the tract, pass through a wonderful windfall. Strike a maple forest. Good land for two miles. Then pass through a white cedar swamp. Then through pine & hemlock timber. Two miles logged off above Power's shanty on the road. Go to the shanty of Power's. Take dinner. Get up the team. Come on to Blodget's. Burn a torch light. Dark & rainy. Get to Blodget's stay all night.**

24   Fair. **Come on through Big Rapids. Stop see Mr. Fuller. Then to Roger's. Take dinner, then on to Newago, stay all night.**

25   Fair. **Come on to see Mr. Wood's prairie lands. Take dinner to a Dutchman's log house. Buy two deer skins. Arrive at Mr. Wood's at 10 pm in Grand Rapids.**

26   Fair SW. **Stay to Wood's until after dinner, then go to Andrew Hood's. They live in a good log house, have a good farm - small barn. He raised 320 bushels of good wheat. Has 92 acres of land. Has 4 smart children. Stay all night.**

---

[342] From "Coeymans and the Past" by Edward D. Giddings, 1973: Wesley Blaisdell died October 22, 1864. He was a graduate in medicine and served as brigade surgeon during the Civill War. He died at Fortress Monroe of yellow fever, on his way to rejoin the service after a leave of absence at New Orleans.

27   Rainy. **Mr. Hood, Bridget, Anthony & I go to see plaster beds on the west side of Grand River owned by Converse & Co.** It is a cave underground and the extent now covers about 3 acres. It is lit up by lamps and supported by pillars and large oak posts. The bed now worked is 10 ft. thick and the crust above is 3 ft. thick, which holds the earth above. The plaster is blasted out and carried out of the cave to the mill by rail cars. It is an interesting sight. We brought holme some fine specimens. Then we go back to Mr. Wood's, stay all night.

28   Cloudy. **Anthony & I start for holme at 9 o'clock am. Arrive at Detroit at 6 PM. Find Mr. Wood. Go to Mr. Ingraham's to tea. Go with Mr. Wood to the church where the Synod meet. Then to Russell house stay all night - very large hotel.**

29   Go to Depot. Take Great Western cars at 6½ am and arrive at Suspension Bridge in the evening. Fair weather come on and arrive at Albany in morning 5¾ am.

30   Lowry. **Take breakfast at R. Siles & stay in Albany. Dine at Dr. Jones.** Walk around the city. Go and see John Cutter's Stable. Take cars to Schodack. Then cross the river in rowboat. Arrive holme at 7 pm.

November 1864

1   Fair, cold NW. Dig potatoes. **Wm. Keller & Jane Seabridge, George Johnson & Emma Ryon get married.**

2   Fair NW. Help I Gregory dig potatoes. George, Levi & myself. **Dr. W. Blaisdell died about this time**.

3   Fair, cold. Freeze hard. We all hands help Mr. Gregory dig potatoes. John Cronk, Augustus Cronk & Lady, Mrs. John Mull here, visit.

4   Rain nearly all day. Husk corn.

5   Cold, cloudy NW. **Husk corn. Dig potatoes. Attend a political meeting at Clark's Hotel**.

6   Fair SW. Go to Meeting in the evening.

7   Rainy, wet. Husk corn all day. Go to river in evening.

8   Rainy, wet. **Send off potatoes to New York. Attend election**.

9   Cloudy, wet. Work around house. Husk corn.

10 Rainy, wet. **Wife & Levi go to Poughkeepsie.**[343]

11 Fair NW. **I go with Anthony [to] survey Ed VanOrden's farm**.

12 Fair. Draw corn & manure.

13 Cold, snow NW. Miss Cook here from Meeting.

14 Cold NW. **Put apples in cellar. Send off 8 barrels. Miss VanBuren come with Wife's sewing machine**.

15 Snow SW. Put away corn. Mrs. T. Civill here.

16 Fair NW. Very cold. **I go to Athens then to Hudson, attend RR suit for E. VanOrden. Stay all night to Bagley's Hotel**.

---

343   Levi is now 19 years old. We believe Sarah Ann was looking for a place to further his education.

17 Rainy. Come holme with boat. Split slats; husk corn.

18 Cloudy NW. Finish corn. Press hay. **Get my beef from Herkimer**.

19 Fair. Press hay all day.

20 Fair. Go to Meeting.

21 Rainy. **Draw 40 bales hay to boat**. Press [hay]. Help I. Gregory. Butcher my old cow Sally.

22 Cloudy NW. Press hay. Split slats. Miss VanBuren here.

23 Fair. Heavy west wind. Press hay all day.

24 Fair. Press hay.

25 Fair. Press hay. Get out slats.

26 Fair SW. Press & draw hay. Caroline Hotaling here. Go to river.

27 Cloudy. Go to Meeting and then to Mrs. Wilson's. **Edward Blaisdell, Euphemia and Dr. Aiken here, call**.[344]

28 Cloudy rainy. Press hay. **I put up 18 gallons wine for Mr. Bancroft**.

29 Cloudy SW. Press hay. Wm. Bagley here.

30 Fair NW. Press hay. Trade mare Topsy with Mr. Lasher. Go to river.

December 1864

1   Fair. Press hay. John Wilson come to work here. Mr. R.A. Alger here.

2   Fair. Press hay.

3   Cloudy and rainy. Draw away hay. Get out slats. Press hay.

4   Fair NW. Go to Meeting. Call to Seabridge's.

5   Fair NW. Press hay. Get slat timber.

6   Cloudy, rainy. Press & draw hay.

7   Rain NW cold. Press hay. Dominie Ackerly Son & their Wives here visit.

8   Fair cold NW. Press hay.

9   Fair, very cold NW. Press & draw hay.

10 Snow all day. Press hay.

11 Snow, but milder. Go to Meeting. McKee call.

12 Cold NW. Draw hay; kill hogs.

13 Cold NW. Boil cows' feet. Work around.

14 Fair SW warm. Cut up hogs. Go to river – all froze up.

15 Fair. Cold forenoon, cloudy. Go to river. Cut up my pork in evening.

16 Fair. Go to N. Baltimore. Draw wood.

17 Cloudy misty. Go to Albany, get lots of things.

---

[344] Edward and Euphemia are two of Wesley's children.

18   Fair. Go to Meeting. Call to I. Gregory's.

19   Rainy. Levi paint sleigh. I work in the shop.

20   Cold NW. Work in shop. Go with Teneyck Schoonmaker on his farm.

21   Snow day. Work in shop. Go with Willis, see his farm.

22   Very cold NW. Cut wood. Go to river.

23   Fair, very cold. Go to Coxsackie with P. Seabridge. **Bible class meet here this evening**.

24   Fair, SW cold. Fix my well. James White help.

25   Fair. Go to Meeting.

26   Thawy SW. Take out potatoes. Fix my well. Go to river.

27   Thawy foggy. **William Akely died**. I go to Albany.

28   Foggy rainy. I work in the shop.

29   Cloudy NW overcast. Go after pine timber Under Hill. Work around house.

30   Fair SW. Get horses shod. Go to river.

31   Snow all day. Levi & Mary Seabridge here. Get my new overcoat from New Baltimore.

January 1865

1   Cold NW. Go to Meeting.

2   Fair, cold SW. Draw wood. Mr. Brandow here. Lots of calls.

3   Fair. **Survey for Uncle Garry Hotaling**. Go to river.

4   Fair, cold NW. **I take Levi to Poughkeepsie to Mr. Bisbee's school at College Hill.**[345] **Stay to supper & all night & Breakfast.**

5   Fair SW. Call at Seabridge's store. Dine with William Seabridge.

6   Rainy. Go to Greenville to A. Fancher's. Stay all night.

7   Snowy, very cold. Stop to Williamson's, get my rents. Come holme.

8   Cold NW. Stay in house. Am unwell.

9   Fair, cold. **Survey for A.E. Willis**. Go to river.

10   Rain. **Attend RR Lawsuit for A.E. Willis**.

11   Fair, cold. Very slippery. Pay my tax.

12   Fair, cold NW. Attend Plank Road meeting. Children & Wife attend donation.

13   Fair, pleasant NW. Go to river. Lay around.

14   Snow all day. **Go and see RR Bridge**. Attend P.R. Meeting. Dominie Patterson here. Attend Quarterly Meeting.

15   Fair, cold. Go to Meeting. Call to P. Seabridge.

---

[345] The Poughkeepsie Journal 18 July 2017 indicates that the Poughkeepsie Collegiate School, which later became the Riverview Military Academy, was run by Otis Bisbee.

16 Fair, very cold. **Attend funeral sermon of Dr. Blaisdell**. Go to river.

17 Fair. Willis & Lady, self & Wife, J.W. Jolly & Lady go to Martina Lysher's Bethlehem visit. Very pleasant time.

18 Fair. **Draw ice**. Mrs. Dr. Fredenburgh here.

19 Fair, cold SW. Visit to J. Reynolds all day and evening – good time.

20 Fair, very cold. **Go to RR Bridge**. Widow Charlotte & Mary VanSlyck here.

21 Fair, very cold. We go to Ed Hubbel's visit. Have a good time.

22 Cloudy SW. Go to Meeting.

23 Snow all day. Clean up oats. SW.

24 Fair, cold NW. Clean up oats. Go to river.

25 Fair, cold NW. Take out my hams. Go to river.

26 Fair, cold SW. **I take a sleigh load, go to Andrew J. TenEyck's, visit all day**.

27 Fair NW. Go to river. **Take sley load to E. VanOrden's visit**. Hang up my hams.

28 Very cold. Stay about house. Go to Meeting.

29 Fair, cold. Pay note & interest to Dr. Fredenburgh & B. Teneyck & A. Bronk.

30 Fair, pleasant. **Paint Bobsleighs**. Go to Gerry Robertson's. Mary go along.

31 Fair SW. A.N. Briggs & Lady, J. Reynolds & Lady, E. Stanton & Lady here visit.

February 1865

1 Cloudy SW. Go to river twice. Cold night.

2 Fair, cold NW. All hands go to J.W. Jolly, visit all day. Have a good time.

3 Fair, cold SW. All hands go to Uncle Garry's, visit.

4 Cloudy, little stormy. Boys & I go to Ten Eyk Huyck's.

5 Fair, cold NW. Go to Meeting. Call to I. Gregory's.

6 Fair, cold NW. Go to river.

7 Cloudy NW. I take Wife and Mrs. T. Civill, go to Albany. Come **home** in snowstorm.[346] **Great ride to Kinderhook today**.

8 Six in. snow. I and Harry go to Mr. Matson's in Schodack. Pay my tax.

9 Fair, cold NW. **Attend visiting party at A.E. Willis**.

10 Fair, cold NW. **Attend visiting party to A.N. Briggs. Party large**.

11 Fair, cold. **Fix school room. Attend another visiting party to A.E. Willis. Have a very good time**.

12 Very, cold NW. Stay at home all day.

13 Very, cold. Go to river, do nothing.

---

[346] This is the first time "home" is spelled this way.

14 Fair SW. Grows warmer. I go to river.

15 Fair W. I draw wood. Visit at night to James Trego, stay late. I take Briggs family along. Snowy in evening.

16 Cloudy. Work at sleigh box. I go under the hill, get wood.

17 Fair. **Attend Festival at Coeymans Academy**. Stay late, have a good time. Draw wood.

18 Fair. Go to river. Attend J.M. Weymouth Vendue. Draw wood. Mr. L. Matson & Son here. I sell him my colt for $125.

19 Fair, cold NW. Go to Meeting. Call to P. Seabridge's & to I Gregory's.

20 Fair. Draw wood. Mrs. Briggs & Hannah call.

21 Fair NW. Draw wood. Go to James Lawton's visit.

22 Cloudy SW. Draw wood for I. Gregory. I take a load. Go to Henry Springstead's visit.

23 Warm, thawy. Draw wood for Gregory. I take a load of furniture to Schodack Center for John M. Weymouth. Widow Charlotte & Aunt Sarah Ann here.[347]

24 **Attend a very large party at Mr. Raymond's in New Baltimore. Have a very nice time, Briggs family along. Leave at 4 ½ o'clock AM.**

25 Fair. Get horses shod. **Attend party to J. Jack's**.

26 Fair. Go to Civill's call. Go to Martin VanSlyck's to tea. Stay all night. Very rainy.

27 Fair, cold. Visit to M. VanSlyck's, come home.

28 Fair. Stay about house all day. **Attend Debate in eve**.

March 1865

1 Cloudy. Go to river. Draw hay. **Attend a party to John McElroy in evening**.

2 Cloudy. Draw hay, posts. Snowy in afternoon.

3 Rainy day. Go to river.

4 Cloudy rainy. Attend P. Long's Vendue. **Attend party to J.J. Colvin's in eve**.

5 Fair, NW cold. Go to Meeting. Call on J. Lawton.

6 Fair. Take apples to I. Schoonmaker's. Draw up Vendue stuff from J.M. Weymouth's & P. Long's.

7 Fair, heavy SW. Work around. Go to river.

8 South wind. **Take potatoes out of hole. Send 8 bbls. to Keller and Johnson's**. Rev. Ackerly and Family, T. Civill & Lady, Jack & Lady, H. Springstead & Lady, J. Clement & Lady, J.M. Harris & Lady. McKee, Springstead & Kate Carroll visit here.

9 Rainy. Work in shop. Go to river. Visit to A.S. VanDerzee. **Bible Class meet here**.

10 Snowy morning. Turns very cold NW. Go to river.

11 Cold SW. **Go to Crosswell & Robb's Mill** and to river.

---

[347] At this point in Fletcher's diary the handwriting changes to Anthony's. Fletcher continued his diary, but he did not get it recopied to his journal before he died on 25 October 1865.

12	Very cold NW. Go to Meeting. **Willard Pond and Kate Teneyck get married**.
13	Fair, cold SW. Fix door at barn.
14	Fair SW. John Wilson begins work here. Mrs. VanBenthuyzen Son & Daughter here.
15	Cloudy SW. Go to river. Work in shop.
16	Foggy, rainy, sunshine. Go to river. **Ice start. High water**.
17	Snowy, clears off. **Ice leaves. Steamboat**. A.N. Briggs and Lady here.
18	Fair. N & S wind. Go to river. Miss Ackerly, Mr. Sparrow and Sister here. Miss Coonley also.
19	Fair, pleasant NW. Go to Meeting. Call to Gregory's.
20	Warmer SW. Make fence on Gregory's lot. Go to river. **Miss Mary Jenkins died**.
21	Foggy, warm. Make fence. **Attend Debate. Dan Baker Jr. and Miss Powell get married**.
22	Fair SW. **Attend funeral of Mary Jenkins**. Make fence.
23	Cloudy, squally. Heavy NW. Make fence. E. Stanton calls.
24	I take Mrs. VanBenthuysen and Family to Schodack. Boys cut wood.
25	Fair, NW cold. **Tony & I survey Lawton and Whitbeck's farm**. Boys move Jacob Race. Cut wood.
26	Fair, cold NW. Go to Meeting. Call to Civill's.
27	Fair, cool NW. Make fence.
28	Fair. Make fence. Settle with P.J. Long.
29	Fair SW. Make fence. Mrs. A. Briggs, Mrs. A.N. Briggs & Mrs. Andrew Hotaling & child here.
30	Rainy day. Work around house.
31	Rainy. Stay about the house.

April 1865

1	Fair NW. Collect money. Pay interest and bills. Go to Hollow.
2	Fair, cold NW. Go to Meeting. Call to H. Neepen's. Go to cemetery.
3	Fair, pleasant SW. **Work at Music Hall all day.**
4	Cloudy SW. Work at Music Hall.
5	Cloudy SW. Make fence. **Levi comes home**.
6	Cloudy, misty. Make fence. SW.
7	Rainy. Make fence. SW turns NW. **John Rogers died**.
8	Fair, cold. M.V. Willis and I go to Coxsackie. Make fence, take out potatoes.

9   Fair, cold NW. **Attend funeral of John Rogers**. Doct. VanAntwerp, Daniel, Mr. Adams & Lady here.

10 Rainy. Go to river. Work around the house.

11 Fair & cloudy. Get horses shod. Sow grass seed. Doct. VanAntwerp leave. **Ritey** comes. Mrs. Pearce comes here.[348]

12 Rainy. Cut wood. **Fix Beetles**.[349]

Beetle

13 Fair, cold NW. Make fence. **Have a large party for Levi's benefit. Mrs. Dr. Jones, Charlie & Emma here visit. Lib & Carrie Hotaling here. Party break up 3 am.**

14 Fair NW. Make fence. **President Abe Lincoln killed**.[350]

15 Rainy SW. Plow. Sow Grass seed. Trim trees. Charlie Jones, Emma and Eliza Phelps leave.

16 Fair. Go to Meeting. Call to H. Neefen's.

17 Fair, cool NW. Plow all day. **Send boards to Jerry Robinson's – 800 feet**.

18 Cloudy SW. Go to Jerry Robinson's with 6 bunches shingles. Plow. Get hinges.

19 Fair NW. Take two loads shingles to J. Robinson's. Plow. Mrs. Jones & Mrs. Pearce leave.

20 Rainy. Go with two loads boards to Jerry Robinson's.

21 Rainy. Cut wood. Dig ditch. Go to Robinson; bring carpenters home.

22 Cloudy. Cut wood. Make fence. Go with Mr. Brady on hill.

23 Fair, cold. Go to Meeting and vineyard. NW.

24 Fair, cold NW. **Sow 14 bushels oats**. Plow AM. Go to river. Attend lecture at Hall.

25 Very fair. **Sow 10 bushels oats**. Fix Music Hall. Send off calf.

26 Fair SW. **Go to Albany, take Wife, Tony & the Civill's to funeral of Abe Lincoln**.[351] Sow 6 bushels of oats.

27 Fair SW. Plow. Make fence. Go Under Hill.

28 Hot. Plow. Fix cutting box. Go to river.

29 Rainy. Go to river. Attend Kennedy's Vendue.

30 Fair, cool NW. Go to vineyard. Call to H. Neefen's. A.E. Willis call.

Lincoln's Funeral Railroad Car

May 1865

1   Rainy. Plow. Make fence. Draw manure to vineyard. Go to river. Get fish.

2   Fair. Make fence. Trim trees. Fix Hall.

---

348 Sarah Ann's sister, Maria, who was married to Dr. VanAntwerp was called Marite, which later gets shortened to Ritey.

349 A beetle is a heavy mallet typically with wooden heads used for ramming and crushing.

350 President Lincoln was shot on the 14th. He died the next day.

351 President Lincoln's funeral procession passed through Albany. His body lay in state in the New York State Capitol Building on April 26, 1865.

3   Fair NW. Plow. Take out potatoes. Go to E. Crum's. Examine premise for R.R. Lawsuit. **Draw sawdust for icehouse**.

4   Fair NW. Plow. Harrow. Dig stone. A. Fancher here.

5   Cloudy, rainy. Plow. Work in shop.

6   Rainy. Cut wood. Work in shop. Go to river.

7   Fair, cold NW. Go to Meeting. Call to Neefen's.

8   Cloudy SW. Plow. Plant potatoes. **Take W. Lawton's smoke house home I made for him. He to pay me $10.**

9   Rainy. Work in shop. Go to river.

10 Cloudy SW. Press hay.

11 Cloudy, rainy. **Attend R.R. Lawsuit of Crum's**. Clean cellar. Make boxes.

12 Fair NW. Lay wall. Cut wood. Fix gate.

13 Fair NW. Lay wall all day.

14 Fair. Go to Meeting. Wm. Bagley here.

15 Fair, warm. Work Under Hill. Cultivate ground. Plant potatoes for I. Gregory.

16 Fair. Plow. Plant potatoes. Work at corn ground.

17 Fair, hot SW. Plant corn. **Attend to Revenue collector**.

18 Rainy. Work in shop. Go to river. Very wet.

19 Rainy. Press hay. Saw wood. Go to river.

20 Rainy. Cut wood. Make fence. Go to river.

21 Cloudy, misty SW. Go to Meeting. Wm. Bagley Jr. here.

22 Cloudy. Work in barnyard. Press hay. Go to Mull's, get fish.

23 Fair, cold NW. Clean and salt fish. Plant corn. Plow.

24 Fair, cool NW. Finish plant corn. Plow.

25 Fair, NW warm. Mrs. A. VanSlyck, Mrs. Niver and Carrie Hotaling here. Work at potatoes, beans.

26 Fair, cool NW. Plant beans. Make fence.

27 Fair. Make fence. Plant Neefen's garden.

28 Rainy. Call to Neefen's.

29 Rainy. Cut wood. **Go to Blacksmith's at C. Square**.[352]

30 Fair, cold NW. Make fence. Trego Girls here.

31 Fair, warm. I cut posts. Make fence.

---

[352] Coeymans Square is now a part of the Village of Ravena.

June 1865

1 Fair, warm NW. Make fence. Plow.

2 Overcast, clears off. Go Under Hill. Make fence. Plow. Dr. Spoor here.

3 Fair, hot. Go to Albany to meet Dr. Clute's girls. Stay all night. Take Dr. Spoon along.

4 Fair, hot. Come home. Find Dr. Clute's girls here. Go to vineyard.

5 Cloudy and rainy. Draw off wine. Work on road Under Hill. Dr. Spoor here. I go to river.

6 Fair SW. Fill blind drains. Plow. Hoe corn.

7 Fair. Help J. Noonen plant potatoes. Hoe corn.

8 Fair. Go to Albany, buy mare of P. VanDerzee for $45. Gave receipt to pay in 30 days. Put the mare to Mr. Mosher's horse.

9 Warm. Hoe corn. Fix up sledge. Carrie Hotaling here.

10 Rainy. Make and hang Barn doors at Big meadow. Cut wood.

11 Fair. I go to Meeting. Call to Neefen's. Go to vineyard.

12 Fair SW. Draw gravel. Go Under Hill, get calf.

13 Fair NW. Draw manure. Go to James' Corner to tanner; take calf skin. Kill calf.

14 Fair. Draw gravel on Dist. Road. Fix barn & Music Hall.

15[353] Cloudy SW. Get horses shod. Hoe corn. Go to river.

16 Little rainy. Clears off. Hoe corn. **Levi comes home**. Uncle Garry & Lady here. Mrs. Enos & child & Caroline VanAntwerp here.

17 Fair SW. Very warm. Hoe corn. **Take a bath**.

18 Hot SW. Go Under Hill with boys. Call to Neefen's.

19 Cloudy. Draw hay & manure. **Levi leaves**. Go to river.

20 Warm, little shower. Draw manure. Dr. Spoor here.

21 Fair. **I & Anthony go to Herkimer to D. Bly's**.

22[354] **Survey out land I sold to Bly.**

23 Fair, sunny. **Go to H Sperl's. Start the sawmill.**

24 Fair, hot. **D. Bly took us to Poland to see cheese factory. They make cheese from 100 cows. Stop at Cold Brook.**

25 Hot. **Go around the land. Stop at D. Bly's.**

26 Rainy day. Mrs. William Bagley & Son here.

---

[353] Andrew Johnson became the 17th President following the death of Abraham Lincoln, who was shot the previous day by John Wilkes Booth, a Confederate sympathizer.

[354] The 22 June 1865 New York Census lists the following residents: Fletcher (48), Sarah Ann (45), Levi (19) student, Anthony (16), Maria Hotaling (70) mother-in-law, Angelina Jackson (30) servant, Elizabeth Hallenbeck (18) servant, John Jackson 10/12 boarder, Harry Vanderzee (16) boarder, Mary Vanderzee (19) boarder.

27   Fair. Sow Indian wheat.

28   Fair. **Survey Ogden Farm.** Sow Indian wheat. Hoe corn.

29   Fair SW. Hill corn. **Go to Albany on Referee Suit of heirs of Dr. Blaisdell.**

30   Fair hot. Finish hoe corn. **Toney & I go to Greenville to survey Dr. Blaisdell's farm. Stay all night at Chas. Seabridge's.**

July 1865

1   Rainy day. **We survey Dr. Blaisdell's farm.** Got very wet.

2   Rainy morning. Clears off. Come home.

3   Fair. **I take Ant[355] & Harry, go to Albany.** Go Under Hill. Mrs. Wm. Bagley & Son leave.

4   Fair, very warm. **Attend celebration in Catholic Grove.** Uncle Garry & Elizabeth here, visit.

5   Fair, cool NW. I take Wife and Clute girl to R.H. VanBergen's in Coxsackie. Cradle rye. Help Gregory. Miss McCabe here.

6   Fair. Work in rye. Draw in 3½ loads.

7   Fair NW. Work at rye. Wife and Ant go to Albany.

8   Fair. Work at rye. Miss McCabe leave.

9   Fair cool NW. Go to Meeting & vineyard. J. Lawton & E. Blaisdell call.

10   Fair SW. Work in rye.

11   Rain AM. Clears off. Work in rye pm.

12   Fair SW. **Work in rye. Draw 13 loads, work hard.**

13   Fair SW. Plow I. Noonen's potatoes piece. Work in rye & grass. Wm. Cadon here. **Attend raising of Crum's barn.**

14   Fair. Work in hay. Finish rye. Wm. Cadon leaves.

15   Fair. Work in hay. Elida & Mrs. VanSlyck here. Chas. Jones here.

16   Fair. Go to Meeting. Call to Neefen's.

17   Fair, cool NW. John mows ½ day. **Wife & Ant go to Poughkeepsie.** Gregory has 3 bushels of my rye.

18   Fair SW. Work in hay. Boys go Under Hill.

19   Cloudy & showery. **Levi comes home.**[356]

20   Fair SW. Work in hay.

21   Fair. Work in hay.

22   Rainy morning; clears off. Work in hay. H. VanDerzee, **Wife & Ant come home.**

---

[355] We assume "Ant" is a nickname for son Anthony (aka Tony).

[356] Evidently Levi did not return to Bisbee's school in Poughkeepsie. The Poughkeepsie Collegiate School's founder, Charles Bartlett, died in 1865 leaving the school in limbo. It was restarted in 1867 by Otis Bisbee, a teacher at the Poughkeepsie Collegiate School, as the Riverview Military Academy. This may have been the reason for Levi's return to home.

23	Fair, warm. Go to vineyard. Wallas call.
24	Fair. Work in hay.
25	Rainy PM. Work in hay. VanDerzee leave.
26	Cloudy NW. Showery. Work in hay & oats.
27	Fair NW. Work in hay & oats.
28	Fair. Work in hay. Chas. Jones & Emma here. Clute girls & Mrs. VanBergen here.
29	Fair. Work in hay and oats.
30	Fair cool day. Call at Neefen's & Civill's.

August 1865

1	Fair SW. Work in hay & oats.
2	Fair SW. Work in hay. Lib & Mary Pelts here.
3	Showery. Work in hay & oats.
4	Showery. Work in hay.
5	Cloudy. Work in hay ½ day. Lizzie & Carrie Silcock & Rev. Mr. Pattison here.
6	Hot. Go to Quarterly Meeting in N. Baltimore. Call at Civill's.
7	Cloudy morning. Clears off. Work in hay.
8	Fair. Work in hay & oats. Johnny Silcock Jr. here.
9	Fair. Work in hay. Mrs. R.H. VanBergen here.
10	Fair morning, cloudy after. Finish hay. Mrs. VanBergen leave.
11	Cloudy. Work around house. Go to river.
12	Fair NW. **Take girls, boys, Wife, all hands, go to cave up to Jerimiah Robison's**. Go to river.
13	Fair day, hot. Walk around. Willis call. I call to Neefen's.
14	Fair. Dig ditch, draw dirt.
15	Fair SW. Dig ditches. **Mr. Morgan here from Kentucky**.
16	Fair morning. Cloudy after & a little shower. Dig ditches.
17	Fair NW. Draw dirt. Wife, Levi & Ant with the Clute girls go to Saratoga.
18	Fair, dry. Go to Greenville. Dine with J.G. Williamson. Take tea to J.B. Waldron's & start to A. Fancher's.
19	Fair, hot. Come home. Leave wool to T.E. Huyck. Wife come home.
20	Hot, dry weather, SW. Go to vineyard. Willis calls.
21	Fair, hot. Draw dirt from ditch Under Hill.
22	Rainy afternoon. Plow. Go to river. Clute girls leave for Coxsackie.
23	Fair, cool NW. Plow Under Hill. [Negro] Wench here. John J. Silcock here.
24	Fair, cool. Plow. J.J. Silcock and children leave.

25	Fair, cool NW. Plow. Sow rye. Pick stone. Chas. Jones here.
26	Fair SW. Harrow rye. Dig blind ditches. Draw stone.
27	Fair, dry NW. Prof. McKee call. We walk on railroad to Ben Hotaling's.
28	Fair, cool NW. Roll rye ground. Dig and fill blind ditches. Dr. Spoor here.
29	Fair NW. Finish sowing and ditching Under Hill.
30	Fair, very dry. Plow. Cut Indian wheat.
31	Fair, dry. Cut Indian wheat. Plow. Fix roller.

September 1865

1	Fair, SW warm. I take Wife, H. Neefen and Lady, go to Greenville, see the Ferris farm. Boys plow. Cloudy in eve, NW.
2	Fair. **Attend sale of the real estate of Dr. Blaisdell. Buy the wood lot farm of 53 acres for $800**. Johnson Smith, Silas Hunt and Wilkson here to dinner. **Make arrangement with Silas Hunt to sell my purchase for $900.**
3	Fair, warm SW. Call at Neefen's. Go to church.
4	Fair, hot. Draw 1 load of muck. Fix roller.
5	Fair. Plow. Fix roller & grape boxes.
6	Rain. Cut up corn. Plow. Go to river.
7	Fair. Plow. I go to Albany. **Send deed mortgage & bond to Henry Sperl for David Bly.**
8	Rainy afternoon. Get broom corn seed from Island.
9	Misty morning. **Go to Catskill on the Coeymans 6 Band Excursion - good time**. Boys plow.
10	Cloudy SW. Go Under Hill & to vineyard.
11	Fair SW. Cut up corn. Harrow rye ground.
12	Fair, hot. Sow rye. Little shower last night.
13	Rainy, clears off SW. Harrow rye ground. Cut up corn.
14	Fair SW. Sow rye. Cut up corn. Take tea to Mr. Civill's. Shower in eve.
15	**Go to Greenville to survey lot bought of Dr. Blaisdell.**
16	Fair. **Survey lot. Stay to Silas Hunt's.**
17	Fair. **Go to Jacob Story's. Stay all day. Walk about.**
18	**Rain all day steady. Stay in house.**
19	**Survey land. Go back to J.W. Story's.**
20	Fair. **Go to Cairo. Attend Green County Fair. Very poor. Come home in eve.**
21	Fair SW. Sow grass seed. **Take 7 boxes grapes to New Baltimore Barge**. Roll land.
22	Fair NW. Thresh Indian wheat. Plow. Roll land.
23	Fair. Thresh & clean Indian wheat. H. VanDerzee & Marite come. Catharine Pierce here.

24 Fair SW. Go to vineyard & Under Hill. Call on Willis.

25 Fair. Work at grapes. **Samuel King died**. Mary VanSlyck here.

26 Fair, cool NW. **Attend funeral of S. King**. Draw away grapes. VanDerzee leave.

27 Fair SW. I go to Baltimore. John thresh rye. Anne & Mary Bagley here. Miss Pierce leaves.

28 Fair. Draw grapes to N. Baltimore. Sow rye.

29 Fair. Finish sowing rye. Mrs. Clement, Eliza, J.M. Harris, John Clement & Lady, Mrs. E. Stanton & Daughter, Mrs. T. Civill, Ann Brace. A.B. Hotaling & lady here.

30 Fair SW. Finish sowing rye. Go after grape boxes to Baltimore.

October 1865

1 Fair SW. Go to Meeting and Under Hill. Call to H. Neefen's. Willis calls.

2 Fair, cold NW. Pick apples Under Hill.

3 Fair cold NW. Send off grapes. Pick apples. Marite leave, Dr. Spoor here.

4 Fair. I take Wife to Albany.

5 Fair, cold. Finish drawing corn. Take grapes to Baltimore. Shower in eve.

6 Fair cold NW. Husk corn. Dig potatoes.

7 Fair. Husk corn. **I & Toney survey for Willis**.

8 Fair. Call to Neefen's. Go to vineyard. Willis calls.

9 Fair. **Am sick**. Boys husk corn.

10 Fair pleasant. Boys husk corn. **I am sick**. I draw away grapes.

11 Cold NW. **I am in house all day sick**. Boys husk

12[357] Cold NW. **I am in house unwell**. Boys husk corn.

13 Cold NW. **Father is quite sick**. Boys husk in am. Dig potatoes and draw the for Gregory.

14 Cold, hard frost. Boys put away corn. **Father is no better**. Boys dig potatoes. Dr. N. Clute of Louisville, KY here.

15 Rain hard all day. A.E. Willis & Neefen call. **Father is no better**.

16 Fair. **Father said he was better**. Boys husk corn. Dr. Clute go to Coxsackie.

17 Fair. Boys dig potatoes. **Father said he was a little better**. Dr. Fredenburgh & A.E. Willis call.

18 Rain a little. Boys finish potatoes and husking corn. **Father no better**. Em Hotaling here.

19 Rainy. Boys thresh. John Jackson did not work. Partial eclipse of sun today. **Father no better**.

20 Fair. Boys go after slat timber. **Father gets no better**. Lydia VanSlyck here on visit. A.N. Briggs calls. **Dr. Mosher here 3 times**.

21 Fair. Hail a little. Boys draw slat timber. **Father no better. Dr. Mosher here twice. Civill call.**

---

[357] This was Fletcher's last entry. The remainder was kept by Anthony.

22	Fair. Dr. Mosher, Dr. Ed Blaisdell, T. Civil, Noble H. Johnson, A.E. Willis & Lady, J.M. Harris, Uncle Garry & Wife call. Father no better. A.N. Briggs call in evening.
23	Fair. Levi goes to Albany to telegraph Dr. VanAntwerp & Wife to come up. They arrive here about 11 o'clock pm. Dr. Mosher here 5 times. Mother employs John Hazelton to set up with Father. He was taken much worse about 3 o'clock last night. Harry went after Dr. Mosher, who came & stayed two hours. Dr. VanAntwerp says there is no hope for him. A.N. Briggs, J.N. Briggs, Trego & Wife call.
24	Father is worse. Great many people call.
25	Father died this morning at 10 o'clock.[358] Dr. VanAntwerp went to Albany to purchase Father's coffin. Boys work around house. Fair day.
26	Fair. Boys work around house, make preparations for Father's funeral.
27	Stormy, snow all day hard. Father's Funeral today. Rev. Mr. Pattison preached. House crowded.

---

[358] Fletcher was only 48 years old when he died. We have no information regarding the cause of his death.

Deaths

22 October 1843 – Anthony Houghtaling
19 March 1844 – Cornelius VanAntwerp
24 March 1844 – Betsy Teneyck
9 June 1844- Daniel Goldsmith
17 September 1844 – Peleg Sherman's Son
20 October 1844 – Andrew Houghtaling's Wife
19 March 1845 – Barbary Carhart
22 March 1845 – Aleas Steenburgh
9 April 1845 – Maria Houghtaling
1 September 1845 – Maria Cronk
7 November 1845 – Jan VanBergen
22 January 1846 – Mrs. Ackerman
18 February 1846 – Mrs. Honse Teneyck
25 March 1846 – Mrs. Albert Jackson
12 April 1846 – Joseph Hazelton
1 May 1846 – Anthony Teneyck
20 February 1847 – Henry Niles
21 February 1847 – John Colvin's child
26 June 1847 – Mr. Scribus
1 December 1847 – Eliza Lawton
2 December 1847 – Sarah Camp
14 December 1847 – J. Hauenstien's Child
12 January 1848 – Old Mrs. Teneyck
26 January 1848 – Harriet Blaisdell
21 February 1848 – Mrs. John Hauenstien
24 February 1848 – John Roseboom
30 April 1848 – Mrs. Stacy
24 June 1848 – Julius Blaisdell
17 August 1848 – G. Holbrox Child
23 August 1848 – Benzilla Nelson
4 October 1848 – Barent Ryon
11 November 1848 – Abram VanBergen
15 November – B.E. Holmes
1 December 1848 – Luzan VanBergen
13 March 1849 – Rees Whitman
6 April 1849 – Conrad VanDalpsen's Child
17 May 1849 – Joseph Blaisdell
12 June 1849 – Peter Cook
24 June 1849 – John Bronk
29 June 1849 – Peter Ostrander's Daughter
5 December 1849 – Cornelius Ryon's Child
2 March 1850 – Mrs. Phillip Pelts
30 April 1850 – Mrs. Wm Wilkins
7 August 1850 – A.E. Willis's Child
4 September 1850 – Caty Houghtaling
9 September 1850 – Mrs. Elias Holmes
14 November 1850 – Gardner Lawton
17 December 1850 – Old Mrs. Barton
22 December 1850 – Emma Sherman
16 January 1851 – James White's Child

30 January 1851 – Christina VanAntwerp
2 February 1851 – Samuel Jolly
18 May 1851 – Jane Springstead
20 May 1851 – Old Mr. Purdy
31 May 1851 – Henriette Willis
3 September 1851 – John McCarty
4 October 1851 – John McDonald
22 December 1851 – Mrs. Tombs
21 January 1852 – Egbert Clement
4 February 1852 – Henry Sperle's Child
14 February 1852 – B.E. Holmes' Child
1 April 1852 – Chatham Johnson
13 April 1852 – Miriam Waldsome
24 May 1852 – Anthony M. VanBergen
1 October 1852 – Hiram Ayres
9 December 1852 – Mrs. Dyer
17 December 1852 – Mrs. Thomas A. Houghtaling
5 January 1853 – Lawrence Fises
23 January 1853 – Anthony Bradwell
30 April 1853 – Mrs. Stephen Gould
21 June 1853 – Mrs. McGregor
21 August 1853 – Mr. A.E. Willis's Child
23 August 1853 – Dutch Frederick's Child
24 August 1853 – Charles Barrett's Child
25 August 1853 – Jonathan McElroy's Son
27 September 1853 – Salmon VanAntwerp's Child
29 October 1853 – William Lawson
8 December 1853 – Mrs. James Stephenson
9 December 1853 – Andrew Sickler
15 April 1854 – Andrew Teneyck
17 April 1854 – Mrs. Haydock
25 July 1854 – Mrs. Southwick
27 July 1854 – Mrs. Parmentus family of 5
12 August 1854 – Cate Lawton
10 November 1854 – Cate VanAntwerp
21 December 1854 – Nelson Agan, J. Teal's Child
17 February 1855 – Margaret Blaisdell
24 March 1855 – Peter VanAntwerp
26 March 1855 – Sally Teneyck
2 April 1855 – John Sperl
17 April 1855 – Henry Applebee
5 May 1855 – A. Jackson's Child
7 May 1855 – Catherine Hotaling
1 June 1855 – L. Hathaway
12 July 1855 – William Southwick
25 July 1855 – Mrs. Joslin
26 August 1855 – M.G. VanBergen
1 December 1855 – Chris Sickler
11 January 1856 – Mrs. Thomas Gould
25 January 1856 – John Mosher
4 February 1856 – Granny Sherwood
22 February 1856 – Dedrick Lawton

29 April 1856 – Old Mr. Tuttle
6 May 1856 – Charles Barrett
30 August 1856 – J. Selkirk
1 September 1856 – Peter W. VanBergen
7 October 1856 – Mrs. Peter Long
25 October 1856 – Barent Houghtaling
10 December 1856 – Mrs. Salmon (Maria) VanAntwerp
24 December 1856 – Mrs. Barent Ryon
1 February 1857 – Catharine VanSlyck
5 April 1857 – Newton Briggs
13 May 1857 – Mrs. Caroline Scott
15 May 1857 – William Lawson
2 June 1857 – Stephen Ostrander
3 June 1857 – Harman VanDerzee
20 June 1857 – Edward H. VanSlyck
26 June 1857 – Mrs. John Hazelton
4 July 1857 – William L. Marcy
15 July 1857 – Arthur McClasky
15 August 1857 – John Sickler
23 March 1858 – Olly Lawton
3 April 1858 – Mrs. Robert Martin
14 April 1858 – Martin VanBergen, Michel Niven
14 July 1858 – Mrs. Teal
15 July 1858 – Daniel Shear's Child
20 September 1858 – A.E. Willis's Child
21 October 1858 – Salmon VanAntwerp
26 October 1858 – Andrew Whitbeck
23 November 1858 – Abram Verplank
20 December 1858 – Rev. Hugh Jolly
7 March 1859 – George Harris' Child
13 March 1859 – Henry Niles Child
9 April 1859 – Mrs. VanAntwerp
7 September 1859 – Mrs. Cornelius Demond
1 October 1859 – Mrs. Barnum, Jacob Sickles
20 October 1859 – Mrs. William Bushants
1 December 1859 – Washington Irving
27 December 1859 – Anthony VanBergen
28 December 1859 – William Civill
25 January 1860 – Edward Baker
24 February 1860 – Old Mrs. Gibbens
27 February 1860 Mrs. Thomas Penton
9 April 1860 – Gilbert Cronk
13 April 1860 – Albert Hotaling
12 July 1860 – Richard Lawton
16 August 1860 – Sarah Willis
31 August 1860 – A. Borkman
5 September 1860 – Old Mrs. Bronk, Sam Teneyck, John Teal's Child
6 September 1860 – Mary Farr Johnstone Blaisdell
10 January 1861 – Barent Mull
17 January 1861 – Old Mrs. Jolly
10 February 1861 – Rachel Gregory's Boy
19 February 1861 – William Bushants

10 April 1861 – Daniel Carhart
2 August 1861 – Catharine Hotaling
27 August 1861 – Helen Keller
28 August 1861 – John Ziegler's Child
5 October 1861 – George Wilson
17 October 1861 – Old Mr. Teats
20 November 1861 – Edward Gibbens
22 November 1861 – Kit Sickels
3 December 1861 – I. VanDerzee
10 August 1862 – Leonard Blodget
29 August 1862 – Willie Stilwell
28 September 1862 – Mrs. Capt. Miller
23 January 1863 – Jemima Hotaling
17 April 1863 – Catharine Hathaway
14 July 1863 – I. Southard
30 July 1863 – George Sickler
11 August 1863 – James Sherman
19 September 1863 – William F. Cronk
30 September 1863 – Mrs. John Sickles
10 October 1863 – James Schofield
4 November 1863 – Mrs. John Anderson's Children (fire)
19 November 1863 – Mrs. Widow Gedney
5 December 1863 – Tommy Colvin
12 December 1863 – William Winnie
20 December 1863 – U.B. Willis
4 January 1864 – Elias Holmes
3 February 1864 – John Gibbens' Daughter
13 February 1864 – Peter Holbrook
4 March 1864 – Patrick Minick
22 March 1864 – Jane Eliza Clement
8 April 1864 – Mrs. Stilwell
2 June 1864 – Phillip Winnie
22 October 1864 – Wesley Blaisdell (yellow fever)
27 December 1864 – William Akely
20 March 1865 – Mary Jenkins
7 April 1865 – John Rogers
15 April 1865 – Abraham Lincoln
25 September 1865 – Samuel King
25 October 1865 – Fletcher Blaisdell

Photos

Sarah Ann Houghtaling Blaisdell

Fletcher Blaisdell

Mary Farr Johnstone Blaisdell

Levi Blaisdell I

Maria VanBergen Houghtaling

Anthony Houghtaling

Harriet Blaisdell

Levi and Anthony Blaisdell

Fletcher and Sarah Ann Blaisdell's Home

Sarah Ann Blaisdell

Fletcher Blaisdell

Levi Blaisdell II

Anthony Blaisdell

Dr. Wesley Blaisdell

Maria (Marite) Houghtaling VanAntwerp

Theophilus Civill

Caroline Brace Civill

Closing Acknowledgements

This project has taken the better part of five years to complete. It grew in scope from being a summary of Fletcher's journal to a complete day by day account with numerous footnotes and photographs to elaborate activities that we didn't fully understand or that we thought would be helpful to future readers.[359] In that process we developed an admiration for the man and a better understanding of what life was like nearly two centuries ago.

We are indebted to many kind people who helped us as we worked our way through Fletcher's journal: family members who typed early drafts and provided photographs of ancestral portraits; our spouses, Edgar and Betsy, for reviewing sections of the book; our cousin, Laura Palmer, for providing names of places that no longer exist in the Greenville area; Sally Civill Phillips for providing information about the Civill family; our sister, Mary Granato, for providing facts that we had forgotten; Barbara Pape Hardy, for her critique of the Preface; Marc Peckham, Hudson River historian, and Joe Boehlke, President of the Ravena Coeymans Historical Society, who graciously answered our many questions and gave us new insights about the history of the river and the local area.

---

[359] Much of the information for the footnotes and photographs was obtained from Google and Wikipedia searches.

In conclusion, we had a good time working together and we hope that the Fletcher Blaisdell's diaries spark interest in local history and genealogy.

John Blaisdell & Linda Blaisdell Roosa